After
the
Coup

The **ISEAS – Yusof Ishak Institute** (formerly Institute of Southeast Asian Studies) is an autonomous organization established in 1968. It is a regional centre dedicated to the study of socio-political, security, and economic trends and developments in Southeast Asia and its wider geostrategic and economic environment. The Institute's research programmes are grouped under Regional Economic Studies (RES), Regional Strategic and Political Studies (RSPS), and Regional Social and Cultural Studies (RSCS). The Institute is also home to the ASEAN Studies Centre (ASC), the Nalanda-Sriwijaya Centre (NSC), and the Singapore APEC Study Centre.

ISEAS Publishing, an established academic press, has issued more than two thousand books and journals. It is the largest scholarly publisher of research about Southeast Asia from within the region. ISEAS Publishing works with many other academic and trade publishers and distributors to disseminate important research and analyses from and about Southeast Asia to the rest of the world.

After the Coup

The National Council for Peace and Order Era and the Future of Thailand

Edited by

Michael J. Montesano • Terence Chong • Mark Heng

ISEAS YUSOF ISHAK INSTITUTE

First published in Singapore in 2019 by
ISEAS Publishing
30 Heng Mui Keng Terrace
Singapore 119614
E-mail: publish@iseas.edu.sg
Website: <http://bookshop.iseas.edu.sg>

The responsibility for facts and opinions in this publication rests exclusively with the authors and their interpretations do not necessarily reflect the views or the policy of the publisher or its supporters.

ISEAS Library Cataloguing-in-Publication Data

After the Coup : The National Council for Peace and Order Era and the Future of Thailand / edited by Michael J. Montesano, Terence Chong and Mark Heng.
1. Thailand—Politics and government—1988–
2. Thailand—History—Coup d'état, 2014.
3. Democracy—Thailand.
I. Montesano, Michael J., editor.
II. Chong, Terence, editor.
III. Heng, Mark, editor.
DS575 A25   2018

ISBN 978-981-4818-98-8 (soft cover)
ISBN 978-981-4843-05-8 (e-book, PDF)

Typeset by Superskill Graphics Pte Ltd
Printed in Singapore by Mainland Press Pte Ltd

Contents

About the Contributors

Aim Sinpeng is Lecturer in the Department of Government and International Relations, The University of Sydney.

Anusorn Unno is Dean of the Faculty of Sociology and Anthropology, Thammasat University, and Associate Professor in the same faculty.

Chanon Techasunthornwat is Lecturer in the Faculty of Economics, Thammasat University.

Terence Chong is Deputy Director of the ISEAS – Yusof Ishak Institute, and Senior Fellow in its Regional Social & Cultural Studies Programme.

Mark Heng was formerly Research Officer in the ISEAS – Yusof Ishak Institute's Nalanda-Sriwijaya Centre and Regional Social & Cultural Studies Programme.

Kwanchit Sasiwongsaroj is Associate Professor in the Research Institute for Languages and Cultures of Asia, Mahidol University.

Duncan McCargo is Professor in the School of Politics and International Studies, University of Leeds, and Visiting Professor in the Department of Political Science, Columbia University.

Michael Montesano is Coordinator, Thailand Studies Programme, and Co-Coordinator, Myanmar Studies Programme, ISEAS – Yusof Ishak Institute.

Porphant Ouyyanont is Professor in the School of Economics, Sukhothai Thammathirat Open University.

Prajak Kongkirati is Assistant Professor in the Faculty of Political Science, Thammasat University.

Puangthong Pawakapan is Associate Professor in the Faculty of Political Science, Chulalongkorn University.

Rungrawee Chalermsripinyorat is a doctoral candidate in the Department of Political and Social Change, Coral Bell School of Asia Pacific Affairs, ANU College of Asia and the Pacific, The Australian National University.

Saowanee Alexander is Assistant Professor in the Faculty of Liberal Arts, Ubon Ratchathani University.

Surachart Bamrungsuk is Professor in the Faculty of Political Science, Chulalongkorn University.

Tanet Charoenmuang is Professor in the Faculty of Political Science and Public Administration, Chiang Mai University.

Thongchai Winichakul is Senior Researcher at the Institute of Developing Economies (IDE-JETRO), and Emeritus Professor of History at the University of Wisconsin-Madison.

Thorn Pitidol is Lecturer in the Faculty of Economics, Thammasat University.

Viengrat Nethipo is Associate Professor in the Faculty of Political Science, Chulalongkorn University.

Wimonsiri Hemtanon is Lecturer in the Humanities and Language Division and Director of the Intercultural Studies and Languages Program, Mahidol University International College.

Youngyut Burasit is Assistant Professor in the Research Institute for Languages and Cultures of Asia, Mahidol University.

1

Introduction: Thai Realities and Possibilities after the 22 May Coup

Michael J. Montesano

The *coup d'état* staged by Thailand's military under the leadership of army commander General Prayut Chanocha on 22 May 2014 inaugurated the country's longest period of naked dictatorship in half a century.

Even before the duration of this spell of authoritarian rule in Bangkok became clear, other factors had already distinguished the 22 May putsch and its aftermath. For one, the campaign of political repression and ideological transformation launched by the self-proclaimed National Council for Peace and Order (NCPO, *Khana raksa khwamsangop haeng chat*) junta that seized power in the coup represented a notable break with what had followed Thai coups of the recent past. Above all, that campaign made this coup very different from the coup of 19 September 2006, which had ousted Thaksin Shinawatra from the premiership, and it left many observers of Thai affairs concerned that the junta was determined to entrench long-term military domination of the country and its politics.

A second factor shaped observers' understandings of the NCPO, of its project and of the prospects for the success of that project from early on. Even at the time of the junta's seizure of power, it was evident that the end of the long life and long reign of King Bhumibol Adulyadej was near. In the event, the king passed away, at the age of eighty-eight, on 13 October 2016, after seventy years as Thailand's sovereign. His son Vajiralongkorn succeeded him, fully four and a half decades after being designated crown prince (Handley 2006, p. 249).

In social, political, cultural, economic, institutional, demographic and other terms, the Thailand that the new king inherited was a different country from that of 1946, from that of the decades of counter-insurgency in which his father had redefined the role of the Thai monarchy, from that of the heyday of Bhumibol's reign in the 1980s and 1990s, and even from that which had first elected Thaksin to the premiership in January 2001. The events of the decade and half since that election had left the NCPO, a segment of the Thai military, more broadly and a number of civilian interests that backed the junta and its seizure of power determined to pursue a certain vision of Thailand's political and social orders. In pursuing that vision, the junta needed even from the earliest days of its dictatorship to attend to its relations with the then heir to the throne and to anticipate his own vision for the role of monarchy in the Thailand of the twenty-first century.

This book speaks above all to the plausibility of these visions. Its chapters concern conditions in Thailand in the period following the 22 May 2014 coup in Bangkok. They serve collectively to document and to analyse the realities and possibilities that obtained in the country in that period, along with the historical factors that accounted for those realities and possibilities.

The origins of the volume lie in the Thailand Forum conference held at the Institute of Southeast Asian Studies — then soon to be rechristened the ISEAS – Yusof Ishak Institute — in Singapore on 27 and 28 July 2015. That conference brought together fourteen scholars, all but one from Thailand, to present papers on panels addressing political developments and the monarchy, economic and social change, decentralization, regionalism, and culture and society. All but two of the chapters in this book originated as papers presented on those panels. While Viengrat Nethipo was unable to join the conference, she nevertheless graciously offered the chapter on decentralization published here for inclusion in the book. And while the conference organizers' oversight meant that the July 2015 gathering featured no presentation on the long-running crisis in Thailand's far-southern region of Patani, Rungrawee Chalermsripinyorat subsequently agreed with great kindness to prepare for us the chapter on that crisis that appears here. Similarly, neither Chanon Techasunthornwat nor Wimonsiri Hemtanon attended the Thailand Forum, but they joined conference participants Thorn Pitidol and Aim Sinpeng, respectively, in co-authoring chapters for this volume. Youngyut Burasit did the same in the case of the chapter co-authored with conference participant Kwanchit Sasiwongsaroj. We regret the absence from the book of chapters on decentralization and on the politics of contemporary Thai Buddhism by, respectively, Achakorn Wongpreedee and Katewadee Kulabkaew, each of whom joined us at ISEAS for the Thailand Forum conference.

Terence Chong, Mark Heng and I would like to thank former ISEAS Director Tan Chin Tiong for his unstinting support for the Institute's Thailand Studies Programme, Betty Tan for her impossible-to-match efficiency in organizing the Thailand Forum conference and Puangthong Pawakapan for her invaluable advice in helping us identify conference participants. The willingness of Jacob Ricks, Cassey Lee, Francis Hutchinson and Su-Ann Oh to moderate sessions of the Thailand Forum conference helped make it the success that it was. In the home stretch of work on this volume, the unfailing commitment to ISEAS's mission and unflagging backing of Ng Kok Kiong and Stephen Logan at ISEAS Publishing were what made it possible for it to appear.

Above all, we thank the contributors to this volume — for the privilege of publishing their work, for their unfailing cooperation and for their patience. That cooperation and that patience have meant that we made new friends and gained valued colleagues in our work on this book. We also had the chance to enjoy once more the intellectual companion-ship of some dear old friends. It is of particular satisfaction to me personally that this volume includes a chapter by Surachart Bamrungsuk, who demonstrated unforgettable kindness to me when I undertook dissertation research in provincial Thailand — and specifically in its remarkable Lower North — a quarter-century ago.

In a special note of thanks, Terence and I thank our third co-editor Mark for the skill and thoughtfulness with which he has steered this volume towards completion. We wish him well in all of his post-ISEAS undertakings.

Writing in early 2016, a savvy observer of contemporary Thailand labelled the military seizure of state power nearly two years earlier one "among a select group of Thai coups which aim to shift the trajectory of the country's politics". That observer, Chris Baker, ranked its ambitiousness alongside that of the coups of 1932, 1976 and 1957 (Baker 2016, pp. 388–89).

The NCPO's effort to "set up an elaborate machinery to restructure the country's political system" (Baker 2016, p. 390), to introduce "lasting new political arrangements" (McCargo 2015c, p. 337), in the year or so following the coup made its ambitiousness clear. At the centre of this effort lay an ideologically sophisticated programme of depoliticization (Montesano 2015; McCargo 2015c, p. 346).

Thailand's military inherited from its experience of domestic counter-insurgency between the 1960s and the early 1980s a conception of its relationship to "the people" (*prachachon*) in a system of "democracy" that did not require politicians or parties (Montesano 2015, pp. 6ff.). In the late 1990s, the Thai Army made this conception explicit by tweaking the slogan of "Nation, Religion, King" (*chat satsana phramahakasat*) introduced early in the century by King Vajiravudh (r. 1910–25) and adopting "For Nation, Religion, King and People" (*phuea chat sat kasat lae prachachon*) as its own slogan (McCargo 2015b, p. 343). It was this latter slogan that appeared on Thai viewers' screens when they tuned into the weekly television broadcasts that NCPO leader General Prayut Chanocha made starting shortly after his coup (Montesano 2015, p. 1). In announcements concerning matters ranging from the suppression of the media to economic policies and the governance of state enterprises and even the state of Thai Buddhism, the announcements of the junta also repeatedly and consistently invoked "the people" (Montesano 2015, pp. 3–4).

These invocations, like the army slogan introduced in the late 1990s, bespoke a corporatist vision of politics, grounded in organic "mutuality" between the military and the undifferentiated mass that composed "the people" of Thailand (Montesano 2015, p. 10; McCargo 2015b, pp. 342, 344).[1] Through the programme of depoliticization that this vision implied, Duncan McCargo observed, "Thailand's political divides were expected to be wished/washed away by rebranding the entire population as 'the people', subordinated to the greater needs of the nation, religion and monarchy, and acting under military tutelage" (McCargo 2015b, p. 345).[2] And this expectation of tutelage in the aftermath of the May 2014 coup unmistakably suggested both frankly praetorian ambitions (Montesano 2015) and integralism masquerading as an interest in "reconciliation" (Ministry of Foreign Affairs 2014).

Less than a year into the NCPO junta's quasi-integralist experiment, McCargo already saw its ultimate failure as a foregone conclusion. "In the long term", he wrote, "depoliticizing the public sphere of such a vibrant country as Thailand surely lies beyond the realm of the possible" (McCargo 2015c, p. 352). This dismissal of the fundamental ambition of the most recent dictatorship to hold power in Bangkok as unrealistic represented a hopeful, even optimistic, assertion. Its emphasis on Thailand's vibrancy would certainly ring true to many outside observers of and stakeholders in the country. That vibrancy doubtless led many of those observers and stakeholders to engage with Thailand in the first place and to remain engaged with it over time.

McCargo's hopeful early prognostication that the NCPO junta's effort to make *solitudinem* pass for *pacem* was doomed glosses the present volume well. The contributions that follow document social and political dynamism and complexity whose susceptibility to long-term authoritarian effacement would appear far-fetched. These contributions do, that is, bespeak vibrancy, not least in Thai intellectual life. At the same time, to satisfy ourselves with viewing them as merely reflective of Thailand's continuing and undeniably appealing vibrancy would not be to do justice to the contributions' collective import. The term "vibrancy" remains essentially descriptive, rather than explanatory. While it sounds right, and seems to capture something essential, its invocation does not amount to an analysis — let alone a guide for observers and stakeholders concerned with the future of Thailand.

The chapters that follow build on McCargo's recognition of the lack of fit between Thailand's dynamism and complexity, on the one hand, and the NCPO's early designs for the country, on the other, to shed light on the forces that the junta's programme of depoliticization would shut down. They thus both lay bare the elements of Thailand's long-running crisis that the current spell of dispiriting dictatorship has failed to address and suggest some of the contours of the country's future.

Federico Ferrara has pointed out that influential understandings of those elements and those contours have focused on three sets of explanatory logic. One stresses the incompatibility of "Western" political forms and institutions with Thailand and its "culture, history, and tradition" (Ferrara 2015, p. 268) to account for the chronic political instability that has so often resulted in authoritarian rule. A second roots that instability in the alleged backwardness of Thailand's provincial electorate, relative to the "modern" middle class of its primate city and capital (Ferrara 2015, p. 270). And the third stresses class conflict (Ferrara 2015, p. 273). Deftly refuting each of these logics in the crucial closing chapter of one of the most important English-language monographs on Thailand and its politics to appear in many decades,[3] Ferrara proposes an alternative, more comprehensive, explanatory logic. That logic centres on "identity conflict", on the contest over "the structure of the Thai nation and [their members'] place in it" among groups defined — and self-defined — with reference to such factors as "social status, regional origin, and political ideas" (Ferrara 2015, pp. 274–75).

Ferrara stresses that "modernization" — "the profound socio-economic transformations [that] the country has experienced since the 1960s" — has been a socially inclusive, indiscriminate, process (Ferrara 2015, p. 273). It has not made some elements of society "modern" while leaving others "backward". It has reshaped "the aspirations and self-image of Thai citizens" of all backgrounds and origins, even while failing to level the "social hierarchy" that those distinctions structure (Ferrara 2015, p. 273).[4] Ferrara's argument thus places the country among those in which, far from playing a sociologically homogenizing role or from reducing differences in society to those defined by class, modernization has for all its pervasiveness increased the salience of multifaceted identities.[5]

The present volume serves to affirm Ferrara's assertion of the need to understand Thailand's twenty-first-century crisis as a conflict among bearers of a range of "collective identities" (Ferrara 2015, p. 252). That assertion has, in turn, a number of implications for our understanding of the chapters in the volume. One is that the country's observed vibrancy is strongly related to the interaction of social, regional and ideological identities. Conflict has been the prevalent recent form of that interaction. Furthermore, efforts in the course of the past half-century to supress the claims of certain identity groups in the name of "Thai-style democracy" have amounted to "structural violence", and an emphasis on "Thainess" to delegitimize historically subaltern groups' identities has amounted to "cultural violence" (Ferrara 2015, pp. 181, 182). Considered with reference to the specific context of the period after May 2014, Ferrara's assertion concerning identity conflict also serves to expose the NCPO junta's appeals to "the people" and its aspirations for integralist depoliticization of Thai society for what they are: attempts to deny, and to do still further violence to, the diversity of identities that has become so pronounced in the past two decades. But the junta's recourse to repression has highlighted the weakness of those appeals and attempts and, perhaps, their futility (Ferrara 2015, p. 292).

The significance of conflict among collective social identities in explaining the early-twenty-first-century Thai crisis of which the NCPO dictatorship is only the latest phase makes Thorn Pitidol's and Chanon Techasunthornwat's chapter in this volume particularly valuable. The chapter draws on careful statistical analysis and on interviews with members of Thailand's Bangkok-centred upper middle class to offer nothing less than the history of one of the identities central to that conflict. This class emerged in the period of economic liberalization and rapid growth from the mid-1980s, years that also saw its fortunes diverge from those of the emerging lower middle class whose members have come since the turn of the century to pose the greatest challenge to the country's established social and political order. But material success alone did not define the new upper middle class. Rather, its identity has been centred on its members' strong sense of having earned their success, on their attachment to political order and on their associating the aspirations of the Thai lower middle class with allegedly corrupt conduct on the part of politicians. The perceived threat to its status embodied in those aspirations accounted for the upper middle class's support for the 2013–14 campaign of the People's Democratic Reform Committee (PDRC)[6] to drive the government of Prime Minister Yingluck Shinawatra from power and for its turn against democracy more generally.

Thorn and Chanon argue that factors including the presence of members of the new lower middle class in urban centres as well as in the countryside render obsolete understandings of political conflict in Thailand that stress the country's urban-rural divide. Anek Laothamatas's influential book chapter on "A Tale of Two Democracies", with its stress on the sophistication of the middle-class urban electorate and the venality and backwardness of rural voters (Anek 1996), has informed those time-worn understandings. Instead of the centrality to Thailand's political troubles of those two geographically distinct electorates, Thorn and Chanon stress that of the contest between "contemporary Thailand's two middle classes".[7] The vision of political order on the part of the upper middle class that they delineate makes unmistakable the degree to which that contest represents an identity conflict.

Other contributors to this volume reinforce Thorn's and Chanon's message. Anusorn Unno's chapter treats an identity group whose members also supported the PDRC in the push to oust Yingluck that led to the May 2014 coup. In its analysis of the political views and activities of people from the Upper South of Thailand resident in Bangkok, it affirms Thorn's and Chanon's observation concerning the inadequacy of understanding Thai politics through the lens of a simple urban-rural divide. At the same time, however, it joins Ferrara in affirming the importance of regional attachments as a factor in defining collective identities in contemporary Thailand. Anusorn offers a reassessment of scholarship that has held that Upper Southern Thais are "anti-state" in their political orientation.[8] Examining the historical relationship of the Upper South with the Siamese and later the Thai monarchy, he casts the participation in the PDRC's protests of people with roots in that part of the country as an example of the "regionalization" of nationalism and of support for the dominant state ideology. His chapter, like Thorn's and Chanon's, thus points both to the evolution of a particular political identity and, more generally, to the dynamism of collective identities in Thailand — the latter a reality certain to figure in the country's future.

Far more than that of the Upper South, the regional identity of Thailand's Northeast, or Isan, has been the subject of considerable scholarly attention.[9] Saowanee's and McCargo's chapter notes the region's historical recalcitrance towards and dispiriting subordination in the Bangkok-centric political order, its "distinctly Lao identity" and the broad support among its inhabitants for Thaksin Shinawatra and the Red side of Thailand's political divide.[10] This history served as background to the revulsion and even, repression notwithstanding, the occasional defiance among people in the region that followed the May 2014 putsch. The authors' fieldwork makes clear that the quiescence that the NCPO junta appeared to bring to the Northeast both resulted from its creepy intimidation tactics and came, ultimately, from the barrels of its guns. But they also offer a more fundamental observation about Isan identity and Thailand's long-term political crisis. Calling attention to the origins outside the Northeast of all of the leading Red Shirt figures of the past decade, they argue that persistent relegation of the region and its people to inferior status in the Thai social and political orders has resulted in an identity that, while strong, nevertheless lacks confidence and ambition. Their tentative diagnosis of "heroic failure" provokes pathos.

Also a bastion of considerable support for native son Thaksin and the Red side of the country's great political schism, Northern Thailand, or

Lanna, is another region of the country with a pronounced historical and sociocultural identity.[11] The clear position of the majority of the North's electorate in the political conflict of this century notwithstanding, the region and its identity have far more often been the objects of admiration than of the scorn suffered by the Northeast. Like Saowanee's and McCargo's chapter on the Northeast, Tanet Charoenmuang's chapter on the North in the year after the coup also addresses apparent quiescence during that period. "Why was there so little resistance to the coup?", he asks. "Why were there so few Red Shirt protests", contrary to expectations shaped by the levels of organization and activity previously evident in Northern Thailand?

Tanet's exceedingly well-informed answers to these questions open up a novel perspective on the course of Thailand's identity conflict. His chapter argues that, to be sure, a robust Red Shirt identity with a strong regionalist or Lanna element emerged out of the turmoil that affected Thailand from 2005 onwards. However, despite considerable activity in support of the Yingluck government during the period of PDRC protests against it, at neither the national nor regional nor local level did Northern Red Shirts develop the bases for effective resistance to the dictatorship that NCPO rule brought to Thailand. The ability to hold demonstrations in Bangkok was one thing, but Tanet's fieldwork in the North revealed a Red Shirt failure in the period before the coup "to strengthen local democracy or to address the country's backward structural arrangements". This failure both explains the lack of effective or widespread resistance to the NCPO junta and highlights the means that parties to Thailand's identity conflict must be prepared to adopt in order to fight their corner.

Elements in the Malay-Muslim population of Patani, in the Lower South of Thailand, have repeatedly taken up arms to fight their own corner, in what is arguably the most dramatic and tragic manifestation of identity conflict that the country has witnessed in modern times.[12] McCargo has referred to the renewed violence that has scarred the region since the first years of the present century and to the fumbling search for a solution — whether military or political — to armed conflict there as a "play within a play" (McCargo 2012a, p. 4). The geographical setting of the Patani conflict is on the far periphery of the country, in provinces along the Thai-Malaysian border that only a tiny proportion of the inhabitants of Bangkok have ever visited or will ever visit. But that conflict has, McCargo notes, long centred on the very same questions that the political struggles at the national level have made pressing in the past decade and a half. "[W]hat is the basis of the country's legitimacy?" How does that legitimacy relate to the interplay of the national identity — of putatively shared and homogenous "Thainess" — on the one hand and the range of in fact "disparate identities" so evident in the country on the other (McCargo 2012*a*, p. 5)?

In tracing efforts to pursue a formal peace dialogue on Patani with the facilitation of Malaysia from the time of the Yingluck government, Rungrawee Chalermsripinyorat's chapter in this volume addresses the conflict in Thailand's Deep South in a fresh and fruitful way. Perhaps surprisingly, the NCPO dictatorship opted to continue attempts at dialogue initiated by the government that its coup had toppled in May 2014. But Rungrawee's account of those attempts and of the difficulties with which they met underlines the extent to which disparate identities could remain a source of conflict rather than a welcome mark of vibrancy or a prod to adaptation. While the perpetrators of violence against the Thai state in the region did not make for easy negotiating partners, the NCPO revealed nervousness and defensiveness bordering on desperation in its reluctance even to call those partners by a proper name. Similarly, its skittishness about potentially constructive foreign involvement in a matter touching on national identity and claims to unity, along with its fear that meaningful devolution of administrative authority might pose a challenge to that presumed unity, suggested the fragility of its outlook and perhaps of the order in which that outlook was grounded.

Identities may serve as vessels for interests, and the media as channels for the expression of interests by means short of conflict. In the wake of the seizure of state power on the part of a faction of the Thai military in 1991 and its violent but futile attempt to perpetuate its hold on power after elections the following year, Thailand embarked on a programme of media reform and liberalization. That programme held out the promise of a plural, more open, media sector — one conducive to the constructive expression of diverse interests in society. Aim Sinpeng and Wimonsiri Hemtanon explain the frustration of the reforms of the 1990s, due not least to the economic pressures on the sector in which the Asian Financial Crisis of 1997 resulted. The *coups d'état* of 2006 and 2014 only intensified the political pressure to which Thaksin Shinawatra had submitted the Thai media during his 2001–6 premiership. They ushered in what Aim and

Wimonsiri characterize as a return of military influence over the media. The same period saw another development on which these scholars place particular emphasis, the deepening partisanship of the media. Their chapter argues that that partisanship extended to the country's burgeoning social media sector. That sector became a significant arena for political conflict, albeit an arena in which the 2007 Computer-Related Crime Act and enforcement of the law on *lèse majesté* served to repress free expression. For both the traditional media and social media, the NCPO dictatorship proved particularly repressive.

The account of thwarted reform, renewed repression and stark partisanship of the Thai media that Aim and Wimonsiri offer exemplifies the vicious cycle in which Thailand has found itself since just after the turn of the century. The impulse to repress the media underlines, again, post-coup governments' recognition of the fragility of the long-established socio-political order in the country. At the same time, the partisanship that has come to define Thailand's media landscape makes clear the depth of the divides in which identity conflicts have resulted. Those divides mean that, rather than embodying the dynamic features of a plural order, Thai media have become, in Aim's and Wimonsiri's telling, weaponized.

In treating another example of frustrated reform and missed opportunity to prevent difference from giving rise to conflict, Viengrat Nethipo tells a strikingly similar story. The measures taken in the area of administrative decentralization to the provincial, municipal and sub-district (*tambon*) levels following the promulgation of Thailand's 1997 constitution introduced a fundamental modification of the bureaucratic, colonial-model regime of territorial control that had long defined Thai life.[13] Inevitably, then, it triggered a campaign of counter-decentralization, one that seemed to culminate in the policies adopted by the NCPO dictatorship.[14]

But the account of Thailand's decentralization in Viengrat's chapter includes another crucial element. In the face of the manifestly differing interests of provincial Thais and many Bangkokians, and in the context of historical patterns of clientelism in the politics of the Thai provinces, decentralization had a potential akin to that of media reform. In taking decision-making and resources out of the hands of officials dispatched from the capital and giving local power brokers an opening to enter formal politics at the sub-district or provincial level, it embodied a chance to reduce the grievances of the residents of the provinces and to head off conflict over resources. In the event, as Viengrat argues, the effect was rather different. Impelling provincial people to take an active interest in politics, decentralization complemented the policies of Prime Minister Thaksin in making those people feel like citizens rather than subjects. It thus pitched them into the national political conflict rooted over Thai identity and the place in the Thai order of people with disparate identities.

Both Aim's and Wimonsiri's analysis of partisanship in the Thai media and Viengrat's explanation of administrative reform's role in the creation of partisan citizens confirm that the impetus for the conflicts into which this century has plunged Thailand long predate the period since 2001. They point to cleavages long fudged, papered over or suppressed.

In contrast to those contributors, Surachart Bamrungsuk treats the absence of reform, but his chapter also points to the duration of identity conflict. Thailand's leading scholar of what would in other contexts be called civil-military relations, Surachart contextualizes the aftermath of the May 2014 coup both in a saga of the country's interminable failure to introduce military reform and in a contemporary period of dramatic social transformation. The challenge of what his chapter calls "the changing relationship among elites, the middle class and the masses" that defines this period accounts for the Thai Army's defensive recourse to an integralist, depoliticizing vision. It also makes all the more anachronistic the persistent lack of military professionalism and of subordination of the armed forces to civilian control in Thailand. This persistence undergirds more than just the politicization of the Thai military and the repeated political interventions on its part that Surachart chronicles. It also explains the army's status as one more among the identity groups in conflict in Thailand, and thus exposes the cynical and self-serving nature of the NCPO dictatorship's early, failed programme of depoliticization.

Since the late 1950s, it has been impossible to assess the political role of the Thai military, or its pursuit of its interests, without reference to its partnership with the Thai monarchy. In the four decades following King Bhumibol's intervention in the events of October 1973, the palace served as the senior partner in what was the most important relationship in Thai politics. But Paul Chambers and Napisa Waitoolkiat have argued that, by 2006 and the years thereafter, "the balance in the relationship" showed signs of change and that, in the aftermath of the 2014 coup, that change was unmistakable (Chambers and Napisa 2016, pp. 434, 438, 439).

We must understand this change against the backdrop of two factors. One is the long final illness of the late king, along with the advanced age of the palace's indispensable agent Privy Council Chairman Prem Tinsulanon (Chambers and Napisa 2016, pp. 436, 438).[15] The other is the surfacing of identity conflict in Thai society from the early years of the present century. While it predated these developments, the army's introduction of a slogan in the late 1990s that stressed its own direct commitment to "the people" aligned well with its transition from a previously subordinate position in its partnership with the palace.[16] Whether King Vajiralongkorn's consolidation of his grip on the monarchy, and perhaps on the Thai military and state, would bring yet another transition in the relationship has remained an important question.[17]

Thongchai Winichakul's chapter in this volume allows us to appreciate the stakes in changes in the decades-old partnership of monarchy and military. He begins the chapter by noting the astonishing persistence of conventional understandings of Thai politics grounded in the naïve idea "that democratization is the struggle against the military to entrench the supremacy of elections and civilian rule". He holds that this understanding misapprehends the long-term reality in the country of "a form of guided democracy" in which the functioning of the monarchy as a politically active "power bloc" has vitiated the substance of electoral rule. Terming this regime type "royal democracy", Thongchai argues that it rests on the transmogrification of a programme of ideological hegemony that Thai monarchists began to craft in the late 1940s as a means of counter-revolution against the toppling of the absolute monarchy on 24 June 1932. The result of that transmogrification was, from the 1970s onward, a pervasive "public culture" of "hyper-royalism" (Thongchai 2016). Along with the media and the law on *lèse majesté*, the military, the bureaucracy, the judiciary, the Privy Council, the Crown Property Bureau and — Thongchai pointedly notes — important elements of civil society and non-governmental organizations have served as the buttresses of royal democracy in Thailand.

Even had that political form not depended on the ambiguous fusion of monarch, in the person of King Bhumibol, and monarchy, what Thongchai calls "a changing society and changing political demography" would have thrown royal democracy into the "predicament" that it faced by the last years of the late sovereign's life. The earliest phase of King Vajiralongkorn's reign has, ironically, confronted that political order with a challenge of a very different sort, in the form of starker, more open assertions of royal power than were the norm in his father's time. The NCPO junta has complied with those assertions of power, whose effect may, Thongchai writes, be "to drop the cloak of democracy and to show the face of a semi-monarchical kingdom more openly".

Thongchai questions the viability of such a regime. The years ahead may put his scepticism to the test, for the start of the new reign has already begun to give the Thai monarchy a very different identity. Events such as the new king's 28 July birthday may continue to see recourse to forms of official and quasi-official public celebration that his father's long reign made familiar. Nevertheless, abrupt change in the institutional identity of the monarchy has, for many observers — even in royalist circles — proved arresting in its unfamiliarity. It does not simply exceed the change in which both very different times and the personal differences between, say, a sovereign who did not leave his kingdom for the last half-century of his life and reign (Crossette 1989) and one who appears to live mainly in Bavaria would necessarily result. In many respects it suggests a determination to repudiate 24 June 1932 and to restore royal absolutism in the management of at least some domains of Thai affairs.[18] These suggestions run in the opposite direction to the evolution in institutional identity that not only changing times but also the examples of the European monarchies that successive Chakri monarchs have sought, at least superficially, to emulate would lead one to expect. Or was that expectation naïve all along?

It is not in any case clear that royal agency or the state of the partnership between palace and military deserve the greatest weight among factors shaping our ideas about the place of monarchy in the Thailand of the future. Well before Vajiralongkorn's reign began, the identity conflicts that had come to the surface in Thailand had already undermined the carefully constructed royal hegemony of the decades since Bhumibol acceded to the throne after the tragic death of his brother Ananda Mahidol in 1946. "Anonymous" has argued that, particularly after the military seizure of power in Bangkok in September 2006, it was the longstanding hegemony of Thai royalism itself that engendered on the Red side of the country's identity divide a sense of betrayal of the expectations of relations between the monarchy and its subjects. Resultant expressions of anti-royalism thus drew with bitter sarcasm on motifs historically employed and invoked to celebrate King Bhumibol (Anonymous 2018).

While not so intense in either substance or expression, a comparable effect was evident in foreign press coverage of the Thai monarchy during the same period. That press had long subscribed to an understanding of the monarchy and its putatively benevolent, modernizing role that essentially reflected royal hegemony in the country. It projected that understanding internationally and thus helped to propagate a version of Thai national identity very much to the liking of elites in Bangkok. In fact, awareness of foreign admiration for King Bhumibol and the Thai monarchy powerfully reinforced confidence at home in that hegemony and in the social and political order that it structured.

In 1988, the active and distinguished Foreign Correspondents Club of Thailand confirmed the prominence, and the largely positive treatment, of Bhumibol and his activities in the international press with the release of a collection of articles that had appeared across the decades (Gray, Everingham and Wrigley 1988). That volume, *The King of Thailand in World Focus*, appeared in the year of grand celebrations to mark Bhumibol's becoming the longest reigning monarch in Thai history. As Puangthong Pawakapan notes in her contribution to this book, two decades later, the year after even grander celebrations of Bhumibol's completion of six decades on the throne, the club released a second, updated edition of the book (Gray and Faulder 2007). But times had changed. Foreign journalists in Bangkok were now in direct contact with Thais of a wider range of identities and backgrounds, in a more complex society, than in the past. They had read former *Far Eastern Economic Review* Bangkok correspondent Paul Handley's "landmark" 2006 biography of Bhumibol (Handley 2006). Professional responsibility alone meant that their coverage captured the partisan role of the monarchy and of royalist elites in the political conflict that had overtaken the country in the new century. The result was a rather decisive change in treatment of Thailand's most important institution and of its leading figure in the foreign press — a change that, Puangthong suggests, had a substantial impact on understandings of Thailand in foreign capitals.

In a short recent essay "On the Thai Monarchy" published in the prestigious, traditionalist *Journal of the Siam Society*, William Klausner reminds us that the long reign of the late king saw monarch and monarchy come to shape Thai identity on many levels at the same time. He argues that, even posthumously, Bhumibol "remains an integral part of each individual Thai identity and of the national identity" (Klausner 2018, p. 317).[19] To resort to clumsy phrasing, a comparable effect long served in the definition of

Thailand's "international identity", too. By October 2016, however, that latter effect had long since faded, as Puangthong makes clear.[20] Both for Thais and for the swelling numbers of non-Thais who claim an interest or stake in the country, the emergence of "Bangkok as a globalized city" (Baker 2016, p. 402) and the parallel globalization of "Thainess" and of contests over its meaning are destined to have the strongest effect in defining the country's international identity in the future.

Klausner's essay omits all mention of King Vajiralongkorn, or Rama X. Instead, its final sentence looks ahead by referring to the late King Bhumibol and by averring, "It may be expected that more than a few Thais will develop future strategies to assure that they will continue to remain under King Rama IX's protection and beneficence" (Klausner 2018, p. 317). As we look ahead to both the short- and long-term future of Thailand in this volume, some of the tests that such future strategies will face are clear.

At the time of writing, political actors in Thailand were increasingly focused on the prospect of long-delayed parliamentary elections in the first half of 2019. Oddly enough, this included even actors who rated the odds that palace, army or some combination of the two would in fact not allow voters to go to the polls at greater than even.

The emerging picture was not one of successful depoliticization, plausible integralism or even remotely viable praetorian tutelage. Instead, a 2017 constitution designed to produce a lower house of parliament with members drawn from numerous medium-sized parties (Prajak 2018, p. 365) looked likely to result in the sort of messy electoral contests that characterized Thailand during most of the final two decades of the twentieth century. Charges of official pressure on former members of parliament to sign on with a party that would serve, either officially or on a de facto basis, as an electoral vehicle supporting General Prayut's retention of the premiership were just one reminder that messiness could easily fade into grubbiness rather than embody vibrancy (*Bangkok Post*, 31 July 2018).

Prajak Kongkirati has traced the performance and fates of "military parties" in Thailand since they first emerged in the 1950s. He notes the historical correlation between those parties' presence on the electoral landscape and "unfree and unfair" polls (Prajak 2018, p. 374). The constraints that the NCPO placed on the August 2016 referendum on the current constitution (Chookiat 2017, p. 357) suggested that this correlation was worth bearing in mind in the run-up to elections in 2019. Prajak also notes the political clumsiness and poor party discipline that have characterized military parties in the past, along with Thai soldiers' record of electoral "misconduct and manipulation" and the popular dissent that these have provoked (Prajak 2018, p. 374). Historical precedent thus suggested that efforts to secure the premiership for General Prayut or perhaps for another member of the NCPO junta following coming elections were a recipe for instability rather than quiescence.

The situation was striking. The junta had enjoyed a long period of total political control. It had armed itself with a constitution that would give an upper house of its own choosing a role in selecting the next prime minister (Prajak 2018, p. 364). It could impose severe and arbitrary constraints on parties and campaigning. Nevertheless, it found itself nervously confronting the unpredictability of electoral politics. This outcome made both the depoliticizing pretensions of its early days in power and its determination to impose a legally binding Twenty-Year National Strategy on the country (Pongphisoot 2018, p. 347) appear slightly absurd.

But impressions of absurdity were misleading. The political climate in mid-2018 Thailand remained sinister. The dictatorship had not stepped back from repression and petty intimidation. This conduct was almost certain to continue, and perhaps to grow in intensity, as campaigning began and polls drew nearer. Also sinister was the authorities' persistent lack of interest in getting to the bottom of the mysterious disappearance in April 2017 of a plaque commemorating the replacement of the absolute monarchy with a constitutional order in 1932. At the time of its disappearance, that plaque had been embedded in the Royal Plaza (*lan phrarup*) in Bangkok's Dusit district for eight decades (Murdoch 2017). Its theft underlined that among the many dimensions of Thailand's identity conflict numbered the divide between those who viewed elections as a basis for political legitimacy and popular sovereignty and those who viewed them as a merely formal and perhaps troublesome exercise in political legitimation.

In his chapter in the present volume, Prajak makes clear the threat that Thailand's identity conflict poses to the legacy of 1932 and the vision of popular sovereignty with which many in the country, of all walks of life, have increasingly come to invest that legacy in very explicit ways. The chapter examines the relationship between violence and electoral politics since the 1970s. It argues that, while "the royal-military alliance" used state violence against those who challenged its ideological hegemony in the middle years of that decade, the following thirty years saw the "privatization" of violence as tool for use among competitors for election to parliament. The change in patterns of political violence in Thailand was a significant one.

But not, perhaps, a lasting one. Like "Anonymous", Puangthong and others, Prajak sees 2006 as a watershed year in the story of Thailand's troubles. Thereafter, his chapter observes, ideological factors again accounted for patterns of political violence in Thailand. The Thai military used substantial force to suppress Red Shirt protests in April and May of 2010. Clashes and confrontations on streets of Bangkok, involving elements on both the Red and Yellow sides of the country's political divide, occurred in the second half of 2008, in April 2009 and in late 2013 and the first half of 2014. Supplanting narrow political rivalries as a source of violence, Thailand's broad identity conflict became an often bloody struggle in the past dozen years. Dwelling on the violence that characterized the PDRC's disruption of the national elections of February 2014, Prajak terms the group's and its supporters' "animosity towards the elections ... an unprecedented development", one that "broke apart the peaceful and democratic means by which the public could decide who had the right to govern". With the coup that soon followed, this development leads him to express a fear of political violence in Thailand, "possibly for years to come".

Prajak's worries call attention, again, to the failure of NCPO efforts to impose a sustainable state of solitude or quiescence on the country. Further, if the right of the governed to select those who will govern does indeed become an issue of long-term future concern, it will join other issues of importance whose resolution will determine the future of Thailand.

This volume does not include, unfortunately, a chapter on Thailand's relationship with the People's Republic of China. But Porphant Ouyyanont's contribution to the volume and that of Kwanchit Sasiwongsaroj and Youngyut Burasit examine a pair of issues that, like that relationship, will shape the future of Thailand by shaping the individual and collective identities of Thais and in fact the national identity itself.

The sustained "boom" that Thailand knew in the years after 1985 resulted in "a different country" — in "the politics, the social changes, and the popular culture" (Pasuk and Baker 1998, p. 1). Even more than the 1997 "bust" that brought the period to an end and prepared the ground for the ensuing rise of Thaksin Shinawatra, the boom years represent the essential background to the identity conflict that has grown so sharp and so evident in the present century. They remain central to the way that many in Thailand see themselves and their compatriots and expect themselves and their country to be seen by the rest of the world.

Porphant's chapter addresses Thailand's transition to slower economic growth after 1997. The country has historically relied on low-cost labour. Scholars, observers and stakeholders have for decades recognized its failures in the area of human capital development.[21] The role of these realities in making Thailand "one of the most unequal societies in Asia" (Pasuk and Baker 2016, p. 1), not least in the context of the transformation of a largely agricultural economy to one focussed on manufacturing and especially services, are unsurprising. But inequality has also set the stage for conflict. Both, on one side, "pattern[s] of privilege" — to recall Thorn's and Chanon's chapter in this volume — and, on the other, the belief that one lacks access to "good education, a fair trial, and a decent chance in life" (Pasuk and Baker 2016, p. 1) have proved constitutive of identities in Thailand. Complementing Saowanee's and McCargo's chapter and also Tanet's, Porphant calls attention to the regional dimension of inequality in the country. To use a term now very much in vogue on American university campuses, identity divides in Thailand exemplify "intersectionality"; that is, indeed, the point of Ferrara's emphasis on identity conflict.

Porphant notes an additional factor in the pattern of slow growth that has come to define the Thai economy. While he does not refer explicitly to fears that Thailand has fallen into the "middle-income trap", with all the implications for stagnation and frustrated expectations that that fate might bring, he shares with many students of the contemporary Thai economy[22] a concern with a lack of the technological innovation necessary to improve its competitiveness.

This concern and those relating to the labour force notwithstanding, Porphant is relatively sanguine about Thailand's adjustment to a period of slower growth. Tourism and other service sectors continue to hold much promise. "Structural change in Thai agriculture", a transition to higher value-added in the sector and diversification of the rural economy more generally give him confidence in the future. So, too, does the promise of increased cross-border trade associated with ASEAN Economic Community. By definition, peripheral parts of Thailand are destined to play a leading role in that trade. And scholars have for some years called attention to the emergence of the "cosmopolitan villagers", "middle-class peasants" and "urbanized villagers" of Thailand's new lower middle class in which the diversification to which Porphant refers has resulted (Keyes 2014; Walker

2012; Naruemon and McCargo 2011). Even in an era of slower growth in the national economy, the dynamism of provincial Thai economies has important implications for socio-economic change and the evolution of identities.

Porphant's sanguine outlook extends even to Thailand's low rates of human fertility, which, he avers, will drive wages up, impel greater use of capital in the farm sector and lead to increased per capita investment in the education of children. Kwanchit Sasiwongsaroj's and Youngyut Burasit's chapter paints a less rosy picture of demographic trends in Thailand. In clear and sobering detail, its authors chart the range of challenges with which rapid ageing will present the country. Most importantly, they call attention to the interaction of the rapid growth of the proportion of Thais aged more than sixty-five years and a number of other developments.

These developments include the range of healthcare and welfare policies, some targeting the elderly, introduced by various Thai governments in the past quarter-century.

Those policies and the demand that they meet put Thaksinite "populism" and the inability of subsequent anti-Thaksinite governments to reverse the associated policies into valuable perspective. Of course, the costs of such policies, and thus the impact of rapid ageing on the Thai economy, will only mount. Other relevant developments include, inevitably, disparities in services available to elderly people in rural and urban Thailand and changing values and family structures in Thai society.

In the simplest terms, Thailand will, like today's Japan, be a very different — and perhaps less vibrant — place when fewer and fewer of its people are young, and as the fiscal burden of caring for greater and greater numbers of elderly people mounts. This difference will affect Thais' understanding of their society and their sense of the possible. In addition to its broad impact on individual, collective and national identities, it will also — as Kwanchit's and Youngyut's vivid chapter makes clear — shape the stakes in conflicts and compromises in the Thai political order.

In the concluding chapter of this volume, Terence Chong makes the invaluable point that Thailand has not reached an "end of history". Neither the sinister putsch announced to members of Thailand's political class at the Army Club on 22 May 2014, the death of King Bhumibol at Siriraj Hospital on the Thonburi bank of the Chao Phraya River on 13 October two years later, the coming official coronation rites for King Vajiralongkorn nor the elections anticipated for some time in 2019 will have been able to reconcile the forces that have stirred Thailand during this century. More importantly, none of these events could "freeze" or stabilize those forces. Like the identities with which they are interwoven, and like "Thai" identity itself, they will remain in flux.

Serhat Ünaldi, author of the striking *Working towards the Monarchy: The Politics of Space in Downtown Bangkok* (Ünaldi 2016*b*), considers "inevitable ... the emergence of a political system that gives expression to the demands and aspirations of the Thai people rather than those of the select few" (Ünaldi 2016*a*, p. 318). Federico Ferrara himself largely shares this Whig view of contemporary Thai history, rooted in "ongoing socio-economic change", the waning effectiveness of state repression and "the rise of ... [an] alternative, 'counterhegemonic' vision of the nation's structure and future" to which "a solid plurality of the electorate" subscribes (Ferrara 2015, p. 276). His faith in modernization strong, Ferrara emphasizes the lack of fit between "the country's diversity and ongoing social change" (Ferrara 2015, p. 270).

After the Coup parts ways with these scholars, but not because its contributors or we editors necessarily take issue with their scholarship, their hopes or even their conclusions. Rather, it is because the volume is not an exercise in soothsaying. Terence Chong, Mark Heng and I have sought here simply to offer readers concerned with the future of Thailand an understanding of the realities and possibilities that will shape that future. Not least, that future will emerge from the unfolding of conflicts over identity. We present the chapters that follow, prepared by a distinguished group of Thai intellectuals, with confidence that they offer perspectives on those conflicts that will prove stimulating, enlightening and useful.

Notes

1. This implicit "Army-people mutuality" (Montesano 2015, p. 10) appeared in the period after the 2014 coup to represent a challenge to the established, similarly integralist, Thai concept of *ratchaprachasamasai* or "king-people mutuality" whose importance the work of Michael Connors has so fruitfully recognized; see, for example, Connors (2008). This newer variant of mutuality thus epitomized what appeared to be the aspirational praetorianism of the NCPO junta at that time.

2. It is important to note that these corporatist and depoliticizing urges, with their integralist and even *völkisch* conception of "the people", were by no means confined to the Thai military. Suthep Thaugsuban invoked a strikingly

similar vision, centred on "the great mass of the people" (*muanmahaprachachon*), in leading the demonstrations against the government of Prime Minister Yingluck Shinawatra that culminated in the NCPO putsch. See, for example, *The Sunday Nation* (2014) and Nidhi (2013*b*).

3. See Montesano (2016).

4. Also see Ferrara (2015, pp. 263ff.).

5. See Sandhu (1986, p. iii).

6. That is, *Khanakammakan prachachon phuea kanplianplaeng prathet thai hai pen prachathippatai thi sombun an mi phramahakasat songpen pramuk* (literally, "the people's committee for the transformation of Thailand into a total democracy with the king as head of state").

7. On the contemporary Thai lower middle class, also see Naruemon and McCargo (2011).

8. See Askew (2008, pp. 52ff.).

9. Keyes (1967) pioneered this study; he surveys long-term developments in Isan in Keyes (2014). Kamala (1997), Dararat (2003), Pattana (2012) and Platt (2013) are also particularly enlightening.

10. This Isan identity is one that has long since ceased to be strictly rural or even provincial; witness its centrality to the make-up of working- and lower-middle-class Bangkok. Naruemon and McCargo (2011, pp. 7, 15–16) call attention to the increasing blurriness of the urban-rural divide, as it applies not only to the population of the Thai capital but also to major provincial centres.

11. See, for example, Easum (2013, esp. pp. 213ff.).

12. See Surin (1985) and McCargo (2008).

13. On the origins of this regime, see Tej (1977).

14. In fact, Viengrat paints a more complicated picture, in which the junta's National Reform Council (*sapha patirup haeng chat*) actually harboured a pro-centralization faction. This wrinkle highlights the extremely ambiguous nature of the reformism behind the 1997 constitution; see McCargo (1998).

15. On General Prem's long-term role as the central node in Thailand's "network monarchy", see McCargo (2005).

16. Also see Chambers and Napisa (2016, p. 441n4).

17. See McCargo (2018).

18. For a discussion of this development as it relates to Buddhism, see Khemthong (2018), and, on control of the Crown Property Bureau, see Reuters (2017) and Associated Press (2018).

19. In a recent article on the Thai television drama *Bupphesanniwat*, Patrick Jory addresses the possibility that members of Thailand's urban upper middle and middle classes may be coming implicitly to distinguish their continued loyalty to the monarchy as an institution or as an idea from their loyalty to "their kings" as individuals. At the same time, he suggests, they may be refocusing

their "moral yearnings ... away from the monarchy [and] towards a more religiously-inclined nationalism" (Jory 2018, pp. 453–54).

20. In another striking illustration of this revised understanding, and of the fact that the prominence of its monarchy had come to reflect negatively rather than positively on Thailand's national identity, a recent overview of Indonesian politics since the fall of Soeharto's New Order refers casually and in an utterly matter-of-fact way to "the kingdom's infamous *lèse majesté* laws" (Davidson 2018, p. 3).

21. See Sirilaksana (1993).

22. See, for example, Patarapong (2018).

2

The Rise of the Thai Upper Middle Class and its Turn against Democracy

Thorn Pitidol and Chanon Techasunthornwat

The upper middle class, the social group between the upper class and the lower middle class, comprises mainly professionals, senior-level employees of firms and business-owners.[1] This class has contributed in crucial ways to Thailand's current political crisis. Taking active roles in the People's Alliance for Democracy (PAD) movement of 2005–8 and in the People's Democratic Reform Committee (PDRC) movement of 2013–14, its members opposed former prime minister Thaksin Shinawatra and his political allies. While they claimed to be struggling for a more substantive form of democracy, they in fact contributed to the Thai military's return to power, and they have since become the main support base for the current military regime in Thailand. One can therefore raise crucial questions about the political stance of the Thai upper middle class, and especially about the emergence of its members' antagonistic perception of electoral democracy, and the conditions that have influenced this perception.

This chapter undertakes two major tasks. The first task is to pursue a quantitative analysis of socio-economic data to describe the development of the Thai upper middle class. The goal is to place this development in the broader context of Thai society and to understand the group's socio-economic characteristics in order to provide insight into the conditions that have shaped the Thai upper middle class's attitudes towards democracy. The second task of this chapter is to build on that insight. The chapter draws on interviews with fifteen members of the Thai upper middle class, all older than fifty years of age, and selected to represent various segments of that class. In-depth interviews with these respondents covered the trajectories of their lives and the development of their political perspectives in the changing socio-economic context. The goal was to understand conditions that have influenced their turn against democracy.

The chapter begins by contextualizing the shifting political stance of the Thai upper middle class with a literature review that sets the scope of the chapter's investigation. It then offers a quantitative socio-economic analysis of the rise of the Thai upper middle class from the 1980s to the present. A qualitative examination of the lives and political perspectives of the Thai upper middle class follows that quantitative analysis.

The main argument of the chapter is that the fundamental trans-formation of the Thai upper middle class occurred in the 1980s. It was between the mid-1980s and the mid-1990s that the members of that class experienced a rapid increase in their economic status, and that they were thus able to solidify their position as an upper middle class. It was also during the 1980s, especially under the semi-democratic regime of Prem Tinsulanon, that the Thai upper middle class formed its attachment to authoritarianism. This attachment arose through its members' adoption of a normative vision that prioritized order, morality and royalism in Thai politics. The perception that the conditions proposed in this vision were under threat, especially from the political changes that accompanied the premiership of Thaksin Shinawatra, drove the eventual turn of members of the Thai upper middle class against democracy.

The Thai Middle Class and Democracy

Having once viewed the Thai upper middle class as a positive force for democratization, scholars now perceive that class as an ally of authoritarianism. Before the rise of the Thai lower middle class to its current position of social and political influence during the first decade of this century, the Thai upper middle class was known simply as "the middle class". Benedict Anderson saw this old "middle class" in the mid-1970s as one with a deep sense of insecurity, one whose members were willing to resort to undemocratic and violent means to counter perceived threats to their newly attained economic status (Anderson 1977, pp. 17–18). In the mid-1990s, a different perception of the middle class emerged. The Thai middle class was heralded for its role in the 1992 protests against the military rule, and perceived as a force for Thai democracy. Anek Laothamatas's seminal work, "A Tale of Two Democracies" (1996), exemplified this portrayal. With Thailand apparently moving away from authoritarianism at the time, Anek argued that the Thai middle class was a leading player in the country's democratization and portrayed the middle class as a progressive force that utilized Western forms of political engagement with the government and other institutions. It prioritized policies, ideologies and the morality and competence of politicians over paternalistic politics. This picture of the middle class contrasted with the portrayal of another key group in Thailand's apparently emerging democracy of the time: rural dwellers who were, according to Anek, deeply rooted in "patron-client" relations and beholden to elected representatives who could reciprocate their own and their families' support. Anek argued that, in order for Thai democracy to mature, the Thai middle class should have more influence in shaping national politics and electing governments.

Anek may have been guilty of painting too positive a picture of the Thai middle class, no doubt in the context of the political developments of the mid-1990s. Even in that same context, other scholars remained unconvinced of the potential of the Thai middle class to serve as a force for democracy. In the view of these scholars, what that class desired was not democracy. Its members actually wanted freedom to pursue their business activities (Preecha 1993, p. 84), and they prioritized political stability as a means of protecting their economic interests (Voravidh 1993, p. 139). Moreover, the middle class also saw itself as allied to the monarchy and the aristocracy. Its members would not side with the lower classes in demanding equality in political rights (Nidhi 1993, pp. 62–64; Ockey 2001, p. 329).

Interestingly, in another study of the Thai middle class of this earlier era, published in 1993, Anek had himself raised questions about the potential of the Thai middle class to serve as force for democracy. He had argued that the excitement of some scholars in the wake of the middle-class uprising against the military in the early 1990s had led them to overlook the fact that, prior to those events, the Thai middle class had also been supportive of the military in its attempts to take power (Anek 1993, p. 43). Furthermore, Anek had asserted that the Thai middle class had a limited commitment to democracy since its members remained dissatisfied with the imperfections of Thai democracy, especially the dysfunctionality of politicians and of the parliamentary system (ibid., p. 44). As time passed, it was likely that the Thai middle class would turn against democratic government again and that it would thus open the way for the military to come back to power (ibid., p. 44).

Thailand's political development from the mid-1990s onward seems to have justified Anek's 1993 warning against taking the democratic potential of the Thai middle class for granted. From the mid-2000s, as the old middle class became an upper middle class, its members were propelled by their discontent with Thaksin Shinawatra to follow a path that took them further and further away from support for democracy. They attributed their opposition to Thaksin and his political allies to his abuse of power and to his alleged corruption. Thai intellectuals who defended as democratic the agenda of mass movements against Thaksin, even after those movements began to oppose democratic elections, claimed that the Thai upper middle class sought to promote substantive democracy by limiting the power of the majority and of elected governments (see, for example, Surin 2013).

However, a more balanced assessment of the Thai upper middle class's political stance since the mid-2000s would note that it had actually turned its back on the basic principles of democracy. Both the PAD and PDRC movements had numerous aspects that one cannot reconcile with democracy. They mobilized nationalist and royalist politics as crucial means to arouse opposition to Thaksin and attempted to delegitimize and disrupt the most fundamental process of democracy, elections.[2] Their leaders openly rejected the electoral rights of the rural poor.[3] Most importantly, the Thai upper middle class's acceptance of and support for the military regime installed by the coup of 22 May 2014 provides adequate evidence to counter any claim that its members have been striving for any form of democracy.

The latest portrayal of the Thai upper middle class in the face of the country's changing political context is that of a group whose members distrust democracy and yearn for authoritarianism. Furthermore, by the mid-2000s, it was no longer possible to sustain Anek's 1996 depiction of Thai politics as characterized by a division between rural dwellers and the urban middle class. One would do better in this context to see Thai politics as comprised of a division between the two middle classes, consisting of the "upper middle class" and the "lower middle class".

The entry of many rural dwellers into the ranks of the "lower middle class" (Apichat et al. 2013, p. 144) explains how the divide between the rural and urban became less important than that between the upper middle and the lower middle classes. It is no longer possible to see Thai rural society as "backward" or "enclosed", because significant parts of it have integrated with urban society, as rural dwellers migrate either temporarily or permanently to urban areas in search of work opportunities. This rural–urban migration has not only increased the wealth of rural dwellers but also transformed the character of urban spaces. Meanwhile, farmers have also diversified their sources of income, learned to be more entrepreneurial and have come to rely more on opportunities to earn money outside their proverbial villages (Nidhi 2013*a*; Rigg and Sakunee 2001, pp. 956–57; Walker 2012, p. 8).[4] The rise in the fortunes of these rural dwellers and their emergence as a new "lower middle class" have had a substantial impact on Thai politics and coincided with the support of members of that class for Thaksin Shinawatra and the Red Shirt movement.

The emergence of the Thai lower middle class also suggests that the importance of patron-client relations in Thai rural society has declined. The significance of Thaksin's pro-poor policies may be that lower-middle-class voters actually pay attention to policies at the national level. It may mean that they are not merely susceptible to largesse from local patrons, as the common portrayal has long had it (Apichat et al. 2013, p. 144; Walker 2012, p. 9). Yet those Thais whom scholars previously labelled as members of the middle class perceive the class transition affecting rural dwellers in negative terms. They have made a transition of their own, to become a new "upper middle class", many of whose members have also become the supporters of political parties and movements opposing Thaksin. The prolonged political crisis in the country has been due, to a significant degree, to the nature of the tensions between contemporary Thailand's two middle classes.

Existing Explanations for the Anti-Democratic Stance of the Thai Upper Middle Class

A growing number of countries across the world face a situation similar to Thailand's in seeing their middle classes turn against democracy. This phenomenon has posed a crucial challenge to the conventional perception, encapsulated in the so-called modernization approach that sees the rise of the middle class as conducive to democratization (Chen and Lu 2011, p. 706; Hattori et al. 2003, p. 129). Democratic crises in many countries have led to an alternative approach to explaining the relationship between the middle class and democracy, called the contingent approach (Rueschemeyer et al. 1992). This approach postulates that the orientation of the middle class towards democracy is in fact contingent upon a number of socio-political and socio-economic conditions. These conditions include, for example, the middle class's dependence on the state, the middle class's political alliances with other classes and the middle class's perception of its own well-being and of threats to its position.

The contingent approach is appropriate to explaining the political experience of Thailand. However, a clear understanding of the set of conditions that affect the relationship between the Thai upper middle class and democracy remains elusive. Existing literature on the issue is divided into two schools, each pointing to a different set of conditions. The first array of explanations puts the focus on the "squeezed" position of the Thai upper middle class; the second emphasizes the effect of its socio-economic success under authoritarianism.

A crucial insight into the first array of explanations for the relationship between the Thai upper middle class and democracy came from the prominent Thai historian and public intellectual Nidhi Eoseewong. In trying to explain the social origins of PAD and PDRC supporters, Nidhi argues that the "squeezed growing path" (*honthang toepto thi khapkhaep*) propelled the Thai upper middle class to a political stance of support for those movements. He adopts the notion of "marginal elites" (*chonchan nam chaikhop*) to explain this process, pointing out that the growth in the socio-economic status of the Thai upper middle class has been met with only limited opportunity to progress further upward. Nidhi explains that, despite the Thai upper middle class's having successfully achieved a rise in its levels of economic and educational attainment in recent decades, its members still cannot attain the advantages that the Thai elites possess. Those elites still hold or dictate access to high-ranking positions in the business sector, in the bureaucracy and even in the arts and literature. This situation causes the Thai upper middle class to feel "squeezed", as its members need to compete vigorously for limited chances to progress upward. Their frustrations over this position eventually led them to form or sign on to the PAD and the PDRC movements (Nidhi 2015).

Marc Saxer (2014a, 2014c) has offered a similar explanation. Saxer terms the position that the Thai upper middle class had to endure before turning against democracy as a "sandwiched position"; it faced abusive elites on one side and the newly emancipated lower middle class and politically transformed rural poor on another side (Saxer 2014a, p. 8). Although the class's members called for democratization to help protect themselves from elites, they also found themselves a minority under institutionalized democracy. The relationship between dominant politicians and their lower-middle-class and rural-poor power base marginalized the Thai upper middle class, causing its members to condemn that relationship as immoral and dangerous to the country. Its members condemn rural electorates as "the poor getting greedy" and criticize pro-poor policies as an attempt to "buy votes" from the uneducated poor (ibid., p. 8). They sided with elites in calling for the disenfranchisement of the perceived "uneducated poor", which would only be possible by suspending electoral democracy.

The second array of explanations for the relationship between the Thai upper middle class and democracy points to the growth of this class under authoritarian regimes as the factor leading to its members' attachment to authoritarianism today, and to their eventual turn against democracy (Attachak 2014; Ünaldi 2014b). Serhat Ünaldi explains that the growth of the Thai upper middle class under a developmental authoritarian regime led to its attachment to authoritarianism. This attachment to authoritarianism happened not only in Thailand. It also occurred in other Southeast Asian countries that followed a similar path, such as Indonesia (Ünaldi 2014b). Pushed by their disenchantment with corruption-prone democracy, the upper middle class in these countries feels nostalgic for the perceived good old days of effective authoritarianism. Its members' yearning for authoritarianism is rooted in the role of developmental regimes led by military dictators in fostering their current socio-economic status. More importantly, it was under authoritarian rule that the identities of members of the upper middle class were shaped. This experience eventually caused them to develop a "symbiotic relationship" with authoritarianism. Ünaldi argues that the attachment to authoritarianism of the upper middle class has had a more prominent effect when its members have confronted political change that enabled the lower classes to dominate democracy (ibid.). The upper middle class feels threatened by such change, and it becomes defensive and reactionary. In Thailand, its members have thus turned to a military regime to resist the change.

Both arrays of explanations share the perception that the increasingly dominant political role of the lower class was a catalyst that turned the Thai upper middle class against democracy. However, the first array points to the antithetical relationship between the upper middle class and Thai elites as a crucial contributing factor, while the second looks rather to the importance of an earlier past connection between upper middle class and authoritarianism. In the following two sections, the chapter provides further insight into the rise of the Thai upper middle class and its turn against democracy, through an exploration of empirical evidence. It also tries to evaluate the relevance of the different explanations, and to enrich the explanation that proves most relevant to the empirical data.

Describing the Rise of the Thai Upper Middle Class

This section applies quantitative analysis to provide insight into the rise of the Thai upper middle class. The section starts by explaining the data set used and the methodology applied to categorize the Thai upper middle class. It then depicts the manner in which the Thai upper middle class has, relative to other classes, including the lower middle class, expanded in the past three decades. In addition, the section sheds light on the changing geographical location, educational attainment and employment profile of members of the Thai upper middle class.

Data and Methodology

The empirical analysis in this study relies on the socio-economic survey (SES) data set collected by Thailand's National Statistical Office (NSO).[5] This data set was collected every five years starting in 1957, and then biennially from 1986; data have been collected annually since 2006. Each survey round asks more than ten thousand households for general demographic and socio-economic information. In addition to household-level information, every household member was also asked to specify such individual characteristics as gender, age, educational attainment and occupation. This study analyses the SES data set from 1981 to 2013. It breaks these years into seven periods, using data from eight survey rounds, in order to emphasize differences along the developmental path of the Thai upper middle class. Figure 2.1 describes the time periods and the sample sizes of the surveys in each period.

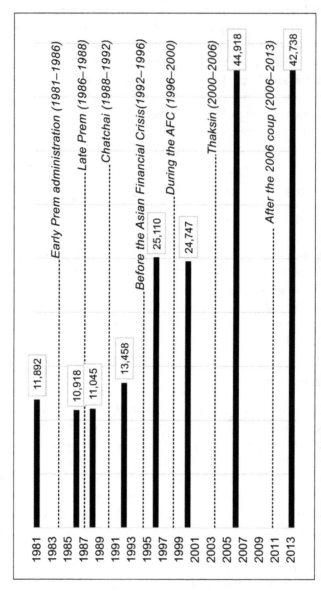

FIGURE 2.1 Sample size of Thai Socio-Economic Survey, 1981–2013 (selected rounds)

Source: Authors' calculation using the Thai SES data set.

Prior studies have proposed a variety of means to define the middle class. Funatsu and Kagoya (2003, p. 245) define the upper middle class as white-collar workers who are employed in professional, technical, administrative-managerial or non-routine clerical jobs. Chun (2010, p. 4) specifies the middle class as people with expenditures of US$2–US$20 per day, on a 2005 purchasing power parity basis. By the latter definition, 86 per cent of the Thai population belonged to the middle class in 2004.

Economic studies to identify the middle class use two main approaches, the relative and the absolute approach. The relative approach uses multiples of the median income as thresholds to identify the middle class. For example, Birdsall, Graham and Pettinato (2000, p. 3) identify the middle class as those who earn between 0.75 and 1.25 times the median income. The problem with this method is that the level of income of the middle class population in different countries may be very different. Cross-country comparison of the middle classes using this approach would be inappropriate (Ferreira et al. 2013, p. 31). Barro (1999) and Easterly (2001), on the other hand, identify the middle class using cut-off numbers based on income quintiles or deciles. The obvious downside of this method is that it enumerates a constant proportion of the population as middle class over time. This is not always the case in reality.

The absolute approach, on the other hand, is more commonly used in the economic literature. It overcomes the comparability problem posed by the relative approach. The absolute approach specifies the middle-class income threshold using a range of standardized international dollars, such as purchasing power parity. The absolute threshold method implicitly takes into account the poverty measurement by assuming that the middle class has a higher living standard than people living under the poverty line. Banerjee and Duflo (2008, p. 4) define the middle class as those households living with an expenditure per capita of US$2–US$10 a day. They illustrated the significantly different consumption, occupational and investment patterns that distinguish the middle class from the poor, who live on less than US$1 or US$2 a day.

To address concerns about the steady relative size of the middle class and about the arbitrary nature of absolute thresholds, this chapter employs a hybrid approach suggested by Birdsall (2010). This approach recognizes poverty as absolute but wealth as relative. The chapter combines the use of the relative measure of the ninety-fifth percentile in the income distribution as the upper bound to define the middle class with the use of the absolute poverty income threshold calculated by the National Economic and Social Development Board to define the lower bound. Specifically, 1.1 times the official poverty line is set to distinguish the poor and the middle-class population. This modification is less arbitrary because the rationale for setting the lower bound is based on the national poverty line.[6]

Furthermore, to sort the middle class into subgroups — that is, the upper and lower middle classes — the chapter subscribes to the hypothesis that the Thai middle classes are comprised of the upper, old rich or elite, class and the lower, emerging or working, middle class (Apichat et al. 2013, p. 36). The "k-means clustering" technique is employed to partition a sample into homogeneous subgroups (MacKay 2003). Table 2.1 reports the thresholds for each class, as determined by the value of its consumption. The next section explores the evolution of socio-economic aspects of the upper middle class over time.

The Rise of the Thai Upper Middle Class

Figure 2.2 shows that the number of Thais in both the lower and upper middle classes has increased over time, with the exception of the period of the Asian Financial Crisis of 1997 to 2000. This expansion has corresponded with a reduction in the incidence of poverty. By 2013, the Thai upper middle class accounted for 21 per cent of the total population, while the lower middle class accounted for 54 per cent.

The rate of growth of the upper middle class proved highest during the final two years of Prem Tinsulanon's administration (1980–88), when it grew by 11 per cent annually, and during the four years preceding the Asian Financial Crisis, when it grew by 10 per cent annually. After the recovery from the crisis, the growth rate of the upper middle class was moderate, at 6 per cent during 2000–2006. The rate has since declined further. This slower pattern of growth also characterizes the lower middle class, as poverty reduction had already been substantially achieved in Thailand by the early 2000s.

To examine the ways in which people in the upper middle class have built their fortunes since 1981, the analysis here focuses only on individuals born before 1967. This means that in 1981 they were fifteen years old or older and thus presumably capable of participating in the workforce. The prospect for economic advancement in their lives came mostly after 1981. Figure 2.3 charts an index of real monthly household

TABLE 2.1

Consumption thresholds (Thai baht, in 2013 values), 1981–2013

		1981	1986	1988	1992	1996	2000	2006	2013
Lowest class	Max	3,317	3,318	3,318	3,341	3,397	3,360	3,332	3,405
	Mean	1,368	1,332	1,364	1,465	1,563	1,550	1,755	2,113
	Med	1,252	1,202	1,259	1,392	1,518	1,490	1,721	2,114
	Min	267	130	238	273	350	307	245	550
Lower middle class	Max	3,548	3,816	4,131	5,163	5,119	5,146	6,396	7,007
	Mean	2,687	2,886	2,988	3,351	3,248	3,339	3,897	4,371
	Med	2,676	2,953	3,000	3,283	3,128	3,247	3,742	4,198
	Min	1,794	1,798	1,802	1,873	1,865	1,955	2,052	2,374
Upper middle class	Max	5,256	5,729	6,658	9,477	10,003	9,689	13,276	14,870
	Mean	4,268	4,559	5,101	6,767	6,850	6,798	8,748	9,649
	Med	4,209	4,428	4,947	6,559	6,607	6,534	8,290	9,165
	Min	3,549	3,821	4,134	5,167	5,120	5,148	6,398	7,008
Top 5 per cent class	Max	147,788	150,655	127,873	185,238	388,963	130,428	151,960	234,643
	Mean	8,460	9,275	12,507	16,657	17,995	16,024	21,163	22,408
	Med	6,758	7,462	9,186	13,220	14,285	12,772	17,551	18,985
	Min	5,258	5,732	6,673	9,480	10,006	9,691	13,278	14,873

Source: Authors' calculation using the Thai SES data set.
Note: In 2013, the average exchange rate was 30.7 THB = 1 USD (Bank of Thailand).

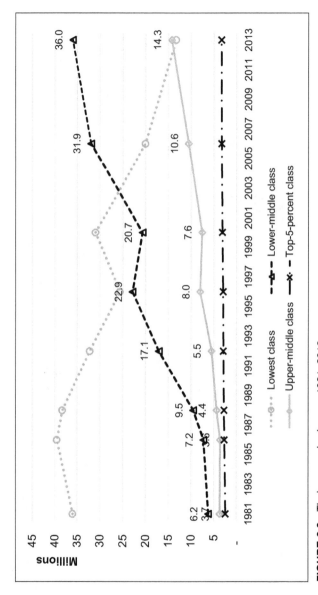

FIGURE 2.2 Thai economic classes, 1981–2013

Source: Authors' calculation using the Thai SES data set.

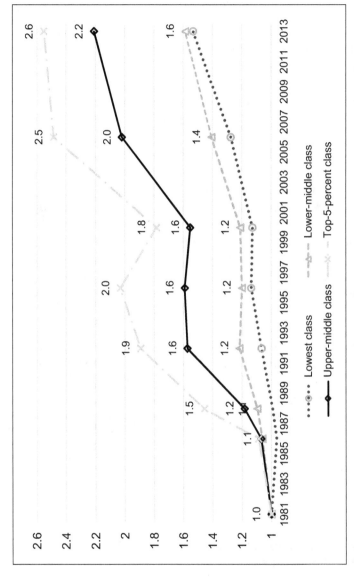

FIGURE 2.3 Index of real monthly household consumption per head (fixed composition) by class, 1981–2013
Source: Authors' tabulation using Thai SES data.

consumption per head by class. The index is calculated using a fixed educational composition for each class, as of 1981. This technique means that the class's average consumption is not affected by changes in within-class educational attainment over time.

The figure indicates that before the Asian Financial Crisis the consumption or welfare of members of the upper classes always grew faster than that of the lower classes. However, the Asian Financial Crisis affected the high-performing classes most severely. During the post-crisis period, the consumption indices of the upper classes increased markedly, before the global financial crisis of 2008 led to renewed stagnation. In general, the consumption levels of the upper classes are more sensitive to macroeconomic conditions than those of the lower classes.

In addition, the divergence between the lower and upper middle classes' welfare first becomes apparent in 1986, when the rate of growth of Thailand's gross domestic product peaked at 9.4 per cent annually during the latter period of the government of Prem Tinsulanon. This divergence became more prominent during the government of Chatchai Chunhawan (1988–91). The growth paths of the lower and upper middle classes were subsequently parallel. We can thus conclude that the major event resulting in the long-term distinction between the lower and upper middle classes in Thailand occurred roughly during the high-growth period of 1986–92.

Three principal factors drove the post-1986 boom: the depreciation of the U.S. dollar in relation to other currencies after the Plaza Accord of September 1985; foreign direct investment, especially from then-emerging Taiwan and Hong Kong; and oil prices that were continually low relative to the prices of major Thai export commodities (Warr and Bhanupong 1996, p. 44). These factors served to create an economic environment more advantageous to the upper middle class than to the lower middle class. The next section examines the socio-economic characteristics of the upper middle class and explains the reasons that members of the upper middle class were in a better position to benefit from the country's economic growth during the post-1986 period.

Transformations Associated with the Rise of the Thai Upper Middle Class

Figure 2.4 compares the proportions of Thailand's total population in the upper middle class in 1981 and in 2013 across regions. Bangkok is the

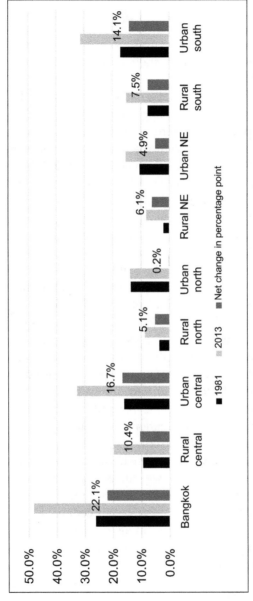

FIGURE 2.4 Proportion of total population (people born before 1967) in the upper middle class in each region, 1981 and 2013

Source: Authors' tabulation using Thai SES data.

region in which the proportion of the upper middle class grew most, by 22 per cent during those three decades. It was followed by urban areas in Central Thailand, at 17 per cent, and in the South, at 14 per cent, and then by rural areas in Central Thailand, at 10 per cent, and in the South, at 8 per cent. Neither urban nor rural areas in the North or Northeast saw such high rates of growth in their upper-middle-class populations during the period.

In 2013, Bangkok and Central Thailand were home to the highest concentrations of members of the upper middle class. In Bangkok, about 47 per cent of the population were members of the upper middle class in that year, and about 33 per cent members of the lower middle class. In contrast, in rural areas of the Northeast, only about 8 per cent of the population were upper middle class, while about 61 per cent were lower middle class. When paired with the results of the 2011 general election and of the Bangkok metropolitan elections of 2013, these numbers affirm the hypothesis that members of the lower middle class have been the main supporters of the Red Shirts, while members of the upper middle class have been the main supporters of the Yellow Shirts.

Panels A and B in Figure 2.5 depict the number of members of the upper middle class by educational attainment. To distinguish, albeit roughly, between two generations, Panel A uses samples of people born before 1967, while Panel B uses samples of people born in or after 1967. The figure shows that members of the upper middle class born before 1967 tend to have lower educational attainments than those born from 1967 onward; the majority of the former had only primary school education. However, when compared with the lower middle class, these people still have higher average levels of educational attainment. Overall, the upper middle class is better endowed with education than the lower middle class.[7]

When considering the younger generation of the upper middle class using the data shown in Panel B, we can see a significant improvement in educational attainment. Educational attainment at the secondary and tertiary levels characterize 42 and 41 per cent of the upper-middle-class population, respectively. One can also observe a similar pattern of improvement among members of the lower middle class. However, the share of the members of that class with tertiary education is, at 15 per cent, still far below that of the upper middle class.

During the 1981–92 period, workers left agriculture for other sectors, especially services. The job pattern of the Thai upper middle class also

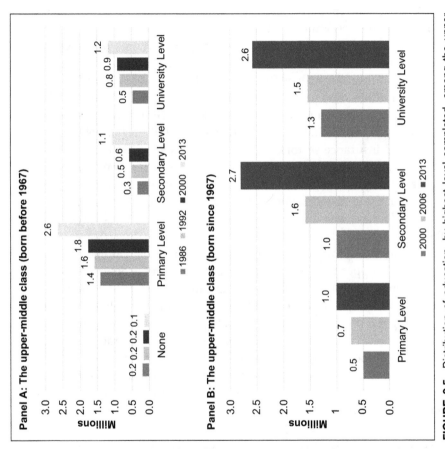

FIGURE 2.5 Distribution of education, by highest level completed, among the upper middle class

Source: Authors' tabulation using Thai SES data.

traced this course. According to the data presented in Figure 2.6, the Thai economy has witnessed a shift of people out of work as farmers and labourers to work as employees in clerical support, service and sales; as entrepreneurs, including employers and self-employed workers; and as professionals, including managers, professionals, and technicians and associate professionals.[8] However, after the Asian Financial Crisis, only employment as entrepreneurs and professionals increased rapidly among members of the upper middle class.

Upper-middle-class entrepreneurs usually own more sophisticated businesses than the small businesses owned by entrepreneurial members of the lower middle class, such as fruit stalls and beauty salons. In addition, the upper middle class comprises a large proportion of professionals. Members of the upper middle class in the service sector are more likely to be employed in jobs that require high levels of skill, such as jobs in the financial and insurance sectors, the information and technology sectors, real estate, and the education service sector. As these sectors benefited most from the country's post-1986 macroeconomic development in the form of financial and trade liberalization and foreign investment, members of the upper middle class were in a better position to thrive than were members of the lower middle class.

In summary, along the path of Thai economic development since 1981, the Thai upper middle class has achieved greater economic success than the lower middle class. Its members caught the train on the high-growth track because they were better educated and more likely to live in Bangkok, the centre of economic development, where well-paid jobs, sources of finance and business opportunities were concentrated. During the 1988–96 period, the job composition of the upper middle class shifted away from one that saw a majority involved in agriculture to one composed principally of employees. After the Asian Financial Crisis, the majority became entrepreneurs and professionals.

Understanding the Turn of the Thai Upper Middle Class against Democracy

This section draws on interviews with selected representatives of the Thai upper middle class. The analysis is inspired by a life-stories approach, which tries to elicit information from the exploration of trajectories and of changing conditions in life, such as education, work, social status and

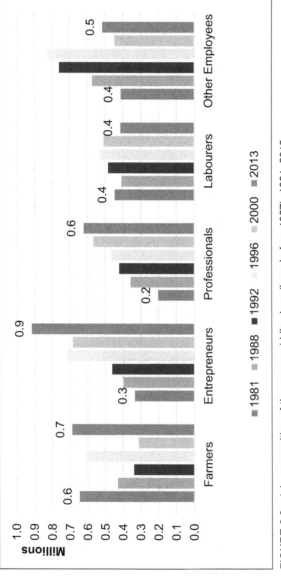

FIGURE 2.6 Job composition of the upper middle class (born before 1967), 1981–2013

Source: Authors' tabulation using Thai SES data.

political perspective (see Bertaux and Kohli 1984, pp. 216–18). Building on the treatment of the socio-economic transformation associated with the rise of the Thai upper middle class in the previous section, this section looks primarily at the political perspective that members of that class developed in the course of that transformation and in changing political contexts. It aims to use this information to gain insight into the conditions that have influenced the turn against democracy among members of the Thai upper middle class.

The section's data cover fifteen individuals representing different sections of the Thai upper middle class. The information about their lives and their political ideas is derived from in-depth interviews. To make possible the examination of longer life-paths, all of the representatives were aged at least fifty years old at the time of the interview. They comprised seven males and eight females. Out of fifteen, six were entrepreneurs, five were or had been high-ranking professionals in the corporate sector, two were civil servants, one was a senior-level employee in a state-owned enterprise and one a retired university professor. All of them had participated in the PDRC protests, were supportive of the 22 May 2014 coup and supported the military rule in Thailand that followed in its wake.

The section begins by exploring the respondents' depiction of their own rise in socio-economic status, of the ways in which it shaped their political perspectives. It then explores the development of their perception of the problems and threats that accompany democracy and concludes by analysing the conditions that turned the Thai upper middle class against democracy.

Socio-Economic Rise and the Formation of Political Perspectives

The interviews started with the request that these selected representatives of the Thai upper middle class narrate their life stories. The interviewees' stories resonated with the analysis offered in the previous section. A common theme of achievement in education and success in jobs characterized these stories. All the interviewees attained at least a bachelor's degree, and almost half held master's degrees. Such an achievement was considerable when contrasted to their descriptions of their parents, whom they described as having rarely attained education at even the secondary level. Their achievements in education were followed with successes in finding employment or building businesses. In accordance with the findings of the previous section, their careers or businesses benefited in some way from the liberalization of the Thai economy. Interviewees in the private sector had opportunities to find employment with multinational corporations or companies that grew as a result of international trade or financial liberalization. Those who operated their own businesses benefited from the relocation of the operations of foreign firms to Thailand.

Success in education and work were the aspects of life that gave the interviewees a valuable sense of identity, of being someone who had managed to rise above others. We asked the interviewees about factors that may have contributed to their achievements, starting with their ethnic background and its importance. A few interviewees who identified themselves as ethnically Thai mentioned their connection with the Thai aristocracy or upper class, but they emphasized this connection for its effect in shaping the ethical value that they attached to concepts such as "self-sufficiency" (*khwamphophiang*) or "respect for hierarchy" (*kankhaorop phuyai*).

When asked whether they thought that government policies had contributed to their success, most interviewees disagreed strikingly. Although a few acknowledged the role of government policies in helping their businesses, most still put more weight on their ability to reap benefits from available opportunities. Many asserted that government involvement in the economy was undesirable, signifying their limited recognition of the advantages that they may have received from government policies. These answers indicated a crucial aspect of the perception that members of the Thai upper middle class have towards their own prosperity and achievements. They understand their successes as coming mostly as the result of their own ability and efforts. The significance of such factors as ethnicity is reduced to a matter of just ethical values taught by parents or ancestors, while the crucial importance of government policies has gone almost unrecognized. It could be that their experience of constantly increasing prosperity and opportunity had not led them to see much beyond themselves as individuals making their best efforts to seize that opportunity.

Hence, when asked whether they perceived, or felt frustrated by, social barriers that elites had imposed on their ability to enjoy growth, most interviewees pointed out that they actually did not feel such barriers. They argued that they were satisfied with what they had attained, and that there was plenty of opportunity in Thai society, enough for everyone to prosper. A few interviewees, who expressed some regret over a lack of success, believed that they could have achieved even more in their lives if they had tried harder. These answers confirm the observation that members of the Thai upper middle class perceive their lives above all in terms of individual effort and success, with little recognition of broader factors aiding or impeding them.

We next asked the interviewees about their political experiences, in order to understand the formation of their political perspectives. In contrast to the extensive descriptions of their education and work, they rarely had stories to tell about their political experiences. All the interviewees explained that, from the time of their youth until the early stages of their careers, they had no interest in politics. "Chat" and "Suwan", both the sons of ethnic Chinese parents, pointed out that Chinese did not want to get involved in Thai politics. Most interviewees said that, influenced by their parents, they only focused on studying hard so that they could eventually build a good career. Their lack of interest in politics in the past seems to have been connected to their perception that the politics of earlier eras was different from the politics of the present. "Phet" and "Nat" depicted politics in the past as "uneventful" (mai mi arai). In describing the 14 October 1973 student uprising, Nat, the owner of an import business, said,

> 14 October and what happens these days are not the same. In the past there were not intervening factors, but today there are bombs and interventions from a third party. If we compare 14 October to the present, 14 October is like an innocent child, while politics in the present is no longer an innocent child.[9]

These answers indicate that members of the Thai upper middle class perceive a more or less "depoliticized" (mai pen kanmueang) past, when little was happening and conflicts and problems were much less prevalent than in the present. Nevertheless, they do not mean that their experience of an era of perceived depoliticization left the interviewees without perspectives on politics. Examination of their characterizations of the politics of the past reveals a normative perception of politics that developed in their youth and early careers.

Many interviewees had the viewpoint that "order" (khwamsangopriaproi) was desirable in politics. "Phu", now a high-ranking employee in a private enterprise, explained his dislike from a young age of political conflict and protest. "I did not care about political events. I only cared about studying. I disliked it when people came out on the street to protest. I wanted them to stick to rules.... Why could not they just go and settle things in the parliament?"[10]

The interviewees' experience of putative depoliticization tended to be related to their perception that a central element in politics was the "moral traits" (*khwammikhunnatham*) of government leaders. Asked about their memory of governments in the past, most interviewees cited their positive impression of times under Prem Tinsulanon and Chuan Leekpai (prime minister, 1992–95 and 1997–2001). They did not recall such times as eras of economic growth, but rather as ordinary periods during which Thailand had leaders with the right "moral quality".

The most crucial aspect of the interviewees' perception of politics in the past related to the basis of their love for and loyalty to the late Thai king. All interviewees pointed to their love for King Bhumibol Adulyadej as something fostered in their youth, especially by learning about his devotion to the Thai people from watching coverage of royal activities on the television news. A number of the interviewees also pointed to their families and the educational institutions that they had attended as contributing to their attachment to the Thai royal family. A notable aspect of their perspective on the king was their memories of the events of May 1992, events that many interviewees cited as the first time that they became interested in politics. They recalled King Bhumibol's role in resolving the conflict of that time. A number of interviewees vividly remembered the televised episode during which the king instructed protest leader Chamlong Srimueang and leader of the military-backed government Suchinda Kraprayoon, both prostrated before him, to end the conflict. As Suwan recalled, the king was in that instance like an "adult" (*phuyai*) telling the kids (*dek-dek*) to stop their quarrel.

These answers indicated in a fundamental way how members of the Thai upper middle class formed their political perspective, even during the times in which they claimed to have had no interest in politics. It was through their own path to affluence, when most of them focused mostly on individual achievements, that they developed an attachment to a normative vision of politics that valued "order", "morality in leaders" and "love for the king". It is worth noting that their normative vision resembled to a large extent the vision of Thai society promoted by the Thai government in the 1980s, especially during the semi-democratic regime of Prem Tinsulanon. According to Pasuk and Baker, this vision portrayed Thailand as having a pyramidal governmental, political and social structure. At the top of the pyramid was the benevolent king who enjoyed absolute power, while the bureaucracy featured in this structure as assistants to the king, and at the bottom of this structure were villagers. The stability of this system was desirable, and it was thought to depend on the peaceful and contented nature of the villagers (Pasuk and Baker 1995, p. 319). This normative vision played a crucial role in the Thai upper middle class's turn against democracy.

Perceptions of Problems and Threats under Democracy

We asked the interviewees about their perceptions of problems and threats in Thai politics. The problems that they most commonly identified included corruption and populist policies. Their dissatisfaction with corruption came both from their direct experience of encountering corruption in their business dealings or work and from seeing their friends accumulate wealth through political connections. They related populist policies, such as Prime Minister Yingluck Shinawatra's rice-pledging scheme and first-time car buyer programme, to the growing influence of consumerism and money in Thai society.

It is worth noting, however, that interviewees' explanations of these problems frequently featured contradictions and inconsistencies. "Phot", a senior employee in a state-owned enterprise, criticized populist policies but admitted that she also participated in the first-time car buyer programme. Nat, a businesswoman operating an import firm, expressed her anger with politicians' corruption. However, she also said that she wanted one of her children to be a policeman or a soldier, as that would bring essential connections to help the operation of her business.

In this sense, interviewees' frustration with corruption and populist policies appeared to reflect their discontent with another major matter. It is notable that, in explaining these problems, the interviewees always related them to the rise to power of one particular politician, Thaksin Shinawatra. Resentment of changes that they perceived to arise during Thaksin's time underpinned their anger with corruption and populist policies.

All the interviewees saw Thaksin's rise to power as heralding a political transformation that allowed politicians and businessmen, both perceived as groups of immoral actors that sought to pursue their self-interests and wealth, to gain power. They perceived Thaksin as combining the immorality of both politicians and businessmen, as a politician who turned Thailand into his own business. Nat explained, "Thai politics has not been the same since Thaksin. Thaksin is a person who takes everything like business. He also took Thailand as business. That is wrong."[11]

Nat and most of the other interviewees cited the privatization of state-owned enterprises and the 2006 sale of Shin Corporation to Singapore's Temasek Holdings as Thaksin's most glaring acts of corruption. In each case, they believe that he had sought personal benefit from the sale of the country's assets. They also believed that Thaksin had caused an increase in corruption on the part of other politicians, especially by administering the country like a business. Phet, a high-ranking employee of a multinational corporation, argued that Thaksin had also inspired other politicians to search for legal loopholes and thus made them more inclined towards corruption.

Most interviewees also identified Thaksin's populist policies as another major threat to Thailand. They regarded these policies not simply as economic policies that lacked sustainability but as Thaksin's means of destroying appropriate morality, especially among Thai villagers. "Nu", a senior government employee, argued,

> Thaksin may have brought about a good economy during his time. But deep beneath the surface of the good economy were troubles for the future. Looking at the first-time car buyer programme[12] as an example, cars are not necessary goods; people should instead be given accommodation.... Thaksin's policies caused people to spend lavishly, becoming materialist and hedonist. The grass roots were the victims. His policies contrasted directly with the king's sufficiency economy concept[13] that teaches people to catch fish [rather than being given fish].[14]

These answers indicate that, among members of the Thai upper middle class, changes perceived to have been brought about by Thaksin are the essence of the political problems that propelled their turn against democracy. These changes were especially problematic because they contrasted with the normative vision of politics to which members of that class were attached. The rise of politicians seen as pursuing self-interest was incompatible with their vision of bureaucrats who served the king, and they considered populist policies disruptive of the content nature of villagers.

One issue, viewed by most interviewees as Thaksin's most crucial problem, best reflects the clash between the Thai upper middle class's normative vision of politics and the changes that came about during the Thaksin era. This issue was the former premier's alleged disloyalty to King Bhumibol. Most interviewees cited this issue as a decisive factor in turning them against Thaksin. They interpreted Thaksin's populist policies as an indication that he tried to deviate from the king's philosophy of sufficiency economy. They saw Thaksin as bent on accumulating power, building himself up as the "god" to the poor and trying to match the appeal of King Bhumibol. The inclination of many interviewees to believe rumours about Thaksin's misbehaviour towards the king was striking. Phet, for example, cited a story that Thaksin chose to attend a fashion show instead of a royal ceremony as evidence of his disloyalty to the monarch. Moreover, there was also a tendency among interviewees to compare Thaksin directly with King Bhumibol. "Som" stated, "Thaksin and the king cannot coexist. The king believes in the sufficiency economy, but Thaksin does not. This makes me feel angry with Thaksin."[15] Such comparisons were another indication that the changes of the Thaksin era threatened interviewees' vision of politics with the king at the centre.

Intertwined with the interviewees' perception of Thaksin as a threat was their perception of Thaksin's supporters, comprised of rural and lower class voters and the Red Shirts. In the minds of most of the interviewees, Thaksin's supporters had traits that contrasted directly with the traits that the interviewees valued and that they ascribed to themselves, such as a high level of education and a strong work ethic. They cited people's lack of education as the source of Thaksin's popularity among the rural poor, as it had enabled him to exert leadership over them by means of inaccurate information. As Som explained,

> Thaksin's votes came from the money he used. There were satellite receivers distributed in rural provinces ... and they [Thaksin supporters] were controlled by receiving one-sided information. We have enough education to know that he lies, but what about those who have low education?[16]

All the interviewees stressed a lack of education among Thaksin's supporters as evidence that elections in Thailand lack legitimacy; the uneducated simply succumb to vote buying. The interviewees' perception of the inferiority of Thaksin's supporters was also related to their resentment of his populist policies. They viewed those supporters as people who always "rely on government support" (ro khwamchuailuea chak ratthaban), for which people like the interviewees must pay with their taxes. Phu compared the two groups by saying, "People of different colours are totally different. The reds have always been the recipients of everything, and they have always asked for support. The blues have always been the givers; they work and pay taxes."[17]

The interviewees' perception of the inferiority of Thaksin's supporters was compounded by their identifying Red Shirts as violent and vulgar. A number of interviewees attributed this view to encounters with Red Shirts during their weeks-long protests in Bangkok in 2010. "Phit", an employee of a financial company, recalled, "as for the Red Shirts, it is more that I am frightened of them … I don't care that they came out for Thaksin.… The type of people who join the Red Shirts are just scary. They acted in a frightening way … like thugs [anthaphan]."[18]

Still, it is worth noting that when we asked many interviewees about their attitudes towards the poor in general, their answers contrasted with their attitudes towards the Red Shirts and towards Thaksin's supporters. A number of interviewees expressed some sympathy towards the poor, recognizing that there are many in Thailand who lacked adequate opportunities. This contrast may indicate that what members of the Thai upper middle class actually resent is not the poor or members of the lower class per se, but these groups' access to the political arena. They feel animosity towards the increasing importance of connections between the poor and politicians, as epitomized by the relationship between Thaksin and the Red Shirts. Phot said, for example, that politicians should not help the poor in Thailand. For politicians will only seek to exploit the poor to the politicians' own benefit. The poor should instead rely for help on the generosity and solidarity that exist aplenty in Thai society.

At the end of the interviews, we asked about the way forward for Thai politics. Most of the interviewees said that they wanted the current military regime to stay in power for many years to come. Some said that they simply did not want Thaksin coming back to power, and preferred to "freeze" (chae khaeng) Thai politics until they could be sure that such a thing would not happen. Others stated that Thai democracy should be reformed by educating voters and, more importantly, by effecting a change towards "controlled democracy" (prachathippatai thi thukkhuapkhum) that will no longer allow politicians to pursue their own self-interest.

Explaining the Turn of the Thai Upper Middle Class against Democracy

The interview data reveal the nature of the transformation that has influenced the turn against democracy among members of the Thai upper middle class. The transformation arose when the putative depoliticization of the era of the Thai upper middle class's socio-economic rise encountered changes due to democratization, in the form of Thaksin's rise to power and the lower class's domination of politics. The findings indicate that, despite their apolitical stance during the time of their class's socio-economic rise, members of the Thai upper middle class also developed during that time a normative view that subsequently propelled their resentment of the political change to come. Their normative view of politics is characterized by their preference for "orderly" politics — free of conflicts or chaos, and administered by leaders with moral values who, most crucially, must be loyal to the highest power in Thai politics, the king. Moreover, the stability of this politics rests upon villagers' contentment with what they already have.

In this light, the findings of this chapter are to some extent aligned with the argument made by Ünaldi (2014b), that the turn of the Thai middle class against democracy is associated with an attachment to authoritarianism. However, this chapter also suggests that recognition of its economic benefits is not the root cause of the attachment of members of the Thai upper middle class to authoritarianism. Rather, that attachment is grounded above all in the formation of their normative view of politics under authoritarian regimes, and particularly under the semi-democracy of Prem Tinsulanon (Attachak 2014, pp. 48–49).

The turn of the Thai upper middle class against democracy came about mostly because political change threatened that class's normative political ideals. Its members' problematizing of corruption and populist policies related mainly to Thaksin. It suggested that they did not understand these issues simply as problems in their own right. Rather, corruption and populism were problematic because they pointed to the infiltration or undermining of "moral politics" in the minds of members of the upper middle class. Their identification of Thaksin as the major threat to moral politics was signified by their willingness to identify his government as a grave danger to King Bhumibol.

The interview findings presented here are rather inconsistent with Nidhi's depiction of members of the Thai upper middle class as marginalized elites frustrated by a lack of upward mobility (Nidhi 2015). The representatives of the Thai upper middle class interviewed did not feel resentment towards elites. Moreover, they did not perceive their opportunities to be limited. They placed more emphasis on their satisfaction with the achievements that they had already made. On the other hand, their contempt for the lower class arose mainly from resentment of the recent political relevance of that class, and of its role as a power base for allegedly greedy and immoral politicians. In assuming that role, the lower class is breaking out of its position of contentment at the base of the Thai social hierarchy, a position in which members of the upper middle class desire to see it remain. Against this background, members of the Thai upper middle class are also propelled to assert their superiority to the lower class. They identify the members of that class as having inferior traits, such as low levels of education, dependence on the support of others, and vulgarity. In this context, it is clear that it is only when the normative vision of politics to which its members subscribe begins to lose its significance or traction will the Thai upper middle class align itself more with democracy.

Conclusion

The transformation of Thai society and of the Thai economy in recent decades has contributed to political tensions between the newly emerging lower middle class and a somewhat older upper middle class. Members of the Thai upper middle class have become a force opposed to democracy, supporting the return of military rule to Thailand. Existing explanations point to two conditions that may influence this turn against democracy: the class's "squeezed" position between the elites and the lower classes and an attachment to authoritarianism rooted in economic success under the authoritarian regimes of the past. This chapter aims to shed further light on the socio-economic rise of the Thai upper middle class and on the conditions that have influenced its members' turn against democracy.

Through a quantitative analysis of socio-economic data, this chapter found that the Thai upper middle class grew fastest between the mid-1980s and the mid-1990s. Its growth coincided with the period in which the Thai government pursued policies of economic liberalization, and its members' rise in socio-economic status is correlated with their attainment of high levels of education and with their increased access to occupations in such sectors as entrepreneurship, management, finance and the professions. The Thai upper middle class, especially those of its members living in Bangkok, was in a position to reap benefits from economic liberalization and the eventual expansion of the Thai economy. Using interviews with selected representatives of the Thai upper middle class, the chapter found that members of that class also saw their success in education and work as crucial aspects of their identity. They viewed these achievements as the result of their own efforts, and held the perspective that Thai society had offered opportunities for everyone to attain similar success. During the time of their rise in socio-economic status, and although they described themselves as having been apolitical people living in an era of depoliticization, they nevertheless formed a normative perception of politics. This perception assigned central value to such features of political life as order, personal moral qualities and, most importantly, loyalty to King Bhumibol. The perception of a threat to these conditions has been the principal influence in turning members of the Thai upper middle class against democracy. They identify this threat with Thaksin's rise to power. They interpret that rise as a change that saw immoral politicians challenge and take power away from the benevolent king and his loyal bureaucrats.

The chapter's findings are in agreement with the argument that an attachment to authoritarianism among members of the Thai upper middle class played a crucial role in turning them against democracy, but it also suggests that their construction of a subjective view of "moral politics", rather than their association of authoritarianism with economic advancement, substantially shaped that stance. The chapter also finds that members of the Thai upper middle class, perhaps still focused on their own recent achievements, have yet to form a critical perception of the Thai elite's privileged position. Their turn against democracy, while primarily a reaction against political change that contradicts their view of political morality, is also related to the attempt on the part of members of the upper middle class to affirm their perception of themselves as people who have achieved a superior position in Thai society, especially in relation to the lower classes whose increasing political significance they resent. Until members of the Thai upper middle class start to scrutinize their own normative perception of politics, their current stance towards democracy is unlikely to change.

Acknowledgements

This research is a part of the research project on *"'Kanmueang khon di' khwamkhit patibatkan lae attalak thangkanmueang khong phusanapsanun 'khabuankan plianplaeng prathet thai'"* ("Good People's Politics": Political Thoughts, Practices and Identities of the "Change Thailand Movements" Supporters), supported by the Thailand Research Fund. We appreciate valuable comments from other researchers involved in the project and from members of the project's external advisory committee, especially Kasian Tejapira, Attachak Sattayanurak, Pasuk Phongpaichit, Pitch Pongsawat and Chusak Pattarakulvanit. We are also indebted to Jiraporn Plangpraphan for her advice on data, Trin Aiyara for his suggestions on the literature review and Thanasak Jenmana for his research assistance. We are very grateful to Michael Montesano, Terence Chong and the editorial team at the ISEAS – Yusof Ishak Institute for their assistance and comments.

Interviews

Interviewees listed by pseudonym; all interviews were conducted in Bangkok.

Nat, 7 April 2015, owner of an import business, female.
Som, 13 April 2015, retired university professor, female.
Suwan, 1 May 2015, owner of a textile business, male.
Phet, 2 May 2015, employee of an information technology company, female.
Pit, 9 June 2015, employee of an insurance firm, male.
Phloi, 9 June 2015, employee of an insurance firm, female.
Phu, 8 July 2015, employee of a company in the energy sector, male.
Phrae, 15 August 2015, former employee of a trading company, female.
Nu, 20 August 2015, official in the Ministry of Industry, female.
Chat, 26 August 2015, owner of a construction equipment business, male
Mon, 5 April 2016, official in the Ministry of Public Health, female.
Kiat, 11 May 2016, owner of a food processing business, male.
Thana, 20 May 2016, owner of an agriculture-sector business, male.
Phot, 28 May 2016, employee of a state-owned enterprise, female.
Wit, 1 June 2016, owner of a jewellery business, male.

Notes

1. This definition draws on Lamont (1992, p. xvii).
2. One of the most notable actions of the PDRC was its disruption of Thailand's general elections on 2 February 2014.
3. For example, Chitpas Kridakorn (Bhirombhakdi), a famous personality among the PDRC leaders, gave an interview to Agence France-Presse in which she remarked, "The problem … is that many Thais lack a 'true understanding of democracy' … especially in the rural areas" (*The Japan Times*, 16 December 2013). Seri Wongmontha, a famous celebrity in the PDRC movement, said in reference to the large number of voters who voted for the Phuea Thai party, "We have 15 millions [*sic*] who lack quality, and 300,000 who have quality". (*Matichon*, 20 December 2013).
4. For example, a survey of the rural Tambon Thung Sadok sub-district of Chiang Mai province, conducted by Rigg and Sukunee in 2001, found that almost half of the income earned came from non-farming sources. Many families in Thung Sadok, especially the poorer ones, relied on members of their families leaving to earn income elsewhere, such as working in the factories or finding jobs in the city (Rigg and Sukunee 2001).
5. The authors obtained and used raw data from the NSO with its permission. The survey rounds used in this paper date from 1981, 1986, 1988, 1992, 1996, 2000, 2006 and 2013. The NSO released the data a year after each survey round.
6. To make up for the missing poverty line during 1981–86, the authors use the inflation rate to project the 1988 poverty line backward.
7. Note that the rising number of workers with primary educations in 1996 was due to a massive reduction in the number of people living in poverty, which resulted in an increasing number in the middle class. The 2013 surge in members of the upper middle class with only primary school educations is another aberration, caused by the rice-pledging scheme implemented by the government of Yingluck Shinawatra during 2011–12. This scheme greatly increased income among some rice farmers, pushing them temporarily into the upper middle class category.
8. Technicians and associate professionals, according to the International Labour Organization, are those who perform mostly technical and related tasks connected with research and the application of scientific or artistic concepts and operational methods, government and business regulations, and who teach at certain educational levels (see International Labour Organization 2004).
9. Interview with Nat, 7 April 2015.
10. Interview with Phu, 8 July 2015.
11. Interview with Nat, 7 April 2015.

12. The Yingluck government implemented the first-time car buyer programme between October 2011 and December 2012. Under the programme, buyers of cars with a price of less than 1 million baht and a maximum engine size of 1.5 litres were entitled to tax rebates equivalent to 10 per cent of the car's price. To be entitled to the rebate, a buyer also needed to hold single-ownership of the car for a minimum period of five years.

13. The sufficiency economy (*setthakit phophiang*) was an idea raised by King Bhumibol in his 1997 birthday speech. Set against the background of the Asian Financial Crisis, the idea prioritized the development of "an economy where people are self-reliant and have an adequate livelihood for themselves" (Grossman et al. 2015, p. 34).

14. Interview with Nu, 20 August 2015.

15. Interview with Som, 13 April 2015.

16. Ibid.

17. Interview with Phu, 8 July 2015; his use of the term "blues" (*si fa*) was meant to refer to supporters of the PDRC.

18. Interview with Phit, 9 June 2015.

3

"We the Southerners Come to Protect the Nation and the King": Southerners' Political Rise and Regional Nationalism in Thailand

Anusorn Unno

Two enduring popular images characterize the People's Democratic Reform Committee (PDRC), which led the rallies against the government of Prime Minister Yingluck Shinawatra in late 2013 and early 2014 that culminated in the 22 May coup.[1] The first is that it was supported by Bangkok residents, especially the "educated urban middle class" and celebrities. Images of the PDRC's mid-day "Bangkok Shutdown" (*patibatkan pit krung thep*) rallies gaining the support of thousands of "office people" in Bangkok's business and commercial centres were widespread, as were images of celebrities taking part in and holding cultural activities at PDRC rallies. The second is Southerners' support for the movement, that of both those travelling from the region to attend rallies in the capital and those residing in Bangkok. Images of tents offering Southern Thai food for free at PDRC rallies were highlighted, along with images of hundreds of Southerners taking trains to Bangkok to attend those rallies. These two popular images combined to create one of the PDRC as an alliance of Bangkokians and Southerners.[2]

Such an alliance is of crucial importance to Thai politics for three reasons. First, it highlights the birth of a new "political actor". While Bangkokians have as a group been a dominant actor in Thai politics for decades — from the "Black May" of 1992 through the anti-Thaksin People's Alliance for Democracy (PAD) in 2005–6 and 2008–11 — Southerners had never been the backbone or stood at the forefront of any political uprising until they vigorously took part in the rallies of the PDRC. Second, the alliance challenges the "Two Democracies" theory once widely held among observers of Thai politics.[3] Rather than acting as rural people who voted for a government destined to be overthrown by Bangkokians, Southerners working through the PDRC joined Bangkokians in ousting the government voted in by people in and from the North and the Northeast. Third, the alliance challenged the notion long held among scholars, especially Thai scholars, of Southern Thailand. Instead of being "anti-state" with regionalism as a backdrop, Southerners emerged as champions of royal nationalism under the PDRC. "We the Southerners come to protect the nation and the king" is what one of them said with great pride when asked why she attended the PDRC's rallies.[4]

Taking a cue from the appearance of this Bangkok-Southern alliance, this chapter examines the ways in which people from the South became a new political actor under the auspices of the PDRC and how they, in conjunction with other political actors, are likely to shape Thai politics in the near and mid-term future. The chapter also examines how Southerners think of the Thai state and of their relationship to it, as well as how they have become champions of royal nationalism while retaining a sense of regionalism.

Getting Involved with Political Uprisings: Black May 1992 and the PAD

Prior to the emergence of the PDRC, Southern Thais had been involved in two major political uprisings. The first was the Black May 1992 incident. Opposed to General Suchinda Kraprayoon's assumption of the premiership, some Southerners joined the protests in Bangkok led by Major General Chamlong Srimuang against General Suchinda. They called themselves the United Front of People Guarding Democracy (*naewruam prachachon phithak prachathippatai*) and wore black headbands bearing the group's name as their symbol. Most of the members of this group were Nakhon Si Thammarat natives who had resided in Bangkok's Huai Khwang

District and worked in the tailoring business there for decades (Khamnun 2006, pp. 211–12). Despite their strong commitment to the anti-Suchinda cause, however, these Southerners constituted only a small portion of the protestors of May 1992, most of whom were drawn from Bangkok's middle class. Their role in the protest was not prominent. As a result, they have hardly been mentioned in discussions of the protests, which, in addition to Black May, have alternatively been dubbed "The Middle Class Mob" and "The Mobile Phone Mob" to reflect the identity of the apparent majority of the protestors.

Given the growth of "participatory democracy" and the stability of parliamentary politics in the post-1992 period, these Southerners and the group into which they organized themselves seem to have disappeared from Thai politics for more than a decade. It was not until Sondhi Limthongkul led the mass protests against Prime Minister Thaksin Shinawatra under

FIGURE 3.1 Sondhi Limthongkul wearing a yellow scarf, a symbol of loyalty to King Bhumibol and now to King Vajiralongkorn too, as he spoke at a PAD rally.
Source: Photo by Don Sambandaraksa, "Sondhi tells the crowd to move to Democracy Monument", https://www.flickr.com/photos/49353237@N00/105404069/. © Don Sambandaraksa. Licensed under the Creative Commons Attribution-ShareAlike 2.0 licence: https://creativecommons.org/licenses/by-sa/2.0/legalcode.

FIGURE 3.2 PAD rally participants with "protest kits" associated with the king, primarily including "clapping hands" and yellow scarves printed with statements expressing reverence for the monarch.
Source: Photo courtesy of *Prachatai*, 31 May 2012, https://prachatai.com/journal/2012/05/40769

FIGURE 3.3 PAD rally participants dressed in yellow t-shirts with symbols of the king and holding banners in protest against the American ambassador's alleged intervention in the country's internal affairs.
Source: Photo courtesy of Sa-nguang Khumrungroj.

the banner of the PAD in the first half of 2006 that they took part in a political uprising again. Initially, they again called themselves the United Front of People Guarding Democracy, as in 1992. For example, when the PAD marched from Sanam Luang to Government House on 14 March 2006, members of this group formed a row holding up a cloth banner with the statement "United Front of People Guarding Democracy, mighty headband cloth, hunt the dictator". Later, perhaps after being tasked with providing security for the PAD leaders and their headquarters at Ban Phra Athit, they began to call themselves the Srivijaya Warriors (*nakrop siwichai*).[5] They also wore black t-shirts with a symbol of Jatukham Rammathep, Nakhon Si Thammarat's guardian spirits, on the chest to signify their Southern origins (Khamnun 2006, pp. 214–15). Despite being tasked with specific duties and dressed in clothing with symbols of the South, however, these Southerners received little attention in the media. It was not until they performed a spectacular and daunting operation during the second round of the PAD rallies that they became widely known to the public as the Srivijaya Warriors.

The PAD resumed its rallies after the 23 December 2007 election, won by the People's Power Party. The party then formed a new government, which was in the eyes of the PAD the proxy of former prime minister Thaksin. The Srivijaya Warriors joined the PAD again, but this time with a more noticeable identity. They were dressed in black — jeans, t-shirts and cloth headbands — and their t-shirts bore "Srivijaya". As part of the PAD guards, which comprised men from state enterprises, the Dharma Army and various NGOs, they were tasked with patrolling the rally sites (Matichon Press 2008, pp. 61–62). It was through this task that the Srivijaya Warriors became widely known. Convinced that there might be "ill-intentioned" or "third-party" persons infiltrating the rallies, the Srivijaya Warriors often performed their duty with aggression and intimidation, even against ordinary rally-goers and reporters. This led to many complaints against them, many of which were made through the media and in public (ibid., p. 66).

The Srivijaya Warriors' infamy reached its peak after their siege of the National Broadcasting Services of Thailand, a television station owned and operated by the state. After several rounds of "whistle-blowing",[6] Sondhi made a public announcement that he would "blow the whistle" for the last time on 26 August 2008, but he did not reveal what the plan was. It was kept secret even among the rally-goers, until the early morning of the day itself, when television news broadcast images of almost one hundred men storming and occupying the station. These men, most with their faces covered, called themselves the Srivijaya Warriors and said that they were part of the People's Army to Rescue the Nation (*kongthap prachachon ku chat*), which would launch operations on that day. However, the police later detained eighty-two of them in possession not only of weapons such as knives but also of the addictive Kratom leaves consumed by many in the South (Matichon Press 2008, pp. 99–109). This operation not only brought the Srivijaya Warriors to public attention but also gave the PAD a bad name. It belied PAD claims of adhering to non-violence and civil disobedience.

According to Kittichai Saisa-at, the PAD Guards' leader and a Nakhon Si Thammarat native, the Srivijaya Warriors "are people from the South and Southerners who earn their living in Bangkok, such as tailors, factory workers" (Matichon Press 2008, p. 66). Despite their claims to be volunteers making personal sacrifices, it was said that the Srivijaya Warriors were highly organized. On the one hand, they were said to be recruited by PAD local leaders. Thus, for example, the Srivijaya Warriors from Nakhon Si Thammarat's Pak Phanang District were under the command of the Pak Phanang River Basin PAD, led by Damrong Yotarak. On the other hand, they were said to be recruited by Democrat Party politicians; some politicians and their "men" came to send the Srivijaya Warriors and other Southerners off to Bangkok at train stations. In addition, then, to the spectacular and daunting Srivijaya Warriors, other Southerners also played crucial roles in the PAD.

First among these other Southerners was the PAD leadership itself. Although initiated by Sondhi, the PAD could not have been formed without the cooperation of leaders from a number of important sectors in Thai society. Apart from Sondhi, a businessman, the four other PAD leaders included retired Major General Chamlong Srimuang, representing the Santi Asoke Buddhist sect; Pipob Thongchai, representing the NGO sector; Somkiat Pongpaiboon, representing academics; and Somsak Kosaisuk, representing state enterprise workers' unions (Matichon Press 2008, pp. 21–22). It was through Somsak, a Nakhon Si Thammarat native, that some five hundred men from state enterprise workers' unions were recruited into the PAD Guards, headed by Kittichai (ibid., pp. 61–62). Importantly, two of the three second-tier PAD leaders were Southerners: Sawit Kaewwan, Phatthalung native, and Samran Rodpetch, a Nakhon

Si Thammarat native (ibid., p. 112). This is not to mention the fact that Sondhi's "close men" included many Southerners: Surawit Wirawan, Pithan Phuetmongkon and Pannarot Buakhli.

The second additional group of Southerners to play a role in the PAD came from the Democrat Party. The Democrat Party was an ally of the PAD from the first round of its rallies. On 18 November 2005, Democrat leader Abhisit Vejjajiva, along with the party's key members, met Sondhi at Ban Phra Athit for discussions and to give support (*MGR Online*, 18 November 2005). However, the alliance was not crucial until the PAD launched the second round of its rallies in 2008, which a large number of Democrat Party politicians, many of them Southerners, joined. For example, Samran Rodpetch, one of the three second-tier PAD leaders and a failed Democrat Party candidate for parliament, delivered frequent speeches from the stage at PAD rallies. Though he was a member of parliament for Nakhon Ratchasima in the Northeast, Songkhla native Phichet Phatthanachot was another Southerner who spoke from the stage. This was in addition to those who "facilitated" Southerners' travel from the region to Bangkok, many of them Democrat Party politicians.

Third were the speakers at PAD rallies. These included a large number of Southerners from various sectors and groups. The most important were Sawit Kaewwan, a state enterprise workers' union activist; Puwadol Songprasert, a university professor and leading historian of Southern Thailand; Arom Meechai, a schoolteacher; Banchong Nasae, an NGO worker; and Watchara Petthong, a former student activist. Moreover, one of the other two PAD Guard leaders, Natser Yima, is a Songkhla native.

Despite the crucial roles that they played on behalf of the PAD, as Srivijaya Warrior guards, leaders, speakers at rallies, facilitators and supporters, Southerners were hardly perceived as a crucial part of or a group central to the identity of the alliance. Like Black May, the PAD was seen as a political movement dominated by Bangkok's middle class. It was not until the later rise of the PDRC that Southerners came to be viewed as an integral part of a political movement, alongside the "educated middle-class" Bangkokians.

A New Political Actor is Born: The PDRC

The PDRC is a political movement aimed at eliminating the "Thaksin regime" from Thai politics and establishing a new political order based on morality. It was formed on 29 November 2013 by Suthep Thaugsuban, Democrat Party secretary general, who appointed himself as the PDRC secretary general of the council (Chonthira 2014, pp. 39–40). Given that the Democrat Party is often portrayed as the "party of the southerners" (Askew 2008, pp. xii, 41–62) and that Suthep himself is a native of Surat Thani and long-time member of parliament for the province, the PDRC was associated with Southerners from the start. Southerners also constituted a large portion of the participants in PDRC rallies. We may thus understand the PDRC as the first political movement in modern Thai history in which Southerners played crucial roles.

Many Southerners who joined the PDRC were first-time rally-goers. Lom, for example, a resident of Nakhon Si Thammarat's Cha-uat District, told me that she had never thought that she would go to Bangkok to protest against the government at the age of fifty-nine. She had only finished primary school and spent most of her life in rubber plantations and paddy fields. She had never thought about "playing local politics", even though she attached importance to national politics as she was fond of the Democrat Party. When the PAD launched rallies against Thaksin in 2005, she only followed the news from afar, even as she agreed with its causes. It was not until the PDRC staged rallies against the Yingluck government in Bangkok that she decided to join.[7]

It should also be noted that before joining the PDRC rallies in Bangkok, Lom had demonstrated the same reluctance to participate in rallies that she believed were organized by "outsiders". For example, she had supported but did not participate in the protests over rubber prices that took place in Cha-uat District. Despite agreeing with their cause and their tactics, she was content to observe the protestors from her motorcycle because she believed that the protests were organized primarily by "outsiders" who had connections with the PAD. In fact, some Democrat Party politicians were highly involved in these protests.

In contrast, Lom participated in the protests over rubber prices that blocked the railroad near Ban Tun railway station on the grounds that it was organized by local people. She did not, however, mention to me the fact that some Democrat Party politicians whom she supported were backers of that protest. She said that, in addition to attending the protest that blocked the rail line, together with her sons and daughters-in-law she cooked food at home and took it to the protest site to give to the protestors. "It was fun at the moment" is what she said in her recollection of this protest.[8]

FIGURE 3.4 Khlong Chan Flat 19.
Source: Author's photograph.

FIGURE 3.5 Roadside market at Khlong Chan Flats.
Source: Author's photograph.

Rom, a Trang native who ran a roadside food stall at the National Housing Authority's Khlong Chan Flats in Bangkok's Bang Kapi District, had never participated in any political uprising before 2013 either, in spite of having resided in Bangkok for almost three decades. She said that attending rallies against the Yingluck government after it passed its controversial Amnesty Bill on 1 November of that year was the first time that she took part in political mobilization. However, rather than the PDRC itself, she preferred joining the protests of the Students' and Peoples' Network for Thailand's Reform or SNT (*khrueakhai naksueksa prachachon patirup prathet thai*) — an ally of the PDRC that had also been associated with the PAD — in spite of the fact that she was a Democrat Party supporter and had never identified with the PAD. This was because,

> The PDRC rallies are boring. Most activities are the leaders' speeches on stage, and they don't move much. But the SNT rallies are focused on mobility. They move from one place to another using the word "paying a visit"[9] in so doing. They are much more fun and exciting. So I joined them although there might be danger, and I am not PAD.[10]

Rom added that it did not matter to her which group — the PDRC or the SNT — she joined because, for her, they shared the same goals: eliminating corrupt politicians and protecting the monarchy. In addition, she sometimes joined the PDRC rallies when they conducted "paying a visit" activities at government offices.

Although some Southerners, especially those residing in Bangkok, had joined political movements, especially the PAD, in the past, their participation in such movements had remained limited. For example, Pum, the 44-year-old manager of Building 18 at the Khlong Chan Flats and also a motorcycle taxi terminal manager, said that he had joined PAD rallies, but only as an "observer".

> I only rode a motorcycle to the PAD rally sites to see what was going on and to follow the situation. But I didn't go every day because I didn't have any task I was responsible for. I was just an observer, not an important person in the crowd. But for the PDRC I was tasked with a duty. I went to the rally sites almost every day and sometimes slept there too. It is the first time that I fully joined the crowd.[11]

Interestingly enough, some Southern PAD members joined the PDRC instead of the SNT. Ek, a 33-year-old resident of the Khlong Chan Flats whose household registration is in Nakhon Si Thammarat, is a case in point. Ek said that he followed Sondhi from the very beginning of the latter's campaign because he wanted information on how Thaksin was cheating and corrupt, especially in matters of tax evasion. He also joined the PAD's campaign to "Vote NO" in the 2007 election because,

> I don't like any politician. I feel so sure that no politicians, when they are in power, will keep their promises. They speak a flowery language and almost prostrate themselves to us when they solicit votes. But after they win the election and have their seats in the parliament, they don't see people's heads. So I don't vote them. I vote NO instead.[12]

However, Ek attended the PDRC rallies led by former Democrat Party politicians primarily because he saw little choice, and because the SNT differed from the PAD.

> I didn't join the SNT because it is too "hard core". This [SNT] is violent, and I don't like this kind of crowd. So I joined the PDRC instead. But let me make myself clear: I personally don't like the PDRC's leader, Suthep. But at the moment Thailand had no leader to fight Thaksin. Suthep can do this because he is powerful in the Democrat Party and knows how to organize crowds.[13]

In other words, Southerners who joined the PDRC rallies were a diverse group. Some travelled from the South and others had resided and worked in Bangkok for decades. Some participated in political rallies in Bangkok for the first time in their lives, and others had previously joined political rallies such as those of the PAD in Bangkok as observers. If political participation was the pull factor for joining the PDRC, then what was the push factor that drove Southerners to the movement?

Reasons to Join the PDRC

When asked why they joined the PDRC rallies, Southerners answered with three major reasons. First, they wanted to protect the nation from being "robbed" by corrupt politicians like Thaksin and his clique. Although they were not satisfied with Yingluck, who was accused of being corrupt in such areas as her government's rice-pledging scheme,[14] they were aware that the accusation alone was not enough to justify the overthrow of her government. Instead, it was the Phuea Thai Party government's attempt to pass its Amnesty Bill that was the last straw and that offered them the opportunity for political mobilization.

Pum, for example, said that he kept a suspicious eye on the Yingluck government since its first day in power. He believed that all politicians were corrupt, even when it came to such small matters as labelling their names on assistance bags during the great floods of 2011, in spite of the fact that other persons, groups and organizations had donated the food and supplies that those bags contained. This was particularly the case for Thaksin, who was in his view the most corrupt of politicians. He cited Thaksin's tax evasion[15] as evidence. As a result, he was angry when he learned of the Yingluck government's plan for the Amnesty Bill that would in effect acquit Thaksin of all wrongdoing, including his alleged tax evasion. He proceeded to participate in rallies against the Yingluck government beginning from the first one at the Samsen railway station on 31 October 2013. He did so because passing "the amnesty bill is unacceptable. How could we teach our children, if someone did wrong and is not punished or [even] becomes [portrayed as someone] who is right?"[16]

The second reason that Southerners gave for participating in the PDRC rallies was to protect the monarchy from being insulted or eliminated by the Red Shirts,[17] whom they believed to be associated with the Phuea Thai Party. In fact, Pum and many other Southerners interviewed said that their main reason for joining the PDRC was to protect the monarchy from being insulted by the Red Shirts. Some even swore that they would do harm to those insulting King Bhumibol Adulyadej if they met them on the street. Ek, the PAD member, is a case in point.

The Red Shirts attack the monarchy. You can find the attacks and the insults on the Web and in clips. Sometimes they are rude. Personally, if I meet them on the street, I don't care if I have to go to jail for hurting them. Like "Tang Achiwa",[18] if I meet him I swear I am willing to go to jail. Why did he do that? He is just a kid. How could he insult his majesty the king? What did he get from doing that? Didn't he know how much the king does for us the Thai people? I have seen the king working hard since I was born and since before I can remember. Is there any politician working hard like him? But you are loyal to the politicians. Are you out of your mind? Can't you think? Those crooked politicians have no right to be compared to the king. The king is above us. Who are you, not respecting but insulting him? I will hurt them if I meet them on the street. I swear.[19]

The third reason for Southern support for the PDRC also related to the Red Shirts. It was to protect the country from being "burnt down" by the Red Shirts. Lom, for example, said, with apparent reference to the events of May 2010, that she grew worried watching the chaos and burning buildings in Bangkok on television, and that she joined the PDRC rallies three and a half years later when she learnt that they had been organized to stop the Red Shirts.

> I was so worried when watching TV. Buildings were burnt down. Chaos was everywhere in Bangkok, also in the provinces. They burnt the provincial halls in the North and the Northeast. It looked like our country was going to collapse. I thought I must do something to prevent this from happening. So when I found out that the PDRC was holding rallies in Bangkok which were also aimed to protect the country from being destroyed by the Red Shirts, I decided to go to Bangkok to join the rallies.[20]

In addition to these reasons, however, political affiliation — especially with the Democrat Party — played a crucial role in determining these Southerners' participation in the PDRC rallies. It structured the ways that they travelled to, and the part that they took in, the rallies.

Going to and Taking Part in the PDRC Rallies

Southerners reached the PDRC rally sites in three different ways. The first was simply on their own, as was the case for most Bangkok Southerners. Rom, for example, went to the rally sites by herself — sometimes on motorcycle and at other times by taking the Khlong Saen Saep express boat, the route of which starts from Wat Sibunrueang Pier opposite the site of the Khlong Chan Flats and ends at Phan Fa Lilat Pier next to the rally site at Ratchadamnoen Avenue. She usually went to the rallies alone, but she sometimes made the trip with her close friends. She added that the number of Southerners taking the express boat from the Khlong Chan Flats to the rally site was so large that "the boat was so full that there was not even a spot to stand".[21] Ek went to the rally site without help as well, and mostly alone, as he called himself "a free man", to confirm that he was not under the PDRC leaders' influence — especially that of Suthep — and was not hired to join the rallies.[22]

People making their way to the rallies independently also included those from the South. Lom said that she went to Bangkok three times by herself, each time by train. The first time, she travelled with her neighbour, without making many arrangements, as she was so restless and did not

FIGURE 3.6   Wat Sibunrueang Pier.
Source: Author's photograph.

know anyone else participating in the rallies. The second and third times, when she knew of rally-goers from nearby villages in Cha-uat District, she travelled in a group.[23]

Lom used her own money for travel; no one, and especially not local politicians, supported her. She could afford this because travel by third-class train was free of charge and she also had few expenses while she was at the rallies; a variety of free food was provided for the rally-goers, and makeshift shelters were available. Lom said that, because it did not cost her much, "I could go to Bangkok to join the rallies several times".[24]

The second type of travel by which Southerners reached the rallies was loosely or informally arranged, as was often the case for Bangkok Southerners who had close ties to Democrat Party politicians. Pum was a case in point. Pum said that he no longer solicited votes for Democrat Party politicians after he moved to Bangkok, but he still maintained relationships with some of them in the South. During the clashes with the Red Shirts in 2011–13, he joined anti-Red groups as a member of the "vanguard" on his own, either alone or with close friends. However, after learning that Suthep would stage a protest against the Yingluck government at the Samsen railway station for passing the Amnesty Bill, Pum and his friends and acquaintances from the Khlong Chan Flats formed a group called the "Khlong Chan Flats 18–19 Free Men's Group" (*klum serichon flaet khlong chan 18–19*) and joined the protest as a group. At the rally he also met the secretary of a Democrat Party politician whom he knew. Talking with this secretary led to an arrangement for Pum and his group to join the PDRC rallies.

> At Samsen I had a chance to meet a secretary of Witthaya [Kaewparadai, a Democrat Party politician from Nakhon Si Thammarat] whom I have known since I lived in the South. The secretary is also a Pak Phanang native like me. So it makes it easy to get connected. When the PDRC held rallies afterwards, I brought our group to join through an arrangement with the secretary. We went to the rallies ourselves and he told us what our tasks and responsibility were.[25]

The third means of travelling to PDRC rallies was more formally arranged, as was the case for many of those travelling from the South. Thong, a Cha-uat resident, said that although most villagers travelled to Bangkok on their own by free train, many from Cha-uat went to Bangkok on buses provided by Democrat Party politicians in the area. He added that there were leaflets informing local people of the departure points and times. Anyone who wanted to go just had to write her or his name

FIGURE 3.7   PDRC rally at the Victory Monument, 22 December 2013.
Source: Photo courtesy of *Prachatai*, 23 December 2013, https://prachatai.com/journal/2013/12/50604

FIGURE 3.8   PDRC rally at Ratchaprasong Intersection, 13 January 2014.
Source: Photo courtesy of *Prachatai*, 13 January 2014, https://prachatai.com/journal/2012/05/40769

FIGURE 3.9   PDRC rally heading to Government House, 9 December 2013.
Source: Photo courtesy of *Prachatai*, 21 December 2013, https://prachatai.com/journal/2013/05/50577

and present her or his identity card. They sometimes had to pay a little bit for transportation — roughly 500–1,000 baht — but sometimes not. It depended on the capacity of the "sponsors", who were Democrat Party politicians and local businessmen. These trips lasted between three and seven days. The Southerners who joined them did not have to pay for food or shelter while at the rallies. Thong also noted that while ordinary villagers slept at the rally sites, some of their leaders slept in hotels with financial support from Democrat Party politicians.[26]

How Southerners travelled to the rally sites partly shaped the ways in which they took part in the rallies. Those who went to the rally sites by themselves chose how to participate in the rallies on their own. They usually sat and walked around the rally sites. Sometimes they talked to and made friends with other rally-goers, especially their fellow Southerners. Lom, for example, said that she and her friends got off the train at the Samsen railway station and walked with the crowds, blowing whistles along the way, to the rally site at Ratchadamnoen Avenue. In addition to sitting and listening to the leaders giving speeches on the stage, she walked around the rally site to see what was going on. In particular, she loved to stop by the tents of Southerners and to talk to them. "I got a lot of new friends in the rally", she said.[27]

Similarly, Rom said that although she had a connection with the "Khlong Chan Flats 18–19 Free Men's Group", she preferred going to the rallies alone or with close friends to going in a group because it gave her more freedom to choose what kind of activities she joined. In addition to participating in "paying a visit" activities, which exposed her to the risks of tear gas and rubber bullets, she walked around the rally sites and stopped by tents that provided Southern food for free.

> I felt like being in the South. There were a lot of Southerners at the rally sites. They spoke the Southern [Thai] language and ate Southern food. Sometimes I heard them play Southern music and shadow puppet VCDs. We had the same ideology because we were Southerners. It made me feel like being with relatives at home in the South.[28]

In contrast, those who joined the rallies in groups had specific tasks to perform. Pum said that joining the rallies as a member of the "Khlong Chan Flats 18–19 Free Men's Group" changed the ways in which he took part in the rallies. From being a "vanguard" member, he became a "volunteer" tasked with providing food and water to rally-goers in general and taking care of fellow group members in particular.

After we formed a group and joined the rallies as a group, my role in the rallies changed. I was not a member of the vanguard anymore. I became a volunteer tasked with providing food, water and other supplies to the rally-goers. This is what Witthaya's secretary tasked us to do in joining the rallies and we are OK with it. This task is important because there are many people at the rallies. I was also responsible for taking care of relatives and friends from the South. Sometimes I drove them to the rally sites with my motorcycle and had them participate in the rallies as members of the group. I also need to take care of them with food, water and clothes when they were in the rally sites.[29]

Similarly, Ek said that many Southerners who went to the rally sites through the arrangement of Democrat Party politicians were assigned certain tasks. Some, especially young men, were assigned roles as security guards, whereas women were tasked with cooking food and providing primary healthcare to rally-goers. He said he was not tasked with any duty because, "I joined the rallies as a free man."[30]

Achievements and their Limits

The Southerners mentioned here believed that they achieved what they wanted in joining the PDRC rallies. Their ultimate goal was to overthrow the Yingluck government on the grounds that it attempted to acquit Thaksin of wrongdoing, and especially of corruption in the form of tax evasion. They believed that their aim of protecting the country from being "robbed" by corrupt politicians, which included Yingluck, as in the case of her rice-pledging scheme, had been achieved. The military coup of 22 May 2014 was for them the "military intervention" to overthrow the "corrupt" government for which they had called. As Rom put it,

We wanted to stop the Yingluck government from robbing the country, from helping acquit her brother Thaksin of wrongdoings. We proposed several ways of doing so, including calling for the military to step in. So we are fine with the revolution [military coup] because it overthrew the Yingluck government as we wanted.[31]

Similarly, those who wanted to protect the monarchy from being insulted and to punish those who had insulted it also believed that their aim had been achieved. Ek, for example, said that although he was not very happy with the way that the rallies ended, as many problems were still unresolved, he was pleased that those who had insulted the monarchy were put in jail.[32]

I didn't feel very happy much. Indifferent. Just felt relieved. This might be because of my experience with the 2006 coup … that everything was still the same afterwards. Problems still existed. So I didn't feel happy or anything. But there is one thing that makes me happy and [that makes me] feel that what I did was worthwhile. It is the arrest of those insulting the monarchy. Just this is enough for me, because prior to this [the] police didn't do anything with them.[33]

The situation was similar for those Southern protestors who wanted to stop the Red Shirts from "burning down the city". Pum, for example, said that the country was now peaceful and back to normal, as there was no *"tho nam liang"* or secret pipeline channelling financial support from Thaksin to the Red Shirts. And this was precisely because, he believed, the military had been able to bring the Red Shirts under control. He did not, however, know for sure whether the Red Shirts had simply gone underground.[34] Likewise, Ek said that one of the things that made him feel reassured was that the military coup had helped to bring the country back to normalcy or order.

Prior to the coup, the police did nothing. They can't arrest those involved in gunfights. But after the military stepped in and declared martial law, tons of war weapons were found and confiscated, and many Red Shirt people were arrested. Now the country is back in order again.[35]

Although their main goals had been achieved, some of these Southerners nevertheless remained dissatisfied with the situation after the May 2014 coup. Pum, despite his close connection with Democrat Party politicians and his support for the National Council for Peace and Order (NCPO) coup, said that the coup-appointed government had not effectively addressed Thailand's problems. Rubber prices, which had led Southerners to take to the streets even before the advent of the PDRC, were still in decline (Fredrickson 2013). From 80 baht per kilogram during the Yingluck government, the price was now down to 40 baht per kilogram. He wondered why the NCPO government did not do anything to solve the problem by, for example, buying and processing rubber rather than exporting it all in raw form. The other problem that Pum thought the government did not solve related to energy prices, especially those of cooking gas.

I think we overlooked the energy price issue. Now people feel that the government didn't help them. The government continually increases the energy prices. Are you pleasing the capitalists? I asked the government about the capitalists in PTT [Petroleum Authority of Thailand]. Are you pleasing them? I know those working at the PTT. They have very high monthly salaries. Damn it! They also get five, six, seven, ten months bonus. But we are getting poorer and poorer. Are we paying for higher cooking gas prices just for them to get more bonuses? The cooking gas prices continually increase but the government didn't do anything. They actually need to take action on this. They need to control the cooking gas price. You increase other prices; people don't care. But you increase the cooking gas price; it affects everyone because every household uses it. They are basic things you need to get under control. If the government doesn't take care of the energy prices well, maybe someday people will take to the street and I may join them.[36]

Ek also wondered where the PDRC leaders were when it came to the energy price problem. He wished that they would say something, especially when there was a rumour that the government would give a natural gas concession to the private sector. He disagreed with the plan as he thought that energy was a "treasure of the nation" (*sombat chat*). However, he was not sure whether he and other rally-goers would be able to oppose the plan, partly because, he thought, the energy sector involved many "generals" who in one way or another had close ties to those who staged the coup and were now in the junta-appointed government. He added,

> Now I follow the news on the PAD's TV channel, which investigates the issue deeply and provides dense information. But the Blue Sky Channel of the PDRC or the Democratic Party doesn't touch the issue. They just lick the military.[37]

What these Bangkok Southerners do now is to "wait and see" how the NCPO government will solve Thailand's problems, especially its economic problems. They have no plans to stage protests against the government, even if the situation worsens. In terms of politics, they thought that the country was not ready for elections, as the process of solving its problems was not finished yet. As Pum put it,

> I don't think that it is time for an election. If we allow it to happen, they [the Phuea Thai Party] will come back again. Problems will arise because the process of solving [problems] is not done yet. We need to amend the constitution first and then proceed with the Yingluck case before moving further. If we hold the election now, chaos will surely happen.[38]

Most informants in the South did not follow news on the political situation after the military coup. They believed that their urgent mission — overthrowing the Yingluck government and stopping the Red Shirts — was accomplished and that they could as a result return home to living their normal lives and earning a living. They thought that the nation was now saved and that the rest of what needed doing, especially "peace and order maintenance", could be left to the military and to the government that it had appointed. As Lom put it,

> I didn't follow the news much after I returned home and after the revolution [coup]. I wanted to oust the Yingluck government and to save the nation. They are done because the military came in to do it. Although the rubber price is not good, we need to bear it. Suthep also told us to remain calm and wait, as our government is solving the problems for us. When he came to the temple nearby as a monk,[39] I went there and made merit with him. He told us that now the government and the military are solving the problems, they are helping the nation and we need to give them support.[40]

Nationalism Regionalized

Southerners have long been said to be critical of or opposed to the Thai state, with their specific personality and the economy and geography of their region given as an explanation. In terms of personality, they have been stereotyped as obstinate, freedom loving and loyal (Narong 2001, p. 15; Akhom 2000, p. 52). In terms of economics, they are argued to have become involved with the market economy before the advent of the state and thus to be able to rely on themselves (Nidhi 2005, p. 30), or are seen as "bourgeois" and not in need of help from the state (Charun, n.d., p. 9). The distance and difficulty of travel in the past (Sangop 1989, pp. 9–10) have made it difficult for the state fully to control the South or its residents, and the latter in turn enjoyed considerable freedom in their interactions with the state (Akhom 2000, pp. 53–66). In this light, Southerners may be said to be more committed to the region and regionalism than to the nation-state and nationalism.

However, the political engagements and responses of the Southerners featured in this chapter may contradict these stereotypes. For example, the fact that Southerners joined the PDRC to protect the nation and a king who was in a sense the embodiment of the nation clearly suggest that they are not as opposed to the state as they are often made out to be. In other words, could Southerners in fact never have been opposed to the state at all? And could their political engagement through the PDRC be evidence of their sense of nationalism? The juncture between the PAD and PDRC provides a starting point to examine these questions.

In general terms, the PAD and PDRC had many things in common. They both took Thaksin's corruption and alleged disloyalty to the monarchy as the causes of Thailand's problems. Both also saw the rescue of the nation and protection of the monarchy as their goals. However, two features differentiated them. First was the dominant symbol that each employed. The PAD employed royal symbols from the start. That is, in late 2005, Sondhi led mass rallies called the "Yellow Shirt Mob" with "royal prerogative" (*pharatcha-amnat*)[41] as a main issue. The rallies collected names to petition King Bhumibol to step in and replace Prime Minister Thaksin (Khamnun 2006, pp. 127–35). Once the PAD was formed in early 2006, its dominant colour was yellow and the statement printed on its best-selling yellow shirts during the period was "We will fight for the king" (*rao cha su phuea nai luang*) (Matichon Press 2008, p. 53). In addition, the PAD sometimes associated itself with the queen, using her "birthday colour" of blue as a symbol. This was quite different from the PDRC. Although claiming to want to rescue the nation and protect the king, the PDRC dissociated itself from the monarch and instead tied itself only to the nation, as seen in its various uses of the national flag. This difference is also evident in the change in its English name — from the original People's Committee for Absolute Democracy with the King as Head of State or PCDA, which is close to the Thai name of "*Khanakammakan prachachon phuea kanplianplaeng prathet thai hai pen prachathippatai thi sombun anmi phramahakasat songpen pramuk*", to the People's Democratic Reform Committee or PDRC. The latter English name made no reference to the king. Two reasons account for such a change. First was the attempt to prevent the monarchy from becoming more "contaminated" by politics, as in the case of the PAD, in the eyes of the international community. Second was the belief that the nation could be best exploited politically by casting it as the "perfect victim" of the Yingluck government, since it was hard to make a case that that government had insulted or defamed the monarchy.

A second feature that differentiated the PDRC from the PAD was that the former associated itself so evidently with Southerners. Sondhi, a man of Chinese descent, often associated the PAD with Bangkok Chinese. This was because Bangkok Chinese constituted a large portion of PAD rally-goers and because many of them, especially merchants and businessmen in Bangkok's Chinatown, were big donors to the PAD (Matichon Press 2008, p. 42). In 2008, and with a Thaksinite government again in power, Sondhi launched a campaign under the banner of "Chinese Descendants Love the Nation" (*luk chin rak chat*), and the best-selling yellow shirts during that period were those screened with "Chinese Descendants Love the Nation" (ibid., p. 53).[42] All this is quite different from the PDRC and its calls for support from Southerners. For example, on 17 December 2013, Suthep announced from the stage at a rally that "The PDRC assigned me to be its representative to inform brothers that the next appointment to drive out Yingluck was scheduled for this Sunday, December 22. After this announcement, I ask brothers, especially in the South, to pack bags and be prepared for travel" (*Prachatai*, 17 December 2013). This cry for help, directed at Southerners, proved one of the main causes that brought many from the South to join the political rallies in Bangkok for the first time. Ping, a Phuket native, was a case in point.

Ping said that one of the reasons that she went to join PDRC rallies in Bangkok was that Suthep, to whom she felt close, directly called for help from Southerners. She added that she sometimes felt alienated from the PAD, even though she supported it, because it was so strongly associated with ethnic Chinese in Bangkok.

> I am a rustic and not rich like Chinese in Bangkok. Sondhi is a wealthy Chinese businessman and always talks about people of Chinese descendent rescuing the nation. He talked to Chinese in Bangkok, in Yaowarat. So I sometimes felt alienated from the PAD, although I agree with it. I might feel uncomfortable and not know how to behave myself if I attended the PAD rallies. So when Suthep led the PDRC and called for help from us the Southerners, I went [to] join him. I didn't feel alienated from the PDRC.[43]

It should be noted that a sense of kinship and localism was also a consequence of Suthep's transformation as PDRC leader from Democrat Party secretary general and member of parliament to "Uncle *Kamnan*". This transformation worked to create a sense of localism and kinship. While serving as the "arm and leg" of provincial government, *kamnan* or sub-district heads are also local leaders. To call Suthep "*kamnan*" after he resigned his posts as Democrat Party secretary general and member of parliament was to associate him with the local role that he had once had. On the other hand, to call Suthep "uncle" or *lung* is to render him a

FIGURE 3.10   Suthep Thaugsuban showing the colours of the Thai flag during a PDRC rally.
Source: Photo courtesy of *Prachatai*, 15 December 2013, https://prachatai.com/journal/2013/12/50438

FIGURE 3.11   Goods with the colours of the Thai flag on sale at a PDRC rally site at Siam Square.
Source: Photo courtesy of *Prachatai*, 23 December 2013, https://prachatai.com/journal/2013/12/50604

FIGURE 3.12   PDRC rally participants displaying the colours of the Thai flag.
Source: Photo courtesy of *Prachatai*, 13 January 2014, https://prachatai.com/journal/01/51133

kinsman. The identity of "Uncle *Kamnan*" signified both a respected local leader and an intimate relative at the same time. What Suthep did as leader of the PDRC was therefore not to launch the campaign of an urbanite to save the nation, as in the case of the PAD. It was, rather, a campaign on the part of a local leader who was also a relative with whom one could easily associate. As a result, many in the South came to join the PDRC in Bangkok after being called on by Suthep. They understood their mission as "to help Uncle *Kamnan* rescue the nation". This combination of kinship, appeals to regional identity and a sense of obligation to the state made the PDRC attractive to Southerners. In other words, it was a regionalized form of nationalism that partly drove Southerners to join the PDRC rallies in Bangkok.

It should also be noted that loyalty to the monarchy was an additional and powerful reason for Southerners joining PDRC rallies. San, a Nakhon Si Thammarat native who called himself a "Yellow Shirt", said that Thailand was lucky because it had a king doing so much for the Thai people and the country that, he added, "Without the king, the Thai nation couldn't exist."[44] Similarly, Phot, another Nakhon Si Thammarat native, appreciated how tirelessly the king had dedicated himself to the Thai people and, as a result, he added, "We Southerners love the king."[45]

The ways that San associated the nation and Phot associated Southerners with the king was in a sense an effect of two related political manoeuvres. On the one hand, it was an effect of the state's attempt to restore the king's status and authority, a process that started in the early 1960s and culminated in the 1990s. This attempt made the king, among other things, the embodiment or centre of the nation and a highly revered god-like monarch. On the other hand, it was an effect of the Democrat Party's attempts to associate itself with the monarchy, to *"hon chao"*, in political contests and conflicts. The notion of "Southerner" — in itself partly an invention of the Democrat Party (Askew 2008, pp. 41–62) — is then expanded to cover love, reverence and loyalty towards the monarchy. It is thus understandable why Southerners subject to these two political manoeuvres thought of King Bhumibol as an embodiment or centre of the nation and why they love, revere and were loyal to the king.

It should also be noted that the history of the region in relation to the Siamese kingdom has also shaped Southerners' thinking and their feelings about the monarchy. Although Southern principalities, especially Nakhon Si Thammarat, attempted to liberate themselves from Siam during the Ayutthaya Period when they had the chance, these attempts were undertaken by ad hoc political allies that were more often than not in conflict with one another. They had nothing to do with regionalism (Yongyut 2007, p. 46). In addition, these principalities sometimes tried to cling to Siam in order to empower themselves in their competition with one another. Therefore, although uniting under the leadership of Nakhon Si Thammarat to liberate themselves when Siam was defeated by Burma in 1767, no other Southern principalities helped Nakhon Si Thammarat when King Taksin attacked thereafter; some even associated themselves with King Taksin. Importantly, in the subsequent Rattanakosin period, Siam consolidated its relationship with the South through marriages and adoptions. This strategy, when combined with its military forces, meant that there have been no rebellions against Siam in the region since then (Nidhi 2007, pp. 93–101). The South then has had a good relationship with Siam for more than two centuries.

In addition to political history, religion — Buddhism — also plays a crucial role in this relationship. Lankan or Theravada Buddhism spread into Thailand via Nakhon Si Thammarat. This development resulted on the one hand in the building of many temples in the South. Nakhon Si Thammarat emerged as the centre of Buddhism in the region. On the other hand, it created a coherent society and thus a means through which Siam could govern the South (Yongyut 2007, pp. 30–31). It also gives great pride to Southerners — especially Nakhon Si Thammarat natives, who see themselves as residents of a centre of Buddhism.

To these considerations, one must add contemporary Southerners' view of the Thai state and its authorities. In their understanding, the Thai state means government agencies and "master" means government officials and politicians. But the rhetoric of "No Fighting the Masters, No End to Poverty" or *"Mai rop nai mai hai chon"*, which was widespread among local intellectuals and NGOs two decades ago, cast government officials and politicians as "enemies" but did not apply to the monarchy. On the contrary, the political manoeuvres mentioned above, in conjunction with their relative lack of involvement in wars between rulers of Southern principalities and Siam, mean that Southerners do not find it difficult to adopt the state's ideology or to be part of the nation when it is embodied by the king. As San, a Nakhon Si Thammarat native, put it,

> We are fine with the nation, religion and the monarch because we are in the land of Buddhism, and the king is the most charismatic person because he did good deeds in his past lives and he deserves the prerogative.[46]

Royal nationalism thus finds fertile soil in the South.[47]

Conclusion

Southerners' political rise through the PDRC brought major changes to Thai politics. Challenging the cliché that rural people vote governments in only for the urban middle class to overthrow them, Southerners, in cooperation with Bangkok's middle class, overthrew a government that had been elected primarily by people in the North and the Northeast. They also challenged the oft-cited notion of Southerners as anti-state regionalists, for they emerged as champions of nationalism who still took pride in their region. In particular, these changes paved a way for a return to military rule, starting with the May 2014 coup and culminating in a military government that was determined to ensure military domination of Thai politics for years to come.

Most of the Southerners who joined the PDRC thought that their mission — to help "Uncle *Kamnan*" rescue the nation — had been accomplished. Although some were dissatisfied with the situation after the coup, they did not stage protests but rather opted to wait and see how the government would solve problems and carry out promised reforms. In addition, although some began to criticize the PDRC leadership, many still admired its leaders, especially Suthep. They continued to follow their lead in spite of the worsening conditions on the economic front in particular. Taken together, most of the Southerners interviewed remained supporters of the PDRC, the NCPO government and the military. That the five provinces in which the greatest percentages of voters supported adoption of the NCPO's 2016 draft constitution in the referendum of 7 August 2016 were in the upper South, where it received backing from some eighty-five per cent of those who cast ballots, is the latest indicator of their support (Office of the Election Commission 2016).[48]

Notes

1. This chapter draws on the research project on "'Phom cha pai chuai phinong rao ratthaban khicho thamrai prachachon': khwamkhit lae patibatkan 'kanmueang khon di' khong khon tai yaithin nai krung thep" ("I Will Go Help My Brothers. The Corrupt Government Hurts the People": Thoughts and Practices on "Good People's Politics" among Migrant Southerners in Bangkok) (Chalita 2016), under the series of research projects on "'Kanmueang khon di': khwamkhit patipatkan lae attalak khong phu sanapsanun 'khabuankan plianplaeng prathet thai'" ("The Politics of Good People": The Thought, Practices, and Identities of Supporters of the "Change Thailand Movement"), of which I serve as co-head. The research project was carried out in 2015 at the National Housing Authority's Khlong Chan Flats in Bangkok's Bang Kapi District, where the majority of the residents are Southerners. Eighteen key informants were interviewed and the names used in the chapter are pseudonyms. In addition, eight more Southerners were interviewed in three villages in the south – Mai Siap village of Na Khon Si Thammarat's Cha-uat District, Ban Kho village of Nakhon Si Thammarat's Hua Sai District and Pa Khlok village of Phuket's Thalang District. The names given for these respondents also are pseudonyms.

2. A preliminary survey found that 54 per cent of the PDRC rally-goers resided in Bangkok and its vicinity and the remaining 46 per cent in the provinces, including fully 38 per cent of rally-goers surveyed who lived in the South (The Asia Foundation 2014). Please note that "the South" under discussion here is the Buddhist-majority provinces of Upper Southern Thailand, rather than the Muslim-majority Lower or "Deep" South of the former sultanate of Patani.

3. In his "Tale of Two Democracies" theory, Anek (1996) states that rural people, who are stereotypically poor and uneducated, view democracy as a means to gain immediate benefits, whereas the "educated urban middle class" view it in terms of ideology, policy and competence. He argues that rural people with their majority vote the government in, only for the urban middle class with its economic power and social status to overthrow the government.

4. Interview with Lom, a 59-year-old rubber farmer, Mai Siap village, Cha-uat District, Nakhon Si Thammarat, 12 April 2015.

5. Part of the territory of what some scholars believe was a kingdom called Srivijaya, extant during the seventh to thirteenth centuries of the Christian Era, covered Southern Thailand. Some have argued that its alleged "capital" was located in Chaiya District of Surat Thani province. After the putative kingdom's collapse, this view of history holds, part of the kingdom's territory was restored and established as the Nakhon Si Thammarat kingdom, with its capital at Nakhon Si Thammarat. On the history of Srivijaya, see Munoz (2006). Southern Thais, and especially Nakhon Si Thammarat residents, are proud of their connection to the kingdom of Srivijaya. As a result, they identified themselves with it when joining the PAD.

6. PAD leaders, and especially Sondhi, blew whistles on stage to call on the assembled PAD supporters to make major moves.

7. Interview with Lom, 12 April 2015.

8. Ibid.

9. "Paying a visit" (*pai yiam*) is part of Thai culture and has a sense of intimacy and of the existence of a bond. However, the phrase is used by the PDRC with a sense of threat and intimidation. This involved having thousands of PDRC supporters "visit" or in fact surround the offices of government agencies with which the PDRC was not satisfied.

10. Interview with Rom, a 59-year-old food stall owner, Khlong Chan Flats, Bangkok, 23 March 2015.

11. Interview with Pum, Khlong Chan Flats, Bangkok, 10 April 2015.

12. Interview with Ek, a 33-year-old private company employee, Khlong Chan Flats, Bangkok, 25 March 2015.

13. Interview with Ek, 25 March 2015.

14. The rice-pledging scheme (*khrongkan rap chamnam khao*) was a programme of the Yingluck Shinawatra government under which farmers sold rice to the government at a particular price, with the right to reclaim the rice if the market price later exceeded that price. It aimed to help farmers but was branded as deeply corrupt. Although it is not clear how Yingluck was involved with the corruption, she was held responsible for it and has faced trial.

15. Thaksin was accused of tax evasion because he sold shares of his corporation worth more than a billion dollars to foreign investors without paying taxes.

However, after years of prosecution, the attorney general decided not to appeal the case to the Supreme Court on 26 September 2011, resulting in Thaksin's exoneration in the case.

16. Interview with Pum, 10 April 2015.

17. Although the Red Shirts primarily comprised United Front of Democracy Against Dictatorship (UDD) leaders, members and supporters, they also include individuals, groups and organizations that do not identify themselves with the UDD and are critical of the UDD, especially its leaders, on some issues. For scholarly work on the Red Shirts, see, for example, Apichat et al. (2013).

18. "Tang Achiwa" is an alias of Ekapop Luera, a former student activist accused of defaming the monarchy when he spoke at a Red Shirt rally at Ratchamangkala Stadium in late 2013. He fled Thailand shortly after the military coup of 2014 and has been granted political asylum in New Zealand.

19. Interview with Ek, 25 March 2015.

20. Interview with Lom, 12 April 2015.

21. Interview with Rom, 23 March 2015.

22. Interview with Ek, 25 March 2015.

23. Interview with Lom, 12 April 2015.

24. Ibid.

25. Interview with Pum, 10 April 2015.

26. Interview with Thong, a 41-year-old rubber farmer, Mai Siap village, Cha-uat District, Nakhon Si Thammarat, 15 April 2015.

27. Interview with Lom, 12 April 2015.

28. Interview with Rom, 23 March 2015.

29. Interview with Pum, 10 April 2015.

30. Interview with Ek, 25 March 2015.

31. Interview with Rom, 23 March 2015.

32. After the coup of 2014, the number of cases in which people have been charged under article 112 of the Thai criminal code, relating to *lèse majesté*, has increased (Thai Lawyers for Human Rights 2016). This increase has on the one hand something to do with the increasing number of those criticizing the monarchy's involvement with political conflicts and on the other hand with the heavy-handed measures of the government placed in power by the NCPO junta (ibid.).

33. Interview with Ed, 25 March 2015.

34. Interview with Pum, 10 April 2015.

35. Interview with Ek, 25 March 2015.

36. Interview with Pum, 10 April 2015.

37. Interview with Ek, 25 March 2015.

38. Interview with Pum, 10 April 2015.

39. On 15 July 2014, or about two months after the coup, Suthep was secretly

ordained at Tha Sai temple in Kanchanadit District of Surat Thani province and moved to stay at Thannamlai temple or Wat Suan Mok in Chaiya District of the same province. He left the monkhood on 28 July 2015 at Traithammaram temple in Mueang District of Surat Thani. He had been ordained as a monk for one year and thirteen days, during which time he performed religious duties such as holding *kathin* ceremonies in Southern temples. Lom attended one such ceremony.

40. Interview with Lom, 12 April 2015.

41. Royal prerogative is the king's power, which surpasses laws and due process. It is often called upon in political crises during which laws and due process are seen as unable to solve problems.

42. Adopting a term that referred to the children of male Chinese immigrants and Thai women in the era before mass female Chinese immigration to Siam, Sondhi called himself and the majority of Bangkok PAD supporters *"luk chin"*. The term previously had a negative connotation because the Thai nation was associated with the Thai race, and Thai nationalism as created and promoted by King Vajiravudh took the Chinese as its enemy. Chinese immigrants and descendants had to hide their identity or assimilate into Thai society and culture. However, changes in Thai politics and the growth of the urban middle class, most of whom are of Chinese descent, in recent decades began to give the term a positive meaning. Members of the new urban middle class not only tried to learn about Chinese culture and invoked their Chinese ethnicity but also reimagined their Chinese-Siamese identity and the Thai imagined community. The new Thai imagined community is composed of peoples of diverse ethnicities and cultures, including Chinese, with the king as the focus of their loyalty (Kasian 1994, pp. 8–15, 32–35). Aware of this new Chinese identity and Thai imagined community, Sondhi took *"luk chin"* as an identity for Bangkok PAD supporters. *"Luk chin"* status is no longer contradictory to being part of the Thai nation. People of that status are able to preserve Chinese identity while being members of the Thai nation (Chai-anan 2008).

43. Interview with Ping, a 52-year-old wage labourer, Pa Khlok village, Thalang district, Phuket 25 October 2014.

44. Interview with San, a 65-year-old retired fishery-sector businessman, Ban Kho village, 15 April 2015.

45. Interview with Phot, a 51-year-old fisherman, Ban Kho village, Hua Sai District, Nakhon Si Thammarat 15 April 2015.

46. Interview with San, 15 April 2015.

47. It should be noted that nationalism does not necessarily stand in contrast to regionalism. Henley (1996, pp. 17–18) maintains that, while certain characteristics — demands for equity rather than self-sufficiency, and for

autonomy rather than freedom — distinguish regionalism from nationalism, there is continuity between regional and national identities as well as a threshold between them. The questions at hand are therefore what the threshold is and what accounts for this continuity. One of the goals of this chapter is an examination of these questions.

48. In marked contrast, the three predominantly Malay-Muslim provinces of the far South voted overwhelmingly against the 2016 charter.

4

Exit, Voice, (Dis)loyalty?
Northeast Thailand after the 2014 Coup

Saowanee T. Alexander and Duncan McCargo

We are now entering the era of Lao civilization...

Interview, Khon Kaen, 9 June 2015

The informants in this Red Shirt community seemed deadly serious. Bangkok and the whole of the Central Plains would soon be under water, thanks to climate change. Khorat would become a port city, and the Thai capital would move to Khon Kaen. Already, many people from Southern and Central Thailand had bought plots of land in Isan, ready to pull up stakes once the waters rose. Those from the rest of the country would be welcome to move to Isan, the villagers hastened to add, but their ominous references to the 2004 tsunami suggested that *le déluge* might conveniently sweep away large swathes of Thailand's population. *Yuk lao siwilai*, however, was already upon us, evinced by the superior 4G phones and imminent Chinese-built high speed trains of Laos itself. Thai dominance was over, and it was only a matter of time — less than seven years, one speaker insisted — before nature took its course.[1]

The apocalyptic discourse of *yuk lao siwilai* or the era of Lao civilization works on many levels. It contains an implicit triumphalism: the underdog will finally have its day, as the predominantly Lao population of the Northeast, or Isan, gains the upper hand over long-dominant Bangkok. The discourse also plays on the extraordinary range of national anxieties that have plagued Thailand in the new millennium, including those relating to the royal succession; concerns that the country's pre-eminent position in mainland Southeast Asia is threatened by dynamic rivals, notably Myanmar and Vietnam, and by the emerging new regional order of ASEAN Economic Community; and deep-rooted if unreasonable fears, inflamed by colour-coded political divisions, that Thailand's arbitrary borders contain within them the seeds of frustration and dissent that could sprout into secessionism and an eventual re-drawing of the national map (Darin 2012, pp. 34–35).

For better or worse, *yuk lao siwilai* is an extremely crude example of wish fulfilment, a collective fantasy that Isan could triumph over Bangkok without the need to lift a finger. It is a narrative that reflects an unequal power relationship, in which Isan/Lao attempts to resist Bangkok/Thai dominance have proved a heroic failure for centuries. In the months leading up to the 22 May 2014 coup in Bangkok, secessionist sentiments were widespread in the North and Northeast, the strongholds of the Red Shirts, a self-proclaimed anti-coup, pro-democracy movement. In March 2014, there were reports of banners hung in various locations in the North that read, "This country has no justice for me, I want to partition the country and set up a Lanna state" (*The Nation*, 4 March 2014; also, Fuller 2014*b*). Online comments about the banners echoed such secessionist sentiments, reflecting widespread dreams about exiting the Thai state. Like the notion of *yuk lao siwilai*, this discourse reflected a venting of frustrations rather than a serious demand for separation, expressing a feeling of *noi chai* — or feeling hurt or neglected — as a result of repeated acts of injustice and neglect.

Military commanders and senior bureaucrats found cause for alarm in the expression of such sentiments, which they viewed as subversive, even treasonous. In the same month, the Red Shirt movement accused the military and its allies of spreading malicious rumours about secessionist plots.[2] Just ten days before the coup, a conservative group in the Isan province of Ubon Ratchathani submitted a letter to the military claiming that Red Shirt groups were harbouring a secessionist movement (*Thai rat*, 14 March 2014). The soldiers quickly agreed to forward the letter to their superiors. On some level, such rumours fuelled the determination of the military to "restore order" and "return happiness to the people" by first staging a coup, and then following up with extensive measures of suppression.

Power relations between Bangkok and the Northeast in the wake of the 2014 military coup are a continuation of longstanding tensions. While broadly accepting a Thai-prescribed identity, the nearly twenty million Isan-Lao inhabitants have long felt resentful about the persistent condescension shown towards them by Bangkokians and others. Such resentment is not only expressed politically: as we argue elsewhere, the unequal Isan-Bangkok relationship is seen in daily-life practices, some as mundane as linguistic choices in verbal transactions (Saowanee and McCargo 2014, pp. 82–83). The history of villagers' migration to Bangkok in search of work with better income is a long history of inequality (Enos 1970, pp. 20–25).

Over the past hundred years, Northeasterners have joined forces in support of movements — previous causes included *phu mi bun* rebels, secessionism, communism and non-governmental organization activism — that ultimately petered out or were violently suppressed by the Thai state. Mass demonstrations in 2009 and 2010 in Bangkok on the part of members of the Red Shirt movement were simply the latest incarnation of a recurrent pattern. The protestors demanded the then military-installed prime minister to step down and call a general election. At the core of the Red Shirt protests were groups of urbanized villagers with relatively low income levels but upward social aspirations, many of whom hailed from or had roots in the North and Northeast (Naruemon and McCargo 2011, pp. 1000–1009). Urbanized villagers straddle the divide between the city and the countryside, often working in towns while officially registered as rural residents. Most of the protestors were not revolutionaries demanding an overhaul of the Thai state. Rather, they were people who aspired to achieve middle-class living standards, to share more in the benefits of Thailand's rapid economic development since the early 1960s and to secure the right to express themselves politically. The violent suppression of the 2010 Red Shirt protests in Bangkok, in which nearly one hundred people were killed, mainly by the military, showed that the Bangkok-centred power and its military allies would not tolerate any challenge from provinces lightly.

Of the 81 civilian deaths related to the military crackdown on the Red Shirts between April and May 2010, 36 victims, or 44 per cent, were registered residents of Isan provinces (People's Information Center 2012, pp. 673–716). Some of these were actually living and working in Bangkok, such as Phan Khamkong and Inplaeng Thetwong, taxi drivers from Yasothon and Ubon Ratchathani, respectively (ibid., pp. 690, 695). At least 469 individuals in Isan were arrested for offences allegedly committed in the region during and after the 2010 protests in Bangkok (ibid., p. 391).[3] The great majority of those arrested were later charged and convicted. Arrest warrants outnumbered actual arrests. In Ubon Ratchathani alone, over 400 warrants were issued (*Matichon*, 4 June 2010), but only 90 individuals were arrested, charged and convicted. About 300 warrants are still outstanding,[4] and 4 Ubon Red Shirts are in prison, serving at least thirty-three years each for charges related to arson at the Ubon Ratchathani provincial hall on 19 May 2010.[5]

In the wake of the dark days of 2010, Red Shirt groups in the Northeast focused on community-building and profile-raising. One strand of this activity was the creation of a network of so-called "Red Shirt villages", allegedly numbering more than twenty thousand communities. Many of these self-proclaimed "democracy villages" also engaged in state-supported activities such as anti-drug campaigns. Anon Saennan, a former associate of the prominent Udon Thani Red Shirt leader Khwanchai Phraiphana initiated the village network (*Nangsue khumue kanpoetmuban suea daeng phuea prachathippatai*, n.d.). Later on, the United Front for Democracy against Dictatorship (UDD), a national organization supporting the political cause of controversial former prime minister Thaksin Shinawatra, sought to co-opt the Red Shirt village movement for its own purposes, resulting in a bitter power struggle. Khwanchai distanced himself from the initiative, preferring to engage in acts of political theatre, such as masterminding the ordination of 999 Isan Red Shirts into the monkhood at the beginning of 2012.[6] Moreover, the majority of Isan Red Shirt groups described themselves as *daeng itsara*, independent Red Shirts not directly linked to the UDD. They typically concentrated on firming up their support base through access to community radio stations linked to savings co-operatives and other self-help projects, which were able to draw on significant levels of state funding during the 2011–14 Yingluck Shinawatra administration.

From late 2013 onwards, anti-Yingluck protest groups spearheaded by the People's Democratic Reform Committee (PDRC) caused extensive disruption to life in the Thai capital. Facing mounting political pressure, Yingluck dissolved parliament and called for a general election. The poll was held on 2 February 2014. However, the PDRC successfully blocked many polling stations in Bangkok and provinces in the Upper South. The

Constitutional Court subsequently annulled the election, claiming that the polling process had not taken place nationwide (International Crisis Group 2014, p. 15). The conflicts continued. The 22 May coup finally quelled the political cacophony of street rallies and violent clashes.[7] Even in the Northeastern stronghold of the Red Shirts, who had proclaimed their ardent opposition to military intervention, protests ended almost immediately.

What happened to the dissenting voices of Isan people? This chapter offers an overview of resistance in Isan after the 2014 military coup, explains the historical background to that resistance and looks at prospects for the future. It is based on field research conducted between May 2014 and June 2015, primarily in Ubon Ratchathani province. We conducted additional research in Mahasarakham, Sakon Nakhon, Mukdahan, Roi Et, Udon Thani, Khon Kaen and Si Saket provinces, and we have included observations of public daily interactions, documentary analysis of news reports and interviews with informants from different backgrounds, including political activists, self-proclaimed apolitical individuals and both former and serving politicians.

This chapter argues that post-2014 coup resistance in Isan, or the lack thereof, represented yet another instance of a long struggle under way since the region became part of what is now Thailand. On one level, the struggle shows the tenacity of Isan's people in their quest to gain Bangkok's recognition of their legitimacy. On another level, the struggle underscores a lack of Isan-born leaders to challenge Bangkok's power.

Historical Tensions

The Northeast of Thailand consists of twenty-two provinces with a population of nearly nineteen million, or 28.8 per cent of the entire population of the country (National Statistical Office 2010). As the most populous region of Thailand, the Northeast is highly significant in electoral terms. To understand its role in Thailand's ongoing political conflicts, we need first to look into its past.

At the time in which Bangkok sought to integrate the Northeastern region into Siam, it was predominantly populated not by Siamese but by ethnic Lao from various sub-groups and, in the southern part of the region, by ethnic Khmer.[8] Nevertheless, the transformation of the Northeast into what came to be known as Isan went relatively smoothly, paving the way for its integration into Thailand, largely because of shared linguistic and cultural similarities.[9] The modernization of Siam originated with King Chulalongkorn's reforms, undertaken in response to Western colonial threats from the early 1890s onward (Sujit 2000, pp. 99–100). By consolidating power over the periphery in the hands of the Siamese monarchy, the reforms themselves amounted to a nationalist policy aimed at making Siam look like a modern state. Their core goal was safeguarding the Chakri dynasty; however, they did nothing to improve the socio-economic well-being of Isan people.

From the outset, the Northeast has played a special role in Siam's and then Thailand's political order, as a recalcitrant region deeply attached to a distinctly Lao identity and to a distinct forest tradition of Theravada Buddhism, which Bangkok has sought systematically both to suppress and to co-opt (Kamala 1997, pp. 172–93). Over the past hundred years, the region has witnessed failed attempts to challenge Thai/Siamese power. Political instability and economic hardship caused the Holy Man's Rebellion (*kabot phu mi bun*) in Isan at the turn of the twentieth century. Lasting only less than a year during 1901–2, the widespread uprising ended in violent suppression by Siam-appointed local overlords (Sila 1992, pp. 274–84). A number of Isan political leaders, including Tiang Sirikhan, a member of parliament for Sakon Nakhon province; Thong-in Phuriphat, an MP for Ubon Ratchathani; Chamlong Daorueang, an MP for Mahasarakham; and Thawin Udon, an MP for Roi Et, were leading figures in the Isan wing of the Seri Thai or Free Thai movement against Japan during the Second World War. They worked closely with Pridi Phanomyong, a French-educated lawyer and leading figure among the plotters of the 1932 coup that ended absolute monarchy, both during and after the war, when Pridi briefly became prime minister. These MPs were active in calling for more benefits for the region's populace, greater resources for rural development in the Isan region and advocating decentralization policies (Charnvit 2001, pp. 168–69).

In late 1947, a Coup Group comprising high-ranking military officers and under the nominal leadership of wartime premier Field Marshal Po. Phibunsongkhram seized power in Bangkok. The Coup Group then conducted a purge of pro-Pridi Isan political leaders, whom it accused of being anti-government, communists and downright secessionists. Thim Phuriphat, Thong-in's brother, was arrested in February 1948 for plotting to establish an independent state in Isan.[10] In 1949, while Thim was incarcerated, the government accused Thong-in, Chamlong, Thawin and another non-Isan politician — all members of parliament and former ministers under Pridi's premiership — of planning a secessionist rebellion. They were brutally murdered while in police custody (Thak 2007, p. 39). In 1952, the police also allegedly murdered Tiang and two other former Seri Thai members (ibid., p. 61). In the years that followed, Krong Chandawong, a progressive member of parliament from Sakon Nakhon, became yet another victim of the campaign of persecution. He too faced accusations of treason and communism. Krong's famous last words before his 1961 execution, *"phadetkan chong phinat prachathippatai chong charoen"* (down with dictatorship, long live democracy), are still popular among Thai pro-democracy activists today.[11]

During the Cold War, Isan became a stronghold of the Communist Party of Thailand (CPT), with villagers in border provinces actively engaged in armed activity against the Thai state.[12] Some of those previously regarded as Seri Thai heroes became villainous communists in the eyes of the state. With the assistance of the United States from the 1960s onwards, the Thai state fought and eventually defeated the CPT in the early 1980s. Using a "political offensive" strategy, the military turned former CPT members into *phu ruam phatthana chat thai* (fellow developers of the Thai nation), rewarding them with participation in development projects and financial compensation. Despite these co-optation measures, some former CPT activists have retained a residual attachment to communist ideologies and have sought to continue their struggles through alternative means ranging from the NGO movement to support for the Red Shirts (Naruemon and McCargo 2011, pp. 1000–1001).

After the end of the Cold War, the region did not see any political leaders of the same stature as the Isan members of parliament of the Pridi era. Nonetheless, throughout the 1980s and 1990s, a variety of socio-economic issues gave rise to protests against the Bangkok state. For instance, displaced and affected villagers vehemently opposed the construction of the controversial Pak Mun Dam in Ubon Ratchathani. The villagers joined the Assembly of the Poor, an organized movement formed by grass-roots people and NGO activists in order to address socio-economic problems.[13] The Pak Mun Dam protest group has been campaigning against the dam project ever since, albeit with very little success. Throughout the 1990s, demonstrators associated with the Small Scale Farmers' Federation of Isan and the Assembly of the

Poor staged mass rallies concerning livelihood issues in central Bangkok virtually annually, most notably the Ninety-Nine-Day Protest outside Government House in 1997.

One consequence of the adoption of the 1997 Thai constitution, which reflected a range of competing and sometimes contradictory agendas, was to strengthen parliament and give Isan voters the chance to flex their muscles electorally. General elections held in 2001 and 2005 handed Thaksin Shinawatra, a former police officer-turned-tycoon-turned-politician, the premiership, giving him greater power and popularity than any elected civilian in Thailand's political history. Isan was a stronghold for Thaksin supporters. To his supporters, Thaksin's populist policies and hands-on approach offered a dramatic change to Thai politics:[14] they considered him the first leader who addressed their problems and aspirations with policies that bettered their living conditions. A highly controversial figure in the eyes of the elite establishment and of many urban middle-class voters, who came to see him as self-serving and authoritarian, Thaksin found himself ousted by means of a military coup on 19 September 2006. But the coup failed to undermine support for pro-Thaksin parties, which won convincing victories in the 2007 and 2011 Thai general elections. The 2006 coup also led to the beginning of the colour-coded politics of anti-Thaksinite, royalist Yellow Shirts versus Thaksinite Red Shirts. Their attachment to Thaksin and to the parties that he founded turned many ordinary Northeasterners into political activists who have emerged as significant players in Thailand's rally politics since the 2006 coup.[15] They held prolonged, large-scale street protests in Bangkok in 2009 and 2010 (International Crisis Group 2010a, pp. 2–6).

The Red Shirt movement, like pro-Thaksin parties, has strongholds in Isan and the North, while the Yellow Shirt movement, like the Democrat Party, was strongest in Bangkok, parts of the Central Plains and the Upper South. Red Shirt supporters claimed to fight for democracy and justice. The Red Shirt movement is nevertheless heterogeneous, composed of factions with ideological differences on certain political issues. For example, at the height of the movement in 2010–12, there were eight or nine rival Red Shirt groups in Ubon Ratchathani alone. The core leadership of the movement, the UDD, is closely tied to the Phuea Thai Party and very much influenced by Thaksin, who has lived in self-imposed exile since 2008. More progressive factions of the movement do exist, but they have little influence over the movement's decision-making on strategy and planning, let alone mobilizing power. Between the 2006 and 2014 coups, the Red Shirts mobilized an unprecedented number of Isan people to join its protests. While it was during this period that Isan people took on new roles as political activists, these protests also claimed the lives and freedom of many. Any victories that they scored proved short-lived.

The long-standing tensions and struggles outlined above stemmed from inequalities that Isan people have had to endure in Thai society. The hierarchical nature of Thai society is an obstacle to ordinary people's participation in democratic development (Rigg 1991, pp. 199–211). Drawing upon her analysis of powerful political figures in Thai history, Saichon Satayanurak has shown that the concept of "Thainess", which is based upon the nation-religion-king trinity, forms the core of the Thai nationalist discourse. She argues that the concept of Thainess idealizes virtue, legitimizes social hierarchy and leads people to view politics as a dirty business (Saichon 2005, esp. pp. 7–9). As she argues, Thainess was used to denounce the general election in 1957 as a "dirty election", and it formed the basis of military rule that supported and strengthened conditions of structural inequality. To make her case about how members of the ruling elite, such as former prime minister Kukrit Pramoj, praised the role of the military in politics, Saichon observes that Kukrit's 1957 definition of "the monarchy" sought to make Thais accept the power of the military, which allegedly demonstrated the utmost loyalty to the king and ruled the country under the monarchy's close supervision. He also sought to portray the monarchy as a moral anchor and urged people to accept hierarchical power relationships, promoting a deep popular awareness of *thi tam thi sung* (what is low and what is high) (ibid., p. 15). Such notions of social inequality have become deeply ingrained in Thai politics: the traditional elite look down on civilian politicians as morally inferior to military officers and civil — in Thai, royal — servants.

The regions of Thailand are structurally subordinated to the political dominance of the capital city. His examination of writings of travelling members of the Siamese elite in the nineteenth century has led Thongchai Winichakul (2000, p. 41) to argue that, in the eyes of the rulers, not all Siamese subjects were equal. The *khon bannok* or country people of Isan were "docile others", assigned to a more favourable category than *khon pa* or wild people living in remote forested areas (Thongchai 2000, pp. 48–50). Both *khon bannok* and *khon pa* were others within — Siamese subjects but yet different and inferior. Such patronizing attitudes persist in modern-day politics. As Thongchai further observes, Bangkok residents and the media determine the dominant view of democracy, while vilifying provincial people for allegedly selling their votes to corrupt provincial politicians (ibid., p. 56).

The discourses of Thainess and of the others within work in concert to maintain social and political inequality and to shore up this status quo. Many Bangkokians and others trapped in a dichotomous good-versus-evil approach to politics have thus rejected any political movement linked to pro-Thaksin elements. To many such people, Thaksin is "bad". The Red Shirts were bad because they were corrupted by Thaksin's populist policies, and those concerned about their public image should not be sympathetic towards "bad people". As a largely pro-Thaksin region, Isan is viewed as a stronghold for those who oppose the politics of virtue. Northeasterners, as speakers on the PDRC stages repeatedly argued, are ignorant, vulnerable and susceptible to vote buying and manipulation by unscrupulous politicians.[16]

Isan after the 2014 Military Coup

Suppression in Isan started with the nationally televised coup announcement on 22 May 2014 after the military's ominous declaration of martial law two days earlier. Within twenty-four hours of the announcement of the coup, the National Council for Peace and Order (NCPO), under the leadership of General Prayut Chanocha, issued a series of orders summoning individuals, both civilians and government officials, to report to designated military compounds.[17] Most of those summoned were pro-Thaksin politicians and Red Shirt activists or sympathizers (*Thai rat*, 25 July 2014). They faced Hirschman's classic choice among exit, voice and loyalty (Hirschman 1970). The military demanded that those summoned make professions of loyalty, often by signing what many euphemistically called "MOUs"— for "memoranda of understanding"— according to which they pledged to refrain from political activity and from making public statements critical of the junta. The great majority agreed to do so. A smaller number, including some who had not been formally called in, chose to flee the country, mainly for Laos or Cambodia, though a few made it as far as Europe and the United States. Some scholars and activists who were already abroad either delayed their returns or decided not to go back to Thailand at all. Those who fled faced the prospect of a potentially indefinite period of absence.[18] The middle path — continuing to voice open criticism of the regime — was the road least taken.

After a few days, the army released many of those who had surrendered, though it charged some with serious crimes. For example, Prasit Chaisisa, a former Red Shirt leader and Phuea Thai MP from Surin, was sentenced to two and a half years in prison for insulting the monarchy (*Thai rat*, 3 December 2014). In another less publicized case, an Isan Red Shirt activist on the summons list committed suicide a day after his name appeared on national television. Instead of surrendering to the military, on the early morning of 2 June 2014, Sarawut Phuthonyothin decided to shoot himself. During a subsequent meeting with Ubon Ratchathani academics, whom the army had summoned to a local military base, a soldier trivialized Sarawut's demise as that of a "local politician" with "political problems", as if the pressures of a televised summons were unrelated to his suicide.[19]

Many Red Shirt leaders enjoyed good relations with army units in their home provinces; in the wake of the coup, the military sent special units from different areas to arrest key targets, since regional army commanders did not trust the local military to round them up. One Red Shirt leader explained that, while she and her husband were in hiding in the days following the coup, right after fleeing the Aksa rally site in Bangkok at which the Red Shirts had gathered to protest against the PDRC just before the coup, a group of fourteen soldiers armed with assault rifles visited their house and asked their children their whereabouts. Acting on orders from their commander, these soldiers had travelled almost four hundred kilometres from their base in another province just to arrest this woman. Instead of turning herself in either in her home province or in the distant province to which the local military unit had summoned her, this Red Shirt leader opted to report to a sympathetic army commander in a third province an hour's drive away.

In addition to direct threats to individuals, the NCPO issued clear orders calling for the media and the general public not to criticize its actions. One Isan Red Shirt leader, not affiliated with Phuea Thai or the UDD, recalled being detained along with four other leaders — some from the UDD, others from independent groups — on the grounds of a provincial military base for six days. While there, they signed an "MOU" with the NCPO. A local Red Shirt leader who was detained on a military base after turning himself in observed that Yellow Shirt leaders who turned themselves in did not, in contrast, then suffer detention.[20] After their release, Red Shirt leaders had to report to the base every Monday; many were still doing so at the time of writing. For a few months after the coup, armed military personnel frequently visited their homes and questioned any visitors. The underlying message was to remind Red Shirts that they were under surveillance and so to encourage them to remain quiet.[21]

Purportedly Red-leaning university lecturers in the Northeast received invitations for a "discussion" at a provincial army base. They were asked to cooperate with the NCPO by not "taking part in any political activity", "keeping an eye on anti-junta activity among students" and "waiting until the NCPO organizes a reform forum".[22] Despite the military's "soft" approach to the academics, the act of summoning them in for a talk in itself raised concern over their freedom.[23] Isan university lecturers in general found themselves in trouble when trying to host academic fora or talks. Universities circulated orders demanding NCPO approval in advance of academic events that concerned politics.[24] A lecturer from Mahasarakham University faced investigation on suspicions that he had hung up a banner sporting an anti-junta message (*Prachatai*, 5 March 2015). Another Mahasarakham lecturer was investigated for his alleged connections with student protestors (*Matichon*, 16 June 2015).

A harsher suppressive approach involved arrests — as opposed to summons, visits or invitations — and serious criminal charges. The most widely publicized case involved the arrests of twenty-two alleged Red Shirt activists on 23 May 2014 in Khon Kaen. Authorities accused them of organizing a subversive plot against the military junta, a plot that the latter labelled the "Khon Kaen Model" (MCOT, 25 June 2014). Those arrested were detained without bail and later charged with terrorism and national-security-related offenses.[25] Authorities subsequently arrested four additional people. All twenty-six defendants went before the Khon Kaen military court in a turn of events that raised grave concerns about the quality of justice they would receive (*Prachatai*, 19 March 2015). The harsh treatment of this "Khon Kaen Model" group, many of them ordinary villagers professing complete innocence, exemplified the hard-line modes of operation that the military reserved for uppity Isan people whom it construed as a threat, echoing the persecution of supposedly secessionist Isan MPs in earlier decades (Thai Lawyers for Human Rights 2015).

Another common form of suppression was "attitude adjustment" programming concentrated at major army bases such as one in Nakhon

Ratchasima, the very same Khorat seen as a future port by the prophets of *yuk lao siwilai*. Those whom the military had earlier summoned were subsequently bused to this base from their home provinces for *kanoprom* or training to promote "peace and stability".[26] During the first few months after the coup, authorities required Red Shirt activists' participation in these activities, though our informants viewed these attitude adjustment activities as a waste of time.[27] As one put it, "It does not matter how many times they take us into 'the room'; our minds will never change. The Yellow Shirts are the same. They will never change their beliefs. We've come this far." Apparently, the army's efforts failed to change the Red Shirts' political convictions.

Citing coup announcements, the NCPO has forbidden the media to criticize the junta's activities (Isra News Agency, 31 July 2014). The junta banned local radio stations from covering politics, and it closed down many Red Shirt stations altogether.[28] Surprisingly, a station run by Khwanchai Praiphana, a prominent Udon Thani Red Shirt leader, remained on air, but was limited to broadcasting popular *luk thung* country music programmes.[29] Mentioning the words "dictator" or even "democracy" in public or on air could land a speaker in trouble. Two Phuea Thai politicians in different provinces who had previously made regular appearances on Red-leaning television channels stated they were being monitored for their use of language at social events, such as weddings and funerals. One had faced reprimand for singing the popular song *Kulap daeng* or "Red Rose", which military officers claimed that he had sung only to incite resistance to the authorities. Some of those summoned were able to negotiate an easing of draconian "MOU" provisions. They might, for example, win release from the requirement that they ask for permission from the military before leaving their home provinces. However, those whose behaviour the military deemed questionable faced additional restrictions. One prominent Red Shirt leader was asked to sign a new "MOU" in February 2015, according to which he had to promise not to wear a red shirt, or even a checked shirt containing red in the pattern.

The NCPO reshuffled and transferred bureaucrats extensively, especially Interior Ministry officials and police officers suspected of holding pro-Thaksin sympathies. Initially using martial law, which it later replaced with the more draconian article 44 of the interim charter, which gave the junta absolute powers to deal with anything it deemed a threat to national security, the junta-backed government claimed to be fighting corruption by targeting problematic government officials (*The Daily Telegraph*, 2 April 2015). It resorted subsequently to more extensive orders for transfers and suspensions from duty, affecting elected and non-elected officials (*Matichon*, 25 June 2015).

Pro–Red Shirt villages were soon virtually clear of Red Shirt paraphernalia. A village in Kalasin province that had displayed several UDD flags at its entrance just days before the coup later sported only the ubiquitous royal and national flags. Some former Red Shirt villages assumed new guises, including re-branding themselves as "mushroom villages" apparently dedicated to the promotion of alternative livelihoods. In similar fashion, some Red Shirt leaders started schemes to market coffee beans and herbal medicine, not least as such activities offered them ways of trying to maintain their personal networks while lying low politically. An Ubon Red Shirt leader, for example, made regular trips to villages throughout the province and held meetings to discuss "business plans" with members of his network. As a prominent leader who had mobilized several hundred protestors to join the 2010 protests and had been under surveillance since the coup, the leader found this time to be an opportunity to prepare himself for eventual elections, or so he hoped.[30]

Silence is Not Loyalty

The NCPO's widespread repressive measures silenced many dissenting voices, especially those of Red Shirts. However, while this heavy-handedness could ensure that there was little overt opposition from the Red Shirts, resistance did continue in subterranean forms.

It is understandable that fear of repercussions meant that Red Shirt activists did not want to resist the junta, as they had been the main targets of the military. Two pro-Thaksin Red Shirt leaders in Ubon Ratchathani, interviewed separately, were both adamant that street rallies did not offer a solution to the country's ongoing political conflicts, whose causes lay deep beneath the surface of public life. One claimed that he might never see democracy in Thailand in his lifetime. He said that, if someone called upon the Red Shirts to stage a protest today or tomorrow, he would definitely not join that protest, regardless of how non-violent it might be. Street rallies might be temporary palliatives, but they would not solve the underlying problems between the two colour-coded camps. The other leader said that he had seen so many lives affected by the 2010 clashes, in which many people were either killed or jailed and families were torn apart. As a result, he did not feel comfortable calling his followers out, not knowing what would happen to them. Most of his followers were older people. He could not afford to leave them vulnerable. These two leaders preferred to wait out military rule, assuming that once an election was called, the voices of Isan people would again be heard.

The authorities had summoned both of these informants, detained them for days and monitored them closely since the coup. Reasons other than concern for their own safety, including the stance of Thaksin Shinawatra himself, may have motivated their decision not to oppose the junta. A number of interviewees, some of whom had spoken directly to Thaksin by phone or Skype, stated that the former prime minister had urged them not to resist the military. Thaksin did not oppose the junta-backed government (*Post Today*, 22 August 2014). Indeed, he had called on Phuea Thai members and Red Shirts to cooperate with the NCPO (*Krungthep thurakit*, 22 August 2014). Phuea Thai told its members simply to "wait" for the junta's rule to end. A Phuea Thai politician expressed frustration over the lack of action from the party's leadership at a time when vote canvassers and voters in local precincts pressed for resistance to the junta. This politician wanted to see the party adopt a stronger pro-democratic stance.[31]

Ordinary Red Shirts were very upset about the coup. During a group interview conducted in Ubon Ratchathani, villager informants became visibly irritated when asked whether the Red Shirt movement was dead, strongly denying that their movement was over. They were adamant that all that they wanted was someone who could lead their rallies against the junta, echoing the region's persistent desire for a strong Isan leader to challenge Bangkok's dominance. If their leaders called for a rally, these villagers said, they would not hesitate to participate. Asked if they themselves had attempted to stage any protest, they nevertheless said, "No". Without some form of leadership, they would not do so. In describing their political frustrations, they used the metaphor of *tin chang yiap pak nok*, or "an elephant's foot crushing a bird's beak", to say that the ruling power used harsh measures of suppression to clamp down on the powerless like them. Similar responses emerged in all our interviews with ordinary Red Shirts.

The silenced Red Shirt movement refrained from staging anti-junta protests, but its supporters continued with life as usual, with resistance reduced to that of quotidian politics. In public places frequented by ordinary people, including markets and train stations in Khon Kaen, Si Saket and Ubon Ratchathani, weathered pro–Red Shirt, anti-Democrat Party and pro–Phuea Thai political messages, on stickers and banners and in graffiti, were still to be found on vehicles and buildings. Some people continued to appear in public wearing red shirts with images of Thaksin's face and UDD logos or slogans.[32] That Isan Red Shirts tried to express their political stance even in such trivial ways showed a continuing desire to remind themselves of the legacy of their unprecedented months-long, fateful protests in Bangkok, though, overall, it was a sorry state of affairs.

"Non-Red" Resistance

Signs of defiance in Isan did not take shape until several months after the 2014 coup. Activists not aligning themselves with any political group took the lead in resistance to the junta. University students and groups working on economic or environmental causes were on the front line in attempts to reclaim space for democracy in the Northeast. A much publicized protest took place on 19 November 2014, when five Khon Kaen University students from the Dao Din group flashed the banned three-fingered salute borrowed from the film *The Hunger Games* right in front of General Prayut Chanocha as he was addressing the audience at the opening ceremony of a government project in Khon Kaen. Dao Din's core interest is in campaigning against development projects that destroy the environment and put local villagers' lives at risk, especially gold mining in Loei province. The three-fingered salute incident marked the beginning of the group's anti-coup campaign. A high-ranking army officer quickly alleged that a local politician had paid the students from Dao Din to protest — an allegation that they fiercely denied (*Krungthep thurakit*, 1 December 2014). The authorities arrested Dao Din members several times, but, because their protests gained both media attention and considerable public sympathy, the junta was not able to apply harsh measures in dealing with them. However, security officers made threats to their parents and academic mentors.[33]

Dao Din students continued to defy the junta authorities while both Thai and international media and human rights organizations kept a close watch on them. On 24 June 2015, the anniversary of the end of the absolute monarchy in 1932, the Dao Din students joined their fellow students in Bangkok to file charges against security officers who had physically abused them while they were in custody after their arrests for participating in a protest at the Bangkok Art and Culture Center on 22 May 2015, held to mark the first anniversary of the 2014 coup. After some hours, with more and ordinary people joining the 24 June demonstration in support of the students, the police finally allowed representatives of the students to file charges (*Matichon*, 24 June 2015). The students' defiant attitude and actions put the police on the spot: in sensitive and highly publicized cases like this one, the military quietly slipped into the background.

Right from the start, the Dao Din students made clear that they were not Red Shirts, even though they supported democracy and elections (*Prachatai English*, 28 November 2014). By linking their concerns to those of disadvantaged villagers, Dao Din was able to claim further legitimacy. A reporter who had followed Dao Din activities confirmed that the students did not want to be associated with the Red Shirts at all. In fact, they were visibly upset when they saw Red Shirts congregating in front of the police station in which they had been detained as a result of their first protest.[34] Dao Din members' negative reaction to the accusation that they were Red Shirts was reminiscent of the posture of a group of well-known law lecturers called Nitirat, who have adamantly denied Red Shirt connections, even though they are anti-military and pro-democracy. The stance adopted by Nitirat and Dao Din reflected the persistent discourse of politics as a dirty business for corrupt politicians.[35] That the media praised anti-junta protests by university students and publicly known intellectuals as legitimate and worthy of endorsement helps perpetuate the belief that political legitimacy belongs only to certain groups in the society. While Dao Din's bold resistance to the power of the NCPO was commendable, the attention gained by this small "apolitical" group testified to the weakness of anti-coup resistance more generally.

Other community activists whose struggles against the state had started long before the coup also held a series of protests. On 14 February 2015, concurrent but unrelated protests took place in the Northeast and in the Thai capital. In Khon Kaen, villagers and NGO supporters protested against state support for the transport of drilling equipment for natural gas wells though a village. In Bangkok, Pak Mun Dam activists confronted security forces.

On 20 March 2015, a group of academics and representatives of Isan villages hosted a public forum in Bangkok focussing on exploitative state-supported development projects in the Northeast. Representatives came from various provinces and from villages affected by gold mining, potash mining and disputes over land rights. Themes addressed included the unequal power relations between Isan and agencies of the centralized Thai state, socio-economic inequality and denial of the right of public participation in the implementation of development projects. The forum concluded with a bold move on the part of participants, who read a manifesto entitled *"Isan mai"* (New Isan). The underlying message of this manifesto was a demand for the right to participate in decision-making about state projects in their communities (*Prachatai*, 20 March 2015).

Less Visible Resistance

While the Red Shirts suddenly turned silent after the coup, complaints about economic hardship became louder. This hardship was an issue that people considered relatively safe to comment about. A Khon Kaen sidewalk stall owner complained of decreasing sales since the 2014 coup. Her choice of reference point was significant, as it implied that the coup had something to do with the deteriorating economy. In her view, responsibility for the recession lay with the military and its supporters. Claiming that she was not Red or Yellow seemed to allow the informant to complain freely. She mentioned that Thaksin and Yingluck's policies had helped poor people. When asked whether other vendors and shop owners in the same area had similar complaints, she said that most of them did. Pointing to a cosmetics shop nearby, she said that the shop owner had been letting go of employees and turning off the air-conditioning in the shop to reduce expenses. She further commented that the conflicts affecting the country were so deep-rooted that an election would not resolve them. Her final remark was, "Under Thaksin, the people were encouraged to be smart, but now the people are encouraged to be utterly stupid." The tone of her remarks and her references to Yingluck's rice pledging scheme and Thaksin's thirty-baht universal healthcare scheme — signature policies of their respective premierships — showed that she had opinions about political developments in spite of her claim to be politically impartial.[36]

Informants were also critical of the constitution-drafting process then being conducted under the auspices of the NCPO. Some Red Shirt supporters still followed politics closely, while others admitted that they were "burned out". An Ubon Ratchathani farmer expressed a lack of interest in following news about constitution drafting. He said that nothing would improve the situation until Thailand was rid of "double standards" — a term commonly used to highlight the differential treatment that Red Shirts believed they experienced at the hands of the justice system. He was also sceptical about elections: all he did was focus on matters of *pak thong*, on bread-and-butter issues. Other informants, who believed that the 2015 draft constitution was so bad that it would not be passed, made similar comments. In the event, the NCPO-appointed National Legislative Assembly rejected the 2015 draft constitution. A popular referendum approved a new draft in August 2016, even as the majority of Isan voters cast their ballots against it.[37]

Even before publication of the 2015 draft constitution, a group of villagers interviewed complained about the provision for an unelected prime minister. One of them commented, "If they will pick *khon nok* [an unelected figure] as the prime minister, then there is no point in holding an election — a waste of budget!"[38] The questionable nature of the constitution-drafting process was another focus of criticism. A community representative who was invited to participate in a public forum held in her province by the Constitution Drafting Committee said that she participated simply because district-level officials had asked her to find some twenty people to attend, offering them participation fees.[39] She commented that she and another attendee had decided not to answer the questionnaire about the draft. She also complained that the people had not initiated the constitution and that there was therefore no point in the people's taking part in its preparation now — not even by offering comments on the draft. While the name of the forum led people to believe that "public voices" would be heard, attendees spent almost the entire event listening to lectures. An Ubon Ratchathani student whose school recruited her entire class to attend the nationally televised forum complained that she was not yet eligible to vote. She thought that the organizers' purpose was to use school students to fill the venue, just so that the forum appeared to have garnered public interest.

Prayut and the military were a regular focus of criticism from informants. In addition to military intervention in politics, informants complained about the huge budget controlled by the military. Prayut's personality was another subject of criticism — a matter not helped by his numerous provocative televised comments. Some villagers claimed that they quickly changed channel to watch Laotian satellite television when Prayut came on the air on Friday nights. Another informant said that he *kliat* (hated) the weekly address and did not watch it. During one interview, Prayut suddenly appeared on the television screen; one of the members of the staff of the office in which we were conducting the interview screamed out his name, leapt up from her seat and immediately turned off the television. An informant who had once served as an army conscript complained that Prayut should have emulated previous coup-makers and declined the premiership. Informants often compared the lack of *khwamsanga-ngam* or grace in the general's rise to power and his patronizing language unfavourably with Yingluck's polite and humble demeanour. Another informant observed that Prayut was the opposite of Yingluck. The informant had expressed dissatisfaction with her when she was in power, but she had never threatened people with imprisonment for criticizing her.

By no means everyone expressed opposition to the coup: support was strongest in urban areas, among government officials and leading beneficiaries of state spending. Banchong Kositchiranan, the long-serving mayor of Roi Et municipality, offered strong support for the NCPO's reform policies, which he claimed were long overdue.[40] While agreeing that military rule was inherently undesirable, Phornchai Khowsurat, the chairman of the Ubon Ratchathani Provincial Administrative Organization, argued that the NCPO's attempts to purge the country of corrupt politicians were laudable.[41] A week after making this comment, Phornchai was one of seventy-one officials removed from office by Prayut under article 44 for alleged corruption (*Matichon*, 25 June 2015). Phornchai's outward show of support for the regime was not enough to save him.

The complaints and criticisms seen in the above examples do not amount to resistance, but they reflect the resentment towards the NCPO government widespread in many parts of Isan. Unwilling to embrace the junta but equally unable to confront it, many Northeasterners confined themselves to whispers of disloyalty — a very muted form of "voice".

Prospects

Recurring themes of anti-establishment discourse in Isan since 2006 are *khwammaipentham* (injustice) and *song mattrathan* (double standards). As one informant put it, "Without justice this country will never get out of the conflicts." Many informants believed that elections might bring a temporary truce but that they would not solve the root cause of Thailand's political problems. A pro–Democrat Party informant in Ubon Ratchathani expressed his concern about the lack of progress after the coup and his dissatisfaction with the junta's approach to solving economic problems. He believed that an election would bring back a civilian government and that the general atmosphere would improve. Others were sceptical about the outcome of any future elections. These sceptics were not only Red Shirts but also those who claimed to be politically impartial. They expressed concern that the elections would not end political conflicts if pro-Thaksin parties won them, in what was the most likely outcome. Pro-Thaksin sentiment still dominated Isan voters' discourse, as one informant observed. Ordinary voters talked about having benefitted from the former prime minister's public policies. This informant further observed that, despite the fact that the Democrat-led government and even the junta implemented policies similar to Thaksin's, the general populace was still not impressed with them. Isan people in general remained fixated on Thaksin as "the first politician" to address their problems. While many observers both inside and outside Thailand have sought to portray the Red Shirt movement as "post-Thaksin" in orientation, the reality was that across Isan most Red Shirts remained resolutely "pro-Thaksin".

The 2006 coup provoked intense anger in Isan, seen in the region's referendum rejection of the 2007 constitution and the strong performance of pro-Thaksin parties across the Northeast in the 2007 and 2011 general elections. The violent suppression of the 2010 Bangkok protests sent many Red Shirts home, shaken but not disheartened. Yingluck's victory in the 2011 elections showed that they still wanted to fight, this time through the ballot boxes. In the wake of the events of 2014 — the failed 2 February elections and subsequent May coup — voters on both sides of the political divide remained sceptical that fresh elections would reset Thailand's troubled politics in a lasting way. In response to a question about whether they thought the people in the region would put up with the junta rule for an extended period of time, one informant noted that ordinary Isan people have long been *cham ot cham thon*, that they had long endured the inevitable, regardless of who served as national leader.

Heroic Failure Revisited?

A long history of Isan resistance formed the backdrop to modes of resistance in the aftermath of the 2014 coup. Inequality has during that history been a major factor driving people to resist the Siamese/Thai state in ways ranging from simple resentment in the face of discrimination to such stronger expressions as rebellions and protests. Yet, to date, one could perhaps best characterize such resistance as a series of heroic failures.

David Brown has observed that the history of Isan is one filled with aspirations without leaders. In his analysis of the place of regionalism in national integration, Brown (1994, p. 190) views the assassinations of the former Seri Thai Isan politicians as great disappointments to Isan people, whose hopes for future prosperity the killings cut short. In a more critical way, Daniel Fineman (1997, p. 9) characterizes the political conflicts that led to the demise of those Isan politicians as those that drew a line between wealthy royalists aspiring to restore power to the monarchy and Isan commoners of humble origins. Earlier still, the stance of the *phu mi bun* rebel leaders reflected the aspirations of some people in the region, though the rebellion also reflected deep ties with territory in what is now Laos. While there were several reasons for the revolt, it was clear that the *phu mi bun* group in Ubon, one of the largest such groups, had a clear aim of being rid of Siamese rule. The group also worked in concert with its allies on the east bank of the Mekong to push out the French administration in power there (Suwit 2014, pp. 181–82, 194). The *phu mi bun* also met their demise at the hands of more powerful political stakeholders. Instead of continuing to rise up after this defeat, ordinary people remained politically dormant for some time, until the pressure built up again at later junctures.

Despite the developments of the past decade, while Northerners and Northeasterners have become actively engaged in politics, no Isan politicians or activists have risen to leading positions in either colour-coded camp — the PDRC or the Red Shirts. The most important UDD leaders were three outspoken southerners, Wira Musikaphong, Nattawut Saikua and Jatuporn Promphan, while Khwanchai Phraiphana, the best known Red Shirt leader in Isan, is a native of Suphanburi province in Central Thailand. Why has Isan failed to produce leaders of its own? Does this failure reflect self-doubt, or a lack of confidence? Does the history of failed attempts at resistance tell us that Isan people largely embrace their inferior status? For most people of the region, exit — whether leaving Thailand or working for Isan's secession — is not a realistic option. Yet full-blooded loyalty to a state that holds them in such low esteem is difficult to sustain; loyalty certainly cannot be secured at gunpoint. Isan people do not like the inequalities imposed on them, and in recent years they have not hesitated to voice their resentment at the ballot box. Some have gone further by protesting on the streets of Bangkok. Nevertheless, they still lack the confidence, not to mention the home-grown leadership, to become more politically ambitious.

The voices of *khon isan* or Isan people became muted after 22 May 2014, but the region will not easily be permanently silenced. Meanwhile, some Northeasterners are quietly hoping that climate change will soon sweep away the problem of Bangkok dominance once and for all.

Acknowledgements

We would like to thank our informants, who were willing to share with us their experiences in spite of grave concerns over potential repercussions. We also thank Michael Montesano and Terence Chong for their valuable comments on an earlier draft of the chapter.

Notes

1. Another version of this introductory section appeared in McCargo (2015*a*).
2. See *Prachatai* (4 March 2014).
3. The figures do not include residents of Isan who were arrested or charged with offences in Bangkok; no detailed information is available for these cases.
4. Interview, Ubon Ratchathani, 16 March 2015.
5. For a discussion of the Ubon provincial hall incident, see Saowanee (2012).
6. Interview, Udon Thani, 10 June 2015.
7. For background, see McCargo (2015*c*).
8. See Grabowsky (1995).
9. See Smalley (1994) for a discussion of how languages in Thailand are arranged on the basis of power and social order.
10. See Suwatsadi (n.d.).
11. A banner containing this maxim was hung from a stand during the annual Chulalongkorn University–Thammasat University football match on 7 February 2015.
12. Interview with a retired security official, 14 June 2015.
13. See Missingham (2003).
14. See McCargo and Ukrist (2005).
15. On rally politics, see McCargo (2012*b*).
16. Field notes, PDRC rallies at Ratchaprasong and Siam intersections, January 2014.

17. For a list of NCPO orders and summons, see Isra News Agency (n.d.).
18. See, for example, the discussion in *The Nation* (13 November 2014).
19. Field notes, 3 June 2014.
20. Interview with a Red Shirt activist detained along with four others, 4 June 2015.
21. Field notes, June–July 2014.
22. Field notes, 3 June 2014.
23. Interview, 3 June 2014.
24. Field notes, August 2014.
25. Details about the case can be found at Freedom of Expression Documentation Center (n.d.).
26. Interview, 3 March 2015.
27. A senior army officer privately confirmed that he believed the attitude adjustment exercises to be wholly ineffective.
28. Interview, 16 June 2015.
29. Interview, 10 June 2015. On *luk thung* music, see Mitchell (2015).
30. Interview, 4 June 2014.
31. Interview, 17 August 2014.
32. Field notes, November 2014 – June 2015.
33. For threats against Dao Din students' parents, see *Prachatai English* (22 May 2015).
34. Interview with reporter, 7 June 2015, Khon Kaen.
35. See Connors (2007, p. 97) and McCargo and Peeradej (2015, pp. 16–18).
36. Interview with a street vendor, Khon Kaen, 6 June 2015.
37. For a relevant discussion, see McCargo, Saowanee and Desatova (2017).
38. Interview with villagers, Ubon Ratchathani, 4 March 2015.
39. Interview with an informant, Ubon Ratchathani, 4 May 2015.
40. Interview, 11 June 2015.
41. Interview, 19 June 2015.

5

The Red Shirts and their Democratic Struggle in Northern Thailand, April 2010 – May 2015

Tanet Charoenmuang

> The deaths of people [at Bangkok's Ratchadamnoen Avenue and Ratchaprasong Intersection] during April and May 2010 brought about "eye-opening" among villagers. They have now understood how the state is ready to use violence and suppress its people ... that the state sees the people's demonstration not just as a call for democracy, but as war. The state sees people as its enemy and intends to destroy them. The killings in Bangkok have transformed those villagers to be fighters who are ready to die for democracy. (Pinkaew 2013, p. 55)

Throughout 2013 and the early part of the following year, the political excitement resulting from each huge Red Shirt demonstration, both in Bangkok and beyond, in support of the elected Yingluck Shinawatra government, led many observers to believe that the Red Shirt movement was a strong democratic force, particularly in the Northeastern and Northern regions of Thailand. These observers believed that the movement was ready to oppose the return of an authoritarian regime by any means, and that the establishment of a government in exile or a division of the country to set up a Federation of Isan-Lanna States or *Sahaphan rat isan-lanna* would be an option if a military coup were staged.

A study of peasants in rural Chiang Mai published by Andrew Walker in 2012, and drawing on fieldwork undertaken since 2005, presented a vivid picture of the transformation both of villager-farmers' outlooks and of rural politics since Thaksin's Thai Rak Thai Party came to power in 2001. It documents many peasants' dissatisfaction with the coup (Walker 2012, p. 209). In addition, two often-quoted works on the Red Shirts in Northeast and Northern Thailand, the first written in November 2013 and published in 2014 (Pinkaew 2013, pp. 51–60) and the second released in September 2014 (Keyes 2014, pp. 175–94), seem to confirm notions concerning the strong political activism of the Red Shirt villagers in these two regions. According to the two studies, especially Pinkaew's, villagers had risen up, had become politically active citizens and brave fighters for democracy, and were ready to protect democracy and to sacrifice their lives for the cause. The importance of Pinkaew's study relates to her having conducted field research with Red Shirt leaders and rank-and-file members in five districts of Chiang Mai province considered the heartland of the Red Shirts in the North: Mueang, Sankamphaeng, Doi Saket, Fang and Mae Ai.

However, because Pinkaew collected those data during 2010 and 2011 — and especially after the Yingluck Shinawatra government assumed office following the elections of July of that latter year — and because another military regime took power in May 2014, the question of what has happened to those Red Shirts and their commitment to struggle, especially in the North and the Northeast, requires attention.

This chapter draws on research in the same districts of Chiang Mai province that Pinkaew studied. However, whereas Pinkaew and her research team did their work in a situation in which spirits were high, in a democratic atmosphere and under a popularly elected and pro–Red Shirt government, I conducted my own research in a totally different milieu. From December 2014 to May 2015, I conducted hastily arranged interviews in coffee shops, hotel lobbies, restaurants, temples and cars. Conversations never took place during any political gatherings because the authorities did not allow any after May 2014. The number of people in each conversation or interview was two, three or, rarely, four; a gathering of, especially, five or more Red Shirts could be a political problem. Notably, several interviews took place in commercial areas in which military units standing guard were within sight. Apart from the study in those districts of Chiang Mai, interviews also covered some parts of the neighbouring provinces of Lamphun, Chiang Rai, Phayao and Phrae as I sought to understand the political nature of the Red Shirt movement as a regional organization.

This chapter seeks to answer the following questions. What happened to the Red Shirts before and after the coup on 22 May 2014? Why was there so little resistance to the coup? Why were there so few Red Shirt protests in the twelve months following the coup? What measures did the military regime deploy against the Red Shirts and other democratic forces in the period following the coup? How can one explain political developments in Northern Thailand since the military coup of September 2006 through the lens of democratization? And what are the prospects for democracy in the Northern region?

A foreign consular official in Chiang Mai asked two reporters ten days after the 22 May coup why there had not been "an armed uprising or a strong and peaceful demonstration against the coup", why the Red Shirts had not blocked all major roads in the North leading to Bangkok and why the Red Shirts had not surrounded all the military camps in the North. Why, to go further, had there been no declaration of an exile government in Chiang Mai or of a Federation of Isan-Lanna States in defence of the elected Yingluck government and democracy?[1]

This chapter assembles scattered data to put forth answers to these questions, hoping to lay a foundation for future studies. It proposes several arguments. First, that the Phuea Thai leadership either failed to understand the fact that political struggle is a war for power and that it therefore did not prepare for any opposition to a coup except by supporting large demonstrations in Bangkok. Second, that apart from solving the economic problems of the people, the Yingluck government did not work on projects to strengthen democratic forces within the country. Whereas the Red Shirt leadership in Bangkok regularly conducted television programmes that discussed political and economic issues and problems, Red Shirt groups in each province were not trained to strengthen local democracy or to address the country's backward structural arrangements and weaken undemocratic structures and practices. The Phuea Thai party and the Red Shirt movement might have thought that another coup was impossible, since each of their demonstrations in Bangkok was so huge.

In contrast, the military continuously sought options to bring down the elected government, and it was prepared to suppress any and all opposition to a coup.

Enlightenment

Unlike the student movement that led to the toppling of the military government of Field Marshal Thanom Kittikhachon in October 1973 and the middle-class uprising against the short-lived government of General Suchinda Kraprayoon in May 1992 — at least as these movements have been understood — the Red Shirt movement for democracy in the 2000s has been a rainbow coalition movement. It consists of people from different classes and professions: farmers and workers, teachers, students, journalists, monks, government officials, policemen, housewives — lower-class people, middle-class people and upper-class people (Apichat 2010, pp. 14–35; Nidhi 2010, pp. 29–30; Pasuk 2010; and Prapas 2010, pp. 36–55). However, the most outstanding characteristic of this movement has been that, whereas most of those who attended the demonstrations staged by those earlier movements were urbanites, the Red Shirts not only attracted many urbanites but also drew many villagers from the countryside, people who had greatly benefited from the policies of the Thaksinite Thai Rak Thai, Phalang Prachachon and Phuea Thai Parties. These policies included, for example, village funds for business and community development, charges of thirty baht for medical treatment, the One Tambon One Product (OTOP) project, deferral of farmers' debts and the suppression of serious drug trafficking.

The process of political education — later referred to as *ta sawang* (eye-opening or enlightenment) — of most Red Shirts did not take place all at once. It was, rather, step by step. However, the policies of the Thai Rak Thai Party government of 2001–5 taught a great number of people that, by electing the right political party which in turn formulated the right policies, the advantages of electoral democracy could be tangible. Thaksin and the Thai Rak Thai Party therefore scored a convincing victory in the general elections of February 2005 and thus set four important Thai political records: a government's completion of its four-year term for the first time since the abolition of the absolute monarchy in 1932, a party's winning re-election for the first time, winning such a landslide victory in a general election, and forming for the first time a single-party government.

A number of Red Shirts came to understand the way that political institutions and the judiciary had brought down elected governments and popular democracy from the political events that followed Thaksin's 2005 electoral victory. These events included, most notably, the dismissal of Phalang Prachachon Party Prime Ministers Samak Sundaravej and Somchai Wongsawat by the Constitutional Court in May and December 2008, respectively, and the Yellow Shirts' seizure of the Government House and the country's two major airports during October and November of the same year. Neither the police nor military forces opposed those seizures or cracked down on them, and the dissolution of the Phalang Prachachon Party and the appointment of Democrat Party leader Abhisit Vejjajiva as prime minister followed. Several major developments after that appointment further enlightened many Red Shirts; namely, the Abhisit government's suppression of Red Shirt demonstrations in April 2009, the lack of reply to petitions to King Bhumibol Adulyadej with thirty thousand Red Shirts' signatures calling for Thaksin's amnesty made in August 2009, and the brutal suppression of Red Shirt demonstrations during March and May 2010. That suppression killed roughly a hundred Red Shirts on Ratchadamnoen Avenue and around the Ratchaprasong Intersection in Bangkok.

In interviews, almost all respondents said that they had learned a great deal from those incidents. They clearly understood why the governments led by Thaksin were toppled time and again, who was behind the dismissal of the elected prime ministers and why anti-government demonstrators had not been prevented from seizing two major airports. They said that they understood clearly who authorized the killings of Red Shirts by American-trained snipers and how the comments of members of the elite classes were in favour of undemocratic practices. Furthermore, because Red Shirt demonstrators had gathered and slept in all parts of the Ratchaprasong area from late March to mid-May 2010, interviewees saw how and from where food and other supplies were transported and sent to soldiers stationed on the top floors of tall buildings in the area, including Chulalongkorn University Hospital, before the snipers began shooting on 13 May 2010.

Through shared information and discussion, grass-roots Red Shirts returned home politically much wiser after their defeat on 19 May 2010. According to them, although they could not say many things in public, they very often discussed sensitive issues among themselves. They now knew who the enemies of democracy were, who ordered the 2014 coup and why Thailand's democracy had been brought down many times in the past sixty years.

The Elected Government's Role

With the very nice appearance of a young lady leader whose brother was well-loved by many members of the lower classes, and with "To solve problems, not to take revenge" and "Thaksin's Ideas, Phuea Thai's Implementation" as her main campaign themes, Thaksin's youngest sister Yingluck scored a comfortable win in the general elections of 3 July 2011. Thanks to electoral support mainly from the lower and middle classes, she could set up another Thaksinite government. However, apart from the continued implementation of earlier policies and the initiation of new policies in the hope of satisfying voters — schemes to assist people in buying their first cars and to allow farmers to mortgage their rice at high prices — this fourth Thaksinite prime minister hardly pursued any solutions to the country's major problems, especially the challenges to Thai democracy.

It is understandable for a newly elected civilian government not to intervene in the affairs of the military, an organization that has staged so many coups and dominated the bureaucracy and the country for such long periods in the past. Moreover, the government in power after the September 2006 coup passed a law that made it more difficult for the defence minister to make major changes within the military.[2] There were no arrests for and only a very slow investigation of the killings at the Red Shirt demonstrations of May 2010, as the Yingluck government was very careful in maintaining good relations with the police, the courts and the military. It did not want to rock the boat (McCargo 2014, p. 417).

However, Thailand has long had a highly centralized state in which education, the sangha, natural resource management, city planning, provincial administration and local government, and the police have all been under the firm control of the central government (Tanet 2006, pp. 60–70). These highly centralized forces have become the backbone of frequent returns to military rule. And the Yingluck government would have done well at least to set up committees to study these centralized administrative structures, their operation and impact and the possibility of reforming them.

That government put aside, for example, a proposal to allocate budgetary authority to schools in localities and provinces rather than keeping it centralized at the Ministry of Education.[3] Similarly, it discarded a proposal to set up a committee to revise the school curriculum to foster a democratic orientation among students. The same was true of the proposal to set up "colleges of democracy" or "colleges of people's empowerment" in all four regions of the country to commemorate the eightieth anniversary of the June 1932 revolution against Siam's absolute monarchy. The elected government neither paid attention to a proposal, put forward by a group of non-governmental organizations, for the direct election of the governors of at least some provinces nor did it formulate a policy to strengthen civil society through people's organizations, community radio stations or village militia groups in defence of democracy.[4]

We may interpret the failure of the Yingluck government to take a role in democratization efforts in six ways. First, leading members of the Phuea Thai Party favoured the postponement of structural reform because any action on that front could upset those who protected the status quo and thus invite untimely opposition. Second, Phuea Thai leaders did not see those reforms as an urgent task or even an important one. Third, those progressive proposals were made neither by Phuea Thai leaders nor by Thaksin, who lived abroad and reportedly made all important decisions on matters of concern to the party, but were rather made by lower-level committees. Fourth, there was little pressure from within the United Alliance for Democracy against Dictatorship (UDD), the Red Shirt movement, the party or other parts of society for those reforms. Fifth, there was no clear leadership within the Phuea Thai Party. With the real leader in exile and Yingluck acting as a caretaker leader who carried out only policies that would maintain the party's popularity among voters, policies to promote structural reform were discarded. Sixth and last, in the absence of the real leader of the party, the contest for cabinet positions was intense. Whereas Thaksin received numerous calls and guests from Thailand daily, Yingluck was busy managing struggles within the party. During the Yingluck government's thirty-four months in office from July 2011 to May 2014, for example, there were four ministers and five deputy ministers of education, each with an average tenure of eight to nine months (Ministry of Education 2015, pp. 4–10), and that was just one ministry.

Activities of Red Shirt Groups and the UDD Leadership

Most activities of the Red Shirt groups in Chiang Mai province from 2011 to early 2014 centred around radio stations and participation in political gatherings. Political education programmes and intelligence-gathering work were minimal. There were Red Shirt groups in every district of Chiang Mai province. The organizational structure of each group was the same, with a president, vice presidents, a secretary, a finance officer and people responsible for political activities. There were no written regulations or clear job descriptions. Because the groups undertook no activities besides holding and attending political rallies in various locations, committee members often met unofficially and conducted discussions. They held very few official meetings. Each Red Shirt group had either registered or unregistered members, but there were few differences between the two, since attending political rallies was the main activity of groups' members.

Although the groups held political classes in the 2011–13 period, these were akin to political rallies. They utilized either a room or a football field, and speakers came from Bangkok. Since Bangkok handled the expenditure for food and drinks, the local group had only to find Red Shirt volunteers to do the cooking. When a group wanted speakers from Bangkok, its committee had to ask for donations from politicians or businessmen in the province. These donations covered the cost of food and beverages, teaching materials, sound systems and sometimes rental for meeting halls. Speakers from Bangkok came on their own and received no per diem for their talks, but were provided with accommodation and food by local organizers. Because at least a thousand people attended one-day political education programmes, it was hard to estimate how much local Red Shirts learned from them. As some Red Shirts in Sankamphaeng and Doi Saket noted, the talks in the morning were good, but photo sessions with famous speakers from Bangkok dominated the afternoon. Furthermore, some attendees came for social gatherings and the opportunity to meet old friends from other districts and provinces. Many of them felt that they had already gained much political education from listening to the daily Red Shirt television programmes broadcast from Bangkok.

The 2006 coup and the suppression of the Red Shirts in 2009 and 2010 led members of the Red Shirt movement to seek ways to fight back. According to the Red Shirts interviewed in all districts in Chiang Mai except

Fang and Mae Ai, two major activities were setting up community radio stations and attending as many Red Shirt rallies as possible. Community Radio 92.5 Mhz broadcast from behind Wat Phra Singh in downtown Chiang Mai. It was run by Petchawat Wattanapongsirikul, an outspoken Red Shirt businessman and leader of the Chiang Mai 51 Group. It was the most important Red Shirt community radio station for three reasons: its downtown location, which people from within and outside the city could visit or take part in any meeting or rally broadcast live from the station; its powerful thousand-kilowatt transmitter, which enabled its signal to reach many districts outside the city of Chiang Mai; and the station's militant stance, which made the Chiang Mai 51 Group the most radical Red Shirt group in the North. Its members were always the first group of Red Shirts to go into action; for example, leading Red Shirts to stage a protest at the Chiang Mai airport when Prime Minister Abhisit visited the city in November 2011. Their animus towards Abhisit was due, not least, to his having been head of government during the periods that saw soldiers and snipers kill more than a hundred Red Shirts on the streets of Bangkok in 2009 and 2010.[5]

The success of Radio 92.5, especially in receiving daily donations and propagating political news and viewpoints to a Red Shirt audience, led Red Shirt groups in other areas to try to emulate it. Between 2009 and 2014, at least four community radio stations operated in Chiang Mai province in addition to Radio 92.5 — in the eastern part of Chiang Mai city, in Sankamphaeng district, in Saraphi and in Fang and Mae-Ai districts. Red Shirts created additional radio stations because the Red Shirt groups in other areas believed that there should not be only one radio station, that they could also have their own radio stations, that the Chiang Mai 51 Group was a closed group and not open to Red Shirts from elsewhere, and that the use of the donations to the Chiang Mai 51 Group was not transparent and the group was thus unaccountable to public scrutiny.[6]

Their second set of activities involved public gatherings, to which they invited prominent Red Shirt leaders to come from Bangkok to speak on the political situation or concepts of democracy. In most cases, Red Shirts also attended political rallies in other districts, other provinces or Bangkok. Whereas the Red Shirt group in Fang and Mae Ai Districts conducted other activities, most notably setting up a co-operative to lend money to small businesses and give money to members during funeral and cremation ceremonies, other Red Shirt groups did not undertake such activities. Three factors accounted for the strength of the Fang and Mae Ai Red Shirt group. First, they had a strong leader, who had experience in political activities in the "liberated zone" controlled by the Communist Party of Thailand during the late 1970s and the early 1980s. Second, Fang and Mae Ai Districts are about 250 kilometres from Chiang Mai city. This distance prevented the Red Shirts there from coming into frequent contact with other Red Shirt groups in and around Chiang Mai city; the Fang-Mae Ai group therefore needed to rely on its own leadership. Third, many farmers in the two districts had waged a long struggle against the use of agricultural chemicals in large orange plantations owned by wealthy businessmen from Bangkok. District-level government officials had no effective authority over this matter. These businessmen's close connections with the central authorities and the centralized administration of natural-resource management in Thailand have permitted them to encroach on forested hills and to turn them into orange plantations. Government officials at the district level have not assisted villagers who have suffered as a result of this encroachment.[7]

According to the interviews, before the rise of the Red Shirt movement, members of parliament and aspiring candidates established networks, involving both canvassers and politically active villagers, to support their campaigns and political parties. Members of these networks received between 200 and 400 baht per meeting to attend political meetings, and canvassers received more to support their efforts to mobilize villagers to vote. The mobilization of Red Shirt supporters drew on this legacy. Red Shirts organized themselves into their own groups in local areas as a means of supporting their parties' leadership in Bangkok. A number of Red Shirts who became politically aware had had no prior political relationships with the MPs from their own areas. The growth of the Red Shirt movement has thus seen two different groups of people in attendance at political gatherings: one mobilized by local Red Shirt groups and another whose members were closely linked to MPs and their electoral campaigns. People close to the Phuea Thai Party received some money for attending rallies and would leave early, while Red Shirts received no money and mostly returned home only when gatherings ended.[8]

Red Shirts received no money for attending political rallies. However, when they attended demonstrations in faraway Bangkok, it was impossible for them to pay for all transportation costs and for their own food since they were people who had to work to earn daily incomes for themselves and their families. Some of them could sacrifice by not working for a few days. Several sources of funds to meet the expenses of joining demonstrations in Bangkok were possible. First, leaders of the Red Shirt group in each district contacted the MP for the constituency or individuals aspiring to run for parliament to request help. Second, each group had money that might prove sufficient to pay for the transportation of some members to Bangkok. The Fang and Mae Ai group, for example, had made money from its activities and secured donations. These funds enabled it fully to support the travel of all those members wishing to go to Bangkok to join demonstrations. Third, funds for travel expenses could come from the organizers of the UDD in Bangkok. This money was sent to Red Shirt leaders in local areas. It included an undisclosed amount sent to the Chiang Mai 51 group, which used its Radio 92.5 Mhz station to call for donations and to mobilize Red Shirts anywhere in Chiang Mai who wanted to attend demonstrations in Bangkok. Some Red Shirts drove down to Bangkok in a group, whether in a pick-up truck owned by a member of the group or in a hired van. In either case, transport was offered to those who needed a ride.

Most participants in the demonstrations in Bangkok were prepared to stay for four or five days before returning home. Other Red Shirts who wanted to take their turn would then replace them. According to the Red Shirts in Mueang Chiang Mai, Doi Saket and Saraphi districts, some local people had relatives or friends in Bangkok with whom they could stay for a day or so, even if Red Shirts mostly slept at the demonstration site. They brought the necessary clothes and some dried food, but for the most part they relied on food prepared by UDD organizers and distributed at the demonstrations. As they gained experience, they travelled to demonstrations in Bangkok without taking food along. Sometimes, the MP and other political aspirants visited them at the demonstration site and gave them financial support.

Asked where the money for food, for the sound system used at the rallies in Bangkok and for all the other organizational work needed to stage those rallies came from, the Red Shirt leaders said that financial support came from the Phuea Thai Party, as donations from rich Red Shirt supporters, from leading members of the party, and possibly a greater portion from Thaksin. As a Red Shirt from Sankamphaeng noted, many Northeastern Red Shirts prepared their own meals at the demonstration site. They preferred Isan food to the food distributed in paper boxes at the demonstration site. These boxes typically held meat curry on top of rice, fried rice, chicken rice or fried noodles — all common food in Central Thailand. They were regularly served three times at the demonstrations. There were Northern Red Shirts who, like Northeasterners, preferred sticky rice, but most Red Shirts from the North were satisfied with the food of the Central region distributed three times a day. They said that they were too lazy to cook or that it was not convenient to cook Northern food at the demonstration site.[9]

The transportation and food expenses are discussed here because of their political relevance, which has several dimensions. First, the more donations were made to each group, the more financial support was given to UDD organizers in Bangkok, and the longer each demonstration — whether in Bangkok or the provinces — lasted. Second, the more dependent each group either at the national or local level was on donors, the more likely some people involved in the demonstrations were to abuse funds by giving false figures for the number of those who travelled to Bangkok and of those who participated and received food each day. This was especially true if the leadership failed to create an efficient system for tracking funds. Third, the more dependent each local group was on donations, the fewer activities it conducted, as its members would always receive support. Similarly, this dependence on donations made it more likely that some leaders might take advantage of donations received from different sources in the absence of effective systems for keeping track of funds. Fourth, the more donations received by the UDD leadership, the more likely it was that the central leadership ran the demonstration and the Red Shirt movement without local participation, especially if leaders from each province did not call for a fully participatory meeting.

These assumptions accord with what the Red Shirt interviewees have disclosed. First, the UDD leadership time and again stressed the importance of big demonstrations, whether in Bangkok or outside the capital, but always under its strong control. Second, in the years since the first big demonstration in Bangkok, held in 2009, there were very few occasions on which Red Shirt leaders from each province and region were called together for decision-making. All important strategies and decisions concerning the Red Shirt movement remained under the almost absolute control of the UDD leadership. Third, no matter how many nights each UDD-led demonstration lasted, all the speakers who appeared during the prime hours from 7 p.m. to midnight were the same. Very few people outside the UDD leadership were invited to speak during this time. Once again, the UDD leadership took control of all political messages conveyed to Red Shirt followers nationwide. Last, one can characterize the political activities and attributes of the UDD in seven ways.

1. Close-knit leadership; the same group of people had controlled the UDD for half a decade, from 2009 to 2014.
2. Very weak participation on the part of Red Shirt leaders from the provinces.
3. The failure to build the Red Shirt movement into a rainbow movement consisting of leaders from other groups; the UDD remained the same.
4. The same leadership's transmission of, admittedly, strong and efficient political messages to the masses.
5. The lack of an open forum for political discussion of the political direction of the democratic movement or its finances and spending.
6. The lack of demonstrated interest on the part of the UDD leadership in expanding and strengthening Red Shirt and democratic forces outside Bangkok, especially in relation to organizational structures.
7. The failure of the open atmosphere under the elected Yingluck government to broaden the discussion of ways to deepen knowledge of democratic principles and of measures to defend democracy from the threat of authoritarianism. Thailand had, after all, seen some seventeen military coups, the Red Shirts' beloved leader remained in exile and the movement had suffered bad defeats in Bangkok in 2009 and 2010; the security of the regime of electoral democracy exemplified by the Yingluck government was not to be taken for granted.[10]

Interviewees in different districts of Chiang Mai said that certain leaders always came from Bangkok to organize each busload of demonstrators. Most Red Shirts in local areas needed not to pay anything. They merely stated the names of those who were to go down to Bangkok at a given time. However, leaders in Chiang Mai did not understand why they were not authorized or empowered to handle this task themselves since they were local people who knew each potential Red Shirt traveller well and who were able to contact the UDD leadership in Bangkok directly. Representatives from Bangkok did not have to come all the way to the North at all.[11]

As each huge Red Shirt demonstration in Bangkok was called and as many Red Shirts from outside Bangkok as possible were mobilized to go to the capital, some local leaders felt that local demonstrations should also be held. Such demonstrations would both allow those who could not go to Bangkok to participate and give local Red Shirts a chance to speak to crowds in the local area. This would be especially important if a coup took place in Bangkok. However, the central leadership insisted that the priority was on, and the decisive battle would be in, Bangkok. At any rate, the Red Shirts in Chiang Mai, Chiang Rai and Phayao did organize some local demonstrations, but the crowds were small, never exceeding a hundred people on any given night. There were three major reasons for these low turnouts. First, most Red Shirts felt that gatherings in Bangkok were much more important and that local gatherings were neither significant nor necessary. Second, most Red Shirts who did not go to Bangkok preferred to stay home watching and listening to the speeches at the Bangkok demonstration sites on television. Third, there were not many local speakers able to attract attention or draw crowds with their eloquence. Sitting comfortably at home, watching television and listening to great speeches live from Bangkok therefore seemed like a better choice.[12]

Local Red Shirt leaders who organized rallies either in front of the Chiang Mai railway station or at the plaza in front of the provincial hall insisted that there be at least one political rally in each province outside Bangkok while there were rallies in Bangkok because these provincial rallies would give local Red Shirts the opportunity to learn to do more things and to improve their skills in organizing. These abilities would make it possible, for example, for them to act as a counter-force all over the country in the event of a military coup in the capital. Local Red Shirts could thus learn how to conduct rallies by collecting donations and assigning work in areas such as giving speeches, operating light and sound systems, security, and intelligence gathering. According to two local leaders interviewed, without learning by doing, it would be impossible to improve the quality of grass-roots work and local activists. Attending a rally or two is necessary, but the returnees should concentrate more on organizing local rallies and sending inexperienced Red Shirts to Bangkok.[13]

Decentralization, Localism and Separatism

Being aware of the independent and proud status of Lanna in the past and of its important strategic location relative to British Burma, the Thai government has made sure that the annexation and domination of Lanna were complete since the era of King Chulalongkorn (r. 1868–1910). The policy of administrative and political over-centralization in effect since the beginning of the twentieth century has been thorough. Use of the Northern Thai written language was not allowed, use of the spoken language was not encouraged, monks and local people had no local autonomy, education was overseen in every respect by the central government, local lords lost their lands and became government servants and Bangkok maintained control over administration at every level. Under such circumstances, the localist revival since the 1950s proved minimal, and institutions of higher education set up in the North followed the Bangkok model in all respects. Local government agencies have had limited power, and calls for the election of provincial governors have always remained subdued (Chamnan 2016, p. 12; Tanet 2011, pp. 208–34).

As all previous governments have benefited from the centralized bureaucracy, they have endorsed localist campaigns only as a means of promoting tourism. In the past two decades, local costumes, handicrafts and dialects have been promoted in government-run ceremonies and festivals and also at fairs for tourists. However, the decentralization in the political, financial, cultural and academic realms has been neglected or suppressed. Amidst the growing unhappiness of Red Shirts in the North over the demonstrations led by Suthep Thaugsuban to oust the elected Yingluck government, there began to be talks about the strengths of local democracy, about the role of localism in defending democracy at the national level and in fostering local economic development, and about preparations for setting up a Federation of Isan-Lanna States to be led by Yingluck and the Phuea Thai Party. According to the leaders of Red Shirt groups in Chiang Mai, Lumphun, Phayao, Chiang Rai and Phrae provinces, those sentiments were growing and began to spread to more Red Shirts, but they were really mere talk and complaint. There were neither plans nor any real follow-through. The local leadership was either mobilizing people to go to join demonstrations in Bangkok or busy with their usual radio programmes and weekly political discussions.[14]

Speculation about and Preparations for a Coup

There were two types of leaders in the Red Shirt movement in Chiang Mai and neighbouring provinces. The first was busy with the radio work and organizing political gatherings, especially sending Red Shirts to attend rallies in Bangkok. The leaders of this type did not think that there would be another coup and felt that the government and the UDD leadership in Bangkok must have better information on the situation and that they would surely instruct Northern Red Shirts on how to cope with the situation. The leaders of the second type, who were active in organizing rallies at the local level, said that they felt that, if the military saw a chance, another coup was always possible. The best evidence, in their view, was the use of armed force against the peaceful and unarmed demonstrators in Bangkok in April 2009 and in April and May 2010.[15]

Different views towards the possibility of a military coup were also found among leaders of the Phuea Thai Party in Bangkok. According to one man who had served as a deputy prime minister in the Yingluck government, because there was no consensus on whether or not there could be another coup and because of the demands of being in government, the Phuea Thai Party had never made preparations to resist a coup; what preparations were made were at best the undertakings of the few people who felt that there could be a coup.[16]

Five or six groups worked to oppose a coup in the provinces of Chiang Mai, Chiang Rai and Phayao. Interviewees said that they knew people who were involved, but that details were not revealed to other Red Shirt groups. The interviewees were not sure what type of opposition those groups were planning. They also expressed dissatisfaction over a lack of financial resources for purchasing just a few firearms to protect themselves in opposing the coup. They were looking for financial support from Phuea Thai MPs, who politely suggested that the Red Shirts should help themselves. The purchase of a gun required at least 20,000 baht, and finances were the biggest problem in the end.[17]

According to a Red Shirt leader in Sansai district of Chiang Mai province, and to another in the Mueang district of Chiang Rai province, a high-level meeting was held in Chiang Mai in mid-October 2013. The secret talks were attended by a leading police officer stationed in the North, two Red Shirt leaders, two leading Northern members of the Phuea Thai Party and a leading member of the party from Bangkok. The major points discussed were the fact that a coup was being planned and opposition would be necessary and that, while the government would discuss tasks for the police and military and for MPs, it would also be necessary to inform Red Shirts so that they could start preparing to oppose a coup.

Confidential telephone numbers were then given to each person present at the meeting, to be used when action to oppose the coup became necessary. This Red Shirt informant tried to call those numbers when martial law was imposed on 20 May 2014, but they were not in service. He tried for several days and failed to reach anyone. Either the plan had been discontinued, or this man was no longer trusted.[18]

As the activities of the People's Democratic Reform Committee (PDRC) led by Suthep Thaugsuban against the Yingluck government increased and the Democrat Party boycotted the elections called by the Yingluck government at the end of 2013, it became clear to several groups of Red Shirts in the North that there could be a military coup or that the situation of political stalemate could drag on as army commander-in-chief General Prayut Chanocha made repeated pledges that the military would not intervene. In four Northern provinces, groups of Red Shirts began to have a strong sense that the military would oust the elected government by force sooner or later.

The situation became complicated after some members of the Assembly for Defense of Democracy (*Sapha pokpong prachathippatai*, AFDD) from Bangkok went to speak at Chiang Mai University in December 2013 and Red Shirts in Chiang Mai and Lamphun set up a Lanna Assembly for the Defence of Democracy (*Sapha pokpong prachathippatai lanna*) to support the AFDD in Northern Thailand. The Thai abbreviation for the name of this new group was "so.po.po.lo.", the same one as that frequently used for the Lao People's Democratic Republic (*Satharanarat prachathippatai prachachon lao*, in Thai). *Manager* newspaper, which had always criticized the UDD, the Red Shirt movement and the Yingluck and Thaksin governments, therefore took the opportunity to allege that the Northern Red Shirt movement was communist (*MGR Online*, 2 March 2014). The situation became even more confrontational after the Democrat Party announced its boycott of the approaching general elections and after several red banners displayed for the first time in downtown Phayao area on 28 January 2014 called for a separate Lanna state. These banners cited the continued injustice that Thailand had caused to the Red Shirts (*MGR Online*, 3 March 2014a; MGR Online VDO 2014; Pantip.com, 29 January 2014).

January saw more red banners with similar contents displayed in Lamphun, Phrae, Nakhon Sawan and Phitsanulok. The following months saw increasing indications of the forces in conflict. For example, on 19 February, over eight thousand village police volunteers marched with red flags and red banners in front of several leading Phuea Thai MPs and Red Shirt leaders from the North and Northeast in Chiang Kham district of Phayao province. Subsequently, on 25 March, three thousand village police volunteers did the same in front of leaders of Phuea Thai, the UDD and the Red Shirts in the Mueang district of the same province (*MGR Online*, 20 February 2014, 3 March 2014*b*). Although the speeches and banners on these occasions had no separatist content but merely stressed the defence of democracy, the rule of law and justice, the show of marching men in the presence of Phuea Thai, UDD and Red Shirt leaders in large numbers could be seen as a defence of democracy and a readiness for political struggle.

Two Red Shirt leaders from different provinces revealed that there were meetings at that time about how to oppose a military coup. If Yingluck were stripped of power by military force, she would be invited to set up a government either in Chiang Mai or in Udon Thani, the Red Shirt stronghold in Isan. Alternatively, there could be headquarters in each of these two regions. Some Red Shirt leaders from the regions met, and a full meeting was to be held in April to decide on concrete measures for opposing an authoritarian regime. Then, in late March, Suporn Attawong, a UDD leader who originally came from the Northeast, set up the National Red Shirt Volunteers Group to Safeguard Democracy (*Klum suea daeng asasamak phitak prachathippatai haeng chat, o.pho.po.cho.*). It accepted pro-democracy fighters from the Northeast to join the group and began with a thousand applicants. On both 5 and 21 April, nearly twenty thousand men, clad in village militia uniforms, marched in the name of the group in Khorat Province, a stronghold of the Red Shirts in the Northeast. At one of these marches, Suporn said that the Red Shirts would oppose any attempt to remove Yingluck from the premiership and fight to uphold democracy. He said that this would not be armed opposition or a separatist struggle; it would only be peaceful defence of democracy (*Thai rat*, 21 April 2014). Although a secret meeting of Red Shirt leaders from the North and Isan in mid-April was called off because of the appearance of many uninvited journalists, it was clear that a number of Red Shirt groups were trying to meet and discuss ways to defend democracy. They were still looking for a common strategy.[19]

Two Red Shirt leaders confirmed that a high-level meeting involving a representative from a "high institution", the military and the Phuea Thai Party took place in Chiang Saen district, Chiang Mai province, on 16 May

2014, six days before the declaration of martial law. They disclosed neither the names of those who attended the meeting nor its agenda and results. The introduction of martial law on 20 May led some Red Shirts to flee across Thailand's borders, but many of these leaders did not think that the military would in fact return to power. As a result, when the news of the coup broke at four o'clock on the afternoon of 22 May, most prominent Phuea Thai leaders were in a meeting at party headquarters. Caught by surprise, many of them tried to leave in taxicabs but found themselves forced by Bangkok's rush hour traffic to disembark from those vehicles and head for home or to safety on foot.[20]

The Eighteenth Military Coup in Eighty-Two Years

Shortly after army commander General Prayut brought to an abrupt end the meeting of representatives of Phuea Thai, the UDD, the Democrat Party and the PDRC at the Army Convention Hall in Bangkok by announcing that he was staging a coup and by detaining government and UDD leaders, including Yingluck, soldiers were dispatched in trucks to round up Red Shirt leaders. They detained thirty to fifty such leaders from each province in military camps. According to Phumjai Chaiya, a Red Shirt leader from Sanpatong district, some eighty kilometres south of Chiang Mai city, three big trucks full of armed soldiers arrived at his home in a remote village and took him to detention in a military camp in Mae Rim district.[21] In Chiang Mai, the Red Shirt leaders were detained for seven days, some in the camp in Mae Rim and others in a camp in Chiang Dao near the Thai-Burmese border. Those Red Shirt leaders whom the soldiers did not find at home were asked to report to provincial military authorities and were detained for seven days. According to a leader in Doi Saket district, at least forty-eight Red Shirt leaders in the central and southern parts of the province were detained at Mae Rim. According to a leader of the Fang and Mae Ai group, twenty-two Red Shirt leaders were detained in the Chiang Dao military camp. The son of a Phuea Thai member of parliament was detained after the coup because the soldiers who went to the family's house could not find the father. They took his son as a substitute. Four days later, the MP reported to the military and replaced his son in detention.[22]

The military posted groups of four to five soldiers in parts of cities and each district in which Red Shirts were located, twenty-four hours a day. In Chiang Mai, for three nights following the coup, groups of anti-coup demonstrators gathered in the city. They lit candles, sang songs and marched to different open spaces in the city. A few demonstrators clad in red shirts or wearing red headbands joined the demonstrations. There were several arrests each night, and there were no more demonstrations afterwards. However, the posting of soldiers around the clock in several downtown areas continued.

The army has a number of intelligence and strategic planning units. They had prepared a weekly report on the political situation for each region on the Yingluck government, Phuea Thai and other parties, and the Red Shirts. These reports attempted to examine every possible dimension of developments in Thailand from a military perspective. One important focus of the reports, requested by superiors, was the strength of the government and of the Red Shirt movement and the possibility of opposition to a military coup. Superiors always asked for reporting on political trends and on strategies and measures that the military could use to control the government and the Red Shirt movement for the sake of national security. According to the interviewee, a general, who described this system of reporting, the military's reports suggested that a coup was always an open option and strategies and measures for staging a coup had long been discussed in military circles.[23]

The Year after the Coup

Apart from banning all political gatherings in support of democracy or in opposition to the military government, the junta allowed only some Red Shirt radio stations to remain open. Their programmes could include only news read from daily newspapers, excluding political commentary in those newspapers. Political discussions were also not allowed. The most militant station in the past, Chiang Mai 51 Radio 92.5 Mhz, broadcast Buddhist dhamma teachings all day. Its most prominent broadcaster, Phetchawat Watthanaphongsirikun, did not speak on air at all. A number of Red Shirts in Chiang Mai missed the chance to listen to the political programmes that they used to listen to every day. They missed the Yingluck government and especially the demonstrations in Bangkok, Chiang Mai and other provinces that they attended. Some had computers at home or mobile phones, and they have set up access to alternative news and ideas from different networks and sources. As Red Shirts turned increasingly to joining clubs of cyclists who rode every morning, or to organizing traditional dance parties in the evening, or to setting up cooperative thrift shops so that they could meet and exchange ideas, they patiently waited for an assignment from the leadership in Bangkok or Chiang Mai.

According to a Red Shirt leader in Fang and Mae Ai districts, "the business of survival is going fine. We must learn how to stay away from trouble at present. Merit-making activities are our main task now. We must face reality." According to a leader of Sankamphaeng Red Shirts, "everybody has to struggle to make ends meet". "It may take several years", the UDD radio station in Bangkok said, "and we must adhere to a peaceful way of struggle."[24]

With regard to opposition to the coup, most Red Shirts said that they were shocked by the incident. They never thought that the government's and the UDD's leadership would be detained. Nor did they think that the active Red Shirts in each district would be detained. Without a clearly defined leadership and with the presence of soldiers in every sub-district, they said that they would have to wait and see how the situation would unfold. When asked again on the first anniversary of the coup, the same people said that, in the previous twelve months, they had met only their close friends to discuss the political situation. As there had not been any action, the Red Shirts would have to wait. A leader of the Fang and Mae Ai Red Shirt group put it best when asked about the direction of the Red Shirts' struggle. He said that the group had continuously carried out political activities in line with parliamentary democracy. He thought that he and his fellow villagers were getting old and had never thought of opposing a coup by means of armed struggle. There might be other groups that adopted such options, but he was not aware of that.

Analysis of the Political Conflicts and Struggle for Power

At least three major events of the past two decades suggest that democracy has a future in Thailand. The first was the two major victories at the polls of the Thai Rak Thai Party under the leadership of Thaksin Shinawatra in January 2001 and February 2005. These victories made possible an unprecedentedly long period of six years of an elected government being in power. The second was the impressive victory of the Phuea Thai Party, led by Thaksin's sister Yingluck, in the elections of July 2011. The third was huge and repeated demonstrations in Bangkok on the part of Red Shirts from all over the country, along with the related phenomenon of the growth of "Red" villages in a number of districts, especially in the North and Northeast. However, as a general put it, the Thai military has never trusted democracy. In the academy, cadets have been taught throughout the past seven decades that the monarchy, national unity and national security matter more than everything else, and that the role of the military is to protect them. As a result, once Thaksin, the Phuea Thai Party and the Red Shirts were branded as anti-monarchy, corrupt and threatening to national unity and security, to stage a coup against them was a duty and an honour. It was therefore not surprising that the military sought ways to topple the elected Yingluck government from power soon after her Phuea Thai Party won the 2011 elections.[25] Suthep Thaugsuban's talking with General Prayut about toppling the Yingluck government many months before the coup reveals much about the military's views and methods.

As UDD leaders worked hard to achieve democracy through peaceful struggle, a hundred Red Shirt demonstrators were killed or injured by snipers' bullets in April and May 2010. However, the Red Shirts continued their non-violent struggle and finally won an important victory for their movement, for Thaksin and for democracy in the July 2011 elections. As Weng Tojirakan, a UDD leader, put it in early July 2015, "We have only one responsibility: we must lead our people to victory without bloodshed or with least losses.... We must strictly adhere to political struggle ... only peaceful struggle."[26] In contrast, the military used a number of tactics, mainly involving force, to overthrow another elected government in 2014.

A feeling of confidence following its election victory of 2011 must have played a big role in shaping the belief of Phuea Thai, the UDD and Red Shirt leaders that a peaceful struggle and pro-people development policies would keep them in power and allow democracy to endure. However, without the organizational strength of the UDD and Red Shirt movement nationwide and with little participation from Red Shirt leaders and representatives from around the country, it is clear that democracy-loving people in Thailand have recourse to only limited forms of political struggle.

When the "Red Village Project" was initiated in the Northeast in mid-2012 and quickly spread to the North, it centred on putting up red flags, red banners, red posters and big pictures of Thaksin in each Red Shirt house and at the entrance of each village. Since most villagers in the North and Northeast supported Thaksin and the Red Shirt movement, there were few problems, besides some government officials' being unhappy because they either were in favour of the Democrat Party or wanted to play a neutral role. However, this project was ultimately akin to political rallies. Whereas the speeches in each political rally could educate listeners, the project gave nothing but a psychological boost to the Red Shirt movement. It involved no other intellectual or practical activities, only the sight of red flags and red banners flying in each participating village.

The huge Red Shirt demonstrations, always thrilling with blood-red oceans of participants, were held time and again in Bangkok and at times outside Bangkok. They made the democratic movement appear strong and well organized. Many Red Shirts — young and old, urban and rural — spoke out for social justice, equality and democracy. A great number of Thai people are now politically active and seem to be ready to defend a democratic regime.

The same could be said concerning the Red Shirts in the Northeast. In the year after the coup, the Isan Red Shirts, considered politically much stronger than those in the North, have been quiet. Whereas most former Phuea Thai members of parliament stayed away from politics and only continued to participate in religious activities with Red Shirt villagers, the Red Shirts in the Northeast were well aware that military units were present in each sub-district and that sub-district chiefs, village headmen and government officials were monitoring the Red Shirt movement and sending reports to military units stationed at the provincial level. In short, the failure of Red Shirt organizations at the provincial and district levels throughout the period of the Yingluck government to prepare to oppose a coup was a major factor in paralysing Red Shirts in the aftermath of the military seizure of power in May 2014. Reliance on the UDD leadership in Bangkok was another major factor in accounting for the inactivity of provincial Red Shirt groups in the year after the coup. The UDD leadership in Bangkok did not make any political move. One could also see that the marches of village police volunteers in the North and Northeast and the secret meetings on a Federation of Isan-Lanna States in February and April were too late, above all in the context of a lack of strong leadership from Bangkok.

There are many ways to strengthen the foundation for a strong and stable democracy. During its first two years in power, the Yingluck government performed well in coping with floods in Central Thailand and in introducing guarantees of higher rice prices for farmers and subsidies for first-time car buyers to satisfy the middle class and stimulate the economy. It is worth noting, however, that the UDD failed to democratize the Red Shirt movement and that the movement was quiet during the twelve months after the coup of May 2014. In fact, the lack of leadership, especially from Bangkok, and of budget allocations from the Phuea Thai Party government for creating and strengthening democratic ideas, culture, practices and institutions meant that the half-decade after 2010 saw little discussion of these topics in the Thai provinces. Once the Abhisit government dissolved parliament and called for general elections in 2011, the Phuea Thai Party, the UDD and the Red Shirt movement joined hands to run a campaign. Once the election was over and the administrative work to run the country began, the UDD leadership chose rallies and television programmes, hoping to work on political education, but did little to restructure and empower the Red Shirt movement as a whole. It is no wonder that the movement of the Red Shirts proved quiescent in responding to the coup. Even after twelve months of an authoritarian regime and with no election date in sight, the Red Shirt movement had hardly played a role in the anti-coup activities of university students and academics that had begun to gain momentum.

As Giles Ungpakorn put it, the response to these developments from "the Red Shirts was a deathly silence" because their leader Thaksin "decided to capitulate to the military" (Giles 2015). At the same time, most left-wing, progressive Red Shirts, whom Thaksin and the UDD leadership had spurned, "refused to organize a coherent alternative political organization to challenge the UDD leaders". So, as Weng Tojirakarn reiterated the UDD's fear that the military would kill Red Shirts, Giles found that in fact the UDD leadership had pulled the plug on the Red Shirt movement. In this regard, as Erik Kuhonta and Aim Sinpeng remarked, the political conflict was "likely to be very protracted" (Kuhonta and Aim 2014a, p. 352). Thailand has in the past half-dozen years seen a major political party and a people's movement struggle not only with how to win re-election but with also how to stay in power and to strengthen the country's democratic regime. It has witnessed the intervention of a military regime that has designed a constitution that cripples democratic forces. The study of the country as a case of late democratization is therefore surely a matter of urgency.

Acknowledgements

The author is grateful for the editorial work and valuable comments of Michael Montesano and for useful earlier comments from Terence Chong.

Notes

1. Interview with a Red Shirt leader in Chiang Mai, 10 December 2014.
2. A law passed after the 2006 coup formed a five-man leadership structure at the Ministry of Defence, comprising the commanders of the army, navy and air force, the supreme commander and the minister of defence. This law made it almost impossible for the minister to undertake major structural changes at the ministry level.
3. Interviews with two high-ranking officials of the Ministry of Education, Bangkok, 21 March 2015. They noted that the Office of the Commission on Basic Education in Bangkok had ordered hundreds of thousands of school uniforms and distributed these to schools across the country; that is, schools at district or provincial levels were not empowered to shoulder this responsibility.
4. Interviews with two advisors to the prime minister, Bangkok, 22 March 2015.
5. Interviews with two leaders of the Chiang Mai 51 Red Shirt group, two Red Shirts from Sankamphaeng district and a Red Shirt from the eastern part of the Mueang district of Chiang Mai, 21–22 December 2014.
6. Interviews with Red Shirt leaders from the eastern part of the Mueang district of Chiang Mai and from Doi Saket, Sansai and Sankamphaeng districts, 22–25 December 2014.
7. Interviews with Red Shirts in Fang and Mae Ai districts, 28–29 December 2014.
8. Interviews with Red Shirts in the San Sai, Mae Rim, Doi Saket, Saraphi and Mueang districts of Chiang Mai, December 2014, and in Chiang Rai and Phayao provinces, January 2015.
9. Interview with two Red Shirt leaders from Sankamphaeng and Saraphi districts, Chiang Mai, 25–26 December 2014.
10. Interviews with Red Shirt leaders in Chiang Mai, Chiang Rai, Phayao, Lamphun and Phrae provinces, December 2014 and March 2015.
11. Interviews with three Red Shirt leaders who had organized rallies at the Chiang Mai railway station and in front of the Chiang Mai provincial hall, 23 March 2015.
12. Interviews with Red Shirt leaders and rank and file in the Sankamphaeng, Saraphi, Doi Saket and Mueang districts of Chiang Mai, March 2015.
13. Interviews with two female Red Shirt leaders in Mueang Chiang Mai and one female Red Shirt leader in Lamphun, April 2015.

14. Interviews with four Red Shirt leaders in Chiang Mai, three in Lamphun, three in Chiang Rai, two in Phayao and two in Phrae, March and April 2015.
15. Interviews with two Red Shirt leaders in the eastern part of the Mueang district of Chiang Mai, March 2015.
16. Interview with a former Phuea Thai Party deputy prime minister, Bangkok, 4 March 2015.
17. Interviews with Red Shirt leaders from the Saraphi and Sansai districts of Chiang Mai and from the Mueang district of Phayao, December 2014 and January 2015.
18. Interview with a Red Shirt leader in the Mueang district of Chiang Mai, 22 December 2014.
19. Interviews with a member of parliament and a Red Shirt leader in Phayao province, 4 January 2015.
20. Interviews with three members of parliament, two from Chiang Mai and one from Lamphun, December 2014.
21. Phumjai Chaiya, a prominent leader of the Red Shirt Chiang Mai 51 Group who later left the group to lead the Red Shirt group in the Sanpatong district of Chiang Mai, died in a motorcycle crash in Phrae in December 2014. Some said that it was an accident but others said that he was followed and that his motorbike was hit from behind by a truck and that his killing was politically motivated. The deaths of four other Red Shirts in the North in the past several years were caused by gunmen.
22. Interviews with four Red Shirt leaders, Chiang Mai, December 2014.
23. Interview with an army general, Bangkok, 24 March 2015.
24. Interview with Fang and Sankamphaeng Red Shirt leaders in Fang and in Sankamphaeng districts, 24–25 December 2014.
25. Interviews with an army general, Bangkok, 24 December 2014 and 20 March 2015.
26. Weng (7 July 2015), in response to Thanathon (6 July 2015).

6

The Shifting Battleground: Peace Dialogue in Thailand's Malay-Muslim South

Rungrawee Chalermsripinyorat

The year 2004 brought a dramatic surge of violence in Thailand's southernmost region, which has now claimed nearly seven thousand lives.[1] In the 2016 Global Terrorism Index, Thailand ranked fifteenth among the 163 countries surveyed for being affected by "terrorism" (Institute for Economics and Peace 2016, pp. 10–11).[2] Despite the relatively high death toll resulting from political conflicts in the southernmost Thai provinces of Pattani, Yala and Narathiwat and adjacent parts of Songkhla, the insurgency there remains at the periphery of public attention both at home and abroad. For almost a decade, the Thai state tried to defeat the militants by suppression and co-optation, but this approach had little effect in putting a permanent end to the conflict. "Negotiation", or *kancheracha*, was a taboo — an idea that the Thai state, and particularly the Thai military, strongly opposed. Nevertheless, a significant policy shift came on 28 February 2013, the day that a formalized peace dialogue between the Bangkok government and the Barisan Revolusi Nasional Melayu Patani (Patani Malay National Revolutionary Front, BRN) was launched. The BRN is an active armed movement seeking to liberate from Thailand what it considers a previously independent sultanate. It is widely perceived to be the strongest among Patani liberation groups in terms of military capability.

This chapter examines how peace initiatives in southern Thailand have unfolded. In particular, I examine how the formalized peace process has changed the dynamic of armed conflict in southern Thailand. The formalized peace dialogue has significantly opened a new front of political contestation and negotiation. It has therefore allowed conflicting parties, particularly the various liberation movements, to bring their grievances concerning ethnic, religious and cultural discrimination and demands for self-governance to bear. It has also allowed them to search for political solutions in a non-violent manner. However, this initiative has encountered challenges from hardliners on both the government and the insurgent sides. The first section of the chapter provides a brief review of state initiatives to establish channels of communication and dialogue with Malay-Muslim insurgents. The chapter then discusses the 2013 formal peace dialogue conducted under the government of Yingluck Shinawatra. The following section examines the resumption of peace dialogue under the military government installed after the May 2014 coup. The chapter concludes with observations on the development of formalized peace dialogue and its prospect for conflict resolution.

I argue that the prospect of ending the violent conflict or achieving a negotiated settlement in the near future is, in light of the military's prolonged intervention in Thai politics, slim. The country's 2017 constitution has granted to the military the power to steer parliamentary politics by means of a senate whose members will be appointees of the junta during the first five years after the next general elections. While permitting Malaysia to continue to play a facilitation role, the military-led government in Bangkok has strongly opposed further third-party involvement in the peace process and demonstrated little serious willingness to make political concessions. No peace agreement is likely to be achieved in the absence of the political will to address the root causes of the conflict and to explore a range of political alternatives.

The Background to Thailand's Southern Conflict

Malay Muslims have embarked on armed resistance against the rulers whom they perceive as "Siamese colonizers" who unjustly conquered and govern Patani. Historically, Thailand's southernmost region was part of the ancient Hindu-Buddhist kingdom of Langkasuka, established sometime in the second century AD. Around the fifteenth century, it went into decline and was replaced by the Patani kingdom.[3] The region soon came into contact with Islam through trade with Arabs and with China, and it became widely known as "one of the cradles of Islam" in Southeast Asia. In 1786, Patani became a tributary of Siam; the liberation movements and some Malay Muslims take that moment as the beginning of "Siamese colonialism" (Che Man 1990, pp. 33–34). However, the region still retained a great deal of autonomy under Thai suzerainty. While other territories in Mainland Southeast Asia fell under the control of European powers, Bangkok further consolidated its power in 1902. At that time, Patani was incorporated into the Thai administrative system and, as a consequence, local leaders lost their powers. In 1909, Patani was formally annexed to Thailand as a result of the signing of an Anglo-Siamese treaty.

Following the annexation of Patani, the Thai state began to implement policies of cultural assimilation in order to incorporate minority Malay Muslims into the nation state. This policy provoked strong resistance, but that resistance remained non-violent. However, state suppression of peaceful campaigns for the rights of minority Malay Muslims led to the emergence of armed resistance in the 1960s. Among the resistance movements were three major separatist groups: the Barisan Nasional Pembebasan Patani (Patani National Liberation Front, BNPP), the Patani United Liberation Organisation (PULO) and the BRN.[4] The armed liberation movements, which reached their zenith in the 1970s and early 1980s, appeared on the surface to dwindle in the ensuing period. The military forces of the BNPP, which changed its name to Barisan Islam Pembebasan Patani (Patani Islamic Liberation Front, BIPP) in 1986, went into decline after the death of their key commander Poh Yeh in the mid-1980s. The BIPP decided to cease military operation in the mid-1990s but it has maintained a small number of armed personnel for defensive purposes.[5] PULO military operations peaked in the late-1970s and early 1980s; its senior commanders received training in Syria and Libya.[6] But internal infighting led the group to split into two factions, New PULO and Old PULO, in the mid-1980s. In 1998, Kuala Lumpur handed over four PULO leaders, including members of both factions, who resided on its soil to the Bangkok authorities and thus dealt a serious blow to the group.

The BRN also suffered from an internal split in the early 1980s. It divided into two factions, called "Congress" and "Coordinate".[7] The

BRN-Congress was more actively involved in military operations in the 1980s, but the pace of those operations gradually declined during the 1990s. Hassan Taib, an important leader of the Coordinate faction, says that the word "Coordinate" was used in the early 1980s for only eight months as a means of reuniting members who did not join the Congress faction and that it has never been used as the movement's official name.[8] While the military strength of other groups declined, the Coordinate faction quietly recruited and trained a new generation of fighters beneath the radar of the Thai authorities, starting in the 1990s. This chapter uses the term BRN to refer to that latter faction, in line with the official name used by its leaders.

The dramatic resurgence of armed resistance in Southern Thailand in 2004 took the Thai state by surprise. While Thailand had experienced rebellion in its predominantly Malay-Muslim southernmost region for several decades, the scale and intensity of violence in the post-2004 period have been unprecedented. Since 2004, nearly seven thousand people have been killed and thirteen thousand injured.[9] Drive-by shootings and bombings have been common modes of insurgents' military operations. Government agents or those perceived to be symbols of the Buddhist-dominated Thai state — members of the security forces, civil servants, participants in village defence forces, Buddhist monks and public school teachers — are prime targets of attacks. Civilians have suffered the heaviest casualties in the past fourteen years.

Peace Initiatives

The underground movement has waged armed resistance behind a veil of secrecy. No group has claimed responsibility for attacks. While rank-and-file members of the movement have been informed of the collective goal of their struggle, most of them have not known the name of the group under whose leadership they have fought. The highly secretive nature of the insurgency long gave the Thai state an excuse to refuse to hold formal peace talks with the insurgents. It could cite the elusive identity of the perpetrators of the violence that plagued the region. Over the years, intelligence reports and the testimony of some ex-militants, together with in-depth research and the investigative reporting of independent analysts and journalists, have come to point in the same direction and to make clear that the BRN has played a central role in the ongoing insurgency in southernmost Thailand.

Despite the clandestine nature of the movement, many third-party actors, both internal and external, have since 2005 made efforts to set up dialogue platforms between the Thai state and Malay-Muslim insurgents. At least four major initiatives to form a dialogue platform preceded the launch of formal peace talks in 2013.

The Langkawi talks were the first concrete post-2004 peace initiative for southern Thailand. Under the leadership of former Malaysian prime minister Mahathir Mohamad, it brought exiled separatist leaders and senior Thai security officials together for meetings on the Malaysian resort island of Langkawi between November 2005 and February 2006. Shazryl Eskay Abdullah, honorary Thai consul on Langkawi, who helped facilitate the meetings, stated that they were an attempt to identify common ground between the two sides. They were designed to reconcile differences, but they did not amount to formal negotiations. No high-ranking representative from the BRN attended the Langkawi talks, even though it was already playing the most important role in the rebellion (Pathan and Ekkarin 2012, p. 76).

The meetings on Langkawi concluded with a set of recommendations titled "Peace Proposal for Southern Thailand". It includes calls for the Thai government to set aside at least 50 per cent of local administrative jobs and uniformed security positions for ethnic Malays. The document also recommended the establishment of a board of review with the power to grant amnesty to Malays convicted of, or charged with, security-related criminal activities. The recommendations were subsequently delivered to the government of Prime Minister Thaksin Shinawatra (Liow and Pathan 2010, pp. 85–86). Thaksin was, however, facing growing anti-government demonstrations led by the People's Alliance for Democracy (*Phanthamit prachachon phuea prachathippatai*), and his government gave no serious consideration to the proposal before the Thai military toppled it by means of an armed putsch in September 2006.

The second initiative to launch talks between the Bangkok state and southern Malay-Muslim rebels was known as the Bogor Talks. Indonesian Vice President Yusuf Kalla led this initiative ahead of the country's 2009 presidential election. He organized a two-day meeting between Thai officials and separatist leaders at the presidential palace in Bogor, West Java, in September 2008. Kwanchat Klahan, a retired general, led the five-member Thai delegation. The insurgent side was represented by fifteen members of the Patani Malay Consultative Congress (Majlis Permesyuaratan Rakyat Melayu Patani, MPRMP). The MPRMP, founded in 1997, is an umbrella organization that is in turn an offshoot of an existing umbrella group, Barisan Bersatu Kemerdekaan Patani (United Front for Patani Independence, Bersatu), established in 1989.[10] The MPRMP's membership is comprised of people from older generations of Patani fighters living abroad, who may still continue their struggle on the diplomatic and political fronts but have little if any role in military operations on the ground.

The Bogor Talks collapsed after Jakarta disclosed the meeting to the media. Indonesian presidential spokesman Dino Patti Djalal told reporters, "we aim to facilitate [the talks] to find a peaceful political solution", but Thai foreign ministry spokesperson Tharit Charungvat officially denied Bangkok's involvement in the talks (Reuters, 21 September 2008). His statement reflected Bangkok's official line on peace talks with southern insurgents: "our position is that the situation in the South is an internal conflict and we will not set up any talks with the militants" (*Bangkok Post*, 22 September 2008). In turn, Yusuf Kalla, who had previously been involved in the Aceh peace process, met with criticism in Indonesia for attempting to use the Bogor initiative to raise his international profile in the run-up to general elections. The talks failed to bear any fruit.

A third initiative was that of the Organisation of the Islamic Conference (OIC, since 2011 the Organisation of Islamic Cooperation). The OIC has continuously expressed concerns over Thailand's southern conflict since 2004. Founded in 1969, the OIC is the second-largest intergovernmental organization after the United Nations; its membership totals fifty-seven countries. It aims to represent the collective voice of the Muslim world and to protect its interests in a spirit of promoting international peace among people of different faiths. The OIC has previous experience in brokering peace in Southeast Asia. From 1975 to 1996, it mediated protracted negotiations between the Philippine government and the Moro National Liberation Front (Rodil 2000, p. 2). The OIC granted observer status to the MNLF in 1977, status that it enjoys until today. The militants in southern Thailand have also tried to gain a similar status, but it has not materialized. With its sizable number of minority Muslims, the government of Thailand was granted observer status by the OIC in 1998. The OIC has arguably become the most significant multilateral forum in which the southern Malay-Muslim liberation movements and Bangkok have competed for legitimacy in the eyes of the international community since the current round of violence began in 2004. The liberation movements have lobbied the OIC to put Thailand's southern conflict on its agenda, whereas Bangkok has waged a diplomatic battle to win the OIC's backing for defining the problem as one with no relation to religion and as a Thai "internal affair". In May 2007, Thailand invited OIC Secretary General Professor Ekmeleddin Ihsanoglu for an official visit to the country.

In late September 2010, the OIC made a move apparently intended to test the possibility that it could play a mediation role in southern Thailand. Senior OIC officials held meetings with exiled Patani leaders in Malaysia and in Saudi Arabia to discuss the situation — a move that raised eyebrows in Bangkok. The BRN-Coordinate reportedly sent an observer to the meeting held in Kuala Lumpur (Pathan and Ekkarin 2012, pp. 102–3). The meetings enraged the Thai government, which expressed strong objection by sending a protest letter to Malaysia through its embassy in Bangkok.[11] The Thai government continued its diplomatic lobbying by inviting a high-level OIC delegation led by Ambassador Sayed Kasim El-Masry, advisor to the organization's secretary general, to visit the country in May 2012. However, the OIC expressed its disappointment with the situation by noting concern over "meagre progress" in southern Thailand in a resolution issued after its annual foreign ministers' meeting four months after the visit. It called on Bangkok to "hold a dialogue with the leaders of Muslims to reach a solution allowing the realization of the legitimate rights of Muslims in Southern Thailand" (Organisation of Islamic Cooperation 2012). Despite this call for dialogue, the OIC did not make any further attempt to play a mediation role in the conflict.

A fourth initiative to arrange dialogue to address the conflict in southernmost Thailand was the process facilitated by the Centre for Humanitarian Dialogue (HD Centre) in Geneva. It has been the most sustained and perhaps the most low-profile effort. Since 2006, the HD Centre has attempted to establish channels of communication between the Thai government and Patani liberation leaders (Vatikiotis 2013). It has partnered with the National Security Council (NSC) on the Thai government side and a faction of PULO led by Kasturi Makota on the liberation movements' side.[12] Although Kasturi has repeatedly offered to hold a dialogue, the Thai government has not attached much importance to his group because of the belief that it plays only a marginal role in the insurgency.

Political turmoil at the national level, caused by the colour-coded battle between pro-establishment and Thaksin-allied forces, has repeatedly disrupted the Geneva process. After the September 2006 coup, Prime Minister Surayut Chulanon, who led the army-installed government, offered an olive branch to the militants by making a public apology for the Thai state's past mistakes and offering to hold talks. Surayut met with Kasturi in Bahrain with the facilitation of the HD Centre towards the end of his premiership in late 2007.[13] However, that premiership was too short for the Bangkok government to make any tangible progress. The subsequent government of Thaksin-allied Samak Sundaravej faced protracted demonstrations led by the Yellow Shirts and largely left policy on the Muslim South in the military's hands. During Samak's premiership, the PULO faction led by Kasturi, which claimed to have some BRN representatives on board in its effort, offered to create a temporary "peace zone" as a confidence-building measure (International Crisis Group 2008, p. 10). The proposal, however, fell on deaf ears in Bangkok.

Effort to create a dialogue platform resumed after Abhisit Vejjajiva, leader of the Democrat Party, formed a new coalition government in late December 2008 after the Thaksinite People's Power Party (*Phak phalang prachachon*) government collapsed following a constitutional court verdict disbanding the party. Kasturi stated that his group and the BRN formed a new umbrella group called the Patani Malay Liberation Movement (PMLM) in January 2010 as part of the search for a political solution to the conflict (International Crisis Group 2010*b*, p. 6). In mid-2010, the PMLM offered to declare a one-month unilateral ceasefire in three districts of Narathiwat province: Cho Airong, Yi-ngo and Ra-ngae. The Abhisit government quietly acknowledged this offer. Kasturi billed the ceasefire as "successful", as only one bombing occurred in the designated zone during the period (Ghosh 2010). Thai security forces, however, rebutted his claim, saying that he had not counted another nine attacks. Towards the end of Abhisit's term, in December 2010, he instructed the NSC to formalize peace dialogue with southern insurgents — a move interpreted as a de facto endorsement of the HD Centre–facilitated Geneva process. A few months later, then NSC Secretary-General Thawil Pleansri told the media that there was a need for the government to hold a dialogue with *phu hen tang chak rat* or people with different views from the state (*Prachatai*, 9 May 2011). It is important to note the change in the term used to refer to those engaged in violence in southern Thailand. That change signified a gradual shift in perceptions of the insurgents. Previously, the terms *phu ko het runraeng* (instigators of violence) or *phu ko khwammaisangop* (instigators of disturbance), each propagated by the military, dominated public perception, particularly in Thailand's mainstream media. This plan was, however, suspended after Thaksin's sister Yingluck assumed the premiership in August 2011, following the election victory of her Phuea Thai Party.

The failure of the Langkawi, Bogor, OIC and Geneva peace initiatives was due mainly to three factors. First, the political turmoil at the national level that Thailand had experienced since the 2006 coup hampered initiatives to address the southern conflict. Governments in Bangkok were short-lived and unstable; it was therefore hard for the Thai government to maintain a consistent and serious effort. Peace initiatives were often neglected or disrupted during these turbulent years. Second, the military, which remains an important force in Thai politics and the southern conflict, strongly opposed the idea of a formalized peace process. It feared that such a move would internationalize the conflict, help elevate the insurgents' political standing and heighten the risk of secession. Third, the Thai state's insistence on keeping the southern conflict an "internal affair" and preventing inter-governmental organizations and foreign governments from engaging in efforts to resolve it also deterred peace initiatives.

The Formalized Peace Dialogue under the Yingluck Government

For nearly a decade, the Thai state's all-out effort to quell the armed liberation movement in the Malay-Muslim South by means of military suppression and political co-optation failed to bring an end to the conflict. The liberation movements proved resilient in the face of counter-insurgency operations, while any peace process remained at the margin of government policies. A significant shift occurred after the Yingluck government requested assistance from Kuala Lumpur to facilitate a peace dialogue. This request represented a reversal of Bangkok's stance towards Kuala Lumpur in matters regarding the South, as the Bangkok government had previously refused any assistance from foreign governments in the efforts to address the conflict there.

Personal discussions between former prime minister Thaksin Shinawatra and Malaysian prime minister Najib Razak in January 2011 kick-started the initiative. A month later, Yingluck held further talks with Najib during her introductory visit to Kuala Lumpur. The Malaysian prime minister stated publicly that Thailand had requested that Malaysia provide assistance in the quest for a long-term solution to the violence in the former country's South (*Bangkok Post*, 21 February 2012). In mid-March, Thaksin held a secret meeting with seventeen separatist leaders in Kuala Lumpur. Two weeks later, major car bombs struck the commercial hub of Hat Yai, in Songkhla province, and the urban centre of Yala, killing fourteen people and injuring more than four hundred (Davis 2012). The military quickly said that the attack might be a response to Thaksin's secret talks, which did not include all insurgent groups (*Matichon Daily*, 3 April 2012).[14] The initiative, however, went ahead. Two officials close to Thaksin — Paradon Phatthanathabut, secretary-general of the National Security Council, and Thawee Sodsong, then secretary-general of the Southern Border Provinces Administrative Centre (SBPAC) — played important roles in it.[15] Months of behind-the-scenes coordination and discussion finally resulted in the launching of the "General Consensus on the Peace Dialogue Process" between the Thai government, represented by Paradon, and the BRN, represented by Hassan Taib, on 28 February 2013 (*Bangkok Post*, 1 March 2013).[16] Hassan signed the document launching the process with the stamp "BRN".

The agreement to launch a formalized peace dialogue had a clear grounding in policy and in the law. The Policy on the Administration and Development of the Southern Border Provinces, 2012–2014 (*nayobai kanborihan lae kanphatthana changwat chaidaen phak tai pho so 2555–2557*) drafted by the NSC, as stipulated in the 2010 SBPAC Act, provided a crucial legal framework for establishing this dialogue (National Security Council 2012). Previously, government officials were afraid that holding peace talks with "criminals" could be deemed illegal and would thus seriously harm their careers. The new policy clearly supported a peace dialogue. One of the nine objectives of the new policy framework stated that the government was obliged to create a conducive atmosphere for dialogue and to guarantee the safety of all stakeholders engaged in this process. This policy direction granted legal protection for state officials to begin a formalized dialogue. The enactment of the SBPAC Act also enabled this civilian-led agency to operate with more autonomy from the military-led Internal Security Operations Command (ISOC), to which it had previously been subordinate.[17] Being a separate legal entity allowed the SBPAC under Thawee's leadership to initiate several new policies, including the peace dialogue, in spite of the military's opposition.

The document laying out the General Consensus included five major points: (1) Paradon, as the NSC secretary-general, was to "head the group supporting favourable environment creation for peace promotion". (2) The Thai government, "Party A", was willing to "engage in peace dialogue with people who have different opinions and ideologies from the state", or "Party B". (3) The process would be undertaken under the framework of the Thai constitution. (4) The government of Malaysia would act as facilitator. (5) All members of the Joint Working Group on Peace Dialogue Process on Southern Thailand (JWG-PDP), set up as a result of this agreement, would enjoy measures to ensure their safety throughout the process. Najib appointed Ahmad Zamzamin bin Hashim, a former chief of the Research Department of the Prime Minister's Office — the Kuala Lumpur government's intelligence agency — to serve as facilitator for the dialogue (Prime Minister's Office of Malaysia 2013).

The first meeting was held in an undisclosed location in Kuala Lumpur on 28 March 2013; it was largely an ice-breaking session. There were nine representatives from the Thai government, led by the NSC chief, and six representatives from the Party B side — five from the BRN and one from PULO.[18] The Thai government called on the BRN to refrain from attacking soft targets, while the BRN representatives spoke at length of historical grievances and called on the Thai government to deliver justice to Malay-Muslims in a "concrete manner".[19]

Shortly before the two parties were scheduled to meet again, Hassan Taib and Abdulkarim Khalid, the two BRN representatives, made their first public appearance via YouTube. They made five demands of the Thai government, which they called "Siamese colonialists" (Muhammad 2013):

1. Allow the Malaysian government to play the role of mediator and not just facilitator.
2. Ensure that the dialogue be held between the Patani people, led by the BRN, and the Siamese colonialists.
3. Allow the Association of Southeast Asian Nations (ASEAN), the OIC and NGOs to witness the peace process.
4. Release all prisoners in security-related cases without conditions and revoke all arrest warrants.
5. Recognize that the BRN is a "liberation" and not a "separatist" movement.

It is important to note the BRN-Coordinate's strategic shift in communications. Having spoken mainly through violence, leaflets and graffiti, it began to use social media as a channel of communication for the first time. The use of YouTube allowed its message to travel beyond the dialogue table and to reach its constituents and the general public. The five demands were later submitted to the Thai government side during the second meeting on 29 April 2013.

On 24 May 2013, Adam Muhammad Noor, the third BRN representative, appeared in a YouTube video clip to clarify further the five demands. He rephrased the fifth point by calling for the Thai government to recognize the *"hak pertuanan"* (sovereign rights) of Patani Malays to Patani land (flyer cryer 2013). Four days later, the BRN released a third statement via YouTube, criticizing the Thai government's disunity in handling the southern conflict and demanding that peace dialogue be declared a "national agenda" (BRNVoices 2013). The definition and implication of the term *hak pertuanan* became a contested issue. In a third meeting of the dialogue partners held on 13 June 2013, the Thai delegation asked for clarification of the five demands, particularly of the meaning of *hak pertuanan*. Party B promised to submit an explanation in writing.

The Thai government wanted at the same time to test Party B's command and control capabilities. In response to the five demands, Bangkok called on Party B to minimize violent attacks during the upcoming month of Ramadan. Party B pledged to respond in ten days' time. On 24 June 2013, Hassan appeared on YouTube demanding seven preconditions in exchange for ceasefire. Bangkok deemed these conditions impossible to meet. Among the demands were the withdrawal from the far South of all troops dispatched from other regions and the removal of local troops from village areas to their bases.[20] Although Bangkok did not agree to such preconditions, the Malaysian facilitator Zamzamin apparently lobbied the BRN to take part in a reduction of violence. This intervention resulted in a statement issued by the JWG-PDP's secretariat on 12 July 2013 — two days after the beginning of Ramadan. The statement announced that the two parties had agreed to "work hard to ensure that Ramadan for 2013 would be a violence-free month to demonstrate the sincerity, commitment and seriousness of both sides in finding solutions to the common problem" (Joint Working Group on Peace Dialogue Process on Southern Thailand 2013).

Although Ramadan 2013 was not entirely peaceful and indeed saw a relatively high number of attacks, a thorough examination of statistics suggested a significant degree of BRN control over fighters on the ground. The scale and scope of attacks corresponded with conversations at the dialogue table. There was a significant drop in violence during the first nine days of Ramadan and then a spike following the deaths of three Malay Muslims with apparent links to the BRN in what was perceived as a violation of the agreement on the part of the Thai government. The ISOC's own statistics include only two incidents attributed to the insurgents between 12 and 20 July 2013. Both were bombing attacks on 17 July, which injured two soldiers and territorial defence volunteers (*o so, asasamak raksa dindaen*).[21] However, violence surged again after the deaths of the three Muslims.[22] On 21 July, insurgents put up dozens of banners and sprayed graffiti on roads across eight districts in Narathiwat, condemning the Thai government for being "deceitful" and demanding that the military leave the region (ASTV Manager Online, 19 July 2013). The attacks intensified during the last nine days of Ramadan. From 31 July to 8 August, there were some thirty-five bombing incidents — a sharp rise from the average of twenty-four a month during the first half of 2013 (Davis 2013).

While the Thai government, Party A to the dialogue, was still unable to come up with a unified and concrete response to Party B's demands, the hardliners in the BRN's military wing appeared to take dominance. On 6 August, two days before the end of Ramadan, the BRN declared on YouTube that the Shura Council, as it called its leadership, had decided to withdraw from the talks, as the Thai government had failed to meet either its five demands or its seven conditions for a peaceful Ramadan. The setting of the announcement in the video clip, uploaded by the Pengistiharan keputusan Majlis Thura BRN (BRN Armed Forces) was different from that of the previous ones. It showed three men wearing balaclavas that covered their faces and holding rifles against a camouflage background. The previous clips had featured the BRN representatives wearing black Malay *songkok* caps with their faces clearly visible (Angkatan Bersenjata-BRN 2013).

The facilitator made further attempts to move the talks forward. Zamzamin travelled to Bangkok in early September in a bid to break the deadlock between the parties. He submitted a document clarifying the BRN's five demands, as requested by the Thai government side. Some observers believed that the facilitation team had mainly prepared the clarification. Suspicions about the extent to which it represented the BRN's thinking were therefore raised.[23] Zamzamin told this author that he assisted Party B in the drafting process, but it was unclear how much he had helped to shape the contents of the clarification.[24] Whatever the case, the document contained an explanation of the definition of *hak pertuanan*. It clarified that Party B "will not demand territorial secession" from Thailand, but instead called for cultural and territorial autonomy.[25] The document also laid out the new composition of Party B to include more parties representing the Patani Malay community, including three BRN members, two PULO members, one member from the BIPP, a legal expert, a historian, an expert on economics and trade and experts on social issues.

The five demands created a dispute among various Thai government agencies, with the military being the most vocal in its opposition to the BRN's proposal. In late October, Bangkok found a diplomatic answer. In a written response submitted through the Malaysian facilitator, it did not give a *yes* or *no* answer but rather stated that it was "willing to discuss" the five demands.[26] However, the nascent peace dialogue was by this point beyond rescue. There was an unfavourable atmosphere on both sides. The BRN's military wing was unwilling to pursue the talks without Bangkok's acquiescence to its five demands. That wing was said to have "abducted" Hassan prior to the meeting scheduled for early December 2013.[27] The meeting was cancelled in light of the growing protests against the Yingluck government led by the People's Democratic Reform Committee (PDRC). Hassan appeared on YouTube on 1 December 2013, making an unusually strong statement to the effect that the BRN aimed "to bring justice and prosperity to Patani in the form of independence ... not peace under the control of Siamese colonialists". He also said that any further dialogue could only be resumed after the Thai government side accepted the BRN's demands as stated in the Shura Council's 6 August declaration. The video clip ended with three invocations of the word *merdeka* (independence) in a harsh tone. None of the previous clips had mentioned this word, and *"mantan delegasi BRN"* (a former BRN delegate) posted this 1 December clip, raising the question of Hassan's removal from the dialogue team. In any case, this dialogue process, facilitated by Kuala Lumpur, finally came to an end with the fall of Yingluck's government. She was forced to step down on 9 December 2013 and to call new elections amid growing anti-government protests under the PDRC's leadership.

The Military-Led Peace Dialogue

Although the peace dialogue pursued under the Yingluck government was short-lived, the idea of a formalized peace process significantly changed

the dynamics of the conflict. It became an apparently essential component
of efforts at conflict resolution in the Deep South. The Thai military, which
expressed strong opposition to the 2013 peace talks, did not completely
abandon the peace dialogue policy after the 22 May 2014 *coup d'état*.
In the context of intensified political turmoil, the PDRC's campaign against
the 2 February 2014 general elections rendered their result inconclusive.
The constitutional court would later annul them. A caretaker government
governed Thailand for more than six months thereafter, and efforts to
organize a new poll faced further opposition from the PDRC. The military
claimed that its coup was due to a need to break the "political impasse".
General Prayut Chan-o-cha, leader of the "National Council for Peace
and Order" (NCPO) junta, took power and assumed the premiership.
To the surprise of many observers, Prayut resumed the peace talks on
the South facilitated by Kuala Lumpur, even though the dialogue teams
that the two sides sent to the talks proved substantially different. On the
Thai government side, the talks became a military-led process, with the
Thaksin-allied bureaucrats who had previously led the Party A delegation
removed from that delegation.[28] There was also a significant change on the
part of Party B, with the formation of a new umbrella organization called
Majlis Syura Patani (Patani Consultative Council, or MARA Patani) that
replaced the BRN as Party B representatives.

The military government in Bangkok set up a new structure to oversee
policies on the southern insurgency. It referred to the peace dialogue
with a new term, *khabuankan phutkhui phuea santisuk* (Dialogue Process
for Peace and Happiness) (Thailand 2014c). Some observers noted that
the replacement of the word *santiphap* (state of peace) with *santisuk*
(peace and happiness) might imply a change in the nature and purpose
of this dialogue. The new terminology echoes the military's campaign to
"bring back happiness" to Thais after years of political polarization.
Two months after the coup, General Prayut, acting as NCPO leader,
issued NCPO Order No. 96/2557, dated 21 July 2014. The order established
a new nineteen-member steering committee to oversee the implementation of policies on the South under the leadership of the army deputy
commander; the committee was to be known as the *Kho Po To*.[29] NCPO
Announcement No. 98/2557, issued on the same day, covered various aspects
of government operations in the South. It announced the establishment
of committees at the policy, policy-to-operational and operational levels.
Prayut, as the NCPO leader, would head the policy-level committee,

while the policy-to-operational level committee was to be led by the chief of the *Kho Po To*. The commander of the Fourth Army Region, who concurrently served as the head of the ISOC's regional forward command, would be in charge of the operational level committee. The announcement also identified four key priority areas. These included mandating the NSC, together with other relevant agencies, to prepare a road map for the "Dialogue Process for Peace and Happiness for southern Thailand".

The NCPO government also set up mechanisms geared towards resumption of peace dialogue, including the appointment of the head of the delegation. Four months after the coup, Prime Ministerial Order 230/2557 led to the formation of a Steering Committee for Peace Dialogue (*Khanakammakan amnuaikanphutkhui phuea santisuk changwat chaidaen phaktai*) tasked with overseeing policies relating to the dialogue and chaired by the prime minister. A Peace Dialogue Panel (*khana phutkhui phuea santisuk changwat chaidaen phaktai*) was set up to lead the Party A delegation, and Area-Based Inter-Agency Coordination Working Groups (*khana prasanngan radap phuenthi*) were tasked with liaison work among government agencies in the South and relevant partners (Deep South Watch 2015).

The establishment of new mechanisms was in preparation for the resumption of the peace dialogue, which officially began after the meeting between Prayut and Najib in Kuala Lumpur on 1 December 2014. The Thai prime minister introduced General Aksara Kerdpol as the new leader of the Thai dialogue team. The Thai military initially wanted to make this new partnership a matter of military-to-military cooperation by having the armies of the two countries be in charge of the dialogue. It preferred a new facilitator from a military background, but its Malaysian counterpart was not receptive to such an idea and Zamzamin was allowed to continue to play the facilitation role.[30]

The liberation movements remained distrustful of the army, and opinions were varied about the pros and cons of being engaged in military-led peace talks. On the day of the resumption of the dialogue, dozens of banners written in Thai, English and Malay appeared across the four southernmost provinces of Thailand. They bore the message, "Is it appropriate to negotiate with government that is the result of a coup? There is no guarantee of sincerity" (*Khaosod English*, 1 December 2014). Abu Hafez Al-Hakim, a senior BIPP member, wrote in an article that there had been serious debate within the movement about the benefits of talking to the junta at this juncture. Members of the movement were concerned that the military would be unwilling to discuss the issue of self-governance for the Malay-Muslim South. Abu Hafez Al-Hakim noted that, in the end, while some Patani liberation movements' leaders were reluctant to join the talks, others were willing to do so, as long as neither party set preconditions (Abu-Hafez Al-Hakim 2014).[31]

Confronted with the BRN leadership's unwillingness to take part in the military-led peace talks, Patani liberation leaders from other smaller groups, along with some individual BRN members, decided to form the new umbrella organization MARA Patani on 15 March 2015 to represent Party B in the resumed Kuala Lumpur peace dialogues (Abu Hafiz Al-Hakim 2015). MARA Patani originally included representatives from five liberation groups: the BIPP, the Gerakan Mujahidin Islam Patani (Patani Islamic Mujahideen Movement, GMIP) and three factions of the PULO: Pulo-P4, Pulo-DSPP and Pulo-MKP (Deep South Journalism School, 31 August 2015). Pulo-P4, led by Shamsuddin Khan, later withdrew in June because of internal disagreements.

MARA Patani made its first public appearance at a press conference in Kuala Lumpur on 27 August 2015, shortly after the third informal meeting between both dialogue parties. Party B used the press conference to state its three preconditions for the talks. It called on the Thai government or Party A to place the dialogue on its national agenda, to recognize MARA Patani as a legitimate party to the dialogue and to guarantee immunity from criminal prosecution for its representatives. The Thai government side held a separate press briefing in Bangkok, at which it called for the establishment of safety zones, for local development and for access to justice for all (Nasueroh and Pimuk 2015). Both parties agreed to start the dialogue anew, beginning with the drafting of terms of reference.[32]

An important question relating to the resumed talks concerned the extent to which the BRN was on board. Some BRN members joined MARA Patani, including Shukri Hari, also part of the 2013 Party B delegation; Awang Jabat, MARA Patani's chairman; and Ahmad Chuwo. However, the involvement of individual members of the BRN did not constitute the official endorsement of the movement's Dewan Pimpinan Parti (Party Leadership Council, DPP).[33] According to BRN sources, Shukri had a mandate to observe discussions in the resumed peace dialogue. However, it was his personal decision to take part in MARA Patani and, as a consequence, he was removed from any active role in the organization.[34] The rift was apparently revealed when Abdulkarim Khalid, another member of the 2013 BRN delegation to the peace talks, appeared on YouTube to read a statement expressing deep mistrust towards the "Siamese colonialists". Speaking on behalf of the BRN's information department, Abdulkarim said that the peace dialogue would lack legitimacy unless Bangkok could guarantee that it would not repeat its previous deceitful behaviour. He called on Bangkok to respect the Patani Malays' rights to self-determination in accordance with the UN General Assembly Resolution 1514 (XV) (Jabatan Penerangan-BRN 2015).[35] His speech made no reference to MARA Patani. In an October interview with security analyst Anthony Davis, four members of the BRN information department, said to have been authorized by the DPP to speak to the media, stated that the current peace dialogue "is discredited and that it should be scrapped in favor of an entirely fresh initiative"; they stressed that the BRN was "categorically not involved" in the dialogue (Davis 2015). While MARA Patani's actual influence over the command and control over the fighters on the ground remained in question, the dialogue went on (Wahari 2015).

What might have been a simple procedure turned out to be highly contentious when the Thai government side in the dialogue proved reluctant to accede to MARA Patani's 27 August preconditions, out of concern that they touched on the matter most feared by the Thai state: the official recognition of Malay-Muslim liberation movements. The two sides set up technical working groups to draft the terms of reference. After three rounds of meetings over a period of five months, the six-page terms of reference were agreed upon on 23 March 2016. While the Thai government had no difficulty affirming that the peace dialogue process was an issue on the national agenda and noting that several national policies and orders confirmed this point, the other two preconditions became points of contention. The Thai government side's technical team, led by Major General Nakrop Bunbuathong, tried to find a way to negotiate for mutually acceptable wording with the counterpart MARA Patani team, led by Shukri. According to General Nakrop, the draft terms of reference agreed upon by the two parties defined Party B as "People with Different Views from the State/ MARA Patani", with a footnote to clarify that Party A referred to Party B as "People with Different Views from the State" and that Party B called itself MARA Patani. The terms of reference made no explicit reference to the issue of immunity, but it was agreed that Party B would be given "protection from detention and prosecution" during passage through and visits to Thai territory for purposes related to the peace effort.[36] Abu Hafez Al-Hakim said that the two sides agreed to note the word "immunity" in the minutes of future meetings, pending further discussion (Abu Hafez Al-Hakim 2016).

While compromise seemed to have been struck at the level of the joint technical working groups, the draft terms of reference faced resistance from various Thai government agencies, notably the NSC and the foreign ministry. MARA Patani came to the meeting held on 27 April 2016 expecting official endorsement of the draft terms of reference, which would have paved the way for the beginning of dialogue on the part of the full panels of representatives of the two parties. To its disappointment, General Aksara instead said that the Thai government side was not ready to endorse the jointly drafted document. A senior Thai journalist, quoting Malaysian sources, said that the Thai prime minister's failure to approve the draft terms of reference had caused his side's decision to delay the endorsement (Isra News Agency, 28 April 2016). This decision came a few weeks after the removal of General Nakrop from the Thai dialogue team amid suspicions that the contents of the terms of reference, in whose drafting he had been the main driving force, led to his removal. However, the general himself explained that his removal was not related to this issue. Rather, his role in the peace dialogue team had ended, as he no longer held the post of deputy director of ISOC's Fifth Operations Coordination Centre.[37] Military sources said that his sacking was primarily related to a dispute between him and the younger brother of then army commander General Teerachai Nakwanich.[38] Whatever the case, General Nakrop's departure from the Thai side's dialogue team was a blow to the revived peace dialogue. Following this surprising move, Abu Hafez Al-Hakim wrote in an unusually harsh tone on his blog that "refusing to accept your dialogue partner by not mentioning the proper name means disrespect and narrow-mindedness. It just shows that one is not truthful in the interaction with one's counterpart" (Abu Hafez Al-Hakim 2016).

With the peace talk stuck in a stalemate, the BRN apparently decided to strike outside its usual theatre of operations. Coordinated bombings and arson in seven provinces of Thailand's Upper South between 10 and 12 August 2016 claimed four lives and injured thirty-six. While the government and police attempted to downplay the possibility that the attacks were the BRN's work, the circumstantial and forensic evidence suggested otherwise. Although the BRN had confined most of its military operations to the southernmost provinces of Thailand, it did have a previous record of attacks outside its traditional theatre of operations. The choice of targets for the August bombings was also in line with the BRN's strategies; the targets included areas of economic significance and of "sinful" activity, along with symbols of the security forces. Most of the areas selected for attack were major tourist sites, such as Phuket, Krabi, Hua Hin in Prachuap Khirikhan province and Khao Lak in Phang Nga province. The shopping malls, discount stores and shops struck also represented hubs of economic activity. Of particular note was the fact that three bombs went off near Phuket's Patong beach, popularly known as a centre of nightlife. In Hua Hin, the bombings took place outside a bar and massage parlour on a lane devoted to nightlife. The Patani fighters apparently considered these entertainment venues, offering covert or open sex services, legitimate targets for military operations. The use of improvised explosive devices in these attacks was also common in attacks staged by the southern insurgents.[39] Police investigations led to the arrest of suspects from the southernmost region of Thailand, even though they remain innocent until proven guilty.

This violence apparently prompted the Thai side in the Kuala Lumpur dialogue to try harder to seek a compromise settlement. In June 2016, Party A had sent a new draft of the terms of reference to Party B through the facilitator. This draft included no mention of the name "MARA Patani" or of immunity. For nearly two months, no progress occurred. It did not seem to be a coincidence that the joint technical working groups reached a compromise settlement on the terms of reference of the resumed dialogue in a 16 August 2016 meeting in Kuala Lumpur, a few days after the bombings in the Upper South.[40] According to MARA Patani, it accepted the new terms drafted by the Thai government side on the condition that the sticking points would be noted in the minutes of the meeting.[41] Two weeks later, four months after the Thai government side's refusal to endorse the jointly drafted terms of reference, the full delegations met in Kuala Lumpur. This time around, MARA Patani made a tactical compromise. On 2 September 2016, both parties agreed to accept the terms of reference proposed by the Party A and to discuss the issue of safety zones in the next phase. However, MARA Patani requested that its concern regarding the question of its recognition as the representative of Party B be noted in the meeting's minutes. The issue of immunity would be discussed during the next phase of the talks.[42]

MARA Patani would again in the next year also face a serious challenge from those speaking in the name of the BRN. After having been silent for a year and a half, the BRN information department issued a statement on 10 April 2017 expressing its desire to hold a peace dialogue with the Thai government, if its three conditions were met. These conditions were, first, that the peace dialogue be based on the willingness of the two negotiating parties and include third parties — meaning the international community — as witnesses and observers; second, that the mediator be credible and impartial and have no conflict of interest; and, third, that the negotiation process be designed by the negotiating parties and agreed upon from the outset and that the mediator facilitate the process according to such agreement. At about the same time, Abdulkarim gave an exclusive interview to the BBC Indonesian Service stressing that the BRN had no involvement in the current peace dialogue and wanted to negotiate with the Thai government in a process involving international observers. He said that the BRN had not joined MARA Patani in that dialogue because it "disagreed with the rules and viewed the process as unequal" (BBC Thai, 11 April 2017; Siregar 2017). The BRN statement contained thinly veiled criticism of the Malaysian facilitator, who was seen to have played a dominant role in the dialogue under the Yingluck government. It suggested the BRN's inclination to explore other facilitators. Most of the demands in the statement in fact reiterated what the BRN had already called for during the time of the Yingluck government.

The 10 April statement came between a pair of rounds of coordinated attacks across the southernmost provinces, meant to display the BRN's military capability. The first round of attacks took place on the night of 6 April and in the early morning of 7 April, during which thirty-one incidents of bombing, arson and shooting struck nineteen districts (*The Nation*, 8 April 2017). These strikes damaged fifty-two electricity pylons and caused widespread blackouts in Pattani but no casualties. Then, on the night of 19 April 2017, twenty-one attacks struck the provinces of Pattani, Narathiwat and Songkhla, most in the form of bomb attacks against the security forces (*The Nation*, 21 April 2017). The coordination of these operations demonstrated the BRN's command and control capability, as did their fighters' refraining from violence during the twelve days between the two rounds of attacks.[43]

Three weeks later, a car bomb exploded in front of the Big C supermarket in Pattani and injured more than sixty people, in what appears to have been a botched operation (ABC News, 10 May 2017). The indiscriminate attack drew widespread condemnation at home and aboard, including the first-ever criticism against a violent attack in southern Thailand from the Parti Islam Se-Malaysia (Abdul Hadi Awang 2017). It is an open secret that a number of fleeing insurgents have sought refuge on the other side of the Thai-Malaysian border. Many of them have taken shelter in the PAS-controlled northern state of Kelantan. PAS has also had a good relationship with the BRN's senior leaders for the past several decades.

In addition to PAS, MARA Patani also denounced the attack.[44] Furthermore, a senior member of the BRN's political wing admitted that it had been responsible for the attack. While the military goal was achieved, the attack was, by this man's own admission, a serious blow to its political objectives.[45]

It was not surprising that the military government in Bangkok immediately rejected the proposal in the BRN statement. Prime Minister Prayut told the media that the BRN should contact the Malaysian facilitator if it wanted to take part in the peace dialogue. Major General Sitthi Trakunwong, secretary of the Thai peace dialogue team, said that Malaysia had done "a good job" as facilitator and that it might not be useful to include many groups in the peace talks. He added that it was not appropriate to bring in international organizations to take part in this "internal affair" (*Thai Post*, 12 April 2017). These remarks reiterated the Thai state's official line that the conflict must remain a domestic issue. According to Hassan, the former Party B delegation leader, the BRN reduced its demands from five to three. It left out the fourth and fifth demands concerning the recognition of the supreme rights of Patani Malays, the release of prisoners detained for security-related offences, and the revocation of arrest warrants. Seen in this light, the BRN had made compromises. It was now demonstrating a willingness to take part in the peace dialogue under no known pressure. However, internationalization remained the issue that most worried Bangkok, and it was unlikely that the military government would accede to BRN's demands. There was also little prospect that the ongoing peace dialogue with MARA Patani would move beyond the confidence-building stage, as the military government's willingness to negotiate on substantive political issues remained a matter of serious doubt.

Observations on the Peace Dialogue in Southern Thailand

The formal peace dialogue between the Thai government and representatives of the Patani fighters, launched nine years after the resurgence of violence in the region, broke new ground. It significantly changed the dynamics of the southern conflict in many respects. Nevertheless, several challenges remain.

First, the BRN does not reject the peace process in principle. However, MARA Patani faces the daunting task of proving its command and control over fighters on the ground and thus fulfilling a significant criterion to demonstrate its legitimacy. According to an insider, MARA Patani has therefore begun an internal dialogue with the BRN leadership in the hope of convincing it to join the dialogue process.[46] Nevertheless, the biggest question concerns whether or not Bangkok would allow international observers to be involved in the current peace dialogue.

Second, the Thai state, particularly the military and foreign ministry, still has a high degree of concern about the possible "internationalization" of the conflict, in spite of the military government's uncharacteristic decision of allowing Malaysia to continue to play a role in the dialogue process. Allowing Kuala Lumpur to serve as facilitator was a significant step forward. It is important to note that this initiative dated to the government of Prime Minister Yingluck — the political opponent of the royalist establishment — and that the military had strongly opposed the initiative at the time. General Prayut, then the army chief, was obliged to follow the government's policy in spite of his disagreement. Thaksin-allied bureaucrats were behind the effort to move this political project on the South forward and their approach was to keep the military at arm's length. The junta's decision to not abandon formal dialogue facilitated by Kuala Lumpur therefore represented reason for cautious optimism. After the 2014 coup, the army had the absolute power to pursue a militarized approach, if it wished. Its decision to participate in talks suggested that it may have realized that it could not win the conflict by military means. However, the post-coup government has provided a reluctant dialogue partner, one still haunted by anxiety about the internationalization of the conflict.

Fear of the internationalization of the conflict in Thailand's Deep South has been a major hindrance to pushing the military-led peace dialogue forward. Even what seems to be a simple issue such as naming Bangkok's dialogue partner in the terms of reference for the dialogue became a highly contested issue and threw the talks into a period of stalemate. Following advice from the Ministry of Foreign Affairs, the Thai military avoided any actions that might allow the situation in the South to be understood as a "non-international armed conflict" in accordance with common article 3 in International Humanitarian Law. For a situation to meet the threshold of a non-international armed conflict, it needs to meet two criteria: hostilities must reach a minimum level of intensity, and the groups involved must possess organized armed forces (Mack and Pejic 2008). The Thai military has tried to conceal the fact that it is indeed confronting an anti-government group or groups with organized armed forces in the South. It barred military commanders in the field from mentioning the BRN's name. Some senior military officers complained that this prohibition prevented soldiers from grasping the true nature of the conflict (Samret, n.d., p. 241). The same underlying consideration accounted for the junta's reluctance officially to recognize the name of MARA Patani. It referred to Party B as "People with Different Views from the State" instead of using the name of the umbrella organization. A senior MARA Patani member said that the Thai government lobbied for the removal of its name from the communiqué of the Thirteenth Islamic Summit of the Heads of State/Government of the OIC Member States issued on 15 April 2016. In the end, "a group of representatives of the Muslim community in the South" replaced "MARA Patani" in that communiqué.[47]

While the parties to the Kuala Lumpur talks struck a compromise in an effort to move the still "unofficial" dialogue process forward, this issue of nomenclature was likely to continue to arise. Nor was the junta receptive to the idea of allowing international bodies, particularly the OIC, to take part in the peace talks. Therefore, it is likely to be difficult to convince the leadership of the BRN to cooperate with this dialogue if Bangkok is unwilling to consider the BRN's latest demands for international observers. Experiences derived from other armed conflicts show that third parties are often instrumental in the success of the peace process, and that success rarely leads to secession. The case of the peace processes between the Indonesian government and Gerakan Aceh Merdeka (Free Aceh Movement) in Aceh and between the Philippine government and the Moro Islamic Liberation Front in Mindanao are cases in point.

Third, if this peace dialogue were to be a meaningful negotiation platform, Bangkok needs to be willing to make genuine political concessions, particularly on the devolution of more administrative powers to the southernmost region of the country. The concept of Thailand as an undivided unitary state has long been upheld as sacrosanct; the 2017 constitution, drafted by a military-appointed committee and endorsed in a tightly controlled referendum, affirms this concept (Thailand 2017a, p. 3).[48] The royalist establishment, particularly the military, has resisted further administrative decentralization, let alone regional autonomy. Some have argued that the military is the real dialogue partner for the Patani liberation movements, as it is the institution that holds de facto power in Thai politics. Nevertheless, it is least likely to make political concessions or to consider any negotiated settlement. After the 2014 coup, the military junta attempted to strengthen the power of the unelected traditional elite and to weaken that of elected political representatives, including local authorities. An NCPO spokesperson reiterated in June 2014 that autonomy for the Deep South would be off the dialogue table (Isra News Agency, 24 June 2014).

As of November 2018, the Kuala Lumpur talks had not begun any substantive discussion, as the process remained in the confidence-building phase. Several months following his return to the Malaysian premiership in May 2018, Mahathir Mohamad tapped former national police inspector-general Abdul Rahim Noor to serve as the new facilitator of the talks on Southern Thailand. Substantial progress before the Thai elections scheduled for February 2019 — and due in any case by May — remained unlikely, however. Yet the provisions of the 2017 Thai constitution that significantly weakened political parties and granted the military substantial control through the appointed senate meant that the army would continue to play a dominant role in Thai politics for at least the first five years after the next general elections (Thailand 2017a, pp. 30, 85).[49] Worse still, General Prayut has expressed an interest in entering politics, and the 2017 constitution allows individuals who are not members of parliament to serve as prime minister. There was therefore little chance that Bangkok's policies on the peace dialogue would change in any significant way following elections. The Bangkok government could consider a wide variety of possible structures of self-governance, perhaps within the framework of greater administrative decentralization for Thailand as a whole. However, continued military domination of Thai politics, albeit under the cloak of civilian rule, will render both of these outcomes unlikely. Peace building in the Deep South perhaps needs to go hand in hand with the democratization effort in Thailand, if it is to succeed.

Acknowledgements

The chapter was written, and updated several times, between 2013 and 2018, a period during which I was closely monitoring the peace dialogue in southern Thailand in various capacities. I would like to thank the British Foreign and Commonwealth Office for its generous support in the form of a Chevening Scholarship, which allowed me to undertake a master's degree in Conflict Resolution in Divided Societies at King's College London in 2012–13. I would like to express my gratitude to Dr Bussabong Chaijaroenwatana, former director of the Institute for Peace Studies at Prince of Songkhla University, and to Dr Srisompob Jitpiromsri of the same university's Faculty of Political Science. Their encouragement and support have been crucial to my intellectual endeavours. Since 2015, I have been a doctoral candidate at the Department of Political and Social Change, Coral Bell School of Asia Pacific Affairs, College of Asia and the Pacific, the Australian National University. I also would like to thank the Thai government for its financial support.

Notes

1. Deep South Incident Database, up to date as of April 2017, in the possession of the author.
2. The survey conducted by the Institute for Economics and Peace provides a comprehensive summary of the key global trends and patterns in terrorism over the last sixteen years, from the beginning of 2000 to the end of 2015. The Global Terrorism Index defines terrorism as "the threatened or actual use of illegal force and violence by a non-state actor to attain a political, economic, religious, or social goal through fear, coercion, or intimidation" (Institute for Economics and Peace 2016, p. 6). The database does not include acts of state terrorism.
3. Note that the names of the historic sultanate of Patani and the modern Thai province of Pattani are spelt differently.
4. For background information on the three major separatist groups, see Che Man (1990) and Surin (1985).
5. Personal communication with a senior BIPP member, June 2017. In the case

of this interview and those cited below for which no locations are given, the author has opted not to disclose the locations in which she met her informants.

6.   Interview with senior PULO leaders, May 2017.

7.   Interview with senior BRN member, 1 August 2016; interview with Hassan Taib, May 2017.

8.   Interview with Hassan Taib, May 2017. Hassan said that the Congress and the Coordinate factions reunited in 2012, but movement insiders said that the Congress faction is de facto defunct. Also see *Prachatai* (20 and 24 June 2013).

9.   Deep South Watch database. As of October 2018, there had been 20,064 security-related incidents in Southern Thailand. A total of 6,877 people have been killed and 13,478 people injured.

10. Bersatu comprises the BIPP, BRN-Congress, PULO and the Patani Mujahidin Movement (Gerakan Mujahidin Patani). The MPRMP had members from six groups — four from Bersatu, BRN (Coordinate) and the Patani Ulama Movement (Gerakan Ulama Patani). However, it has never achieved its mission of uniting the liberation groups, and the BRN (Coordinate) is said to have attended only a few of its meetings. A BIPP senior member said that, although the MPRMP still exists, those remaining with the umbrella group are individuals who have no authority to represent any liberation groups. The BIPP withdrew from the grouping several years ago. Interview with a BIPP senior leader, August 2016.

11. Personal communication with a Malaysian diplomat, Bangkok, June 2011.

12. The 2004 resurgence of violence gave PULO fresh impetus to renew its campaign. In mid-2005, some forty senior PULO members met for a reunification congress in Damascus, Syria. In October 2011, an internal dispute split PULO into two factions. Kasturi led a faction known as PULO-MKP, while Noor Abdul Rahman headed PULO-DSPP. MKP stands for Majlis Kepimpinan Pulo (PULO Supreme Council). It functions as the organization's executive. The faction led by Kasturi and other younger members of PULO used this abbreviation to demonstrate that its legitimacy came from the elected MKP. The DSPP (Dewan Syura Pimpinan Pertubuhan) or "consultative council for organizational leadership" is comprised mostly of members of PULO's older generation. The third faction, called PULO-P4 and led by Shamsuddin Khan, has never reunited with the rest of PULO. Earlier, in the late 1980s, PULO had also divided into two factions, known as the old PULO and new PULO. Shamsuddin stayed with the old PULO, which continued to use the organization's original name in Malay, Pertubuhan Persatuan Pembebasan Patani. Those joining the new PULO changed its Malay name to Pertubuhan Pembebasan Patani Bersatu. The old PULO name in Malay contains four

capital "P" letters, and it is to this that "P4" refers. Interview with a PULO senior leader, December 2016.

13. Personal communication with HD Centre personnel, Bangkok, February 2013.

14. General Prayut Chanocha, then army commander, indirectly criticized Thaksin's move by telling the media that other insurgent groups might stage attacks to compete for supremacy if talks did not include all groups (*Matichon Daily*, 3 April 2012).

15. Thawee was appointed SBPAC secretary-general in October 2011. He replaced Panu Uthairat, who had close ties to the Democrat Party. Paradon replaced Somkiat Boonchu as the NSC's deputy secretary-general in July 2011 before assuming the NSC leadership three months later. Somkiat had been a key person working with the HD Centre in developing the Geneva peace dialogue and his transfer was a major blew to that process.

16. This coverage also provides the full text of the "General Consensus on the Peace Dialogue Process".

17. After the 2006 coup, the Surayut government revamped the structure of bureaucratic organs that Thaksin had set up in the South. He bolstered the role of the ISOC — a counter-insurgency body established in the 1960s to fight against the communists — by enacting the 2008 Internal Security Act. He also revived the SBPAC, originally established in 1984 and dissolved by Thaksin in 2002. Under the terms of the new Internal Security Act, the SBPAC functioned under ISOC supervision. This organizational structure was not conducive to the SBPAC's taking any policy initiative.

18. The five BRN representatives were Hassan Taib, head of the Party B delegation; Adam Muhammad Noor, also known as Fadel; Ustadz Ma Chalong; Shukri Hari and Abdulkarim Khalid. Lukman bin Lima of PULO-DSPP is the only representative from the PULO in this dialogue.

19. Telephone interviews with sources informed about the Thai government–BRN meeting, April 2013.

20. Hassan stated seven preconditions for the reduction of violence during Ramadan on 24 June 2013 via a YouTube video clip (Hassan Taib 2013). Four additional requests were withdrawing regular police and Border Patrol Police from villages in Patani; allowing *O. So.* to take leave so that they could perform religious duties and spend time with their families; completely halting military offensives, road blocks and arrest operations; and refraining from holding Ramadan-related events. In its last request, the BRN called on the Thai prime minister to grant these preconditions formally by 3 July 2013.

21. ISOC data obtained by author. The "Common Understanding" had a retroactive effect and covered the period between 10 July and 18 August 2013 (1 Ramadan 1434 – 10 Syawal 1434).

22. Toleb Sapae-ing, who was being prosecuted for security-related charges, was

killed on 15 July, and Mahyahali Ali, a religious leader believed to have links with the BRN, was assassinated the following day. Rubbing salt into the wound, the security forces shot to kill Masupien Mama, a suspected insurgent, during a raid on his house in Narathiwat on 19 July 2013.

23. See Romadon (2015, p. 198n441). Romadon argues that the document was originally drafted by the Malaysian facilitation team.

24. Personal communication with Zamzamin bin Hashim, Kota Bharu, Malaysia, 18 February 2014.

25. The BRN made concrete demands in the document that it submitted to the Thai government: (a) allowing Patani Malays to practise their way of life, culture and traditional practices based on Islam; (b) establishing an autonomous special administrative region; (c) reserving seats in the Thai parliament for Patani Malay representatives; (d) having a Patani Malay serve as the provincial governor, with one Buddhist and one Muslim deputy governor, in each of the three Malay-Muslim majority provinces; (e) reserving special quotas for Patani Malays among police serving locally; (f) reserving special quotas for Patani Malays in government offices; (g) allowing the Office of Islamic Judges (*qadhi*) to manage Muslim affairs; (h) allowing Malay-language media to operate; and (i) allowing a portion of local taxes and revenues to be returned to the southernmost region. English version of "Explanations on the five (5) preliminary demands of the National Revolutionary Front (BRN) Panel" (n.d.), document obtained by author.

26. Interview with a senior NSC official involved in the peace dialogue, Pattani, September 2013.

27. Interview with a source close to Hassan Taib, 1 August 2016.

28. The NCPO ordered the removal of Thawee, Defence Ministry permanent secretary General Niphat Thonglek, and Police Special Branch superintendent Lieutenant General Saritchai Anekwiang, who spearheaded the peace talks, from their respective posts. Lieutenant General Paradon was removed from the NSC leadership before the coup by court order. The Supreme Administrative Court ruled on 7 March 2014 that the removal of Thawil Pliensri from the post of NSC secretary-general by the Yingluck government in 2011 was unlawful, and he was hence reinstated to the position.

29. The Thai name of this committee is *Khanakammakan khapkhlueankankaekhai panha changwat chaidaen phak tai.*

30. Personal communication with a Malaysian diplomat, Bangkok, September 2015.

31. According to Abu Hafez Al-Hakim, MARA Patani built on the Majlis Amanah Rakyat Patani (Amanah Council for the People of Patani) that the BRN's pro-dialogue faction had launched on 25 October 2014; the abbreviation of this group's name was also MARA.

32. Personal communication with a MARA Patani insider, 29 August 2016.

33. Personal communication with a MARA Patani insider, 23 August 2016.

34. Interview with senior BRN members, May and June 2017.

35. United Nations General Assembly Resolution 1514 (XV) is a declaration on the granting of independence to colonial countries and people, which reaffirms people's rights to self-determination.

36. Interview with Major General Nakrop Bunbuathong, Bangkok, 14 June 2016.

37. Ibid.

38. Telephone interview with military sources, April 2016.

39. For an analysis of the bombings in the Upper South, see Rungrawee (2016).

40. The meeting was scheduled before the Upper South bombings. However, the violence helped push Party A to find a compromise.

41. Interview with MARA Patani representative, 3 November 2016.

42. Personal communication with Abu Hafez Al-Hakim, Northern state of Malaysia, 17 June 2016.

43. Personal communication with a Western diplomat monitoring the southern conflict, Bangkok, 3 June 2017, and interview with a member of the political wing of BRN, July 2017.

44. Abu Hafez Al-Hakim, MARA Patani spokesperson, wrote on his Facebook page on 10 May 2017, "We condemn any act of cowardice that directly inflicts casualties on civilians/non-combatants especially of women and children. The perpetrators must be brought to justice."

45. Interview with a senior member of the BRN's political wing, July 2017.

46. Interview with a Patani liberation movement insider, May 2017.

47. Interview with a MARA Patani representative, 3 November 2016.

48. Section 1 of the 2017 constitution drafted by the military-appointed committee led by Meechai Ruechuphan states that "Thailand is one and an indivisible kingdom".

49. Article 269 of the 2017 constitution stipulates that the 250-member senate will be selected by the NCPO in the initial period after the promulgation of the constitution. The senate's term is five years. After that term has expired, according to article 107, a two-hundred-member senate will be selected from representatives of occupational groups, through a selection process carried out among members of each group at the district, provincial and, ultimately, national levels.

7

Thailand's Zigzag Road to Democracy: Continuity and Change in Military Intervention

Surachart Bamrungsuk

Instead of asking why the military engage in politics,
We ought surely ask why they ever do otherwise.

— Samuel E. Finer
The Man on Horseback (1962, p. 5)

As society changes, so does the role of the military.
In the world of oligarchy, the soldier is a radical;
in the middle-class world, he is a participant and arbiter;
as the mass society looms on the horizon,
he becomes the conservative guardian of the existing order.

— Samuel Huntington
Political Order in Changing Societies (1968, p. 221)

Will the military launch a coup? Will the army overthrow the elected government? Such questions continue to arise regardless of the stage of development in which Thai society finds itself. From 1932 to the present, military intervention in Thai national politics has been a recurring theme, making it necessary for those who want to understand Thai politics to understand the Thai military. Indeed, the role of the military in the country's politics has been a crucial point of contention since the Siamese Revolution of 1932. It remains so because the Thai officer corps remains unreformed and unchanged. From 1932 to the Second World War, to the Cold War and through the post–Cold War era, the military has remained a main actor in Thai politics regardless of changing international circumstances.

Thai politics remains subject to the significant influence of military leaders. Since its break with the palace in 1932 and through its extended record of political intervention in subsequent decades, the Thai officer corps has held an undisputed role as a leading political actor in the country. The military has never proved its professionalism in large-scale warfare; rather, it has engaged only in limited counter-insurgency operations in rural areas. The absence of external security challenges has left the army free to involve itself in political affairs and to become more skilled in political manipulation. Furthermore, the political strength of the army has owed much to the weakness of civil society and of other potential civilian challengers.[1]

This reality suggests that the political preferences of military elites determine whether a democratic transition is possible or not. More fundamentally, the country cannot sustain such a democratic transition unless military elites decide to commit to democratic rule and to abide by government by elected civilians. In other words, the Thai military's support is a basic prerequisite for the emergence of democratic rule.

The Siamese Revolution of 1932 was, of course, not the first time that the Thai military involved itself in politics. Inspired by the Meiji Revolution in Japan and the Hundred Days' Reform movement in China, and in the context of a conflict between Rama VI's much-criticized Wild Tiger Corps (*suea pa*) private army and the regular military, a group of young officers plotted to replace royal absolutism with a limited monarchy. Authorities arrested all of the plotters in 1912, the year of the abolition of the Qing Dynasty and of the establishment of the Republic of China under the presidency of Dr Sun Yat-Sen.[2] Ironically, then, the first attempt at direct political intervention on the part of the Thai military was an ideologically progressive one![3]

In 1932, a group of young civilians and officers calling themselves the People's Party mobilized support from several groups in Siam to establish a constitutional regime. The 1932 Siamese Revolution could be considered the "first wave of democratization" in Thailand.[4] There were, however, many conflicts between the crown and these political newcomers; this period saw the military join the People's Party government to oppose pro-royalist coups. The army thus became the new regime's main instrument for the defence of constitutional rule. Without its support, the regime to which the 1932 revolution gave birth would have collapsed. One may therefore argue that a threefold ideology of nationalism, militarism and constitutionalism infused the Thai military, and that the military hence played a role as "constitutional protector" (Suthachai 2010, p. 76).

With the 1932 revolution the role of the palace diminished and the king was thus brought under the law. It was the end of absolutism, paving the way for a new political order in Thai politics in which the military became an instrument of the government rather than the palace. At the same time, the military was open to influence from members of the military elite such as Field Marshal Po. Phibunsongkhram, whose role after the 1941 Franco-Siamese War became more crucial as his popularity grew among young officers.

During the Second World War, the Bangkok government, under Phibun's leadership, allied Thailand with Japan. The Japanese expansion into Indochina and later to Thailand helped to strengthen his regime and the role of military. After gaining territory from French Indochina with the Tokyo Treaty of 1941, the military was honoured as "territorial fighters",[5] who had repossessed land that Thailand had lost to the French empire in the late 19th century (Surachart 2009, p. 12). Although Thailand was a close ally of Japan during the war, it was not treated like Germany, Italy and Japan after the war ended. The Thai military in the post-war period thus remained more or less unchanged. The British government attempted to pressure the Thai military to reorganize, but Washington treated Thailand as a formerly occupied country. Without American resistance to Britain's ideas, Thailand's post-war military would have come under British management.[6] If the Allies had occupied Thailand and restructured the political system, as was the case in Japan during the American occupation, Thai politics and the role of the country's military would be very different.

The Thai Military and the Cold War

The dawn of the Cold War in Europe led to sharper focus on the expansion of communism from the Soviet Union to Europe and, later, to Asia.

Communism was the primary security threat in the eyes of Western governments, especially after the crises in Greece and Turkey in 1947. The establishment of the People's Republic of China in 1949 and the outbreak of the Korean War in 1950 only compounded perceptions of this threat in Asia.

At the same time, the Thai military elite, supported by royalists, staged a coup in November 1947 (Suchin 2014, pp. 88–111; Suthachai 2010, pp. 100–101), the first successful coup after the Second World War. Although the military elite, and especially Field Marshal Phibun, had been strong supporters of Japan during the war, Western governments allowed them to come back to power and, without foreign intervention, the military government successfully returned to Thai politics (Suchin 2014, pp. 112–37; Suthachai 2010, pp. 65–132). The new international order of the Cold War helped the Thai military to survive as a political actor because the West viewed the Thai military regime as the sort of strong government necessary to fight the communists.

The first sign of this close orientation towards the West was Thailand's decision to sign agreements with the United States on educational and cultural exchange, economic and technical cooperation, and military assistance in 1950. These agreements indicated the new relationship between Field Marshal Po. Phibunsongkhram, a former ally of the Axis powers, and the United States. The Korean War also helped to strengthen the U.S.-Thai relationship. Thailand offered ground troops to join United Nations operations in that conflict, and the country's security policy from the time of the Korean War onward was an indication of its moving towards the West. The Cold War had made the Thai military elite a strategic ally of the West (Surachart 1988, p. 44). The Thai military also gradually moved from being the protector of the constitution to adopting a pro-royalist stance. As in the days of the *ancien régime* and the pre-constitutional era, it viewed the crown and not elected political elites as the sovereign power, underlining the point that the 1947 coup had triggered a new order in Thai politics. This new order saw the revival of the traditional elite and its alliance with the military elite. The latter included senior officers from the 1932 coup group who had long since severed their ties to the People's Party that had taken power in that year (Suthachai 2010, pp. 102–3).

Did these developments signal the end of the first wave of Thai democratization? Because of the Cold War, the military had become a major political actor, but it was not a coherent one, as solidarity among senior officers only existed on paper. The reality was that internal power struggles had contributed to political conflict and led to a series of post-1947 coups and coup attempts.

One of these conflicts among members of the Thai military elite led to a major coup in 1957 under the leadership of Field Marshal Sarit Thanarat. In its aftermath, the military expected to gain control over politics, but it failed. Accordingly, Sarit launched another coup in 1958, hoping, optimistically, to revolutionize the country. Like the 1947 coup, the 1958 coup saw cooperation between military elites and the royalist faction in Thai politics. It thus paved the way for traditional elites to take power. After 1958, the military incorporated royalism as a component of its core ideology and pledged to protect king and country through its anti-communism stance.[7] The spectre of communism also proved an effective justification for military coups during the Cold War, especially in the eyes of Washington (Surachart 1993, p. 184; Thamrongsak 2007, pp. 32–35).

Nevertheless, U.S. geopolitical interests shifted with the Nixon administration, and with this shift came a new policy position with regard to Asia. That administration embarked on its so-called "Vietnamization" policy in the late 1960s and proceeded to re-establish relations with China in 1971–72. Field Marshal Thanom Kittikhachon launched a coup in 1971 in anticipation of the changed landscape resulting from Sino-American rapprochement. He sought to move decisively against the perceived threat of communism to the country, in the context of fears that the United States would withdraw from Asia — and especially from Southeast Asia — and thus leave Thailand to stand alone.

The Second Wave of Democratization

The 1971 coup led to the 1973 student revolution in Bangkok.[8] The coup was viewed as an attempt at military consolidation contrary to liberalizing trends in Thai society. Moreover, the military government faced widespread domestic criticism, especially concerning corruption and military domination of the government. A rising demand for constitutional rule came from all strata of society. The legitimacy of the military regime was challenged when the National Student Center of Thailand began to launch a series of campaigns for a democratic transition. The military regime came to an end when soldiers fired on unarmed demonstrators on 14 October 1973, and the palace and some senior military leaders dissociated themselves from the regime.

These events in turn triggered the "second wave of democratization" in Thailand. This was a period of military retreat from politics, but again there was no organizational or ideological reform of the military. Public will to reform the military was absent in the aftermath of the events of October 1973. Additionally, political change in Thailand was happening concurrently with the beginning of American withdrawal from Vietnam, when the tide of war had shifted in favour of Hanoi. Thai elites, both civilian and military, were concerned mainly about the expansion of communist activities and student activism, which they believed to be a proxy campaign on behalf of the Communist Party of Thailand.

Without military reform and in the context of a weak civil society, military leaders continued to play a major role in post-1973 politics. After the 1973 incident, the military veered to the extreme right in response to the expansion of social activism in the form of cooperation among students, peasants and workers. There was a growing fear of communism among military officers and the country's moneyed elite. The right-wing movement rallied around the conservative ideology of "Nation, Religion, King" and mobilized violently against left-wing groups. The rightists' main strategy was to provoke disorder in order to justify military intervention. In the event, a right-wing attack on students demonstrating at Thammasat University paved the way for a coup, mounted on 6 October 1976 with the ostensible purpose of restoring public order. Military leaders and members of the Thai elite strongly believed that the regime that a coup could introduce was the best means to protect "Nation, Religion, King" from the communist threat. However, the October 1976 putsch turned out to be the bloodiest in Thai history, though it did reflect the palace's suspicion of and disenchantment with liberal and left-wing groups in the country (Kobkua 2003, p. 174).

During the events of 6 October 1976, extreme right-wing groups supported by the military massacred many students. For the conservatives, this violence was a response to the expansion of student and social movements between 1973 and 1976. After the coup, there was repression of the left and also the centre. The atmosphere of obsessive anti-communism in the name of "national security" intensified. As a result, opponents of military intervention fled abroad or went underground. Many of them joined the Communist Party of Thailand in rural areas.

The 1976 coup marked the end of the second wave of democratization and brought about the consolidation of right-wing power to maintain the old order that student radicalism had threatened. The 6 October massacre at Thammasat University and in an adjacent park in the heart of Bangkok made clear the extent to which the elites and the military were ready to move against anyone who planned to challenge the traditional establishment (Bradley et al. 1978, pp. 23–37).

The repression following the coup led reformist officers to begin to realize that the longer a hard-line authoritarian regime was in power, the faster the country would lose its struggle with communist insurgents. That repression served not least to fuel the insurgency. The result was another coup in 1977, an attempt to relieve domestic political pressure.

The coup was part of a dynamic process in which the military's perception towards the opposition changed. The new military regime of General Kriangsak Chamanan promised a more liberal, less repressive approach to government and elections in a year rather than in twelve years. These were held in April 1979. The government pursued a reformist line, easing press censorship, establishing a better relationship with labour unions, offering amnesty to student activists and drafting a new, more liberal constitution. The goal was for this line to slow the tide of communist revolution in Thailand. More importantly it came at a time when external threats to the country seemed newly alarming because of the instability in Khmer Rouge Cambodia that would lead to a Vietnamese invasion of the country in the last week of 1978. The resulting loss of a notional buffer zone between Thailand and Vietnam represented a nightmare come true for Thai security planners.

On the internal political scene, an oil crisis and the resultant increase in the prices of goods and commodities led to mounting criticism of the government from parliament and the public. General Kriangsak was forced to resign in February 1980 following parliamentary debate on his government; he could clearly no longer rely on military support. General Prem Tinsulanon, who had served as Kriangsak's defence minister and as army commander, assumed the premiership in March 1980.

The coup that General Kriangsak led in 1977 also laid the foundation for a so-called "hybrid politics" or "hybrid regime",[9] whereby an elected government was in power under the leadership of the military. In other words, national politics were still guided by military elites. The Prem government faced coup attempts in 1981 and 1985 but survived them. It was unusual that the attempted coups did not succeed, even though the 1981 incident saw a high level of military mobilization to topple the government, spearheaded by a group of middle-ranking officers who controlled main battalions and regiments in the army.

The coup attempts initiated by this "Young Turks"[10] group in 1981 and 1985 failed because of both military factionalism and national political conditions. Few in Thailand wanted to see the country return to the old days of military government. Many observers believed that the age of military coups would become history. At the same time, this period also saw the expansion of the military's role in society. The Thai military moved closer to the "new professionalism" of many officers in Latin America, in a trend that saw officers tend to become more rather than less politicized. Militaries came to play a crucial role in interpreting and dealing with domestic problems. Their highly politicized officers saw managing threats to internal security as their role.[11]

The Thai military believed that it had to move beyond the traditional concept of external defence to tackle internal defence. As a consequence, Thai officers placed more emphasis on internal security and social services in the belief that previous civilian governments had failed to stimulate economic and infrastructural development and that the communists had exploited that failure. The concepts of new professionalism and military guardianship of internal security helped to encourage the expansion of the military's role in domestic affairs.

Its internal security doctrine now led the Thai military to assume control over a wider political sphere. This doctrine led to belief in a fundamental relationship between the military and politics. The army devoted attention to the military's role in counter-insurgency warfare, civic action or civil affairs, and nation-building. Its approach to internal warfare changed, as it focused on internal threats. Prime Ministerial Orders 66/2523 and 65/2525 exemplified this development. Many officers began to study socio-political questions, to think about the social and political conditions that would help to bring an end to revolutionary insurgency. This trend inevitably allowed the military to expand its role in Thai society to a certain degree. Officers assumed the role of "military developmentalists" in order to prevent domestic insurgency. The Thai Army became more concerned with internal political problems, and officers became interested in imposing their own views of political development on governments.[12]

Following the change in military strategy for fighting communism under Prime Ministerial Orders 66/2523[13] and 65/2525, the Thai military began to win the internal war in rural areas. The Thai domino did not fall, as many observers had worried after the fall of Indochina to communism in 1975.

The Third Wave of Democratization

The Thai state's internal war with the Communist Party ended in 1982–83, while on the international stage the Cold War ended in 1989 with the fall of the Berlin Wall and the collapse of communist regimes in Europe. With communism no longer a credible threat to national security, the Thai military and its elite officers had to seek a new ideological rationale to complement nationalism and militarism.

The post–Cold War era ushered in a new strategic environment, not only for Thailand but also for the rest of the world. Governments around the world had to reform and reorganize their militaries in order better to meet the challenges of this new strategic environment. However, the Thai military remained untouched. Although there was no longer a credible threat from the communists, the Thai military retained its structure because of internal politics and organizational inertia.

In the post–Cold War era, the international system entered the era of "globalization", marked by the apparent triumph of liberalism and capitalism (Booth 2014, pp. 94–97). The same winds of change had blown to every corner of the world. With the coming of globalization, authoritarian regimes stepped down in many places. This era also appeared to be one of "democratization", as one of the features of globalization was a "democratic wave". This wave changed the political landscape at both national and international levels in the late twentieth century. Might it also bring the end of the age of military coups in Thailand?

In 1988, the newly elected government under General Chatchai Chunhawan tried to diminish the power of the military in favour of business interests, in a move that triggered conflict between his government and the army. This conflict culminated in another coup, in February 1991 — the first post–Cold War coup in Thailand. The main reason for this coup was not the need to fight communism but rather allegations of massive corruption, of the abuse of power and of a lack of integrity and good governance. Many members of the military elite of the day were "anti-politicians" — mistrustful of elected politicians and opposed to what they perceived to be "parliamentary tyranny" (Suthachai 2008, p. 219). Their views implied that the parliamentary system was a problem in itself. These members of the military elite viewed popular elections and elected politicians as sources of "evil". They subscribed to ideas akin to the concept of "antipolitics" among right-wing officers in Latin America in the 1960s and 1970s. These Latin American officers formed alliances with the conservative elites and technocrats, preferring authoritarian rule over a polity governed by an elected administration.[14] In the case of Thailand, it became clear that the 1991 coup marked a change in the attitude of military elites. Like Peruvian officers before them, the Thai military believed that "the army, drawn from all social classes of the nation, must intervene directly in the management of the affairs of state" (Loveman and Davies 1997, p. 4). Both these militaries viewed themselves as patriotic, self-sacrificing and dedicated to national rather than class interests, unlike self-interested civilians.

Following much political manipulation, one of the coup's leaders, General Suchinda Kraprayoon, became prime minister in early April 1992. The military initially turned to violent suppression of protests against his assumption of the premiership and the army's attempt to consolidate power. It sought to break up the demonstrations on the streets of Bangkok that gained momentum in May 1992. Many casualties resulted, and in consequence the military lost both the battle on the street and the contest for legitimacy and prestige. After this political defeat in May 1992, it had no obvious reason for continued engagement in politics in the narrow sense of the term. A new era in Thai politics, like that following the students' victory in 1973, seemed to dawn in what was a major political defeat for the military.

The 1992 crisis ended in a process of military withdrawal from politics. It seemed decisively to answer the question, "what had military intervention achieved?" Many observers seemed to believe that Thailand's democratization process was on track. Moreover, they tended to believe that the coup in 1991 had been the country's last, since the military had learned its lesson in trying — and failing — to fight against the popular demand for democracy.[15]

The apparent decline of military influence on Thai politics did not, however, change the perception of Thai military elites. Furthermore, military reform was yet again not initiated.[16] Without necessary reforms, the military remained saddled with pre-democratic and Cold War legacies, unable to adapt to evolving politics and the changing world order. The objectives of the military were order, obedience, authority and stability, and the public at large were expected to abide by these objectives whenever the military formed a government. It was clear that military elites were out of step with the concepts of liberalism and democracy. Instead, personality politics was the order of the day in the military. The army commander had the power to mobilize military units to stage a coup. Subordinate officers would comply without hesitation, whether the order was legal or not. Under these conditions, officers believed, the perfection of anti-politics required "nonpolitical leadership and the negation of partisan strife" (Loveman and Davies 1997, p. 8). It required military leadership. And the Thai military considered itself a national guardian, necessary to protect the country from self-interested politicians and corrupt regimes. That is to say, the military must rid national life of the "cancer of elected politics" (Loveman and Davies 1997, p. 13).

In light of the Thai military's conceptions of the most desirable political order, the electoral victories of the Thai Rak Thai Party in 2001, of the People's Power Party in 2007 and of the Phuea Thai Party in 2011 meant little to the military. The elected governments that took power following those elections were unable to control the military, as the concept of civilian control remained far from being the political reality. Instead, a new alliance in opposition to those governments and, effectively, to their base of electoral support was formed among the traditional elites, military leaders and the middle class.

The Third Reverse Wave or the Fourth Wave?

Globally, the middle class has, theoretically, been a major factor in the democratization process (Lipset 1959). However, while members of the Thai middle class were advocates of democracy, as in the case of the 1992 demonstrations against military domination of politics, the Thai middle class has more recently emerged as an advocate of coups in its support of military intervention and of a retreat from popular democracy. The Thai elite and urban middle class have, over the years, become more politically conservative and increasingly concerned about corruption.[17] The issue of corrupt governments and bad governance has thus become an ideal factor for use in mobilizing the middle class in support of coups. They are the "furious middle class", less and less concerned with elections and equality and more and more convinced that democracy breeds immoral politicians. Elections, in the minds of many members of this class, open up opportunities for vote buying, especially in rural areas. In this case, members of the conservative middle class see themselves as the "protectors" of political morality from "dirty" elections and corruption. For the conservatives, this is the "revolt of the middle class" (Kurlantzick 2014). Some take the view that this development is the "fourth wave" of political transition, indicated by democratic retreat (ibid.).

Moreover, the economic development experienced by residents in the North and Northeast of Thailand since the premiership of Thaksin Shinawatra have left them more aware of their rights and power as citizens. The sheer numbers and the voting patterns of people from the North and Northeast indicate that the conservative Democrat Party, supported by many in the urban middle class, cannot win elections, in spite of its bases of support in the capital and the South. The voting power of the North and the Northeast, the main political bases of the Phuea Thai Party, makes it difficult for the Democrats to form a government, forcing it to look for alternatives. The Thai press reported, in fact, that the government of Democrat leader Abhisit Vejjajiva that took office in late 2008 was put together during a meeting held on a military base, under army guidance (Bell 2008). And it was members of the party that organized the demonstrations against the elected Yingluck Shinawatra government that began in late 2013. Their rallies mobilized the middle class, including many conservatives, and successfully prevented the February 2014 elections from taking place through a "Bangkok Shutdown" campaign. That campaign saw government buildings and many streets in the capital occupied. These events culminated in yet another military coup, in May 2014.

The conservative middle class welcomed the 2014 coup, as it did the 2006 coup, because of its concern not only about dirty politics but also about the rising political aspirations of rural people. Economic development has increased political participation in provincial and rural areas of Thailand. This participation resulted in support for the Thai Rak Thai,[18] People's Power and Phuea Thai Parties. Moreover, while the military and members of the middle class viewed populist policies and vote buying as evidence of corruption, for many residents of rural and even urban areas, they were a sign of a government that cared for the poor. Many rural voters appreciated Thaksinite governments' attempts at outreach through a variety of efforts such as subsidized universal healthcare policies, village funds, small and medium enterprise programmes, and the "one subdistrict, one product" scheme and "one district, one scholarship" initiative. For rural voters, democracy was finally "eatable"; that is, relevant to their everyday lives and not merely an abstract concept.

Two Levels of Power Struggle

In recent years, Thailand has seen a new form of political struggle. In the past, the struggle was among elites, both civilian and military. However, a political struggle between the elites and the broader population has made itself increasingly visible. Greater political engagement on the part of rural voters ready to demand their political, economic and environmental rights is seen a threat to the old elites, the military and the middle class.

What is currently happening in Thai politics[19] is thus not only a political transition but also a social transformation, changing the relationship among elites, the middle class and the masses in general. Unlike the Communist Party of Thailand in the past, pro-Thaksin parties have won over residents in the North and Northeast, and this success may serve to entrench the divide in Thai politics.

In this context, the military coup of May 2014 represents an attempt to turn back time to when military regimes played the role of political manager, controlling the opposition, censoring the media and subordinating social movements, including student groups. By not tolerating different ideas and opinions, the military elite today attempts to trade freedom for order. Above all, the coup is meant to preserve the old order.

The Judicial Coup

In addition to military coups, Thai political elites have another means by which to overthrow an elected government — the judiciary.[20] "Judicial activism" was identified as a new mechanism that forced pro-Thaksin parties from political power in 2006 and 2008 through the power of the courts. This past decade may be the first time that the Thai judiciary has been so directly involved in removing administrations. The result has been a more politicized justice system. As Red Shirt supporters have claimed, court verdicts demonstrate a "double standard" because parties in alliance with the elites have not suffered adverse rulings, while the courts have most often ruled against those perceived to be pro-Thaksin (Terwiel 2011, pp. 296–97). Recent years have made clear that the judicial coup or "juristocracy" can operate in parallel to the military coup or "militocracy"

(Surachart 2015). In the future, these two powerful actors will significantly affect Thai politics by combining to control and coordinate political change according to their interests, thus fostering an "illiberal democracy".

Under such conditions, even if elections are allowed to take place in Thailand, there will be constitutional limits. The 2014 coup will lead to another period of hybrid politics, in which military elites attempt to maintain control over political transition. However, there is no guarantee that this transition will result in consolidation or popular consensus, since the military and one section of the political elite have no commitment to democracy. Furthermore, for as long as the Thai caudillos enjoy their current status, a military coup will always be possible.

Conclusion

Democratic regimes cannot survive without their military leaders' commitment to democratic rule. And in Thailand the political preferences of the military have traditionally determined prospects for democratization. For this reason, political crafting (Stepan 2001, pp. 138–58) should be extended to crafting democratic armies supportive of democratic rule, because such armies are crucial prerequisites of democratization. Their existence is a necessary condition, albeit not a sufficient one, for the success of a democratic transition. That existence is conducive to transforming civil-military relations to serve democratic rule. The establishment of civilian control of the military is an important challenge for democratizing and newly democratized countries (Croissant et al. 2012, p. vii). It is especially a challenge for Thailand.[21]

However, creating democratic armies is a difficult task, especially in the Thai context. Military leaders in Thailand, as in Myanmar, will continue to exert their prerogatives and interests after elections. The task for pro-democracy groups is therefore to promote the concept of military subordination to civilian authority and the end of military involvement in politics. In order to accomplish these objectives, military reform must come hand-in-hand with political reform. One cannot be separated from the other. For example, political reforms should lead to new relations and a new protocol between the prime minister and the commander of the army based on rules and regulations. They should lead to the drawing of a clear distinction between the government and military leaders on several issues: military budgets, weapons procurement, arms deployment and defence planning. Military reform, on the other hand, must be carried out to create professional soldiers who are supportive of democratic rule. The aim of military reform is to depoliticize the army and return the officers to the barracks, so to speak. They should not play any political roles, except to vote in elections. They should, at the same time, remain capable enough to accomplish the missions that politicians assign to them (Barany 2012, p. 33).

Finally, a democratic regime must recognize that promoting civilian competence in the area of national defence is indispensable. In a democratic state, defence policy formulation is the business of not only military leaders but also civilian politicians. To play their proper role, the executive and the legislature have to be well informed and also capable of overseeing the armed forces. There are two dimensions of democratic strategy. The first is to increase military professionalism, and the second is to increase civilian knowledge of military matters. Although these goals represent ideals, democratic civil-military relations cannot be achieved without the fulfilment of these conditions. We have to accept the fact that democratic relationships can exist only in a democratic state. The construction of a democratic Thai military has to occur concurrently with the development of Thai democratic governance. These are two sides of the same coin of democratization in Thailand.

Appendix 1
Coups, Attempted Coups and Regime Changes in Thai Politics

Date	Coup	Attempted Coup	Leaders	Reasons
1) 27 February 1912		✓	Capt. Leng Sichan, others	Anti-absolutism
2) 24 June 1932	✓		Col. Phraya Phahon, others	– Transition to constitutionalism – First democratic wave
3) 1 April 1933	✓		Phraya Manopakon, others	– Against People's Party – Anti-communism cited as reason
4) 20 June 1933	✓		Col. Phraya Phahon, others	Counter-coup
5) 11 October 1933		✓	Gen. Prince Bovoradet, others	Return to absolutism
6) 3 August 1935		✓	Sgt. Sawat Mahamat, others	Return to absolutism
7) 29 January 1939		✓	Phraya Song Suradet and Royalists	Return to absolutism
8) 8 November 1947	✓		Field Marshal Po. Phibunsongkhram Lt.Gen. Phin Chunhawan, others	Return of military to politics in post-war era
9) 6 April 1948	✓		Lt.Col. Kan Chamnongphumwet, others	Transition to military rule
10) 1 October 1948		✓	Maj.Gen. Sombun Saranuchit	– Demand for military reform – Against 1947 Coup group
11) 26 February 1949		✓	Pridi Phanomyong and the Free Thai Movement	– Against 1947 coup group – Coup by civilian group from People's Party
12) 29 June 1951		✓	Navy Maj. Manat Charupha, others	Against 1947 coup group (military leaders from navy against army elites)
13) 29 November 1951	✓		Gen. Phin Chunhawan, others	– Anti-communism cited as reason – Return to military rule

continued on next page

Appendix 1 — cont'd

Date	Coup	Attempted Coup	Leaders	Reasons
14) 10 November 1952		✓	Intellectual group	Against military government and its pro-Western policy in Korean War
15) 16 September 1957	✓		Field Marshal Sarit Thanarat	– Military politics – Conflict between army and police elites
16) 20 October 1958	✓		Field Marshal Sarit Thanarat	– Double coup – Transition to authoritarianism
17) 3 December 1964		✓	Air Chief Marshal Nakrop Binsi, others	Military politics (military faction in Air Force)
18) 17 November 1971	✓		Field Marshal Thanom Kittikhachon	– Coup against own government – Anti-communism cited as reason
19) 14 October 1973	✓		Liberal army faction	– Following student uprising – Second democratic wave
20) 6 October 1976	✓		Adm. Sangat Chaloyu, others	– Anti-communism cited as reason – Transition to authoritarianism
21) 26 March 1977		✓	Gen. Chalat Hiransiri, others	Military politics
22) 20 October 1977	✓		Adm. Sangat Chaloyu, Gen. Kriangsak Chamanan, others	Transition to semi-democratic regime under military leadership
23) 1 April 1981		✓	Col. Manun Rupkhachon, others	Military politics
24) 9 September 1985		✓	Col. Manun Rupkhachon, others	Military politics
25) 23 February 1991	✓		Gen. Sunthon Khongsomphong, Gen. Suchinda Kraprayoon, others	– Military politics – Transition to military rule
26) 17 May 1992	✓		People's movement	– Popular demonstration – Third democratic wave
27) 19 September 2006	✓		Gen. Sonthi Bunyaratkalin	Transition to military rule
28) 22 May 2014	✓		Gen. Prayut Chanocha	Transition to military rule

Appendix 2
Successful Coups and Changes of Regime in Thailand

1) The 1932 Revolution   The People's Party revolution
2) The 1933 Coup   The first silent coup
3) The 1933 Coup   The People's Party counter-coup
4) The 1947 Coup   The first coup after the end of the Second World War /
     The first Cold War coup
5) The 1948 Coup   Silent coup to install a military government
6) The 1951 Coup   Silent coup to consolidate military power
7) The 1957 Coup   Coup to install military power, against country's police elite
8) The 1958 Coup   Double coup to consolidate military power
9) The 1971 Coup   Self-coup to consolidate military power
10) The 1973 Incident   Student uprising and coup
11) The 1976 Coup   Coup against student radicalism
12) The 1977 Coup   Coup to liberalize politics
13) The 1991 Coup   Coup to install military power
14) The 1992 Uprising   Popular uprising
15) The 2006 Coup   Coup to install military power
16) The 2014 Coup   Coup to consolidate military power

Appendix 3
Thwarted Coups or Rebellions in Thai Politics

1) 1912   The R.E. 130 Rebellion   *Kabot ro so 130* (กบฏ ร.ศ. 130)
2) 1933   The Borworndej Rebellion   *Kabot Boworadet* (กบฏบวรเดช)
3) 1935   The NCOs Rebellion   *Kabot nai sip* (กบฏนายสิบ)
4) 1939   The 1939 Rebellion   *Kabot 2482* (กบฏ 2482)
5) 1948   The Staff Rebellion   *Kabot senathikan* (กบฏเสนาธิการ)
6) 1949   The Royal Palace Rebellion   *Kabot wang luang* (กบฏวังหลวง)
7) 1951   The Manhattan Rebellion   *Kabot maenhaettan* (กบฏแมนฮัตตัน)
8) 1952   The Peace Rebellion   *Kabot santiphap* (กบฏสันติภาพ)
9) 1964   The 1964 Rebellion   *Kabot 2507* (กบฏ 2507)
10) 1977   The Chalat Rebellion   *Kabot chalat* (กบฏฉลาด)
11) 1981   The Young Turks Rebellion   *Kabot yangtoek* (กบฏยังเติร์ก)
12) 1982   The Second Young Turks   *Kabot yangtoek khrang thi 2*
     (กบฏยังเติร์กครั้งที่ 2)

Appendix 4

Patterns in the Relationship between the Thai Military and Politics

Year	Context	Military Ideology	Civil-Military Relations	Patterns of Regime	Possible Political Problems
(1) 1911	Ro So. 130 Rebellion	• Nationalism • Militarism • Constitutionalism	Absolutism	Absolutism	• Conflict between palace and military
(2) 1932	1932 Revolution	• Nationalism • Militarism • Constitutionalism	Civilian Rule	First Democratic Wave	• Conflict between royalist groups and "new" military • The beginning of democratization
(3) 1947	• Cold War • 1947 Coup	• Nationalism • Militarism • Anti-Communism	Military Dominance		• Increased politicization of military • Loss of military professionalism • Power struggle among military elites • Military rejection of civilian political system
(4) 1973	1973 Student Revolution (October 14 Incident)	• Nationalism • Militarism • Anti-Communism	• Military Withdrawal from Politics • Weak Civilian Rule	Second Democratic Wave	• Experience of open politics after military intervention • Expansion of democratic demands • Military search for new political base

Period	Events	Ideology		Regime Characteristics
(5) 1976	• October 6 Incident • 1976 Coup	• Nationalism • Militarism • Anti-Communism	Military Dominance	Civil-Military Authoritarianism	• Interdependence between military and civilian elites • Army divided among rival elite groups • Instability in absence of either democratic rule or strong authoritarianism • Expansion of Communist Party of Thailand in rural areas
(6) 1977	1977 Coup	• Nationalism • Militarism • Anti-Communism	Military Dominance	Half-Democratic Regime	• Military bureaucratic authoritarianism • "Guided democracy" by military leaders
(7) 1988 1989/ 1990	• 1988 Election • End of half-democratic regime • The end of Cold War	• Nationalism • Militarism • Anti-Communism	Power Sharing	Democratic Transition	• Experience of open politics after military intervention • Expansion of democratic demands • Military search for new political base
(8) 1991	1991 Coup	• Nationalism • Militarism • Anti-Politics	Military Dominance	Military Authoritarianism	• Interdependence between military and civilian elites • Army divided among rival elite groups • Instability in absence of either democratic rule or strong authoritarianism

continued on next page

Appendix 4 — cont'd

Year	Context	Military Ideology	Civil-Military Relations	Patterns of Regime	Possible Political Problems
(9) 1992	Black May Incident (17–24 May 1992)	• Nationalism • Militarism • Anti-Politics	• Military withdrawal from politics • Return to Civilian Rule	Third Democratic Wave	• Democratization may gain momentum that the military cannot control • Democracy is the only game in town
(10) 2001	Election	• Nationalism • Militarism • Anti-Politics	Strong Civilian Government	Third Democratic Wave	• Civilian control over the military
(11) 2006	2006 Coup	• Nationalism • Militarism • Anti-Politics	Military Dominance	Military Authoritarianism	• Interdependence between military and civilian elites • Army is divided among rival elite groups • Instability in absence of either democratic rule or strong authoritarianism
(12) 2007	Election	• Nationalism • Militarism • Anti-Politics	• Power Sharing • Weak Civilian Government	Democratic Transition	• Experience of open politics after military intervention • Expansion of democratic demands • Military search for new political base • Alliance between military and middle class

(13) 2014	2014 Coup	• Nationalism • Militarism • Anti-Politics	Military Dominance	Military Authoritarianism	• Interdependence between military and civilian elites • Army is divided among rival elite groups • Instability in absence of either democratic rule or strong authoritarianism • Strong alliance between military and conservative middle class

Notes

1. For an introduction to the military and Thai politics, see Girling (1981) and Wilson (1962) in English, and Surachart (1998) and Surachart (2000).
2. On inspiration for change drawn from the Meiji Restoration and from the anti-Manchu movement of Dr Sun Yat-Sen in Asia, see Mishra (2013) and Zarrow (2005).
3. For more details, see Atcharaphon (1999).
4. For more details, see Thamrongsak (2000).
5. See Field Marshal Po. Phibunsongkhram's speech to the soldiers and field police on 11 March 1941 in Royal Thai Government (1941, pp. 113–17). The book was partly a celebration of victory over the French military in Indochina and was reprinted by the Thai Army's Directorate of Operations in 2009. Also see Crosby (1973, pp. 95–96). Because of Siam's victory in the Franco-Siamese War in 1941, Major General Phibun was promoted to Field Marshal — the first in the Thai armed forces after the revolution of 1932.
6. After the war, the British and American governments had different policies towards Thailand. The British government wanted to treat Thailand as a defeated country. At the same time, the British government wanted to punish Thailand by demanding reparations and Allied occupation; see Pensri (1999, pp. 204–5).
7. This process is a major theme of Thak (1979).
8. For more details, see Charnvit and Thamrongsak (2013).
9. Wigell (2008) provides a useful framework for classifying political regimes, and for more details on the characteristics of hybrid regimes, see Menocal et al. (2008, pp. 33–36).
10. For more details about this military group, see Chai-anan (1982).
11. On the concept of the new professionalism, see Stepan (1973, pp. 47–53), and for further development of that theme, see Stepan (1988). On the Thai case, see Surachart (1999).
12. On the concepts central to Thai internal security doctrine, see Prime Ministerial Orders 66/2523 and 65/2525 in Appendices 3 and 4 of Surachart (1999), and also Surachart (1998, pp. 72–78).
13. This order ushered in a new era of military involvement in Thai politics, which became more institutionalized and less personalized. See Surachart (1998, pp. 72–78).
14. For an example from the Brazilian case, see Skidmore (1976, pp. 16–19). For another good example of class relationships between elites and the military, see LeoGrande and Robbins (1997, pp. 480–93).
15. For a contrary view, see Surachart (1998, pp. 106–20).
16. On the role of the military after the 1992 May Incident, see ibid.

17. This trend is a major concern of Saxer (2014*b*).
18. On the impact of Thaksin's populist policies, see Pasuk and Baker (2012, pp. 83–96).
19. On political polarization in contemporary Thailand, see Nostitz (2009) and Nostitz (2011).
20. This section draws on Surachart (2014).
21. For more details on Thailand's civil-military relations, see Surachart (2006) and Chambers and Croissant (2010, pp. 63–101).

8

Murder and Regress: Violence and Political Change in Thailand

Prajak Kongkirati

Thailand's electoral politics has changed drastically in the past four decades, and these profound changes have ushered in a new type of political struggle. Since the democratization process began in the late 1970s, electoral politics in Thailand has been tainted by various forms of violent conflict. Apart from targeted assassinations, other forms of election-related violence have included attacks on polling stations on election day, bombing candidates' and vote canvassers' houses, threatening election-related personnel with harm, burning political parties' headquarters, and mass protests following elections. Hundreds of people have died or been injured as a result of these various types of election-related violence. Arising from this history is an important question that calls for investigation: how have the patterns and degree of election-related violence shifted over time? Election-related violence first manifested itself in the 1975 and 1976 elections, during the turbulent period of democratic transition after the 1973 student uprising. The intensity and degree of electoral violence increased in the 1980s and remained relatively constant until the late 1990s. Thai society then observed a sharp rise in violence associated with the 2001 and 2005 elections. Despite predictions that the deep political polarization that occurred after the 2006 military coup would intensify electoral competition and produce higher levels of bloodshed during campaigning and polling, electoral violence actually declined in the 2007 and 2011 elections. Violence increased again, with a new pattern of mass mobilization, in association with the 2014 elections, polls that resulted in the paralysis of the country and eventually paved the way for the military coup of May 2014.

These trends in electoral competition and violence occurred in the context of dramatic political change in Thailand during the past four decades. This chapter aims to provide a broad overview and explanation of the changing landscape of electoral politics since the democratization process began in the 1970s by focusing specifically on political violence in Thai electoral politics. It aims to identify the primary factors, processes and actors that fomented electoral violence. By examining the changes in the characteristics of actors involved in electoral violence in particular, it reflects the shifting mode of electoral competition and terrain of struggle in Thai politics over time. During 1975–76, electoral conflict was a struggle between progressive forces, led by the student movement on the one hand and the conservative elite on the other. State security officers used violent tactics to eliminate and weaken left-wing parties, as the latter were perceived as a political threat. During the long period of unstable parliamentary democracy from the 1980s to the 2000s, patterns of violence shifted to killings between rival politicians who struggled with one another to win elections and exert control over territory in the provinces. From 1976 to 2006, electoral killings reflected the increasing significance of elections as a means of gaining power in Thailand. Electoral democracy enhanced the power of elected politicians, and the value of winning seats in parliament thus reached a point at which politicians were willing to kill opponents who threatened their power.

The political landscape and modes of violence changed dramatically after the 2006 coup, when the traditional elites toppled the popular prime minister Thaksin Shinawatra. Street clashes between opposing mass movements and between the demonstrators and state security forces became the prevailing mode of violence. Violent conflicts were driven by ideological battles between opposing sides over the legitimacy and nature of rule in the country. Political struggle after the 2006 coup became a highly violent zero-sum game. As democratic rule was destroyed, political regression was the result. The turbulence surrounding the February 2014 elections reflected the changing landscape of Thai politics, as traditional elites, supported by the urban middle class, employed violent tactics to undermine the electoral process. Old elites and the urban middle class saw majoritarian democracy and elections as threats to their status and power. They opposed the basic principle of political equality of "one man, one vote". Middle-class protestors' rejection of elections as a legitimate means to win political power paved the way for the coup of May 2014, which returned the country to military rule.

The alliance between the army and the middle class poses the greatest obstacle to democratic development in Thailand in the years ahead. As the fundamental institutions and principles of democracy are under attack, the political future of the country remains uncertain and bleak.

Violence by State Agents and Right-Wing Paramilitary Groups: Turbulent Democratic Transition, Political Polarization and State Crime, 1973–76

The military regime of Thanom Kittikachorn and Praphat Charusathian was brought to an end by the mass uprising led by students in mid-October 1973. During the demonstration, soldiers fired into the crowd of demonstrators, killing 77 and wounding 857 (Charnvit 1993, p. 88). The intervention of King Bhumibol Adulyadej on the side of Thanom's rivals in the Thai military elite and of the students, together with the persistence of the protestors in struggling for democracy even after the initial killings, rendered military suppression ineffective in keeping the junta in power.[1] The 1973 uprising ushered in a highly unstable interim period of civilian democracy. Under the government of Prime Minister Sanya Thammasak, a royalist judge, the country witnessed greater political participation than in any other period before or since. During this period, press censorship virtually disappeared, to the delight of editors, newsmen and readers; the democratic 1974 constitution was promulgated, creating a more open political environment; trade unions were rapidly formed, pressing a host of demands through strikes and marches; and peasant organizations were created to urge land reform. Several left-leaning and socialist political parties were established to compete in the general elections (Anderson 1998, pp. 269–70).

After its success in toppling the authoritarian regime, the nationwide student movement maintained pressure on the new civilian government to sustain constitutional democracy, and it also formed an alliance with peasants and workers to fight for social and economic justice. This progressive alliance, however, threatened the traditional beliefs, economic interests and political power of the privileged classes, including leaders of the army, senior bureaucrats, business tycoons, rural landlords and royalists (Pasuk and Baker 2005, p. 190). The ruling cliques felt that the student-peasant-labour alliance threatened the privileges and power that they had long enjoyed. Some factions in the army were increasingly alarmed by the radical ideas of members of that alliance, which challenged the military's concept of an orderly society and its national security policy. The student movement's campaign for the withdrawal of American troops from Thailand, for instance, was especially threatening to the establishment. Under military dictatorship, government bureaucrats had been accustomed to exercising arbitrary authority, and they had enjoyed virtual immunity from public criticism. After the uprising, they found themselves facing criticism and questions from the poor and the disadvantaged, while rural landlords were frustrated by the peasants' demands for land reform. Many members of the ruling elite considered the civilian governments too weak and incapable of protecting their interests, and they accordingly turned to extra-parliamentary tactics. They created right-wing militias and paramilitary groups to which the military provided leadership and logistical support in order to weaken and disrupt the progressive coalition. State-sponsored assassins carried out a series of clandestine assassinations targeting leaders of peasant, labour and student organizations. During 1974–76, such confrontational and violent tactics by the rightists, combined with government inaction, eventually debilitated the student movement (Prajak 2006, pp. 31–33).

The 1975 and 1976 elections took place in this context of tumultuous ideological struggle between the left and the right. The right-wing movements and conservative elites waged war on burgeoning socialist political parties and their candidates. Unlike the non-violent elections held in previous authoritarian settings, electoral competitions in 1975 and 1976 were unruly and bloodstained. State security agencies and right-wing activists resorted to violence to attack left-wing candidates and their supporters. Electoral violence was, in essence, part of the establishment's larger campaign to eradicate the left-wing movements.

The January 1975 Elections

After the promulgation of a new constitution in October 1974, Prime Minister Sanya dissolved parliament and called for elections on 26 January 1975. The Thai people welcomed the elections with enthusiasm, as they were the first competitive polls held in a democratic setting in many decades. Forty-two political parties competed for 269 seats. The Chart Thai Party, an ultra-right-wing party formed by generals and provincial oligarchs, was prominent among them. Another major party was Kitsangkhom or the Social Action Party, led by Kukrit Pramoj and representing the interests of royalists and national capitalist groups. Most importantly, three major left-wing parties entered the competition for the first time: the Socialist Party of Thailand, the Naeoruam sangkhomniyom (Socialist Front) and Phalang Mai (New Force). These three parties gained popular support from the student-farmer-labour coalition. The elections saw twenty-two parties win seats, but none with clear parliamentary majority, thus leading to the formation of a large and unstable multi-party coalition (Chaowana 2007, pp. 42–43).

The three leftist parties campaigned impressively to win a combined total of thirty-seven seats nationwide. But their success came at a high cost, as several of their workers lost their lives. In the course of the elections there were twelve assassination attempts, six mob clashes and two acts of physical intimidation, resulting in twenty dead and ten wounded Government security forces and the Internal Security Operations Command carried out secretive operations in a large number of villages throughout the country, particularly those in the Northeast, intimidating residents into not voting for progressive parties.[2] The secretary of the Socialist Party, Bunsanong Punyodhayana, told the media that local police threatened to imprison his party's supporters if they voted for socialist candidates (*Prachachat*, 3 January 1975, p. 3). The media and student election monitoring groups reported that the state's heavy interference in the election campaign was "anti-communist psychological warfare", in which the local state apparatus tried to brainwash villagers, accusing all leftist candidates of being communists who conspired to destroy the monarchy, the Buddhist religion and the nation (*Prachachat*, 6 January 1975, p. 3, and 5 February 1975, p. 7).

Violent incidents occurred during the campaign period as well as on the day of the elections. In precincts that were strongholds of the Communist

Party of Thailand or in which Muslim separatist movements were strong, the insurgent groups attempted to disrupt voting by attacking polling stations, assaulting poll workers and stealing ballot boxes. For example, in a remote district of Kanchanaburi province, communist rebels clashed with border patrol police and poll workers, killing one officer and wounding five others. The provincial governor had to change the polling station's location to avoid further attacks (*Thai rat*, 26 January 1975, pp. 1, 2, 16, and 27 January 1975, pp. 1, 2, 16). Casualties resulting from clashes between government forces and insurgents accounted for more than half of the total death toll associated with these elections, demonstrating the significant threat that the insurgency posed to election security. Security personnel figured as both perpetrators and victims of election-related violence. Their heavy interference in electoral processes continued in the next election as they stepped up their violent operations against the socialist parties.

The April 1976 Elections

Facing strong pressure in the form of daily public protests and from among members of his own coalition, Prime Minister Kukrit dissolved parliament on 12 January 1976 and called for general elections on 4 April 1976. The right wing and security forces mounted a full-scale campaign of violence to prevent left-wing parties from winning votes. Their acts of aggression were very effective; incessant death threats, bombings and assassinations paralysed and destroyed the leftists' campaigns. Consequently, the Socialist Party of Thailand, the Naeoruam sangkhomniyom and Phalang Mai suffered a heavy defeat. They won a combined total of only six seats nationwide, compared to their previous thirty-seven, and several of their party personnel and supporters were brutally killed. In total, there were twenty-one violent incidents — nine assassination attempts, two mob clashes, three acts of physical intimidation, six explosions and one arson attack — during the course of the campaign. These incidents left sixteen dead and nineteen wounded. Although the number of incidents and casualties was not significantly greater than that for the 1975 elections, the perpetrators were highly indiscriminate and ruthless this time, making this election more chaotic and terror-ridden.

The main perpetrators of violence in this election were state agents and hired right-wing vigilante groups, and their primary victims were supporters and members of political parties that espoused a socialist ideology. Early in the campaign, a gang of hooligans working for military leaders attacked the Phalang Mai Party's headquarters with grenades. The building was left seriously damaged, but all party staff survived the explosions.[3] In early February, two Phalang Mai parliamentary candidates for Lopburi were shot dead while canvassing for votes. A few days later, on 28 February, Bunsanong Punyodhayana, the Socialist Party secretary-general and a Cornell University–educated Thammasat University professor, was assassinated in central Bangkok while he was driving home (*Prachachat*, 18 February 1976, pp. 1, 12). Many leading public figures denounced this act of what they considered brutal public murder. Puey Ungphakon, the rector of Thammasat, demanded that the government bring the perpetrators to justice and prevent electoral competition from descending into "fighting through bullets" (*Prachachat*, 1 March 1976, p. 12). He further commented, "It [the shooting] was abhorrent and appalling.... political parties were supposed to campaign with non-violent methods. There should have not been shootings or bombings. These [violent methods] degrade democracy" (*Prachachat*, 3 April 1976, p. 12). Boonsanong's shooting demoralized the progressive candidates.

Nevertheless, violent attacks on the part of rightists did not stop. On 24 March, right-wing thugs threw bombs into the crowd at a Phalang Mai campaign rally in Chainat province, instantly killing eight people and injuring ten in one of the most violent incidents in the history of Thai electoral campaigns. After this incident, all candidates affiliated with progressive parties requested government protection, but to no avail. On 28 March, in Udon Thani province, right-wing thugs stormed a campaign activity of the Socialist Party, harassing candidates and voters, burning billboards and attacking campaign vehicles. The head of the party, Somkhit Sisangkhom, had to terminate the party's campaign in the province to avoid further violent attacks. Two days before voting day, in Roi Et province, a Phalang Mai rally suffered an assault by means of grenades, but, fortunately, nobody was injured (*Prachachat*, 2 April 1976, p. 12). Election day in 1976 was as turbulent as the one in 1975. Various kinds of violence occurred, including the burning of and shooting into polling stations, the threatening of voters, bombings, and clashes between the communist and separatist insurgents in the southernmost provinces. From the victim's perspective, Somkhit Sisangkhom, whose Socialist Party won only two seats, lamented, "this election is the dirtiest, cruelest and most barbaric" (*Prachachat*, 4 April 1976, p. 12).

The ultra-right wing's employment of violence and force in the 1976 elections succeeded in wiping the socialist groups off the electoral map. The escalation of rightist violence led to political turmoil and ended with a brutal massacre of students on 6 October 1976. According to police records, forty-three people were killed, several hundred injured, and more than three thousand arrested on that day, with some five thousand more arrested later (Pasuk and Baker 2014, p. 194). One army faction staged a coup, taking power from the elected civilian government that evening, terminating three years of popular democracy and mass mobilization among progressives, and returning Thailand to dictatorship. It was not the mobilization of progressive reformers that was responsible for the breakdown of the country's democratic transition, but rather the violence perpetrated by the royal-military-bureaucratic elites through the deployment of right-wing groups. After 1976, an unprecedented number of radical students, intellectuals and political activists joined the Communist Party of Thailand to wage guerrilla warfare with the Thai state from jungle areas in a deadly civil war that killed thousands of people.

The electoral violence of 1975 and 1976 was inseparable from the royal-military alliance's campaign against its challengers. Electoral and non-electoral violence was closely connected to and mainly motivated by fierce ideological struggle between leftists and rightists. At stake was state power and the ideology that defined the political regime. Essentially, electoral violence was a continuation of state violence by other means. The rapidly changing environment after the democratic dawn in 1973 had turned the electoral tide against the traditional elites. When they realized that they were unlikely to win through popular means, they sought to rely on both electoral and non-electoral violence instead. Before 1973, authoritarian bureaucratic elites had relied on strategies such as imprisonment, unlawful detention, draconian laws and electoral fraud to exclude progressive forces from the electoral sphere and to win elections. These tactics rendered the elections held from 1932 to 1973 both unfree and uncompetitive. They also made the use of violence in these elections unnecessary. However, after the democratic uprising of 1973, the establishment lost its control over electoral processes and the guarantee of electoral victory. Democratic constitutions, civil society and civilian governments had paved the way for more open political participation, more inclusive electoral space and more transparent electoral administration. Therefore, royal-military elites felt that they needed to resort to brute force to eliminate the progressive alliance and to regain control over electoral outcomes.

After 1976, the pattern, logic and methods of electoral violence changed as a result of major political and economic shifts at both the national and local levels. State-sponsored electoral violence disappeared, but privately contracted murders perpetrated by provincial elites came in its place. Electoral violence became more privatized, specifically targeted, locally directed and entrepreneurial.

From Clientelistic to Contract Killers: Electoral Democracy and the Privatization of Violence, 1976–2001

The revival of the parliamentary system and the competitive elections of the 1980s brought with them the frequent assassinations of members of parliament, nouveau riche tycoons, local bosses and vote canvassers. These political killings were private enterprise murders related to national and local electoral competition, with professional gunmen hired by the political and business rivals of the victims. The gunmen comprised professional assassins, former security guards, petty gangsters and moonlighting policemen (Anderson 1998, pp. 171–91; Ockey 2000, pp. 74–96). Violence took place both before and after elections, as candidates and their supporters were threatened by their rivals with kidnapping or murder. Vote canvassers who betrayed a candidate might be killed, and highly successful vote canvassers were sometimes also eliminated by their opponents (Ockey 1998, pp. 39–53). In an attempt to explain this phenomenon, Anderson (1998) argued that the increasing prevalence of politically motivated murders in the late 1980s reflected the high "market value" (pp. 188–89) of MPs in Thailand, and thereby signalled the greater importance of elections in deciding who gained political power.

From the 1980s to the 1990s, the capitalist economy, parliamentary politics and professional gunmen developed hand in hand. The increased demand for coercive force in settling disputes or eliminating rivals in business and politics generated a supply of violence. The existence of "professional gunmen" in Thailand served a specific function, politically and economically. These gunmen specialized in exercising physical force, with violence as a means to an end, a resource and also the final product. With violence as their commodity, these gunmen were "specialists in violence" or "violent specialists" — those "who control [a coercive] means of inflicting damage on person and objects" and command "extensive skills" in using violence (Tilly 2003, pp. 35, 232–33). Before the 1970s, when the Thai bureaucratic state succeeded in controlling extra-state coercion, most violent specialists worked within or on behalf of the government. By the late 1970s, under new political conditions, the Thai state had lost dominant control, and large numbers of specialists in violence operated outside the government. The specialists included "men in uniform" — policemen and soldiers — who started to exercise their coercive power for personal material gain.[4]

A large supply of hired gunmen emerged in the late 1970s. These mercenaries can be classified into two main categories by their degrees of institutionalization, commoditization and independence from provincial bosses. The first category included gunmen working directly under bosses or "bosses' gunmen", and the second, gunmen working for a "den of hired guns" or "a hitmen company".[5] Each type of gunman had a different modus operandi, and an individual gunman could move across categories.[6]

Bosses' Gunmen: Clientelistic Killers

A boss's gunmen were part of his personal network — employees whose task was essentially violent enforcement. Political bosses recruited assassins for protection.[7] The boss's gunmen were mainly local thugs, criminals, former security guards, and moonlighting policemen and military officers. Compared with other types of gunmen, they were well protected by their patrons, who were influential politicians, and being in their employ reduced the chances of being caught or prosecution by state authorities. But politicians' direct employment of gunmen did mean that violence could be easily traced back to them. These assassins were, technically, not guns for hire, and their primary job was to provide security for their boss and/or to help oversee their boss's business empire. Clients who wanted to use the boss's gunmen needed to be the boss's friends (Pongsak 1998, pp. 61–63). Usually, bosses hired out their gunmen-employees only to their associates or to trusted political allies.[8]

Gunmen assumed a specific role in the political networks of politicians in the post-1976 period. Vote canvassers and gunmen were two different types of people with different roles during elections. The task of the former was to manage the election campaign, visit constituents and gather votes, while that of the latter was to provide security for the boss and/or to deploy coercive force against enemies. Under some circumstances, gunmen might become involved more closely in the electoral campaign, in which case their job would be to obstruct or intimidate rival vote canvassers.

> [M]any times vote buying required or was buttressed by coercive force. Because some of our competitors have local thugs, some of whom are armed, blocking us from their territories. So we need to have our own force, either police on our payroll or hoodlums, to show them that we are not afraid. Otherwise you cannot buy votes even though you have plenty of money.[9]

Gunmen and vote canvassers required different skill sets and personalities. There have been only a few cases of people who took on the dual role of assassin and vote broker. On the other hand, there were cases in which politically skilful gunmen were encouraged by their political boss to run in elections, but this practice was rare.[10]

Influential provincial bosses usually employed more than one gunman. Gunmen generally killed without payment, as they already received regular salaries and other benefits from their bosses. In the 1990s, a wealthy boss would pay 1,000–2,000 baht a day to his gunmen. However, sometimes gunmen earned extra pay for difficult jobs or for jobs requested by the boss's friends. Bosses would bail these gunmen out from jail if they were caught by the authorities, with some making payment to the police prior to a murder to ensure that they would not investigate it. If gunmen were imprisoned, bosses would take care of their families.[11] The demise of a boss naturally led to the disintegration of his gang of gunmen. Gunmen had to seek protection and patronage from a new boss or otherwise to become a hired gun (Piak 2004, pp. 33–55).

The operation of bosses' gunmen underwent noticeable change after the mid-1980s, when capitalist development became entrenched and expanded at a rapid rate both nationally and in local settings.[12] The expansion of the market economy in provincial areas in effect eroded the clientelistic relationships that had existed previously. The number of gunmen working under provincial bosses diminished and the boss-gunman relationship became more fragile, unstable and less clientelistic. The patron-client model that has dominated studies of local relations in Thailand is insufficient to understand local political dynamics because it fails to account for the fact that electoral violence has evolved from a *boss* model to a *business* model as a result of rapid economic development.[13] Some gunmen continued to be employed by bosses and operated simultaneously as hired gunmen.

Financial gain, rather than returning a favour or seeking revenge on behalf of bosses, had become the motivation for violence.

The story of the legendary Phet Thamrongdaeng or "Koming" illustrates the shift from clientelistic killings to killing-as-business in Thailand that occurred in the period from the 1980s to the 1990s. Koming started out as a fisherman before he became a gang leader in the central and the southern regions of Thailand. An influential boss-turned-MP in Prachuap Khiri Khan province recruited Koming to work as his right-hand man and to oversee his underground business empire. He excelled at eliminating competition and making handsome profits for his boss, and within a few years Koming had attracted gunmen from the central and southern regions to work for him. With his boss's approval and a large gang of gunmen under his control, Koming developed his own contract killing business. At its peak in the late 1980s, Koming's "killing company" had roughly two hundred gunmen for hire; it was the largest den in the country. This den was located in Prachuap Khiri Khan but took jobs in Bangkok and the central and southern regions of the country. These jobs included many election-related murders in the 1980s and 1990s.[14]

Hired Gunmen: Contract Killers

The involvement of contract hitmen in electoral violence has been reported since the Thai elections of 1975, and by the mid-1980s professional hired guns had taken over many electoral killings. The political murder of a former MP from Samut Songkhram on 16 November 1976 signalled the emergence of private violence. According to the police, the death of the MP was a consequence of political conflict with the candidate whom he opposed during the campaign. The police arrested one of the perpetrators, who confessed that he had received thirty thousand baht to undertake the job, and that his team comprised three members whose team leader was a soldier who had been dismissed from his unit for misconduct. Police investigation determined that these "hired gangs for murder" were also contracted to kill other politicians (*Thai rat*, 17 November 1976, 18 November 1976, 20 November 1976, 30 November 1976).

Hired gunmen are accessible, impersonal, efficient and entrepreneurial, functioning like professional business operators. A hired gunman is akin to a labourer who deploys his skill in the use of force to make a profit. Like members of any profession, hitmen accumulate the necessary skills, develop contacts, build organizations and calculate the cost and benefit of each job. The business of hired gunmen was linked to the growth of organized crime and underground business in Bangkok in the 1950s. Hired guns provided protection for illegal economic activities such as gambling, drug dealing and prostitution by eliminating rivals, troublemakers or "unexpected difficulties" (Suriyan 1989, pp. 5–20). In the late 1970s, contract killing expanded into and became connected with electoral competition, attracting many participants with its lucrative profits. Over time, the hired gun market became better structured, well established and competitive.

The service of professional gunmen brings an important advantage to political bosses as it provides them with cover and with distance from a shooting. Most of the time, the police can trace the murder back only to the gunmen's agents or perhaps to the owner of the hired gun den.[15] Moreover, these dens help to obviate the burden of building and sustaining a standing force of violent followers. Instead of having a hundred gunmen on the payroll, as was the case for "big bosses" in the early 1980s, political bosses in the 1990s generally had only four or five goons.[16]

The hired gun business attracts a wide range of people, including the unemployed, young hoodlums, local thugs, farmers, low-skill workers, taxi and motorcycle drivers, and athletes. It also provides opportunities for corrupt police and military officers. Some state agents condone and profit from the contract killing business by using their professional training in coercion for personal gain. Conversely, clients prefer the service of these state agents or "official violence specialists" because they are not only the calmest and best trained but they also have inside information on the criminal justice process and institutions.[17] Many of them are protected by higher-ranking officers, the so-called "mafia" police or military officers who themselves engage in illegal business. For the government, these "uniformed hitmen" are the most dangerous and difficult to apprehend.[18] Studies reveal that many active and former government violence specialists remain closely engaged in the violence business until the present day. Collusion between state security forces and the violence business runs deep.[19]

The Rise of Thaksin and the Intensification of Electoral Violence, 2001–6

The pattern of electoral violence witnessed in Thailand during the 2001–6 period, when Thaksin Shinawatra served as prime minister, was not dramatically different from that of the period from the 1980s to the 1990s. Political bosses who hired gunmen to assassinate opponents in the run-up to elections continued to perpetrate electoral violence. However, this period saw fiercer electoral competition and a higher degree of electoral violence than in the past. The major factor that contributed to the transformation of Thai politics and the increase in electoral violence during this period was the political ascent of Thaksin Shinawatra and his strong Thai Rak Thai (TRT) party. The TRT introduced party-based and more policy-oriented politics and a new style of electioneering. The political changes brought about by the TRT altered the relationship between political parties and provincial bosses and forced the bosses to adjust their political strategies in order to maintain their power. Thaksin's ambitious goal of building a strong party over a short period of time raised the stakes of electoral competition and therefore compelled provincial bosses to resort to aggressive tactics to defeat their opponents and to protect their political turf.

Thaksin had a different strategy from that of the party leaders of the pre-2001 period. Rather than being satisfied with sharing power with other parties in a multi-party coalition, he sought to form a single-party government with an absolute majority of votes in the parliament. To achieve this goal, he reached out to establish political alliances with prominent provincial bosses in all regions of the country, aware that most Thai MPs represent constituencies located outside Bangkok. The forceful intervention of Thaksin and the TRT tilted the balance of power among provincial politicians. TRT's massive war chest and popular policies attracted many politicians and resulted in large-scale party-switching in favour of the party prior to the 2001 elections. The TRT's financial and political support gave the upper hand to local bosses allied with the party. On the other hand, those provincial politicians and families who refused to cooperate with the TRT had to struggle hard for survival. It was the dynamic of fighting for dominance and survival among members of local elites that produced violent outcomes (Prajak 2014, pp. 392–93).

The TRT's forceful entry on to the volatile local political scene also intensified political divisions and weakened extant patron-client relationships. Vote canvassers were aware of the changing political environment and of voters' mood. As a result, most of them wanted to support the TRT. Things went smoothly in cases in which their bosses agreed to run under the TRT banner, but conflict arose when bosses refused Thaksin's offer to join the party. Many vote canvassers defected from their old bosses to work for the TRT. Clientelistic relationships broke down, and violence erupted. Thaksin's efforts to build a strong political machine to replace the personal clientelistic networks of local elites clearly aggravated local conflicts (Prajak 2014, pp. 394–95).

The volatile situation continued and intensified in the lead-up to the 2005 elections, when the popularity of Thaksin and his party was at its peak. Thaksin announced his party's ambitious goal of winning 75–80 per cent of the seats in parliament. The problem was that the number of politicians wanting to run on the TRT ticket in each province exceeded the number of available seats. Many people were therefore denied the party's support, including several former TRT candidates. The TRT replaced these candidates with stronger new ones. This practice reignited personal conflicts among members of the political elite in many provinces. As a result, electoral competition in 2005 was fraught with defections, betrayals and conflicts within personals networks that led to a large number of violent incidents. It turned out to be one of the most violent elections in modern Thai history.[20]

In interviews, gunmen agreed that 2001–6 was the golden age of the hired gun business.[21] Hired guns' agents were extremely busy, recruiting new hitmen to meet soaring demand. During this period, the market price for hired gunmen to kill an MP ranged from one to five million baht, depending on the degree of the MP's political influence.[22] These prices encouraged a greater number of young hoodlums, the unemployed and moonlighting officers to step into the business. The number of independent gunmen rose. Some rookie gunmen formed small dens comprised of three to four members, offering cut-rate service. Competition for business led to inter-den bloodshed. The violence market in the 2000s became more competitive, fragmented and business-oriented as electoral competition was more competitive and had higher stakes. Patron-client networks controlled by local elites were disrupted and weakened by the emergence of a strong political party and the powerful national leadership presented by Thaksin.

After the 2005 elections, Thaksin and his TRT party reached the peak of their power. The TRT won 377 out of 500 seats in the parliament and became the first party in Thai history to establish a single-party government. Thaksin's political dominance generated fear and perturbation among his opponents, particularly royalist networks and the military, which formed an alliance of the most formidable sources of traditional power in the Thai polity.[23] The royal-military-bureaucratic elite had no ability or willingness to defeat Thaksin in an electoral contest. Its members realized that the only way to unseat Thaksin was by non-electoral, extra-parliamentary means. Eventually, traditional elites staged a coup to eliminate Thaksin in September 2006, the first coup in the fifteen years since the 1991 coup. The consequences of the coup were drastic. From 2006 to 2014, Thai society witnessed a new mode of political contestation. Political struggle shifted from the electoral sphere to the street. State repression and street violence took the place of electoral violence, and mass movements and the military overshadowed politicians.

Military Suppression and Street Politics:
The Militarization and Ideological Struggles of
Electoral Politics after the 2006 Coup

After the 2006 coup, the conflict between the establishment and those aligned with ousted prime minister Thaksin profoundly transformed Thai politics, making political struggle a more ideological one. Electoral competition was no longer dominated by particularistic campaigns based on personality and patronage networks, but was instead marked by attention to policies and by ideological struggle. Thailand was deeply polarized. The fundamental political divide after the coup, which also reflected social divisions, was between anti- and pro-Thaksin elements. Thaksin's opponents resorted to legal tools and coercive force to undermine his political networks. On 30 May 2007, the Constitutional Court dissolved the TRT party and banned 111 party members from any involvement in political affairs for five years.[24] Other former TRT members created a new party called the Phak Palang Prachachon or People's Power Party (PPP) under the leadership of veteran politician Samak Sundaravej to stand in the 2007 elections. Running on a populist policy platform and drawing on Thaksin's popularity, the PPP was victorious and formed a coalition government. However, on 9 September 2008, the Constitutional Court delivered a controversial decision disqualifying Samak from the premiership.[25] The majority of the PPP and coalition parties then voted to make Somchai Wongsawat, a deputy prime minister and brother-in-law of Thaksin, the new premier. Somchai stayed in power for only three months before he was forced to step down in the middle of the occupation of Bangkok's airports by members of the anti-government Yellow Shirt movement under the leadership of media mogul Sondhi Limthongkul and Major General Chamlong Srimuang and after the Constitutional Court dissolved the PPP on charges of electoral misconduct.[26] Immediately after Somchai stepped down, military leaders forced some of Thaksin's allies to switch sides and vote to make Democrat Party leader Abhisit Vejjajiva prime minister.

The removal of Thaksinite prime ministers through the manoeuvring of the palace-army network angered Thaksin's Red Shirt supporters and led to the demonstrations of 2009 and 2010. The Red Shirts thought that unelected actors who did not respect their vote had illegitimately toppled a government that they had elected. The Abhisit government that took power in December 2008 responded to the Red Shirt protests of the following two years with violent crackdowns. The military crackdown of April and May 2010, when the government ordered the army to suppress the Red Shirt demonstrations led by the United Front for Democracy against Dictatorship (UDD) in central Bangkok, marked the culmination of political violence. With an official casualty total of ninety-four people dead and thousands wounded, that crackdown represented the most violent episode of political suppression in modern Thai history.[27]

From 2006 to 2014, Thai national politics was in a state of upheaval, with violent street clashes, mob confrontations, the occupation of government buildings and business premises, and military crackdowns dominating political life. Street violence between opposing mass movements and state officials replaced electoral killings among bosses. The political turmoil caused by the clashes between anti- and pro-Thaksin forces changed the national political landscape and shaped voting behaviour. Voters had different political stances and ideas regarding democratic values, the legitimacy of the coup and royal-army political interference, military suppression and the nature of Thaksin's rule. Thaksin and his party remained popular among the voters in the North and Northeast and among members of Thailand's lower and lower middle classes. While the Democrat Party and the anti-Thaksin movement enjoyed major support in the South, in the wealthy core of Bangkok and among members of the urban middle class, the bitter power struggle between the two sides that crippled governments and paralysed the country had strong effects on Thai people's thinking and understanding. The Thai electorate exercised the franchise more strategically than in the past, in the hope that it could shape national political outcomes by helping one side or the other to gain state power. In general, the political polarization clearly worked in favour of two major contending groups: Thaksinite parties under various names and the Democrat Party. It was detrimental to minor political factions and provincial bosses (Pasuk and Baker 2013, pp. 607–28; Prajak 2013, p. 338). Colour-coded politics and ideological conflict at the national level overrode personal feuds among political bosses and their families at the local level. With this changing mode of conflict, the demand for assassinations during election campaigns decreased, though it did not entirely disappear, as killing candidates or vote canvassers could not substantially alter election results. Voters cast their ballots for the major parties and in support of those parties' ideological stances and policies.

The demand for electoral violence thus slumped after the 2006 coup. Hired gunmen and their agents sought new jobs; some became full-time drug dealers, business enforcers, debt collectors, private security guards or extortionists. Ideological struggles and street violence created new work for mercenaries as security guards for political movements or protest leaders. Some of them were paid to instigate violence and thus to destabilize governments.[28] Violence entrepreneurs and violence specialists found new business opportunities and new clients in this era of political turmoil.

What made the conflict following the 2006 coup more complex and worrying was the use of coercive force by social movements. All movements rhetorically vowed a commitment to non-violent struggle, but some of their actual practices violated the principles of non-violence. One of the notorious novelties of mass social movements was the use of hired thugs and gangsters to take care of security. Many of these hirelings were retired or active-duty uniformed men with military training. They formed paramilitary units working as security guards for the movements and their top leaders. The mobilization style of both the Yellow Shirt and the Red Shirt movements was provocative and confrontational. Although it was true that most of the protestors were unarmed and committed to non-violent practices, the presence of armed elements among them weakened the legitimacy of the movements and made them prone to militarism and violent clashes. Intensified extra-parliamentary conflict in the form of violent interactions between the opposing movements and the state effectively weakened the processes of parliamentary democracy.

Violence by the Masses: The PDRC Protests and the Attack on Electoral Processes and Institutions in 2014

Political life in Thailand saw a brief moment of calm in the wake of the July 2011 elections. The campaign and polling went smoothly, and the conflicting parties accepted the results. The fragile hope shared among observers that the conflict-ridden country could seek a peaceful way forward did not, however, survive the failed elections of February 2014, let alone General Prayut Chanocha's putsch of 22 May of the same year.

After almost three years in power, on 11 March 2011 Prime Minister Abhisit dissolved parliament. He seemingly believed that going to the polls early would prove advantageous to his party and its coalition partners, as they had recently passed the annual budget and still controlled the state apparatus. Thailand's new ideological politics had positive effects on voting behaviour. Ideology now overshadowed personal conflicts among rival provincial bosses, and party branding, policy packages and political ideology shaped voters' choices. The ideological battle between anti- and pro-Thaksin movements dominated the 2011 elections. In the provinces, where the Yellow Shirts or Red Shirts were strong, members of the two groups actively volunteered to assist campaigns, replacing the old money-driven, entrepreneurial vote canvassers. However, the most crucial factor contributing to the relatively peaceful elections of 2011 was the decision of all parties to play by the electoral rules. The Democrat Party leadership did not choose to boycott the elections, as they were confident that they could win the contest. The Phuea Thai Party (PTP) led by Thaksin's sister Yingluck Shinawatra conducted a campaign focused on populist policies and political reconciliation. The Yellow Shirt and Red Shirt movements also refrained from unruly tactics during the campaign. The Yellow Shirts conducted a "Vote No" campaign, asking voters not to cast ballots for any party, whereas the Red Shirts were aware that any disturbance could provide the army with the justification to intervene. Under these favourable conditions, the electoral contest went smoothly, and the electoral victory of the PTP was accepted by its opponents. No violent protests followed the polls (Prajak 2016, pp. 472–73).

By the time of the 2014 elections held under the Yingluck government, the political situation had changed significantly. When the Yingluck government attempted to pass a controversial "blanket" amnesty bill at the end of October 2013, it faced strong opposition from the public.[29]

Democrat Party deputy leader Suthep Thaugsuban led protests against the bill, arguing that it absolved former prime minister Thaksin of his corruption conviction. Meanwhile, the Red Shirts, the UDD and groups of activists also opposed the law because they saw it as providing amnesty to soldiers and to former prime minister Abhisit Vejjajiva and former deputy prime minister Suthep, whom they held responsible for the deaths and injuries suffered during the 2010 crackdown. Widespread opposition forced the government to drop the amnesty bill. Nevertheless, Suthep continued to lead demonstrations, which soon changed their aim from protesting against the amnesty bill to overthrowing the Yingluck government (Prajak 2016, p. 474).

Another conflict that led to the anti-Yingluck protests stemmed from her government's attempt to introduce a constitutional amendment making Thailand's senate a fully elected chamber. On 20 November 2013, the Constitutional Court blocked the proposed amendment, reasoning that the amendment would change the nature of the constitutional monarchy. The PTP insisted that the amendment was constitutional. Under considerable pressure, however, Prime Minister Yingluck was forced to withdraw it. Suthep accused the government of disrespecting the court and of therefore lacking the legitimacy to stay in power.

The anti-government protests led by Suthep gained momentum very quickly. The protest leaders aggravated the conflict by changing their tactics from staging peaceful protests to seizing government offices. On 29 November 2013, the protest leaders formally established an organization named, in English, the People's Democratic Reform Committee (*Khanakammakan prachachon phuea plianplaeng prathet thai hai pen prachathippatai thi sombun an mi phramahakasat songpen pramuk*, PDRC),[30] with Suthep as its secretary-general. The PDRC was a broad coalition movement composed of many groups of people with various political agendas. Their unifying goal was toppling Yingluck and undermining the PTP. Besides Suthep, the core leaders of the PDRC were other former Democrat Party politicians who were close to him (*Thai Post*, 29 November 2013).

The PDRC protest received support from the traditional elite — an influential network of old wealth, aristocrats, technocrats, presidents of university councils, judges, civil society leaders and some business leaders. This group saw the Shinawatras and their party machine as a threat. Resources and protection from the traditional elite made it possible for the PDRC to continue its street protests for several months and paralyse the government (Baker 2016). In terms of mobilization, the PDRC gained support from the urban middle class in Bangkok and Southerners, who were longstanding supporters of the Democrat Party. Despite their differences in socio-economic and educational backgrounds, these two groups shared the same political identity as minority voters in recent elections who felt powerless under the political system dominated by Thaksinite parties. The PDRC employed violent, disruptive and confrontational tactics to destabilize the government. The movement's leaders recruited hired guards, thugs and state security officers to be responsible for violent provocation and confrontation with its opponents (Wassana 2014, pp. 261–453).

The ideological discourse of the PDRC was deeply opposed to electoral democracy. It rejected the legitimacy of the elections as a means to power and as a means of deciding who should govern. The core belief was that Thai society should be governed by the self-proclaimed "good people", installed through appointment, instead of by "bad politicians" elected by the majority of voters who were still poor and uneducated (*Khao sot*, 23 December 2013, pp. 1, 14). The movement's leaders declared an intention to assume sovereign power and to "reform" the country through a non-elected "People's Council". Their main slogan was "reform before elections", and whistles and national flags were chosen as their main symbols, as they presented themselves as righteous and patriotic citizens who desired to "cleanse" Thai society of corrupt politicians and the influence of the ignorant rural masses. Suthep outlined plans for the People's Council to act as a legislative body, amend laws and carry out a reform plan. The council would include four hundred members, three hundred of whom were to be representatives of various professions, while the PDRC would select the rest. According to the PDRC's plan, the country would be "frozen" for two years without elections while the "reform" process took place. The PDRC demanded Yingluck's immediate resignation in order to pave the way for a new government led by an unelected prime minister (*Thai Post*, 29 November 2013).

By 8 December 2013, the political situation had reached a deadlock, when Democrat Party leader Abhisit announced the resignation of the party's 153 party MPs from parliament. This was clearly a move to pressure Prime Minister Yingluck to dissolve the parliament. She did so the next day and called for new elections on 2 February 2014. She hoped that the prospect of elections would bring an end to the street protests and that the polls would restore her party's legitimacy to rule. However, the situation did not unfold as expected, as the Democrat Party boycotted the elections and joined the PDRC in its fight to topple the government. Moreover, the PDRC's leaders announced the organization's rejection of the elections, declaring that its adherents would "not vote under the existing rules" (*Khao sot*, 23 December 2013). Suthep vowed that he would lead the demonstrators to obstruct the elections at any cost because they were illegitimate. The PDRC insisted that its supporters would not end their protests until the People's Council was established and an unelected prime minister appointed. Suthep urged his followers to boycott and disrupt the elections. In the run-up to the February 2014 elections, Thai society witnessed a new form of violence, one never before seen in the country: violent mobilization by a mass movement attacking electoral processes and institutions.

Mass Movement Electoral Violence

Compared to previous general elections, the 2 February 2014 general elections witnessed the highest level of chaos and violence in Thailand's electoral history. This time, almost no violent incidents involved conflict between rival candidates. Rather, they stemmed from conflicts between PDRC protestors and those who supported the elections, and between PDRC supporters and state security officers. The pattern of conflict and violence in the 2014 election was an extension of the colour-coded political conflict outside the electoral arena.

The most common forms of violence during the run-up to the 2014 polls were gun and bomb attacks on protestors, government buildings and political landmarks; threats; and murder attempts. Bomb attacks, targeting a wide range of the population, resulted in the highest numbers of injuries and deaths (Prajak 2016, p. 481). Targeted assassination attempts were less common and were replaced by random shootings in public, resulting in the deaths of many bystanders. Apart from the use of guns and explosives, tear gas and rubber bullets were used by state officials in handling the demonstrators. The violence that occurred during these elections also stemmed from mob clashes resulting from differences in ideologies, which were uncommon in the past.

Violent incidents started on 22 December 2013, when PDRC protestors forcefully occupied six roads in Bangkok (*Khao sot*, 22 December 2013).

On 23 December, the first day of the registration of candidates to run as party-list MPs, PDRC demonstrators occupied all entrance and exit points of the registration venue. On 25 December, the PDRC led a mob to occupy a registration building. Police officers used riot shields to prevent demonstrators from gaining access to the front entrance of that building, causing a clash, while some PDRC demonstrators threw water bottles into the building (*Thai rat*, 24 December 2013, pp. 1, 10, 11, 16, 19). On 26 December, the confrontation turned violent when PDRC leaders lost control of the protestors, with one group storming the building, throwing water bottles, petrol bombs and bricks, and hitting police officers in the process. The confrontation resulted in a total of ninety-six injured (*Prachatai*, 27 December 2013).

In Bangkok, violence continued to erupt in protest areas for several months, causing the deaths and injuries of many PDRC guards and supporters, who were shot or fell victim to bombings. Meanwhile, police officers working in the area, as well as journalists and bystanders, were also attacked by PDRC guards (*Sayam rat*, 11 January 2014, pp. 1, 10). On the day of advance voting, 26 January 2014, chaos erupted nationwide.[31] PDRC leader Suthep Thaugsuban had urged demonstrators to disrupt the voting at all polling stations, and PDRC demonstrators surrounded key polling stations in Bangkok. PDRC protestors also used force to prevent civilians from casting their ballots — an act never before seen in Thailand's history. Some voters who wanted to cast their votes had to climb fences to avoid being attacked by the agitated protestors. At some polling stations, PDRC mobs strangled voters and accusing them of "not having an understanding of democracy" and "lacking love for the nation" (*Matichon*, 27 January 2014). In total, approximately 400,000 people were prevented from exercising their right to vote on the advance voting day because of the disruptions caused by the PDRC (*Krungthep thurakit*, 27 January 2014, pp. 13, 16).

The most spectacularly violent incident took place on 1 February 2014. It highlighted the changing pattern of electoral violence in Thailand. On that day, near the Lak Si intersection in the north of Bangkok, PDRC demonstrators clashed with the Red Shirt group called the "red gaur army" or *"krating daeng"*. The latter group wanted to travel to the Lak Si district office, then surrounded by PDRC protestors, in order to facilitate the transportation of ballot boxes. The two sides exchanged multiple rounds of gunfire at the intersection. The Red Shirt group was out-gunned by a group of men dressed in black, hiding their faces with masks and equipped with military-grade weapons. Appearing at the scene of the gun battle, one gunman concealed an automatic rifle inside a popcorn sack so that it would collect his spent cartridges and prevent investigation. This gunman was later dubbed the "popcorn gunman" by the media. The bullets fired from the gunmen siding with the PDRC severely wounded one bystander, who died seven months later, and less gravely wounded three other people (*Bangkok Post*, 2 February 2014).

Observers pointed out that the professional use of weapons showed that these gunmen must have gone through military or security force training. Suthep stated that these gunmen were not PDRC guards but were "armed troops who protected the demonstrators" (Wassana 2014, p. 429). However, the "popcorn gunman", named Wiwat Yotprasit, was later arrested by the police and sentenced by the Criminal Court to thirty-seven years and four months in jail after being found guilty of murder and illegally possessing an assault weapon and ammunition used in a deadly clash. Wiwat confessed that the PDRC's leaders had hired him to work as a security guard and to disrupt the 2 February elections. At the Lak Si intersection, he was given an order by his team leader to shoot at "whoever pops up" (*Bangkok Post*, 4 March 2016).

Despite Suthep's denial and the court's verdict, PDRC demonstrators praised these gunmen, particularly the "popcorn gunman", as heroes who saved good people's lives from evil people. Songs, poems and souvenirs were produced and shared among PDRC members to celebrate these vigilante "heroes" (*Manager Daily*, 8 February 2014). During the demonstrations, the dehumanizing rhetoric repeatedly used by PDRC leaders on stage and in their media paved the way for the justification of the physical violence perpetrated by their movement's security guards and adherents. The PDRC leadership did not categorically deny the use of violence in disrupting the elections and attacking the government's supporters. On the contrary, they justified the use of violence by referring to a "war between good and evil", as elaborated clearly by monk and PDRC leader Buddha Issara: "We have gathered to protest here in order to use moral force to eradicate them [bad politicians and their supporters] permanently. I just want to assure you all that what you are doing is morally right and in accordance with Buddhist principles."[32]

While professional gunmen hired by influential politicians have carried out acts of violence in previous elections, the perpetrators of violence in the 2014 elections were armed men hired to work for the movement. Their main task was not killing candidates or vote canvassers but obstructing the conduct of voting. Another significant departure from previous elections was the involvement of a mass movement that engaged in violent attacks against voters and electoral processes. In this regard, the PDRC was the first social movement in Thailand directly opposed to the electoral process and to elections as an institution. It challenged not only parties and politicians but democratic principles and parliamentary politics as a whole, as was evident in its rejection of elections as a means to power. The PDRC's rejection of the 2014 elections escalated the prolonged political conflict to another level, one from which it will be difficult for the country to recover. The political battle in Thailand after those elections was an ideological struggle in which political debate did not revolve around parties or policy stances but rather around the fundamental questions of what political regime was good for Thailand and who should have the right to govern.

The final turnout on 2 February was low, with only 20,530,359 — or 47.72 per cent — of a total of 43,024,042 eligible voters casting their ballots. Compared to the high voter turnout of 75.03 per cent for the 3 July 2011 elections, this low turnout made it clear that mob violence in 2014 effectively impeded people's ability to vote. The Election Commission did not approve the election results.[33] After the elections, Suthep announced that he would continue leading the PDRC's protests until the Yingluck government was replaced by the People's Council. Street protests led by the PDRC and the resulting violence continued for over three months and seriously paralysed the country. The army, led by General Prayut Chan-o-cha, staged a coup on 22 May 2014. It thus returned Thailand to authoritarian military rule, claiming that the political situation had reached a dead end. Clearly, it used the political deadlock that the PDRC's protests had staged and engineered as a convenient pretext for the coup.

Conclusion: The Trajectory of Violence and Political Struggle in Thailand

This chapter has examined the relationship between political violence and electoral politics in modern Thailand and its broad implications for the political development of the country. Focusing specifically on election-related violence, the chapter has identified the primary factors, political processes and groups of actors that have caused or instigated violence in elections and explained the changing mode of political struggle in Thailand over time.

Electoral violence from 1975 to 1976 was part of a national and ideological battle between left-wing groups and the state. This violence was inseparable from the royal-military alliance's violent strategy to counter the progressive political forces led by the student movement. Right-wing organizations received advice and were sponsored by state security units and military elites; they were not independent social movements that had their own political agendas to pursue. In essence, violence surrounding election campaigns in this period was a continuation of state violence by other means.

After 1976, the pattern, logic and methods of electoral violence changed as a result of major political and economic shifts at both the national and local levels. State-sponsored electoral violence disappeared, and privately contracted murders perpetrated by members of the provincial elite became mainstream. This was private violence in the public realm of electoral democracy, and it targeted individual actors involved in elections, but not the electoral process or elections as an institution. The main perpetrators of violence were provincial bosses and professional gunmen. Political bosses used their wealth to hire violence specialists to undertake violent acts. From the 1980s, the market for political killings expanded in line with rapid economic development and personal political struggles. Electoral violence has turned out to be more privatized, entrepreneurial and non-ideological. Essentially, electoral violence became instrumental and profane. There was nothing sacred at stake in election-related violence from 1976 to 2006.[34]

After the 2006 coup, the political struggle between supporters and opponents of Thaksin made Thai politics more turbulent, ideological and volatile. Thai society witnessed street clashes, the occupation of government buildings and airports, bombings in public places and violent military crackdowns. The ideological contestation reached its peak in the February 2014 elections. The pattern of violence in those failed elections witnessed the collective and spectacular violence of the mass movement attacking the election. It was violence in the realm of ideological competition that aimed to destroy the prevailing democratic electoral order. The PDRC's animosity towards the elections marked an unprecedented development in the country's protracted political conflict. The mobilization of the PDRC, I argue, posed the most serious challenge to democratic development in Thailand, as it broke apart the peaceful and democratic means by which the public could decide who had the right to govern. The PDRC's disruptive actions resulted in not only physical damage and loss of life but also institutional damage as the group rejected and destroyed the legitimacy of the democratic process as a peaceful mechanism for the transfer of political power. Moreover, the danger posed by the PDRC whistle protests was the most serious because of the occurrence of violent acts stemming from a civic movement and the middle class, both supposedly bastions of support for democracy. The supporters of the PDRC, instead of committing themselves to non-violent struggle, provided an ideological justification for the use of violence on the part of the movement's guards and other members. The prospects for democratic development or a return to democracy in Thailand appear to be dim for now, because the middle class has rejected the most fundamental principles of political equality and majority rule. In the current political crisis in the Siamese kingdom, the middle class has essentially become the social base of authoritarianism rather than democracy. Under repressive military rule, civil liberties are restricted, free speech is censored, criticism is prosecuted and political activity is prohibited. The rule of law has been severely undermined, and rules of the game that all conflicting parties can accept have not been established. The generals have set themselves up as a new ruling group by enhancing their status, the scope of their power, their budgets and their manpower. They plan to maintain their dominance through constitutional design by weakening the majoritarian democracy and undermining the influence of political parties (Puangthong 2015). Thai society remains as polarized as ever, and the coup and repressive military rule have plunged Thailand into a state of uncertainty and potentially violent instability, possibly for years to come.

Notes

1. Divisions within the authoritarian Thanom-Praphat regime can be traced to the late 1960s. The most significant divide was within the army itself, but there were also signs of tension between the army and the palace, especially after the 1971 coup (Prajak 2012, p. 243).
2. In 1967, the Thai government established a strategic unit for counter-insurgency programmes called the Civilian-Police-Military Headquarters. It later evolved into the Communist Suppression Operations Command and subsequently into the Internal Security Operations Command or ISOC (Chai-anan and Morell 1981, pp. 286–87).

3. However, one culprit was accidentally killed by his own grenade (*Prachachat*, 16 February 1976, pp. 1, 12).

4. In general, government violence specialists include military personnel, police, guards, executioners and judicial officers. Non-government violence specialists include private security guards, private police forces, paramilitary forces, militias, vigilante groups, guerrilla fighters, terrorists, thugs, bandits, enforcers, gangsters and mafias. The separation is not always clear-cut, as under certain conditions the government recruits force from outside the state apparatus to carry out its missions. See Nagengast (1994), Sluka (2000) and Tilly (2003).

5. Commonly known in Thai as *sum mue puen rap chang*.

6. Information on bosses' gunmen, hired guns and independent hitmen is mainly drawn from the author's interviews and from Worawat (2010), Dittita (2005), Matichon Criminal News Section (1989, 1995), Special Criminal News Unit (1993) and Research and Development Division, National Police Office, Thailand (2004, 2005).

7. In the same way, Indian political elites recruited wrestlers and local thugs, Russian politicians deployed gang members, and Philippine bosses built coteries of goons to protect their political enclaves. On the case of India, see Brass (1997) and Wilkinson (2006); on the Russian case, see Volkov (2002); on the Philippines, see McCoy (1993).

8. Interview with a former Chonburi boss's gunman, Chonburi, 14 August 2011.

9. Interview with the principle of an underworld protection racket, Bangkok, 6 April 2012.

10. One exceptional case was a prominent gunman nicknamed "Chaikhao", who miraculously progressed from being a boss's gunman to a mayor and subsequently the election campaign leader for the Chart Pattana Party in Chonburi in the September 1992 elections. He was shot dead a few weeks before the general election and therefore had no chance to celebrate the victory of his party. Interview with a former Chonburi boss's gunman, Chonburi, 14 August 2011.

11. Interview with lawyers who had represented gunmen, Phetburi, 18 April 2012.

12. See Brown (2004) and McVey (2000).

13. A partial list of significant works applying the patron-client model to the study of Thailand would include Akin (1969), Johnston (1980), Moreman (1969) and Sharp and Hanks (1978).

14. The police apprehended Koming on 27 September 1992 with 5.4 kilograms of heroin in his possession. He was prosecuted and sentenced for drug trafficking. See Piak (2004, pp. 55–58), Special Criminal News Unit (1993, pp. 5–17) and Suriyan (1989, pp. 59–71).

15. Interview with a senior police officer in the Crime Suppression Division,

Bangkok, 11 April 2012; interview with a senior crime reporter, Bangkok, 11 April 2012.

16. Interview with the principle in a protection racket, Bangkok, 6 April 2012. Only a few eminent bosses, such as one in Phrae and one in Buriram, are willing to build a force larger than twenty to thirty personnel and are capable of doing so.

17. Ibid.

18. The most scandalous case was that of Lieutenant Colonel "Tueng" (his nickname), who gained notoriety in the 1980s as a brutal and corrupt officer through extortion, debt collection and the smuggling of contraband. When the construction business boomed in the 1990s, he protected contractors and helped dishonest land developers evict residents; if residents resisted, he used violence to drive them out and burned their properties. Eventually, he established his own hired gun business, simultaneously assuming the roles of agent and hitman. His crew comprised five to six low-ranking state agents and undertook only high-profile cases. The job that brought him national fame and ended his long, murderous career was the assassination of the Yasothon provincial governor in 2001. Lieutenant Colonel "Tueng" is only one example, among many, of public officers turned (private) contract killers. Interview with a senior police officer in the Crime Suppression Division, Bangkok, 11 April 2012.

19. Ibid.; interviews with two investigative reporters focusing on military affairs, 12 and 20 April 2012. See also Sirirat (2005) and Research and Development Division, National Police Office, Thailand (2004).

20. In total there were 77 violent incidents, causing 30 deaths and injuries to 16 people (Prajak 2013, p. 161).

21. This information draws on a range of anonymous interviews: with a gunman, Chonburi, 14 August 2012; a principle in a protection racket, Bangkok, 6 April 2012; local bosses and gunmen, Nakhon Si Thammarat, 21 and 30 January 2010; a local boss and a gunmen's agent, Nakhon Sawan, 4 and 5 September 2010; a senior police officer in the Crime Suppression Division, Bangkok, 11 April 2012.

22. A gunman who used to work with an influential boss in the eastern region of Thailand told me that he received 3 million baht for assassinating a prominent MP. It was the highest-paid job he had ever done. Normally, he would be paid between 300,000 and 800,000 baht for each murder. Another gunman working in the South gave me similar figures. Interview with a gunman, Chonburi, 14 August 2012; interview with gunman, Nakhon Si Thammarat, 30 January 2010.

23. On the royal-military-bureaucratic elite, see Chambers and Napisa (2016), McCargo (2005) and Mérieau (2016).

24. The court ruled that the TRT's leading members had hired small parties to run in the April 2006 elections in order to make the elections appear competitive and to ensure the legal legitimacy of their results (*Thai rat*, 31 May 2007, p. 1).

25. According to the court's ruling, Samak, by gaining income from appearing in a televised cooking show while he was prime minister, acted in breach of the 2007 constitution. The court ruling led to public debate and wide criticism (*Matichon*, 9 September 2008, p. 1).

26. As had happened to the TRT party, all 109 executive members of the PPP were banned from politics for five years. Besides the PPP, the Constitutional Court also dissolved two other parties (*Thai rat*, 2 December 2007, pp. 1, 16).

27. For accounts of violent confrontations, clashes and crackdowns after the coup, see International Crisis Group (2010a), Nostitz (2009) and Wassana (2009, 2010).

28. A Bangkok-based protection racketeer provided security to Red Shirt demonstrations, and a former gunman from Nakhon Si Thammarat acted as a bodyguard for Yellow Shirt leaders. Interview with the principle in a protection racket, Bangkok, 6 April 2012; interviews with gunmen, Nakhon Si Thammarat, 23 and 30 January 2010.

29. The bill was drafted to pardon not only protestors but also protest movement leaders, those who ordered crackdowns on protestors, former government leaders, and military commanders. It covered the period from 2004 to 2013. This was effectively a "blanket amnesty" for all sides going back to 2004, even though it excluded crimes under article 112 of the Criminal Code relating to *lèse majesté*. The bill passed rather suddenly on the night of 31 October – 1 November 2014, provoking widespread opposition.

30. The Thai name translated as "People's Committee to Change Thailand into a Complete Democracy with the King as Head of State".

31. According to the election law, registered voters who cannot go to vote on election day can register to vote earlier on the advance election day, which is usually held one week before the general election day.

32. This speech was given on 20 November 2015 from PDRC's stage at Ratchadamnoen Avenue (Sompis 2013).

33. Results of the election on 2 February 2014 can be viewed at *Thai rat* (6 February 2014).

34. For the distinction among instrumental, symbolic and sacred violence, I draw on Girard (1977), Kalyvas (2006) and Krishna (2010).

9

Thailand's Politics of Decentralization: Reform and Resistance before and after the May 2014 Coup

Viengrat Nethipo

To determine whether political transformation causes radical and long-lasting change requires attention to the question of whether that transformation has changed the regime or the state (Petras 1989, pp. 26–27). At the regime level, change occurs in government, parliament, electoral rules, political parties and degrees of civic participation. Changes at the regime level often occur as a result of the reform of political institutions, from which a new regime emerges. For instance, when the administrative structure is reformed, state-society relations are re-regulated or the electoral system is changed, regime change is or may be the result. In the context of international interest in democratizing reforms, many states have introduced institutional designs meant to promote democracy. Political change at the state level, while more powerful and consequential, has proved less likely to occur. Petras (1989, p. 26) emphasizes the state's embodiment of "the permanent institution of government and the concomitant ensemble of class relations which have been embedded in these same institutions". It follows that to determine whether political change has the potential to consolidate democracy demands consideration of change at the level of the state.

Decentralization ranks among the most important reforms of a state's political institutions. It entails administrative restructuring that aims to establish efficient, participatory and democratic self-government. According to Sharpe, three principles underpin democratic local governance: liberty, participation and efficient service (Sharpe 1970, p. 156). Any local administration that upholds these values would approach the ideal of local democracy, which is a foundation for a developing democratic regime.

This chapter examines the effects that regime decentralization can have on the characteristics of the state, including those not anticipated by the elites that have supported decentralization. It elaborates on characteristics of the Thai state and, in particular, on interactions between the state and local political actors in rural and provincial areas. Its focus is on political power relations outside Bangkok. The chapter assesses the way in which three basic attributes of the state — a centralized and powerful bureaucracy, deep-rooted clientelism and what I term "hegemonic ideology" — informed decentralization. In turn, these attributes engendered resistance to the process of decentralization itself. That resistance dated from the beginning of the decentralization movement. However, the trend of democratization at the time meant that it took concealed forms. As the counter-democratic movement has gained momentum and eventually prevailed since the overthrow of the Thaksin Shinawatra administration in 2006, attempts at counter-decentralization have resurfaced. They have reached a new peak under the authoritarian regime in power since the May 2014 *coup d'état*.

The Decentralization Movement and Process

Decentralization numbered among the ideals of the democratic and political reform movement undertaken by Thai intellectuals following the Black May incidents of 1992. It emerged as a key item on the agenda in the months after the elections of September 1992 (Tanet 1994, p. 59). Some intellectuals saw decentralization as necessary to the construction of true democracy in Thailand (Anek 2009, p. 1; Anek 2012, p. 28; Tanet

1994, p. 59), while others viewed it as a solution to problems resulting from an over-centralized public administration (Charas 1994, pp. 79–80). Still others advocated decentralization as a means for rural development and grass-roots empowerment (Kanoksak 1994, pp. 336–38; Thirayuth 1993, p. 13). At the same time, international agencies such as the World Bank, which extended loans to many countries for administrative restructuring towards decentralized administration, actively promoted decentralization. Thailand, within the framework of the World Bank's country assistance strategies, was urged to undertake decentralization (Litvack et al. 1998, p. 2).

Despite having no direct influence on the resistant Thai bureaucracy or leading political actors, the World Bank induced the National Economic and Social Development Board (NESDB) to include as one of the objectives of its Seventh National Economic and Social Development Plan (1992–96) the redistribution of government revenues to decentralize and build local administrative financial capacity (National Economic and Social Development Board 1991, p. 119).[1] This goal corresponded to a global trend of encouraging both capitalist development and state efficiency by downsizing the state and devolving authority to local government.

The 1997 Thai constitution reflects the demand for decentralization and other political reforms. The charter's chapter on local administration incorporated an institutional design for decentralization influenced by intellectuals who played important roles in the process of drafting it (Supasawad 2013, p. 63). Chapter 9 of the constitution emphasized autonomy, democracy and participation. Section 284 in the same chapter stipulated that a law and an accompanying plan for decentralization would be enacted to cover, first, the distribution of powers and duties between the state and local administrative organizations and among those organizations; second, the allocation of taxes between the state and local administrative organizations and among those organizations; and, third, the establishment of a committee consisting of representatives of relevant government agencies, representatives of local administrative organizations, and experts to perform the above.

This institutional reform marked the first instance of the decentralization of state power since the establishment of the modern Thai state at the end of the nineteenth century. Although five of the fifteen previous constitutions — those of 1949, 1968, 1974, 1978 and 1991 — had stipulated local self-administration, none of these documents included sufficient provisions to bring about decentralization (Somkhit 1998, pp. 374–75). Moreover, extant acts concerning local administration — the Sanitary District Act of 1952, the Municipality Act of 1953, the Provincial Administrative Organization Act of 1955, the Tambon Administrative Organization Act of 1956 — had failed to provide for democratic organizational structures. Additionally, they included a critical loophole that allowed the provincial administration to retain control over these matters (Somkhit 1998, pp. 361–74).

The passage of the 1997 constitution was followed by the promulgation of the Decentralization Plan and Procedure Act of 1999 (*phraratchabanyat kamnot phaen lae khanton kankrachai amnat hai kae ongkan pokkhrong suanthongthin pho so 2542*).

Nelson attaches particular importance to that latter act, as it provided a concrete basis for the process of decentralization in Thailand. "[I]t stipulates in what time tasks, which are at the moment being performed by the state or by the state's territorial administration, will have to be transferred to local government authorities". These tasks comprised not only "duties for which the state and local governments have overlapping responsibilities, or duties the state performs in local government areas", but also "tasks the state performs in a local government area which have an impact on other local governments, and responsibilities according to government policies" (Nelson 2002, p. 233).

One of the significant concrete provisions in this act concerns revenue allocation. Section 30 stipulates that no less than 20 per cent of government revenue must be allocated to local governments by 2001 and no less than 35 per cent by 2006 (Thailand 1999*b*, section 30, p. 63).

Once the above act was put into effect on 18 November 1999, the National Decentralization Committee (NDC, *khanakammakan krachai amnat su thongthin*) was formed to carry out the process of decentralization according to the terms of the act. The committee declared a Decentralization Plan (*phaen kankrachai-amnat hai kae ongkan pokkhrong suanthongthin*) in 2000 and a First Operational Plan for Decentralization (*phaen patibat kankamnot khanton kankrachai-amnat hai kae ongkan pokkhrong suanthongthin chabap thi 1*) in 2002. These plans appeared to give stability and momentum to the push for decentralization.

The First Operational Plan for Decentralization detailed the process of decentralization. Its main provisions included the expedition of the transfer of work to local administration and the distribution of responsibilities between the central-state and local administration and among organs of the latter. Perhaps the most important provision of the plan concerned the allocation of revenue.

The implementation of this plan gradually changed local administration in Thailand and augmented its power. As of 2004, local administration throughout the country had been organized into municipalities, provincial administrative organizations, sub-district or *tambon* administrative organizations and special administrative organizations (Weerasak 2004, p. 218). The municipality is the local administrative body for urban areas; there were altogether 2,441 municipalities in 2016 (Somkiat and Issakul 2016, p. 7). Depending on population density and income, a municipality can be a sub-district municipality (*thetsaban tambon*), a town municipality (*thetsaban mueang*) or a city municipality (*thetsaban nakhon*). Provincial administrative organizations (*ongkan borihan suanchangwat*) cover the country's seventy-six provinces — exactly the same domain, both pre- and post-decentralization, of the provincial administration under the authority of the Department of Local Administration (*krom songsoem kanpokkhrong thongthin*) of the central interior ministry. Sub-district administrative organizations were established only in non-urban areas; there were 5,334 of them as of 2016 (ibid.). Finally, the Bangkok Metropolitan Administration and Pattaya City are special local administrative organizations. Every local administrative organization has a legislative body or council and an executive team whose members are popularly and directly elected as in a presidential system.

In a number of ways, the new structure of local administration transformed Thai politics at the local level. First, the democratic election of the leadership of local administrative organizations all over the country helped to expand electoral politics. In both urban and rural areas, people became more involved in politics and participated more actively in elections. Unprecedented opportunities for democratic competition among local leaders arose. Second, much of the authority of the central government at the provincial level was transferred to the local administrative organizations. Local politicians came into play as contenders for state power, challenging the central government bureaucrats who had held authority for a century. Although major provincial businesspeople monopolized most local political positions, decentralization nevertheless allowed even minor local leaders and businesspeople to compete for power too. Third, the surge in public budgets turned the local political arena, especially in urban areas, into a sphere of competition for positions in local administrative organizations (Viengrat 2008, p. 60).

For more than a decade, from 1999 to 2014, obstacles to decentralization posed by conservative bureaucrats arose regularly. These obstacles obstructed the implementation of the Operational Plan for Decentralization and led to the failure to meet the requirement of the Decentralization Plan and Procedure Act of 1999 that 35 per cent of total government revenue be allocated to local government entities by 2006. At the beginning of the decentralization process, the national government transferred authority for taxes and duties, along with some subsidies, to local governments, such that they received 20.7 per cent of government revenue in 2001, but the figure remained at only 24 per cent fifteen years later (Somkiat and Issakul 2016, pp. 7–8). Difficulties in complying with the 35 per cent requirement led General Surayut Chulanon's administration to amend the Decentralization Plan and Procedure Act in 2006; acknowledging reality, this amendment removed the time frame for complying with the 35 per cent requirement (*Phraratchbanyat kamnot phaen lae khanton kankrachai-amnat hai kae ongkan pokkhrong suanthongthin pho so 2549*, section 3; Thailand 2006, section 3, p. 1).

Despite these failures, local administrations were thoroughly and freely established across Thailand. More importantly, the allocation of such significant resources from central and provincial government funds to the use of locally elected representatives of Thai voters signified a marked change in state-society relations. The example of an administrative organization in a sub-district with a population of approximately five thousand that found itself managing an annual budget of more than 10 million baht since 2002 suggested the impact of this change.[2]

Thoroughly establishing local government organizations paved the way for local people to engage in politics and in effect created a new political system that has revolutionized Thai politics and power structures in provincial areas for the first time since Thailand became a modern state. The consequences have shaken the characteristics of the Thai state.

The Characteristics of the Thai State

The stable and even rigid characteristics of the Thai state have deeply informed patterns of state-society relations in the country. They have structured state-society relations at the local level, specifically those between centre and periphery, central and local political power-holders, and state power and provincial people. This structure has remained unchanged since the era of modern state formation, through periods of absolute monarchy, constitutional monarchy, military regimes, semi-democratic regimes, numerous *coups d'état*, parliamentary democracy, and eventually an electoral political regime. Unfortunately, while electoral democracy showed signs of altering these characteristics, it confronted a counter-democratic movement. That movement prepared the foundation for the 2014 coup of the National Council for Peace and Order (NCPO, *khana raksa khwamsangop haeng chat*) to return Thailand to authoritarianism and apparently to restore its former state structure.

The modern Thai state's relations with provincial society have had three important dimensions during the course of the development of that state across the past century. First, and most significantly, the Thai state is a centralized state in which the bureaucracy has exercised powerful dominance, even as it has lacked effectiveness and proved incapable of contesting the power of local strongmen closer to their people. The second characteristic, a consequence of the first, is that informal political powers outside the bureaucracy have exercised significant authority. These powers have helped the state to maintain its relationship with society through clientelism. The third characteristic reflects the state's success in constructing an ideology centred on the *chat*, or "nation", and also on the monarchy and the Buddhist religion. However, this notion of *chat* does not represent a community of citizens. Instead, it alludes to a united entity, bound together by the monarchy. The most important pillar of this ideology has been the king; the nation and its security are tied to the king's *barami* or legitimacy to rule.

State Dominance through a Centralized Bureaucracy

In the late nineteenth century, Thailand started establishing a modern state with foundations in the bureaucratic system. This process was one of state building by ruling classes who were pressured by external forces, in the form of the colonization of neighbouring countries by Great Britain and France. At the beginning of the state-building process, the monarchy unsurprisingly centralized and monopolized power around the throne. In the Thai case, several factors intervened to prevent other forces from challenging the monarchy.

First, it was the monarchy itself that had initiated reform, not least with the aim of securing its own status. "A modern administration and tax system would strip wealth and power from the great families and remove the noble class as the mediator between the king and people" (Kullada 2004, p. 41). Hence, reforms allowed the monarch to monopolize power by marginalizing aristocrats, local lords and other private interests who might compete with him for power.

Second, that Siam escaped direct colonization has several effects. External actors did not undertake the process of state building, and the monarch was therefore able to maintain supreme power without interruption. Furthermore, no nationalist movement of citizens was necessary to liberate the nation from colonization. The absence from the political system of actors outside the bureaucracy was the result.

Third, as Chai-anan (2011, p. 2) has emphasized, the modernization process of the Thai monarchy was one of state building, and not nation building. It was an act of resource mobilization aimed at expanding the power of state officials, and not at the inclusion of other groups in political processes. This mobilization of resources from society was intentionally used to construct an administrative structure within the state, and not to establish relations between state mechanisms and other social forces.

Furthermore, the centralization of power was an imperative, as power had previously been diffused throughout the structure of the "galactic polity" (Tambiah 1977). That polity linked the Siamese court in Bangkok to other courts throughout the notional territory of the country (Somkiat 1984, pp. 123–24). However, external factors, in the form of neighbouring colonial states, demanded that Siam clarify its borders in the late nineteenth century and it therefore adopted a modern regime of territorial administration within borders dating to the early twentieth century (Thongchai 2001, pp. 58–59). The new state administration made evident to people living within Siam's borders the power of the king in Bangkok. The central government did not allow local elites beyond those at the village and sub-district levels to share that power. The reform of local government in 1894 shifted power over local administration to the Ministry of Interior (Chai-anan 2011, pp. 59–61). That ministry came to embody the modern state's supreme power over the country, not only by controlling officials within the entire national territory but also by controlling the resources allocated to village headmen chosen by local people.

When the regime changed to a constitutional monarchy after 1932, the bureaucracy grew stronger still. Chai-anan (2011, p. 58) calls this continuity an "old state apparatus in a new political regime". The constitution that the new regime introduced did not articulate these mechanisms of state powers because, again, the purpose of its drafting was to determine power relations between administrative bodies and to transfer power from the king to the cabinet and from the Privy Council to the parliament. Since the constitution did not clarify the authority and political power of the bureaucracy, it allowed the bureaucracy to grow stronger, with the Ministry of Interior continuing to exercise central power rooted in the old regime (Chai-anan 2011, p. 59).

The self-described People's Party or *khana ratsadon* had staged its revolution to change the regime. Despite its goal of creating democracy, it inevitably had to maintain centralization in order to hold on to power. According to Nakarin Mektrairat, the group was concerned with three issues: transforming the king into a figurehead, revoking extraterritorial rights and thus liberating Siam from Western powers by endorsing modern laws, and fostering political nationalism to unite the citizens of the country in spite of differences in regional origins, language and ethnicity (*Prachatai Online*, 21 June 2012). Decentralization and the establishment of new municipalities or reformed municipal government were not high among the priorities of the People's Party.

The first years after 1932 centred on the rearrangement of political relations among members of Siam's elite. The characteristics of the state, especially the relationships between the state and its people, had yet to change. The public administration was operated for mundane governing, not for changing the state's structures.

Changes began to take place during Field Marshal Po. Phibunsongkhram's second premiership between 1948 and 1957. Reform of the bureaucracy began in 1952, with significant changes to administrative structures. The Ministry of Public Health was established, and the structures of ministries were changed in the interest of supporting the national economy (Chai-anan 2011, p. 71). These reforms made the bureaucracy more responsive to central political power while preventing other groups from participating in the political sphere, in what Riggs (1966, pp. 395–96) christened the "bureaucratic polity". Following Field Marshal Sarit Thanarat's *coup d'état* in 1958, a policy of thwarting the participation of political parties, politicians and non-bureaucratic groups further strengthened the still-centralized state and the bureaucratic polity. During this Cold War era of development assisted by the United States, technocratic responsibility for policy planning only made the bureaucracy stronger still (Ninnart 2002, pp. 29–35).

Although parliamentary democracy gained ground during the 1970s and 1980s, the characteristics of the centralized state did not change much. Parliamentary institutions and elections opened opportunities in politics to national- and local-level businesspeople and to local mafias (Anderson 1990, pp. 41–42). It enabled these groups to share a modicum of political power with the centre. They used their newly acquired power to gain further benefits, leaving ordinary people the chance to benefit only as their clients. The powerful bureaucracy remained the centre of state administration.

The centralized Thai state, with the bureaucracy at its core, delivered sustained economic growth to Thailand. However, relations between the state and its citizens were marked by inefficiency and worsening in service delivery from the state to the people, as the next section illustrates.

The Thai State Coexists with Influential Actors

The discussion above makes clear that the idea of the bureaucratic polity powerfully captures the nature of the Thai state, especially before the 1990s. At the same time, the reality was that, with respect to the actual exercise of power in the provinces, the Thai state was not capable of exerting its authority, except through cooperation with local strongmen or *phu mi itthiphon* (men of influence) (Tamada 1991, pp. 457–58).

A large body of scholarship argues for the role of *chao pho* or "godfathers" in local politics in Thailand (see, for example, Ockey 1993 and McVey 2000). The term refers to businessmen who patronize and protect local people in exchange for various forms of support. The clientelistic politics of *chao pho* represented a major phenomenon in Thailand, especially in the 1980s and 1990s. These figures accumulated wealth through businesses dependent on concessions from the state or involvement in illegitimate activities; each required strong connections with high-ranking bureaucrats. At the same time that he accumulated wealth, a *chao pho* also established his leading status in a locality by means of patronage. He could mobilize people more effectively than provincial bureaucrats. Typically, a *chao pho* would use his connections with bureaucrats to benefit his own business then share these benefits with bureaucrats. The mutual interest between *chao pho* and bureaucrats could even result in *chao pho* helping low-ranking government officers by using their connections with higher-ranking officers. In this sense, local power actually mediated centralized power.

At the same time, *chao pho* extended patronage by distributing wealth to their communities and offering various in-kind benefits. Some of this help represented protection against the abusive use of power by bureaucrats. The *chao pho*'s function as patron enabled him powerfully to mobilize people, therefore inevitably leading to his playing an important role in electoral campaigns. This same context saw occasional recourse to violence in order to settle disputes.

Scholarly consensus saw electoral politics as the crucial factor that empowered *chao pho*. Elections opened the way for these figures to play an important role in Thailand's provincial politics (Anderson 1990, pp. 39–40; Pasuk and Baker 2000, p. 38; Sidel 1996, p. 59). At the same time, the most salient structural factor sustaining networks of influence was the ineffectiveness of the state's centralized bureaucratic system. This ineffectiveness was manifest in two areas: the state's inability to deliver services to its citizens, and bureaucrats' lack of competence and capacity. The state's lack of capacity created a multitude of opportunities for clientelism. Bureaucrats' lack of resources, local knowledge and expertise led them to rely on *chao pho* to maintain social order in provincial areas. At the same time, villagers relied on these same figures to meet various needs. Finally, *chao pho* utilized their connections with high-ranking officials to achieve their own vested interests. In a social climate in which the majority of the population lacked access to public resources and in which the existing patronage system and networks of influence played important roles, the accommodation of state power and powerful groups in society perpetuated distinct patterns in Thai political life (Viengrat 2003, p. 451).

A salient characteristic of this pattern of clientelism was that, in contrast to clientelistic exchanges in other societies, the Thai variant limited possibilities for social mobility on the part of the clients. The nature of the bureaucracy — its lack of resources and capacity — fostered a clientelistic exchange in which the *chao pho* traded an ability to help govern for access to bureaucratic connections. However, villagers' and others' connections to *chao pho* represented a static clientelistic resource that they could not transform into opportunities for social mobility. The transfer of the power that derived from one's connections to high-ranking officials or access to powerful positions in government was difficult in such a network. Moreover, the benefits that trickled down to ordinary people worked to make them satisfied and complacent in the knowledge that they were connected to someone who was in turn connected to state authority.[3]

The political decentralization process launched after 1997 brought important changes to this state structure. Decentralization reduced the power of the government in the capital. It thereby decreased the significance of connections between influential persons in the provinces and powerful state officials deployed from Bangkok. This change undermined clientelistic relations between the state and influential people (Viengrat 2008, pp. 73–74). Furthermore, local leaders now had an alternative means of accessing state power in the form of local government positions. It was no longer necessary to maintain the costly and risky structures of patronage that had distinguished *chao pho*.

Once influential persons participated in local election and held elected positions, their relationships with local people gradually changed too. As elected local officials, they were obliged to deliver services according to formal authority, even as they might possess the charisma of the *chao pho*. Allocated public budgets allowed them to deliver patronage without relying upon connections with "high-and-mighty" bureaucrats. Furthermore, since anyone could campaign for elective office, almost anyone could become a local powerhouse without possessing the charisma of a *chao pho*. As a consequence, violence was slowly transformed into electoral battle (Viengrat 2008, pp. 100–101). Decentralization was upending the static nature of the state that had, with its accompanying culture and ideology, persisted for decades.

The Domination of State Oriented Culture and Ideology

The Thai state has long proved successful in maintaining its powerful image. That image has been intertwined with an ideological complex whose supremacy has faced few challenges since the late 1950s.[4] It has crowded out the notion of the nation as a community of citizens, which has not developed in Thailand. The nation is in the sphere of monarchy, which comprises not only the king but also the networks around him (McCargo 2005) and the ideology and culture symbolized by the myths and traditions of the institution (Jackson 2010, pp. 31–35). The national sphere is characterized by the ideology and symbols attached to the monarchy as representative of Thai identity: virtuousness, patriotism, nationalism, loyalty, Buddhism, and so forth.

Notably, the state's success in establishing the monarchy as the centre of collective morality long effaced to a striking degree ideological differences in Thai society and prevented those differences from taking on political significance. The state ideology's privileging of the hegemonic monarchy marginalized politics as a matter remote from the lives of most Thais. It encouraged citizens to view the state as a benevolent dispenser of aid and patronage. Rural citizens, in particular, came to believe that state institutions would benevolently assist them; they did not see service delivery as an obligation of the state.

Numerous projects, of which the 1987 *khrongkan isan khiao* (Green Isan Project) led by the Thai Army stands as an example, deliberately reinforced the image of the aforementioned structure. "Green Isan" was in fact the popular nickname of the project officially called "His Majesty the King's Mercifulness for the Development of Northeastern Region according to His Royal Initiatives" (*Khrongkan nam phrathai chak nailuang phuea kanphatthana phak tawanokchiengnuea tam naeo phraratchdamri*). At the ceremony to launch the project, a convoy of water trucks was put on display in the Royal Plaza in Bangkok, with television coverage of its departure for the Northeast (*Nangsuephim raisapda kongthap* 1991, p. 125). Such ritualistic events were common in the 1980s. This depicted the state's service delivered in the form of social welfare solely through bureaucratic means, as if the state were extending its generosity to the impoverished subjects in a philanthropic sense.

The ability to have an impact made gradually available to the citizenry meant that local democracy saw people realize that their rights carried some weight and that exercising these could actually bring about changes. Although the changes were not guaranteed always to be positive for voters, there was always the opportunity to make things better in the next elections (Viengrat 2015*a*, p. 144). Simultaneously, national politics under the Thai Rak Thai party during 2001–6 featured populist policies that benefitted the lives of the people even more. Their votes held power, and not only for the benefit of politicians eager for access to office. This awareness emerged nationwide, and it reshaped the relationship between political institutions and the people, particularly the rural workers and farmers, in a way that the country had never experienced.

Although the new pattern could not transform the hegemonic state ideology, its emergence challenged various aspects of that ideology. In one respect, it gave political subjects a status closer to that of citizens. It also became a new basis of legitimacy for state power, which had previously been appropriated by the sphere of the monarchy. When Thaksin announced on 14 January 2006 that his legitimacy was upheld by 19 million votes (*MGR Online*, 14 July 2006), this remark critically redefined the sources of legitimate power in Thailand. However, the starkness of this remark obscured a parallel process of redefinition, one that was also inducing influential people, political patrons and powerful local leaders, whose power derived from citizens, to adapt and change accordingly. This process, with the attendant emergence of citizens, posed a tremendous challenge to the Thai state. Decentralization defined this process.

The Red Shirt movement that emerged after the 2006 *coup d'état* is an important illustration of the way in which citizens had a new understanding of the state. Without the awakening that accompanied "becoming citizens", the Red Shirts would have not demanded political justice, equality and the rule of law, and democracy as they did (Buchanan 2013, pp. 66–69). Additionally, although they disguised some of their activities, it was evident that they dared to challenge the legitimacy of the supreme institution of Thai society (Viengrat 2015*b*, p. 187). The formation of citizens is one of the grounds that have convinced the Red Shirts to adopt the discourse of *phrai* (serfs) and *ammat* (aristocrats, royal, elites) that feature in the campaigns of the United Front for Democracy against Dictatorship (*Naeoruam prachathippatai totan phadetkan haeng chat*). In this regard, without the transformation of oneself into a citizen, one never realizes what being a subject is.

The decentralization process that unfolded after 1997 not only created a path for democratization but also revolutionized the state structure, particularly with respect to the Thai state's relationship to Thai citizens. It unsettled elite power at the centre and weakened the bureaucratic system that had comprised the core of the state. It created a new political process, grounded in electoral politics, and thus upset the clientelism that had coexisted with the centralized bureaucratic state. This new political process created channels for local leaders to possess formal power, while restricting opportunities for bureaucrats to gain more power. For this reason, decentralization was resisted in many ways, particularly by the old, powerful bureaucratic forces.

Counter-Decentralization

Decentralization cost the Ministry of Interior, the longstanding core of the centralized state, much of its power. Bureaucrats' reaction to this loss generated counter-decentralization forces, often in disguised form.

These forces emerged even before the reforms of the 1997 constitution. The movement for democratization that followed the Black May incident of 1992 saw the issue of decentralization receiving focused attention from Thai scholars. Some progressive academics even proposed the idea of elected rather than appointed governors, an extremely radical idea in the Thai context.[5]

Although the post-1992 atmosphere made it difficult for opponents of decentralization to mobilize explicitly, they nonetheless made attempts to indirectly thwart the process. The Ministry of Interior launched these events in 1994 by proposing an act on sub-district councils (*sapha tambon*) and sub-district administrative organizations (*ongkan borihan suantambon*) (*Phratchabanyat sapha tambon lae ongkan borihan suantambon pho so 2537*; Thailand 1994). This act provided for the establishment of sub-district councils as legal entities in local administration. However, it did not grant much autonomy to the councils. They remained under the power of provincial administrations. Councils are composed of the *kamnan* or sub-district headman, the village headmen of all villages in the sub-district, the sub-district doctor, and one elective member from each village (ibid., section 7, p. 12). The *nai amphoe* or district officer also has power over the council. He can discharge any member found to be disqualified after an inquiry (ibid., section 12[6], p. 14), and he appoints the council's vice president from among its members (ibid., section 16, p. 15). While on the surface this proposal appeared to promote democratization, in actuality the ministry put it forward as a means to supplant the proposal for elected governors.[6]

However, at the time, any attempt to block the move towards decentralization faced strong headwinds, and the 1997 constitution proved the first Thai constitution clearly to articulate an approach to decentralization by devoting a chapter to the issue. As overtly opposing decentralization directly was not possible, moves for counter-decentralization had to assume different forms, including the penetration and obstruction of the decentralization process.

Bureaucratic Penetration of the Decentralization Process

Bureaucratic penetration of the decentralization process worked through several channels. First, bureaucrats played a dominant role in planning decentralization. The Decentralization Act of 1999 defines the roles and responsibilities of the National Decentralization Committee (Thailand 1999*b*, section 1, pp. 2–5). The NDC was responsible for producing a decentralization plan for submission to the cabinet and the parliament for approval. The plan was to identify, first, a clear distribution of powers and duties between the central state and local administrative organizations and among those organizations and, second, the allocation of taxes and responsibilities among those same entities. The NDC had the chance to define many of the policy parameters for the legal framework for decentralization. It was also charged with implementing the framework and with monitoring outcomes. These roles allowed this committee to recommend to the government the appropriate measures for devolving powers to local governments (Nelson 2002, p. 233). The NDC was composed of thirty-six members, who were to represent the sectors affected by decentralization, including members of the central bureaucracy, such as a deputy prime minister acting as chair; the interior and finance ministers; the permanent secretaries of the Ministries of Interior, Finance, Education, and Health; the secretaries-general of the Office of the Council of State, the Office of the Civil Service Commission, the National Economic and Social Development Board, the Bureau of the Budget and the Department of Local Administration; twelve representatives of local government; and twelve senior "experts" (Weist 2001, p. 199). Supasawad's research indicates that the number of bureaucratic representatives was even larger than this roster suggests, as many of the "experts" were retired Ministry of Interior bureaucrats.[7] Additionally, the representatives of local politicians on the NDC did not, because of a lack of collective action, exercise power significant enough to shape the decentralizing process in favour of local government (Supasawad 2010, pp. 36–37).

Control over Local Administrative Organizations by Provincial Administrative Officers

A number of clauses in the laws governing provincial administration allowed bureaucrats posted by the Ministry of Interior to exercise superior power over local governments. For example, section 77 of the Provincial Administrative Organization Act of 1997 stipulates that

> Provincial governors have the authority to supervise the provincial administrative organizations in the conduct of their work according to laws, regulations, and rules of procedure. To do so, a governor has the power to investigate a provincial administrative organization or to order a provincial administrative organization to clarify actions concerning its operation. In the case that a governor finds that the chief executive of the provincial administrative organization or the deputy chief executive of the provincial administrative organization has executed a duty in a way that is detrimental to the provincial administrative organization or violates laws or regulations, the governor holds the power to suspend that operation and report to the Minister of Interior within fifteen days. The Minister of Interior then has to make a final decision within thirty days. (Thailand 1997, section 77, p. 19)

The next section, section 78, of the same act reads,

> A governor may withdraw the resolution of a provincial administrative organization council if it violates laws or regulations or it is beyond the scope of a provincial administrative organization's authority. (ibid., section 78, p. 20)

The Sub-District Council and Sub-District Administrative Organization Act of 1994 extends to the district officers who supervise and regulate sub-district administrative organizations' powers, similar to those that governors wield over provincial administrative organizations and municipalities according to the 1997 act cited above. However, section 20 of the amended 1999 version of this act states,

> To protect the interests of citizens who reside in the area over which a sub-district administrative organization has authority, the district officer will report his views to the governor, including if he is proposing the dissolution of the sub-district administrative organization council. (*Phraratchabanyat sapha tambon lae ongkan borihan suantambon pho so 2542*; Thailand 1999a, section 20, p. 8)

Section 92 of the same act was amended by section 36 in the Sub-District Council and Sub-District Administrative Organization Act of 2003. It stipulates,

If the chief executive or deputy chief executive of a sub-district administrative organization or chairman or vice chairman of its council appears to act against the security and welfare of the people or neglects to perform her or his duty or performs that duty illegitimately, the district officer must investigate immediately. If the investigation proves the accused guilty, the district officer must propose to the governor that the guilty party be discharged from her or his position. The governor may also investigate further if the situation makes it necessary, and the order of the governor must be final.

(*Phraratchabanyat sapha tambon lae ongkan borihan suantambon pho so 2546*; Thailand 2003, section 36, p. 36)

Because the powers of bureaucrats posted to the provinces by the Ministry of Interior overlap with the jurisdiction of local administrative organizations, the complicated relations between the bureaucrats and the organizations encourage a clientelism that undermines decentralization in substantive ways. In particular, at the level of sub-district administrative organizations, district officers' responsibilities for inspecting sub-district administrative organizations' budgeting processes and expenditures encourages the latter to comply with the wishes of bureaucrats at the district level. Sub-district administrative organizations are required to add a category of funds "supporting the district's operations" to their budgets. Some surrender their emergency budgets to the district office when the district requests it. In a few cases, sub-district administrative organizations have even used these funds to buy vehicles used by district officers.[8]

The Authority of the Department of Local Administration over Local Administrative Organizations

The Department of Local Administration of the Ministry of Interior was established in 2002 with the principal objective of promoting decentralization and supporting local administrative organizations.[9] Other objectives include making and amending regulations and standardizing and supervising the operation of local administrative organizations. Because of the department's regulatory power over local administrative organizations, it has become the most powerful department in the Ministry of Interior. In 2008, it expanded its apparatus to the provincial level by establishing a Provincial Office for Local Administration (*samnakngan songsoem kanpokkhrongthongthin changwat*) in every province as part of the provincial administration (*Kot krasuang baeng suanratchakan krom songsoem kanpokkhrongthongthin krasuang mahatthahao pho so 2552*; Thailand 2008*b*, section 3, p. 4, section 16, p. 7).

The Department of Local Administration has used several tools to make local administrative organizations comply with its directives. One is standardizing the procedures by which they carry out their duties in order to exercise control over them. A second is the allocation of subsidies, which comprise approximately 39.4 per cent of local administrative organizations' total revenue (Somkiat and Issakul 2016, p. 10), to enable the department to determine how they should spend money. These allocations are just one indicator of how the central bureaucracy undermines the fiscal autonomy of local administrative organizations. Using a third tool, the Department of Local Administration issues orders to local administrative organizations via provincial governors throughout the year. The department does not have the formal authority to command local administrative organizations, but it employs provincial administrations and ambiguities in their lines of command to ensure that those organizations follow certain policies determined at the national level.

Obstructing the Devolution of Authority

The obstacles put in the way of the transfer of authority from the national government to local administrative organizations embody an attempt at re-centralization, in the form of prolonging the transitional period by the longest duration possible. The transfer of responsibilities on the part of the Ministries of Public Health and Education epitomize the failure to transfer authority caused by those ministries' attempts to retain power.

The case of public health devolution exemplifies the above obstacles. In adherence to the Decentralization Act of 1999, the NDC appointed a subcommittee for the devolution of duties relating to public health to local organizations, with a mandate to study and assist the process of devolution. The NDC and the Ministry of Public Health agreed that all Primary Health Care Units, which serve as community-level public health service providers, be transferred from the Ministry of Public Health to sub-district administrative organizations by 2010.[10] Accordingly, in 2007, the Ministry of Public Health set up a committee to prepare guidelines for devolution (Office of the Permanent Secretary, Ministry of Public Health 2006). This committee specified criteria for the "readiness" that local administrative organizations needed to demonstrate in order to receive authority for public health tasks that ultimately served to stymy the devolution process. Under the guidelines for devolution developed by the Ministry of Public Health, the devolution of units could occur only when a sub-district administrative organization or municipality met criteria concerning readiness to manage healthcare. It must have received a good governance award and demonstrated a capacity for and commitment to managing healthcare by establishing a public health section and contributing funds to a community health fund.[11] Additionally, at least fifty per cent of a primary healthcare unit's staff, including the head, must support devolution and be willing to become personnel of the local administrative organization rather than of the ministry. A survey of or process of consultation with the community must also be carried out to ensure that there was majority community support for devolution (Hawkins et al. 2009, p. 5).

These criteria posed significant challenges to devolution, with the result that by 2010 — ten years after promulgation of the Decentralization Act — only 28 out of 9,787 public healthcare units in the country had, after considerable difficulties, been transferred (Songkramchai 2012, p. 48).

Moreover, in 2012, the Ministry of Public Health, supported by funds from the government of Abhisit Vejjajiva, redesignated public healthcare units as "sub-district health-promoting hospitals",[12] in a change that made further consideration of their transfer to sub-district administrative organizations more complicated. As of the end of 2016, only 51 primary healthcare units and sub-district health-promoting hospitals had been transferred (Thai Civil Rights and Investigative Journalism 2017).

The case of the thwarted decentralization of public health demonstrates the irreconcilable visions of decentralization of the central and local government administrations in Thailand. The central administration, in this case the Ministry of Public Health, was reluctant to transfer its authority to local administrations, while the latter were eager to grasp new opportunities presented by public health management. The former raised a number of difficulties for the transfer process. First, although the decentralization process was legally completed and accompanying organizational structure created, government agencies failed to implement and enforce the law. Second, the central administration's privileging of expertise and professionalism hindered decentralization. For instance, the longstanding reputation of the Ministry of Public Health for high professional standards discouraged its officers from recognizing the benefits of decentralization (Viengrat 2011, p. 39).

Public health represents just one responsibility among many others to be transferred to local governments that have faced obstruction. Similar problems also confronted devolution in the area of education (Nelson 2002, pp. 239–46).

Re-Centralization under the De-Democratization Process

In the wake of Thailand's political crisis following the 2006 *coup d'état*, counter-democratic movements gained momentum. The movements that delegitimized and ousted Thaksin fiercely condemned the corruption that allegedly tainted Thai politicians. This theme received much emphasis among Thai scholars and the urban middle class. It was reflected in the 2007 constitution, drafted following the coup of the year before. For the first time, a Thai constitution explicitly mentioned provincial administration under central government control (Supasawad 2010, p. 25). Chapter 5 guaranteed the status of the administration.

> The state shall pursue directives in relation to the administration of the state affairs as follows ... 2) to organize the central, provincial, and local administration to the effect of achieving boundaries, powers, duties, and responsibilities that are clear and well-suited to national development, and enabling a province to have a plan and budget of its development in the interest of local residents. (Thailand 2007, section 78:2)

In a 2009 interview, Nakharin Mektrairat stated, "the provision in that statement was inserted by one of the Constitution Drafting Committee members who used to be a senior bureaucrat of the Ministry of Interior and was accepted by the committee as part of a compromise" (Supasawad 2010, p. 26). That is, it sought to entrench the priorities of forces intent on administrative centralization.

The National Legislative Assembly appointed following the coup also amended the Local Government Act of 1914 (Thailand 1914) by cancelling the five-year terms of village headman and sub-district headmen so that they could retain their positions until the retirement age of sixty (Thailand

2008*a*, section 14, p. 98). Fortunately, the proposal to return appointment authority over these positions to provincial governors did not pass the assembly (*Thai rat*, 2 June 2012). Nonetheless, it served as an indicator of the attempt to strengthen the provincial administrations under the control of the Ministry of Interior at the expense of the local administrations to which power had been devolved in the preceding decade. It also offered a sign of things to come in the wake of Thailand's next coup.

After the 2014 Coup: Recentralization Proceeds

The National Council for Peace and Order, the junta that staged Thailand's latest *coup d'état* in May 2014, has signalled through numerous efforts its agenda of reconstructing a centralized state under the control of the national bureaucracy. In fact, the Office of the Permanent Secretary of the Ministry of Defense raised concerns that decentralization might lead to instability and harm the unity of the administration.[13] To halt the decentralization process, the NCPO issued an order on 10 July 2014. The significant points of this order include the following.

(1) If the four-year terms for elected roles in local administrative organizations are completed and come to an end, election to fill them must be deferred. If the remaining occupied seats on a local council are less than half of the body, it must be dissolved.

(2) To appoint new council members after the dissolution of a council, an appointing committee must be formed. The new council's membership must be composed of at least one-third bureaucrats or former bureaucrats from the rank of special expert or C8 or its equivalent or above.[14]

(3) The number of seats on the local councils of sub-district administration organizations is reduced to ten members, those of municipalities of all kinds to twelve members and those of provincial administrative organizations to 50 of their present numbers.

(4) Members of the councils of local administrative organizations are required to be bureaucrats or former bureaucrats from the rank of special expert or C8 or its equivalent and above.

(5) Appointment committees must consist of the provincial governor as a chairman, the provincial prosecutor or anyone appointed by the chief prosecutor, the director of Provincial Election Commission, and the director of the provincial auditor general's office.

The holders of all council elected positions will be selected by a committee, and at least two-thirds of local council members must be either current or former senior bureaucrats.

The appointment committee of each province will be formed by bureaucrats led by the governor, the director of the Provincial Anti-Corruption Commission, the deputy director of the Provincial Security Office (Military), and one private sector representative (the chairman of the provincial chamber of commerce or the provincial branch of the Federation of Thai Industries or the Lawyers Council of Thailand).

(6) Once the members of a local council are selected, the chairman of the appointment committee must appoint the council chairman within three days.

...

(12) The interior minister is responsible for implementing this order and has the authority to issue rules and regulations to enforce this order.

(*Prakat khana raksa khwamsangop haeng chat* 85/2557; Thailand 2014*a*)

Another powerful tool that General Prayut Chanocha, the NCPO's leader and the prime minister, exercises to maintain the junta's power is his ultimate authority under section 44 of the 2014 interim constitution.[15] By November 2017, Prayut had used that authority to issue 176 orders, including orders affecting the local administration. Ten of these orders dismissed officers under investigation for corruption. The dismissals totalled several hundred.[16] As a result, local administrative executives began to exercise great caution in their spending decisions in order to avoid corruption charges. This might also explain the 1.7 billion baht in funds accumulated from local governments' budgets that remained untouched. In November 2017, the junta tried to alter regulations to be able to use these funds for other purposes (Krungthep thurakit 2017).

These NCPO orders saw counter-decentralization and the objective of re-centralization reach a new pinnacle. It formed part of the junta's broad effort to establish an authoritarian regime in the country. At the same time, however, the government has had to incorporate into its programmes members of the elite and middle class who made up the political movement in the past decade that paved the way for its coup. The National Reform Council (NRC, *sapha patirup haeng chat*) was created in October 2014 as required by the interim constitution (Thailand 2014*b*, section 27, p. 9). The NCPO's selection of members of the NRC was a means of allowing other groups to share the junta's political power. Although the NRC was disbanded in September 2015 after it voted against the adoption of the junta's first draft constitution,[17] its extensive debates on decentralization proved noteworthy. These debates split the NRC into two camps. Consisting of former Ministry of Interior bureaucrats who represented the "old" generation, one camp supported re-centralization, while the other camp comprised advocates of decentralization and included scholars and activists.

Those NRC members who promoted decentralization nonetheless agreed on a number of necessary reforms. They sought the creation of a new Committee for Local Administration Reform (*khanakammathikan patirupkanpokkhrongthongthin*), whose membership would include more non-governmental organization representatives and scholars.[18] They also wanted to reform the scale of local government organizations so that all had the scale of sub-district administrative organizations and to merge some into other, larger ones, such as city municipalities. A third reform that this group advocated was decentralization that "went beyond local politicians" by distributing power directly to citizens. This stance reflected an ideology dismissive of electoral politics. Finally, the group proposed giving greater monitoring power to civil society, whose participation would be guided by the Local Development Institute, a foundation with close bureaucratic connections that seeded and funded NGOs.[19]

The positions of the "pro-decentralization" camp of the NRC demonstrated the complex strands of the anti-democratization trend in Thailand. People who had advocated decentralization during the process of drafting the 1997 constitution now exhibited scepticism towards electoral politics, after participating in the anti-Thaksin movement since 2006. They sought to strengthen governance and "people power" but had low levels of trust in politicians and the electoral process. Their willingness to suspend electoral democracy, however, reflects their support for an authoritarian regime.

In August 2016, a referendum approved the second constitution drafted under the auspices of the NCPO, and it was promulgated on 6 April 2017. This charter has had fewer provisions dedicated to local administration than the 1997 document. Although it does not provide clear guidance for decentralization, it nonetheless nominally accords importance to democratic processes. In a slight difference from the earlier charter, section 252 stipulates that local chief executives be selected through elections or the consent of the local council (Thailand 2017a, section 252, p. 75). This section thus affords room for organic laws or enabling legislation to return to the system replaced in 2001 with one in which the chief executives of local administrative organizations were directly elected in an executive system. The content on local government in Thailand's latest constitution does not provide for concrete organizational structure, as the debates on, and expectations of, local administration among the elites who held power after the 2014 coup remained unresolved.

In the process of drafting the organic laws for local administration, the actors are limited to the top organizations: the NCPO, the National Reform Steering Assembly, the National Decentralization Committee and the Department of Local Administration. All of these organizations are indeed under the influence of the NCPO. The National Reform Steering Assembly (NRSA, *sapha khapkhluean kanpatirup prathet*), which replaced the NRC, was established by section 39/2 of the interim constitution to guide the country's reform (Thailand 2014b, section 39).[20] All of the members were appointed by the prime minister.[21] In the National Decentralization Committee, three key figures are from the cabinet: Deputy Prime Minister Wissanu Krea-ngam, who is the chair; Minister of Interior General Anupong Paochinda; and Minister of Finance Apisak Tantivorawong. Obviously, the Department of Local Administration is under the command of its minister General Anupong, the former army commander. However, since the design of the structures for decentralization and local administration are technically complicated, we do not witness direct commands from NCPO in this area. The organizations concerned informally negotiated during the drafting process, but the Department of Local Administration was commissioned by the cabinet to draft the act and present it to Wissanu before approval by the junta's National Legislative Assembly.[22] The politics of the drafting process is interesting and often confusing to the public. News releases by Wissanu or other leading informants were soon followed by further news releases to deny the information. Conflicting reports have concerned the possibility of holding local elections before national elections, abolishing sub-district administrative organizations, reforming local government finance by pulling resources back into the central government budget, and other matters.[23] In this context, the bills to be adopted by the assembly will reflect power relations among actors in the decentralization process under the authoritarian NCPO regime.

Conclusion

The decentralization process under way in Thailand since the late 1990s has significantly transformed the political landscape, especially at the local level. Among the many effects of reforms, the most significant is that on the power of the Ministry of Interior. The ministry, which had dominated local society since the beginnings of the modern Thai state in the 1890s, has faced a critical challenge to its domination for the first time. When the core characteristic of the Thai state — its over-centralized bureaucracy — is challenged, other characteristics are also threatened.

This chapter has examined three characteristics of the Thai state that have informed state-societal relations at the local level over the course of the past two decades. It is clear that the newly established system of local administration has affected the centralized state — the first of those characteristics — as that system has weakened the domination of the Ministry of Interior over society. This development has affected the second characteristic, clientelism. Once the state functions as a service provider, clientelism is no longer necessary. Also, local strongmen begin to exercise formal, rather than informal, power through electoral politics. This change challenges the third characteristic, which is a unifying ideology centred on the monarchy. After one or two post-1997 electoral cycles, Thai voters increasingly came to realize that "Thai-style democracy" had been a regime for subjects, not citizens (Piyabut 2011). This realization was fundamental to the rise of the Red Shirts and to their political understanding.

These changes and challenges meant that a counter-decentralization movement appeared at the same time the decentralization process began to gain momentum. In the context of a mainstream movement centred on democratization, counter-decentralization took on various disguised forms to obstruct the process. Once the de-decentralization process started, it became more open and took on more aggressive forms. The climax of this trend came with the NCPO order to stop all processes relating to decentralization after the *coup d'état*.

Among pro-junta intellectuals, some pro-decentralization figures continued to push the decentralization agenda as members of the National Reform Committee. Although these figures shared the mistrust of electoral politics and national-level politicians, a common quality central to both the Yellow Shirt movement and the NCPO project, they nevertheless thought it desirable to foster small-scale democratic government at the local level.

One only hopes that the members of this pro-decentralization camp will realize that without democracy and electoral politics, decentralization and good governance are impossible.

Acknowledgements

I would like to thank Tamada Yoshifumi, Siripan Nogsuan Sawasdee and Kritdikorn Wongsawangpanich for their comments on and help with earlier drafts of this chapter. I owe immense thanks to Illan Nam for helping me to revise the chapter and offering comments that have been invaluable to its completion.

Notes

1. This is stated in chapter 1 on "Guidelines for Fiscal and Monetary Policies Supporting Income Distribution" of part 3 on "Guidelines for Income and Prosperity Distribution to the Regions and Rural Areas" (National Economic and Social Development Board 1991, p. 119).
2. For example, the sub-district administrative organization in rural Pueai in Ubon Ratchathani province has a registered population of about 7,000, of which only 4,500–5,000 people are actually in residence. This local administrative organization had an annual budget of 7–12 million baht between 2000 and 2006 (Interview with Likhittiya Philaiwong, Pueai sub-district administrative organization permanent secretary, 18 June 2008, Luea-amnat district, Ubon Ratchathani province).
3. In contrast, local machine politics in the United States from the late nineteenth century onwards through the second half of the twentieth century allowed social mobility, albeit at a slow pace, as some low-level members of machines became bosses and lower-ranked bosses achieved higher positions. This was because the inducements in American machines' networks were jobs and political positions, which made social mobility inside these networks possible. This contrast highlights the difference between patronage and clientelism. See, for example, Judd and Swanstrom (2015).
4. The Communist movement of the 1960s and 1970s, defeated by the early 1980s, and perhaps the Southern Thai insurgency of the last dozen years, largely confined by the state to the fringes of the country, have numbered among the few exceptions.
5. Thawin Praison, a Democrat Party politician who advocated decentralization, describes his role and that of others in proposing reform in opposition to the preferences of the Ministry of Interior at that time in Thawin (2014, p. 4).

6. Interview with Charas Suvannamala, 8 March 2015, Bangkok.

7. Another committee crucial to the decentralization process, the National Commission on Local Government Personnel Standards, was similar in that regard. This latter commission in turn oversees other commissions formed at various levels of local government. It has extensive powers over personnel policy, such as the promotion and removal of local officials, salaries and other issues. They too are dominated by members who have bureaucratic backgrounds (Supasawad 2010, p. 18).

8. Interviews with sub-district administrative organization chief executive, 23 June 2008, Pakphun sub-district, Mueang district, Nakhon Si Thammarat province; municipal chief executive, 2 March 2011, Warinchamrap, Ubon Ratchathani province; and sub-district administrative organization chief executive, 17 November 2010, Pingkhong sub-district, Chiang Doa district, Chiang Mai province.

9. It is stated on the website of the Department of Local Administration that "Its main responsibility [is] to promote and support the work of the local administrative organizations (LOAs) through the development and series of advices [sic] on the local development plan, personnel administration, finance, and administration in order to strengthen the capacity and efficiency of the local administrative organizations on public service provision" (Department of Local Administration 2015).

10. Interview with Supphakit Sirilak, 14 May 2010, Ministry of Public Health, Nonthaburi province.

11. This was an initiative of the National Health Security Office taken to encourage local governments to lead and commit resources to disease prevention and health promotion activities, with co-financing from the office.

12. This Ministry of Public Health project cost 50 billion baht; 50 per cent of the budget came from the Abhisit government's "Strong Thailand" (*thai khemkhaeng*) initiative (Thai Civil Rights and Investigative Journalism 2017).

13. "Over decentralization may harm unity in administration because it may cause disputes among various local entities. This [decentralization] leads to inadequate collaboration and conflicts. Therefore, careful control and supervision by the central administration is necessary in order to maintain adequate unity in administration" (Office of the Permanent Secretary, Ministry of Defense 2014, p. 12).

14. The personnel ranking system in the Thai civil service has eleven levels, from the lowest "C1" to the highest "C11". C8 is thus an executive rank. In provincial administration, this rank is approximately that of an early-career district officer (*nai amphoe*).

15. Section 44 reads, "In the event that the Leader of the National Council for

Peace and Order finds necessary for the purpose of reforms in various fields, the promotion of unity and amity amongst people in the Nation, or the prevention, abatement, or suppression of an act which subverts peace and order, national security, the royal throne, the national economy, or official affairs of the State, whether it comes to pass inside or outside the Kingdom, the Leader of the National Council for Peace and Order shall have the power to, upon approval of the National Council for Peace and Order, order, suppress, restrain, or perform whatever act, regardless of whether such an act would produce a legislative, executive, or judicial effect. And it shall be deemed that the order or act, as well as the observance of such an order, is an order, act, or observance that is lawful and constitutional under this Constitution, and is final. However, when it has been done so, a report shall forthwith be submitted to the President of the National Legislative Assembly and the Prime Minister for their acknowledgment" (Thailand 2014).

16. As of December 2017, ten orders on this matter had been issued by the National Council for Peace and Order: 16/2558 (Thailand 2015a), 19/2558 (Thailand 2015b), 1/2559 (Thailand 2016a), 43/2559 (Thailand 2016b), 44/2559 (Thailand 2016c), 50/2559 (Thailand 2016d), 52/2559 (Thailand 2016e), 59/2559 (Thailand 2016f), 35/2560 (Thailand 2017b), and 39/2560 (Thailand 2017c).

17. Section 38 (2) of the Constitution of the Kingdom of Thailand (interim) of 2014 stipulates, "In the event that the Constitution Drafting Committee fails to complete the drafting of a constitution within the time limit fixed in section 34, the Constitution Drafting Committee shall come to an end, and arrangements shall be made for the appointment of a new Constitution Drafting Committee within fifteen days reckoned from the date the Constitution Drafting Committee comes to an end" (Thailand 2014b, section 38 [2]).

18. Interview with Charas Suvannamala, 8 March 2015, Bangkok.

19. Ibid.

20. Section 39 (2) reads, "When the National Reform Council is dissolved under section 38, no further establishment shall be made of a National Reform Council under this Constitution, and a National Reform Steering Assembly shall be established in place of the National Reform Council to proceed to initiate reforms in various fields in accordance with section 27 in continuance of work by the National Reform Council. Herewith, consideration shall be given to expediency and the achievement of reform in the remaining period of time, and paragraph one and paragraph two of section 31 shall apply mutatis mutandis. The National Reform Steering Assembly shall consist of not more than two hundred members appointed by the Prime Minister from persons of Thai nationality by birth and being of not less than thirty-five years of age. The appointment shall be completed within thirty days from the date the National Reform Council is dissolved" (Thailand 2015c, section 39).

21. Judging from the name list, the tentative composition of 200 members include 60 former NRC members, 20 former bureaucrats, 20 active bureaucrats, 50 military men, 10 jurists, 10 scholars, 10 businessmen, and 20 others.

22. Interview with an officer of the Department of Local Administration, 3 December 2017, Bangkok.

23. While plans to abolish sub-district administrative organizations have been reported (*Post Today*, 27 February 2017), the prime minister denied them (*Post Today*, 6 September 2017).

10

Change and Continuity in the Politics of the Media after the Coup

Aim Sinpeng and Wimonsiri Hemtanon

Nearly two decades ago, Duncan McCargo argued that the Thai media constituted "a political space in which different elite groups have sought to advance their interests and views" (McCargo 2000, p. 166). This chapter assesses patterns of continuity and change in the relationship between the media, both traditional and social,[1] and politics in Thailand in the inter-coup period between 2006 and 2014 and the post-coup period since 2014. Using McCargo's analysis of the Thai press as a departure point, we focus on the period of the last decade for three reasons. First, Thailand experienced unprecedented levels of political and social upheaval — marked by prolonged and violent street protests, significant political instability and two military *coups d'état* — during that decade. Second, the proliferation of information and communications technology for mass consumption in the 2010s has led to an expansion of space for civic engagement. Third, the military government has sought since 2014 to institutionalize information controls in ways that would have a negative impact on future relations between the state and the media. We therefore evaluate and analyse how this period of heightened political conflict, on the one hand, and the rapid expansion of social media use, on the other, have fostered change or demonstrated continuity in the dominance of political elites, including the National Council for Peace and Order (NCPO, *khana raksa khwamsangop haeng chat*) junta, over the media landscape.

We advance two claims in this chapter. First, political elites have continued to exert control and influence over traditional and social media in three major ways: (1) establishing new institutions to reduce media independence, (2) taking direct ownership of media outlets in order to advance their political agenda, and (3) shaping the content and discourse of both traditional and social media through state channels.[2] Specifically, we argue that the Thai military and its conservative-royalist allies made a comeback in exerting dominance over the media during two recent periods of authoritarian rule, 2006–7 and 2014–15. The creation of new institutions to govern both traditional and social media — most notably the constitution of 2006 and the 2007 Computer-Related Crime Act (CCA) — constrained media independence and press freedom in ways that allowed political elites to re-exert their dominance. Of particular use to government agencies and the military, these institutions were not created to advance the interest of the public or to protect freedom of press and of expression. Instead, their purpose was to subject expression and the media to greater state control. The expansion and increased availability of information and communications technology have also provided opportunities for political elites to assume ownership of media outlets and content producers and thus to advance their own interests. Moreover, traditional and social media outlets that represented views in opposition to the existing power holders, such as the ruling government, have experienced continued harassment or sometimes the outright suppression of free speech.

Our second claim is that the intense political conflicts in Thailand during the past decade have deepened the partisanship of the media. This chapter addresses the strictly "political dimension", the relationship between media organizations and political parties or groups.[3] The Thai media, especially print media, have long been subject to some degree of "influence", whether political or commercial, but few respected media outlets consistently toed the line of a particular political faction. By the mid-2000s, however, a number of major print media outlets and television and radio stations fell clearly into camps divided along partisan lines to an extent unparalleled even just a decade earlier. Partisan elites also exploited the growing popularity of social media by mobilizing their own supporters on platforms such as Facebook. The potential of social media to "democratize" the polity by expanding opportunities for political engagement and reducing the gap between the elites and others in society was met with restrictive cyber regulations following the 2006 military takeover.[4] Such authoritarian reversals and illiberal political environments more generally have hamstrung the impact of new media in challenging the dominance of political elites in the media arena. In the short to medium term, the expansion of Internet access and growth in new media usage is unlikely to contribute significantly to meaningful political change in Thailand. The institutional constraints that limit press freedom and civil liberties will, that is, militate against the greater engagement of citizens via those media.

The Limits of Media Reforms, 1992–2001

Thailand has come a long way from the "mobile phone mob" of Black May in 1992. Following the anti-military mobilization against General Suchinda Kraprayoon's attempt to become prime minister and the crackdown on protestors that it provoked, the state of the Thai media, along with a host of other political and social issues, stood at the forefront of the country's reform agenda. Anti-Suchinda activists envisioned a progressive role for the media, in which it would cease to be an instrument of the state and instead reflect the voices of the people. They saw the dominance of the military over various parts of the traditional media as an impediment to a more democratic and open Thailand. Black May revealed the danger of the state monopoly over television — the most popular form of media — as it facilitated information control during times of political crisis. Mobile phones were important tools for communication and mobilization, particularly as the government tightened its grip on the censorship of traditional media (Rungmani 2010). Older technologies also played a role as some anti-government activists resorted to faxing scripts to radio stations so that the latter could update their audience on the crackdown in Bangkok (Supinya 2013).

The Black May activists pushed for a series of media reforms in the 1990s, reforms designed to open up space for a more independent media sector. It was during this time that academics, professional journalists and pro-reform activists sought to increase the role of the people in shaping policy on the mass media.[5] According to Pirongrong Ramasoota, media activists and academics saw three issues as instrumental to media reform: the allocation of radio frequencies to non-state actors, the creation of media that served the public good, and improvement in the overall climate of press freedom (Pirongrong 2013, pp. 42–23).

The 1990s represented a hopeful period for those determined to see media liberalization in Thailand. Following the Black May events, the media took more seriously their role as a watchdog "monitoring the conduct of government officials" (Francke 1995, p. 109). Reporting in the print media contributed to the downfall of Chuan Leekpai's government in 1995, after exposing the land reform scandals involving a high-profile member of the prime minister's Democrat Party (McCargo 1999, p. 551). Through subsequent governments, the media did not waver in their efforts to investigate government affairs, especially corruption cases. A crucial moment for "free media" in Thailand was the advent of the 1997 constitution, which sought to reduce avenues for state intervention in the media, while increasing the number of both private and independent media actors (Pirongrong 2013, p. 43). Media activists, journalists and academics, who had long advocated for freeing the broadcast media from their status as mere instruments of the state, celebrated the inclusion of articles 39, 40 and 41 in the 1997 constitution.[6] Article 39 specifically prohibited closure of the press and censorship of news by the state except "by virtue of the provisions of the law specifically enacted for the purpose of maintaining the security of the State".[7] State officials were not to censor news, television or broadcasting of any kind unless the country was in a "state of war".[8] The state would also redistribute telecommunication frequencies to new private players, and it was encouraged to provide them with subsidies to reduce state dominance in the media space, according to article 40. Private media outlets would enjoy freedom of expression without fear of government interference, as per article 41. Boonlert Kachayuthadej, a renowned journalist who participated in the drafting of the 1997 constitution, argued that the protection of freedom of expression enshrined in this constitution referred not just to the media but also the general public — a poignant distinction from previous constitutions (Boonlert 2010). Despite the major step forward in safeguarding freedom of the press that the 1997 constitution represented, Boonlert admitted that it remained unclear whether changes in the constitution would lead to genuine changes in practice (ibid.).

The effort during the 1990s to liberalize the Thai media was initially successful, as media freedom improved significantly in the mid-1990s.

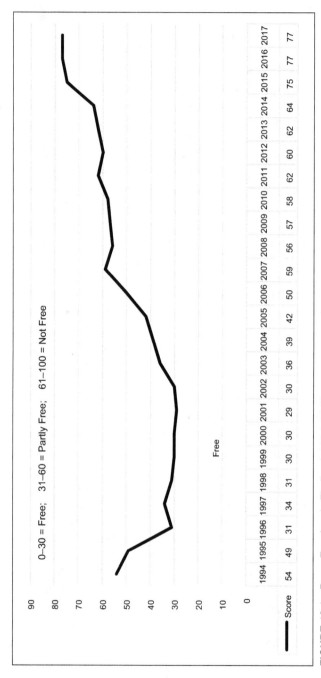

FIGURE 10.1 Press Freedom in Thailand, 1994–2017

Source: Adapted from Freedom House's annual ratings of press freedom (Freedom House 2017).

Freedom House ranked the press in Thailand as "free" between 1999 and 2002 — the first period that the country had achieved this status in twenty years — as a result of increasing media engagement in investigative journalism and in spite of continuing low levels of political interference in press freedom through bribery.[9] Yet, a general decline in press freedom from 2003 onwards followed the more liberal media environment of this brief period; the steepest declines came in the aftermath of the military takeovers of 2006 and 2014. Despite the country's return to formal democratic politics after the 2007 and 2011 elections, the media no longer enjoyed the levels of press freedom of the late 1990s. When the number of prosecutions in cases relating to information and communications technology climbed after Yingluck Shinawatra's election as prime minister in 2011, Reporters Without Borders dubbed Thailand an "enemy of the Internet" (Reporters Without Borders, 12 March 2012). By 2015, Thailand's press freedom was ranked among the worst in Southeast Asia (Freedom House 2015a) — a sad development for a nation whose media had been dubbed among the "freest" in Asia in the 1990s (Suthichai 2012).

Among traditional media, the print media had in fact benefitted the most from press liberalization. During the 1990s, mainstream newspapers received praise for helping to bring down the Suchinda government by decrying state censorship and repression. "The image of the Thai press as the courageous guardian of liberty and democracy contains a great deal of truth", argued McCargo (2000, p. 13). At the same time, he emphasized that the media were not a unitary actor and that any attempt to analyse the media must take into consideration the nuances of specific contexts. Moreover, the print media had undergone rapid commercialization during the economic boom years of the late 1980s and 1990s, and journalists could not report openly on the state of the national economy leading up to the Asian Financial Crisis in 1997 for fear of losing advertising and investors (Lewis 2006). Widely criticized for failing to report on the financial bubble, the print media responded by exposing a number of high-profile corruption scandals during the period of the second Chuan Leekpai government of 1997–2001.[10] The print media sector itself also saw thousands of journalists laid off, while more newspapers went out of business in the aftermath of the financial crisis (Kavi 2002, p. 256). This latter development provided the opportunity for large media corporations to consolidate the industry.[11] Consequently, while the economic downturn weakened the print sector as a whole, certain individual players were able to strengthen their market share and expand their businesses to include broadcasting, radio and cable television (Ubonrat 1997). In essence, that sector engaged in successful economic rather than political liberalization, as evinced in high growth in advertising revenues and increased corporate ownership prior to the 1997 financial crash (ibid.). While the state was willing to deregulate on the commercial side and to allow more private players into the media industry, it sought to maintain the status quo by directly and indirectly controlling news content and censorship (ibid., pp. 65–66). The print media were largely preoccupied with increasing revenue and neither interested nor in a position to raise politically sensitive issues without significant political backing after the 1997 financial crisis (McCargo 2000, p. 13).

The birth and death of Thailand's first independent television station, iTV, demonstrated the limits of media reforms in the years after Black May. The combination of the disastrous impacts of the financial crisis and frequent changes in government meant that political elites lacked the will to pursue legislation to further the media reform process, and it became very difficult for the media to resist commercial interests. iTV initially represented a source of hope among media activists. It embodied for them the possibility of creating an outlet for broadcast news free of state, government and commercial intervention. At the time, most of the free-to-air channels remained either military- or government-owned.[12] In 1995, the Siam Commercial Bank and its major shareholder the Crown Property Bureau helped to establish iTV and brought in a team of news producers from the Nation Media Group — publisher of The Nation newspaper — to create an independent channel that would focus on delivering critical, investigative news programmes. In 2000, however, after the 1997 financial crisis and mismanagement of the company, Shin Corporation took over the bank's shares in iTV in order to help restore its financial stability. Shin Corporation belonged, of course, to the family of soon-to-be prime minister Thaksin Shinawatra. Many of the journalists at iTV protested its owning shares in the channel, which they regarded as compromising the integrity of news reporting, particularly if Thaksin succeeded in becoming the country's leader (Nity 2007). During the campaign for the January 2001 elections, amidst accusations of his improper asset management and share dealing (Mitton 2000), some iTV journalists and editors rebelled against what they saw as Thaksin's interference in the reporting of the scandals and campaign (Pasuk and Baker 2009, p. 149). More than twenty employees of the channel were subsequently sacked following Thaksin's election victory, while several more met the same fate when pursuing "critical reporting" on Thaksin and his government in later years.[13]

The demise of iTV came after the 2006 coup, when the military-backed government of Prime Minister Surayut Chulanon changed its name to Thailand Independent Television (TITV) and put it under the direct control of the government's Public Relations Department (*krom prachasamphan*). TITV eventually underwent another transformation in early 2008, when it took its current form, as the Thai Public Broadcasting Service (Thai PBS), under the leadership of a mixed group of notable Thaksin opponents and academics.[14] Many in media circles saw the establishment of Thai PBS as a "political move" meant to reassert the control of the state and the military and reduce the influence of the Shinawatra family, the previous major shareholders of iTV, in the wake of the coup (Jom 2013). Ultimately, in succumbing to both commercial and political interventions, iTV failed to live up to expectations that it would serve as a "truly independent" television channel.

The Mobilization of Opposition Media, 2001–6

The iTV "rebellion" against Thaksin's interference in many ways set the tone for the mobilization of opposition media during his administrations from 2001 to 2006. As McCargo and Ukrit argue, the takeover of iTV "signalled a controversial new departure for [Thaksin's telecommunications businesses], provoking a bitter conflict between Thaksin, his political rivals, the media and democratic activists" (McCargo and Ukrit 2005, p. 47). Indeed, the first media outlet to come out strongly against Thaksin's government was *The Nation*, whose journalists had strongly criticized Shin Corp's management of iTV journalists. Tepchai Yong, a former editor of *The Nation* who was actively involved with the production of news content at iTV, said that Thaksin often told the media not to criticize the government and to let it do its job for the nation (Ubonrat 2002). When the media continued to criticize the government, Thaksin employed both legal and financial intimidation against media critics. The National Anti-Corruption Commission "suddenly" investigated executives of the Nation Media Group, which owned *The Nation*, *Thai Post* and *Naewna* newspapers, all of which had been critical of the Thaksin government (ibid.). The government claimed, "someone asked us to look into their financial accounts", but gave no justifiable reason for this investigation (*Matichon*,

2 June 2002). The Thaksin government also threatened the Assumption University or "ABAC" Poll, and attempts were made to eliminate the coverage of politics on UBC cable channel 8.[15] As the situation continued to worsen for media opponents of the government, Shin Corp launched a 400 million baht lawsuit against media activist Supinya Klangarong and the *Thai Post* on the grounds of defamation (Keya 2007). Supinya, who led the Committee for Media Reform (*Khanakammakan patirup sue*) at the time, was investigating alleged conflicts of interest relating to Thaksin, his Thai Rak Thai party (TRT) and Shin Corp.[16] As pressure against media critics mounted, the Thai Journalists' Association made a public statement condemning the government for cracking down on media independence through the abuse of state power, personal wealth and connections, and intimidation (*Thai rat*, 3 January 2003). In 2004, towards the end of the first Thaksin government, opposition broadened to include civil society organizations, labour groups, religious groups, academics and factions of the political elite.[17]

The final straw, which prompted the street mobilization of Thaksin's opponents, including those from the media sector, came when a popular talk show, "Thailand Weekly" (*Mueang thai raisapda*), was cancelled. Its host Sondhi Limthongkul, owner of the multimedia Manager Group and a former supporter of Thaksin, had begun regularly to criticize the TRT government soon after it won re-election in 2005.[18] The popularity of the programme — aired on a public channel, Channel 9 — surged as Sondhi openly and consistently criticized TRT policies and Thaksin's leadership.[19] The response from the government was harsh and swift. There was first a reduction in airtime from five days to three days a week, then the abrupt cancellation of the programme (Thoettam 2008, p. 38). Taking "Thailand Weekly" off the air turned out to be a grave mistake. The popularity of its host soared, giving rise to "the Sonthi phenomenon" (*prakottakan Sondhi*), which solidified his position as Thaksin's arch-enemy. Sondhi and his Manager Media crew capitalized on this surge of support, which was good for business, to continue the "mobile" version of his talk show (*Mueang thai raisapda sanchon*), first at Thammasat University and then at public parks. These events drew hundreds of thousands of audience members.[20] Sondhi was not the first outspoken critic of Thaksin, but his power and ability to draw crowds was in large part due to his ownership of the media outlets and his willingness to put those outlets at his own disposal.[21] "Sonthi is the most important leader of the top ranks of the *phanthamit*", admitted Suriyasai Katasila. He was referring to the anti-Thaksin People's

Alliance for Democracy (*Phanthamit prachachon phuea prachathippatai*, PAD), in whose secretariat he served. "He owns the media and he gets to frame the movement the way he sees fit ... and he has the funds."[22]

The mobilization of opposition media against Thaksin culminated in further politicization of some important media outlets. The leadership of the Manager Group in the anti-Thaksin mobilization, and to a lesser extent that of the Nation Media Group, went far beyond taking a political stance against the government — they became the opposition movement.[23] When Sondhi became the leader of the PAD, the Manager Group transformed into a political entity, and his media became instruments to serve his political ends. The PAD, or the Yellow Shirts, was a loose grouping of opponents of the Thaksin government that had been gathering steam since the early 2000s. It included media activists, opposition media, teachers, labour unions and Sondhi supporters among others.[24] Sondhi was among the most powerful individuals in the PAD movement as he was able to push his own agenda in the offline and online media and in books and other materials published by Manager's Ban Phra Athit Press. When state television stations had no space for him, he resorted to using satellite television to air his own channel, ASTV. Indeed, Sondhi was chosen to be one of the five top leaders of the PAD because of his position as a "media mogul",[25] which was crucial to the recruitment of members, the dissemination of information, and efforts at fundraising and mobilization (Khamnun 2006, p. 280). Manager staff worked for the PAD during and between rallies. They employed the company's resources to sustain the movement's activities. Manager print, online and social media vehicles allowed PAD leaders to issue their demands and coordinate their activities with the public at large (*MGR Online*, 28 July 2008). Instead of being silenced or marginalized, media outlets that opposed the Thaksin government became more politicized and empowered as the overall climate of dissent towards the ruling party intensified. By the time of the September 2006 coup, both *The Nation* and Manager publications ran a series of articles heralding the overthrow of the "Thaksin regime" (*MGR Online*, 20 September 2006).

The Partisanship of the Media and the Return of Military Dominance, 2006–15

The period following the September 2006 coup saw two major changes in the media landscape: partisanship on the part of the media and the return of military dominance over the media. The growing political divides between pro- and anti-Thaksin forces in the aftermath of the 2006 putsch led feuding elites to manipulate and capture the media as their main tools for political mobilization. The majority of the traditional media, along with social media, were torn between partisans on two sides: conservative royalists and pro-democracy or pro-Thaksin groups. At one end of the spectrum, opponents of Thaksin broadly supported the conservative-royalist agenda, which favoured strengthening the role of the monarchy and the military in politics.[26] As a crucial part of this broader agenda, the PAD heightened its activity and increased mobilization again after allies of Thaksin came back to power through the electoral victories of the People's Power Party (*Phak phalang prachachon*) in December 2007 and the Phuea Thai Party in July 2011.[27] Depending largely on the Manager Group and its allies, such as *The Nation* and new media outlets such as Kapook.com, the Seri Thai web board and Facebook, the yellow-leaning media united to undermine individuals and groups that could be linked to Thaksin and his family (*Khom chat luek*, 19 September 2012). The PAD continued its strategy of street protests, which culminated in a 193-day rally in 2008 — all aired via satellite television (*MGR Online*, 31 December 2008) — and further rallies again in 2009 (*Prachatai*, 30 September 2009). Following the decline of the PAD in 2011,[28] the People's Democratic Reform Committee (PDRC)[29] emerged to defend the conservative-royalist agenda and to push for the return of the military to power and the temporary cessation of electoral politics. The PDRC was under the leadership of members of the opposition Democrat Party and, instead of relying on PAD media resources, party leaders created their own: Blue Sky TV (*Sai lo fa*), which aired on satellite television and via YouTube.[30]

On the other end of the ideological spectrum were supporters of Thaksin, which included groups that were pro-majoritarian, pro-democracy and simply pro-Thaksin. The United Front for Democracy against Dictatorship (*Naeoruam prachathippatai totan phadetkan*, UDD) or Red Shirts formed in response to the September 2006 coup and the dismantling of the Thai Rak Thai Party. The Red Shirts represented what Taylor describes as "a number of broad interest groups brought together by a desire to see full representative democracy" (Taylor 2011, p. 3). The UDD saw much of the mainstream media toe the conservative-royalist line, and felt it necessary to create its own media outlets to counter the "double standard" in Thai society.[31] After the emergence of the movement, a plethora of print, online and social media, satellite television and local radio stations

TABLE 10.1
Selected Media by Partisanship (2006–15)

	Yellow/Yellow-Leaning (conservative-royalist)	Red/Red-Leaning (pro-majoritarian, pro-democracy, pro-Thaksin)
Television (broadcast, satellite, cable)	Channel 5 Channel 9 Channel 11 Blue Sky TV* ASTV The Nation	UDD Today* DNN* Voice TV Spring News People Channel* Asia Update PTV* DTV* Peace TV*
Newspapers/ Magazines	*Phu chatkan* (Manager) *ASTV* *The Bangkok Post* *Sayam rat* *Deli niu* *Post Today* *Thai Post* *The Nation* *Naeona* *Kom chat luek* *Positioning Magazine*	*Khao sot* *Prachathat** *Thai Red News** *D Magazine** *Truth Today** *Thong Daeng Magazine** *Bangkok Today** *Matichon* *Voice of Thaksin**
New Media (blogs, web boards, online news)	Kapook News Chao Praya News Thai-ASEAN News Seri Thai Web Board	Ratchaprasong News Same Sky* Thai E-News UDD Red Blog*

Notes: This is not an exhaustive list. *No longer in operation as of January 2016.
Source: Compiled by authors.[32]

proliferated. The Red Shirt media were instrumental in the successive electoral victories of the Thaksin-aligned People's Power and Phuea Thai Parties. They allowed Thaksin to maintain and expand his influence while in exile and to mobilize supporters prior to elections and major rallies. The main means of direct communication between Thaksin and his supporters was via a satellite phone-in, which he conducted regularly to shore up support for his political interests. For instance, Thaksin held a series of phone-in sessions outlining election campaign strategies to Phuea Thai candidates in the lead-up to the 2011 elections (BaBeBurin 2009). At the grass-roots level, the Red Shirt movement relied heavily for mobilization on the "Wira-Nattawut-Chatuphon" appearing on People's Television talk shows and subsequently in a series of Truth Today (*Khwamching wanni*) rallies between 2008 and 2009.[33] Wira Musikhaphong, Chatuphon Phromphan and Nattawut Saikuea became "the face" of the movement, whose popularity galvanized the Red Shirts into action to bring back Thaksin, returning his allies to power and releasing Red Shirt political prisoners (*Sayam rat*, 24 June 2011). In May 2010, during the premiership of Democrat Abhisit Vejjajiva, the UDD launched its biggest protests in Bangkok following the verdict of Thailand's supreme court ordering the seizure of assets worth 1.4 billion baht from Thaksin. These protests ended in a bloody crackdown by the military (Weaver and Gabatt 2010).

Although the partisanship of the media deepened as both the Yellow and Red Shirt camps mobilized their supporters for political ends during the period between the 2006 and 2014 coups, the May 2014 coup ushered in systematic repression and marginalization of the Red Shirt media. The vast majority of the media outlets associated with the Red Shirts were no longer in operation by January 2016, even though many of them had functioned for only a few years. The few that survived altered their programming to become "more mainstream" and to demonstrate in good faith that they were not instruments of Thaksinite political machines. For example, in April 2015 the junta suddenly revoked the permit of a Red Shirt satellite channel, Peace TV, on the grounds that one of its programmes, hosted by prominent Red Shirt leader Chatuphon Prompan, could be a threat to national security (*Prachachat thurakit*, 1 May 2015). Chatuphon then moved his talk show to a new YouTube channel and Peace TV was able to resume its broadcasting (PEACE TV, 16 July 2015). A number of Red Shirt radio stations had no choice but to cease their activities, and the military continued to monitor the movements of some of the prominent radio hosts (*Deli niu*, 22 May 2014).

The military-backed government of General Prayut Chanocha sought to "neutralize" the highly polarized politics of the previous decade by silencing and cracking down on only the Red end of the political spectrum. The end result was an illusion that the media scene had become less polarized simply because many of the Red Shirt media outlets could no longer exist. To make matters worse, the partisanship of the media during this period had already dented public confidence in the credibility of the media, in their ability to deliver unbiased, non-partisan views. A 2013 poll revealed that an overwhelming 75 per cent of respondents believed that the media did not present "the whole truth" and that 65 per cent believed that the integrity of the media was compromised (Bangkok University Research Center 2013).

The decade from 2006 saw the Thai military reassert its influence over the media in important ways.

First, it created a number of new institutional mechanisms to reassert state control over the ownership structure and content production of the media. In concrete terms, the media came to reduce the political power of Thaksin's allies, strengthen the conservative-royalist camp and reduce media partisanship. The 2006 coup and the abrogation of the 1997 constitution that accompanied it not only spelled the end of aspirations for media liberalization among reformers but it also created new institutional frameworks for the return of military dominance of the media at a level not seen since before the pre-reform period in the 1990s. While media activists argued that Thaksin's vast political and financial influence compromised media integrity, his government did not have the power to intervene in the same way that the military could during intervals of authoritarian rule. The government installed after the 2006 coup established new institutions and constitutional frameworks that would limit and constrain freedom of speech and press. The 2007 constitution included a new article, article 48, that prohibited holders of public office from owning or having stakes in the newspaper, radio, television and telecommunications businesses. While other articles from the 1997 charter that were important to media reformers remained in the new document, in practical terms article 48 specifically targeted Thaksin and his family's involvement in the telecommunications and media sectors. When Thaksin's brother-in-law Somchai Wongsawat and his sisters Yaowapha Wongsawat and Yingluck Shinawatra assumed posts in the People's Power and Phuea Thai Parties, they had to sell their stakes in firms operating in the telecommunications sector (*MGR Online*, 23 September 2008). Members of the Shinawatra family can own and operate a media company as long as they do not hold political office.[34] Article 46 of the 2007 constitution did not permit individuals holding political office to intervene in the reporting of news or the expression of opinion by the media. In reality, however, despite the return of electoral democracy in late 2008, freedom of the press was in continual decline in the years leading up to the 2014 coup. Reports indicated that journalists faced intimidation and persecution from those in power.[35]

Second, the governments installed following the 2006 and 2014 coups expanded state-directed Internet censorship and consolidated channels for online information control. In 2007, the post-coup government established an unprecedented legal framework to institutionalize Internet censorship policy with the promulgation of the Computer Crime Act (*phraratchabanyat wa duai kankratham khwamphit kiaokap khomphiotoe*, CCA). This act would prove potent in constraining the behaviour of Internet users and service providers through the regulatory framework that it introduced. Enforcement of the CCA has had a series of consequences for Thai cyberspace: legalizing the blocking of Internet content; holding intermediaries and Internet content providers liable for violations, whether they commit those violations directly or not; and creating a log file of Internet traffic to expose the identities of net users (Pirongrong 2011).

Empowered by the CCA, the Thai state has used a combination of direct and indirect means to impose Internet controls and significantly to raise the costs to both individuals and firms of any potential violation of the computer regulations. To strengthen the state's grip on information control further, the Prayut government that took power in May 2014 sought to consolidate all the Internet gateways into a single government-controlled point, to allow additional policing of online information flow (Ramsey 2015). Despite an outcry among Internet users,[36] the government committed 20 billion baht to "improve Internet broadband service" in early 2016 — a move seen by critics as a way to pursue its single gateway plan (Sasiwan 2016).

Moreover, the military and the conservative-royalist political elites exploited the deep political divides in Thailand by means of normative discourses about what constituted "appropriate" behaviour online. Its flagship programme, the Cyber Scouts (*luk suea saiboe*), promoted ethical and moral conduct online and was meant to ensure the "monitoring [of] behaviour that was a danger to the security of the country by means of information technology and communications systems" (Cyber Scout Thailand, n.d.). At a Cyber Scout camp aptly named "Fight Bad Web" (*kanprachum phuchiaochan chapho dan kanchatkan wep sai thi mai mosom*), hundreds of eleven-year-old volunteers learned to monitor cyberspace and report websites containing pornography, involving gambling or narcotics, or expressing *lèse-majesté* to the Ministry of Information and

TABLE 10.2
State Cyber Crime Suppression Programmes and their Estimated Budgets

Institution/Programme	Estimated/Reported Budget (baht)	Administrative Unit
Central Censorship Budget, 2010 (Sarinee 2012)	76,300,000	Ministry of Information and Communications Technology (MICT)
Project on Computer Crime Watch, 2008–9	Unknown	CAT Telecom Public Co. Ltd., Telecom of Thailand Co. Ltd. (TOT)
Internet Security Operation Centre (ISOC), 2009–11 (*Thai rat*, 20 February 2009)	80,000,000	MICT, TOT
Cyber Scout, 2010–present	At least 17,000,000	MICT
Cyber Security Operation Centre (CSOC), 2011–present	At least 3,600,000	MICT
Committee for the Monitoring of Illegal and Improper Dissemination of Information and Communication Technology, 2011–Present (*MGR Online*, 12 January 2012)	Unknown	Prime Minister's Office
Technological Crime Suppression Division (TCSD), 2009–Present (*Prachatai*, 25 January 2016)	At least 1,000,000	National Police Office
ICT Community, 2009–Present (Sarinee 2012)	28,900,000	MICT

Source: Adapted from Aim (2013b).

Communications Technology (MICT). For their efforts, the MICT awarded volunteers with a portrait of King Bhumibol (*Prachatai*, 1 December 2011). These programmes represented powerful tools that enabled the state to shape the discourse on appropriate online behaviour. They also reinforced other coercive measures to assert control over the Internet.

The exertion of state dominance over the media following the 2006 coup was so great that press freedom and freedom of expression more generally would not in the six years following the restoration of electoral democracy in 2008 return to the same level as in the pre-coup period. Indeed, the democratically elected governments of the inter-coup period chose to continue some of the policies designed to suppress freedom introduced after the 2006 coup, such as criminal prosecutions under the CCA. The subsequent 2014 military putsch was a "nail in the coffin" for media activists and reformers, not only because authoritarian rule was so antithetical to freedom of speech but also because the government that took power after that coup was more active in controlling the media. Media control figured among the greatest concerns of the NCPO in the days after it seized power from the Yingluck government on 22 May 2014. In those early days, at least ten of the NCPO's announcements involved some form of media ban or restrictions on freedom of expression.[37] Reporting or dissemination of publications and information that would undermine internal peace and order was prohibited; broadcast, radio and satellite services had to suspend their programmes and air only approved material from the military; politically aligned media, television and radio stations had to suspend their operations; and the state would monitor all information in cyberspace to prevent threats to peace and order.

While the military relaxed some of these measures after a few months, media content and press ownership remained subject to the dictates of the Prayut government, which would not hesitate to remove material that might represent a threat to its stability. In November 2014, the military government forced a reporter from the public and "independent" channel Thai PBS off the air for being critical of the ruling junta (*The Nation*, 15 November 2014). She was the host of the *Siang prachachon tong fang kon patirup* (People's Voices that Need to Be Heard before Reform) programme. Thai PBS subsequently received a fine for reporting on an anti-coup activity on the part of university students, activity that later led to their arrest (Thai PBS, 6 July 2015). Military officers showed up at the home of a *Prachatai* reporter to "invite" the journalist to discuss the infographics that she had created to raise awareness among the public about online actions that could violate CCA and the law on *lèse majesté* (*Khao sot*, 27 October 2015). In the view of media activists during the reform heyday of the 1990s, the media had lost the independence and credibility that it had demonstrated a decade earlier. "The media no longer serve the public ... but rather elites and their political and business interests", said Jom Petpradap, a former journalist involved with the iTV in the pre-Thaksin era but who was living in exile (ibid.). Supinya Klangnarong, a media activist working for the independent media regulator the National Broadcasting and Telecommunications Commission (*Khanakammakan kitchakan krachaisiang kitchakanthorathat lae kitchakan thorakhamanakhom haeng chat*, NBTC), was dismayed by the future of media in Thailand under the military's thumb.

> The power to reform the media is in the hands of the military and the Ministry of Industry. I mean the military because the president of the NBTC is in the military and within the organization there are five retired military officers. The "super board" that monitors the NBTC is staffed with soldiers; two out of its five presidents are drawn from the military too. (Supinya 2013)

From the vantage point of Supinya, media "reform" under military rule was not about empowering citizens or the protection of public interest, but rather about the military's business interests (ibid.).

Social Media and Political Change: Opportunities and Constraints

Could resistance to the media dominance of political elites, particularly the military, come from social media? Social media should have the greatest potential to undermine state mechanisms curbing media freedom. Unlike traditional media, they create what Jenkins (2006, p. 7) calls a "participatory culture" in which consumers are transformed into participants and producers of content. Because of their interactive, two-way communication characteristics, new media allow more freedom, space and time for content production. This is in stark contrast to passive forms of traditional media and their consumption: watching television, listening to radio or reading newspapers. Unlike reporters in traditional media, participants in social media need not wait for instructions from the editors or the distribution of news according to a publication schedule (Chuwat 2011, pp. 38–39).

Platforms such as Facebook, YouTube and Twitter require users to generate information, sometimes by sharing mainstream media news, but other times by producing news and sharing opinions themselves. This two-way communication can empower ordinary people by giving them a platform to express their opinions, as long as they have access to the Internet (*Prachatai*, 16 June 2015). These networked forms of communication are different from traditional media in ways that, again, should make state control difficult because of the sheer volume of online communication and the presumed anonymity of Internet users. Thailand offers a good case for examining the extent to which the Internet is indeed a "liberation technology" (Diamond 2010), and the extent to which it succumbs to the same manipulation by political elites that affects traditional media. During the decade of political turmoil between 2005 and 2015, Internet penetration in Thailand grew rapidly, from 15 per cent to more than 40 per cent. More than 90 per cent of Internet users reportedly had Facebook accounts, representing one of the world's highest per capita rates of Facebook usage (Saiyai 2013). With millions of Thais on Facebook, even as the political crisis continued to rage on the streets of Bangkok and elsewhere, could this social media platform provide space for civic engagement and potentially undermine state dominance over the media?

On the basis of this preliminary analysis, we argue that the extent to which social media can challenge state dominance of the media in cyberspace has remained limited and will remain limited in the foreseeable future. This is not to say that political participation online does not matter. In so far as social media provide new platforms for political expression on the part of individuals who may not have alternative avenues to express themselves, they certainly do matter. However, we must be careful in differentiating between the availability and the impact of social media in the political realm. Social media have not played a meaningful role in inducing political change in formal institutions — the constitution, government, regime, legislature or cabinet — for three reasons.

First, social media emerged and became a popular tool for communication during a time of limited freedom of press and speech. This meant that social media have operated within a constrained public sphere from the beginning. Authoritarian governments, particularly the government of Prime Minister Surayut Chulanon installed after the 2006 coup, created new institutions to govern the Internet and limit citizen's rights in cyberspace through legal provisions such as the CCA and

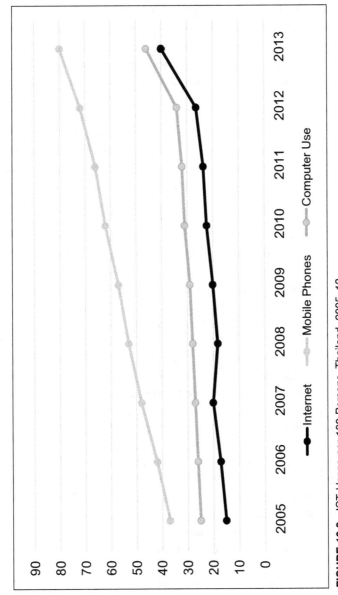

FIGURE 10.2 ICT Usage per 100 Persons, Thailand, 2005–13
Source: National Statistical Office (n.d.).

enforcement of the law of *lèse majesté*. Policymakers saw the governance of Internet use through the lenses of national security and political conflict. Internet and media rights groups have long complained about the improper use of article 14(1) of the CCA, which stipulates punishment for individuals who falsify electronic information and threaten public safety or the nation, to silence critics of the government.[38] A notorious recent case involving the use of the article saw the Thai navy sue *Phuketwan*, an online news outlet operating on the southern resort island of Phuket, for defamation under the CCA. At issue was the site's republication of an award-winning Reuters article that accused the navy of being involved in the smuggling of Rohingya refugees from Myanmar (Murdoch 2015). *Phuketwan*'s Chutima Sidasathian and Alan Morrison fought the charge and eventually won, in a case that could have landed them in prison for seven years. According to iLaw, an Internet rights group, the original purpose of article 14(1) was to protect the public from fraudulent websites, not to threaten media freedom, but it has increasingly been used to sue online media outlets for defamation since the CCA came into effect (iLaw 2014).

Second, the lethal combination of the CCA, allegations of defamation, and enforcement of the law of *lèse majesté* has enabled the punishment and silencing of opposition to the military and the conservative-royalist elites, with supporters of Thaksin Shinawatra, the Red Shirts or anyone that the state considers a potential threat to the monarchy as the primary targets. According to an iLaw report, CCA charges of defamation and *lèse majesté* account for nearly half of all the offences prosecuted under the act.[39]

The Seri Thai Movement (*Khabuankan seri thai*), a pro-monarchy political group, has encouraged its eighty thousand members to defend the monarchy by reporting *lèse majesté* violators through its Facebook page and popular Web board.[40] The Seri Thai Web board even offered information about whom to contact at the MICT to report *lèse majesté* violations online. In another example of abuse of the CCA for political purposes, PAD member Wiputh Sukprasert, who went by the online name of "I Pad", was responsible for filing sixteen complaints accusing individuals, including some high-profile journalists, of committing computer crimes (*Thai Free News*, 24 May 2012). Critics of the state's Internet policy referred to this vigilante regulation of cyberspace as "cyber witch hunting" and argued that it further compounded the already repressive Internet environment in Thailand (Siriwut 2012).

TABLE 10.3
Computer Crime Act Cases, 2007–14

Types of CCA Cases	2007–11	2012	2013	2014
Defamation	100	0	9	9
System-related offence	47	1	1	0
Lèse Majesté	40	11	10	18
Fraud	31		1	1
Pornography/Obscenity	31		1	
Illegal program	12			
National security	6		4	
Other	58	2	1	4
Total cases	**325**	**14**	**27**	**32**

Source: Thai Netizen Network (2012, 2013, 2014, 2015a).[41]

Filtering and blocking URLs was another means by which the state controlled the content of and traffic on websites deemed threats to national security. A report conducted by the Citizen Lab showed that, from 22 to 26 May 2014, in the immediate aftermath of the coup, the authorities blocked the URLs of fifty-six websites and social media accounts with political content (Senft et al. 2014). The NCPO also summoned the executives of fifty-one Internet service providers and "asked for cooperation" in monitoring and reporting any "inappropriate" behaviour online that would create disharmony in the society by submitting a list of URLs to be blocked within one hour of the occurrence of such behaviour to the MICT, cyber police or the NBTC (*Prachachat thurakit*, 21 May 2014).

Third, political engagement online through social media platforms during the decade of turmoil beginning in 2015 provided new avenues for polarization rather than neutral spaces for engagement among groups across the political divide. A survey of the most "liked" Facebook groups relating to politics clearly demonstrated the prominence of groups that either supported the conservative royalist and Yellow Shirt camp or the Thaksinite and Red Shirt camp. They had garnered far more support than student or activist groups that were pro-democracy but non-partisan. The non-partisan blue groups, despite constant online activities and frequent campaigning, elicited far less support than either the Red or Yellow Shirt groups, such as UDD Thailand or V for Thailand. A study of five partisan Facebook groups in 2014 also showed that the vast majority of people on either side of the political divide only interacted with others on the same side. The result was an "echo chamber" on social media (Groemping 2014). This deep partisanship was partly a reflection of societal divisions, but it also resulted in part from political movements' reliance on social media as some of their main tools for mobilization. The PDRC's media campaigns during its protest rallies against the Yingluck government from late 2013 until the May 2014 coup included a twenty-four-hour satellite television channel, Bluesky TV,[42] very popular Facebook pages, opposition media outlets, a website,[43] magazines,[44] radio stations, and supporters very active on social networks. The public Facebook page that PDRC leader Suthep Thaugsuban maintained when he served as a member of parliament had only thirty thousand "likes" as of March 2013. After he assumed the leadership of the PDRC, his page's popularity grew by 6,000 per cent to nearly two million "likes" just a year later. Suthep's Facebook page ranked as the twenty-sixth most popular Facebook page in Thailand, while both Yingluck's and Panthongtae Shinawatra's accounts were even more popular, according to a social media ranking agency, Zocialrank.

Conclusion

This chapter provides an overview of the relationship between politics and the media landscape during Thailand's decade of political upheaval from 2005 to 2015. It also offers a background account of the media liberalization and reform period of the 1990s, following the 1991 coup and the collapse of the military government the following year. Political influence, especially from the military and its conservative-royalist allies will continue to permeate the media, both traditional and social, in the near future. The decade on which the chapter focuses saw a resurgence of the dominance of political elites in the media. While promising at the outset, the reform efforts designed to free the Thai media from political intervention proved short-lived and superficial. Following the 1997 financial crisis and the subsequent consolidation of the media industry, business interests superseded reform ideals, and the further legislative and institutional change required to free the media from interference did not materialize. With media outlets on shaky financial ground, both business and political interests permeated the sector, as some media owners entered

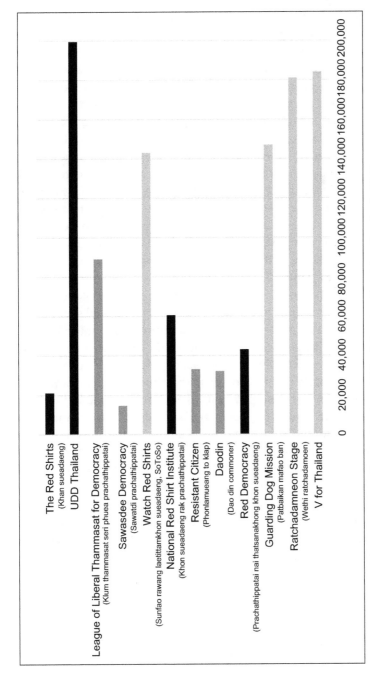

FIGURE 10.3   Political Pages/Groups and the Number of "Likes" that they Earned on Facebook, 2015

Note: Coded according to their political allegiance. Light grey: conservative-royalist; pro-PAD/PDRC/Multi-Coloured; Dark grey: pro-majoritarianism, pro-Thaksin; Black: pro-democracy/anti-coup, progressive.

Source: compiled from Facebook.

politics themselves and as political actors became media owners, further attenuating the space for independent media.

The Thaksin administrations from 2001 to 2006 were particularly hostile to opposition media. Political leaders used direct and indirect means to marginalize, censor and silence critics of the government and of their business interests. Opposition media became mobilized and deeply partisan, as some outlets became active players in the movement that would oust Thaksin from power. Following the September 2006 coup, new institutions to govern the media in ways that strengthened the position of the state and the military vis-à-vis the media came into existence. The inter-coup period saw the continued suppression of media freedom and the dominance of military and state elites, in spite of the return of electoral democracy; at the same time, partisanship in the media deepened. The media faced a near complete blackout by the time the military declared martial law as a prelude to the May 2014 coup, demonstrating the ability of political elites to "shut off" the media at will.

Political influence, especially from the military and its conservative-royalist allies, will continue to permeate both traditional and social media in the post-May 2014 era. Social media, as tools for communication, have the potential to challenge conservative dominance of Internet governance. By virtue of being a free, fast, personalized and anonymous form of communication, social media can offer Thai Internet users new space for collective action with the potential to undermine state authority in cyberspace. Yet the power of social media to foster such change faces significant institutional constraints in Thailand. The most important obstacles to social media acting as a technology of liberation are the institutions created to limit Internet freedom, notably the CCA of 2007, whose amendment in 2017 further curtailed freedom of speech online. The amendment, according to a media watchdog, gives "unfettered authority" to the state to "restrict free speech, engage in surveillance, conduct warrantless searches of personal data and undermine freedoms to utilize encryption and anonymity" (Electronic Government Agency 2017). Furthermore, the lack of clarity concerning the kinds of content whose dissemination is prohibited leaves the power of "interpretation" in the hands of state authorities (Thai Netizen Network 2015b). Other institutions, such as the cybercrime police or the Cyber Scouts, will remain in place long after elections return to Thailand to ensure that the conservative-royalist agenda continues to permeate the Thai cyberspace.

Acknowledgements

We would like to acknowledge the Sydney Southeast Asian Centre at the University of Sydney for the funding provided to make this collaborative chapter possible.

Notes

1. For the purpose of this chapter, traditional media refer to such forms as television, radio, newspapers, magazines, newsletters and other print publications. Social media refer to forms of digital media that are personalized and networked. They include blogs, wikis, podcasts, picture/video/music-sharing sites and Web fora. Definitions are drawn from the Electronic Frontier Foundation (2009).
2. References to "political elites" include not only individuals in political office but also state actors in the political arena, such as the military.
3. This is a narrow analysis of partisanship of the media, only addressing the political dimension. McCargo (2000) looks at a broader definition of partisanship, which also includes the relationship between the press and commercial business interests.
4. See Chadwick (2006), Benkler (2006) and Shirky (2008).
5. This included representatives from the Thai Journalists Association and the Thai Broadcast Journalists Association, coinciding with the expansion of civil society organizations.
6. The Black May activists then pushed for a series of media reforms in the 1990s designed to open up space for a more independent media sector. It was during this time that academics, professional journalists and pro-reform activists sought to increase citizens' role in shaping policy on the mass media.
7. In Thai, "*wen tae doi asai amnat tam botbanyat haengkotmaichapho phuea raksa khwammankhong haeng rat*".
8. In Thai, "*wen tae chakratam nai rawang wela thi prathet yu nai phawa songkhram rue kanrop*".
9. Since Freedom House began its rankings in 1980, it has rated Thailand "free" only five times: in 1993, 1999, 2000, 2001 and 2002. Its methodology rates a country's level of press freedom with reference to the legal, political and economic environments and how conducive they are to media independence. For a full description of the methodology, see Freedom House (2015*b*).
10. Chuan Leekpai served as prime minister for a second time from September 1997 to February 2001.
11. The 1997 financial crisis particularly affected business-oriented press, whose

revenue relied heavily on business advertisements. For further discussion, see Pongpat (2017).

12. For example, Channels 5, 9, and 11.

13. This incident was referred to in the Thai press as the "iTV Rebellion"; see Thailand Political Database (2008).

14. For example, Kaewsruang Athipoh, an academic but also an active supporter of the PAD; Tepchai Yong, a reporter at *The Nation* who became well-known for reporting on corruption scandals during the Thaksin administration; and Apichart Tongyoo, who was a former press secretary of the Mahachon Party.

15. The channel was run by *The Nation* at the time; see Phongphiphat (2012).

16. In her blog post, she listed all of the cases relating to conflicts of interest concerning Thaksin, his party and his family business that she was investigating (Supinya 2005). She and the *Thai Post* eventually won the lawsuit.

17. For a list of some of Thaksin's early opponents, see Aim (2013*a*).

18. See Sondhi and Sarocha (2005*a*, 2005*b*, 2006) for a collection of publications of *Mueang thai raisapda* that outlined the key topics that were covered in the programme. There was a clear shift in Sondhi's attitude towards the government in 2005, when the programme became critical and negative.

19. An ABAC poll showed that one in three respondents in Bangkok followed this programme (*Positioning Magazine*, 5 December 2005).

20. One of the biggest rallies was the one held on 4 February 2006.

21. For example, Choemsak Pinthong — a former senator, public intellectual and talk show host — had been critical of Thaksin since 2002. He published a series of articles by academics, activists and respected individuals from different sectors who were critical of Thai Rak Thai policies in his book series *Ru than thaksin*, which ran to four volumes; see Choemsak (2004*a*, 2004*b*, 2004*c*, 2006).

22. Suriyasai Katasila, personal communication, 22 December 2012.

23. The media had taken a stance on opposing a government before, as for example during the Black May incident.

24. For a full list of groups that formed the People's Alliance for Democracy, see Aim (2013*c*).

25. This happened in spite of the fact that Sondhi was considered an "outsider" by other PAD leaders, who were all drawn from the civil society sector.

26. For further discussion, see McCargo (2005); the special journal issue edited by Michael K. Connors and Kevin Hewison, "Thailand and the "Good Coup" (2008); and Montesano, Pavin and Aekapol (2012).

27. For an extensive discussion of the Yellow Shirts, see the special journal issue edited by Erik Martinez Kuhonta and Aim Sinpeng (2014*b*), and Kengkij and Hewison (2009).

28. The PAD as a movement declined partly as a result of rifts among its leaders

and a gradual loss of public support, particularly once the Democrat Party assumed leadership of the government in December 2008.

29. In fact, the Thai name of this organization, *Khanakammakan prachachon phuea kanplianplaeng prathet thai hai pen prachathippatai thi sombun an mi phramahakasat songpen pramuk*, is more accurately rendered as the People's Committee for Absolute Democracy with the King as Head of State.

30. Following the 2014 coup, the name was changed to *"Fa wan mai"* (BLUESKYCHANNEL 2018).

31. Pitch Pongsawat (2010) discussed the issue of a double standard in the reporting on the PAD rallies and UDD rallies, arguing that coverage of the latter was negative and judgmental.

32. This list does not include media that do not fall neatly into the two camps, such as *Thai rat*, *Prachatai* and *Krungthep thurakit*, OK Nation, Isra News, and Thai PBS. For a reference list of "Red" media, see Muthita (2009), and, on "Yellow" media, see *Positioning Magazine* (5 November 2008).

33. Wira Musikaphong, Chatuphon Phromphan and Nattawut Saikuea (the "Trio") emerged as Red Shirt leaders through their talk and comedy show "Truth Today" (*Sam kloe*) in 2008. The programme was meant to mobilize Thaksin supporters to oppose the military-installed government and to continue the fight for justice. The show was initially broadcast on People's Television via satellite, and then via DTV. "Truth Today" was hugely popular and had a mass following, helping to raise the profile of the Trio.

34. For example, VoiceTV is run and managed by Thaksin's son, Panthongtae Shinawatra, and one of his daughters, Pinthongta Shinawatra.

35. See Freedom House annual reports on Thailand in the area of press freedom (Freedom House 2018).

36. There are several petitions and forums in opposition to the single gateway plan. This community on Facebook has nearly thirty thousand likes (Kamhaeng, n.d.).

37. For a full list of NCPO press releases, see National Council for Peace and Order (n.d.).

38. For the full iLaw report, see Sawatree et al. (2013).

39. For the full iLaw report, see Sawatree et al. (2014).

40. See examples of the discussion among Seri Thai Movement members on the issue of finding violators of the law on *lèse majesté* on their Web board Serithai Movement (n.d.) and Serithai Forum (n.d.).

41. There are two sources on CCA-related cases, those of the Thai Netizen Network and of iLaw. We found discrepancies in iLaw reporting and have chosen to use the Thai Netizen Network data.

42. Its website is BLUESKYCHANNEL (2018).

43. For example, Reformthai (n.d.).

44. For example, Lips Magazine (n.d.).

11

Thailand's Royal Democracy in Crisis

Thongchai Winichakul

Observers typically use one of two conventional discourses of democratization to explain the May 2014 coup in Thailand. First is the "vicious cycle" discourse that posits a repeated cycle of military coups, followed by new constitutions, and then general elections. The elected government proceeds to fail, whether because of challenges from the communists, challenges to the monarchy, corruption scandals or a combination of these factors. This failure leads to yet another coup. This discourse was most prevalent between the 1950s and the 1980s, when coups were more frequent. From 1992 to 2006, when electoral democracy was more stable, another discourse — that of "linear progress" — became more popular. This discourse characterized Thailand's history of democratization as one of linear progression beginning from the end of the absolute monarchy in 1932, with milestones such as the 1973 popular uprising that ended twenty-three years of military rule and the 1992 uprising that seemed to put military rule to rest.[1] However, the occurrence of two coups in less than ten years, in 2006 and 2014, undermined the second discourse and revived the idea of the vicious cycle as an explanation for the state of Thai democracy.

The two discourses have one thing in common: an understanding that democratization is the struggle against the military to entrench the supremacy of elections and civilian rule. This struggle is a common political experience for Thais, especially those born in the 1940s or somewhat later and coming of age in the late 1950s or the 1960s. Likewise, during the past fifty years, Thais have conventionally understood their monarchy as being "above" politics, always neutral in the ideological struggles and politicking between political parties and within the government.

By "monarchy", I mean a social institution and entity that is active in cultural, social, economic and political life, like any other institution or entity. Duncan McCargo (2005) shows that the "royal institution", as it is often called, is a network of non-monolithic groups and individuals whose interests rely on, and who derive legitimacy from, their varying associations with the king. This "network monarchy" is thus a larger entity than the king or even the palace. Nonetheless, as this chapter argues, the charismatic king himself was indispensable and indeed pivotal to the success or failure of this network monarchy.[2]

Scholars have argued that the 2006 and 2014 coups, in various ways, concerned the royal succession (Marshall 2014; Pavin 2014a, 2014b and 2015). The reign of King Bhumibol Adulyadej (1946–2016) was the source of privilege, patronage and power for monarchists. By the first decade of the twenty-first century, that reign was clearly coming to an end, while former prime minister Thaksin Shinawatra was, thanks to his wealth, power and popularity, perceived as a potential threat to the royalist elite in the post-Bhumibol era. In my view, these two coups were attempts by a coalition of royalists to secure control and influence over the succession.

But why did the succession matter so much to Thai royalists? For that matter, why does succession in countries with constitutional monarchies such as England, Denmark and Japan not lead to political crises like the one that engulfed Thailand during much of the first decade and a half of this century? To be sure, the legal procedures and frameworks for succession were not the problem, for they were clearly established. One might be prompted to think that the wealth of the Thai crown, which is among the richest in the world,[3] raised the stake of the succession considerably. This chapter argues that the power and relevance of the monarchy in the Thai political system is more important to the politics of succession than the wealth of the crown. For, while a constitutional monarchy in a democratic country may not enjoy effective political influence or economic relevance, let alone real authority or power, the same has certainly not been the case for Thailand under what I call "royal democracy".

Royal democracy is a form of guided democracy — an ostensibly democratic polity, but one in which the electorate and elected authority do not have substantive power because true power remains in the hands of the monarchic institution. The formal name for this system in Thailand, "the Democratic Regime with the Monarch as the Head of the State", is quite a revealing euphemism for a political system in which the formal parliamentary system comes under the authority of the unelected monarchy. The Thai monarchy is a political power bloc that has been active throughout modern history and that was able by the mid-1970s to establish a pattern of royal democracy. While previous studies have focused on the palace's interventions at various significant moments in Thai politics (McCargo 2005, pp. 503–14; Kobkua 2003, pp. 168–80), this chapter seeks to explain how royal democracy operated in an ostensibly normal democratic system, thanks primarily to royal hegemony entirely dependent on the charisma of King Bhumibol. It further asserts that the political turmoil in Thailand since 2006 has essentially been a crisis of royal democracy triggered by the challenge from electoral democracy and the end of the Bhumibol era. This chapter concludes with a discussion of the prospects of royal democracy and the possibility of praetorianism.

The History of Thailand's Royal Democracy[4]

Thailand's democratization process goes beyond the contest between military rule and a democratically elected administration. It also concerns the predicament of the monarchy's power and role in a democratic era, a predicament that has arisen from its "unfinished" transition from absolute monarchy after the revolution of 1932 (Ferrara 2015). For this reason, we cannot speak about democratization in Thailand without taking the monarchy into account.

As Ferrara (2012) has brilliantly explained, the revolution by the People's Party that ended the absolute monarchy in 1932 unravelled because of that group's compromise with the monarchists, which allowed the latter to reassert their power and led to counter-revolutionary moves in many forms, including a violent insurrection in 1933. By 1938, the monarchists' attempts at subversion had been quelled. Although the monarchy was not abolished, it was agreed that the king must be "above" politics in the sense that he must not involve himself therein, that he must refrain from politicking, as was stipulated in the 1932 constitution.[5] The rule of members of the People's Party lasted only fifteen years, from 1932 to 1947. As a result of the conflict within the People's Party before and during the Second World War, the monarchists were able to conspire with the army to topple the government with a military coup in November 1947. This coup paved the way for the monarchists' return to the circle of power, albeit as the less influential partner of the military for the next twenty-six years.

With Bhumibol's accession to the throne in 1946, the monarchists embarked on a long-term project to position the monarchy to play a role in a democratic setting. They needed to create a new monarchy, of a type that Thailand never had before, as part of their blueprint for a future royal democracy. They also laid down other foundations for royal democracy. First and foremost was the 1949 constitution, which stipulated that Thailand's political system was to be known as "the Democratic Regime with the Monarchy as the Head of the State", in a phrase coined by Seni Pramoj as chairman of the committee that drafted the 1949 constitution. This expression proved a euphemism for the royalist guided democracy that has operated under every Thai constitution since that time. Second, the 1949 constitution also created the Privy Council, the king's advisory body. Eventually, the Privy Council became a crucial mechanism for the actual operation of royal authority over elected authority. The 1949 constitution also provided for mechanisms to limit elected authority, such as the powerful appointed upper house. Third, in 1948, new legal provisions governing the Crown Property Bureau (CPB, *samnakgan sapsin suan phramahakasat*) were introduced. As we shall see later in this chapter, the authority to manage, make decisions about and have access to the crown's wealth was returned from the government to the monarchy. Finally, but importantly, this period marked the beginning of the reign of King Bhumibol, a successful personification of the ideal monarch who was groomed under the fecund conditions for the promotion of hyper-royalism in subsequent decades. Without the charismatic Bhumibol, the fortunes of royal democracy would have been different.

The actual construction of the new monarchy described above began in the early 1960s, on the one hand under the royalist military regimes of Sarit Thanarat (1958–63) and Thanom Kittikhachon (1963–73) and on the other as part of the United States government's anti-communist agenda. This agenda recognized the monarchy as the most potent politico-cultural weapon for counter-insurgency in Thailand (Handley 2006, pp. 135–79; Hyun 2014). Together, these regimes and Washington constructed a people's monarch, a popular figure who cared for and served the people and who became active in areas of public affairs that were not overtly political or ideological, including anti-narcotic programmes, care for upland minorities, agricultural and rural development, and education and welfare for the poor, especially in rural areas. As a result of the monarch's engagement in such social welfare programmes, the popularity of King Bhumibol and his family began to grow rapidly from the 1960s, becoming the basis for his cult of personality and for monarchical hegemony in subsequent decades.

The turning point for the monarchy was the popular uprising against military rule in 1973. The same event that saw a triumph for the people also marked the moment in which the monarchy attained political authority to match that of the military. On this occasion, the royal family, in casual dress, came out of its residence to show sympathy for the demonstrators who sought refuge inside the palace grounds. King Bhumibol's intervention to stop violence on the streets of Bangkok later that same day eventually became emblematic of the monarch's political role as a benevolent stabilizer, even if he did not intervene in the massacres of 1976 and 2010. The symbolism of the 1973 display of sympathy and of royal intervention marked the beginning of the era of royalist guided democracy.

Between 1973 and 1992, parliamentary democracy took root in Thailand, albeit under the auspices of the powerful military (Likhit 2003, pp. 213–95). During this period, however, observers of Thai politics tended to overlook the position of the palace, and to see it as being in fact "above" the contention between the military and popular democracy. This position allowed the monarchy to appear as a source of legitimacy and as such a determining factor in major political issues that the success or failure of a coup often depended on the palace's blessing. With the adroit positioning of the monarchy as neutral and beyond politics, its political leverage rose rapidly, while the military lost legitimacy as a political force. If the 1991 coup signified the last hurrah of military dominance in Thai politics, the 1992 popular revolt marked its end. The widely circulated picture of King Bhumibol on a sofa with the leaders of the junta and the revolt prostrating themselves obediently before him came to symbolize the power relations in Thai politics in the decades that followed. Growing in popularity and legitimacy since 1973, the dominance of the monarchy was now unquestioned.

During the 1980s and 1990s, royalism and liberalism in Thailand appeared to be growing in tandem, prompting Connors (2007) to describe it as an era of "royal liberalism". However, the reality was that electoral democracy came under the benevolent guidance of the monarchy and prospered as long as it did not pose a threat to the latter. Moreover, when it did, putative royal liberalism quickly dissipated (Connors 2008), because the relationship between royalism and democracy was a marriage of convenience, if not a mirage.

Royal Hegemony or Modern *Barami*

The success of royal democracy relied primarily on royal hegemony — on, that is, consensual leadership and uncoerced compliance (Kasian 2016, pp. 226–28). That hegemony was founded on the cultural capital of the monarchy as modified to suit modern and democratic values. The main repository of the monarchy's cultural capital has been the royal-nationalist ideology, which attributes every virtue of Siamese civilization to the monarchy. Formulated under the absolute monarchy in the 1900s–1920s period, this ideology and the accompanying historiography have been modified. Nevertheless, they have remained unchallenged, even after the 1932 revolution (Thongchai 2011). Drawn from this ideology, the two particularly significant intertwining elements that formed the basis for royal hegemony were the cult of King Bhumibol and hyper-royalist culture. A king is divine according to Hindu-Buddhist tradition. He possesses the great moral power — *barami* in Thai, *parami* in Pali, *paramita* in Sanskrit — that is innate to an extraordinary person who has achieved supremely virtuous accomplishments, or "the Great Perfections", in a previous life (Jory 2016). This stock of supreme *barami* elevates him to the status of monarch in this life. It places him above the need for office, law, social contract or any social relations. It enables someone like the late King Bhumibol to accomplish what an ordinary person cannot.[6] This idea of divine kingship with *barami* survived the transition to modernity, as it had been transformed to suit contemporary conditions. King Chulalongkorn, was, for example, a modernizer, and yet he is worshipped as a divine king even in the present day (Stengs 2009). The *barami* of the monarchy was thus adjusted to suit contemporary conditions.

Allegedly based on old Siamese conceptions, and as Prince Dhani Nivat proposed in 1946, kingship should have three characteristics: sacredness, righteousness and the quality of being the people's king. Beginning with a quotation from Malinowski about the lasting value of a sacred tradition, the prince described the ancient Hindu concept of divine kingship as a pillar of Siamese monarchy. The ideal Buddhist king is a *Dhammaracha*, literally a "righteous king", who assumes power by "election" or popular consent, following the Buddhist concept of *Mahasammati*, or the Great Elect (Dhani 1946, p. 101). This king must, however, observe the ten virtues for kingship — in Thai, the *thotsaphitratchatham* — in order to acquire a high level of *barami*. Dhani argued strongly that Thai kings never claim to be high priests or highly divine figures. Instead,

> ... the old Thai have their own traditions of kingship. The monarch was of course the people's leader in battle; but he was also in peace-time their father ... [who] was accessible to his people, for we are told by an old inscription that in front of the royal palace of Sukhothai there used to be a gong hung up for people to go and beat upon whenever they wanted personal help and redress. The custom survived with slight modifications all through the centuries down to the change of regime in 1932. (Dhani 1946, p. 94)

The last of these elements was quite novel. In order to frame the relationship between king and his subjects, Dhani looked to a stone inscription allegedly dating from the thirteenth century, which told the story of the benevolent King Ramkhamhaeng of Sukhothai who cared for his people as would a father. Royalist intellectuals of the time strongly propagated this idea of the Sukhothai monarch, including during the drafting of the 1949 constitution (Santisuk 2012, pp. 173, 203–4). Over the years, they developed this virtue further until it became central to the cult of King Bhumibol.[7]

Such virtues and the revival of many Brahmanic rituals went into weaving a public persona for the king from the late 1950s onward (Thak 2007, pp. 210–14; Bowie 1997, pp. 87–91). During King Bhumibol's long reign, the monarchy became more sacralized, even as it grew increasingly tied to Thai capitalism at the same time (Gray 1986; Jackson 2010). However, the cornerstone of Bhumibol's modern version of *barami* was his persona as a Dhammaracha and as the people's king, both of which were captured in his coronation dictum in 1950: "I shall reign by righteousness for the benefits and happiness of the Siamese people."[8] Note the words righteousness (*dharma*) and people or masses (*mahachon*, literally "people at large") in the same sentence. True to his word, King Bhumibol initiated thousands of royal development projects aimed at helping the poor, particularly minorities and those in rural areas (Chanida 2007), thereby shoring up his reputation as the people's monarch.

The proliferation of television and print media from the early 1960s onwards was also vital for the promotion of the cult of King Bhumibol. Ordinary Thais witnessed the selfless monarch with their own eyes, often with maps, pens or a notebook in hand; a camera and sometimes a pair of binoculars around his neck; complete with beads of sweat on his face. In an era in which "politics has become (visually) representational" (Morris 2009, p. 124), the frequency of the king's visibility and the effects of such spectacles as royal ceremonies went into the making of the cult of a semi-divine Bhumibol.

Meanwhile, political factors provided the right conditions for the growth of the Bhumibol cult. First, after the 1973 uprising that toppled the military dictatorship, the political legitimacy and power of the military was in relative decline. Nevertheless, not since 1932 has the Thai monarchy exercised power and influence free from the shadow of the army. Second, with the success of revolutions in Indochina in 1975, the monarchy truly believed that it was under serious threat from communism. Third, in the wake of the 1973 uprising, the Thai radical movement grew rapidly. Not only were the communist states now on Thailand's eastern borders, but in the royalists' view they were also right in its front- and backyards. Under these conditions it was urgent for the monarchy to exert its influence to fight communism. The conjuncture of these supporting factors and putatively urgent needs resulted in what I call "hyper-royalism".

As I have elaborated elsewhere (Thongchai 2016, pp. 7–11), the characteristics of hyper-royalism are as follows. First, it is the permeation of royalism in everyday life and the increased demand for the expression of loyalty to the monarchy. Extravagant public displays of royal symbols and platitudes are encouraged and found everywhere. The annual celebrations for royal birthdays, which began in the 1960s, have been reinforced by the added significance of the king and queen as the figurative parents of all Thais.[9] Second, hyper-royalism indulges in exaggeration and exaltation. Members of the royal family are often touted by royalists and their acolytes as being at the top of every field, from sports, fashion and acting to scientific research, academic achievement, the arts and social service. Hyperbole becomes normative; eulogies become truth. Academics may earn recognition and promotion by composing hagiographies of the king and royals.[10] Every virtue in the nation must be credited to the king. Even the winning of an Olympic medal was attributed to Bhumibol's *barami*.[11]

Third, the control of public discourse on the monarchy protects hyper-royalism. Section 112 of the Thai Criminal Code reads, "Whoever defames, insults or threatens the King, Queen, the Heir-apparent or the Regent shall be punished with imprisonment of three to fifteen years." Scholars have observed that this law is problematic in every aspect, from procedure, enforcement and severity of punishment to its interpretation (Streckfuss 2011). The ambiguity of the law makes it impossible to know what is or is not permissible and, as a consequence, a climate of fear is pervasive. When royalism is akin to religion, detractors become blasphemers.

Fourth, and crucially, the manufacture and encouragement of hyper-royalism have not been exclusive to the palace or state. Civil society has actively involved itself in the production and circulation of hyper-royalism while participating in the suppression of critics of the monarchy. Hyper-royalism is not simply manipulated by an Orwellian state. It is a public culture. Reverence rooted in royal hegemony is not limited to the royal family but also extended to members of the Privy Council, judges, palace associates and even royal pets. However, hyper-royalism is never absolute. The ridiculous exaltations, coupled with the suppressive law, have merely pushed unspeakable views underground. Gossip about royalty is widespread and parallels hyper-royalism. Hyper-royalism breeds anti-monarchism (Thongchai 2014, pp. 97–98).

Royal Democracy at Work

Royal democracy has not been another form of absolute monarchy. It is democracy in which the elected government and legislature ostensibly operate normally but in which in reality the power of the elected bodies is restricted by various means to parameters prescribed by the monarchy. A government's popular mandate is valued as long as it remains within the boundaries drawn by the monarchy. After all, the monarchy needs an effective manager to run the state under its guidance, prompting the chairman of the Privy Council once to liken the elected government to a jockey who rides but does not own the horse (*MGR Online*, 14 July 2006).

The royalists' and other elites' distrust of the elected authority and their distaste for populist politicians can be traced back over a century to powerful kings and princes who argued that democracy was not appropriate for Siam because people trusted the king (Chulalongkorn 1989, pp. 131–32)[12] and were thus not ready for a representative government (Batson 1974, p. 18). The public generally perceives politicians as corrupt and self-interested (Thongchai 2008, pp. 24–27). The pervading sentiment among royalists and members of the elite is that ordinary people remain uneducated and ignorant, and therefore vulnerable to deception by politicians. The country required guidance on the part of moral or "good" people, especially the monarchy.

With its hegemony in place from the 1970s onwards, the monarchy has exercised power over state affairs in spite of the absence of formal authority to do so. Critics have usually pointed to its occasional political interventions, especially the palace's support of coups and the appointments of men close to King Bhumibol as prime minister at critical times, such as in 1973, 1976 and 1992. In fact, the monarchy's political actions have gone beyond these interventions. They have extended to the exercise of informal authority and influence over the administrative system. Nonetheless, even when such interventions have been made known to the public, they have usually been seen positively as a moral power reining in a corrupt government. When faced with royal intervention, the elected authority has usually complied. The channels for advice, guidance and interference from "above" have been built into the formal system of administration by law and custom. In other words, royal democracy is a political system that integrates the informal power of the monarchy, as an institution "above" the elected authority, into the regular political system. Over the years, the forms, issues and frequency of the monarchy's exercise of informal authority have varied according to changing situations. The primary functionaries serving the monarchy have come from the army, particular parts of the bureaucracy, the judiciary and, at the top, the Privy Council. The roles and significance of various functionaries may vary over time, but they have not strayed far from the arrangements described below.[13]

The Army

The Thai Army has been the key to the monarchy's power over the elected authority and bureaucracy. Since 1973 the palace has been actively involved in the appointment of almost every army commander-in-chief. Although the palace's choice has not always prevailed, every army chief must at least meet the palace's approval. This approval is often by proxy. General Prem Tinsulanon, the palace's choice for army chief in 1978–80 and former prime minister (1980–88), has been a member of the Privy Council since 1988. Prem, in representing the palace, has had a say in the selection of the country's army chiefs ever since the early 1980s. Every year before the annual reshuffling of the top army commanders, the top brass of the armed forces would pay him a visit; this practice does not seem to be perceived as a political transgression or conflict of interest.

Nevertheless, the relationship between the monarchy and the armed forces goes deeper than the former's control of the chiefs of the latter's service branches. Bhumibol long maintained an interest in the well-being and honour of the military. King Bhumibol renamed the Army Cadet School in 1948 to associate the school and the army with the great King Chulalongkorn. From Army Cadet School (*rongrian nai roi thahan bok*), it became and remains the Chulachomklao Royal Military Academy (CRMA, *rongrian nairoi phra chunlachomklao*). King Bhumibol also continued a tradition dating to 1928 in which each graduate from the various military schools received a sword from the king himself.[14] Even when King Bhumibol was in hospital, the tradition was upheld by Princess Sirindhorn, who had been professor at the CRMA since 1980.[15] Most, if not all, of the graduates of the academy who have since risen to senior army posts in that time were once her students. In a country in which teachers are revered, the importance of having the most respected member of the royal family other than the king himself as a teacher has enormous significance. In return, since 1961 the Thai armed forces have organized ceremonies each year to swear allegiance to the throne (Thak 2007, p. 210), and there is no comparable ritual for the state or the nation. Since the ascendency of the monarchy from the 1970s onwards, the military has promoted its guardian status in line with the ideology that the nation and monarchy embody each other. Hyper-royalism does not diminish the significance and honour of the armed forces, but it does put them in a position of subservience to the monarchy. When the political crisis intensified in 2006, the military publically declared quite bluntly that they were "soldiers of the king".[16]

The Bureaucracy

The monarchy has influence over three basic facets of the bureaucracy; namely, personnel, policy and programmes, and budgets. Apart from military chiefs, the monarchy, in the broad sense, usually secures personnel in a number of key positions within the bureaucracy that on the one hand serve the monarchy's needs and on the other keeps the elected authority in check. While my informants stressed that these positions may vary depending on the monarchy's needs at the time, some of them are mainstays, such as those of the top bureaucrats in the Ministry of Foreign Affairs, the Ministry of Interior, and the Ministry of Agriculture. The director of the Irrigation Department was normally King Bhumibol's man, too — vital to many royal projects, including the construction of dams and water management. The holders of other positions whose incumbents were necessary to similar projects also tended to be close to the late king. The interests of particular members of the royal family in areas outside politics have sometimes been a reason for intervention in high-ranking appointments. As revealed in the scandalous purges of the unwanted members of the entourage of the then crown prince in early 2015, many members of that entourage occupied high positions in the army and the police force. The three informants who were former cabinet ministers noted that these appointments were rarely the result of direct or explicit commands. Rather, suggestions, hints and signals from members of the Privy Council, and occasionally from King Bhumibol or other members of the royal family themselves, were more common. Ministers from the ranks of elected members of parliament would comply most of the time.

An elected government must also come to terms with ongoing public programmes in the bureaucracy. These include several thousand royally initiated projects and those initiated by government agencies that are trying to associate themselves with the network monarchy. Thailand remains a bureaucratic polity to the extent that the opportunity for an elected government to introduce new policies is limited. In fact, some elected governments, such as those led by the Democrat Party, have preferred to abide by the decisions of the bureaucratic establishment and only to implement new policies or programmes that would not disrupt the normal business of the bureaucracy. In other words, under the parameters of guided democracy, it has been the bureaucracy that runs the administration rather than the other way round.

The Thaksin administration (2001–6) attempted to implement several new policies for various purposes, many of which unsettled the establishment. A good example was the effort on the part of the Thaksin government to change the status quo in the administration of the Malay-Muslim-majority southern border provinces, with its serious consequences (McCargo 2005, pp. 514–16).[17] The government also tried to alter the century-old system of centralized administration. Whether the new policies of the Thaksin government benefitted the people is for debate elsewhere. The point here is that senior bureaucrats did not like the Thaksin administration (GotoKnow 2006) because, in the words of Pasuk and Baker (2009), it "began to change [the] operating methods and culture" (p. 173) of the "deadweight of bureaucracy" (p. 354), trying to "transform the bureaucracy by reorientation to business thinking and methods (p. 355)". As one of my informants observed, officials set up road blocks to hinder the government's efforts, mainly by citing legal and budgetary limitations. The reshuffling of personnel was therefore unavoidable for an administration determined to fulfil its promises to the electorate. This situation led to increasing tension between the elected authorities and the establishment.

The monarchy's unmatched hegemony and the weight of authoritarian rule have meant that the bureaucracy usually complies with the initiatives of the monarchy and the military. In addition, the palace has created a number of mechanisms to coordinate government agencies across several ministries to serve its purposes, such as the Office of the Royal Development Projects Board (RDPB, *samnakngan khanakammakan phiset phuea prasan ngan khrongkan an nueang ma chak phraratchadamri*). This mechanism has been placed virtually above government authority. Direct palace intervention has not been unusual either. One incident illustrates the palace's power over the bureaucracy. In 1995, a major flooding disaster occurred in Bangkok, during the government of the elected Prime Minister Banharn Silpa-archa. In response, King Bhumibol called a televised meeting of relevant top bureaucrats from various agencies and instructed them on how to tackle the disaster. These bureaucrats listened obediently, but more telling was the conspicuous exclusion of elected ministers, the formal bosses of these bureaucrats, from the meeting (Somkiat 2011). This episode was a rare occasion in which the palace's intervention was publicized. The public's response to the televised episode was overwhelmingly positive, glorifying the direct intervention as evidence of the monarch's care for his people. According to two informants whom I have interviewed, similar meetings and direct communication between the palace and government offices have often taken place without being televised.

The bureaucracy's budget reflects its programmes and priorities. Apart from salaries, which make up the biggest portion of that budget, the rest of the funds are allocated to existing programmes, as discussed above. This leaves little for new policies initiated by elected governments, leading them to seek external sources of funds. The Thaksin government funded (or planned to fund) its prime projects; namely, the village funds scheme, thirty-baht medical services, the "One Tambon, One Product" project and the high-speed train project, among others, by seeking extra-budgetary resources and by reforming the budgetary system. However, in the words of Suehiro (2014, p. 299), "Thaksin's ambitious reforms ultimately collapsed because they were too radical and too speedy for all the people including the royalists, the military, government officers, as well as conservatives." In contrast, according to the World Bank, in the same period (2001–5), Thailand spent 7–8 per cent of its annual budget on the military. After the 2006 coup, the military's budget rose even more sharply, growing by 135 per cent during 2006–15 (Saksith 2014). Meanwhile, Thailand's monarchy is one of the most expensive in the world, with costs not significantly lower than the British monarchy in spite of the difference in the sizes of the Thai and British economies and the annual budgets of the two countries.[18] Finally, it should be noted that the palace has rarely intervened in economic or budgetary matters. Nevertheless, during the crisis that has gripped Thailand since 2006, a number of important government economic policies and projects have been disrupted or cancelled by the so-called independent bodies discussed below.

The Judiciary

The judiciary has played an active role in working against elected governments since 2006, if not earlier. Prasong (2008) has documented how *tulakanphiwat* — the judicialization of politics or, more neutrally, judicial review — became a crucial and politically transformative factor in the last decade. The judiciary took unprecedented action against the elected government before the 2006 coup, toppled two governments in 2008, protected leaders of the royalist movement, and assured the apparent end of Thaksin's political career. It did so not only through decisions in several court cases that were politicized but also through the new powers given to them by the 2007 constitution. That charter gave the top echelon of the judiciary and other pseudo-judicial bodies mentioned below enormous authority over the selection and accountability of elected officials.

It is surprising that the Thai judiciary largely escaped the attention of political observers and scholars alike before 2006. There are a small number of studies of the Thai judiciary, but they are not very useful to an effort to understand how the judiciary has assumed such a prominent role. On the one hand, some scholars suggest that the modern Thai judiciary, founded under the absolute monarchy, survived the 1932 revolution almost unscathed (Dressel 2012, p. 82). On the other, some people in the legal profession argue that the People's Party tried to change the judiciary so that it would suit the democratic era by establishing both Thammasat University as a new centre of legal education and a new judicial commission in 1934.[19] According to this latter view, royal hegemony over the judiciary began after 1947, especially under the influence of Sanya Thammasak, one of the most influential figures in the history of the Thai judiciary, who was the permanent secretary of the Ministry of Justice in 1953–58, president of the Supreme Court in 1963–67 and a member of the Privy Council in 1968–2002. He served as chairman of the Privy Council in 1975–98.[20]

Members of the judiciary believe in their special relationship with the monarchy because, in the words of Sanya that became a maxim for judges, the judiciary acts on behalf (or in the name) of the monarch.[21] King Bhumibol also gave them special honours and privileges that no other state agency received. For instance, every judge had an audience with Bhumibol at the start of his or her career to receive his or her robes from the monarch, a practice continued even during the king's illness in his final years.[22] Therefore, judges believe that they are superior to the elected authority and to ordinary people, a belief generally shared by the Thai public. Such institutional practices undermine the basic principle of the separation of powers among the executive, legislative and judicial branches. Drawing legitimacy from the monarchy, members of the Thai judiciary believe that it should be completely immune to the elected authority and, as it turns out, that it is in fact completely independent from, and not accountable to, the public. Even elected figures, as I found during recent research, believe that they should not be involved in the affairs of judges. That the judiciary is not accountable to the people has never been an issue in Thailand. Moreover, as a consequence of royal hegemony, the late king long made all appointments, even to the lower courts.

The common perception that politics is dirty and politicians are corrupt is often amplified by the contrast between elected institutions and more noble ones endowed with moral power, such as the monarchy and the judiciary. Therefore, in the middle of the tense political crisis of mid-2006, King Bhumibol advised the Thai judiciary to intervene in order to bring about a resolution. It was an unprecedented historical moment. At the time, the Thaksin government had dissolved the parliament amidst widespread dissatisfaction embodied in some of the biggest anti-government movements in the country's history. It seemed probable that an election would assure Thaksin's return to power. However, the polls of 2 April were highly controversial in many ways. The result was a pervasive legitimacy crisis, and political deadlock. During an audience with new judges in April 2006, and in an intervention that no one had anticipated, Bhumibol said,

> Right now, it is the worst crisis in the world.... [I] ask the judges to help. People have hope in the judiciary ...[that] the judiciary is uncorrupted and knowledgeable.... If the country does not follow the rule of law,... it will not survive.... The judges should do something urgently. Otherwise, the country may fall. (Prasong 2008, p. 32)

The judiciary took this advice to heart, initiating a series of unprecedented actions. Between 2006 and 2014, Thai courts, including the Constitutional Court, which is strictly speaking not a normal part of the judiciary but has been treated as such,[23] nullified two elections, protected two anti-election movements, disqualified two prime ministers, dissolved five political parties, banned 224 politicians from political activities, obstructed governments' policies, persecuted elected leaders for following their election promises, and more (Prasong 2008). The 2007 constitution gave the judiciary the unprecedented power of having representatives on the committees charged with selecting the members of the Constitutional Court, the National Anti-Corruption Commission, the Election Commission, the Senate and other bodies. The 2016 constitution retains this special judicial power. The allegedly clean, superior and inviolable stature of Thai judges lends them the moral credibility to oversee the political system, but they are highly political precisely because they are perceived as non-political.

Independent Bodies

Another set of mechanisms that have acted to limit the power of the elected authority are the so-called "independent" bodies, such as the National Anti-Corruption Commission, the Ombudsman, the Election Commission and the National Human Rights Commission. They were either created under the 1997 constitution or made more powerful than previously under the terms of that charter. The goal was to enable them to rein in and hold elected governments accountable and have authority previously belonging to elected governments, such as for the supervision of elections. The Constitutional Court, though considered part of the judiciary, is one of these independent bodies. While good governance is the ostensible reason that such bodies should be autonomous from elected authorities, they have in fact been used by those "above" politics to topple several elected governments since 2006 and to derail democratization efforts (Kasian 2015). The 2007 constitution made the judiciary responsible for the selection of the members of these bodies, thus creating a loop of unelected, unaccountable individuals proclaimed clean, moral and "above" politics. Besides, despite the suspension of constitutions in the aftermath of recent coups, these independent bodies have been authorized by the regimes that took power after those coups to continue their operations. They are due to play their intended roles under the 2016 constitution and as long as royal democracy endures.

The Privy Council

The main mechanism of royal democracy has been the Privy Council. Established in its current form in 1949, though at the time with a more limited role than in the last decades of King Bhumibol's reign (Somchai 2015, pp. 15–48), the Privy Council expanded its role and spread its informal authority, especially from 1991 (Thanapol and Chaithawat 2015, pp. 664–67). We may get an idea of the areas in which the Privy Council has had keen interest by examining the profiles of the last nineteen councillors under the reign of King Bhumibol (Privy Council 2011).[24] They comprised experts in military and security affairs, foreign affairs, legal matters, water management and irrigation, and probably economics, but with a focus on the crown's business. It seems that these are the areas to which the Privy Council has paid close attention. Only a few councillors have lacked expertise in these areas, including a former university president and, more interestingly, five council members known to have had conflicts with the Thaksin government. Two of them were appointed to the council almost immediately after being fired from their positions by Thaksin (Thanapol and Chaithawat 2015, pp. 68–69). After Bhumibol died, the members of the

Privy Council resigned. King Vajiralongkorn reappointed some of them, including Privy Council chairman General Prem, and appointed several new members with military backgrounds.

Officially, the Privy Council's role is to "deliberate and submit its views on all matters in which the government requests the king's signature" (Grossman and Faulder 2011, p. 319). As described by one of the councillors, the council's responsibilities seem routine and non-political, including overseeing royal projects and representing the king at various functions (ibid., pp. 319–22). In reality, at least in the last few decades of Bhumibol's reign, the council's tasks expanded to include the supervision of royal democracy. According to my informants, who confirm political gossip, the Privy Council has scrutinized important appointments, including those of military commanders-in-chief, permanent secretaries of ministries, other high-ranking positions in the bureaucracy and all of the judges of the high courts. The council has also communicated with government offices on various matters and carefully examined the laws that have passed the legislature for the king's signature. In practice, the government, judiciary and legislative offices have worked with the Privy Council regularly before state matters have been submitted for the king's signature. In other words, the Privy Council may influence such state matters by offering advice or sending signals to government offices in order, as it is often said, to avoid situations that might "irritate His Majesty".[25] The relevant government bodies have usually complied in order to avoid unnecessary trouble. In this way, the Privy Council has virtually had the power to endorse or to block important decisions taken by the government.[26]

Little publicly available information sheds light on the inner workings of the Privy Council, apart from the fact that it has held weekly meetings and that it worked closely with King Bhumibol. We have not known, for instance, when councillors were expressing their own opinions, acting on their own interests or on behalf of the late king. Such ambiguity, a characteristic of the operation of the network monarchy through a "politics of fudge and obfuscation" (McCargo 2005, p. 506), has worked to their advantage. It has given authority to their words and actions in the eyes of the public. Recently, many people have misunderstood that the *lèse majesté* law also protects the members of the Privy Council.[27] These advisors have thus become members of the extended royal family.

Direct interventions from the monarchy have not been limited to occasional critical issues. As a matter of custom, the prime minister of every government, elected or otherwise, was scheduled to have an audience with King Bhumibol at least once a month, during which royal advice would be offered directly to the premier. This advice might come in the form of mere guidance, or as specific and concrete instructions on particular projects and political decisions.

The Crown Property Bureau

Another important mechanism of royal democracy has been the Crown Property Bureau. The emergence of the CPB in its current form probably began with the creation of its legal framework in 1948. This framework returned control of the bureau to the monarchy; it had been under government control since the 1932 revolution (Pharut 2014, pp. 188–98). According to the 1948 CPB Act, the king has the power to appoint the majority of the CPB board and its director. Furthermore, the use of CPB resources and income is totally at the discretion of the king (Porphant 2015, pp. 18–19). The CPB Act also created a distinctive legal status exclusive to the CPB as a juristic person that is not a government agency, not a state enterprise, and not a private business or a public company (Pharut 2014, pp. 200–203; Somsak 2014). This unique status ultimately freed the CPB from government and public scrutiny, even as it gave advantages and privileges to the CPB in its expansion of business and power from 1948 to 1997 (Porphant 2014, pp. 262–307). The CPB also benefitted in questionable ways from the support of the government and taxpayers after the 1997 financial crisis (Porphant 2014, pp. 323–24, and 2015, pp. 26–27).

The CPB is one of the most powerful capitalist entities in the country, if not the most powerful. Although it was not the personal property of King Bhumibol, its resources and incomes could be used at his discretion, totally free from government or public accountability.

Others

Last, but also very important, is the royalist network in civil society. As mentioned earlier, public participation in and production of royalism are important elements of hyper-royalism. Perhaps ideologically and also for political and material reasons, any association with the royals has been beneficial. This subject is enormously complex and it awaits further study. Suffice it to say, however, that the royal network in civil society grew to be extremely extensive during King Bhumibol's reign. It reached perhaps into almost every quarter of the public sphere. The royalist network has also been strong in educational institutions and academic circles, the healthcare professions, the arts and culture community, journalism and the media and even — perhaps especially — among non-governmental organization activists. The nodes of royalist power extend throughout Thailand's social relations.

In addition, this extensive network has not been created by the monarchists alone. Civic groups love royal connections. They have become part of the network voluntarily, and for their own benefit. However, like other aspects of hyper-royalism, it has been ambiguous and unclear whether the royalism of this widespread network has been for the monarchy as an institution, regardless of who the king is, or if it was only for Bhumibol. The years ahead will make the answer to this question clearer.

Royal Democracy in Crisis

Discourses on the Thai monarchy have usually conflated the individual and the institution. This is unsurprising since royal hegemony as described thus far, together with the length of Bhumibol's reign, created a fusion of the "monarch/y" (Thongchai 2014, pp. 81–82). Royal hegemony and royal democracy have been social and political institutions successfully built upon the foundation of one king's reign. However, this success has paradoxically foreshadowed their failure because these institutions have relied on an irreplaceable individual.

The political turmoil since 2006 reflected the predicament of royal democracy. At the root of the crisis were two conflicts. One pitted a changing society and changing political demography against an obstinate establishment, and the other the rural and semi-urban population that supported electoral democracy against the upper classes residing mostly in Bangkok that favoured royal democracy. Thaksin recognized these changes and took advantage of them to boost his personal popularity among large numbers of Thais, with resultant concern among the monarchists. The widespread saying, to the effect that "in four years Thaksin accomplished what the monarchy had been doing for forty years", is a personalization of the structural conflict, regardless of its truth.

Coinciding with Thaksin's rise was the deterioration of King Bhumibol's health. In the meantime, many Thais saw the king's chosen successor as a less-than-ideal monarch who might undermine the royal hegemony built up over years. The coups in 2006 and 2014 can be seen as efforts on the part of the monarchists to take control of the state and country in order to remove perceived threats to royal democracy.

Although the reason given by the military and its supporters for the latest two coups was to remove corrupt politicians, only a small number of them, particularly the Shinawatras, were targeted. The junta's targets also included non-politicians who fought to defend electoral democracy but who may not have necessarily supported the Shinawatras. Intellectuals, for example, faced repeated intimidation and were summoned by the junta that seized power in 2014 to "readjust their attitudes" because many of them had criticized the royalists for derailing democracy. Since the 2006 coup, the number of people charged with *lèse majesté* has skyrocketed, with the targeting becoming more indiscriminate, the lack of due process worse, the interpretations of the law more outrageous and the severity of punishment for a crime of expression more severe (Streckfuss 2014, pp. 119–30). Even an unfavourable comment on a historical king was punishable (*Prachatai*, 14 November 2013).[28] In addition, the government installed following the September 2006 coup enacted the Computer Crime Act of 2007 to suppress critics of the monarchy in cyberspace. However, instead of eliminating critics of the monarchy, this suppression generated more dissent. Critics are no longer limited to small circles of intelligentsia, as in previous periods; many common folk who used to hold royalist views now believe that the palace played an important role in supporting the most recent two coups, and probably also in the killings of 2010 (Thongchai 2014, pp. 92–97; Ünaldi 2014c).

The King Has Died, but Royal Democracy Has Not (Yet)

As I mentioned at the beginning of this chapter, the end of a monarch's reign should not have much impact on a country's political system if the monarchy has truly been uninvolved in politics. But this latter is not the case for royal democracy in Thailand. The military mounted the 2014 coup primarily to ready political conditions for the new king and post-Bhumibol royal democracy. After a long bout of illness, King Bhumibol died on 13 October 2016. Will his longstanding indispensability to royal democracy mean that the political regime over which he had presided in recent decades come to an end? What are the prospects for the Thai political system in Thailand during the reign of King Vajiralongkorn, Rama X?

Royalist guided democracy will continue. The system and the operations that have been institutionalized in recent decades will live on. Nevertheless, the whole system requires a monarch with a significant endowment of *barami* who can provide moral authority and legitimacy for its operations. Otherwise, it is likely to fall into decline. Despite the reputation of the new king, whether it will be possible to fashion for Vajiralongkorn a monarchy similar to that of his father remains an open question.

The military junta that seized power in 2014, which rules by fear and measures of severe suppression, succeeded in quelling its opponents and critics of the monarchy. The 2017 constitution assures that elected governments will be weak, fragile and under the control of unelected bodies; in this respect, it is even stronger than the 2007 constitution. The monarchy may have more power than at any time since the end of the absolute monarchy. This power will lie not only in the usual mechanisms of the monarchists but also in the monarchy's active involvement in politics, already exemplified by King Vajiralongkorn's demand for revision of the 2017 constitution. The government acceded to this demand. Royal democracy under that constitution appears set to drop the cloak of democracy and to show the face of a semi-monarchical kingdom openly.

Is this trend good for the country? How long can rule of this kind survive before the next political crisis takes place? How long will it last if the *barami* of the new king is inadequate to justify an authoritarian regime? Perhaps observers of Thai politics should take a look at the history of the former absolute monarchy and study the reason that the revolution to end it took place in 1932, twenty-two years after the death of King Chulalongkorn.

Acknowledgements

I am grateful to many people for the contributions that they have in many ways made to the research for this chapter, especially those who provided insights about the Thai legal and judicial systems and the informants (who asked not to be named) for their candid interviews. They are in no way responsible for the views, interpretations and analysis of this chapter.

Notes

1. This first discourse was initially articulated by Chai-anan Samudavanija (1982, pp. 1–5), who subsequently elaborated on it in extensive writings in Thai. These included a textbook (Chai-anan 1989) reprinted several times. He later modified the concept to some extent, after the notion of the vicious cycle became better known. The second discourse has been more common among those scholars and observers who believe in progress towards democratization, such as Suthachai (1993). Charnvit and Thamrongsak (2009, pp. 7–8) state that since the late 1980s, critical studies of history have helped observers to get over the idea of the vicious cycle.

2. This chapter uses the term "monarchy" in this sense throughout, in contrast with the monarch, king, queen, prince, princess, and so on for those individuals. Another term, the "palace", is ambiguous but justifiably so. It serves as a spatial metaphor to denote a collective.

3. See Serafin (2007). Similar rankings have appeared every year since the publication of this one.

4. This section draws on Thongchai (2008, pp. 12–21).

5. See article 11 of the 1932 constitution and the discussion on article 11 on the website of King Prajadhipok's Institute (2016).

6. Scholars of Theravada Buddhism and specialists on Thailand often translate *barami* as "charisma". I do not translate the word here because, as useful as a translation might be, the differences between the two concepts remain significant. Of relevance to this chapter are the following considerations. First, *barami* is generated from religious or moral acts, while charisma is not necessarily so. *Barami* is moral power. Second, while charisma enables a person to do something, the *barami* of a king engenders a kingdom's prosperity or calamity by itself, even when the king does not do anything. The state of his kingdom always reflects the level of his *barami*. Third, the two terms are based on the fundamentally different concepts of power/potency/authority and rule/state/polity. Charisma is modern, often Weberian, and *barami* pre-modern and Hindu-Buddhist.

7. This idea was so popular that military governments tried to claim to follow the father-children rule as well. It was the key concept framing the dictatorship of Field Marshal Sarit Thanarat during 1957–63 (Thak 1979, pp. 111–39). But Bhumibol and the monarchists exploited this concept much more successfully and over a much longer period than any soldier did.

8. This statement is widely known in Thailand and can be found in many sources. However, the translations can be slightly different. For example, Anand Panyarachun translates it as "We shall reign with righteousness …" (Grossman 2011, p. 11). The *Bangkok Post* has it as "We shall rule with righteousness …

happiness of the people of Siam" (Grossman 2009, p. 49). Note that "reign" and "rule" are translated from the Thai word *khrong*. The translation in the text above is my own.

9. In 1960, the Sarit government changed Thailand's national day from 24 June, the day of the revolution in 1932, to King Bhumibol's birthday on 5 December because 24 June was reportedly "inappropriate in many ways" (Grossman 2009, p. 111). Queen Sirikit's birthday celebration was also declared the annual "Mother's Day" in 1976 and King Bhumibol's as "Father's Day" in 1980. Birthday celebrations became grander at every tenth anniversary and every twelve-year cycle for each of them. See Thongchai (2016, p. 7) for a partial list of special royal occasions since 1976, each of which involved grand celebrations and year-long activities nationwide.

10. See, for example, Kanok (1988).

11. This neo-tradition started with the first Olympic gold medallist from Thailand in 1996, Somluck Khamsing. He told a story concerning the role of the king's *barami* in the form of the latter's picture in helping him win the medal. Once he knew that he won the boxing bout, he raised the picture of the king high above his head. Upon his return he had an audience with King Bhumibol and offered his gold medal to the king. Since then, most Thai Olympic medallists have raised a picture of King Bhumibol when they have won and offered their medals to the king on their return to Thailand, even though Bhumibol reportedly kept only Somluck's medal and returned the others to the Olympian winners. See Thai PBS News (2016) and *Clipdet yangni ko mi nailok* Channel (2016).

12. The original document was written in 1903.

13. Apart from documentary sources, the information in this section on how royal democracy operates comes from interviews with five informants. Three of them are former cabinet ministers, the fourth a senior judge on one of the highest courts in Thailand and the fifth a scholar with expertise on judicial affairs. Except the fifth, who is close to fifty years old, all of these informants are in their early sixties. All are male. I conducted these interviews — one session with each of the first three informants and two sessions with each of the other two — in October and December 2015. Whenever possible, I corroborated the specific information that a given informant shared either with another informant or other informants, with documentary sources or press reports bearing on the issue at hand, or with both.

14. King Prajadhipok (r. 1925–35) started this tradition at the army cadet school in 1928 (CRMA 1967, pp. 118–19). After a hiatus after 1932, King Bhumibol revived it for the first time in 1950, and continued it in all but just a few years. The records of the king's speeches show that Bhumibol presided over the ceremony at least since 1950 (Office of His Majesty's Principal Private

Secretary 2016). They are missing mention of such ceremonies only for 1962 and 1965, either because there was no ceremony or simply because no record has survived.

15. This information derives from an online search for news of these ceremonies in recent years. King Bhumibol presided over the ceremony until 2009. From 2010, Princess Sirindhorn did so on his behalf at the CRMA and the police academy, the then crown prince did the same for the air force academy and Princess Chulabhorn presided at the naval academy.

16. In Thai, "*thahan khong phra racha*"; the phrase is derived from the original "*thahan khong phrachaoyuhua*", which has the same meaning. It was used by General Prem, the chairman of the Privy Council, former army chief and former prime minister, on 14 July 2006. In his lecture at the CRMA during the tense weeks leading up to the 2006 coup, Prem implicitly rebuked Prime Minister Thaksin and asserted that the military's undivided loyalty belonged to the king, not to the government (*MGR Online*, 14 July 2006). The phrase subsequently gained great currency as the movement against Thaksin grew stronger.

17. It is believed that these included the outbreak of violence from 2004. King Bhumibol immediately appointed the ousted head of the special administrative entity responsible for the southern Malay-Muslim-majority provinces to the Privy Council.

18. According to Jotman (2008), the Thai Royal Household cost Thai taxpayers US$65 million in 2008, while the British monarchy cost British taxpayers US$74 million. See also the annual budgets for the Bureau of the Thai Royal Household (1997–2008) in *Fa diaokan* ("Ratchawong thi khachaijai phaeng thisut nai lok" 2008, p. 21), a translation from English of Jotman (2008). However, the total expenditure on the monarchy is difficult to compile because, in addition to the Royal Household budget, its expenses are also allocated to various government agencies. For instance, they appear in the police and defence budgets as expenses for security matters, and in the budgets of other ministries for various royal projects.

19. Two informants agreed on this point. See also "Phraratchabanyat rabiap kharatchakan tulakan phutthasakkarat 2477" (Thailand 1935); this law stipulated specifically that the founder of Thammasat University, Pridi Phanomyong, was a member of the judicial commission (ibid., p. 254). I have yet to study the impact of this law and how it was abolished.

20. This is a view shared by two informants, both members of the legal profession. Recent research by Kritphatchara Somanawat also supports this view; see the report on this research by *Prachatai* (26 April 2016). Sanya's career and his various roles in serving royalist democracy are too important for the brief account here to do justice to them. Suffice it to note that he was also on the committee investigating the death of King Rama VIII in 1946, was the dean

of the Faculty of Law at Thammasat University in 1968–71 and rector of the university in 1971–73. King Bhumibol hand-picked him to serve as prime minister in 1973–75. See Wimonphan (2003) for a hagiographic biography.

21. *"Kharatchakan fai tulakan ... thamngan nai phraboromaphithai phramahakasat"* said Sanya Thammasak in 1967, before his retirement as the president of the Supreme Court (Wimolphan 2003, p. 128).

22. This information derives from an online search for news in recent years. The new judges had an audience with King Bhumibol every year without exception, even when he was in hospital. The last time was on 14 December 2015, ten months before the king died.

23. Legally speaking, the Constitutional Court is one of the "independent bodies" created for the first time by the 1997 constitution. Unlike regular courts, its judges have expertise relevant to constitutional matters, but are not required to pass the examination for judges. Instead, they are selected by designated authorities, such as the Senate or a selection committee, and then appointed by the king. They also serve for a limited term, unlike judges, who serve until retirement. Nevertheless, this court has been treated as part of the judiciary. Perhaps the most important indication of this fact is that the members of the Constitutional Court attended audiences with King Bhumibol at the same time that the members of other branches of the judiciary did. For the history and recent roles of the Constitutional Court, see Mérieau (2016).

24. See also Thanapol (2015) and Thanapol and Chaithawat (2015) for brief profiles of every councillor since 1949, including the current ones, and for an analysis of the composition of the Privy Council. The collective profile of the council, and therefore its purview, has changed over time.

25. In Thai, *rakhai bueang phra yukonlabat*, literally "to irritate His Majesty's feet". There is no law regarding this transgression. Nonetheless, in an era of hyper-royalism, it has become one of the most serious transgressions that one may commit against the monarch.

26. Nidhi (2012, pp. 42, 45) shares this observation.

27. In 2007, after a demonstration against Prem, there were calls for the police to charge the leaders of the demonstration for violating article 112 (*Bangkok Post*, 5 April 2007). After the police declined to do so because the law did not cover the members of the Privy Council, some members of the Legislative Council proposed amendment of article 112 to cover them (*Prachatai*, 8 October 2007). However, the proposed amendment did not move forward. In July 2015, a year after the 2014 coup, the officer serving as army commander at the time announced that he would file a charge of violation of article 112 against Thaksin for his criticism of Prem. The charge was ultimately filed, though not under article 112.

28. See the full record of the court's deliberation in Supreme Court, Thailand (2015).

12

The Foreign Press and its Changing Perceptions of the Thai Monarchy

Puangthong Pawakapan

In comparison to its neighbours, Thailand has long given the impression of being a stable and unified country. Its monarchy has been seen as a vital force behind this stability, and when the Cold War ended the kingdom was expected to be a key driver of regional economic cooperation and a model for democratization in the region. However, the portrayal of Thailand in major foreign press outlets in this century has told a different story. It has depicted a country that has been in deep crisis since the *coup d'état* that overthrew the elected government of Thaksin Shinawatra in September 2006, with a solution still nowhere in sight. The coup that overthrew the Phuea Thai Party government in May 2014 swept away any fragile opportunity for Thailand carefully to build a functioning democracy.

Foreign press coverage of the leading players' role in the conflict has changed, too. This change has been most evident in journalists' increasingly frequent challenges to the long-accepted mainstream narrative of the Thai monarchy. Discussion of the role and objectives of traditional elites and of Thailand's draconian *lèse majesté* law began to appear more frequently, while news coverage of and op-ed articles on the royal institution became increasingly critical. The titles of articles in the foreign press that appeared after the 2006 coup themselves conveyed this newly critical tone towards the monarchy: "As Thai Monarchy's Power Wanes, King Still Revered" by the Associated Press (25 May 2010); "Thailand's King Sees His Influence Fading" in *The New York Times* (Mydans and Fuller 2010); "Thai Monarch Is a Factor in Dispute" in *The Wall Street Journal* (Wright 2014); "The King and Its Crisis: A Right Royal Mess" in *The Economist* (4 December 2008*b*); and "Thailand, A Coup, the Crown and the Two Middle Classes" in *The Diplomat* (Ünaldi 2014*a*).

While constructing itself in the image of traditional Buddhist-Brahmin kingship, the Thai monarchy has also presented itself as international and cosmopolitan. Since the era of King Chulalongkorn (r. 1868–1910), the institution has deeply and openly concerned itself with its international image, with successive monarchs fashioning themselves according to European norms. Western-style etiquette, dress, habitation, patronage and pageantry have long since made their way into the Thai court and been on display in both the domestic and international arenas (Peleggi 2002). The elegant images of King Bhumibol Adulyadej and his consort Queen Sirikit taken during their extensive overseas travels in the early 1960s have been reproduced continually at home, while the invitation to royalty from twenty-five countries to join the grand celebration of the late King Bhumibol's sixtieth year on the throne in June 2006 (Associated Press, 13 June 2006) reflected the Thai monarchists' yearning for global prestige. Moreover, monarchists have shown themselves to be sensitive to negative perceptions on the part of the international community, and they have tried to defend the royal institution through publications and interviews. The publication of a big, thick volume on *King Bhumibol Adulyadej: A Life's Work* (Grossman and Faulder 2011), prepared under the chairmanship of former prime minister Anand Panyarachun, represented just one attempt to refute Paul Handley's landmark book *The King Never Smiles: A Biography of Thailand's King Bhumibol Adulyadej* (Handley 2006).[1] Even before the appearance of the latter book, when monarchists learned that Yale University Press would publish Handley's work, they sent Bowornsak Uwanno, a royalist legal expert, to persuade the press to delay the publication until after the celebration of the sixtieth anniversary of the king's reign. Yale complied (McCargo 2007, p. 136).

This chapter examines the foreign press's changing perception of the Thai monarchy. With the passing of the much-loved King Bhumibol in October 2016 and the accession of his son to the throne as King Vajiralongkorn, Thailand now finds itself between the end of an era and the consolidation of a new reign. It is therefore opportune critically to survey the relationship between the foreign press and Thai royal politics. The chapter argues that Western journalists have covered the monarchists more unfavourably since the 2006 coup, and it examines both the ways that post-2006 developments have affected the foreign media's perception of the monarchy and the ways that the media have responded to the monarchists' arguments.

To begin, it is necessary to compare dominant perceptions of the foreign media towards the Thai monarchy before and after the 2006 coup. The sources for this study include articles in major foreign press outlets and interviews with eight Thailand-based foreign journalists and one security expert, whose identities Thailand's *lèse majesté* law leads the author not to disclose.[2]

Discourse on the Monarchy before the 2006 Coup

When the late King Bhumibol marked sixty years on the throne in June 2006, most if not all of the foreign media reporting from Bangkok embraced the official narrative of the monarch and monarchy as pure and benevolent. They described the king in positive terms such as "the most beloved and revered king", "the embodiment of the nation's spirit", "the supreme moral authority", "the peacemaker", "the unifying force", "the development monarch", "the pillar of stability" and "the democratic king". In short, the devoted monarch was a great blessing for the Thais. These terms of praise appeared in a collection, *The King of Thailand in World Focus*, edited by two veteran journalists, Denis D. Gray and Dominic Faulder, and published in new editions by the Foreign Correspondents' Club of Thailand in 2007 and 2008 to celebrate the sixtieth anniversary of the start of the king's reign (Gray and Faulder 2008, cover and pp. 53, 162, 185, 202, 204). This edition of the book carried 167 selected news pieces from 56 different media agencies around the world that had appeared between 1946 and 2006. This book was an updated edition of a 1988 volume published under the same title, which the club had released to celebrate the king's sixtieth birthday and his achieving the status of the longest-reigning monarch in Thai history. The collection represented "The world's longest-reigning monarch seen through the eyes of foreign journalists and photographers, spanning nearly eight decades of turmoil and triumph" (Gray and Faulder 2008, dust jacket). These books are clear and collective evidence of the positive view of King Bhumibol and his monarchy that the foreign press corps in Bangkok had long taken.

Although the image of the benevolent king had largely prevailed in the foreign press up to the first decade of the twenty-first century, not all of its reports agreed with the official narrative that the monarchy was "above politics" — a characterization usually taken to mean that the palace kept itself distant from the hustle and bustle of national politics and that the king himself remained neutral in his stance towards political parties and other contenders for power. The influence and political role of the monarchy had not gone unnoticed among Western journalists, especially during the Cold War, when the monarchists manoeuvred to restore the dominant role that they had lost with the end of the absolute monarchy in 1932. As early as the 1960s, foreign journalists pointed out rather openly that royal endorsement was the main source of legitimacy for governments, especially military regimes. These observations suggested that these journalists had more freedom and space than the Thai media to discuss the monarchy. This relative freedom was possibly due to the fact that their readers were mostly either not Thais or members of the Thai elite, and also to the fact that foreign news media penetration at the time was still limited. For example, in a 1960 article, "The King of Siam", *The Observer*, a British publication, explained to readers the history of tension between King Bhumibol and Field Marshal Po. Phibunsongkhram, who had been an obstacle to the former's public role until Field Marshal Sarit Thanarat seized power from Phibun in a coup in 1957. The king's good relationship with Sarit significantly transformed the role of the constitutional monarchy. The king's developing interest in politics and his new appeal to the populace became increasingly noticeable. The article concluded that "the basis of Thai rule therefore remains the King and the ruling military group" (*The Observer*, 17 July 1960). In 1966, *Time* magazine also illuminated the importance of the monarchy's powerful status to the country's security and stability. *Time* explicitly stated that the king had tacitly supported Sarit's military takeover. As a result, "partly in gratitude, partly [to] rally public support for his own rule, Sarit consciously set out to build up the image of the tall, spare king and his comely queen". Sarit and the king worked closely together to develop the country. By the time of the military regime of Field Marshals Thanom Kittikhachon and Praphat

Charusathian (1963–73), the growing power of the king made him "more than ever the throne behind the power". The king and queen, working as a team, took every opportunity to identify themselves with Thailand and its progress (*Time*, 27 May 1966).

Foreign journalists were well aware that the monarchy played an essential role in United States–sponsored anti-communist operations in Thailand. King Bhumibol's tireless visits to the countryside and the initiation and promotion of numerous rural development programmes were vital components of the monarchy's image. The royal institution became a symbol of "Thainess" and thus resistance to communist invasion.[3] The king's endorsement, in the form of speeches and overseas trips, also assisted in building up popular support for Thai military cooperation with the United States during the Second Indochina War. *Time* magazine pointed out that, because of the king's moral authority, his message to the Thai people regarding the importance of Thailand's military cooperation with the United States during the war helped to alleviate tension between Thais and the increasing numbers of American soldiers stationed at bases in the country. Even officials of the United States Information Service (USIS) in Bangkok, who were actively involved in anti-communist psychological operations and propaganda, concluded that "USIS funds could not be better employed than in spreading the likeness of His Majesty" (*Time*, 27 May 1966).

Students of Thailand have learned from the pioneering academic work of Thak Chaloemtiarana (1979) and Kobkua Suwannthat-Pian (2003) of the partnership among the king, Sarit, and the United States. Foreign journalists also observed from the 1960s onwards the effect of this relationship in transforming the role and power of the monarchy in Thai politics. For example, *The Observer* noted that the king appeared to be happier during Sarit's government than during Phibun's. "Relations between government and king eased. Consultations between them became more frequent. The stifling atmosphere of the past lifted and the King began to loosen up" (*The Observer*, 17 July 1960). Another matter that the foreign press invariably emphasized was King Bhumibol's six decades of unfaltering commitment to improve the livelihood of the poor in remote areas through numerous royal projects,[4] with *The King of Thailand in World's Focus* devoting an entire chapter to those projects.

Naturally, foreign journalists covering Thailand during the Cold War were aware that the Thai monarchy did not strictly fit the Western concept of a constitutional monarchy or remain strictly above politics. They did not, however, view this situation as a serious problem. A 1981 piece in the *Far Eastern Economic Review* offered a straightforward analysis of the palace's position as the most important factor determining the success or failure of political factions. This article appeared after a failed coup mounted by the "Young Turks" faction of the Thai army against the government of General Prem Tinsulanond in April of that year. It analysed the influential role of King Bhumibol in this crisis. The magazine told its readers that, as the Young Turks staged their coup, the king had departed from Bangkok in the early hours of the morning to join Prem in the northeastern centre of Nakhon Ratchasima or Khorat. The action "spelled the death knell for the Young Turks's coup attempt. Although the king made no public comment during the affair, his mere presence at Khorat decisively tipped the balance in Prem's favour, bestowing on him continued legitimacy" (*Far Eastern Economic Review* [hereafter *FEER*], 19–25 June 1981). In hindsight, the palace's role in the failed coup was interpreted as support for the Prem government and also for the democratic process.

While this article in the *Far Eastern Economic Review* noted that the habit of political interference might not be positive for the royal institution, it did not examine the issue critically. Instead, the article reiterated that "the King as symbol of the nation could, however, stay far above the political world only so long as there was a person or institution able to provide the country with effective and tolerable government", such as that of Sarit or, later, Prem (ibid.). However, when military regimes were corrupt and oppressive beyond the point of being tolerable, like that of Thanom and Praphat in the early 1970s and that of Suchinda Kraprayoon in the early 1990s, the king would intervene, or so the foreign press had it. He would be a just and timely arbiter, stepping in before society experienced great damage. The monarchy was cast as impartial and without selfish interests. Unlike constitutional monarchies elsewhere, much foreign reporting stressed that the king drew authority from his own merit and actions in pursuit of the well-being of his subjects. He had succeeded in achieving a supreme moral authority (*FEER*, 18 October 1974; *Time*, 1 June 1992). In other words, the monarchy might not be strictly *above* politics, but it was certainly not a party to political conflict. Foreign media thus embraced and heralded the justification and the alleged uniqueness of Thailand's constitutional monarchy.

However, the foreign press proved inconsistent when it came to rationalizing the relationship between the palace and the successive military regimes. On the one hand, it always viewed the monarchy in a positive light and stressed that the king's approval was crucial to regime legitimacy. On the other hand, it assessed authoritarian military regimes critically, in spite of the military's royal-nationalist ideology and commitment to protect the monarchy. Sarit's government had allowed the palace to consolidate its power and prestige. The view of the Western press was that Thai society could not depend on self-serving military leaders, but that the king could, in contrast, "restrain an unscrupulous successor to the marshal. Therefore, the stronger King Bhumibol emerged, the better the guarantee for Thailand's internal equilibrium" (*The Observer*, 17 July 1960). The foreign press thus presented King Bhumibol as being a democratic monarch in spite of his corrupt and anti-democratic military allies.

The popular uprising against the Thanom-Praphat regime in October 1973 sealed the idea of King Bhumibol as a defender of democracy, an idea that the foreign press largely adopted and promoted. The palace's intervention on 14 October, its willingness to shelter people fleeing violent military suppression, and the collapse of the Thanom-Praphat regime seemed to demonstrate that the king stood by his people and democracy (Associated Press, 17 October 1973).

The foreign press would have little to say about the palace's position on the massacre of Thai students by right-wing groups in October 1976 or the simultaneous ouster of the civilian government. Rather, in reinforcing the image of a democracy-loving monarch, it made royal intervention to end the violence following military suppression of anti-Suchinda demonstrators in May 1992 a favourite reference for the foreign press. It reproduced again and again a photograph of King Bhumibol reprimanding the two antagonists in the crisis, General Suchinda himself and Chamlong Simueang, as both prostrated themselves on the floor in front of him.

Interestingly, Western scholars focusing on Thailand during the Cold War shared perceptions similar to those of most foreign journalists. In a provocative and influential article, Benedict Anderson pointed out that, rather than making it the subject of critical examination, Thailand specialists tended to see the monarchy as one more example of the uniqueness of Thai society (Anderson 1978). He wrote that Western, and above all American, scholars of his own generation had a tendency to approach Southeast Asian societies through the lens of indigenous culture and nationalism and thus in opposition to colonial powers. In the case of Thai studies, they viewed the Chakri dynasty as playing a historical role in modernizing and building the Thai nation. Western Thailand specialists were thus reinforcing what Thongchai Winichakul (2001) would later term "royal nationalism".

Western journalists appeared to work along this same line. Three months after the student uprising of October 1973, the *Far Eastern Economic Review* placed King Bhumibol on the same pedestal with other anti-colonial nationalist leaders in Southeast Asia. "Southeast Asia has thrown up many remarkable men — Ho Chi Minh, Sihanouk, General Giap. I wouldn't have dreamed of saying it a few months ago, but King Bhumibol may wind up being remembered as the most remarkable of them all" (*FEER*, 17 December 1973). All this suggests that Thailand scholars and foreign journalists were complicit in reinforcing each other's perception of the monarchy.

One reason for this perception of the monarchy was the belief that, in the face of corrupt military leaders and the threat of communism, Thailand needed a benign, authoritative and unifying figure to lead the country, especially if it was to emerge as a democracy. This role was one that King Bhumibol could apparently fill.[5] Therefore, the foreign press voluntarily assisted in the careful construction of the benign image of King Bhumibol in the international arena. However, it failed to analyse the ways in which the monarchy's partnership with military leaders essentially strengthened military rule; Thailand still confronts the legacy of that partnership.

The period between 1992 and 2006 appeared to be one in which King Bhumibol's power and moral authority reached their zenith. Elected governments were in power in Bangkok, and, though all of them — save that of Thaksin Shinawatra (2001–5) — failed to last a full four-year parliamentary term, the country was relatively stable. Most journalists believed that coups in Thailand were a thing of the past. There were no political crises demanding royal intervention. Foreign journalists arriving in Thailand during this period tended to accept the view that the monarchy was above politics, or at least not a key player. Moreover, the palace's inconspicuous role made it difficult for journalists to find concrete evidence pointing to significant political intervention. On the contrary, members of the royal family were mainly involved in development projects.[6] The foreign press did not regard King Bhumibol's annual birthday speech or the advice that he offered to government leaders and top civil servants on special occasions interventions but, rather, caring gestures from the nation's father that politicians must heed.

However, by mid-2006 Thailand's political situation had become increasingly volatile. The Constitutional Court had invalidated the elections held in April of that year and the attacks of the Yellow-Shirt People's Alliance for Democracy's (PAD or *Phanthamit prachachon phuea prachathipatai*) on Thaksin were increasing in ferocity. In the meantime, the country geared up to celebrate the sixtieth anniversary of King Bhumibol's accession to the throne. The foreign press corps joined in to pay tribute to the king. Many of its members still firmly believed that he, as the figure with the greatest moral authority in the country, would pull Thailand through its political crisis (Gray and Faulder 2008, pp. 198–205). Denis Gray summed up the nearly universal admiration that the king had achieved by observing, "King Bhumibol has consistently enjoyed the kind of press most world leaders can only command in their daydreams" (Gray and Faulder 2008, p. 15). However, things started to change after the coup in 2006.

Discourse on the Monarchy after the 2006 Coup

Initially, several Western media outlets viewed the 2006 coup as a typical Thai way of bringing about swift political change. Some of their analyses sounded like the work of apologists for the junta. For example, the *Financial Times* placed all the blame on Thaksin by citing King Bhumibol's birthday speech of 2001, which warned of disaster for the country due to arrogance, egotism, conflict and the double standards of politicians. Thaksin had failed to pay sufficient attention to the king's warning — an unpardonable act in the eyes of many Thais (*Financial Times*, 23 September 2006). Similarly, *The Spectator* believed that the coup would probably succeed because of Thaksin's repeated errors and because it had the tacit approval of the popular monarch. "The people, like their monarch, understand the limits of democracy and the boundless advantages of flexibility in a turbulent world" (*The Spectator*, 23 September 2006). According to the BBC, the coup happened because of Thaksin's abrasive and divisive leadership. With Thaksin's huge wealth and popularity among rural voters in mind, military leaders saw the coup as the only way to get rid of him, it said (BBC, 20 September 2006). Some media sources did not make excuses for the junta, but nevertheless did not show any disapproval of its putsch (Hookway, Barta and Solomon 2006). They hardly criticized the Yellow Shirts' call for the military to topple the elected government.

A Bangkok-based foreign journalist told me frankly that there was even a sense of relief among his colleagues, as the coup had finally put an end to the prolonged street protests, confrontations and impasse.[7] However, *The Economist* (21 September 2006*a*) disapproved of the 2006 coup and believed that the actions of "spoiled" Yellow Shirt protestors had struck a deep blow to a still-fragile democratic system.

Right after the coup, the dominant image of Thaksin in most of the foreign press was that of an elected leader popular among the poor and rural voters because of his policies focused on the poor and on the rural sector. However, these same policies alienated urban middle-class voters and the intelligentsia, who believed that they benefitted Thaksin's business empire and patronage network. Moreover, Thaksin had interfered in and disabled the independent agencies intended to serve as checks and balances on the government. Freedom of expression was compromised because of his intolerance of media criticism. His harsh anti-drug campaign and handling of the three southern Muslim-dominated provinces grossly violated human rights. Nepotism in the army, serving to boost members of his network, further antagonized his opponents among the top brass. These were the major factors, many foreign journalists believed, contributing to his downfall (*The New York Times*, 20 September 2006).[8] It should be noted that the image of Thaksin as an abusive authoritarian and self-serving politician still prevails in most foreign publications.

Although much of the foreign press saw that King Bhumibol's endorsement granted legitimacy to the junta, its members did not necessarily suspect that the royal institution was behind the putsch. The press viewed royal endorsement as a mere formality that the palace was required to grant to a government. However, Duncan McCargo's formulation of the idea of the "network monarchy" would soon lead journalists to understand the political role of the palace in a new light. The network monarchy is centred on the palace and involves active interventions in the political process by the palace and its proxies, not least under the guidance of former premier and current Privy Council chairman Prem. It exercises considerable influence over and through other political institutions, including the parliament, the military and the judiciary (McCargo 2005).

Immediately after the September 2006 coup, *The Economist* identified Prem's role in an orchestrated attempt to undermine Thaksin's government. Prem's notorious speech to military cadets in early 2006, asserting that the armed forces served the king and not the government of the day offered clear evidence of this attempt, even though *The Economist* (21 September 2006*a* and 21 September 2006*b*) remained uncertain about the palace's role in the coup. However, by December 2008, it pinpointed Thaksin's popularity among rural people as a point of contention between him and the palace, which had felt threatened. It believed that the monarchists, including Queen Sirikit, were behind the anti-Thaksin movement. The magazine was the first to touch upon the crisis of royal succession, suggesting that Thaksin's financial generosity to the then crown prince, which helped to explain the former prime minister's influence, had caused distrust among the network monarchy. Despite what the celebrated term "the democratic monarch" commonly used to describe King Bhumibol implied, recognition of his role in Thailand's delayed democratization had begun (*The Economist*, 4 December 2008*b*). This recognition challenged the fairy-tale version of history in which the late king never did wrong, stayed above politics and only ever intervened on the side of democracy (*The Economist*, 4 December 2008*a*).

In April 2009, *The Economist* (16 April 2009) published an article titled, "The Trouble with the King", with the sub-title, "Nobody can say it in public, but the Thai monarchy, invisible during the latest crisis, is at its heart". Then, in March 2010, the magazine again stated that the crisis of succession and the monarchists' anxiety over Thaksin's expansive role were the real reasons for the coup of three and a half years earlier (*The Economist*, 18 March 2010). Similarly, after the coup of 22 May 2014, *The Economist* (24 May 2014) boldly suggested that it was a collaborative undertaking among the Democrat Party's Suthep Thaugksuban, the civil servants who had supported the protests against Thaksin, the army, the judiciary and the court surrounding King Bhumibol.[9]

Following *The Economist*, other foreign press outlets also gradually started to discuss the role of the network monarchy and of the monarchy itself more openly. In May 2010, *The New York Times* suggested that the 2006 coup had had the tacit approval of the Privy Council and other members of the elite who saw in Thaksin and his broad base of popular support a challenge to their power (Mydans 2006; Mydans and Fuller 2010). *The Wall Street Journal* (Wright 2014) pointed out that the king was a factor in the dispute because the two feuding political factions — one representing the urban establishment and the other a populist movement with roots in the rural heartlands — tried to publicly court the palace's support and sought to use his name to their advantage.

Foreign journalists' and commentators' increasingly unsympathetic assessment of the monarchy had clearly gained momentum after the 2006 coup. It was the result of several factors and incidents, as discussed below.

New Generation, New Sources

The majority of foreign correspondents working in Thailand in recent years had started to cover Thailand only after the 1997 economic crisis. They witnessed Thaksin's abuse of power and they perceived him as an authoritarian leader. Although they recognized the reverence of Thais for King Bhumibol, they were not uncritical of traditional elites. This was especially true when events clearly challenged the prevailing narrative centred on royal benevolence. All eight journalists and one security analyst interviewed pointed out that, after the 2006 coup, they had focused more on the monarchy simply because numerous incidents connected the palace to the unfolding events of the day. These incidents aroused the curiosity of journalists. The events that they were witnessing suggested that a refusal to address the political role of the monarchy would have made their reports implausible, even unprofessional.

The foreign press has enjoyed more diverse information sources in the last twenty years than during the Cold War, when leading informants were largely limited to members of the Bangkok elite. Today, the foreign press reflects the voices of politicians, academics, mass leaders, and people in both the Red and Yellow camps in Bangkok and the provinces. Their varied and at times conflicting opinions, aspirations and even resentments have shown foreign journalists that Thailand is not a simple, unified or homogenous society and that major political institutions and elites are facing a crisis of legitimacy.

The more open discussions, diversity of opinions and availability of information on the monarchy have been additional important factors leading to foreign journalists' more critical coverage of the Thai monarchy. Paul Handley's landmark 2006 book, *The King Never Smiles*, profoundly challenged the conventional view of the role and power of the monarchy. The Thai authorities' decision to ban the book only served to arouse interest among journalists. Handley offered insights into an institution that thrived on secrecy by connecting the dots to explain the means by which that institution dominated Thailand's political landscape.[10] His book broke the taboo on critical writing about the monarchy and became an important source of historical background information on the monarchy for many foreign journalists.[11]

The work of Andrew MacGregor Marshall, a former Reuters journalist, also had an impact on discussion of the monarchy in the foreign press. In June 2011, Marshall resigned from the agency after it refused to run a series of long articles that he had written. Soon afterward, he self-published *Thailand's Moment of Truth* (Marshall 2011*a* and 2011*b*), in which he analysed the role of the monarchy in Thai politics. The book drew on hundreds of leaked United States diplomatic cables that WikiLeaks later released to the public. This material confirmed the elite's anxiety over royal succession and the palace's political position (Rex 2011). In 2014, Marshall published another book, *A Kingdom in Crisis: Thailand's Struggle for Democracy in the Twenty-First Century*, which the Thai police banned for its anti-monarchy sentiments (*Bangkok Post*, 13 November 2014). The leaked classified information in the book confirmed much that journalists had long suspected.

Marshall's extensive use of social media also stimulated interest in the monarchy and provided a venue for discussion of its realities and its role. The rise of the Internet and social media broke the monopoly of conventional news reporting on Thailand. New outlets offered intriguing material and exposed readers to ideas that were previously difficult to publish in the mainstream press. Their content often excited the public and thus made it impossible for mainstream media to ignore them. In addition, foreign media outlets increasingly published critical assessments by Thailand specialists such as Duncan McCargo, David Streckfuss, Michael Montesano, Patrick Jory, Thongchai Winichakul and Pavin Chachavalpongpun, in the form of op-ed articles and interviews (*The Economist*, 18 March 2010 and 3 February 2011; Fuller 2014*a*). It thus became common for the foreign press to observe that anxiety over succession, following the looming death of King Bhumibol, was one of the root causes of the country's protracted political turbulence.[12]

The Yellow Shirt Movement

The PAD, led by the media mogul Sondhi Limthongkul and the retired right-wing lieutenant general Chamlong Simueang during the anti-Thaksin campaign, was in fact the first party in Thailand's recent history of strife to shine the spotlight on the royal institution. Although some journalists had doubts about the PAD's credentials even prior to the coup, they nevertheless still tended to see it as a legitimate popular movement against the authoritarian government of Thaksin. However, after the coup succeeded in ousting the prime minister, the PAD's actual political objective became crystal-clear to foreign journalists.[13] The PAD's constant references to the monarchy in speeches and through symbols, as it sought to build legitimacy for its push against Thaksin's faction, served as an invitation for the foreign press to scrutinize the group's links with the palace. PAD members donned yellow shirts, wearing the colour associated with the day of the week on which King Bhumibol had been born, and, later, light blue scarfs, used to symbolize Queen Sirikit's birthday. Sondhi claimed to have received the latter through palace connections (Somsak 2008). Moreover, in the name of defending the monarchy, the PAD's leaders employed the divisive rhetoric of "us" against "them", so that anyone who disagreed with the PAD was cast as an opponent of the monarchy. This rhetoric implied that the Red Shirts or those sympathetic to the Red Shirts were opponents of the monarchy. While most of the Thai media refrained from analysing the PAD's claim to have royal support, foreign journalists found it necessary to explain why the monarchy had become connected to the campaign against an elected government. In making the monarchy the centrepiece of their movement, PAD leaders were the first openly to drag the institution into the political conflict, thus undermining the official narrative that placed the monarchy above politics.[14]

The PAD's behaviour after 2006 undermined its credibility as a democratic force. This behaviour included actions such as seizing Government House and Bangkok's international airports in 2008, threatening and harassing journalists, calling for the military to overthrow the Thaksinite governments of Samak Suntharawet and Somchai Wongsawat and introducing the idea of a 70:30 ratio of members of parliament appointed from professional groups to elected members.

The foreign press began to describe the PAD as an anti-democratic force, "a loose coalition of businessmen, academics and monarchists who want to scrap Thailand's one-person, one-vote democracy in favour of a system where the majority of parliament is appointed by professional and social groups" (Barta 2008); a not-so-peaceful "right-wing protest movement" that "has a political agenda that contradicts its name" and enjoyed "the impunity … to break the law" (*The Albion Monitor*, n.d.); a group that wanted to return Thailand to "old, pre-democracy politics with a mostly unelected parliament and power for the army to intervene" (*The Economist*, 26 August 2008); and a group that, "[d]espite the name,… is actually campaigning for an end to democracy" (BBC, 26 August 2008). When those who claimed to be the king's men behaved in democratically dubious ways, their actions also cast the palace in a poor light.

The Democrat Party and the PDRC

The Democrat Party's founding political ideology was a royalist-conservative one. Its principal founder, Khuang Aphaiwong, considered Pridi Phanomyong, the intellectual leader of the 1932 revolution against Siam's absolute monarchy, an arch-rival. The party sought to create the impression that Pridi was the mastermind behind King Ananda Mahidol's death in 1946 by having a party member shout out in a crowded theatre that Pridi had killed the king. However, by the 1990s, under the leadership of Chuan Leekpai, the Democrat Party had apparently evolved into a tribune of democracy. Chuan had been an outspoken opponent of the "National Peace-Keeping Council" junta that seized power from the elected government of Chatchai Chunhavan on 23 February 1991. Chuan's "Mr Clean" image as an educated, well-mannered man with a strong commitment to parliamentary politics defined the new image of the party in the local and foreign media. It was an image that was perfectly maintained by Abhisit Vejjajiva, whose quasi-aristocratic background and overseas education helped to retain the party's middle-class supporters.

Notwithstanding this evolution, with the rise of Thaksin the Democrat Party once again became the favourite ally of the royalists and the military, representing the royalists' ideology and interests via parliamentary politics. The behaviour of Abhisit and other Democrat leaders from 2006 onwards led *The Economist* to point out that "the Democrats, the parliamentary opposition, are opportunists, cheering on the PAD while seemingly hoping for another royally approved coup to land the government in their lap" (*The Economist*, 4 December 2008*b*).

The Democrat Party reached its nadir in the eyes of foreign journalists when its leaders decided to abandon parliamentary politics and practise street politics, often associated with undemocratic goals and sometimes with the use of violent methods to overthrow rivals. The opportunity for the Democrats arose in early November 2013, after the Phuea Thai Party pushed through a blanket amnesty bill, which would have pardoned individuals and political groups for various charges made against them since 2004; those covered included former prime minister Thaksin. The bill caused outrage across the political spectrum. The Democrats and the Yellow Shirt leaders immediately organized demonstrations (*Bangkok Post*, 3 November 2013). The protests continued even as the Phuea Thai Party dropped the bill. Their objective became the removal of Prime Minister Yingluck Shinawatra. Demonstrations under the auspices of a self-styled "People's Democratic Reform Committee" (PDRC, *Khanakammakan prachachon phuea plianplaeng prathet thai hai pen prachathipatai thi somboon an mi phramahakasat songpenpramuk*) launched by Suthep Thaugsuban, deputy leader of the Democrat Party, gained massive support from the Bangkok middle class and from Southerners. Suthep announced a plan to create an unelected "People's Council" to replace the existing parliamentary system (*Khaosod English*, 12 December 2013). He would choose its members himself. With the aim of creating a situation in which Thailand was a failed state, PDRC demonstrators occupied government offices, blocked major road intersections, held daily mass rallies in central Bangkok and obstructed polling places during the general elections held on 2 February 2014 in Southern provinces and the capital. Many celebrity speakers participating in PDRC rallies openly insulted rural voters for being ignorant, easily bribed and unqualified to make political decisions via the ballot box. Speakers argued that the one man, one vote principle was for these reasons unsuitable for Thailand. The PDRC's armed security guards took the law into their hands, carrying weapons, harassing and injuring members of the police and passers-by. A fierce gunfight in the Laksi suburb of Bangkok on 1 February 2014 revealed to the public how heavily armed the PDRC guards were. Democrat Party leaders claimed that the PDRC had no relationship with the party, as Suthep and some of the group's other leaders had resigned from the party prior to the creation of the PDRC. The party continued to assert a strong commitment to democratic principles, but the foreign press met this flimsy claim with considerable suspicion.

Time (Campbell 2013) summed up the Democrats' behaviour with an article titled, "Thailand's Democrat Party is Hilariously Misnamed", while *The Sydney Morning Herald* (4 February 2014) used a similar headline, "Thai Elections: Opposition are Democrats in Name Only". *Time* (Campbell 2013) added that, when it came to democracy, the Democrat Party was among its worst practitioners. An editorial in *Forbes* (3 February 2014) slammed the PDRC's Yellow Shirt protestors for acting like Mussolini's

Black Shirts. The article said that the party did not have the capability to formulate policies to win the hearts and minds of the rural voters in the North and Northeast of Thailand, and that it ruthlessly called upon powerful allies, such as the military and judiciary, to undermine its rivals. *The Wall Street Journal* (3 February 2014) strongly criticized the Democrats for their actions, saying that "their path to power lies through street demagoguery and lawyers rather than the ballot box". The Associated Press (cited in Al Jazeera America, 21 December 2013) saw the Democrats' boycott of the 2014 election as a recurrence of their 2006 electoral boycott, which "helped destabilize the government and paved the way for a military *coup* that ousted the then-Prime Minister Thaksin". It can be said that this last sentiment has become a shared perception of the Democrats (*The Economist*, 6 May 2014; Head 2014; *The New York Times*, 3 February 2014; *The Wall Street Journal*, 23 December 2013).

The Palace

The claim by Yellow Shirt leaders that they enjoyed support from the monarchy would not have been credible but for specific actions on the part of the palace and its inner circle. For example, on 13 October 2008, Queen Sirikit, accompanied by her youngest daughter Princess Chulabhon Walailak, attended the funeral of 28-year-old female PAD protestor Angkana Radappanyawut. Angkana had been killed in a clash with the police when PAD supporters tried to obstruct the new prime minister Somchai Wongsawat, Thaksin's brother-in-law, from reaching parliament to deliver a policy statement. The queen reportedly told Angkana's father that "Angkana was a good girl, she helped protect the country and the monarchy." She also reportedly said that "the King was informed of the matters and the donation to the family was the King's contribution" (*The Nation*, 14 October 2008). Reuters promptly asserted that the queen was "giving explicit royal backing to a five-month street campaign to oust the elected government" (Chalathip 2008). The Red Shirts termed the date of the queen's attendance at the funeral "National Awakening Day" (*Wan ta sawang haeng chat*) (Thongchai 2014), and the incident did indeed prove an eye-opener for many foreign journalists.[15] The queen's presence and her unambiguous message to the family of the deceased made the palace's view of the political conflict and of the PAD obvious to the press. The foreign press has since that time frequently referred to the funeral incident as evidence of the palace's participation in the conflict that has polarized Thailand (Rex 2011).

The coups of 2006 and 2014 also significantly altered foreign journalists' views of the relationship between the monarchy and other institutions. One such relationship was that with the military, which many in the foreign press corps came to see as symbiotic. Defending the monarchy has become the military's *raison d'être*. In return, the alliance greatly legitimized the Thai Army, and did much to empower it to interfere in politics. As *The Economist* (4 December 2008*b*) put it,

> The army is a big part of the country's predicament. Its generals believe they have a right to remove any government that incurs its, or the palace's, displeasure — taking its cue from the monarchy that has approved so many of its coups. These two obstacles to Thailand's democratic development are inextricably interlinked.

Another crucial relationship is that between the monarchy and the judiciary. What foreign journalists term "judicial coups" and the politicization of the judiciary have also been linked to the palace's intervention in Thai politics. In April 2006, King Bhumibol gave a speech to judges of the Administrative and Supreme Courts (*san pokkhrong* and *san dika*), asking that the Thai judiciary help resolve the political impasse and growing tension in the streets. Within weeks, the Constitutional Court annulled the results of the recent parliamentary election of April of that year, which Thaksin's Thai Rak Thai Party had won. Since then, Thai courts have consistently ruled against Thaksinite factions. These rulings have included invalidating election results, banning the Thaksinite Thai Rak Thai and Phalang Prachachon Parties, suspending the political rights of more than a hundred executive committee members of these and smaller political parties for a period of five years, obstructing the Phuea Thai Party government's attempt to amend the 2007 constitution, sacking Prime Minister Samak Suntharawet for accepting a fee for appearing on a televised cooking programme and dismissing Yingluck for removing the head of the National Security Council. As a result, the foreign press came to view Thailand's judiciary, along with such allegedly independent organizations as the National Anti-Corruption Commission, as institutional tools of the monarchists in their effort to subvert electoral democracy (*The Economist*, 4 December 2008*b*; *The Wall Street Journal*, 3 February 2014 and 7 May 2014).[16]

The foreign press also began to discuss members of the royal family more openly. It frequently brought up the unpopularity of then crown prince Vajiralongkorn after the 2006 coup, not to titillate readers with accounts of the colourful scandals surrounding him but rather to address the challenge that succession might pose for the monarchy. Its role in politics had, after all, been possible because the majority of Thai people came from the 1970s onwards to accept King Bhumibol as a man with moral authority. The new king would lack that authority, and King Bhumibol's health made this lack a source of anxiety, especially for the entrenched royalist elite. An unpopular king would diminish the popular appeal of the monarchy and its networks of power, thus tipping the balance of power in Thailand in favour not only of Thaksinite forces but also of the Thai electorate more broadly. The monarchists' belief that Thaksin was gaining influence over the then crown prince was one of the causes of the country's ongoing conflict. It was a factor of which many foreign journalists were well aware.[17]

Princess Chulabhon, the youngest daughter of King Bhumibol, was another member of the royal family who attracted the scrutiny of the foreign press. The leaked American cables indicated that it was she who had persuaded the queen to attend Angkana's funeral. She had also told a television host that the episodes of arson that accompanied the end of the Red Shirt protests against the Abhisit government in May 2010 had brought great sorrow to the king and the queen. These remarks broke the palace's silence over the conflict (*Prachatai*, 4 July 2011). In addition, during the PDRC campaign of protests to topple Yingluck Shinawatra in early 2014, Princess Chulabhon posted several photographs of herself on social media with hair braids and bracelets of red, blue and white. These colours of Thailand's national flag were closely associated with the PDRC, and her posts prompted *The Independent* to title its analysis, "Thai princess uses social media to 'Declare war': Photos posted by Princess Chulabhorn Mahidol widely interpreted as a sign of her support for anti-government protesters" (Rex 2014). Both the anti-government and pro-government elements circulated these photographs of Princess Chulabhon widely. The anti-government side happily convinced themselves that the palace was on their side.

While the actions of members of the royal family and the network monarchy thrilled the Yellow Shirts, they inevitably disappointed the Red Shirts. Journalists started to pick up the collective disappointment expressed discreetly in various forms and at various venues. Such increasingly explicit sentiments exacerbated the monarchists' anxieties. Although most journalists interviewed believed that the majority of Red Shirt supporters still held the late king in high regard and dismissed monarchists' fear of republicanism as paranoia, they admitted that the Abhisit government's violent crackdown on the Red Shirts in 2010 devastated the Red Shirts and their supporters. Many Red Shirts had expected King Bhumibol to mediate between the protestors and the government in order to end the crackdown, as had happened in 1992. They were disappointed.

The *Lèse Majesté* Law: When Constraint Becomes an Invitation

The 1908 Thai law on *lèse majesté*, section 112 of the Criminal Code, stipulates that anyone who defames, insults or threatens the king, the queen, the heir apparent or the regent will be subject to punishment of from three to fifteen years' imprisonment per count. The number of *lèse majesté* cases rose from fewer than ten cases per year before 2006 to more than four hundred in 2010 (Streckfuss 2014, p. 119). Of all the political issues to confront Thailand in the period since 2006, *lèse majesté* has drawn the most international attention to the Thai monarchy. In early March 2009 and again in February 2012, over a hundred acclaimed international scholars and dignitaries signed letters expressing concern over abuse of the charge of *lèse majesté* and calling for a reform of the law governing *lèse majesté* to Prime Ministers Abhisit and Yingluck, respectively. The United Nations Human Rights Commission, the European Union, the government of the United States and human rights groups have issued public statements concerning harsh punishment for *lèse majesté* and the effect of the law on *lèse majesté* in undermining freedom of expression in Thailand. In recent years, Western embassies have also engaged Thai authorities behind the scenes to offer ideas on reform of the law (Crispin 2011). But the establishment has shown no signs of yielding, and Thai academics and social activists who have campaigned for reform have been accused of participating in a conspiracy against the monarchy.

In response to worldwide criticism of abuse of the law on *lèse majesté* for political gain and of its effect in constraining freedom of expression, Bowornsak Uwanno diligently produced a number of English-language articles explaining its role. He argued, in essence, that Thailand and its culture were unique, that its monarchy was both above politics and central to Thai history and culture, that King Bhumibol was a righteous king who had tirelessly devoted himself to the well-being of Thais. He further argued that the law carried a harsh sentence because it was rooted in Thai culture and that Thais would never allow anyone unfairly to criticize the king whom they saw as their father. Bowornsak even claimed that having the world's harshest *lèse majesté* law was Thailand's cultural right, one that other democratic countries must respect. He accused Westerners who criticized the law of "ethical dictatorship", of being guilty of imposing their own beliefs and standards on Thai society. He asserted that such "ethical absolutism" was unacceptable to Thai society (Bowornsak 2009*a*, 2009*b*, 2009*c* and 2014).[18]

Bowornsak's culturalist argument is a familiar one, the standard argument of Thai monarchists for many decades. The difference was that in the past the number of people facing *lèse majesté* charges was small and thus did not attract much international attention. However, after the 2006 coup, the enforcement and exploitation of the law by various groups for political ends made it difficult for foreign journalists to buy into the culturalist claim. The monarchists seemed unable to come to terms with the fact that their culturalist argument had lost its spell and was no longer convincing to liberal-minded people.

David Streckfuss has thoroughly studied the Thai law against *lèse majesté* and the problems that it poses.[19] This chapter only highlights the dimensions of those problems relevant to the discussion at hand. In legal terms, Thai authorities argue that the law on *lèse majesté* protects the rights of the monarchy, just as libel law protects private individuals (Ministry of Foreign Affairs, Thailand, n.d.). However, it is well known that, under the *lèse majesté* law, defendants are not allowed to prove whether the allegedly defamatory content is factual (*The Nation*, 20 July 2012). The enforcement and interpretation of the law simply falls short of international legal standards, and it is for this reason that liberal journalists find it hard to respect (*The Economist*, 3 February 2011). Moreover, the majority of people charged with *lèse majesté* have been connected in some way either to the Red Shirt movement, to Thaksin or to opposition to the 2006 coup and the military regime that followed. It has thus been difficult not to perceive charges against them as exploitation of the law on the part of monarchists as part of an effort to silence their opponents and critics.

The lack of transparency in the management of the Crown Property Bureau was another issue that foreign journalists came to highlight. The 2008 claim in *Forbes* that King Bhumibol was the richest monarch in the world stirred up considerable international interest. It was therefore natural for sceptical journalists to ask questions concerning the ownership of the bureau's assets, its legal status and its management. But, here again, the law on *lèse majesté* hampered efforts to cover these matters, and the treatment of the Crown Property Bureau in the book *King Bhumibol Adulyadej: A Life's Work* failed to clear these questions up (*Forbes*, 20 January 2012). The foreign press came routinely to describe Thailand's *lèse majesté* law as draconian and to note that, curiously and alarmingly, it allowed any Thai citizen to file a complaint with the police anywhere in the kingdom. This provision opened the law to abuse for political purposes or as a means of taking personal vengeance.[20] Foreign journalists became fully aware of the dangers of the law after the BBC's Jonathan Head was charged with *lèse majesté* in May 2008. Again in 2009, a female Yellow Shirt supporter filed a complaint charging the board of the Foreign Correspondents Club of Thailand for selling a digital video disc recording of a speech by a former leader of the Red Shirts' United Front for Democracy against Dictatorship Chakkraphop Penkhae that allegedly defamed the king.

Long before 2006, generations of foreign journalists arriving in Thailand had quickly learned from their colleagues and contacts that writing critically about the monarchy was off limits. Moreover, big news companies had always worried about being closed down or expelled from Thailand; at a time when Bangkok served as a base for reporting on Thailand's then relatively closed neighbours in Indochina and Myanmar, this consideration carried particular weight.[21] However, the heavy use of this law after 2006 only invited a new generation of foreign journalists to pay greater attention to it.[22] While rumours and gossip surrounding the palace remained murky and difficult to report on, *lèse majesté* cases presented clear facts for reporters to investigate and cover.

It was clear after 2006 that the role and power of the Thai monarchy had become crucial factors for understanding the country and its long-running conflict. Yet the law on *lèse majesté* prohibited free and open discussion. The challenge for journalists was to write about the monarchy without being prosecuted. And, while they had to be tactful in referring to the palace, their coverage of the monarchy appeared more frequently and its analyses became more straightforward than ever before.[23]

Many foreign journalists remained perplexed by the failure of Thai authorities to heed the words in a speech that King Bhumibol delivered in 2005, in which he pointed out that he himself was not perfect, that he was open to criticism, and that charging people under the *lèse majesté* law troubled him. The king had certainly been aware of the negative attention that the *lèse majesté* law brought to Thailand and to his monarchy. "Foreign countries see Thailand as a country where people cannot criticize the King; otherwise they will go to jail. This puts the King in trouble."[24] While many foreign journalists believed that these words were sincere, they had had no impact on the application of the law on *lèse majesté*. Indeed, the number of cases filed under this law would skyrocket in the years after the king delivered this speech. This turn of events led foreign journalists to attribute the heavy use of the defamation law to the determination of members of the network monarchy and of Yellow Shirt politicians to advance or defend their own interests. They believed that, although the palace may not have explicitly consented to charging Thai subjects with *lèse majesté*, the royal institution clearly benefitted from the law. Furthermore, what was good for the institution was, after all, good for the enduring power of leading courtiers.[25] However, it is worth pointing out that circumstances in 2005, when the late king made the speech in question, were different from those after the 2006 coup. In 2005 King Bhumibol was in some ways at the zenith of his reign, and the number of *lèse majesté* cases was still low. Polarization had not yet overtaken Thai society, and the stance of the members of the palace and the network monarchy was not obvious. After the 2006 coup, it was impossible to imagine politicians or senior courtiers possessing the courage to reform the law.[26]

Conclusion

Negative news coverage of Thailand's traditional elite has ramifications beyond the country's shores. Throughout the Cold War, the United States considered Thailand's traditional elite trusted allies in the struggle against communism. However, post-2006 news coverage highlighted the anti-democratic behaviour of Thai monarchists and their intransigent position in opposition to majoritarian democracy, which had become a hindrance to reconciliation and economic development. Such coverage, if it continues during the new reign, is likely to convince the Western community to reconsider its relations with the country's conservative elites.

Perhaps the consequences of Thailand's political crisis are already evident. Comparing the reactions of the international community to the September 2006 and May 2014 coups, one could observe a change in attitude. In 2006, a U.S. State Department spokesman noted that Washington "look[ed] to the Thai people to resolve their political differences in a peaceful manner and in accord with the principles of democracy and the rule of law" (Bloomberg, 19 September 2006). The American response was not a harsh one. It appeared to be a standard line for its long-term ally in Southeast Asia. However, the latest military coup drew stronger criticism from foreign governments. The United States, the European Union and Australia were the most vocal in urging the military junta to restore civilian government immediately. Washington announced after the coup that it had suspended US$8.2 million in security-related funds to Thailand as well as a U.S.-sponsored firearms training programme and a study trip for senior Thai police officers (*Bangkok Post*, 25 June 2014). While in 2006 the United States froze military aid to Thailand until the junta held an election a year later, the 2014 coup prompted noticeably stronger reactions and criticism from then secretary of state John Kerry and secretary of defense Chuck Hagel. Washington even threatened to move Cobra Gold, one of its biggest annual military exercises and a key element in American strategy in Asia, to Australia. In January 2015, then assistant secretary of state for East Asian and Pacific affairs Daniel Russel drew fierce reactions from Thai monarchists and nationalists when he boldly criticized the judicial unfairness and undemocratic practices to which Yingluck had been subjected (*Bangkok Post*, 27 January 2015). The European Union suspended high-level official visits and postponed the signing of the Partnership and Cooperation Agreement in 2014, while Australia downgraded its diplomatic and military ties with Thailand, imposed a travel ban on the leaders of the junta and cut defence cooperation (*The Guardian*, 30 May 2014). Eventually, the United States, Australia and the European Union refrained from imposing further serious sanctions against the military government for fear of forfeiting their interests in and influence over Thailand to China.

Some analysts simply saw the reaction of these Western nations as consistent with their championing of democratic values, even as they were inconsistent in the application of such values to other non-democratic regimes (Tay 2014). In reality, the response of the West to the 2014 coup in Thailand went beyond the desire to spread liberal ideology. Instead, it reflected a more profound change in perceptions of the ruling elite in Thailand. This change began years before the 2014 coup, when concern over the politicization of the palace, the role of the old establishment in the ongoing colour-coded conflict, and their impact on regional stability and development grew (Kurlantzick 2012). Most notable was the view of the American ambassador to Thailand at the time, Eric John, that the monarchy would lose its moral authority in light of Queen Sirikit's attendance at the funeral of the Yellow Shirt supporter in 2008.

This chapter argues that, prior to 2006, the foreign press, like its domestic counterpart, wrote about the late king and "Thai-style" constitutional monarchy as bulwarks against communism and corrupt military leaders and politicians. The foreign press was instrumental in constructing a benign image of King Bhumibol in the international arena, and was thus complicit in entrenching the power of the monarchy. However, the political coverage of Thailand changed after 2006. The foreign press began to see the monarchy, and especially its closest courtiers, as a crucial factor in the conflict that now engulfed Thailand. While the monarchists often blame Thaksin and the Red Shirts for undermining the legitimacy of the monarchy, foreign journalists have pointed to the anti-democratic behaviour of the royalist camp. They view the establishment's fear of losing power and its inability to adapt to socio-political change as obstacles to democratization and conflict resolution. Meanwhile, the decades-old culturalist defence of the monarchy's uniqueness has become untenable. Despite the risk of draconian defamation charges, foreign journalists continue to push the boundary of this taboo topic. With the passing of the much-beloved King Bhumibol and the start of a new reign in a country that remained under military dictatorship, the conventional view of the monarchy as a unifying force could no longer be taken for granted.

Acknowledgements

I would like to express my special appreciation to Michael Montesano, Terence Chong, Thongchai Winichakul, Tyrell Haberkorn and Patrick Jory for their support and for comments on earlier versions of this chapter.

Notes

1. Other such attempts included Suchit and Prudhisan (2012) and Office of the National Identity Board (2009).
2. Names of interviewees given here are thus pseudonyms.
3. For a study of the role of the monarchy in American psychological operations, see Nattapol (2011, pp. 94–166).
4. The royal projects began as an initiative of King Bhumibol in 1969. They have

covered a wide range of issues, such as problems of deforestation, poverty eradication in rural areas and targeting opium production by promoting alternative crops.

5. Interview with Dane G., Bangkok, 25 June 2015. Dane G. moved to Thailand in the 1970s. He works for an American news agency.

6. Electronic mail correspondence with P. Friendly on 16 and 23 May 2015. P. Friendly arrived in Thailand in 1987 to work for a weekly Asian news magazine and left Thailand before 2006.

7. Interview with Tim Ferdinand, Bangkok, 29 September 2014. Ferdinand works for one of the biggest American media outlets, with a daily readership of more than a million people.

8. Interview with Marty M., Bangkok, Thailand, 6 September 2014; interview with Niel G., Bangkok, 29 September 2014. Marty M. started covering Thailand in 2001. He works for a non-profit global news agency. Niel G. has covered Thailand since 2002 and works for an Asian English-language media outlet with a circulation of over 350,000.

9. Similar analyses can be found in Kinder (2014) and Head (2014).

10. Interview with Marty M.

11. Interview with Sim L., Singapore, 14 November 2014. Sim L. started covering Thailand in 1995 for a British weekly magazine with a circulation of over 1.5 million in print and another 100,000 in paid digital subscribers.

12. Interview with M. Winner, Bangkok, 28 November 2014. M. Winner is a political analyst for a non-profit advocacy organization who has worked in Thailand since 1993.

13. Interview with Marty M.

14. Ibid.; interview with Niel G.; and interview with William G., Bangkok, 1 October 2014. William G. arrived in Thailand in 2001 and works for a European newspaper, the daily circulation of which is above 140,000.

15. Interviews with journalists Marty M., Niel G. and William G.; and interview with Kran P., Bangkok, 1 October 2014.

16. It is noteworthy that, before the September 2006 coup, some Western press outlets viewed the advice that the king offered to the judges in April of that year in a positive light. *The Washington Post* (28 May 2006) quoted the royalist Anand Panyarachun saying, "When there is a political void, when there is a real imminent threat to democratic rule, then he [the king] would use his reserve power to show the way, to provide the guiding light or possible answer to a crisis". *The Financial Times* (23 September 2006) praised the king's having "denounced the bizarre April election — boycotted by the opposition — as 'undemocratic', which prompted the courts to annul the vote".

17. Interviews with Marty M., Niel G., Tim Ferdinand, William G. and Kran P.

18. Also see Suchit and Prudhisan (2012) and National Identity Office (2009).

19. See Streckfuss (2014).

20. Interviews with Marty M., Niel G., Tim Ferdinand, William G. and Kran P.

21. Communication with Paul H. via email between 2 May 2015 and 23 May 2015. Paul H. was in the 1990s a reporter working from Bangkok for a weekly magazine with a Southeast Asia focus. He wrote extensively about the Thai monarchy and no longer lives in Thailand.

22. Interviews with Marty M., Niel G. and Tim Ferdinand, 29 September 2014.

23. Interviews with Marty M. and Tim Ferdinand.

24. See King Bhumubol's Speech of 4 December 2006 at phraezila (2007).

25. Interviews with Tim Ferdinand and Marty M.

26. Interview with Tim Ferdinand.

13

Thai Economic Growth: Retrospect and Prospect

Porphant Ouyyanont

Viewed in retrospect, the Asian economic crisis of 1997 marks a watershed in the pattern of long-term Thai economic growth. Prior to the crisis, Thailand had experienced a lengthy period of significant growth, but the growth rate has subsequently shown a sharp decline. At the present time it seems that slower growth will characterize the Thai economy, at least for the next decade or so.

The purpose of this chapter is to explore aspects of this slower growth. In particular, it analyses the structural changes in the Thai economy that underlie this trend, and also suggests that there are positive features of the Thai economy that will sustain its growth, albeit at moderate rates, in the future.

It is well known, of course, that gross domestic product (GDP) statistics are a blunt instrument for depicting a true picture of economic attainment. Nonetheless, GDP data are the best indicator for the purposes of assessing long-term change and drawing international comparisons, and the chapter therefore uses GDP statistics to give an overall picture of the performance of the Thai economy. Table 13.1 presents figures relevant to long-term trends.

TABLE 13.1
Thailand: Rates of Growth of GDP and GDP per capita, 1951–2014

Period	Real GDP Growth	Real GDP Growth per capita
1951–1986	6.5	3.9
1987–1996	9.2	8.0
1997–1999	–6.1	–7.1
2000–2003	4.0	3.3
2004–2014	4.1	3.2
1951–2014	6.6	4.8

Sources: Warr (2005, p. 5); NESDB (n.d.).

Since the crisis of 1997, Thailand's economic growth rate has been only moderate, and much lower than in the decade before the crisis. Thailand's medium-term growth, as measured by the thirteen-year moving average of annual GDP growth rates during the 2000–2014 period, has been only about 4 per cent. This is a sharp decrease from the 7 per cent or higher that was obtained during the 1963–93 period (NESDB, n.d.).

Short-term factors have certainly contributed to slow economic growth since the late 1990s. The crisis itself was one factor, and there have also been political turmoil, the tsunami of 2004, Southern separatism, the 2008 global economic crisis, various periods of drought and flooding, and most recently the Bangkok bomb blast of August 2015, with its adverse impact on foreign capital inflows and tourism.

International factors have affected, and continue to affect, Thai growth too. The slowdown in China's economy is one factor, and another is the present economic difficulties faced by Russia. The former has considerable repercussions for inward investment, trade and tourism. The latter has had a particularly serious effect on tourism and property markets. For example, in 2015 the number of Russian tourists to Thailand dropped by nearly half to only 884,000 compared with 1.6 million in 2014. This is because of the plunge in oil prices and the weakening value of the rouble (*Bangkok Post*, 1 June 2016).

These short-term factors notwithstanding, however, it seems clear that slower growth is likely to become a characteristic of the Thai economy for the foreseeable future. Moreover, Thai growth looks set to lag behind that of other countries in the region, as Table 13.2 suggests.

TABLE 13.2
GDP Growth, East Asia and the Pacific

Unit: %	2013	2014	Forecast		
			2015	2016	2017
East Asia and Pacific	6.1	6.0	5.0	6.0	6.0
China	7.7	7.4	7.1	7.0	6.0
Indonesia	5.6	5.0	5.2	5.5	5.5
Malaysia	4.7	6.0	4.7	5.0	5.1
Philippines	7.2	6.1	6.5	6.5	6.3
Thailand	2.9	0.7	3.5	4.0	4.0
Vietnam	5.5	6.0	6.0	6.2	6.5
Cambodia	7.4	7.0	6.9	6.9	6.8
Laos	8.5	7.5	6.4	7.0	7.0
Myanmar	8.3	8.5	8.5	8.2	8.0
Mongolia	11.6	7.8	4.4	4.2	3.9
Fiji	4.6	3.8	2.5	2.4	2.6
Papua New Guinea	5.5	7.5	16.0	5.0	2.4
Solomon Islands	3.0	0.1	3.5	3.5	3.5
Timor-Leste	5.4	6.6	6.8	6.9	7.0
Developing East Asia and Pacific excluding China	5.2	4.6	5.1	5.4	5.4
ASEAN	**5.0**	**4.4**	**4.9**	**5.1**	**5.2**
World	**2.5**	**2.6**	**2.9**	**3.2**	**3.2**

Source: World Bank (2015a, p. 23).

Several sources offer confirmation of the rather gloomy prospects for Thai growth. Various economists have noted that Thai GDP growth will remain below its full potential, estimated at 4–5 per cent (Suttinee 2015). The economy grew at only 2.9 per cent in 2013 and 0.7 per cent in 2014. In 2015, the National Economic and Social Development Board (NESDB) cut its GDP growth forecast for the year to 3–4 per cent from an earlier prediction of 3.5–4.5 per cent (ibid.). It lowered its export growth forecast to 0.2 per cent from 3.5 per cent (ibid.). The Bank of Thailand also cut its 2015 growth forecast from its previous level of 3.8 per cent to 3.0 per cent (ibid.). According to a World Bank forecast, Thai GDP will grow at 4 per cent in 2016. Other 2016 forecasts come from the Ministry of Finance (2016), 3.5 per cent; the National Economic and Social Development Board (NESDB 2016), 3.0–3.5 per cent; and Asian Development Bank (2016), 3.0 per cent.

I will turn shortly to the underlying structural factors that form the background to lower secular growth. However, we should also note, as is elaborated later in this chapter, that a period of slower growth also coexists with positive features of Thai economic development. Demographic factors will allow for increases in per capita production, and lower rates of population growth will encourage investment in labour-saving technology; agriculture is already adapting to changing circumstances through diversification, the growth of agribusiness, a higher-quality labour force, and new and more productive enterprises in rural villages. Moreover, slower growth will reduce many environmental problems, which have been a striking feature of earlier heady growth, or at least delay their onset.

Slow Growth after 1997

Among the structural and fundamental factors that underlie slow growth in Thailand, we may single out the reduced supply of cheap labour, the low quality of the labour force, and weak technological capacity and capability.

Cheap Labour

Cheap labour, together with an inflow of foreign capital, fuelled the boom before 1997. However, the period of growth based on cheap labour is now at an end. Cheap labour has been significant in increasing the competitiveness of Thai manufacturing. Thailand's fast-growing manufacturing sector concentrated on labour-intensive commodities, such as textiles, clothing or leather goods, before the 1990s. Low urban wages raised profit margins in the commercial and industrial sectors.

As far as can be judged, real wages in Bangkok probably stagnated or even declined in the years between 1960 and 1980, but from the early 1980s real wages in both Bangkok and the provinces dramatically increased (Nipon 2007, pp. 72–107; National Statistical Office, n.d.). A Thailand Development Research Institute (TDRI) study shows that from 1982 to 1996, real wages roughly doubled, with the increase heavily concentrated in the years after 1990 (Warr 2005, p. 24). Thereafter, real wages continued to increase after 1997, even in the difficult 1996–2002 period, at an average annual rate of 9 per cent (Warr 2005, p. 124).

Workers in Bangkok generally earn much higher wages than those in the primate cities of most other Association of Southeast Asian Nations

(ASEAN) countries, especially those in the poorest countries in the region: Cambodia, Vietnam, Laos and Myanmar. In 2011, for example, monthly wages of factory workers in Bangkok averaged US$286, while the figures for Jakarta, Ho Chi Minh City and Yangon were US$209, US$130 and US$68, respectively (Somkiat et al. 2013, p. 17). The continued rise in relative labour costs will hurt Thai competitiveness, particularly in labour-intensive industries. Between 2005 and 2014, real wages for unskilled labour in the manufacturing sector rose at a rate of around 4–5 per cent annually.[1]

The hypothesis that cheap labour can promote growth has been prominent in the economic development literature since the 1950s. Thailand approximated such a model, in which labour with low or zero marginal productivity in the rural sector can be drawn to the more productive urban or manufacturing sector. Eventually, marginal productivity rates in the two sectors, and hence real wages, will tend towards equality. Thus, rural–urban migration is a mechanism for adjusting the disequilibrium between the urban and rural labour markets. A high wage differential brings rural migrants into the urban or "modern" sector with no loss of output, since there is a surplus of unemployed or underemployed labour in the rural sector (Zarembka 1972). Wage differentials will continue to attract rural migrants until uncertainties over finding high-wage employment in the modern sector begin to dissuade potential migrants (Todaro 1969, p. 139).

Demographic patterns can also influence wage rates. In Thailand, despite population increases, the annual population growth rate has shown a significant decline, especially after the early 1970s. The annual population growth rate was 2.70 per cent from 1960 to 1970, 1.10 per cent from 1990 to 2000, and 0.72 per cent from 2000 to 2010 (National Statistical Office 1962, 1973, 1990, 2000 and 2010b). Low population growth rates were influenced largely by rising incomes and the effectiveness of family planning programmes from the early 1970s onward. The total fertility rate in Thailand had steadily declined. In 1964/65, there was an average of 6.3 live births among women of childbearing age; the figure dropped to 2.11 and 1.4 in 1987 and 2012, respectively (Somboon 2012, p. 57; UNICEF 2013). The current population growth rate is largely a lag effect from earlier trends of population growth, and recent data show that fertility rates are in fact slightly below replacement level. This situation is all the more astonishing in a country in which the population is, at least officially, still largely rural.

The late 1980s saw significant changes in the Thai rural workforce that also affected wages in the countryside. There was a large-scale movement of young workers out of the agricultural sector and from rural areas, spurred by the very high rates of economic growth achieved at the end of the 1980s. This movement naturally caused a rise in real wage rates in the countryside. Figures for foreign capital inflows in those years indicate the extent of the boom in manufacturing, centred on Bangkok. Somboon noted that "foreign direct investment increased by 67 per cent in 1986, 360 per cent in 1987, and 140 per cent in 1988. In 1987, Japanese investment approved by the Board of Investment exceeded the cumulative investment in Thailand since the 1960s" (Somboon 2012, p. 148). The exodus of agricultural labour was concentrated, both in time and in the age group of workers principally affected. According to Ammar (2004), "most of the movement was among men and women in the 15–24 years old group between 1989 and 1998. The agriculture sector lost almost half of its workers in this age group within these years" (Nipon 2007, p. 6, citing Ammar 2004). Since then, the Thai rural labour force has declined only gradually, and, "between 1999–2005, the decline in the number of 15–24-year-old farm workforce dropped little more than 0.6 million persons. The decline is mainly attributed to the increase in number of students and non agricultural employment in the rural areas" (Nipon 2007, p. 8). This growth in the numbers of students in rural areas in the 1990s was partly due to the extension of compulsory education from primary to secondary education; the establishment of new provincial universities was also a factor (ibid., p. 9).

Shortages of labour have been felt throughout Thailand, and in all major sectors of the Thai economy. In some areas of agricultural production, such as fisheries and rubber, labour shortages have resulted in a reliance on immigrant labour. In some parts of the country, especially the South, many of the migrants have come from Myanmar. In the 2000–2010 period, the unskilled labour force from Myanmar increased almost fourfold, from 724,000 to 2,673,000 (Somchai 2014, p. 14). In fact, these figures are underestimates, since they do not include undocumented workers. A TDRI study estimates that there were some 932,255 illegal immigrants in Thailand in 2010, with around 80 per cent coming from Myanmar (Srawooth and Yongyuth 2012). One finds Burmese labourers in many industrial and service sectors, including construction, domestic work, cloth and clothing production and sales, food vending, retail and wholesale trade, hawking, and general manufacturing and trade (Somkiat et al. 2013, p. 15).

Low fertility rates and outmigration have not only tended to increase wages for unskilled labour in rural areas, but they have also resulted in the ageing of the agricultural population. One National Statistical Office survey found that the proportion of farmers aged sixty years and more increased from 2.5 per cent in 1984 to 3.3 per cent in 2005 (*Bangkok Business News*, 2 July 2013). Another survey by the Department of Community Development showed that in 2009 the proportion of the population older than sixty formed about 9.7 per cent of the entire village population in the country (Department of Community Development 2009). The ageing workforce will have significant implications for the Thai rural economy and for the future system of support for the elderly.

A United Nations projection suggests that Thailand will become a "completely aged" society around 2025, when one fifth of its population will be aged sixty or older (Somkiat and Nonnarit, p. 5). In 2014, one tenth of the total population was aged sixty and older (ibid., p. 5). In comparison with other Asian countries, Thailand will become a completely aged society faster than most, with the exceptions being Japan, South Korea and Singapore. As the birth rate in Thailand declines, the country's total population is predicted to decrease from 68 million in 2015 to about 63.8 million by 2045, in a situation likely to create a severe shortage of labour (ibid., p. 5).

Under conditions of increasing real wages, Thailand's export industries, especially those in highly labour-intensive sectors, will be particularly vulnerable. This is because such industries often face highly competitive international markets for their products; they cannot pass increased labour costs on in the form of increased prices.

The Quality of the Labour Force

One of the most serious problems facing Thailand is likely to be the quality of its labour force. Despite various attempts by successive governments to expand and improve education at every level, especially after 1992, the results have not been satisfactory. Thailand may thus face a chronic shortage of skilled labour. In 2010, of the total Thai labour force of 38.6 million, more than half or 20.8 million had only primary education of six years or less (National Statistical Office 2010b). This means that Thailand's comparative advantage lies in its unskilled labour force. Although the literacy rate of the population is impressive, and in fact the highest in Southeast Asia, there has been a significant drop in school enrolment after the completion of the six years of primary school that were compulsory until 1999. Many more students gave up their studies after the first level of secondary school, an additional three years of education (Kermel-Torrès 2004, p. 176).

Low standards and high variability in educational quality also characterize the Thai educational system. Enrolment rates have increased rapidly in recent decades, but the quality of education remains low, not least when international comparisons are made. Moreover, students from Bangkok and other urban areas generally receive higher-quality education and have a higher chance of being admitted to the best universities than those from the provinces.

The very high proportion of unskilled labour in the Thai labour force is not conducive to an industrial structure that requires more skilled labour to increase labour productivity. Somboon argues that, "as industrialization proceeds, the unskilled and low-skilled labour force should become smaller compared to high-skilled labour, including managers, professionals, and white-collar workers. This enhances a country's capacity to acquire and make use of advanced technology which, in turn, brings about the productivity growth" (Somboon 2012, pp. 151–52). However, Thailand's labour supply is still largely composed of unskilled labour.

Thailand's education system is also unsuitable to prepare graduates for the labour market, which is increasingly facing global competition. Such relevant skills as the use of information technology, communication skills and leadership are lacking. Government plans to emphasize vocational education to serve the growing industrial sector have yet to receive high priority. Thus, both semi-skilled and skilled labour remains in short supply, and a recent study noted that "Thailand's educational system does not equip graduates with the skills required by industries and the labour market" (Pasuk and Pornthep 2013, p. 19).

Technological Capability

Thailand's industrial development has not emphasized developing its own technological capability, but rather focuses on suppressing wages to enhance competitiveness in the global market. Investment in research and development has long remained very low, averaging around 0.2 per cent of GDP annually for years (Somchai 2012, p. 16).

Industrialization by means of cheap labour has discouraged innovation and development towards a higher level of technology. Productivity has, in consequence, remained low, and a large part of the population has low-income levels and a low quality of life. Income inequality also grew for many years. A low level of technological capability will leave the economy increasingly vulnerable, as Thailand is now more dependent on the ebbs and flows of the world economy. The future of Thai industrialization is uncertain, given the present difficulties in the international economy.

For the reasons noted above, the Thai economy seems to have lost its competitiveness in the global economy. In the International Institute for Management Development ranking of international competitiveness, Thailand fell from the position of 13 among 61 countries in 2011 to 27 in 2012; in the following three years it ranked 27, 29 and 30 (*Bangkok Post*, July 2015, p. 9).

Inequality

During the lengthy period of significant economic growth after the 1950s, poverty in Thailand declined significantly. For example, in 2011 about 10 per cent of the rural population and 2.1 per cent of the urban population were below the poverty line, compared with figures of 52.6 and 25.3 per cent for 1986 (Medhi 1986, pp. 5–21; Somchai 2004; NESDB 2015*a*, pp. 1–6). As Table 13.3 indicates, figures for regional GDP per head showed a widening gap between regions. In 1960, average per capita incomes for the whole kingdom were about double those for the Northeast; in 1989 the ratio was 2.67, increasing to 2.71 in 2012. Significant differences also existed among regions. The ratio in per capita income between Bangkok and the Northeast rose from a ratio of 5.5 in 1960 to 8.03 in 1989; it was still 5.27 in 2012. The ratio in per capita income between the Central region and the Northeast rose from 2.42 in 1960 to 2.55 in 1989, and jumped to 8.78 in 2012 (Table 13.3).

The Northeast has long been not only a region of relative poverty and deprivation but also one of low per capita incomes, high levels of rural employment, small family farms, low agricultural productivity, high levels of out-migration and low standards in the provision of education and health services. A wide variety of statistical indicators demonstrate the inequalities and gaps in the provision of social services, including hospitals and schools, between the Northeast and other regions.

TABLE 13.3
Regional GDP per Head, 1960–2012 (baht) (market prices)

	1960	1980	1989	2012
Bangkok Region	5,715	45,300	96,239	361,639
Central	2,537	20,647	30,587	259,306
North	1,458	10,511	18,833	93,067
Northeast	1,046	6,294	11,981	68,514
South	2,594	14,052	21,955	126,178
Whole Kingdom	2,056	15,280	32,028	185,807

Source: Falkus (1999, p. 131); NESDB, n.d.

In 2010, twelve of the fifteen provinces with the lowest per capita GDP in the country were located in the Northeast, the remaining three being in the North. Among northeastern provinces there are also substantial differences between prosperous ones such as Khorat or Khon Kaen and poor ones like Nong Bua Lamphu or Amnat Charoen. In 2012, for example, GDP per head in Nong Bua Lamphu and Amnat Charoen, respectively, was 41,400 baht and 49,000 baht; for Khorat the figure was 95,000 baht and for Khon Kaen 106,600 baht (NESDB, n.d.).

Education levels in the northeastern countryside were low compared with other regions, despite improvements after 1992. In the mid-1990s, less than 15 per cent of primary school children in the Northeast went on to secondary education (Kermel-Torrès 2004, p. 180). Although opportunities expanded, the quality of education in the Northeast has always been lower than elsewhere. Given the basic educational disadvantages of the Northeast, the chances for students to enter prestigious universities were very limited. In addition, inadequate education inhibits the movement of labour from low- to high-productivity occupations. The effect is to impede economic growth in Thailand — an issue that was raised at the opening of this chapter.

Inequality remains one of the major problems of Thai society. The disturbances associated with pro- and anti-Thaksin Shinawatra factions in the last dozen years can be usefully viewed through the lens of regional inequality. The advent of Thaksin in 2001, his overthrow in 2006, the violent disturbances of 2010, and the May 2014 military coup have all focused attention on the Northeast region. Pro-Thaksin political parties and the "Red Shirts" were heavily, though not exclusively, associated with popular support from the Northeast. Of course, as it accounts for a third of the country's population, a one man, one vote system gives potentially enormous political power to that region.

The striking feature of this conflict is that it appears to have a very definite regional core, despite the nationwide relevance of many of the issues involved. While it is simplistic to see the conflict in stark regional and class terms —in terms, that is, of a rich Bangkok-centred elite versus a poor rural Northeast — a regional perspective on the conflict does highlight matters for reflection. In other words, low agricultural productivity, a lack of alternate occupations and limited education help account for large rural populations in certain regions of Thailand. Furthermore, the continuing presence of these populations has an obvious influence on an electoral system based on universal suffrage.

In view of the support that Thaksin has enjoyed in all regions of the country save the South, it is worth asking why he, the pro-Thaksin People's Power Party (*Phak phalang prachachon*), the Phuea Thai Party formed after his ouster in 2006 and the abolition of the Thai Rak Thai Party should be so firmly associated with the Northeast. Three reasons may be suggested. First, in terms of sheer numbers, the Northeast controls more parliamentary seats than any other region because of the size of its electorate. Second, the most obvious examples of vote buying and vote rigging often came from the Northeast. Third, when the Red Shirt movement developed after the September 2006 coup, many Northeasterners and the forms of entertainment that they favoured seemed to predominate at its rallies.

Socio-economic differentiation is also an important aspect of the Thai rural economy. As agricultural production has become more capital-intensive, increased integration with the market economy has tended to sharpen socio-economic differentiation in the countryside. For example, Thippawal explored agricultural diversification in upland environments of Nakhon Pathom Province in Central Thailand. In these places, "land concentration in hands of a few capitalists is more frequent ... than in predominantly rice growing areas, because sugarcane cultivation lends itself to economies of scale and can be managed with hired labour" (Thippawal 2003, p. 151).

Likely Consequences of a Slow-down in the Rate of GDP Growth

Generally speaking, continued economic growth is important for Thailand's development. High economic growth helps to reduce poverty and provides resources that can be used to finance improvements in healthcare, education and infrastructure. It can also yield resources to combat other economic and social problems, such as environmental degradation. Thailand retains a large rural labour force. In 2010, around 56 per cent of the population lived in rural areas (National Statistical Office 2010*b*). Economic growth, especially if centred on the industrial and service sectors, can offer off-farm jobs for migrants from rural areas.

However, economic growth can also have adverse effects. In the period of high growth before 1997, rapid industrialization led to considerable environmental damage. Such damage included shrinking forest areas and the adverse effects of deforestation and the depletion of other natural resources. One study noted that ninety million *rai* of forests were cleared between 1960 and 1990, at an average rate of three million *rai* per year (Somboon 2012, p. 149).[2] It is therefore hardly surprising that Thailand has had one of the most rapid rates of deforestation in the world since the 1950s, partly because Thailand's export-oriented industrialization relied very much on the exploitation of natural resources.

In my view, an average growth rate of 3–4 per cent annually is perfectly manageable and would not prevent the smooth development of the Thai economy. Such moderate growth has been the pattern since the 1997 crisis, and growth will probably remain at this level in the next decade or so. We should not, then, be overly concerned about the future if Thai GDP growth continues at this rate during this period. Three major factors substantiate this conclusion: the continued low rate of fertility, comparative advantages possessed by the Thai economy, and border trade and the establishment of the ASEAN Economic Community (AEC).

The Continued Low Rate of Fertility

Although Thai GDP will grow more slowly, a low birth rate will also continue to characterize the country. This combination will in turn lead to higher per capita incomes, with families able to devote more expenditure to each child, including on education. Higher incomes should bring greater savings and higher rates of investment. According to one survey from the Health Insurance System Research Office, in 2015 households caring for elderly relatives spent at least 7,620 baht per month on them, or 28 per cent of the average monthly household income of 26,915 baht. (Fraser 2016). With the continued transformation from a rural to an urban economy, family size will continue to drop. The decline will result from a number of factors, including the rise in women's education levels and employment rates that accompany increased income; we may expect, therefore, that women will postpone raising families.

The impact of the low fertility rate can already be seen in rural areas of Thailand. Low fertility, together with outmigration from the villages, has brought higher wages in rural areas. In response to higher wages, farmers utilize more farm machinery to replace expensive labour. The number of agricultural machines — such as tractors, threshing machines, water pumps and other equipment — increased throughout rural Thailand. Farm mechanization was particularly rapid in the irrigated areas of the Central Plains. Somporn's and Hossain's study of the dynamics of rice farming in the Chao Phraya Delta between 1987 and 1998 concluded that, "As a consequence of labour saving technology [farm mechanization], the total amount of labour use per hectare in rice farming activities declined significantly in all production environments" (Somporn and Hossain 2003, p. 122). Mechanization played a significant role in inducing farmers to use hired labour instead of family labour. As Somboon notes, "this change is inevitably associated with an increase in the value of the wife's time. The opportunity cost of employing children as capital good is increasing" (Somboon 2012, p. 61). Changes in the rural labour market, caused partly by low fertility rates, have certainly benefited Thai economic development. These benefits have come in the forms of both increased agricultural productivity and the social benefits of reduced child labour. Low fertility rates also lead to a greater cultivated area per head, and may lead to more investment in enlarged commercial farms.

Comparative Advantages of the Thai Economy

There are a number of comparative advantages of the Thai economy that mitigate the consequences of the slowdown in growth, and that also indicate potential for further growth and development. These advantages include large foreign income earnings from agricultural exports, a very low rate of open unemployment in the agricultural sector, high regional and provincial labour mobility, growing value added in agricultural production, a strong service sector and the buoyancy of tourism.

In the past two decades or so, economic growth has occurred at a moderate rate. Nevertheless, the agricultural sector, while contributing only around 10 per cent of GDP (NESDB, n.d.), has continued to play an important role in Thai economic development. Agricultural production ensures food security and provides income, both directly and indirectly, to a large portion of the population; 40 per cent of the Thai labour force is engaged in this sector (National Statistical Office, n.d.). Rural areas can supply labour for the urban industrial and service sectors, and agriculture represents a large source of foreign income earning. Rural Thailand also provides national stability and retains valuable cultural and social dimensions.

The agricultural sector has seen much regional specialization, with the practice of single-crop farming increasing. Specialization results in lower average production costs and increased innovation. On the Central Plains, irrigated rice cultivation predominates, but rice production is declining in favour of the cultivation of crops for the metropolitan market. Such crops include market garden produce and tree crops, including grapes, rose apples, lemons, asparagus, vegetables and guava, which often require considerable investment (Cheyroux 2003, pp. 157–76). One study noted, "The effects of urban growth [in the central region] can also be seen, to a lesser extent in the surrounding provinces and some provinces in the Eastern Seaboard. The proximity of export infrastructure and the size of the markets have favoured development of new products that are highly integrated into agro-industry and are added to more traditional crops (rice and upland crops)" (Kermel-Torrès 2004, p. 104). High-yielding rice varieties are also available to farmers in this region. On the Central Plains, the percentage of single-crop holdings has remained virtually the same since the 1960s, but the share of holdings specializing in perennial crops, vegetables and flowers has increased, while that of paddy farms has declined (Nipon 2007, p. 50).

The North, Northeast and West are highly specialized in crop cultivation. The crop share of agricultural value added — the increase in the economic value of a commodity resulting from production processes — in the North increased from 74 per cent in 1981 to over 90 per cent in 2013 (Office of Agricultural Statistics 2014). One possible explanation is that the North, with the smallest household landholdings in the country, is less suitable for agricultural activities other than vegetables and high-value fruit crops (Nipon 2007, p. 50). With a plentiful supply of surface water, many farmers in the region can grow several crops in one year. The North is fortunate in that "local people developed a communal irrigation system using water from rivers and streams; this system allows higher paddy yields than in other regions and dry-season cultivation of crops such as soybeans" (Shigetomi 2004, p. 301). The West is dominated by upland crops and rice.

In the Northeast, the major crops are rice, cassava and sugar cane. Agricultural production is concentrated on crops, which in early 2004 accounted for 80.5 per cent of agricultural value added, while livestock accounted for 16.8 per cent (Office of Agricultural Statistics 2012). Because of poor soil and limited irrigation, rice yields in the region are low. Most rice cultivated is glutinous, and mainly for domestic consumption. Farmers in upland areas grow cassava, sugar cane and rubber; rubber cultivation in the region grew rapidly from the 1990s. Northeastern agricultural households are more dependent on rice than those in other regions. A decade ago, only 13 per cent of Northeastern farmers specialized in non-rice crops, such as cassava and maize or fruits and vegetables — the lowest share in the country (NESDB and World Bank 2005, p. 140).

In the South, farmers have specialized in the production of rubber, oil palm and fruit and in aquaculture, but the region is generally not suitable for the substantial cultivation of rice and upland crops. Because of the higher value-added of its agricultural products compared with rice and other upland crops, the South is the only region of the country in which the proportion of agricultural income exceeds non-agricultural income (Office of Agricultural Statistics, n.d.).

Structural change in Thai agriculture has been in part a response to higher wages. It has resulted in a more intensive approach to increasing agricultural output. It involves a greater application of capital and technology and it links agriculture to Thailand's processes of urbanization and export-oriented industrialization. This set of changes is particularly associated with agribusiness. Intensive livestock rearing, aquaculture, horticulture and fruit growing show increasing vertical integration between upstream inputs and downstream processing industries. Exports of agro-industrial products, which include canned seafood, canned fruits, canned vegetables, cane sugar and molasses, have grown impressively. Their share in total exports of food and agricultural products grew from 24 per cent in 1988 to almost 40 per cent in 2012 (Bank of Thailand, *Quarterly Bulletin*, various issues). Thailand has developed agribusiness to a greater degree than any other Southeast Asian nation, and the industry is dominated by large corporate enterprises, which includes the giant multinational Charoen Pokphand group.

As rural Thailand has experienced rapid economic transformation, farm families have adjusted to the changes and have been able to survive on the land. It should be emphasized that the growth of the service sector — including such small-scale activities as grocery stores; food stalls; motorcycle and tractor repair shops; television, radio and electronic repair shops; small construction firms; and a host of other kinds of workshops — has been very rapid, as Table 13.4 shows. Remittances from migrants have sustained this growth, and they have become increasingly important as major sources of employment for own-account workers and unpaid family workers.

The data in Table 13.4 confirm that the rural household economy and rural families have turned their attention to various forms of non-agricultural activity in order to be able to survive on the land. Rural people have shown a remarkable capacity to adapt to changing conditions while at the same time conserving their established patterns of behaviour and their particular modes of survival. Indeed, peasant workers, far from disappearing, have been increasingly central to the Thai village economy. They have provided the workforce and often the entrepreneurship behind the expansion of a multitude of new small businesses.

The service sector, especially activities associated with tourism, embodies another comparative advantage of the Thai economy. The service sector has contributed significantly to the Thai economy by generating between 49 and 57 per cent of GDP during the period 1993–2013 (NESDB, n.d.). The share of employment in the service sector has increased significantly, from about 41 per cent of total employment in 1998 to 50 per cent in 2014 (National Statistical Office, n.d.). Tourism generates the largest share of the sector's contribution to GDP, and it provides an exceptionally large share of employment in the sector. In 2013, tourism made more than double the contribution of the financial services sector to GDP, which stood at 8 per cent, and three times the mining sector's contribution of 4.9 per cent (World Travel and Tourism Council 2013). Tourism sustained a total of 5.3 million jobs, directly and indirectly, and it directly supported nearly twice as many jobs as the education sector (ibid.). Tourism has grown rapidly and it has made an important contribution to economic growth. We may note that in 2013, income from tourism was 75 per cent of Thailand's total income from services, and 12.2 per cent of total exports (ibid.). Between 2000 and 2013, tourism expanded 258 per cent, at a rate virtually identical to that of exports of goods and services (ibid.).

TABLE 13.4
Small Shops in Villages, 1992–2011

Year	Number of villages	Grocery store/small restaurants	Agricultural selling input shop	Vehicle repair shop	Radio and television shop	Electronic repair shop	Welding shops	Small construction firms	Artisan workshops
1999	63,239	272,415	9,032	50,155	8,881	6,080	10,695	1,212	1,697
2001	66,193	292,420	15,366	59,449	10,117	7,301	12,497	4,503	6,443
2005	69,110	326,758	15,949	58,204	12,287	n/a	16,601	9,125	n/a
2009	71,130	327,152	20,606	62,311	25,587	15,587	17,413	11,368	n/a
2011	71,137	317,025	19,969	70,557	n/a	14,518	16,171	10,321	12,359

Source: Department of Community Development data set.

The share of tourism in total GDP increased from 6 per cent in the late 1990s to 10 per cent in 2014 (Tourism Authority of Thailand, n.d.). Because of its importance, the government pays particular attention to supporting the tourism sector with various policies and measures, including tourist infrastructure development and promotional campaigns (Kermel-Torrès 2004, p. 132).

Table 13.5 shows the growth in foreign tourist numbers during the 2000–2014 period. In 2014, despite the disturbed political situation in Thailand, the number of foreign visitors was 24.7 million, and they generated an income of 1.13 trillion baht. In 2013 Thailand earned 1.47 trillion baht and ranked seventh among the world's top tourist destinations (NESDB 2015b, p. 10).

Many factors lie behind the development of Thailand's tourist industry. Bangkok is a major hub for air travel in Asia, and international air routes extend to Bangkok and also to some provincial centres. Bangkok has grown rapidly in importance as a tourist centre, and many international airlines use Bangkok as a convenient stopping place for refuelling. Flying times to the major centres of mainland Southeast Asia, such as Yangon, Mandalay, Kuala Lumpur, Vientiane, Phnom Penh and Saigon, are about one hour,

TABLE 13.5
Numbers of Foreign Visitors to Thailand, 2000–2014

Year	Number of Foreign Visitors (millions)
2000	9.57
2001	10.13
2003	10.0
2004	11.73
2006	13.82
2007	14.46
2008	14.58
2009	14.15
2010	19.23
2011	15.93
2012	22.35
2013	26.54
2014	24.70

Source: World Bank (2015b) and NESDB (2015b, p. 10).

while Hong Kong, Singapore and Calcutta are about two hours distant, and Delhi, Jakarta and Manila about four hours.

Other attractions possessed by Thailand include those of a historical and cultural nature, modern and vibrant shopping centres, a wide range of hotel accommodation, and striking sea coasts with many attractive resorts. Increasingly, tourists are travelling beyond the traditional centres of Bangkok, Chiang Mai, Phuket and Pattaya to more distant locations, while the decline of the Thai baht following the 1997 crisis also boosted foreign arrivals.

Tourism benefits many other sectors of the economy, and the domestic economy can supply all but the most specialized needs of the average tourist. Benefits from tourism are spreading increasingly to the provinces. Thus, for example, Hua Hin and Cha Am have developed into a new urban agglomeration because of the tourist industry. In the early 2000s, this urban area contained over 300,000 people, not including tourists themselves; it was one of the larger urban agglomerations in Thailand (Webster 2005, p. 293). The Hua Hin and Cha Am urban region received about 7 million tourists a year at that time — some 4 million Thais and 3 million foreigners (Webster 2005, p. 299).

As well as tourism, other branches of the service sector also help to generate income growth and employment. These include spas, hospitals and other healthcare services, and restaurants.

Cross-Border Trade and the AEC

The full establishment of the AEC from 2015 onwards will have important implications for the integration of ASEAN member states into a regional economy. The AEC creates opportunities for flows of goods, capital and technology to fuel more rapid economic growth, for increased access to goods and services, and for the development of trade, logistics and tourism hubs.

Because of its strategic location, Thailand stands to benefit from the AEC. Thirty-three of its seventy-seven provinces border neighbouring countries. Thailand lies at the intersection of several economic corridors, including the East-West corridor connecting Myanmar, Thailand, Laos and Vietnam; the North-South corridor connecting the southern provinces of China, Myanmar, Thailand, Laos and Malaysia; and the Southern corridor connecting the Dawei deep sea port in Myanmar, the

Laem Chabang deep sea port in Thailand, and Cambodia. Thailand has shown an interest in developing these economic corridors and has tried to set up border economic zones and regional development hubs along them, with the aim of developing relatively poor areas through mutual cooperation. The idea is that by shifting agricultural processing and labour-intensive manufacturing to border economic zones, Thai industries could benefit from cheap labour and resources from neighbouring countries, while neighbouring countries could benefit from job creation and the development of consumer markets.[3]

Because of differences in the level of economic development and infrastructure, among other factors, the AEC may benefit Thailand more than poorer countries such as Laos, Cambodia and Myanmar. Thailand is more developed, with better infrastructure and logistics and more advanced technology, and its economy is largely an industrial one, with the non-agricultural share of GDP reaching around 90 per cent. By comparison, for instance, Laos faces obstacles that will limit gains from improved integration with its neighbours. Its economy remains largely concentrated on subsistence and agriculture, in spite of recent strides in industrial development. Most domestic private production consists of small-scale enterprises, with low levels of technology and competitiveness. Transport costs are high, and the growth of the economy relies on the utilization of natural resources. These obstacles will limit the opportunities for Laos to capture gains from trade from the AEC, and the same will apply to Cambodia and Myanmar.

It is encouraging that over the last decade, Thailand's trade with neighbouring countries, especially cross-border trade, has grown rapidly. Cross-border trade has played an increasingly important role in Thailand's exports and economic growth. In 2014, Thailand's border trade with neighbouring countries rose to 990 billion baht, with exports accounting for 590 billion baht or 8 per cent of the country's total exports. This figure is close to the level of exports to major markets, such as the United States, the European Union and Japan (Export-Import Bank of Thailand 2015).

Among the factors promoting the growth of cross-border trade is a significant rise in per capita incomes in Cambodia, Laos and Myanmar. Thailand's trade promotion policy, including the establishment of Special Economic Development Zones (SEZs), has also proved important (ibid., p. 2). Ten provinces have been designated in the first phase of SEZs, including Tak, Mukdahan, Songkhla, Sa Kaeo, Trat, Nong Khai, Chiang Rai,

Nakhon Phanom, Narathiwat and Kanchanaburi. In 2015 the government hoped to open two SEZs in Mae Sot and Ayanyaprathet. It has also considered establishing zones dedicated to particular industries, such as innovation, high technology, and research and development (*Bangkok Post*, July 2015, p. 54). However, by mid-2016 the two SEZs mentioned above were not in operation yet. In 2016, Chonburi, Chacheongsao and Rayong in the Eastern region were designated as SEZs as well (*Thai rat*, 31 May 2016).

The growth of cross-border trade has produced changes in Thailand's border provinces, and even in provinces only situated in proximity to international borders. There have been more international tourists, greater investment in land and property, and rising land prices. The governments of Khon Kaen, Mahasarakham and Roi Et, in cooperation with the Northeastern Strategic Institute of Khon Kaen University, created a regional industrial cluster plan for 2005–8 based on the Greater Mekong Subregion and Ayeyawady–Chao Phraya–Mekong Economic Cooperation Strategy frameworks. The aim is for Khon Kaen to take advantage of its location to become a logistics hub with an inland container depot. As part of this plan, a container yard has been established adjacent to the Khon Kaen railway station.

It is expected that, as the AEC comes into full effect, Thailand will experience many benefits. Development will be decentralized, with more regional employment as a result of industrial relocation, reduced rates of rural–urban migration and lower rates of regional income inequality.

Conclusion

The high growth rates achieved by Thailand before 1997 seem to have come to an end. However, the undesirable effects of more moderate growth of some 3–4 per cent a year should not be exaggerated. Some factors leading to slower growth are external, such as weak export demand and a decline in private sector investment. Lower demand from the United States, China and Europe not only affects Thailand but is also felt throughout the international economy, and this situation will persist into the near future.

The Thai economy is still growing, and growth will be sustainable in the context of a low population growth rate that will help to raise per capita incomes, and an agricultural sector that will produce more high-value crops with links to agribusiness. Agriculture will support growing exports and urbanization. Growing tourism will provide more jobs and greater incomes, with benefits from decentralization. Therefore, Thailand can sustain economic growth at moderate rates, in spite of continued weak demand from world markets.

Acknowledgements

I am very grateful to the late Professor Malcolm Falkus for kindly reading through the draft version of this chapter and commenting on many points of it. Special thanks also go to Dr Michael Montesano and Dr Terence Chong for their editorial work and helpful comments on the chapter.

Notes

1. Calculated from the Thai labour force survey (National Statistical Office, n.d.) and consumer Price index (National Statistical Office, *Statistical Yearbook of Thailand*, various years).
2. One *rai* equals 1600 square metres.
3. See, for example, Tsuneishi (2007 and 2008).

14

Features and Challenges of an Ageing Population in Thailand

Kwanchit Sasiwongsaroj and Youngyut Burasit

The world is experiencing an increase in the number of elderly people, aged sixty and over. There were approximately 841 million aged people worldwide in 2005, and this number is projected to increase to more than two billion in 2050 (United Nations 2013a, p. 75). While this global trend is more advanced in developed countries, where life expectancy is greater and healthcare better, it has also recently become apparent in developing countries whose economies have enjoyed rapid economic growth (Kinsella and Phillips 2005). Projections show that the percentage of the ageing population in developing countries will soar by 140 per cent within the next two decades (United Nations 2007).

Asia is on the path of demographic transition towards an ageing population. More than half of the world's population aged sixty-five and over is in Asia, and Asia will become the "oldest" region in the world in the next few decades (Menon and Melendez-Nakamura 2009, p. 2). Within Asia, East Asian countries have become ageing societies more rapidly and have a higher proportion of elderly than Southeast Asian countries. However, "population ageing"[1] in the latter is projected to increase at a more rapid rate during the next five decades (Mujahid 2006, p. 5).

The phenomenon of population ageing has caught the world's attention, as it generates many challenges and significantly affects local, regional and global health and economic conditions (McCall 2001; Norton 2000). More advanced ageing countries have witnessed challenges in the areas of long-term care (Wiener and Tilly 2002, pp. 777–78), the financial sustainability of pension systems and the well-being of the elderly (Beard et al. 2011, pp. 18–20; Restrepo and Rozental 1994, pp. 1328–33).

Although demographic transformation is widespread, the change varies in degree and pace among countries and regions. Ageing has proceeded more gradually in developed countries, thus affording them decades to introduce policies and infrastructure to deal with this change. On the other hand, developing countries face a particular set of challenges; namely, the predicament of getting old before getting rich and having less time, fewer resources and less technology to adapt to the many implications of demographic change (Bloom et al. 2011, pp. 31–32). The question that this chapter poses is, what are the specific features of Thailand's ageing population, the challenges that it poses, and their long-term socio-economic and political consequences?

The Features of Population Ageing in Thailand

Among Southeast Asian countries, Thailand ranks second after Singapore with the highest percentage of elderly people (United Nations 2015, p. 30). It is markedly different from the majority of the countries in the Greater Mekong Sub-region. According to official figures, Thailand has been an ageing society since 2005 (National Statistical Office 2008). Estimates from the United Nations (2007) indicate that the percentage of people aged sixty-five and over in Thailand has increased from 5.0 per cent in 1950 to 8.4 per cent in 2000 and will continue to increase to 27.1 per cent by 2050. These estimates mean that Thailand will become "a super-aged society"[2] in the next thirty years. The percentage of the Thai population aged sixty-five and over will increase at a faster rate than both the Asian and world averages; see Figure 14.1.

The Rapid Transition to an Ageing Society

Ageing has proceeded more gradually in developed countries. It took many decades for Western nations to make the transition to ageing societies. For

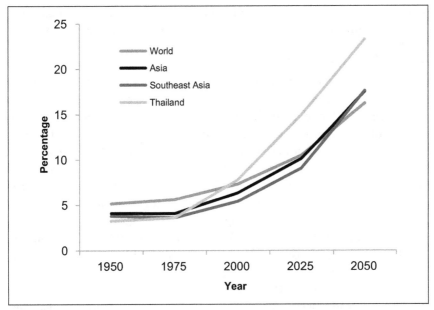

FIGURE 14.1   Population Aged 65 and Over in Thailand Relative to Global and Regional Trends, 1950–2050
Source: United Nations (2007).

example, it took 115, 85 and 69 years for the proportion of population aged sixty-five or older in France, Sweden and the United States, respectively, to increase from 7 to 14 per cent. On the contrary, the same increase occurred in just 22 years in Thailand (Kinsella and Phillips 2005, p. 15).

The rapid ageing experienced by Thailand is due primarily to remarkable improvements in the healthcare system and successful government campaigns for birth control. Thailand's total fertility rate (TFR)[3] has declined from 6.4 in the mid-1960s to 1.9 in the mid-1990s (Sutthichai et al. 1993, p. 377). These developments have resulted in declining mortality and fertility rates, respectively.

Extension of Lifespan

The life expectancy of Thais has also increased. According to the National Statistical Office (1970 and 2006), life expectancy at birth increased by between fourteen and fifteen years between 1965 and 2005, and it is projected to rise to 82.3 years for females and 77.2 years for males by 2040; see Figure 14.2. Among older Thais, women outnumber men. They constitute the majority of Thailand's older population and live longer than men by approximately five to six years (United Nations 2013*b*; also see Figure 14.2). Needless to say, significant longevity prolongs the duration of care, social security and welfare payments for aged people.

Between 2010 and 2040, the proportion of "the oldest-old" — people aged eighty or older — in Thailand will almost double to about 19.1 per cent (National Economic and Social Development Board 2014). The greater proportion of women to men in the population becomes more pronounced as people's age advances, especially beyond seventy (Knodel et al. 2015, p. 19). The oldest-old are the fastest growing segment of all population groups as defined by age; see Figure 14.3. This growth is one of the main challenges that Thailand will have to confront as a large portion of people become more susceptible to disease and disabilities under ongoing economic constraints.

The age structure in Thailand has changed gradually. The country's low TFR will lead to a shrinking of the working-age population in decades to come, while the aged population continues to increase.[4] This pattern will result in a situation in which fewer working adults have to support the physical and healthcare, pensions and social security benefits of more elderly people, either directly through family support mechanisms or indirectly through taxation (Ingham et al. 2009, p. 223). Figure 14.4 shows the upward trend in the old-age dependency ratio from 10.7 per cent in 1994 to 22.3 per cent in 2014.[5] The latter figure translates to approximately one hundred working adults being required to take care of twenty-two older persons. Conversely, the potential support ratio has progressively decreased.[6] Currently, four persons of working age have the capacity to take care of one older person (National Statistical Office 2014). This raises concerns over old-age dependency.

Challenges Posed by Population Ageing

Health Challenges

As population ageing is directly related to issues of physical deterioration, the foremost challenge facing Thailand is that of providing adequate healthcare for older adults. The elderly are at higher risk of disease and

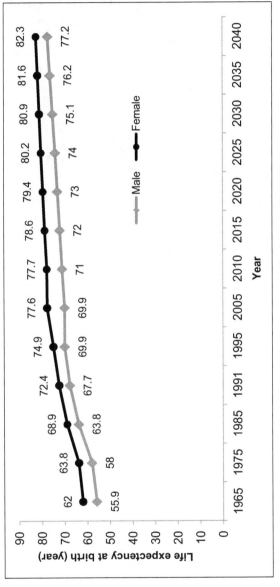

FIGURE 14.2 Estimation and Projection of Life Expectancy in Thailand, 1965–2040

Sources: National Statistical Office (1970 and 2006); United Nations (2013*b*).

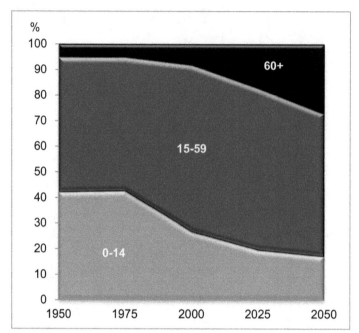

FIGURE 14.3   Share of Population in Thailand Aged 65 or Older, 1950–2050
Source: United Nations (2007).

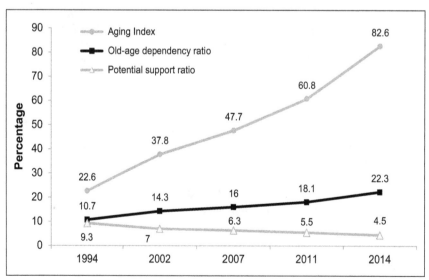

FIGURE 14.4   Aging Index, Old-age Dependency Ratio and Potential Support Ratio in Thailand, 1994–2014
Source: National Statistical Office (2014*b*).

disability. A middle-income country like Thailand must address questions such as whether the Thai elderly will live longer with good health or more illness, disability and dependency and how ageing will affect healthcare costs.

Generally, the ageing process is associated with numerous pathologies at the cellular, tissue and organ levels. Moreover, the most devastating aspect is the decline of brain functions (Gkikas et al. 2014, pp. 1–2). Increasing age normally comes with increased degeneration and consequently leads to frailty and subsequent dependency. Older adults living with dependency will become a big burden for Thailand in the near future.

Chronic Diseases

The current situation and trends related to the health status of older Thais are crucial to answering the questions posed above. According to the National Survey of Older Persons (National Statistical Office 2011b) and Health Survey of Thai Elders (Department of Health 2013), the percentage of elderly persons who reported their health as "poor" to "very poor" has decreased gradually from 25.9 in 1994 to 16.0 in 2013. A steady improvement in self-rated health recorded in five rounds of surveys may be due to advances in medical technology and improvements in the Thai healthcare system over recent decades. However, degenerative and chronic diseases, which accounted for leading causes of death and disability worldwide, are more likely to increase with age. Projections made by the World Health Organization suggest that deaths from chronic diseases such as cancer, hypertension, cardiovascular diseases and diabetes were projected to increase by 17 per cent, from 35 million to 41 million globally by 2015 (World Health Organization 2005).

The patterns of chronic diseases reported among the Thai elderly are similar to those in developed countries, with the most common being hypertension and diabetes mellitus. Both are important risk factors for cardiovascular and cerebrovascular diseases (Department of Health 2013, pp. 20–24). The prevalence of these diseases among older Thais increased significantly between 1994 and 2013, as Table 14.1 indicates. The prevalence of hypertension was 41.4 per cent and 18.2 per cent for diabetes mellitus. These rates were rather close to reported cases in American and Japanese elders (Avendano et al. 2009, p. 542; Ishine et al. 2005, p. 45). However, many elderly Thais could not control their blood sugar levels (55 per cent) and blood pressure (43 per cent) (Department of Health 2013, pp. 21, 23). Additionally, and not surprisingly, ageing people usually suffer from at least one chronic disease. Numerous chronic diseases are a major risk

TABLE 14.1
Percentage of the Elderly in Thailand Self-reporting Poor Health
and Chronic Disease, 1994–2013

	1994	2002	2007	2011	2013
Poor to very poor health	25.9	24.3	24.3	15.9	16.0
Hypertension	25.0	20.0	31.7	33.7	41.4
Diabetes	5.0	8.3	13.3	15.0	18.2
Heart disease	9.2	7.2	7.0	4.8	N/A
Cancer	0.5	0.5	0.5	0.9	N/A

Sources: National Statistical Office (1994, 2002, 2007*b*, 2011*b*, and 2014*b*); Department of Health (2013).

factor for other ailments, such as hypertension leading to cerebrovascular disease (Halpin et al. 2010, p. 123). Diabetes mellitus is a major risk factor for heart disease, strokes, hypertension, metabolic syndrome and end-stage renal disease (Martinez-Hervas et al. 2008, pp. 212–13). Co-morbidity is commonly found among older adults in ageing and aged societies. For example, approximately 74 to 90 per cent of aged Canadians reported having at least one chronic condition, and about one quarter were affected by two or more of these conditions (Smith 2012, p. 2). Similarly, the Thai Ministry of Public Health (Department of Health 2013, p. 12) reported that 95 per cent of older Thais were living with at least one chronic disease. Chronic disease among the elderly may consequently lead to poor health and represent a burden on care and financial support.

Physical Impairment: Disability

Elderly individuals are susceptible not only to chronic diseases but also to declining functional ability. Physical impairment is typically caused by degeneration, illness or injury. It relates to inability to perform such basic activities of daily living as walking, feeding oneself, dressing oneself, using the toilet and grooming. It also relates to difficulties in performing instrumental or advanced activities of daily living such as interacting with other people, financial management and participation in social activities (World Health Organization 2003).

Although functional ability naturally declines with age, some comparative studies reveal significant differences in the pace of decline in both basic and advanced activities of daily living between elderly people in developed and developing countries. The latter group reports a greater rate of decline than the former group. According to cross-national studies, older Thais and their counterparts in other Southeast Asian countries were less likely to conduct basic and advanced activities of daily living independently than Japanese of the same age group; see Table 14.2 (Ishine et al. 2005, p. 118; Ishine et al. 2006, p. 44; Wada et al. 2005, p. 171). Despite the older Thais being significantly younger than their Japanese counterparts, the study found that the former needed more help and care than Japanese elderly. The discrepancies may be due to differences in economic status, infrastructure and education level. It is supposed that economic and social development might play as important a role as healthcare improvement in delaying the onset and diminishing the severity of disability in older Thai adults.

Furthermore, a national survey of disability noted that the number of elderly Thais with disabilities has increased gradually during the decade covered, from 5.8 per cent in 2001 to 21.4 per cent in 2012 (National Statistical Office 2013). The three most common disabilities reported by the Ministry of Public Health in 2013 were mobility, vision and hearing impairment at 43 per cent, 27 per cent and 4.6 per cent, respectively (Department of Health 2013).

Reduced physical activity is also linked to poorer health among the elderly. Some twenty-five chronic diseases are directly associated with physical inactivity (Smith 2012, p. 23). The growing number of oldest-old in Thailand with the simultaneous presence of two or more chronic diseases will pose serious difficulties in the forms of financing healthcare costs and meeting the massive demand for long-term care.

TABLE 14.2
Cross-national Comparisons, Basic and Advanced Activities of Daily Living

	Thailand (Khon Kaen)	Indonesia (Karawan)	Vietnam (Ngọc Quan)	Japan (Sonobe)
Mean age	68.2	72.1	71.2	71.7
Independence in basic activities (%)	52.2	69.8	55.8	89.2
Independence in advanced activities (%)	29.7	4.3	34.2	58.3

Sources: Wada et al. (2005, p. 171); Ishine et al. (2005, p. 118); Ishine et al. (2006, p. 44).

Age-Related Memory Impairments: Dementia

Another health challenge of concern for Thailand's ageing society is age-related memory impairment. Dementia,[7] or "senility", is one of the major causes of disability and dependency among older people worldwide (World Health Organization 2003). The cause of most dementia remains unknown, and there is no effective treatment for this disorder. Dementia is a challenge that must be faced in health and social care worldwide, particularly with the rapidly expanding segment of the oldest-old group (Kinsella and Phillips 2005, p. 21). As experienced in more advanced ageing countries, dementia has a profound impact on patients and their families. The care of dementia patients demands considerable resources. According to the World Alzheimer Report, the total estimated worldwide cost of dementia was US$604 billion in 2010, with 70 per cent incurred in Western Europe and North America (Wimo and Prince 2010, p. 5). These costs account for around 1 per cent of the world's gross domestic product (ibid.). To better comprehend the economic impact of dementia, if dementia care were a country, it would be the world's eighteenth-largest economy, ranking between Turkey and Indonesia (ibid.). Costs are attributed to informal care, the direct costs of social care and the direct costs of medical care (ibid., p. 5).

The estimated number of people with dementia worldwide in 2015 was 46.8 million, and the estimated incidence rate about one new case every three seconds (Prince et al. 2015, pp. 22–23). The number of affected people will double every twenty years to 81.1 million by 2040. More than half of those with dementia (60 per cent) are in developing countries, and this figure is likely to rise to 71 per cent by 2040 (Ferri et al. 2005, p. 4). The prevalence of Thai elderly with dementia reported in a survey undertaken in 2008–9 was 12.4 per cent (Duangruedee 2014). Older women accounted for a greater percentage of dementia cases than older men — 15.1 per cent and 9.8 per cent, respectively (ibid., p. 43). Moreover, the number of elderly Thais with dementia was predicted to increase twofold from 2001 to 2020 (Ferri et al. 2005, p. 12).

Although the number of elderly with dementia in Thailand is relatively low compared to developed countries, problems related to dementia are evident. A report by the Ministry of Social Development and Human Security (Ammar et al. 2006) reveals that among the elderly reported to have wandered away from their homes, 63 per cent were suffering from dementia at the time, and most of their family members were unaware that they were affected by the disease. Notwithstanding this, the issue is not yet of serious concern for policymakers. Instead, the current challenge faced in confronting the dementia epidemic is limited resources for diagnosing and treating the disease. Additionally, Thailand has had little time to develop comprehensive systems of social protection and of health and social care, while bad health habits among older Thais, including smoking and the consumption of alcohol, and the rising incidence of such chronic diseases as type 2 diabetes, hypertension and obesity (Department of Health 2013) will accelerate the severity of dementia in Thailand.

Healthcare Services

Ageing is likely to influence healthcare patterns because the elderly face a higher risk of co-morbidity and physical or cognitive dysfunction. The healthcare system therefore needs to provide appropriate and sufficient services to respond to the demands of an ageing population. However, the relevant systems in most developing countries are ill-prepared for such demands.

After some decades of improvement in the healthcare system and technological advancements in Thailand, good healthcare services now cover all communities throughout the country (Suwit 2002). Prior to emerging as an ageing society, Thailand had focused primarily on maternal and child health together with infectious diseases. Since seniors have started to make up an increasing share of the total population, healthcare for the aged has become a critical concern for the government. Geriatric clinics have been established as part of state services, and training in geriatric medicine has been imparted to healthcare providers. Additionally, convenient and rapid access to healthcare services for the elderly supplements regular governmental health services. Although many health resources and programmes have been developed to serve the elderly, they remain limited. The efficiency of some of these resources and programmes awaits verification (Jiraporn and Sutthichai 2008).

Thailand has to deal with not only the burden of chronic diseases but also infectious diseases, which remain the major cause of morbidity and mortality among Thai people. Although the rate of deaths associated with infectious diseases had declined fivefold from 1958 to the mid-1990s, a reversal of this trend was reported in the late twentieth century. The mortality rate from emerging and re-emerging infectious diseases such as Aids, tuberculosis and pneumonia increased (Suchunya et al. 2012). Thailand has had to shoulder a double burden, while certain problems in the health service system, such as a shortage of professional medical staff and inequitable health resource allocation between urban areas — predominantly the Bangkok metropolis — and rural areas, remain unsolved. Compared to other Southeast Asian countries, Thailand has relatively few physicians in relation to the number of patients; see Figure 14.5. This shortage has an impact on the effectiveness, efficiency and quality of care. Besides the limited number of physicians, a study has demonstrated an uneven distribution of medical personnel, with one third of doctors, or 34.7 per cent, and almost half of dentists, or 49.2 per cent, concentrated in the Bangkok metropolitan region (Ministry of Public Health 2010, pp. 18–19). Furthermore, a report from the Ministry of Public Health revealed the maldistribution of medical technologies and the healthcare budget. Although medical technologies constituted a rapidly increasing slice of the national budget, very few medical instruments have been made available in provincial areas (Suwit 2002 and 2011). This maldistribution reflects the problem of the centralization of the public sector management system. As population ageing becomes a nationwide phenomenon, the health service system will need to develop accordingly.

Healthcare Costs

From 1980 to 2004, healthcare expenses in the United States grew faster than the economy as a whole, rising from 9 per cent of GDP to 16 per cent. By 2002, approximately 36 per cent of total personal healthcare expenses were spent for older age groups (Stanton and Rutherford 2006). This situation is a consequence of the ageing population and the accelerating pace of medical innovation. Health expenditure for the elderly in Thailand is projected to increase almost fourfold by 2022 (Health Information System Development Office 2011).

Although health expenditure in Thailand is lower than certain Southeast Asian countries, it was the highest in terms of percentage of GDP; see Table 14.3. More than half of health expenditure came from out-of-pocket payments, thus making healthcare less accessible for the Thai elderly, among whom reports reveal financial insecurity. Almost half of the population has no retirement pension, and only 35.8 per cent of older

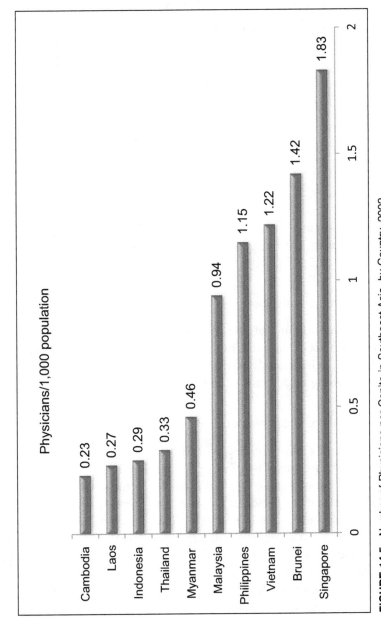

FIGURE 14.5 Number of Physicians per Capita in Southeast Asia, by Country, 2002
Source: Central Intelligence Agency (2012).

TABLE 14.3
Health Expenditures among Southeast Asian Countries

Country	Health expenditure per capita (USD)		Percentage of GDP		Proportion (Govt.: household)	
	1998	2007	1998	2007	1998	2007
Thailand	112	282	6.1	6.4	33 : 67	42 : 58
Indonesia	54	82	2.7	2.2	26 : 75	55 : 46
The Philippines	144	130	3.6	3.9	42 : 58	38 : 65
Malaysia	168	604	2.5	4.4	58 : 42	44 : 57
Singapore	744	1,643	3.6	3.1	35 : 65	33 : 67

Sources: Suwit (2002, p. 328, and 2011, p. 290).

persons have savings (National Statistical Office 2011b). Additionally, household debt in Thailand is also extremely high, at 84.7 per cent of GDP (Sukritta 2015).

Socio-economic Challenges

The progressive ageing of the elderly population leads to greater dependency on social support, more social risks and increased demand for services. The challenges posed by an ageing society include the need to develop lifelong opportunities and services.

The Vulnerability of Older Women

Elderly women are more vulnerable and disadvantaged with respect to virtually all dimensions of well-being (United Nations Population Fund 2012, p. 28). Socio-economic status is a crucial factor in determining the quality of life of an older person. It is evident that there is a gender disparity in socio-economic status among elderly Thais. A recent national survey reveals that elderly women report illiteracy and low levels of educational attainment more frequently than men. The literacy rate is 79.9 per cent for women and 90.1 per cent for men (National Statistical Office 2014, p. 10). However, the educational level and literacy rate of the Thai population has improved greatly over the past eighty years. The gender gap in literacy and education levels is therefore narrower among the younger-old than the older-old (Knodel and Napaporn 2008a, p. 7). Illiteracy or low education levels limit the ability of older persons to take part in economic activities. Notably, older Thai women are more likely to be living under the poverty line than men.[8] About 24.7 per cent of women have an annual income of less than 20,000 baht compared to 17.7 per cent of men. Furthermore, insufficient income for daily living is more pronounced among elderly women than among their male counterparts — 15.7 per cent and 13.8 per cent, respectively (National Statistical Office 2014, p. 12).

Marital status can also make women more vulnerable, as spouses are generally primary sources of material, social and emotional support and of care in times of illness or frailty. Only 46 per cent of elderly women are currently married and living with a spouse compared to 79 per cent of elderly men. Older women also outnumber men in living alone, particularly at very old ages; the figures are 5.5 per cent and 2.0 per cent, respectively. Furthermore, almost half of older women — 43.2 per cent — are widowed; this figure is three times higher than that for older men (National Statistical Office 2014, p. 9).

A combination of age and low socio-economic status also puts older women at increased risk of violence and abuse. Although the literature is limited, a survey on violence released by the Ministry of Social Development and Human Security (2010, p. 19) reported that older women were at twice the risk of abuse relative to older men; rates of abuse were 3.6 per cent and 1.8 per cent, respectively. Despite the presence of various specific disadvantages confronting the elderly, government policies relating to ageing are generally gender-neutral, and gender and ageing issues rarely are linked.

Support and Care for the Aged

Informal Support from the Family

Support and care for elderly parents by adult children is one of the most basic virtues universally found in diverse cultures. Most elderly people in Asia have traditionally relied on their children or on other family members to provide financial support and care. These responsibilities are "a moral obligation", widely known as "filial piety" (Stuifbergen and Van Delden 2011, p. 64).

In principle, filial piety is a fundamental norm in Thai society. According to Buddhist beliefs, the concept of karma means that good deeds bring good returns and bad deeds bring bad returns (Prayudh Payutto 1993).

The value of "being grateful" is influenced by this belief. Many Thais have been socialized to value this quality of gratitude. A person should acknowledge or be conscious of their indebtedness to the persons who have shown them goodness or given them assistance and try to repay the debt of gratitude whenever opportunities arise. Accordingly, parents are perceived as benefactors who make sacrifices to raise their children, while children owe a debt of gratitude to their parents and repay this debt by caring for their parents in old age. Children who fail to pay parents back in this way are believed to have sinned and will suffer consequences in return (Tassana 1999, p. 97). This belief certainly influences the thoughts and actions of people in Thailand. However, economic and social situations have changed in ways that raise questions about the future of filial care, particularly long-term care.

National surveys undertaken from 1994 to 2014 indicate that adult children are the main source of economic support and care for elderly Thais; some 80 per cent of the elderly reported receiving income from their children. Apart from financial support, adult children also provide non-monetary material support — food, goods and clothing — to their parents; see Figure 14.6. They also continue to make up a significant proportion of caregivers in all the surveys; see Figure 14.7. However, the percentage of the elderly who received financial support from their children decreased slightly from 87.6 per cent in 1994 to 84.8 per cent in 2014, and a much more significant decline was found in the percentage of older persons citing their children as their main source of income, from 54.1 to 36.8 per cent (Knodel et al. 2015, pp. 54, 66).

This trend may be due to significant changes in patterns of living arrangements among the Thai elderly. Intergenerational social and economic exchanges within the family closely linked to living arrangements significantly contribute to elderly persons' well-being. Living with adult children is viewed as an essential way for ageing parents to meet their needs for support and assistance (Knodel and Napaporn 2008*b*). Older Thais are less likely to live with their adult children than in the past. The percentage of those living with their children has fallen by approximately 20 per cent over the past twenty-five years. The Thai elderly are now more likely to live with their spouses or to stay alone; see Figure 14.8.

The value attached to "being grateful" also seems to have declined. Consecutive national surveys indicate trends of decreasing "repayment of gratitude". The percentage of people who reported practising such

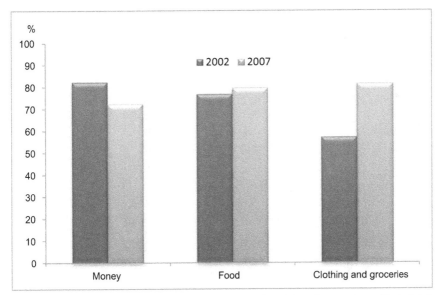

FIGURE 14.6 Percentage of Elderly Reported as Receiving Support from Their Adult Children
Sources: National Statistical Office (2002 and 2007*b*).

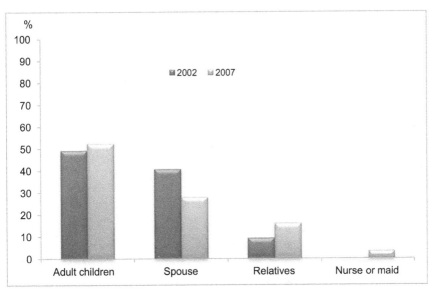

FIGURE 14.7 Key Caregiver for Elderly Persons, 2002 and 2007
Source: National Statistical Office (2002 and 2007*b*).

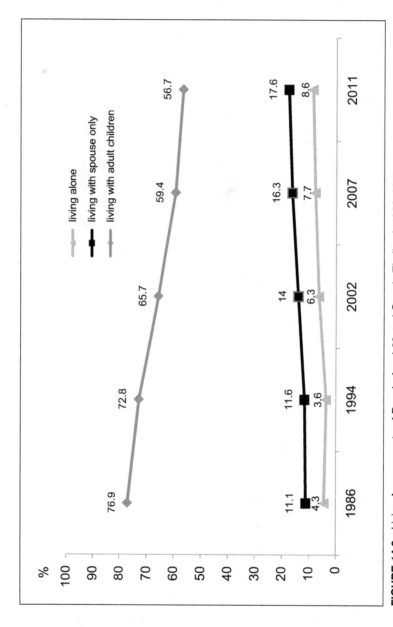

FIGURE 14.8 Living Arrangements of People Aged 60 and Over in Thailand, 1986–2011
Sources: Knodel and Napaporn (2008a and 2008b); National Statistical Office (2011b).

repayment declined slightly from 98.6 per cent in 2005 to 96.0 per cent in 2011 (National Statistical Office 2005 and 2011*b*). Fortunately, most people in Thailand — 91.7 per cent — report disagreeing with the idea of sending elderly to live in a home for the aged or elsewhere, and very few — 6.2 per cent — perceive the elderly as a burden for the family (National Statistical Office 2011*b*).

Formal Support from the Government

Since the early 1980s, the Thai government has responded to population ageing with various social programmes designed to meet the needs of elderly people (Medhi 2007, p. 26). However, significant challenges to the further development of some schemes persist.

Universal health coverage is a free medical care programme for the disadvantaged elderly initiated in 1989 and extended to cover all elderly in 1992. In 2007, the scheme was modified to serve as a universal healthcare system with no minimum premium payment for each visit (Knodel and Napaphon 2008*b*, p. 98). The scheme has broadened access to health services and helped to reduce the financial burden of meeting healthcare expenses for the elderly.

There are still significant gaps with regard to non-medical costs and social support in facilitating access to and utilization of healthcare services (Sutayut and Sondergaard 2016). These gaps affect poor elderly individuals and those in the oldest-old group in particular. The elderly poor who live on the universal old age allowance alone, the bedridden elderly and the poor elderly with mobility constraints are the most vulnerable. A World Bank study (ibid.) reveals that the lack of access to health services under the universal care scheme is due to the dependence on the availability of caretakers and relatives for taking elderly patients to healthcare facilities. Additionally, a lack of public or affordable transportation is the most important barrier to access to healthcare services among the elderly in rural areas. These findings reflect the complexity of the problems among elderly people who face multiple disadvantages.

Welfare Allowance

In 1993, the Department of Public Welfare initiated a financial assistance programme designed to provide monthly subsistence allowances of

200 baht for indigent old persons (Knodel and Napaporn 2008*b*, p. 98). Since 2006, the programme has served as one offering a universal old age allowance of 500 baht per month to all people aged 60 and over ineligible to receive other pensions from state agencies, state enterprises or local government organizations. In 2009 the programme began to operate on a multiple monthly-rate system, with the amount of monthly allowances depending on the age of recipients. The young-old between 60 and 69 years of age receive 600 baht per month, the middle-old between 70 and 79 years receive 700 baht, and the oldest-old between 80 and 89 years and those older than 90 years of age receive 800 and 1000 baht per month, respectively. These amounts fall below the standard of living in Thailand (Sutayut and Sondergaard 2016, p. 24). However, the universal coverage of the old-age allowance system contributed substantially to government expenditures, costing 10.83 billion baht in 2007 and 36.00 billion baht in 2011. Its cost is projected to increase to 133.26 billion baht by 2021 (Thailand Development Research Institute and Ministry for Social Development and Human Security 2012, pp. 44, 48).

Seven years after the government decided to make the old-age allowance a universal entitlement, the Ministry of Finance considered withdrawing the allowance from older people with monthly incomes of more than 9,000 baht or total assets of more than 3 million baht; their intention was to steer budgetary resources to those seniors most in need and to reduce the burden on state spending. The announcement met with extensive public criticism, as the old-age allowance helps to reduce income inequality among older people. Many recipients spend part of the allowance on health-related costs such as transportation to hospital and basic medicines for minor illnesses (Knox-Vydmanov and Usa 2016). Therefore, the government recently reconsidered the programme and has developed plans to increase the living allowance for the elderly to 1,500 or 2,000 baht, to meet a minimum standard of living, at an estimated cost of 2 billion baht a year (Wichit 2017).

Intended to support the indigent elderly, the old age allowance programme is non-contributory. Its funding comes solely from the government, and a growing proportion of aged people in the population will increase the cost of the programme. Its sustainability is thus a matter of debate; long-term security for the aged may entail mounting budget deficits for Thailand.

Cultural Challenges

While the economic and biomedical challenges posed by an ageing population are often discussed, the cultural challenges have been rarely considered until recently. One of these cultural challenges is ageism. Robert Butler coined the term "ageism", which he defined as "a process of systematic stereotyping and discrimination against people because they are old" (Butler 1996, p. 35). A number of studies in Western countries have identified widespread ageism. A survey conducted in the United States showed that the majority of older Americans faced ageism and that over half of these incidents were reported to have occurred "more than once". The most frequent types of ageism were disrespect shown for older people, and people making assumptions about ailments or frailty caused by age (Palmore 2001, p. 573). Apart from self-reported ageism, people close to the elderly — such as family members, caretakers and neighbours — reported that they had held negative attitudes about ageing, in confirmation of a generally ageist worldview (Dobbs et al. 2008, p. 521).

Confucianism, a set of Chinese cultural beliefs that has influenced many countries in Asia, emphasizes the importance of family and social harmony. Living with respect and dignity in old age is, in principle, greatly appreciated in Asian culture. Thai society is organized according to hierarchical traditions and patronage, where older persons usually enjoy high status because of their valuable contributions. They are viewed as sources of wisdom and good role models for younger generations (Saowapa et al. 2007). Cultural norms of respecting the elderly are a part of the Thai social code. On 13 April, Thailand marks National Older Persons' Day to highlight the importance of older persons. A recent national survey on social perceptions of ageing (National Statistical Office 2011a) illustrated a high proportion of positive attitudes; see Table 14.4.

Nevertheless, and in spite of the social status enjoyed by the elderly, their perceived value to society has been on the decline, particularly among teenagers; see Figure 14.9. Teenagers view the elderly as old-fashioned, difficult to understand, hard to please and boring (National Statistical Office 2011a). In this respect, ageism in Thailand is as commonplace as it is in the West; see Table 14.5. Age discrimination is experienced most by the female elderly and the oldest-old group. It has an impact on the self-esteem and well-being of the elderly (El Bcheraoui and Adib 2015, pp. 29–32; Minichiello et al. 2000, pp. 261–66). Meanwhile, these kinds of

TABLE 14.4
Percentage of Thai People Aged 13 and Over Who Agree to Statements
Reflecting Positive Social Perceptions towards Aging People

Positive social perception	Total	Urban	Rural
Propagating cultural traditions to younger generations	95.4	94.3	96.0
Having a lot of valuable experiences	95.0	94.8	95.1
Being a good example	94.0	93.5	94.2
Having ability to benefit family and community	93.7	93.4	93.9

Source: National Statistical Office (2011*a*).

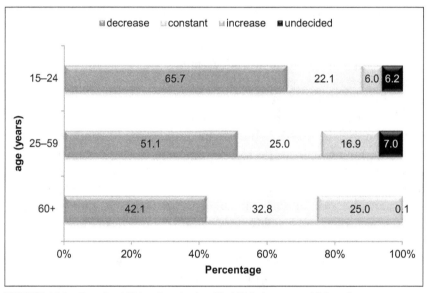

FIGURE 14.9   Perceived Value Attached to Thai Elderly among All Age Groups
Source: National Economic and Social Development Board (2014, p. 20).

social perceptions towards ageing have also influenced societal behaviour and care for older people (Pasupathi and Löckenhoff 2004).

Conclusion

Although Thailand has only become an ageing society in the past decade and begun to experience the early stages of the demographic transition,

TABLE 14.5
Self-reported Experience of Ageism among the Thai Elderly

Experience of ageism	Total	Sex		Age group (years)		
		Male	Female	60–69	70–79	80+
I was denied employment because of old age (%)	30.2	28.1	31.9	28.7	30.3	36.3
I heard a joke that poked fun at old people (%)	34.4	37.9	31.7	33.8	33.6	28.9
I was excluded from social activities (%)	25.4	22.8	27.5	21.6	28.2	34.5
My opinion or idea was overlooked because of old age (%)	29.5	26.7	31.7	25.6	34.0	35.4
I was ignored by a waiter or waitress because of old age (%)	19.7	18.7	20.5	17.0	21.2	27.4

Source: National Economic and Social Development Board (2014, p. 21).

the astonishing rate of the increase in its ageing population requires urgent attention. Fortunately, as a second-wave ageing society, Thailand has taken advantage of medical knowledge and technologies in care for the aged found in developed countries. There are, however, complex challenges that require solutions. The high incidence of chronic diseases with poor health literacy and unhealthy behaviour related to diet, tobacco and alcohol consumption, and the lack of exercise among older Thai adults, may increase the rates and severity of co-morbidity and the early onset of disability that lead to massive demand for long-term care and exploding healthcare costs. Nevertheless, while Thailand has provided universal health coverage since 2002, offering all Thais access to health services, the capacity and quality of care remain unequal between urban and rural areas. Lack of access to healthcare services for older persons who have no caretaker, lower incomes and the impact of disability all figure in this gap. Age-related health problems require specific expertise and care, both of which are concentrated in the metropolitan region. This situation suggests that the country must address the over-centralization of the public health sector management system.

Another important consideration is gender disparity. Various aspects of vulnerability are more likely to affect older Thai women than older Thai men. Government policies related to ageing should put more emphasis on the issue of gender. Finally, long-term security for the elderly under universal social programmes remains a cause for concern. A system designed with considerations of financial sustainability in mind is a priority.

Notes

1. Population ageing is defined as the increasing proportion of older persons (60 years and over) in the total population (United Nations Population Fund 2006, p. 2).
2. A super-aged society is one in which the proportion of the population aged 65 or older exceeds twenty per cent of the total.
3. The total fertility rate is the average number of children a woman would bear over the course of her lifetime if current age-specific fertility rates remained constant throughout her childbearing years, normally between the ages of 15 and 49 (United Nations 2002, p. 42).
4. The aging index is a demographic indicator used to measure the rate at which a population ages; it is measured as the number of people in old age (60 or older) per hundred people under 15 years of age in a given population (United Nations 2002, p. 41).
5. The old-age dependency ratio describes the burden of supporting older persons placed on the working population, measured as the number of elderly people (60 or older) per one hundred persons aged 15 to 59 years (United Nations 2002, p. 41).
6. The potential support ratio is the number of persons aged 15 to 59 for every person aged 60 or older (United Nations 2002, p. 42).
7. Dementia is "a syndrome in which there is deterioration in memory, thinking, behaviour and the ability to perform everyday activities" (World Health Organization 2017).
8. The 2015 poverty line in Thailand was 2,644 baht per head per month or 31,728 baht per year (National Statistical Office 2015).

15

Conclusion: Thailand in Transition

Terence Chong

As tourists to Bangkok hurtle down the highway from Suvarnabhumi Airport into the city, one particularly forbidding sign will flash by them. Written both in English and Thai, it says, "It is wrong to use Buddha as a decoration or tattoo. Means no respect [*sic*]. Don't buy or sell Buddha." This is perhaps no surprise, given the status of Buddhism as the country's de facto national religion, not to mention the ubiquitous commodification of Buddha images for all manner of business from bars and bistros to club music and fashion. So one may be forgiven for believing that the government is serious about clamping down on the crass popularization and export of Buddhist iconography. After all, it strictly prohibits the export of any Buddha images without written permission while imposing an export ban on parts of Buddha such as the head, hands or feet (*Bangkok Post*, 30 June 2013). Moreover, although trinket-sized images do not require government permission for export, only a maximum of five pieces are allowed per person. Not least, such rulings have firm footing in the legitimate need to prosecute looters who remove pieces from Buddhist monuments and archaeological sites around the country.

However, later that evening, as the very same tourists stroll down Sukhumvit Road or traverse cavernous shopping purgatories like MBK

Centre, it will become strikingly obvious that Buddha statues of varying sizes are as popular as $20 Rolexes and even cheaper aphrodisiacs lining the streets. Buddha heads the size of watermelons for your dining table, Buddha masks for your wall, Buddha paintings in colour or black and white, Buddha smiling, laughing, lying prone, in wood, bronze, silver, on t-shirts, are arranged openly for your perusal. Asking your friendly neighbourhood vendor if her Buddha products have had prior approval from the government will win you, at best, a patronizing smile or, at worse, a derisive snort. Furthermore, if you are brave enough to test her patience even further, you can ask whether they know where to seek export permits for your purchase.

By the end of the evening, our tourist friends will have realized two things. First, there are sensible rules and regulations in Thailand. Many may have strong rationales behind them and are, for the most part, well thought out. This culture of bureaucracy is evident in almost every part of Thai society, even when the country is in political transition. In fact, the institutions and bureaucratic procedures in place have a variety of uses beyond what they were intended for, such as offering a veneer of law and order, stability and civil coherence to citizens and outsiders alike in a society pulsating with the forces of demographic, economic and political shifts.

Second, Thais will always find a way to survive. Faced with bureaucratic contradictions and onerous directives in everyday life, they do what all people do — ignore, negotiate, select or flout so that they can move on. Whether it is selling Buddha iconography or tolerating military coups and street blockades, the pragmatism of the Thais seeps through. There is enough cultural and social diversity — from regional identities in the Northeast and the South, agrarian and manufacturing industries, or socio-economic divides between Bangkok and the rest of the country — to ensure that a routine resilience is built into communal groups as they navigate everyday hardships and frequent transitions emanating from the capital.

Nevertheless, beyond the realities of everyday life, Thailand is again confronting uncertainty. A new king whose role in politics and public life is not yet clear, a prime minister who continually kicks the electoral can down the street, and the exiled Shinawatras who probably do not believe in going gently into the good night. This politicking is not just symptomatic of conflicting interests but, more importantly, points to fundamental shifts in the key institutions that have shaped Thailand's political history through the decades.

The chapters in this volume have collectively demonstrated that Thai political life continues to revolve around three institutions; namely, the military, the monarchy and the establishment elites and capitalists. The reader will see that contemporary Thai politics has been a complex story of these three institutions' negotiation with one another and of the popular vote occasionally interrupting their partnership. The political transitions in Thailand over the decades have been triggered in one way or another by this jostling of institutional interests. However, Thailand's political transitions cannot be explained solely as the struggle of self-interests. These interests, diverse as they are, continue to hold sway in public discourse because they appeal to an amorphous concept of "Thai culture", or the Thai-way-of-doing-things.

The ideological and moral contradictions arising from this three-way negotiation, such as bloody coups, denial of popular will, curtailed political freedoms, and an ever-changing constitution, have generally been attributed to the primacy of an ambiguous form of Thai culture. Or, more specifically, the need to respect Thai sensitivity and values which, though unfamiliar to Western liberal sensitivities, must always supersede democratic institutions and norms in order to preserve "Thainess" and cultural sovereignty.

The selective extrapolation of cultural values for political objectives is, of course, not new. In this case, "Thai culture" or "Thai sensitivities" serve as an ideological mechanism for those vested in the status quo to resist good governance, bureaucratic transparency, an even playing field, popular votes and political accountability. Moreover, there are a variety of well-trodden reasons for privileging this type of nativism. The rural voters are simple minded and easily led astray by populist politicians, it is said. These politicians are corrupt, and the military needs to step in from time to time to purge these bad hats for the sake of the country. Furthermore, of course, the ace card: it is the will of the king, whose moral authority cannot be surpassed, that political change takes place.

This ideological mechanism is the main cog in so-called "Thai-style democracy". Thai-style democracy is "the denial of popular sovereignty, the repudiation of majority rule, and the advocacy of hierarchical over egalitarian understandings of 'the nation'" (Ferrara 2014, p. 19). This hierarchical understanding of the nation is necessary because of the deep-seated belief that "elections are not adequate grounds for legitimizing governments in Thailand, because rural and less-educated voters are not sufficiently politically mature" (Askew 2010, p. 11).

And it has been effective because it is often cloaked as the struggle to challenge Western or foreign political ideologies, most frequently liberal democracy, which are not completely suitable for Thais, or Asians for that matter. The enduring appeal of Thai-style democracy comes from the way it is framed as an "us versus them" debate. For example, in justifying the September 2006 overthrow of Prime Minister Thaksin Shinawatra, Surin Maisrikrod perpetuates the clinical division between the protagonists in the coup and a Western-style democracy. "In other words, these opposing views could appropriately be termed the Thai versus Western views of the coup, which is in a way quite consistent with contending views in other areas, such as culture and economics" (Surin 2007, p. 352). Such expressions of political nativism have been effective in creating unwarranted binaries in an erroneous diagnosis of the complex struggle among actors such as the military, palace, judiciary, politicians, establishment elite, and capital owners, all of whom seek to advance their own interests.

One sees echoes of the "Asian values" discourse of the 1990s in such arguments. Like Thai-style democracy, the Asian values discourse also sought to present a specifically Southeast Asian alternative to Western-style democracy. Like Thai-style democracy, the Asian values discourse privileged local culture and values over Western-centric institutions, regarding the latter as that which needed to be tweaked and modified to suit local histories, politics and norms.

Like Thai-style democracy, proponents of Asian values emphasized the type of "collective identity" discussed by Federico Ferrara (2015) and by Michael Montesano in the introductory chapter of this volume. Moreover, like all forms of collective identities, essentialist character traits and politically expedient values come to the fore while heterogeneity and complexity recede into the background. This emphasis was hardly neutral either; it especially privileged deference to authority, hard work and the subjugation of individual interests to communal ones as somehow particularly "Asian". Like the discourse of Thai-style democracy, that of Asian values refined its Occidentalist habit over the years by cataloguing the various moral deficiencies and political failures of the West. However, unlike Thai-style democracy, where denying the will of the people as expressed by the popular vote in order to save them from themselves meant restoring the status quo, Asian values privileged capital and the market economy. It is unclear if promoters of Thai-style democracy ever envisioned anything beyond safeguarding the traditions, powers and institutions of the establishment, while it can be argued that the allure of the "Asian values" discourse was its description of an Asian modernity in which industrialization and economic development could be achieved under authoritarian or semi-liberal governments.

But Thai-style democracy predates the Asian values discourse. According to Federico Ferrara (2014, p. 26ff.), the seeds of this political concept were sown after Field Marshal Sarit Thanarat ousted Field Marshal Po. Phibunsongkhram from the Thai premiership in 1957. Civil liberties were curtailed while political rights, such as freedom of speech and association, were restricted. Domestic conglomerates were protected from external competition as the military government suppressed labour movements or any attempt by rural workers to agitate for better working conditions. Run-of-the-mill authoritarianism so far. Then came two factors that characterized this emerging Thai-style democracy.

First, Sarit tightened the palace-military relationship, with the former initially as a junior partner. This saw unelected government officials, especially military officers, enjoy a stronger grip over power. These officials, whose dominance of the Thai political order Riggs (1966) termed the "bureaucratic polity", emerged as the country's ruling class, responsible for making key political and national decisions. According to Chambers (2018), this development set in place a pattern of "authoritarian neo-monarchism" in which the state would selectively leverage the power of the military and the prestige of monarchy for its own interests (p. 40). As Ferrara (2014) observes, the reconciliation of the two institutions that were "mostly at loggerheads over the previous quarter century" was not difficult partly because of "the weakness of the opposition, deprived of many of its leading personalities through arrests, exile, and murder" (p. 27). This reconciliation allowed the military elite to align itself ideologically with the monarchy by vowing to protect the king (Thak 2007, pp. 205–6), therefore enjoying renewed legitimacy and purpose even in the 1980s, when the communist threat was fading.

Second, and perhaps more crucial, was the elevation of the monarch over the constitution. Sarit sought to deify the young King Bhumibol because he "saw the restoration of the monarch's mystique, prestige, and power a source of legitimacy more potent than the pretence of constitutionalism and elections" (Ferrara 2014, p. 27). The centrality of the monarch in Thai-style democracy therefore became a powerful means to end any political debate in so far as one only needed to purport to speak on behalf of the king. Or, as Pattana Kitiarsa argues,

> Since Western-style democracy was introduced to Thailand through the 1932 revolution by the People's Party, the nation (*chat*) preceded democracy (*prachathipatai*), but the monarchy has always prevailed above all symbolic national pillars including *satsana* (Buddhism) and *ratthathamanun* (the constitution). Thais would try by all means to glorify or defend the king and the nation, even if they have to halt the development of democracy. (Pattana 2006, p. 6)

In short, Thai-style democracy, along with its later renderings, is an ideological and nativist construct that allows the interests of the monarchy, military, bureaucrats and capitalists to be served. It strengthens the foundations on which collective social identities can be manufactured, politicized and deployed for specific interests. Nevertheless, it is a construct that will do little to halt the deeper, more profound changes that are taking place in Thai society, changes that the contributors to this volume have pointed out.

Political consciousness among rural and working-class voters has been entrenched over the last two decades. Former prime minister Thaksin's engagement of villagers, peasants and small traders beyond Bangkok has given them a sense of political empowerment, which has brought them into conflict with the middle and upper middle classes in Bangkok once believed to be the stewards of democracy. Policies such as funds for village development and business, the One Tambon One Product scheme, thirty-baht medical fees, deferral of farm debts and the clampdown on the drugs trade by successive Thaksinite parties like Thai Rak Thai and Phuea Thai have ensured that political empowerment has been accompanied by economic empowerment. The Bangkok upper middle class's response to the growing voice of the rural and working-class voters was to infantilize them, as the run-up to the 2014 coup demonstrated. It is unclear if this derogative treatment will continue to hold sway in the mid- to long-term. The most important questions looking ahead would be how these rural and working-class voters can be further mobilized, how they perceive the upper middle class in Bangkok and the way that its members portray them, and whether the national economy continues to develop in favour of the upper middle class.

Another central question is what type of relationship will evolve between King Vajiralongkorn and the Thai military. The unfolding partnership between the new king and the military will have ramifications on the balance of power-sharing between these institutions. Will he be content with the current arrangement or will he take his cue from his great-great-grandfather King Mongkut (r. 1851–68), who established the military as a permanent force in part to quell challenges from regional rivals (Chambers 2018, p. 39)? King Vajiralongkorn may endeavour to remould the mission and goal of the military to align it in service of the palace. The mysterious 2017 disappearance of an eighty-year-old bronze plaque commemorating the end of absolute monarchy in 1932 may hold a clue. Embedded in the road of the Royal Plaza, in front of the Ananta Samakhom Throne Hall in Bangkok, it read, "Here at dawn on 24th June 1932, we the People's Party gave birth to the constitution for the progress of the nation." The 1932 plaque was replaced by another celebrating the monarchy. The new plaque reads, "Long Live Siam forever. Happy, fresh-faced citizens are the power of the land." It also carries the motto of the ruling Chakri dynasty: "Loyalty and love to the Buddhist Triple Gem, the State, one's family, and an honest heart for the King are good tools for the prosperity of the state" (Pavin 2017). This replacement occurred just before the king signed and witnessed a new constitution.

Another trend to watch out for is the country's ageing population. According to United Nations data, over 27 per cent of Thailand's population will be sixty years old or older by 2030 (United Nations 2015, p. 11). Thailand's population is ageing at a much faster rate than most developed countries because of factors such as its relatively low total fertility rate of 1.9, improvements in healthcare and increased life expectancy. The ageing population will pose challenges to the government, including providing adequate and affordable healthcare for the elderly, providing financial support for that group and finding a role for its members in the workforce.

These socio-political trends and their impact on collective identities will continue to shape Thai society in the years to come. After all, these collective identities can only be sustained by the values, interests and beliefs that communities attribute to themselves. Whether it is the upper middle class's belief that its members are deserving of their material success because of their hard work, the communities in the Northeast and the South who believe they have been systematically exploited and marginalized by Bangkok, the monarchists who cannot imagine national politics without royal institutions in play, or the military who have taken it upon themselves to be the guardians of Thai society, these socio-political identities are driven by narratives that will come into conflict with one another. How the country's institutions and leaders respond to these conflicts will determine if the transitions to come will warrant another volume like this one.

Bibliography

ABC News. "Car Bomb Attack outside Busy Pattani Supermarket in Thailand Injures at Least 60". 10 May 2017 <http://www.abc.net.au/news/2017-05-10/car-bomb-attack-outside-thailand-supermarket-injures-60/8512732> (accessed 6 December 2017).

Abdul Hadi Awang. "PAS Condemns Bombing of Supermarket in Southern Thailand". *Buletin Online*, 12 May 2017 <http://buletinonline.net/v7/index.php/pas-condemns-bombing-supermarket-southern-thailand/> (accessed 6 December 2017).

Abu Hafez Al-Hakim (pseud.). "The Peace Talk Resumes?" *Deep South Watch*, 4 December 2014 <https://www.deepsouthwatch.org/node/6485> (accessed 6 December 2017).

———. "What is MARA Patani?" *Deep South Watch*, 26 May 2015 <https://www.deepsouthwatch.org/en/node/7211> (accessed 6 December 2017).

———. "Dissecting the T-O-R". *Deep South Watch*, 19 May 2016 <https://www.deepsouthwatch.org/node/8733> (accessed 6 December 2017).

Aim Sinpeng. "Party-Movement Coalition in Thailand's Political Conflict (2005–2011)". In *Contemporary Socio-Cultural and Political Perspectives on Thailand*, edited by Pranee Liamputtong, pp. 157–68. Dordrecht: Springer, 2013a.

———. "State Repression in Cyberspace: The Case of Thailand". *Asian Politics & Policy* 5, no. 3 (July 2013b): 421–40.

———. "The Power of Political Movement and the Collapse of Democracy in Thailand". Doctoral dissertation, University of British Columbia, 2013c.

Akhom Detthongkhum. *Hua chueak wua chon* [The knot of the fighting bull]. Bangkok: Thailand Research Fund, 2000.

Akin Rabibhadana. "The Organization of Thai Society in the Early Bangkok Period, 1728–1873". Southeast Asia Program Data Paper Series, no. 74. Ithaca: Southeast Asia Program, Cornell University, 1969.

Al Jazeera America. "Thai Opposition to Boycott 2014 Election". 21 December 2013 <http://america.aljazeera.com/articles/2013/12/21/thai-opposition-toboycott2014election.html> (accessed 27 February 2017).

The Albion Monitor. "Thailand Government Falls as Court Bans Ruling Party". n.d. <http://www.monitor.net/monitor/0812a/copyright/thaigovernmentfalls. html> (accessed 29 October 2014).

Ammar Siamwalla. "The Old Age of the Agricultural Sector: The Past and Future of Thai Rural Areas". Paper presented at the 2004 Thailand Development Research Institute (TDRI) Year-end Conference on "Twenty Years of Thailand's Socio-Economic Situation: In Retrospect and a Forecast", 27–28 November 2004, Pattaya, Thailand.

Ammar Siamwalla, Worawan Chandoevwit, Niramon Suthamkit, Kullaporn Unnanon, Suwimon Fakthong, Bowornpun Achakul, and Patanayut Santiyanon. "Kanpramoen khwamsiang lae khwamprobang thangsangkhom kanwat phawa khwamyakrai lae khwamprobang sangkhom su naeothang nam pai patibat dai nai prathet thai" [Risk assessment and social vulnerability: The measurement of poverty and social vulnerability for the purpose of guidelines for implementation in Thailand]. Thailand Development Research Institute, 31 January 2006 <http://tdri.or.th/wp-content/uploads/2012/12/h103.pdf> (accessed 10 October 2017).

Anderson, Benedict R.O'G. "Withdrawal Symptoms: Social and Cultural Aspects of the October 6 Coup". *Bulletin of Concerned Asian Scholars* 9, no. 3 (July–September 1977): 13–31.

———. "Studies of the Thai State: The State of Thai Studies". In *The Study of Thailand*, edited by Eliezer B. Ayal, pp. 193–247. Athens: Ohio University Center for International Studies, 1978.

———. "Murder and Progress in Modern Siam". *New Left Review* I/181 (May–June 1990): 33–48.

———. *The Spectre of Comparisons: Nationalism, Southeast Asia, and the World*. New York: Verso, 1998.

Anek Laothamatas. "Rue pen yak thi phueng tuen chonchan klang kap kanmueang thai" [Sleeping giant awakens? The middle class in Thai politics]. *Thammasat Journal* 19, no. 1 (1993): 43–68.

———. "A Tale of Two Democracies: Conflicting Perceptions of Elections and Democracy in Thailand". In *The Politics of Elections in Southeast Asia*, edited by Robert H. Taylor, pp. 201–23. Washington: Woodrow Wilson Center Press and Cambridge University Press, 1996.

———. *Praethin plianthan sang kanpokkhrong thongthin hai pen prachathippatai* [Transforming localities, changing bases: Building democratic local governments]. Bangkok: Thammasat University Press, 2009.

———. "Prachatippatai thi prachachon pokkhrong ton eng" [Democracy in which people govern themselves]. *Warasan sathaban watthanatham lae sinlapa mahawitthayalai sinakharinwirot* [Journal of the Institute of Arts and Culture Research of Srinakharinwirot University] 12, no. 2 (2012): 26–30.

Angkatan Bersenjata-BRN. "Pengistiharan keputusan Majlis Thura BRN" [Declaration on the resolution of the BRN's Shura Council]. YouTube, 6 August 2013 <https://www.youtube.com/watch?v=8JE9NiawBL8> (accessed 6 December 2017).

Anonymous. "Anti-Royalism in Thailand Since 2006: Ideological Shifts and Resistance". *Journal of Contemporary Asia* 48, no. 3 (2018): 363–94.

Apichat Satitniramai. "Suea daeng khue khrai mop toemngoen phrai rue chonchan klang mai kap tangphraeng sangkhom thai" [Who are the Red Shirts — a crowd for hire, serfs, or a new middle class? And Thailand's crossroads], pp. 14–35. *Daeng thamai?* [Why red?], edited by Pinyo Traisuriyadhamma. Bangkok: Open Books, 2010.

Apichat Sathitniramai, Yukti Mukdawijitra, and Niti Pawakapan. *Thopthuan phumithat kanmueang thai* [Re-examining the political landscape of Thailand]. Chiang Mai: Public Policy Studies Institute, 2013.

The Asia Foundation. *Profile of the "Bangkok Shutdown" Protesters: A Survey of Anti-Government PDRC Demonstrators in Bangkok.* Bangkok: The Asia Foundation, 2014.

Asian Development Bank. "Thailand: Economy". 2016 <http://www.adb.org/countries/thailand/economy> (accessed 9 November 2016).

Askew, Marc. *Performing Political Identity: The Democrat Party in Southern Thailand.* Chiang Mai: Silkworm Books, 2008.

———. "Introduction". In *Legitimacy Crisis in Thailand*, edited by Marc Askew, pp. 1–29. Chiang Mai: Silkworm Books, 2010.

Associated Press. "The Students' Revolt". 17 October 1973. In *The King of Thailand in World Focus*, edited by Denis D. Gray and Dominic Faulder, pp. 90–91. Singapore: Editions Didier Millet, 2008.

———. "World's Royals Hit Bangkok Tourist Trail". 13 June 2006. In *The King of Thailand in World Focus*, edited by Denis D. Gray and Dominic Faulder, pp. 201–2. Singapore: Editions Didier Millet, 2008.

———. "As Thai Monarchy's Power Wanes, King Still Revered". *The Jakarta Post*, 25 May 2010.

———. "Thai King Signs Royal Family's $30bn Fortune over to Himself". *The Guardian*, 17 June 2018 <https://www.theguardian.com/world/2018/jun/17/thai-king-signs-royal-familys-30bn-fortune-over-to-himself> (accessed 23 August 2018).

ASTV Manager Online. "Wisaman 'Masuphian Mama' mue buem thahan cho-airong dap kha banphak" [Masupien Mama, allegedly behind bomb attack against soldiers in Cho Airong, killed at his house]. 19 July 2013 <https://www.manager.co.th/South/ViewNews.aspx?NewsID=9560000089022> (accessed 6 December 2017).

Atcharaphon Kamutphitsamai. *Kabot ro so 130: kabot phuea prachathippatai naeokhit thahan mai* [The Ro So Rebellion: Rebellion for democracy and the thinking of the new military], 2nd ed. Bangkok: Amarinwichakan, 1999.

Attachak Sattayanurak. *Prachathippatai khon thai mai thaokan* [Democracy: Inequality among Thais]. Bangkok: Matichon Books, 2014.

Avendano, Mauricio, Maria Glymour, James Banks, and Johan P. Mackenbach. "Health Disadvantage in US Adults Aged 50 to 74 Years: A comparison of the health of rich and poor Americans with that of Europeans". *American Journal of Public Health* 99, no. 3 (March 2009): 540–48.

BaBeBurin. "Thaksin fon in phuea thai" [Thaksin's phone-in to Phuea Thai]. *Sanook!,* 23 February 2009 <http://video.sanook.com/player/403184/> (accessed 21 March 2018).

Baker, Chris. "The 2014 Thai *Coup* and Some Roots of Authoritarianism". *Journal of Contemporary Asia* 46, no. 3 (2016): 388–404.

Banerjee, Abhijit V., and Esther Duflo. "What Is Middle Class about the Middle Classes around the World?" *Journal of Economic Perspectives* 22, no. 2 (Spring 2008): 3–28.

Bangkok Business News. "Raengngan kaset nai prathet thai" [Agricultural labour in Thailand]. 2 July 2013 <http://www.bangkokbiznews.com/blog/detail/514538> (accessed 9 November 2016).

Bangkok Post. "Authorities Close in on Prem's Foes". 5 April 2007.

———. "Govt 'Not Party' to Peace Talks". 22 September 2008.

———. "Yingluck, Najib Vow to Tackle Insurgency". 21 February 2012.

———. "Parties Agree Dialogue Terms". 1 March 2013.

———. "Exporting Buddha". 30 June 2013 <https://www.bangkokpost.com/print/357587/> (accessed 1 August 2018).

———. "Pheu Thai Says Amnesty Bill Lawful; Other Disagree". 3 November 2013.

———. "Washington Considers Moving Cobra Gold". 25 June 2014.

———. "Thailand Police Chief Bans Book; A Kingdom in Crisis". 13 November 2014.

———. "U.S. Warns on Political 'Fairness'". 27 January 2015.

———. *Bangkok Post Economic Review, 2015 Mid-year Edition*. July 2015 <http://www.bangkokpost.com/epaper/special-issue/20151> (accessed 9 November 2016).

———. "Thailand a Top Destination for Russians this Year". 1 June 2016 <http://www.bangkokpost.com/business/tourism-and-transport/997889/thailand-a-top-destination-for-russians-this-year> (accessed 9 November 2016).

———. "Thanathorn May Face Computer Crime Charges". 31 July 2018 <https://www.bangkokpost.com/news/politics/1513298/thanathorn-may-face-computer-crime-charges> (accessed 23 August 2018).

Bangkok University Research Center. "Phon samruat rueang 'krungthep pho ruam patirup prathet thai patirup sue phuea lot khwamkhatyaeng'" [Results on "Bangkok Poll joins in reforming Thailand: Media reform for conflict reduction"]. 18 October 2013 <http://bangkokpoll.bu.ac.th/poll/result/doc/poll706.pdf> (accessed 21 March 2018).

Bank of Thailand. *Quarterly Bulletin*. Bangkok: Bank of Thailand, various issues.

Barany, Zoltan. *The Soldier and the Changing State: Building Democratic Armies in Africa, Asia, Europe, and the Americas*. Princeton, New Jersey: Princeton University Press, 2012.

Barro, Robert J. "Determinants of Democracy". *Journal of Political Economy* 107, no. 6 (December 1999): 158–83.

Barta, Patrick. "Thai Protests Heighten Crisis". *The Wall Street Journal*, 26 November 2008 <www.wsj.com/articles/SB122762440088656477> (accessed 27 February 2017).

Batson, Benjamin. *Siam's Political Future: Documents from the End of Absolute Monarchy*. Ithaca: Cornell Southeast Asia Program, 1974.

BBC (British Broadcasting Corporation). "Q&A: Thailand's Coup Impact". 20 September 2006 <http://news.bbc.co.uk/2/hi/asia-pacific/5362878.stm> (accessed 27 February 2017).

————. "Thai Protesters 'Want New Coup'". 26 August 2008 <http://news.bbc.co.uk/2/hi/asia-pacific/7581565.stm> (accessed 27 February 2017).

BBC Thai. "Bi a en kho nanachat ruam sangketkan cheracha santiphap doitrong kap thai" [BRN calls on international community to observe peace negotiations with Thailand]. 11 April 2017 <http://www.bbc.com/thai/39560844> (accessed 6 December 2017).

Beard, John R., Simon Biggs, David E. Bloom, Linda P. Fried, Paul Hogan, Alexandre Kalache, and S. Jay Olshansky, eds. *Global Population Ageing: Peril or Promise*. Geneva: World Economic Forum, 2011.

Bell, Thomas. "Thai Army to 'Help Voters Love' the Government". *The Telegraph*, 18 December 2008 <http://www.telegraph.co.uk/news/worldnews/asia/thailand/3831672/Thai-army-to-help-voters-love-the-government.html> (accessed 30 November 2017).

Benkler, Yochai. *The Wealth of Networks: How Social Production Transforms Markets and Freedom*. New Haven: Yale University Press, 2006.

Bertaux, Daniel, and Martin Kohli. "The Life Story Approach: A Continental View". *Annual Review of Sociology* 10 (1984): 215–37.

Birdsall, Nancy. "The (Indispensable) Middle Class in Developing Countries; or, the Rich and the Rest, not the Poor and the Rest". In *Equity and Growth in a Globalizing World*, edited by Ravi Kanbur and Michael Spence, pp. 157–87. Washington, DC: World Bank, 2010.

Birdsall, Nancy, Carol Graham, and Stefano Pettinato. "Stuck in the Tunnel: Is Globalization Muddling the Middle Class?" *Working Papers*, no. 14 (August 2000). Washington, DC: Center on Social and Economic Dynamics, Brookings Institution, 2000.

Bloom, David E., David Canning, and Günther Fink. "Implications of Population Aging for Economic Growth". NBER Working Papers, no. 16705 (January 2011). Cambridge: National Bureau of Economic Research, 2011.

Bloomberg. "Thai Military, Police Say They Have Seized Bangkok". 19 September 2006 <http://www.bloomberg.com/apps/news?pid=newsarchive&sid=aaiO h9GgOtL4&refer=asia> (accessed 10 September 2014).

BLUESKYCHANNEL. "Fa wan mai" [Sky of a new day]. 2018 <http://www.fahwonmai.tv/> (accessed 21 March 2018).

Boonlert Kachayuthadej. "Seriphap sue — seriphap prachachon upasak thi khat to chettanarom" [Press freedom — civil liberties and impediments to the principle]. Isra News Agency, 4 February 2010 <http://www.isranews.org/component/content/article/14058-2010-02-04-05-29-28.html> (accessed 21 March 2018).

Booth, Ken. *International Relations*. London: Hodder & Stoughton, 2014.

Bowie, Katherine. *Rituals of National Loyalty*. New York: Columbia University Press, 1997.

Bowornsak Uwanno. "The Law of Inviolability in Thailand". *Bangkok Post*, 7 April 2009a.

———. "Thai Culture and the Law on Lese Majeste". *Bangkok Post*, 8 April 2009b.

———. "*Lese Majeste*: Abuse and Benevolence". *Bangkok Post*, 9 April 2009c.

———. "Ten Principles of a Righteous King and the King of Thailand". *Thailand Today*, 3 April 2014 <http://m.thailandtoday.in.th/monarchy/elibrary/article/167> (accessed 27 February 2017).

Bradley, William, David Morrell, David Szanton, and Stephen Young. *Thailand, Domino by Default? The 1976 Coup and Implications for United States Policy with an Epilogue on the October 1977 Coup*. Athens: Southeast Asia Program, Center for International Studies, Ohio University, 1978.

Brass, Paul R. *Theft of an Idol: Text and Context in the Representation of Collective Violence*. Princeton, New Jersey: Princeton University Press, 1997.

BRNVoices. "Pengisytiharan dari Barisan Revolusi Nasional Melayu Patani (B.R.N.) K – 3" [Declaration of the Patani-Malay National Revolutionary Front (BRN) – No. 3]. YouTube, 28 May 2013 <https://www.youtube.com/watch?v=9vCoPDi80Rc> (accessed 6 December 2017).

Brown, Andrew. *Labour, Politics and the State in Industrializing Thailand*. London: RoutledgeCurzon, 2004.

Brown, David. *The State and Ethnic Politics in Southeast Asia*. New York: Routledge, 1994.

Buchanan, James. "Translating Thailand's Protests: An Analysis of Red Shirt Rhetoric". *Austrian Journal of South-East Asian Studies* 6, no. 1 (2013): 60–80.

Butler, Robert. "Ageism". In *The Encyclopedia of Aging*, 2nd ed., edited by George L. Maddox, pp. 38–39. New York: Springer, 1996.

Campbell, Charlie. "Thailand's Democrat Party is Hilariously Misnamed". *Time*, 28 November 2013 <http://world.time.com/2013/11/28/thailands-democrat-party-is-hilariously-misnamed/> (accessed 27 February 2017).

Central Intelligence Agency, United States. *CIA World Factbook*. Langley: Central Intelligence Agency, 2012.

Chadwick, Andrew. *Internet Politics: States, Citizens, and New Communication Technologies*. Oxford: Oxford University Press, 2006.

Chai-anan Samudavanija. *The Thai Young Turks*. Singapore: Institute of Southeast Asian Studies, 1982.

―――. "Thailand: A Stable Semi-Democracy". In *Democracy in Developing Countries*, vol. 3, *Asia*, edited by Larry Diamond, Juan J. Linz, and Seymour M. Lipset, pp. 305–46. London: Adamantine Press, 1989.

―――. "Luk chin rak chat" [Chinese descendants who love the nation]. *MGR Online*, 17 August 2008 <http://www.manager.co.th/Daily/ViewNews.aspx?NewsID=9510000097001> (accessed 28 October 2016).

―――. *Nueng roi pi haeng kanpatirup rabop ratchakan wiwatthanakan khong amnat rat lae amnat kanmueang* [100 years of bureaucratic reform: The development of state power and political power]. Bangkok: Institute of Public Policy Studies, 2011.

Chai-anan Samudavanija and David Morell. *Political Conflict in Thailand: Reform, Reaction, Revolution*. Cambridge: Oelgeschlager, Gunn & Hain, 1981.

Chaithawat Tulathon, ed. *Phraphrom chuai amnuai hai chuencham setthakit kanmueang wa duai sapsin suan phramahakasat lang 2475* [The god Brahma helps make things juicy: The politics and economics of crown property since 1932]. Nonthaburi: Fa diaokan, 2014.

Chalathip Thirasoonthrakul. "Thai Queen Weighs in with Anti-Government Protesters". Reuters, 13 October 2008 <http://www.reuters.com/article/us-thailand-protest-idUSTRE49C56K20081013?feedType=RSS&feedName=worldNews> (accessed 27 February 2017).

Chalita Bundhuwong. "'I Will Go Help My Brothers; The Corrupt Government Hurt People': Thoughts and Practices on 'Good Man's Politics' of Bangkok Migrant Southerners". Unpublished research report, 2016.

Chambers, Paul. "In the Land of Democratic Rollback: Military Authoritarianism and Monarchical Primacy in Thailand". In *National Security, Statecentricity and Governance in East Asia*, edited by Brendon Howe, pp. 37–60. London: Palgrave Macmillan, 2018.

Chambers, Paul, and Aurel Croissant, eds. *Democracy under Stress: Civil-Military Relations in South and Southeast Asia*. Bangkok: Institute of Security and

International Studies, Faculty of Political Science, Chulalongkorn University, 2010.

Chambers, Paul, and Napisa Waitoolkiat. "The Resilience of Monarchised Military in Thailand". *Journal of Contemporary Asia* 46, no. 3 (2016): 425–44.

Chamnan Chanrueang. "Changwat chatkaneng nawattakam khong phak prachasangkhom" [Self-administered provinces: An innovation of civil society]. *Krungthep thurakit*, 13 April 2016.

Chanida Chitbundid. *Khrongkan an nueang ma chak phraratchadamri kansathapana phraratcha-amnatnam nai phrabatsomdetphrachaoyuhua* [The royal projects: The making of royal hegemony]. Bangkok: The Foundation for the Promotion of Social Sciences and Humanities Textbooks Projects, 2007.

Chaowana Traimat. *Khomun phuenthan 75 pi prachathippatai thai 2475–2550* [Basic information about 75 years of Thai democracy, 1932–2007]. Bangkok: Institute of Public Policy Studies, 2007.

Charas Suvannamala. "Kankrachai amnat thangkanmueang lae kanklang su thongthin nai thotsawat na" [The devolution of authority and finances to localilities in the next decade]. In *Kankrachai amnat yangrai sang prachathippatai* [How to devolve power to build democracy], edited by Pasuk Phongpaichit and Sungsidh Piriyarangsan, pp. 77–99. Bangkok: Political Economy Center, Chulalongkorn University, 1994.

Charnvit Kasetsiri. *14 October 1973: A Historical Record*, translated by Benedict R.O'G. Anderson. Bangkok: Thammasat University, 1993.

———, ed. *Prawat kanmueang thai 2475–2500* [A history of Thai politics, 1932–57], rev. ed. Bangkok: Foundation for the Promotion of Social Sciences and Humanities Textbooks Project, 2001.

Charnvit Kasetsiri and Thamrongsak Petchlert-anan. *Patiwat 2475: The 1932 Revolution in Siam*. Bangkok: Foundation for the Promotion of Social Sciences and Humanities Textbook Project, 2009.

———, eds. *Tula-tula: sangkhom rat thai kap khwamrunraeng thangkanmueang* [October–October: The Thai state and society and political violence]. Bangkok: Foundation for the Promotion of Social Sciences and Humanities Textbooks Project, 2013.

Charun Yuthong. "Watthanatham thangkanmueang khong thongthin pak tai" [The political culture of the southern region]. Unpublished paper, n.d.

Che Man, Wan Kadir. *Muslim Separatism: The Moros of Southern Philippines and the Malays of Southern Thailand*. Singapore: Oxford University Press, 1990.

Chen Jie and Lu Chunlong. "Democratization and the Middle Class in China: The Middle Class's Attitudes toward Democracy". *Political Research Quarterly* 64, no. 3 (September 2011): 705–19.

Cheyroux, Blandine. "Fruit and Vegetables in Thailand's Rice Bowl: The Agricultural Development of Poldered Raised Bed Systems in Damnoen Saduak Area".

In *Thailand's Rice Bowl: Perspectives on Agricultural and Social Change in the Chao Phraya Delta*, edited by François Molle and Thippawal Srijantr, pp. 157–76. Bangkok: White Lotus, 2003.

Choemsak Pinthong. *Ru than Thaksin* [Keeping up with Thaksin]. Bangkok: Kho Khit Duai Khon Press, 2004*a*.

―――. *Ru than Thaksin 2 thueng ma nuea mek ko ru thao than* [Keeping up with Thaksin 2: Seeing through his tricks]. Bangkok: Kho Khit Duai Khon Press, 2004*b*.

―――. *Ru than Thaksin 3 Minority Reports ruam phon khon chai thueng* [Keeping up with Thaksin 3: Minority Reports bring together the work of courageous people]. Bangkok: Kho Khit Duai Khon Press, 2004*c*.

―――. *Ru than Thaksin 4: The insiders khon wong nai thaksin* [Keeping up with Thaksin 4: The insiders, those inside Thaksin's circle]. Bangkok: Kho Khit Duai Khon Press, 2006.

Chonthira Sattayawatthana. *Prakottakan phalang muan mahaprachachon* [The phenomenon of the force of the great mass of the people]. Pathum Thani: Rangsit University Press, 2014.

Chookiat Panaspornprasit. "Thailand: The Historical and Indefinite Transitions". In *Southeast Asian Affairs 2017*, edited by Daljit Singh and Malcolm Cook, pp. 353–66. Singapore: ISEAS – Yusof Ishak Institute, 2017.

Chulachomklao Royal Military Academy. *Prawat rongrian nairoi phra chunlachomklao* [History of the Chulachomklao Royal Military Academy]. Bangkok: Chulachomklao Royal Military Academy, 1967.

King Chulalongkorn. "Wa duai khwamsamakkhi" [On unity]. In *Ekkasan kanmueang kanpokkhrong thai* [Documents in Thai politics and administration], edited by Chai-Anan Samudavanija and Khattiya Kannasutra, pp. 127–35. Bangkok: Social Science Association of Thailand, 1989.

Chun, Natalie. "Middle Class Size in the Past, Present, and Future: A Description of Trends in Asia". ADB Economics Working Paper Series, no. 217 (September 2010) <http://hdl.handle.net/11540/1562> (accessed 21 April 2017).

Chuwat Rerksirisuk. *Born to be Democracy*. Bangkok: Prachatai Bookclub, 2011.

Clipdet yangni ko mi nai lok Channel. "Somluck Khamsing lao thueng nailuang yang prathap chai" [Somlak Khamsing's impressive recollections about the King]. YouTube, 4 November 2016 <https://www.youtube.com/watch?v=h3rvIq0q0rY> (accessed 16 February 2017).

Connors, Michael Kelly. *Democracy and National Identity in Thailand*. Copenhagen: NIAS Press, 2007.

―――. "Article of Faith: The Failure of Royal Liberalism in Thailand". *Journal of Contemporary Asia* 38, no. 1 (February 2008): 143–65.

Connors, Michael Kelly, and Kevin Hewison, eds. "Thailand's 'Good Coup':

The Fall of Thaksin, the Military and Democracy". Special issue, *Journal of Contemporary Asia* 38, no. 1 (February 2008): 1–189.

Crispin, Shawn W. "Royal Contradictions in Thailand". *Asia Times Online*, 13 December 2011 <www.atimes.com/atimes/Southeast_Asia/ML13Ae01.html> (accessed 27 February 2017).

Croissant, Aurel, David Kuehn, and Philip Lorenz. *Breaking with the Past? Civil-Military Relations in the Emerging Democracies of East Asia*. Honolulu: East-West Center, 2012.

Crosby, Josiah. *Siam: The Crossroads*. New York: AMS Press, 1973.

Crossette, Barbara. "King Bhumibol's Reign". *The New York Times*, 21 May 1989 <https://www.nytimes.com/1989/05/21/magazine/king-bhumibol-s-reign.html> (accessed 23 August 2018).

Cyber Scout Thailand. "About". Facebook, n.d. <https://www.facebook.com/pg/cyberscoutthailand/about/> (accessed 21 March 2018).

The Daily Telegraph. "Thai Junta Replaces Martial Law with Absolute Power". 2 April 2015 <http://www.telegraph.co.uk/news/worldnews/asia/thailand/11510666/Thai-junta-replaces-martial-law-with-absolute-power.html> (accessed 10 February 2017).

Dararat Mettarikanon. *Kanmueang thai song fang khong kanruamklum thangkanmueang khong so so isan pho so 2476–2492* [Politics on two banks of the Mekong: The formation of the Isan group of members of parliament, 1933/4–1949]. Bangkok: Sinlapawatthanatham, 2003.

Darin Inmuean. "Duncan McCargo: Mong kanmueang thai chak mummong baep lang ananikhom" [Duncan McCargo: Looking at Thai politics from a postcolonial perspective]. *Fa Diaokan* 10, no. 1 (2012): 20–35.

Davidson, Jamie S. *Indonesia: Twenty Years of Democracy*. Cambridge Elements: Politics and Society in Southeast Asia. Cambridge: Cambridge University Press, 2018.

Davis, Anthony. "Explosive Escalation of Thai Insurgency". *Asia Times*, 6 April 2012 <http://www.atimes.com/atimes/Southeast_Asia/ND06Ae04.html> (accessed 29 December 2017).

———. "Brief: Separatists Strike — The Ramadan Offensive in Southern Thailand". *IHS Jane's Terrorism & Security Monitor* 13, no. 8 (August 2013).

———. "Southern Thai Insurgents Stake out Peace Terms". *Nikkei Asian Review*, 11 October 2015 <https://asia.nikkei.com/Politics-Economy/Policy-Politics/Southern-Thai-insurgents-stake-out-peace-terms> (accessed 6 December 2017).

Deep South Journalism School. "Tham-top kham to kham muea MARA Patani phop suemuanchon thai khrang raek" [Asking and answering word-for-word: When MARA Patani first met the Thai media]. *Deep South Watch*, 31 August 2015 <https://www.deepsouthwatch.org/ms/node/7547> (accessed 6 December 2017).

Deep South Watch. "Khamsang samnak nayokratthamontri thi 230/2557 rueang kanchattang konkai khapkhluean krabuankan phutkhui phuea santisuk changwat chaidaen phaktai" [Prime ministerial order 230/2557 on the establishment of mechanisms to steer the dialogue process for peace in the southern border provinces]. 1 November 2015 <http://www.deepsouthwatch. org/node/7717> (accessed 6 December 2017).

Deli niu. "Rai ngao 'Khwanchai Phraiphana' lang thahan khao khum sathani witthayu daeng" [Not a trace of "Khwanchai Phraiphanna" after soldiers raid a Red Shirt radio station]. 22 May 2014 <https://www.dailynews.co.th/ regional/239544> (accessed 21 March 2018).

Department of Community Development, Thailand. Muban chonnabot thai chak khomun phuenthan radap muban [Villages in rural Thailand, from basic village-level data]. Bangkok: Ministry of Interior, 2009.

Department of Health, Thailand. "Raingan kansamruat sukhaphawa phu sungayu thai pi 2556" [Report on a survey of the health status of Thai elderly, 2013]. Bangkok: Ministry of Public Health, 2013.

Department of Local Administration. "History". 2015 <http://www.dla.go.th/en/ index.jsp> (accessed 21 February 2018).

Prince Dhani Nivat. "The Old Siamese Conception of Monarchy". Journal of the Siam Society 32, no. 2 (1946): 91–106.

Diamond, Larry. "Liberation Technology". Journal of Democracy 21, no. 3 (July 2010): 69–83.

Dittita Tititampruk. "Kankhaosu wongkan mue puen rap chang sueksa chapho korani phutongkhang rueancham klang bang khwang" [Entering the circles of contract killers: A case study of prisoners in Bang Kwang Central Prison]. Master's thesis, Thammasat University, 2005.

Dobbs, Debra, J. Kevin Eckert, Bob Rubinstein, Lynn Keimig, Leanne Clark, Ann Christine Frankowski, and Sheryl Zimmerman. "An Ethnographic Study of Stigma and Ageism in Residential Care or Assisted Living". Gerontologist 48, no. 4 (August 2008): 517–26.

Dressel, Björn. "Thailand: Judicialization of Politics or Politicization of the Judiciary?" In The Judicialization of Politics in Asia, edited by Björn Dressel. London: Routledge, 2012: 79–97.

Duangruedee Lasuka. "Dementia in Thailand: Current Situation". Paper presented at the International Symposium on Current Issues in Dementia and Dementia Care in East Asia, 2 March 2013. Osaka University, 2014.

Easterly, William. "The Middle Class Consensus and Economic Development". Journal of Economic Growth 6, no. 4 (December 2001): 317–35.

Easum, Taylor M. "A Thorn in Bangkok's Side: Khruba Sriwichai, Sacred Space and the Last Stand of the Premodern Chiang Mai State". South East Asia Research 21, no. 2 (June 2013): 211–36.

The Economist. "Soldiers in Power: Thailand's Dangerous Coup". 21 September 2006*a* <www.economist.com/node/7942244> (accessed 27 February 2017).

———. "Thailand's Military Coup: Old Soldiers, Old Habits". 21 September 2006*b* <www.economist.com/node/7944306> (accessed 27 February 2017).

———. "Thailand: Under Siege". 26 August 2008 <www.economist.com/node/11998386> (accessed 27 February 2017).

———. "Thailand's Monarchy: The King and Them". 4 December 2008*a* <www.economist.com/node/12724832> (accessed 27 February 2017).

———. "The King and Its Crisis: A Right Royal Mess". 4 December 2008*b* <www.economist.com/node/12724800> (accessed 27 February 2017).

———. "Banyan: The Trouble with the King". 16 April 2009 <www.economist.com/node/13496103> (accessed 27 February 2017).

———. "Thailand's Succession: As Father Fades, His Children Fight". 18 March 2010 <www.economist.com/node/15718981> (accessed 27 February 2017).

———. "Thailand's Monarchy: When More is Less". 3 February 2011 <www.economist.com/node/18073343> (accessed 27 February 2017).

———. "The Future of Thailand's Elite: Helplessly Hoping". 6 May 2014 <www.economist.com/blogs/banyan/2014/05/future-thailands-elite> (accessed 27 February 2017).

———. "Thailand's Coup: The Path to the Throne". 24 May 2014 <http://www.economist.com/news/asia/21602759-sudden-move-army-brings-only-near-term-calm-path-throne> (accessed 27 February 2017).

———. "Politics in Thailand: Vacuum Power". 17 May 2018, pp. 17–18.

El Bcheraoui, Charbel, Salim Abid, and Nicole Chapuis-Lucciani. "Perception of Ageism and Self-Esteem among Lebanese Elders at Home and Abroad". *Journal Medical Libanais* 63, no. 1 (January–March 2015): 27–33.

Electronic Frontier Foundation. "Definition of Media". 24 November 2009 <https://www.eff.org/files/filenode/social_network/media_def_resp.pdf> (accessed 21 March 2018).

Electronic Government Agency. "Phraratchabanyat waduai kankratham khwamphit kiaokap khomphiutoe (chabap thi 2) pho so 2560 thi ma lae sara samkhan" [The origins and content of the Computer Crimes Act (second version) of 2017]. 12 January 2017 <https://www.ega.or.th/upload/download/file_ce8c32197b28a5d438136a3bd8252b7c.pdf> (accessed 17 April 2018).

Enos, John. *Modeling the Economic Development of a Poorly Endowed Region: The Northeast of Thailand.* Santa Monica: RAND Corporation, 1970.

Export-Import Bank of Thailand. "EXIM Thailand Promotes Cross-border Trade and Investment Catering for AEC and Rising Purchasing Power in Neighboring Countries". 27 May 2015 <http://www.exim.go.th/Doc/adn/5800005241_0.pdf> (accessed 9 November 2016).

Falkus, Malcolm. "Income Inequality and Uncertain Democracy in Thailand".

In *Growth, Distribution and Political Change: Studies in the Economies of East and Southeast Asia*, edited by Ryoshin Minami, Kwan S. Kim, and Malcolm Falkus, pp. 114–42. London: Palgrave Macmillan, 1999.

FEER (*Far Eastern Economic Review*). "Bhumibol: Asian Phenomenon". 17 December 1973. In *The King of Thailand in World Focus*, edited by Denis D. Gray and Dominic Faulder, pp. 156–57. Singapore: Editions Didier Millet, 2008.

———. "King Bhumibol: 'Politics is a Filthy Business'". 18 October 1974. In *The King of Thailand in World Focus*, edited by Denis D. Gray and Dominic Faulder, pp. 47–49. Singapore: Editions Didier Millet, 2008.

———. "The Power Wielded by a Constitutional Monarchy". 19–25 June 1981. In *The King of Thailand in World Focus*, edited by Denis D. Gray and Dominic Faulder, pp. 96–99. Singapore: Editions Didier Millet, 2008.

Ferrara, Federico. "The Legend of King Prajadhipok: Tall Tales and Stubborn Facts on the Seventh Reign in Siam". *Journal of Southeast Asian Studies* 43, no. 1 (February 2012): 4–31.

———. "Unfinished Business: The Contagion of Conflict over a Century of Thai Political Development". In *"Good Coup Gone Bad": Thailand's Political Developments since Thaksin's Downfall*, edited by Pavin Chachavalpongpun, pp. 17–46. Singapore: Institute of Southeast Asian Studies, 2014.

———. *The Political Development of Modern Thailand*. Cambridge: Cambridge University Press, 2015.

Ferreira, Francisco H.G., Julian Messina, Jamele Rigolini, Luis-Felipe López-Calva, Maria Ana Lugo, and Renos Vakis. *Economic Mobility and the Rise of the Latin American Middle Class*. Washington, DC: World Bank, 2013.

Ferri, Cleusa P. "Global Prevalence of Dementia: A Delphi Consensus Study". *Lancet* 17, no. 366 (December 2005): 2112–17.

Financial Times. "King Bhumibol Adulyadej: The Reserved Yet Revered Monarch is Seen as the Turbulent Country's Spiritual Authority", 23 September 2006. In *The King of Thailand in World Focus*, edited by Denis D. Gray and Dominic Faulder, pp. 114–15. Singapore: Editions Didier Millet, 2008.

Fineman, Daniel. *A Special Relationship: The United States and Military Government in Thailand, 1947–1958*. Honolulu: University of Hawai'i Press, 1997.

Finer, Samuel E. *The Man on Horseback: The Role of the Military in Politics*. New York: Praeger, 1962.

flyer cryer. "penjelasan 5 tuntutan awal : BRN 29.04.2013" [Clarification: Five initial demands on 29 April 2013]. YouTube, 24 May 2013 <https://www.youtube.com/watch?v=x6r5WxFlBlY> (accessed 6 December 2017).

Forbes. "In Thailand, a Rare Peek at His Majesty's Balance Sheet". 20 January 2012.

———. "'Yellow Shirt' Protestors Act like Mussolini's Black Shirts". 3 February 2014.

Francke, Warren. "The Evolving Watchdog: The Media's Role in Government Ethics". *Annals of the American Academy of Political and Social Science* 537 (January 1995): 109–21.

Fraser, Isabelle. "Thailand's Ageing Population Adds Cost to Family Budgets". Angloinfo World: Expat Life (blog), 6 May 2016 <http://blogs.angloinfo. com/angloinfo-world-expat-life/2016/05/06/thailands-ageing-population-adds-cost-to-family-budgets/> (accessed 9 November 2016).

Fredrickson, Terry. "Rubber Protests Continue". *Bangkok Post*, 28 August 2013 <http://www.bangkokpost.com/learning/advanced/366792/rubber-protests-continue> (accessed 28 October 2016).

Freedom House. "Freedom of the Press 2015: Harsh Laws and Violence Drive Global Decline". *Freedom of the Press 2015*, April 2015a <https://freedomhouse. org/sites/default/files/FreedomofthePress_2015_FINAL.pdf> (accessed 21 March 2018).

———. "Methodology". *Freedom of the Press 2015*, April 2015b <https:// freedomhouse.org/report/freedom-press-2015/methodology> (accessed 21 March 2018).

———. "Freedom of the Press (FOTP) Data: Editions 1980–2017". *Freedom of the Press Data*, 2017 <https://freedomhouse.org/sites/default/files/FOTP1980-FOTP2017_Public-Data.xlsx> (accessed 21 March 2018).

———. "About *Freedom of the Press*". *Freedom of the Press*, 2018 <https:// freedomhouse.org/report-types/freedom-press> (accessed 21 March 2018).

Freedom of Expression Documentation Center. "Khon Kaen moden" [The Khon Kaen model]. *Than khomun khadi* [Legal case database], n.d. <http://freedom. ilaw.or.th/case/590#allegation_1> (accessed 10 February 2017).

Fuller, Thomas. "In Thailand, Growing Intolerance for Dissent Drives Many to More Authoritarian Nations". *The New York Times*, 6 June 2014a <https://www. nytimes.com/2014/06/07/world/asia/in-thailand-a-growing-intolerance-for-dissent.html> (accessed 27 February 2017).

———. "Thailand's Political Tensions are Rekindling Ethnic and Regional Divisions". *The New York Times*, 12 April 2014b <http://www.nytimes.com/2014/04/13/world/asia/thailands-political-tensions-are-rekindling-ethnic-and-regional-divisions.html> (accessed 10 February 2017).

Funatsu Tsuruyo and Kazuhiro Kagoya. "The Middle Classes in Thailand: The Rise of the Urban Intellectual Elite and their Social Consciousness". *Developing Economies* 41, no. 2 (June 2003): 243–63.

Ghosh, Nirmal. "Thai Rebels 'Ready for Talks with Gov't'". *The Straits Times*, 10 August 2010.

Giles Ji Ungpakorn. "The Demise of the Red Shirts?" *Uglytruth-Thailand*, 5 July 2015 <https://uglytruththailand.wordpress.com/2015/07/05/the-demise-of-the-red-shirts/> (accessed 9 October 2017).

Girard, René. *Violence and the Sacred*, translated by Patrick Gregory. Baltimore: Johns Hopkins University Press, 1977.

Girling, John L.S. *Thailand: Society and Politics*. Ithaca: Cornell University Press, 1981.

Gkikas, Ilias, Dionysia Petratou, and Nektarios Tavernarakis. "Longevity Pathways and Memory Aging". *Frontiers in Genetics* 5, no. 155 (June 2014): 1–10.

GotoKnow. "Phon wichai rabu kharatchakan thai rusuek toktam sut yuk 'Thaksin'" [Results of research showing that the Thai civil service felt most in decline in the Thaksin era]. *Sarup khao prachamwan khong hong samut krom banchi klang* [Daily news summary, comptroller general's department library], 9 August 2006 <https://www.gotoknow.org/posts/43645> (accessed 16 February 2017).

Grabowsky, Volker. *Regions and National Integration in Thailand (1892–1992)*. DeKalb: Northern Illinois University Center for Southeast Asian Studies, 1995.

Gray, Christine. "Thailand: The Soteriological State in the 1970s". PhD dissertation, Department of Anthropology, University of Chicago, 1986.

Gray, Denis D., John Everingham, and Owen P. Wrigley, eds. *The King of Thailand in World Focus*. Bangkok: Foreign Correspondents Club of Thailand, 1988.

Gray, Denis D., and Dominic Faulder, eds. *The King of Thailand in World Focus: Articles and Images from the International Press, 1946–2006*, 2nd ed. Singapore: Editions Didier Millet, 2007.

———, eds. *The King of Thailand in World Focus: Articles and Images from the International Press 1946–2008*, 3rd ed. Singapore: Editions Didier Millet, 2008.

Groemping, Max "'Echo Chambers': Partisan Facebook Groups during the 2014 Thai Election". *Asia Pacific Media Educator* 24, no. 1 (September 2014): 39–59.

Grossman, Nicholas, ed. *Chronicles of Thailand: Headline News since 1946*. Bangkok: *Bangkok Post* and Editions Didier Millet, 2009.

Grossman, Nicholas, and Dominic Faulder, eds. *King Bhumibol Adulyadej, A Life's Work: Thailand's Monarchy in Perspective*. Bangkok: Editions Didier Millet, 2011.

Grossman, Nicholas, Apiradee Treerutkuarkul, and Jim Algie, eds. *Thailand's Sustainable Development Sourcebook: Issues & Information, Ideas & Inspiration*. Bangkok: Editions Didier Millet, 2015.

The Guardian. "Australia Downgrades Ties with Thailand after Military Coup". 30 May 2014 <www.theguardian.com/world/2014/may/31/australia-downgrades-ties-with-thailand-after-military-coup> (accessed 5 September 2014).

Halpin, Helen, Maria M. Morales-Suárez-Varela, and Jose M. Martin-Moreno. "Chronic Disease Prevention and the New Public Health". *Public Health Reviews* 32, no. 1 (June 2010): 120–54.

Handley, Paul. *The King Never Smiles: A Biography of Thailand's King Bhumibol Adulyadej*. New Haven: Yale University Press, 2006.

Hasan Taib. "Pengistiharan dari Barisan Revolusi Nasional Melayu Patani (B.R.N) K – 4" [Declaration of the Patani-Malay National Revolutionary Front (BRN) – No. 4]. YouTube, 24 June 2013 <https://www.youtube.com/watch?v=EC5hYrI5Grg> (accessed 6 December 2017).

Hattori Tamio, Funatsu Tsuruyo, and Torii Takashi. "Introduction: The Emergence of the Asian Middle Classes and Their Characteristics". *Developing Economies* 41, no. 2 (June 2003): 129–39.

Hawkins, Loraine, Jaruayporn Srisasalux, and Sutayut Osornprasop. *Devolution of Health Centers and Hospital Autonomy in Thailand: A Rapid Assessment*. Washington, DC: HSRI and World Bank, 2009.

Head, Jonathan. "Where is Thailand Heading after Protests?" British Broadcasting Corporation, 7 March 2014 <www.bbc.com/news/world-asia-26467100> (accessed 27 February 2017).

Health Information System Development Office. "Mo so pho so phoei kha raksa phayaban 3 kongthun mi naeonom phueng phop khon kae chai borikan maksut" [Foundation for research on and development of the Thai aged announces that medical care costs on a spiking trend, finds that the elderly use services the most]. *News Update*, 21 January 2011 <http://www.hiso.or.th/hiso/ghealth/newsx2245.php> (accessed 16 October 2017).

Henley, David E.F. *Nationalism and Regionalism in a Colonial Context*. Leiden: Royal Institute of Linguistics and Anthropology, 1996.

Hirschman, Albert O. *Exit, Voice, and Loyalty: Responses to Decline in Firms, Organizations, and States*. Cambridge: Harvard University Press, 1970.

Hookway, James, Patrick Barta, and Jay Solomon. "Coup Ousting Thailand's Premier Tests Democracy in Key U.S. Ally". *The Wall Street Journal*, 20 September 2006 <www.wsj.com/articles/SB115867950942167569> (accessed 27 February 2017).

Huntington, Samuel P. *Political Order in Changing Societies*. New Haven: Yale University Press, 1968.

Hyun Sinae. "Indigenizing the Cold War: Nation-Building by the Border Patrol Police of Thailand, 1945–1980". PhD dissertation, Department of History, University of Wisconsin-Madison, 2014.

iLaw. "Pho ro bo khomphiutoe mattra 14(1) ya raeng phit khanan samrap kanminpramat onlai" [The Computer Crime Act's Article 14(1) the wrong medication for online defamation]. 26 August 2014 <https://freedom.ilaw.or.th/blog/พรบคอมพิวเตอร์ฯ-มาตรา-141-ยาแรงผิดขนานสำหรับการหมิ่นประมาทออนไลน์> (accessed 17 April 2018).

Ingham, Barbara, Andrejs Chirijevskis, and Fiona Carmichael. "Implications of an Increasing Old-age Dependency Ratio: The UK and Latvian Experiences Compared". *Pensions* 14, no. 4 (November 2009): 221–30.

Institute for Economics and Peace. "Global Terrorism Index 2016". *Reports*, November 2016 <http://visionofhumanity.org/app/uploads/2017/02/Global-Terrorism-Index-2016.pdf> (accessed 6 December 2017).

International Crisis Group. "Thailand: Political Turmoil and the Southern Insurgency". *Asia Briefing*, no. 80 (28 August 2008).

———. "Bridging Thailand's Deep Divide". *Asia Report*, no. 192 (5 July 2010*a*) <https://www.crisisgroup.org/asia/south-east-asia/thailand/bridging-thailand-s-deep-divide> (accessed 10 February 2017).

———. "Stalemate in Southern Thailand". *Asia Briefing*, no. 113 (3 November 2010*b*).

———. "A Coup Ordained? Thailand's Prospect for Stability". *Asia Report*, no. 263 (3 December 2014) <https://www.crisisgroup.org/asia/south-east-asia/thailand/coup-ordained-thailand-s-prospects-stability> (accessed 10 February 2017).

International Labour Organization. "Major Group 3: Technicians and Associate Professionals". *International Standard Classification of Occupations*, 18 September 2004 <http://www.ilo.org/public/english/bureau/stat/isco/isco88/3.htm> (accessed 21 April 2017).

Ishine Masayuki, Sakagami Teiji, Sakamoto Ryouta, Wada Taizo, Kovit Khampitak, Fushida Mutsuko, Kawakita Toshiko, Okumiya Kiyohito, Kita Toru, and Matsubayashi Kozo. "Comprehensive Geriatric Assessment for Community-Dwelling Elderly in Asia Compared with Those in Japan: VII. Khon Khen in Thailand". *Geriatrics & Gerontology International* 6, no. 1 (March 2006): 40–48.

Ishine Masayuki, Wada Taizo, Sakagami Teiji, Pham Tien Duna, Tranc Duc Vienh, Kawakita Toshiko, Fushida Mutsuko, Okumiya Kiyohito, Kita Toru, and Matsubayashi Kozo. "Comprehensive Geriatric Assessment for Community-Dwelling Elderly in Asia Compared with Those in Japan: III. Phuto in Vietnam". *Geriatrics & Gerontology International* 5, no. 2 (June 2005): 115–21.

Isra News Agency. "Winthai chaeng pom phutkhui santiphap yan rat thai nuengdiao mai mi pokkhrong phiset" [Winthai clarifies peace talk, Thailand a unitary state, autonomy not possible]. 24 June 2014.

———. "Kamsang khana raksa kwamsangop haeng chat chabap thi 108/2557" [National Council for Peace and Order, Order Number 108/2557]. 31 July 2014 <http://www.isranews.org/announcement/item/31737-faa_31737.html> (accessed 10 February 2017).

———. "Phutkhui dap fai tai sadut! 'Aksara' pat longnam rang TOR" [Dialogue hits a snag, Aksara refuses to sign TOR]. 28 April 2016.

———. "Ruam prakat khamsang kho so cho." [Collection of NCPO announcements and orders]. n.d. <http://www.isranews.org/announcement.html> (accessed 10 February 2017).

Jabatan Penerangan-BRN. "Perisytiharan Jabatan Penerangan B.R.N" [Announcement of the BRN's information department]. YouTube, 7 September

2015 <https://www.youtube.com/watch?v=lZYnDJ77fyU> (accessed 6 December 2017).

Jackson, Peter A. "Virtual Divinity: A 21st Century Discourse of Thai Royal Influence". In *Saying the Unsayable: Monarchy and Democracy in Thailand*, edited by Søren Ivarsson and Lotte Isager, pp. 29–60. Copenhagen: NIAS Press, 2010.

The Japan Times. "Thai Opposition Torn between Elections and 'People's Revolution'". 16 December 2013 <http://www.japantimes.co.jp/news/2013/12/16/asia-pacific/politics-diplomacy-asia-pacific/thai-opposition-torn-between-elections-and-peoples-revolution/> (accessed 21 April 2017).

Jenkins, Henry. "Confronting the Challenges of Participatory Culture: Media Education for the 21st Century". *Building the Field of Digital Media and Learning*, 2006 <https://www.macfound.org/media/article_pdfs/JENKINS_WHITE_PAPER.PDF> (accessed 22 March 2018).

Jiraporn Kespichayawattana and Sutthichai Jitapunkul. "Health and Health Care System for Older Persons". *Ageing International* 33, nos. 1–4 (December 2008): 28–49.

Johnston, David B. "Bandit, *Nakleng*, and Peasant in Rural Thai Society". *Contributions to Asian Studies* 15 (January 1980): 90–101.

Joint Working Group on Peace Dialogue Process on Southern Thailand (JWG-PDP). "Common Understanding: Ramadan Peace Initiative 2013". 12 July 2013.

Jom Petpradap. "Chak aithiwi thueng thai phi bi et … udomkan 'sue' thi tong sang" [From iTV to Thai PBS … the ideals for media that must be created]. *Media Inside Out*, 23 March 2013 <http://www.mediainsideout.net/columnist/2013/03/118> (accessed 22 March 2018).

Jory, Patrick. *Thailand's Theory of the Monarchy: Vessantara Jataka and the Idea of a Perfect Man*. New York: SUNY Press, 2016.

———. "*Bupphesanniwat* Fever: Gendered Nationalism and Middle-Class Views of Thailand's Political Predicament". *SOJOURN: Journal of Social Issues in Southeast Asia* 33, no. 2 (July 2018): 440–56.

Jotman. "World's Most Expensive Royal Family". 27 February 2008 <http://jotman.blogspot.sg/2008/02/worlds-most-expensive-royal-family.html> (accessed 16 February 2017).

Judd, Dennis R., and Todd Swanstrom. *City Politics*, 9th ed. New York: Routledge, 2015.

Kalyvas, Stathis. *The Logic of Violence in Civil War*. New York: Cambridge University Press, 2006.

Kamala Tiyavanich. *Forest Recollections: Wandering Monks in Twentieth-Century Thailand*. Honolulu: University of Hawai'i Press, 1997.

Kamhaeng. "Phonlamueang totan Single Gateway phuea seriphap lae khwamyuttitham" [Civilians against Single Gateway for freedom and justice].

Facebook, n.d. <https://www.facebook.com/พลเมืองต่อต้าน-Single-Gateway-Thailand-Internet-Firewall-opsinglegateway-424552194421120/> (accessed 22 March 2018).

Kanok Wongtra-ngan. *Naeo phraratchadamri nai kanmueang kanpokkhrong khong phrabatsomdet phrachaoyuhua* [His Majesty's political ideas]. Bangkok: Thai Studies Institute, Chulalongkorn University, 1988.

Kanoksak Keawthep. "Kanphatthana chonnabot phuea kankrachai amnat koranisueksa chak prasopkan khong ongkon chaoban" [Rural development and decentralization: Case studies from the experience of people's organizations]. In *Kankrachai amnat yangrai sang prachathippatai* [How to devolve power to build democracy], edited by Pasuk Phongpaichit and Sungsidh Piriyarangsan, pp. 305–51. Bangkok: Political Economy Center, Chulalongkorn University, 1994.

Kasian Tejapira. *Chintanakan chat thi mai pen chumchon: khon chan klang luk chin kap chatniyom doi rat khong thai* [An imagined nation that is not a community: Middle-class Chinese descendants and Thai state nationalism]. Bangkok: Institute of Journalist Development and Training, Manager Newspaper, 1994.

———. "'Governance' in Thailand". In *A Sarong for Clio: Essays on the Intellectual and Cultural History of Thailand — Inspired by Craig J. Reynolds*, edited by Maurizio Peleggi, pp. 181–96. Ithaca: Cornell Southeast Asia Program Publications, 2015.

———. "The Irony of Democratization and the Decline of Royal Hegemony in Thailand". *Southeast Asian Studies* 5, no. 2 (2016): 219–37.

Kavi Chongkittavorn. "The Media and Access to Information in Thailand". In *The Right to Tell: The Role of Mass Media in Economic Development*, edited by Roumeen Islam, Simeon Djankov, and Caralee McLeish, pp. 255–65. Washington, DC: The World Bank, 2002 <http://documents.worldbank.org/curated/en/957661468780322581/The-right-to-tell-the-role-of-mass-media-in-economic-development> (accessed 22 March 2018).

Kengkij Kitirianglarp and Kevin Hewison. "Social Movements and Political Opposition in Contemporary Thailand". *Pacific Review* 22, no. 4 (September 2009): 451–77.

Kermel-Torrès, Doryane, ed. *Atlas of Thailand: Spatial Structures and Development*. Chiang Mai: Silkworm Books, 2004.

Keya. "Supinya Klangnarong phut khwamching!???" [Supinya Klangnarong telling the truth!???]. *OK Nation*, 10 September 2007 <http://www.oknation.net/blog/keya/2007/09/10/entry-2> (accessed 22 March 2018).

Keyes, Charles F. *Isan: Regionalism in Northeastern Thailand*. Ithaca: Southeast Asia Program, Department of Asian Studies, Cornell University, 1967.

———. *Finding Their Voice: Northeastern Villagers and the Thai State*. Chiang Mai: Silkworm Books, 2014.

Khamnun Sitthisaman. *Prakottakan Sonthi: chak suea si lueang thueng pha phan kho si fa* [The Sondhi phenomenon: From yellow shirts to blue scarves]. Bangkok: Ban Phra Athit Press, 2006.

Khao sot. "Mop ko po po so hue thamrai nakkhao sao chong 3 9 kao kaennam ham phanlawan!" [PDRC leaders prevent mob attacks on Channel 3, 9 News reporters]. 22 December 2013.

———. "Buklom thi samak Thueak nam khatkhwang" [Suthep leads mobs to disrupt candidate registration]. 23 December 2013.

———. "Thahan choen nakkhao 'prachatai' prap khwamkhaochai pom infokrafik mattra 112" [Soldiers invited *"Prachatai"* journalist to discuss the issue of infographics on Article 112]. 27 October 2015 <http://www.khaosod.co.th/view_newsonline.php?newsid=1445961509> (accessed 22 March 2018).

Khaosod English. "Establish People's Council, Or No Election: Suthep". 12 December 2013.

———. "Southern 'Separatist Banners' Dismiss Peace Talks". 1 December 2014 <http://www.khaosodenglish.com/politics/2014/12/01/1417418805/> (accessed 6 December 2017).

Khemthong Tonsakulrungruang. "Thailand's Sangha: Turning Right, Coming Full Circle". *New Mandala: New Perspectives on Southeast Asia,* 7 August 2018 <https://www.newmandala.org/thailands-sangha-turning-right-coming-full-circle/> (accessed 23 August 2018).

Khom chat luek. "6 pi ratthaprahan 2549 chut kamnoet sue mi si" [Six years since the 2006 coup and the emergence of the coloured media]. 19 September 2012 <http://www.komchadluek.net/news/detail/140370> (accessed 22 March 2018).

Kinder, Tabatha. "Who Will Succeed Thailand's King Bhumibol?" *International Business Times,* 7 August 2014 <www.ibtimes.co.uk/who-will-succeed-thailands-king-bhumibol-1460220> (accessed 27 February 2017).

King Prajadhipok's Institute. "Ratthathammanun haeng ratcha-ananachak thai pho so 2475" [The 1932 Thai constitution]. 2016 <http://wiki.kpi.ac.th/index.php?title=รัฐธรรมนูญแห่งราชอาณาจักรไทย_พ.ศ._2475> (accessed 16 February 2017).

Kinsella, Kevin, and David R. Phillips. "Global Aging: The Challenge of Success". *Population Bulletin* 60, no. 1 (March 2005): 1–42.

Klausner, William J. "On the Thai Monarchy". *Journal of the Siam Society* 106 (2018): 315–17.

Knodel, John E., Bussarawan Teerawichitchainan, Vipan Prachuabmoh, and Wiraporn Pothisiri. "The Situation of Thailand's Older Population: An Update Based on the 2014 Survey of Older Persons in Thailand". PSC Report Series, no. 15-847 (October 2015). Ann Arbor: Population Studies Center, University of Michigan, 2015.

Knodel, John E., and Napaporn Chayovan. "Population Ageing and the Well-being of Older Persons in Thailand". *PSC Research Reports*, no. 08-659 (October 2008). Ann Arbor, Michigan: Population Studies Center, University of Michigan, 2008*a*.

———. "Gender and Ageing in Thailand: A Situation Analysis of Older Women and Men". PSC Research Reports, no. 08-664 (December 2008). Ann Arbor: Population Studies Center, University of Michigan, 2008*b*.

Knox-Vydmanov, Charles, and Usa Khiewrord. "Rationing the Old-Age Allowance a Backwards Step". *Bangkok Post*, 27 May 2016 <http://www.bangkokpost.com/print/990397/> (accessed 16 October 2017).

Kobkua Suwannathat-Pian. *Kings, Country and Constitutions: Thailand's Political Development, 1932–2000*. London: RoutledgeCurzon, 2003.

Krishna, Sankarna. "Comparative Assassinations: The Changing Moral Economy of Political Killing in South Asia". In *Political Violence in South and Southeast Asia: Critical Perspectives*, edited by Itty Abraham, Edward Newman, and Meredith L. Weiss, pp. 27–46. Tokyo: United Nations University Press, 2010.

Krungthep thurakit. "Chaos Erupts at Advance Elections". 27 January 2014.

———. "Thaksin yam 'kaennam daeng-phuea thai' ploi kho so cho lui temthi" [Thaksin to 'Red Leaders and Phuea Thai Party': Let NCPO go at full speed]. 22 August 2014 <http://www.bangkokbiznews.com/news/detail/600302> (accessed 10 February 2017).

———. "Daodin to kankhao thahan mua yan mai khoei rap ngoen chu 3 niu" [Dao Din brushes off military claim, insists never flashed 3-finger salute for cash]. 1 December 2014 <http://www.bangkokbiznews.com/news/detail/620796> (accessed 10 February 2017).

———. "Triam dueng ngop o po tho kratun setthakit lot raek 5 muen lan" [Preparing to pull budget from local administrative organizations to stimulate the economy, 50 billion baht for the first phase]. 29 November 2017 <http://www.bangkokbiznews.com/news/detail/783248> (accessed 21 February 2018).

Kuhonta, Erik M., and Aim Sinpeng. "Democratic Regression in Thailand: The Ambivalent Role of Civil Society and Political Institutions", in "The Challenges of Democratic Consolidation in Thailand", edited by Erik M. Kuhonta and Aim Sinpeng, special issue, *Contemporary Southeast Asia* 36, no. 3 (December 2014): 333–55.

———, eds. "The Challenges of Democratic Consolidation in Thailand". Special issue, *Contemporary Southeast Asia* 36, no. 3 (December 2014*b*): 333–466.

Kullada Kesboonchoo Mead. *The Rise and Decline of Thai Absolutism*. London: Routledge, 2004.

Kurlantzick, Joshua. "The King and US". Council on Foreign Relations, 16 November 2012 <http://www.cfr.org/thailand/king-us/p29509> (accessed 27 February 2017).

————. *Democracy in Retreat: The Revolt of the Middle Class and the Worldwide Decline of Representative Government*. New Haven: Yale University Press, 2014.

Lamont, Michèle. *Money, Morals, and Manners: The Culture of the French and the American Upper-Middle Class*. Chicago: University of Chicago Press, 1992.

LeoGrande, William M., and Carla A. Robbins. "Oligarchs and Officers: The Crisis in El Salvador". In *The Politics of Antipolitics: The Military in Latin America*, 2nd ed., edited by Brian Loveman and Thomas M. Davies, pp. 480–500. Lanham, Maryland: Rowman & Littlefield, 1997.

Lewis, Glen. *Virtual Thailand: The Media and Cultural Politics in Thailand, Malaysia and Singapore*. Abingdon, UK: Routledge, 2006.

Likhit Dhiravegin. *Wiwatthanakan kanmueang kanpokkhrong thai* [The development of Thai politics and administration]. Bangkok: Thammasat University Press, 2003.

Liow, Joseph Chinyong, and Don Pathan. *Confronting Ghosts: Thailand's Shapeless Southern Insurgency*. Sydney: Lowy Institute for International Policy, 2010.

Lips Magazine. "LIPS MAGAZINE". Facebook, n.d. <https://www.facebook.com/lipsmag> (accessed 22 March 2018).

Lipset, Seymour M. "Some Social Requisites of Democracy: Economic Development and Political Legitimacy". *American Political Science Review* 53, no. 1 (March 1959): 69–105.

Litvack, Jennie I., Junaid Ahmad, and Richard M. Bird. *Rethinking Decentralization in Developing Countries*. Washington, DC: The World Bank, 1998.

Loveman, Brian, and Thomas M. Davies, eds. *The Politics of Antipolitics: The Military in Latin America*, 2nd ed. Lanham, Maryland: Rowman & Littlefield, 1997.

Mack, Michelle, and Jelena Pejic. "Increasing Respect for International Humanitarian Law in Non-International Armed Conflicts". International Committee of the Red Cross, February 2008 <https://www.icrc.org/sites/default/files/topic/file_plus_list/0923-increasing_respect_for_international_humanitarian_law_in_non-international_armed_conflicts.pdf> (accessed 6 December 2017).

MacKay, David. *Information Theory, Inference, and Learning Algorithms*. Cambridge: Cambridge University Press, 2003.

Marshall, Andrew MacGregor. "Thailand's Moment of Truth: A Secret History of 21st Century Siam (Part One of Four)". *ZENJOURNALIST*, 23 June 2011*a* <http://www.zenjournalist.com/wp-content/uploads/2011/06/thaistory1.1.pdf> (accessed 27 February 2017).

————. "Thailand's Moment of Truth: A Secret History of 21st Century Siam (Part Two of Four)". *ZENJOURNALIST*, 24 June 2011*b* <https://thaistoryblog.files.wordpress.com/2011/06/thaistory2-0.pdf> (accessed 27 February 2017).

————. *A Kingdom in Crisis: Thailand's Struggle for Democracy in the Twenty-First Century*. London: Zed Books, 2014.

Martinez-Hervas, Sergio, Pedro Romero, Enrique B. Hevilla, José T. Real, Antonia

Priego, Jose M. Martin-Moreno, Rafael Carmena, and Juan F. Ascaso. "Classical Cardiovascular Risk Factors According to Fasting Plasma Glucose Levels". *European Journal of International Medicine* 19, no. 3 (May 2008): 209–13.

Matichon. "Patibatkan po po ngo truatsop sapsin sue" [Suspicion over anti-money laundering office: Checking finances of media]. News Center Database, 2 June 2002 <http://www.infoquest.co.th/th/news-services/newscenter/> (accessed 2 June 2012).

———. "Tuean phuwa thua po tho daeng ben pao mung phao so no ngo thongthin DSI leng chap phoem ik 18" [Warning to governors nationwide: Reds shift arson targets to local offices. DSI mulling 18 more arrests]. 4 June 2010 <http://www.matichon.co.th/news_detail.php?newsid=1275668857&catid=01> (accessed 10 February 2017).

———. "Pu bin pluk khwan hat yai Bik Tu tuean pram ratthaban cheracha chon tai" [Yingluck flies to Hat Yai to raise morale, Prayut warns government about talking to southern insurgents]. 3 April 2012.

———. "Thammai matichon sutsapda chabap ni chueng phat hua pok '1 khon 1 siang yang chai kap "khon thai" mai dai'" [Why does this edition of *Matichon Weekly* feature the cover story "1 person, 1 vote cannot yet be used with 'Thai people'"?]. 20 December 2013 <http://www.matichon.co.th/news_detail.php?newsid=1387500777> (accessed 21 April 2017).

———. "Thahan riak tua achan mo mahasarakham sop kiaoyong kap daodin" [Army summons Mahasarakham University lecturer for questioning over links to Dao Din]. 16 June 2015 <http://www.matichon.co.th/news_detail.php?newsid=1434368629> (accessed 10 February 2017).

———. "'Bik Tu' chai mo 44 deng 71" [Big Tu uses article 44 to remove 71 from posts]. 25 June 2015 <http://www.matichon.co.th/news_detail.php?newsid=1435222892> (accessed 10 February 2017).

———. "No so-prachachon salai kanchumnum na so no pathumwan lang chaeng khwamdamnoenkhadi cho no tho" [Students, protesters disband rally in front of Pathumwan Police Station after filing charge against officers]. 24 June 2015 <http://www.matichon.co.th/news_detail.php?newsid=1435129440> (accessed 10 February 2017).

Matichon Criminal News Section. *Pha anachak gotfathoe mueang luang* [Uncovering the empires of the godfathers of the capital]. Bangkok: Matichon, 1989.

———. *Kae roi khadi dang* [Tracing famous criminal cases]. Bangkok: Matichon, 1995.

Matichon Press. *Lap luang luek phanthamit prachachon phuea prachathippatai* [Delving deeply into the secrets of the People's Alliance for Democracy]. Bangkok: Matichon Press, 2008.

McCall, Nelda, ed. *Who Will Pay for Long Term Care? Insights from the Partnership Programs.* Chicago: Health Administration Press, 2001.

McCargo, Duncan. "Alternative Meanings of Political Reform in Contemporary Thailand". *Copenhagen Journal of Asian Studies* 13 (1998): 5–30.

———. "The International Media and the Domestic Political Coverage of the Thai Press". *Modern Asian Studies* 33, no. 3 (July 1999): 551–79.

———. *Politics and the Press in Thailand: Media Machinations*. London: Routledge, 2000.

———. "Network Monarchy and Legitimacy Crises in Thailand". *Pacific Review* 18, no. 4 (December 2005): 499–519.

———. "A Hollow Crown". *New Left Review*, 43 (January–February 2007): 135–44.

———. *Tearing Apart the Land: Islam and Legitimacy in Southern Thailand*. Ithaca: Cornell University Press, 2008.

———. *Mapping National Anxieties: Thailand's Southern Conflict*. Copenhagen: NIAS Press, 2012*a*.

———. "Two Cheers for Rally Politics". In *Bangkok May 2010: Perspectives on a Divided Thailand*, edited by Michael J. Montesano, Pavin Chachavalpongpun, and Aekapol Chongvilaivan, pp. 190–98. Singapore: Institute of Southeast Asian Studies, 2012*b*.

———. "Competing Notions of Judicialization in Thailand". *Contemporary Southeast Asia* 36, no. 3 (December 2014): 417–41.

———. "Passive Resistance in Thailand's Northeast". *Nikkei Asian Review*, 31 August 2015*a* <http://asia.nikkei.com/Viewpoints/Perspectives/Passive-resistance-in-Thailand-s-northeast> (accessed 10 February 2017).

———. "Peopling Thailand's 2015 Draft Constitution". *Contemporary Southeast Asia* 37, no. 3 (December 2015*b*), pp. 329–54.

———. "Thailand in 2014: The Trouble with Magic Swords". In *Southeast Asian Affairs 2015*, edited by Daljit Singh, pp. 337–58. Singapore: Institute of Southeast Asian Studies, 2015*c*.

———. "Finish Line for Century-Old Bangkok Horse Track". *Asia Times*, 12 August 2018 <http://www.atimes.com/article/finish-line-for-century-old-bangkok-horse-track/> (accessed 23 August 2018).

McCargo, Duncan, and Peeradej Tanruangporn. "Branding Dissent: Nitirat, Thailand's Enlightened Jurists". *Journal of Contemporary Asia* 45, no. 3 (2015): 419–42.

McCargo, Duncan, Saowanee T. Alexander, and Petra Desatova. "Ordering Peace: Thailand's 2016 Constitutional Referendum". *Contemporary Southeast Asia* 39, no. 1 (April 2017): 65–95.

McCargo, Duncan, and Ukrist Pathmanand. *The Thaksinization of Thailand*. Copenhagen: NIAS Press, 2005.

McCoy, Alfred, ed. *An Anarchy of Families: State and Family in the Philippines*. Madison: University of Wisconsin Center for Southeast Asian Studies, 1993.

MCOT. "Khayaiphon 'khon kaen moden' chap phutongha phrom awut songkhram chamnuan mak" [Investigation expanded in 'Khon Kaen Model' case, more arrested with many lethal weapons]. 25 June 2014 <http://www.mcot.net/site/content?id=53aa64f6be0470e77e8b45c9> (accessed 10 February 2017).

McVey, Ruth, ed. *Money and Power in Provincial Thailand*. Copenhagen: NIAS Press, 2000.

Medhi Krongkaew. "Thitthang kanphattana chonnabot thai adit patchuban lae anakhot" [The direction of rural development of Thailand: Past, present, and future]. In *The Direction of Thai Economy in the Next Decade*, Annual Symposium, February 1986, pp. 1–94. Bangkok: Faculty of Economics, Thammasat University, 1986.

———. "The Elderly and Their Social Protection in Thailand". Paper presented at the Global Development Network Annual Conference, 16 January 2007, Beijing. Tokyo: Institute for International Cooperation, Japan International Cooperation Agency, 2007.

Menocal, Alina R., Verena Fritz, and Lise Rakner. "Hybrid Regimes and the Challenges of Deepening and Sustaining Democracy in Developing Countries". *South African Journal of International Affairs* 15, no. 1 (June 2008): 29–40.

Menon, Jayant, and Anna Melendez-Nakamura. "Aging in Asia: Trends, Impacts and Responses". Working Paper Series on Regional Economic Integration, no. 25 (February 2009). Mandaluyong, Metro Manila: Asian Development Bank, 2009.

Mérieau, Eugénie. "Thailand's Deep State, Royal Power and the Constitutional Court (1997–2015)". *Journal of Contemporary Asia* 46, no. 3 (2016): 445–66.

MGR Online. "'Aphisit' hai kamlangchi phuchatkan — 'Sonthi' at rat chai 'amnat tamcha' thisut" ["Abhisit" gives encouragement to *Phuchatkan* — "Sondhi" accuses the state of using "malevolent power" to the fullest]. 18 November 2005 <http://www.manager.co.th/Politics/ViewNews.aspx?NewsID=9480000159653> (accessed 28 October 2016).

———. "Thaksin yua phuak babo lai yamwikan – cha hai ok ro chatna saisai!" [Thaksin provokes crazy antics, refusing to resign until next life!]. 14 January 2006 <https://mgronline.com/politics/detail/9490000005298> (accessed 21 February 2018).

———. "Pa Prem yam 'phrachaoyuhua-chat' khue chao khong thahan thae ching" [Papa Prem emphasizes king and nation are real owners of military]. 14 July 2006 <http://www.manager.co.th/Politics/ViewNews.aspx?NewsID=9490000090486> (accessed 22 March 2017).

———. "Lamdap hetkan samkhan – nathi khon lom 'rabop Thaksin'" [The chronology of key events in the overthrow of the Thaksin regime]. 20 September 2006 <http://www.manager.co.th/Politics/ViewNews.aspx?NewsID=9490000118409> (accessed 22 March 2018).

———. "Ruam prakat — thalaengkan phanthamit prachachon phuea

prachathippatai" [A collection of People's Alliance for Democracy press releases]. 28 July 2008 <http://www.manager.co.th/Politics/ViewNews.aspx?NewsID=9510000088721> (accessed 22 March 2018).

———. "Wongsawat tam roi Chinnawat" [Wongsawat following in the steps of the Shinawatras]. 23 September 2008 <http://info.gotomanager.com/news/printnews.aspx?id=73220> (accessed 22 March 2018).

———. "193 wan chaichana khong phanthamit 'banthuek tula dueat'" [193 days of the victory of the PAD; "the bloody October incident"]. 31 December 2008 <http://www.manager.co.th/Politics/ViewNews.aspx?NewsID=9510000153554> (accessed 22 March 2018).

———. "Chaloem yan mai lueak patibat khrai min sathaban phan wep thuklongthot mot" [Chaloem insists no double standard, whoever insults the institution on the web will receive punishment]. 12 January 2012 <http://www.manager.co.th/Politics/ViewNews.aspx?NewsID=9550000004829> (accessed 22 March 2018).

———. "'Adison-pho tho phayao' radom to ro ban top thao sadaeng phalang klang krasae khao kong kamlang suea daeng" [Adison, Phuea Thai man from Phayao, mobilizes village police volunteers to march to show strength in a trend of news on Red Shirt forces]. 20 February 2014 <https://mgronline.com/local/detail/9570000020318> (accessed 23 October 2017).

———. "Raingan: khothetching wa duai so po pa lanna lae krasae yaek prathet" [Report: The facts concerning the Lanna Assembly for the Defence of Democracy and the separatist trend]. 2 March 2014 <http://www.manager.co.th/Local/ViewNews.aspx?NewsID=9570000024084> (accessed 23 October 2017).

———. "Chi 'suea daeng riyam' khit yaek prathet tangtae pi 53 tang muban bang na pan krasae tae choe mai khaeng 'Bik Tu'" ["Riyam Red Shirt' intended to split the country in 2010, set up front villages to foment this trend, but encountered a hard stick in "Big Tu"]. 3 March 2014a <http://www.manager.co.th/Politics/ViewNews.aspx?NewsID=9570000024587> (accessed 9 October 2017).

———. "To ro-thahan wingro chaeng chap khon tit pai 'yaek prathet lanna' klang mueang phayao sam pho bo ko ang mai thueng khan kabot" [Police and army sprint, announce arrest of person who put up poster 'Lanna should secede' in the middle of Phayao town, commander says that it does not rise to the level of rebellion". 3 March 2014b <http://www.manager.co.th/Local/ViewNews.aspx?NewsID=9570000024374> (accessed 23 October 2017).

MGR Online VDO. "2014/02/27 klip den 'suea daeng' lan kho baeng prathet yu kap Thaksin" [2014/02/27 hot clip: Red Shirts demand dividing the country so they can be with Thaksin]. YouTube, 2 March 2014 <https://www.youtube.com/watch?v=gejS-R6t3gY> (accessed 9 October 2017).

Minichiello, Victor, Jan Browne, and Hal Kendig. "Perceptions and Consequences of Ageism: Views of Older People". *Ageing and Society* 20, no. 3 (May 2000): 253–78.

Ministry of Education. *Raingan pracham pi samnakngan khanakammakan kansueksa phuenthan 2558* [Annual report of the office of the commission on basic education]. Bangkok: Ministry of Education, 2015.

Ministry of Finance, Thailand. "Raingan pramankan setthakit thai 2559" [Report of estimates of Thai GDP, 2016]. The Secretariat of the Prime Minister, 28 April 2016 <http://www.thaigov.go.th/index.php/th/news-ministry/2012-08-15-09-16-10/item/102688-รายงานประมาณการเศรษฐกิจไทยปี-2559> (accessed 9 November 2016).

Ministry of Foreign Affairs, Thailand. "One Month Progress Report of NCPO". 5 July 2014 <http://www.mfa.go.th/main/en/media-center/3756/47354-One-month-progress-report-of-NCPO.html> (accessed 23 August 2018).

———. "The Use of the Lèse-majesté Law in Thailand". Royal Thai Embassy, Singapore, n.d. <http://www.thaiembassy.sg/press_media/news-highlights/the-use-of-the-l%C3%A8se-majest%C3%A9-law-in-thailand> (accessed 27 February 2017).

Ministry of Public Health, Thailand. "Country Profile: Thailand. Human Resources for Health", October 2010 <http://www.surveymed.co.th/file_content/article_doc_16.pdf> (accessed 16 October 2017).

Ministry of Social Development and Human Security, Thailand. "Raingan khomun sathannakan khwamrunraeng khong prathet thai tam mattra 17 haeng phraratchabanyat phuthukratha duai khwamrunraeng nai khropkhrua pho so 2550" [Report on violence in Thailand according to article 17 of the Act to Protect Victims of Domestic Violence, B.E. 2550]. 2010 <http://123.242.156.83/society2013/data/UserFiles/File/vio_09.pdf> (accessed 16 October 2017).

Mishra, Ponkaj. *From the Ruins of Empire: The Revolt against the West and the Remaking of Asia*. London: Penguin Books, 2013.

Missingham, Bruce. *The Assembly of the Poor in Thailand: From Local Struggles to National Protest Movement*. Chiang Mai: Silkworm Books, 2003.

Mitchell, James. *Luk Thung: The Culture and Politics of Thailand's Most Popular Music*. Chiang Mai: Silkworm Books, 2015.

Mitton, Roger. "Favorite under the Gun". *Asiaweek*, 6 October 2000 <http://edition.cnn.com/ASIANOW/asiaweek/magazine/2000/1006/nat.thai.html> (accessed 22 March 2018).

Montesano, Michael J. "Praetorianism and 'the People' in Late-Bhumibol Thailand". SEATIDE Online Papers, no. 10 (2015) <http://www.seatide.eu/?content=activitiesandresults&group=3> (accessed 23 August 2018).

———. "BOOK REVIEW: *The Political Development of Modern Thailand* by Federico Ferrara". *SOJOURN: Journal of Social Issues in Southeast Asia* 31, no. 3 (November 2016): 948–53.

Montesano, Michael J., Pavin Chachavalpongpun, and Aekapol Chongvilaivan, eds. *Bangkok, May 2010: Perspectives on a Divided Thailand*. Singapore: Institute of Southeast Asian Studies, 2012.

Moreman, Michael. "A Thai Village Headman as a Synaptic Leader". *Journal of Asian Studies* 28, no. 3 (May 1969): 535–49.

Morris, Rosalind. "Photography and the Power of Images in the History of Power: Notes from Thailand". In *Photographies East: The Camera and Its Histories in East and Southeast Asia*, edited by Rosalind C. Morris, pp. 121–60. Durham, North Carolina: Duke University Press, 2009.

Muhammad Abdullah. "Pengistiharan Barisan Revolusi Nasional Melayu Patani" [Declaration of the Malay-Patani National Revolutionary Front]. YouTube, 26 April 2013 <https://www.youtube.com/watch?v=3XzxHyvRu1U> (accessed 6 December 2017).

Mujahid, Ghazy. *Population Ageing in East and South-East Asia: Current Situation and Emerging Challenges*. Bangkok: UNFPA Country Technical Services Team for East and South-East Asia, 2006.

Munoz, Paul Michel. *Early Kingdoms of the Indonesian Archipelago and the Malay Peninsula*. Singapore: Editions Didier Millet, 2006.

Murdoch, Lindsay. "In Phuketwan Case, Reuters Supports Media Freedom — But from a Distance". *The Sydney Morning Herald*, 31 April 2015 <http://www.smh.com.au/world/in-phuketwan-case-reuters-supports-media-freedom--but-from-a-distance-20150831-gjbhx2.html> (accessed 22 March 2018).

———. "Thailand Censors Debate about Missing Democracy Plaque in Bangkok". *The Sydney Morning Herald*, 4 May 2017 <https://www.smh.com.au/world/thailand-censors-debate-about-missing-democracy-plaque-in-bankgok-20170504-gvynfv.html> (accessed 23 August 2018).

Muthita Chueachang. "Raingan prakottakan nangsuephim khon suea daeng ban saphrang" [Report on the blossoming of Red Shirt newspapers]. *Prachatai*, 30 June 2009 <http://www.prachatai.com/journal/2009/06/24908> (accessed 22 March 2018).

Mydans, Seth. "Thailand Reinterprets the Rules of Democracy, Again". *The International Herald Tribune*, 21 September 2006 <www.nytimes.com/2006/09/21/world/asia/21thailand.html> (accessed 27 February 2017).

Mydans, Seth, and Thomas Fuller. "Thailand's King Sees His Influence Fading". *The New York Times*, 15 May 2010 <www.nytimes.com/2010/05/16/world/asia/16king.html> (accessed 27 February 2017).

Nagengast, Carole. "Violence, Terror, and the Crisis of the State". *Annual Review of Anthropology* 23 (1994): 109–36.

Nangsue khumue kanpoetmuban suea daeng phuea prachathippatai [Handbook for the establishment of Red Shirt villages for democracy]. Udon Thani: Samaphan muban suea daeng phuea prachathippatai haeng prathet thai [Federation of Redshirt Villages for Democracy of Thailand], [2015?].

Nangsuephim raisapda kongthap [Army weekly newspaper]. "Khwamwang mai chiwit lae phonngan khong phon ek Chawalit Yongchaiyut" [New hope: The life and work of General Chaovalit Yongjaiyudh]. Bangkok: *Nangsuephim raisapda kongthap*, 1991.

Narong Bunsuaikhwan. *Withi chiwit khong prachachon nai phuenthi lumnam pak phanang an nueang ma chak kanphatthana khong rat nai phaen phatthana chabap thi 1–8* [The way of life of the people of the Pak Phanang river basin under the impact of national development plans 1–8]. Bangkok: Thailand Research Fund, 2001.

Naruemon Thabchumpon and Duncan McCargo. "Urbanized Villagers in the 2010 Thai Red Shirt Protests: Not Just Poor Farmers?" *Asian Survey* 51, no. 6 (November–December 2011): 993–1018.

Nasueroh and Pimuk Pakkanam. "Thai Delegation, Deep South Rebels Meet in Kuala Lumpur". *BenarNews*, 25 August 2015 <http://www.benarnews.org/english/news/thai/peace-talks-08252015141041.html> (accessed 6 December 2017).

The Nation. "Queen Attends Slain Protester's Cremation". 14 October 2008.

———. "Court Defers *Les Majeste* Case, Defence Advised". 20 July 2012.

———. "Chiang Mai Red Leader Denies Supporting a Lanna State". 4 March 2014 <http://www.nationmultimedia.com/politics/Chiang-Mai-red-leader-denies-supporting-a-Lanna-st-30228306.html> (accessed 10 February 2017).

———. "Anti-Coup Academics Taking Refuge in the United States". 13 November 2014 <http://www.nationmultimedia.com/politics/Anti-coup-academics-taking-refuge-in-the-United-St-30247650.html> (accessed 10 February 2017).

———. "Thai PBS Replaces Programme Host Nattaya after NCPO's Tough Stance". 15 November 2014 <http://www.nationmultimedia.com/politics/Thai-PBS-replaces-programme-host-Nattaya-after-NCP-30247847.html> (accessed 22 March 2018).

———. "Motive Sought for Attacks in Deep South". 8 April 2017 <https://www.pressreader.com/thailand/the-nation/20170408/281479276270589> (accessed 6 December 2017).

———. "Multiple Attacks in Deep South 'Bid to Sow Chaos'". 21 April 2017 <http://www.nationmultimedia.com/detail/national/30312849> (accessed 6 December 2017).

National Council for Peace and Order. "Prakat khamsang khana raksa khwamsangop heang chat" [Announcements of the National Council for Peace and Order]. National Legislative Assembly, n.d. <http://library2.parliament.go.th/giventake/ncpo.html> (accessed 22 March 2018).

National Security Council. "Nayobai kanborihan lae kanphatthana changwat chaidaen phak tai pho so 2555–2557" [The policy on the administration and development of the southern border provinces (2012–2014)]. Deep South Watch,

15 March 2012 <https://www.deepsouthwatch.org/node/3018> (accessed 6 December 2017).

National Statistical Office, Thailand *1960 Population Census, Whole Kingdom*. Bangkok: Office of the Prime Minister, 1962.

———. *Raignan kansamruat kanplianplaeng khong prachakon pi 2507–2510* [Report on the survey of population change, 1964–1967]. Bangkok: National Statistical Office, 1970.

———. *1970 Population and Housing Census, Whole Kingdom*. Bangkok: Office of the Prime Minister, 1973.

———. *1981 Socioeconomic Survey*. Bangkok: National Statistical Office, 1982.

———. *1986 Socioeconomic Survey*. Bangkok: National Statistical Office, 1987.

———. *1988 Socioeconomic Survey*. Bangkok: National Statistical Office, 1989.

———. *1990 Population and Housing Census, Whole Kingdom*. Bangkok: Office of the Prime Minister, 1990.

———. *1992 Socioeconomic Survey*. Bangkok: National Statistical Office, 1993.

———. *Kansamruat prachakon sungayu nai prathet thai pho so 2537* [The 1994 survey of the elderly population in Thailand]. Bangkok: National Statistical Office, 1994.

———. *1996 Socioeconomic Survey*. Bangkok: National Statistical Office, 1997.

———. *2000 Population and Housing Census, Whole Kingdom*. Bangkok: Office of the Prime Minister, 2000.

———. *2000 Socioeconomic Survey*. Bangkok: National Statistical Office, 2001.

———. *Samruat prachakon sungayu nai prathet thai pho so 2545* [The 2002 survey of the elderly population in Thailand]. Bangkok: National Statistical Office, 2002.

———. *Sarup phonkansamruat kankhaoruam kitchakam thangwatthanatham pho so 2548* [Survey of participation in cultural activities, 2005]. Bangkok: National Statistical Office, 2005.

———. "Prachakon lae kheha" [Population and housing], "Kansamruat kanplianplaeng khong prachakon pi 2458–2459" [Thailand survey of population change, 2005–6], 2006 <http://service.nso.go.th/nso/web/survey/surpop2-1-4.html> (accessed 24 October 2017).

———. *2006 Socioeconomic Survey*. Bangkok: National Statistical Office, 2007a.

———. *Samruat prachakon sungayu nai prathet thai pho so 2550* [The 2007 survey of the elderly population in Thailand]. Bangkok: National Statistical Office, 2007b.

———. *Phu sungayu thai 2550 mummong/siangsathon chak khomun sathiti* [Thai elderly 2008: Perspectives and reflections from statistics]. Bangkok: National Statistical Office, 2008.

———. "Botsarup samrap phuborihan sammano prachakon lae kheha pho so 2553" [Executive summary: Population and household census 2010]. National

Census Bureau, 2010*a* <http://popcensus.nso.go.th/file/popcensus-20-12-54.pdf> (accessed 8 February 2017).

———. *2010 Population and Housing Census, Whole Kingdom*. Bangkok: Office of the Prime Minister, 2010*b*.

———. *Kansamruat saphawa thangsangkhom lae watthanatham pho so 2554* [The 2011 survey on social and cultural conditions]. Bangkok: National Statistical Office, 2011*a*.

———. *Samruat prachakon sungayu nai prathet thai pho so 2554 botsarup phuborihan* [The 2011 survey of the elderly population in Thailand: Executive summary]. Bangkok: National Statistical Office, 2011*b*.

———. *Kansamruat khwamphikan pho so 2555* [The 2012 disability survey]. Bangkok: Statistical Forecasting Bureau, National Statistical Office, 2013.

———. *2013 Socioeconomic Survey*. Bangkok: National Statistical Office, 2014*a*.

———. *Samruat prachakon sungayu nai prathet thai pho so 2557 botsarup* [The 2014 survey of the elderly population in Thailand: Executive summary]. National Statistical Office, 2014*b*.

———. "Sen khwamyakchon (dan raichai) chamnaek tam phak lae changwat pho so 2549–2558" [Poverty line (by expenditure) by region and province, 2006–15]. 2015 <http://service.nso.go.th/nso/web/statseries/statseries12.html> (accessed 16 October 2017).

———. "ICT". *Statistical Data*, n.d. <http://web.nso.go.th/en/stat_theme_ict.htm> (accessed 22 March 2018).

———. *Kansamruat phawa kanthamngan khong prachakon* [Labour force survey]. Bangkok: Office of the Prime Minister, n.d. (various years).

Nattapol Chaiching. "Phrabarami pokklao tai ngao insi phaen songkhram chittawitthaya amerikan kap kansang sathaban kasat pen sanyalak haeng chat" [The royal benevolence under the eagle's shadow: American psychological warfare and the making of the monarchy as the national symbol]. *Fa Diaokan* 9, no. 2 (April–June 2011): 94–166.

Nelson, Michael H. "Thailand: Problems with Decentralization?" In *Thailand's New Politics: KPI Yearbook 2001*, edited by Michael H. Nelson, pp. 219–81. Bangkok: King Prajadhipok's Institute and White Lotus Press, 2002.

NESDB (National Economic and Social Development Board, Thailand). "The Seventh National Economic and Social Development Plan (1992–1996)". Bangkok: National Economic and Social Development Board, 1991 <http://www.nesdb.go.th/nesdb_en/ewt_dl_link.php?nid=3782> (accessed 2 March 2018).

———. "Khunkha phu sungayu nai sangkkhom thai" [The value of older persons in Thai society]. *Phawa sangkhom* [Social situation and outlook] 11, no. 2 (2014): 18–22 <http://www.nesdb.go.th/temp_social/data/SocialOutlookQ1-2014.pdf>.

———. *Raingan kanwikhro khwamyakchon lae khwamlueamlam nai prathet thai phi 2556* [Report on the analysis of poverty and inequality in Thailand in 2013]. Bangkok: National Economic and Social Development Board, 2015*a*.

———. "Thongthiao thua thai sang raidai thuathueng" [Travel all over Thailand, income generation all over]. *Warasan setthakit lae sangkhom* [Journal of economy and society] 52, no. 1 (2015*b*): 8–16.

———. "NESDB Economic Report: Thai Economic Performance in Q1 and Outlook for 2016". Macroeconomic Strategy and Planning Office, 16 May 2016 <http://www.nesdb.go.th/article_attach/article_20160516100900.pdf> (accessed 9 November 2016).

———. n.d. <www.nesdb.go.th> (accessed 9 November 2016).

NESDB and the World Bank. "Thailand: Northeast Economic Development Report". World Bank, November 2005 <http://siteresources.worldbank.org/INTTHAILAND/Resources/333200-1097667766090/need_report-2005-eng.pdf> (accessed 9 November 2016).

The New York Times. "With Premier at U.N., Thai Military Stages Coup". 20 September 2006.

———. "Democracy in Thailand, Interrupted". 3 February 2014 <https://www.nytimes.com/2014/02/04/opinion/democracy-in-thailand-interrupted.html> (accessed 27 February 2017).

Nidhi Eoseewong. "Wattanatham khong chonchan klang thai" [The cultural dimensions of the Thai middle class]. In *Chonchan klang bon krasae prachathippatai* [The middle class on the democratic wave], edited by Sungsidh Piriyarangsan and Pasuk Phongpaichit, pp. 49–66. Bangkok: Political Economy Centre, Chulalongkorn University, 1993.

———. "Pak tai ban rao" [The South, our home]. *Matichon sutsapda*, 25–31 March 2005.

———. "Nakhon si thammarat nai ratcha-anachak ayutthaya" [Nakhon Si Thammarat in the Ayutthaya Kingdom]. In *Khapsamut thai nai ratcha-anachak sayam* [The Thai peninsular in the Siamese Kingdom], edited by Yongyut Chuwaen, pp. 65–105. Bangkok: Nakhon Press, 2007.

———. *An kanmueang thai 3 kanmueang suea daeng* [Reading Thai politics 3: The politics of the Red Shirts]. Bangkok: Open Books, 2010.

———. *Phiphak san* [Critical comments on the judiciary]. Bangkok: Matichon Publishing, 2012.

———. "Chonnabot phap thi plian pai" [The changing landscape of Thai rurality]. *Matichon Weekly*, 17 February 2013*a*, p. 28.

———. "Muan mahaprachachon doi Nidhi Eoseewong" [The great mass of the people by Nidhi Eoseewong]. *Matichon Online*, 17 December 2013*b* <http://www.matichon.co.th/news_detail.php?newsid=1387190430> (accessed 4 February 2014).

———. "Thi ma thangsangkhom khong suea lueang salim nokwit" [The social origins of the Yellow Shirts, the ignorant, and the whistle-blowers]. *Matichon sutsapda*, 18 May 2015, p. 20, and 25 May 2015, p. 20.

Ninnart Sinchai. "Saharat amerika kap kanplianplaeng naeonayobai kanphatthana setthakit khong thai nai samai chomphon Sarit Thanarat sueksa phonkrathop thi mi to khrongsang khwamsamphan rawang rat thun ekkachon nai prathet lae thun ekkachon tangprathet" [The United States and change in Thai economic development policy during Sarit's regime: A study of its impact on the structure of relationships among the state, local capital and foreign capital]. Master's thesis, Faculty of Political Science, Chulalongkorn University, 2002. Thai Thesis Database <http://www.thaithesis.org/detail.php?id=1082545001691> (accessed 2 March 2018).

Nipon Poapongsakorn. *Southeast Asian Agriculture and Development Primer Series: Thailand*. Los Baños: Southeast Asian Regional Center for Graduate Study and Research in Agriculture, 2007.

Nity. "Yon roi kabot aithiwi tueanchai khon aithiwi trakun Chin?" [Revisiting the iTV rebellion: Lessons from iTV staff about the Shinawatras?]. *OK Nation*, 8 March 2007 <http://www.oknation.net/blog/nity/2007/03/08/entry-2> (accessed 22 March 2018).

Norton, Edward. "Long Term Care". In *Handbook of Health Economics*, vol. 1, edited by Anthony Culyer and Joseph Newhouse, pp. 955–94. Amsterdam: Elsevier, 2000.

Nostitz, Nick. *Red vs. Yellow*, vol. 1, *Thailand's Crisis of Identity*. Bangkok: White Lotus, 2009.

———. *Red vs. Yellow*, vol. 2, *Thailand's Political Awakening*. Bangkok: White Lotus, 2011.

The Observer. "The King of Siam", 17 July 1960. In *The King of Thailand in World Focus*, edited by Denis D. Gray and Dominic Faulder, pp. 49–51. Singapore: Editions Didier Millet, 2008.

Ockey, James. "Chaopho: Capital Accumulation and Social Welfare in Thailand". *Crossroads: An Interdisciplinary Journal of Southeast Asian Studies* 8, no. 1 (1993): 48–77.

———. "Crime, Society and Politics in Thailand". In *Gangsters and Democracy: Electoral Politics in Southeast Asia*, edited by Carl Trocki, pp. 39–53. Ithaca: Southeast Asia Program, Cornell University, 1998.

———. "The Rise of Local Power in Thailand: Provincial Crime, Elections, and the Bureaucracy". In *Money and Power in Provincial Thailand*, edited by Ruth McVey, pp. 74–96. Singapore: Institute of Southeast Asian Studies, 2000.

———. "On the Expressway, and under It: Representations of the Middle Class, the Poor, and Democracy in Thailand". In *House of Glass: Culture, Modernity, and the State in Southeast Asia*, edited by Yao Souchou, pp. 313–38. Singapore: Institute of Southeast Asian Studies, 2001.

Office of Agricultural Statistics, Thailand. *Agricultural Statistics of Thailand*. Bangkok: Office of Agricultural Statistics, n.d. (various years).

Office of His Majesty's Principal Private Secretary. "Phraratchadamrat lae phraboromaratchowat" [Royal speeches and guidance]. 2016 <http://v1.ohm. go.th/th/monarch/speech> (accessed 16 February 2017).

Office of the Election Commission of Thailand. "7 singha — ok siang prachamati" [7 August — referendum voting]. 2016 <http://www.ect.go.th/th/?page_id=8583> (accessed 10 November 2016).

Office of the National Identity Board, Thailand. *King Bhumibol: Strength of the Land*. Bangkok, 2009.

Office of the Permanent Secretary, Ministry of Defense. *Kropkhwamhen ruampatirup prathet thai dan kanpokkhrong thongthin* [Framework of views on reforming Thailand in the area of local administration]. Bangkok: Office of the Permanent Secretary, Ministry of Defense, 2014.

Office of the Permanent Secretary, Ministry of Public Health. *Khamsang krasuang satharanasuk lekthi 715/2549* [Ministerial decree of the Ministry of Public Health no. 715/2549]. Bangkok: Office of the Permanent Secretary, Ministry of Public Health, 17 December 2006.

Organisation of Islamic Cooperation. "Resolutions on Muslim Communities and Minorities in Non-OIC Member States adopted by the Thirty-Ninth Session of the Council of Foreign Ministers (Session of Solidarity for Sustainable Development). Djibouti — Republic of Djibouti, 01–03 Muharram 1434 (15–17 November 2012)". 15 November 2012 <https://www.oic-oci.org/docdown/?docID=360&refID=26> (accessed 6 December 2017).

Palmore, Erdman. "The Ageism Survey: First Findings". *The Gerontologist* 41, no. 5 (October 2001): 572–75.

Pantip.com. "Talueng pai 'kho yaek prathet' phlo bon saphan loi phahon yothin klang mueang phayao" [Stunning banner "Split the Country Up" on a pedestrian overpass in the middle of Phayao town]. 29 January 2014 <https://pantip.com/topic/31580435> (accessed 9 October 2017).

Pasuk Phongpaichit. "Thopthuan khabuankan thang sangkhom suea lueang suea daeng" [Reviewing social movements – Yellow Shirts, Red Shirts]. *Prachatai*, 18 September 2010 <http://prachatai.com/journal/2010/09/31130> (accessed 9 October 2017).

Pasuk Phongpaichit and Chris Baker. *Thailand: Economy and Politics*. Kuala Lumpur: Oxford University Press, 1995.

———. *Thailand's Boom and Bust*. Chiang Mai: Silkworm Books, 1998.

———. "*Chao Sua, Chao Pho, Chao Thi*: Lords of Thailand's Transition". In *Money and Power in Provincial Thailand*, edited by Ruth McVey, pp. 30–52. Copenhagen and Chiang Mai: NIAS Publishing and Silkworm Books, 2000.

————. *A History of Thailand*. Cambridge: Cambridge University Press, 2005.

————. *Thaksin: The Business of Politics in Thailand*, 2nd ed. Chiang Mai: Silkworm Books, 2009.

————. "Populist Challenge to the Establishment: Thaksin Shinawatra and the Transformation of Thai Politics". In *Routledge Handbook of Southeast Asian Politics*, edited by Richard Robison, pp. 83–96. London: Routledge, 2012.

————. "Reviving Democracy at Thailand's 2011 Election". *Asian Survey* 53, no. 4 (July–August 2013): 607–28.

————. *A History of Thailand*, 3rd ed. Cambridge: Cambridge University Press, 2014.

————. "Introduction". In *Unequal Thailand: Aspects of Income, Wealth and Power*, edited by Pasuk Pongphaichit and Chris Baker, pp. 1–31. Singapore: NUS Press, 2016.

Pasuk Phongpaichit and Pornthep Benyaapikul. *Political Economy Dimension of a Middle Income Trap: Challenges and Opportunities for Policy Reform: Thailand*. Bangkok: Faculty of Economics, Chulalongkorn University, 2013.

Pasupathi, Monisha, and Corinna Löckenhoff. "Ageist Behavior". In *Ageism: Stereotyping and Prejudice against Older Persons*, edited by Todd D. Nelson, pp. 201–46. Boston: MIT Press, 2004.

Patarapong Intarakumnerd. *Mismanaging Innovation Systems: Thailand and the Middle-Income Trap*. Abingdon: Routledge, 2018.

Pathan, Don, and Ekkarin Tuansiri. *Negotiating a Peaceful Coexistence between the Malays of Patani and the Thai State*. Pattani: Patani Forum, 2012.

Pattana Kitiarsa. "In Defense of the Thai-style Democracy". Asia Research Institute, National University of Singapore, 12 October 2006 <https://ari.nus.edu. sg/Assets/repository/files/events/pattana%20paper%20%20edited.pdf> (accessed 1 August 2018).

————. "From Red to Red: An Auto-ethnography of Economic and Political Transitions in a Northeastern Thai Village". In *Bangkok, May 2010: Perspectives on a Divided Thailand*, edited by Michael J. Montesano, Pavin Chachavalpongpun, and Aekapol Chongvilaivan, pp. 230–47. Singapore: Institute of Southeast Asian Studies, 2012.

Pavin Chachavalpongpun, ed. *'Good Coup' Gone Bad: Thailand's Political Developments since Thaksin's Downfall*. Singapore: Institute of Southeast Asian Studies, 2014*a*.

————. "Thailand's Coup and the Royal Succession". *The Strategic Review*, October–December 2014*b* <http://www.sr-indonesia.com/in-the-journal/view/thailand-s-coup-and-the-royal-succession> (accessed 16 February 2017).

————. "Royal Succession, Military Rule Come Together in Thailand". *Nikkei Asian Review*, 21 January 2015 <http://asia.nikkei.com/Politics-Economy/Policy-Politics/Royal-succession-military-rule-come-together-in-Thailand> (accessed 16 February 2017).

————. "The King of Thailand is Jittery about His Image (and His Country's Democratic Past)". *The Washington Post*, 24 May 2017 <https://www.washingtonpost.com/news/democracy-post/wp/2017/05/24/the-king-of-thailand-is-jittery-about-his-image-and-his-countrys-democratic-past> (accessed 1 August 2018).

PEACE TV. "Chatuphon phoei phit thiwi ok akat 20 ko kho" [Chatuphon announces PEACE TV to go on air on July 20]. YouTube, 16 July 2015 <https://www.youtube.com/watch?v=7BZQjrRLyG0> (accessed 22 March 2018).

Peleggi, Maurizio. *Lords of Things: The Fashioning of the Siamese Monarchy's Modern Image*. Honolulu: University of Hawai'i Press, 2002.

Pensri Duke. *Kantangprathet kap ekkarat lae athippatai khong thai tangtae samai ratchakan thi si thueng sinsamai chomphon Po Phibunsongkhram* [Foreign affairs and Thailand's independence and sovereignty: From Rama IX to the end of Field Marshal Plaek Phibunsongkhram's regime]. Bangkok: Royal Institute of Thailand, 1999.

People's Information Center. *Khwamching phuea khwamyuttitham hetkan lae phonkrathop chak kansalai kanchumnum mesa-phruetsapha 53* [Truth for justice: Incidents in and effects of the crowd dispersal in April–May 2010]. Bangkok: People's Information Center, 2012.

Petras, James. "State, Regime and the Democratization Muddle". *Journal of Contemporary Asia* 19, no. 1 (1989): 26–32.

Pharut Phenphayap. "Sapsin suan phramahakasat khue arai?" [What is crown property?]. In *Phraphrom chuai amnuai hai chuencham setthakit kanmueang wa duai sapsin suan phramahakasat lang 2475* [The god Brahma helps make things juicy: The politics and economics of crown property since 1932], edited by Chaithawat Tulathon, pp. 161–203. Nonthaburi: Fa diaokan, 2014.

Phongphiphat Banchanon. "Lok khukhanan khong 'Thakoeng blusakai' lae Sorayut – yong Thaksin?" [The parallel world of "Thakoeng Bluesky" and Sorayut – tied to Thaksin?]. Isra News Agency, 6 October 2012 <https://www.isranews.org/isranews-article/16856-โลกคู่ขนาน-สื่อ-เถกิง-สรยุทธ-ทักษิณ.html> (accessed 22 March 2018).

phraezila. "'If They Get Sent to Prison, I Pardon Them' – Said Thai King". YouTube, 13 April 2007 <https://www.youtube.com/watch?v=1DZD17stiHI> (accessed 27 February 2017).

Piak Chakkrawat. *Mue puen rap chang* [Hired gunmen]. Bangkok: Pailin, 2004.

Pinkaew Luang-aramsri. "Muea phuak khao dai klai pen 'suea daeng' kanmueang muanchon ruamsamai nai changwat chiang mai" [When they have become "Red Shirts": Contemporary mass politics in Chiang Mai Province]. In *Becoming Red: kamnoet lae phatthanakan suea daeng nai chiang mai* [Becoming Red: The birth and development of the Red Shirts in Chiang Mai], edited by Pinkaew Luang-aramsri, pp. 33–65. Chiang Mai: Center for Research and Academic Services, Faculty of Social Sciences, Chiang Mai University, 2013.

Pirongrong Ramasoota. "Internet Politics in Thailand after the 2006 Coup: Regulation by Code and a Contested Ideological Terrain". In *Access Contested: Security, Identity, and Resistance in Asian Cyberspace*, edited by Ronald Deibert, John Palfrey, Rafal Rohozinski, and Jonathan Zittrain, pp. 83–114. Cambridge: MIT Press, 2011.

——. *Phinit sue phinit sangkhom* [Scrutinizing media, scrutinizing society]. Bangkok: Kobfai Publishing Project, 2013.

Pitch Pongsawat. "Khosangket wa duai 'khwamnian' khong sue lae ratthaban" [Observations on the "smoothness" of media and the government]. *Prachatai*, 11 March 2010 <http://prachatai.org/journal/2010/03/28087> (accessed 22 March 2018).

Piyabut Saengkanokkun. "Prachathippatai baepthaithai khue arai" [What is Thai-style democracy?]. *Mthai*, 30 June 2011 <https://talk.mthai.com/politics/144021.html> (accessed 22 February 2018).

Platt, Martin, B. *Isan Writers, Thai Literature: Writing and Regionalism in Modern Thailand*. Singapore: NUS Press, 2013.

Pongpat Bunchanont. "Yon adit 'wikrit sue' pi 2540 'suenami so ko' kwat khonkhao chomnam nap phan" [Re-examining the "media crisis" of 1997: The tsunami that drowned thousands of people in the media]. Thai Journalists Association, 10 August 2017 <http://www.tja.or.th/index.php?option=com_content&view=article&id=4072:-2540-&catid=158:-31-2559-> (accessed 24 April 2018).

Pongphisoot Busbarat. "Thailand in 2017: Stability without Certainties". In *Southeast Asian Affairs 2018*, edited by Malcolm Cook and Daljit Singh, pp. 343–62. Singapore: ISEAS – Yusof Ishak Institute, 2018.

Pongsak Khamphet. "Khrueakhai rabop uppatham sueksa chaopho korani mue puen rap chang" [Patron and client network system: The case of hired gunmen]. Master's thesis, Chulalongkorn University, 1998.

Porphant Ouyanont, "Samnakngan sapsin suan phramahakasat kap botbat kanlongthun thang thurakit" [The Crown Property Bureau and its role in investment in business]. In *Phraphrom chuai amnuai hai chuencham setthakit kanmueang wa duai sapsin suan phramahakasat lang 2475* [The god Brahma helps make things juicy: The politics and economics of crown property since 1932], edited by Chaithawat Tulathon, pp. 245–331. Nonthaburi: Fa diaokan, 2014.

——. *Crown Property Bureau in Thailand and its Role in Political Economy*. Trends in Southeast Asia 2015, no. 13/2015. Singapore: Institute of Southeast Asian Studies, 2015.

Positioning Magazine. "Koranisueksa ABAC pho samruat khon krungthep khatkhan plot raikan chong 9" [The case study of the ABAC poll on the opposition of Bangkokians towards the removal of the Channel 9 programme]. 5 December 2005 <https://positioningmag.com/8154> (accessed 22 March 2018).

————. "Chamlae sue" [Media analysed]. 5 November 2008 <https://positioningmag.com/11353> (accessed 22 March 2018).

Post Today. "Thaksin mai khwang hai ratthaban mai tham ngan" [Thaksin not to obstruct new government]. 22 August 2014 <http://www.posttoday.com/การเมือง/314075/ทักษิณไม่ขวางให้รัฐบาลใหม่ทำงาน> (accessed 10 February 2017).

————. "Ao nae! patirup thongthin yup 'o bo to'" [For sure! Local administration reform: Terminating sub-district administrative organizations]. 27 February 2017 <https://www.posttoday.com/analysis/report/482852> (accessed 22 February 2018).

————. "Pat yup o bo to nayok patiset krasae khao wonsochian yuenyan ratthaban yang mai yup o bo to" [No termination of sub-district administrative organizations, prime minister denies social media news current, confirms government will not yet terminate sub-district administrative organizations]. 6 September 2017 <https://www.posttoday.com/politic/513186> (accessed 22 February 2018).

Prachachat thurakit. "Ko o ro so tang khanakammakan ruam aisithi – ko so tho cho prasan ISP blok wep tam khamsang phainai 1 chuamong" [Peace and Order Maintaining Command established a committee in collaboration with ICT-NBTC to coordinate blocking of websites within 1 hour]. 21 May 2014 <http://www.prachachat.net/news_detail.php?newsid=1400666329> (accessed 22 March 2018).

————. "'Phit thiwi' thuktatsanyan – cho dam riaproi laeo ton song thum khrueng" [PEACE TV cancelled – screen blacked out at 8:30pm]. 1 May 2015 <http://www.prachachat.net/news_detail.php?newsid=1430414898> (accessed 22 March 2018).

Prachatai. "So no cho sanoe phoem thot mo 112 kotmai min khayai khlum ongkhamontri lae ham sanoe khao khadi min" [National Legislative Assembly propose increasing the punishment for article 112 on the *lèse majesté*, extending it to cover privy councillors and to prohibiting reporting on *lèse majesté* cases]. 8 October 2007 <https://prachatai.com/journal/2007/10/14446> (accessed 22 March 2017).

————. "Phanthamit an thalaengkan thuangkhuen phaendin thai thi khao phrawihan (Chamlong)" [PAD's press release on demanding the return of Thai land at Khao Phrawihan (Chamlong)]. 30 September 2009 <http://prachatai.org/journal/2009/09/26034> (accessed 22 March 2018).

————. "Thawin Pliansi lekhathikan so mo cho mai mi arai khatkhong pokkhrong phiset chaidaen tai" [NSC Secretary-General Thawin Pliansi: "No problem with special administration for the South"]. 9 May 2011.

————. "Princess: Country Burning Last Year Brought Great Sorrow to the King and Queen". 4 July 2011 <http://www.prachatai.com/english/node/2406> (accessed 27 February 2017).

———. "Krasuang ICT to yot khrongkan luksuea saiboe phoem laksut phunam – phuborihan" [Ministry of ICT extended cyber scout programme and added additional courses for executives]. 1 December 2011 <http://prachatai.com/journal/2011/12/38109> (accessed 22 March 2018).

———. "Banyakat pho tho mo chumnum yuen sapha thon 4 rang kotmaiprongdong" [Atmosphere as the People's Alliance for Democracy gathers to ask parliament to withdraw the four reconciliation bills]. 31 May 2012 <https://prachatai.com/journal/2012/05/40769> (accessed 3 August 2018).

———. "Exclusive interview with Hassan Taib, BRN leader: Part I". 20 June 2013.

———. "Exclusive interview with Hassan Taib, BRN leader: Part II". 24 June 2013.

———. "Kham phiphaksa khadi min adit kasat phit mo 112" [Court ruling in case of defaming historical kings — guilty on article 112]. 14 November 2013 <https://prachatai.com/journal/2013/11/49805> (accessed 22 March 2017).

———. "Suthep Thueaksuban klao wa mai mi wan hai kanluektang 2 ko pho 57 koetkhuen detkhat" [Suthep Thaugsuban says that the 2 February 2014 elections will never be held]. 15 December 2013 <https://prachatai.com/journal/2013/12/50438> (accessed 3 August 2018).

———. "Suthep nat chumnum yai 22 tho kho — lai Yinglak ok chak raksakannayok" [Suthep schedules a mass gathering for 22 December to drive Yingluck out of the caretaker premiership]. 17 December 2013 <http://prachatai.com/journal/2013/12/50495> (accessed 28 October 2016).

———. "Ko po po so tang 5 wethi yai – 'Seri Wongmontha' chat thap pai ban Yinglak 9.00 no athitni" [United Front for Democracy against Dictatorship sets up five large stages – "Seri Wongmontha" organizes a force to go to Yingluck's house at nine o'clock this Sunday] 21 December 2013 <https://prachatai.com/journal/2013/12/50577> (accessed 3 August 2018).

———. "Pramuanphap chumnum yai ko po po so 'pit krung thep khruengwan' 22 tho kho 56" [Photographs of the gatherings of the United Front for Democracy against Dictatorship to "close Bangkok down for half a day" on 22 December 2013]. 23 December 2013 <https://prachatai.com/journal/2013/12/50604> (accessed 3 August 2018).

———. "Safe and Sound: Taxi Driver Survives STR Attacks". 27 December 2013.

———. "Pramuanphap chatdao krungthep 2014" [Photographs: Bangkok shut-down 2014]. 13 January 2014 <https://prachatai.com/journal/2014/01/51133> (accessed 3 August 2018).

———. "Poet chai so po po lanna sakha sankamphaeng kap khoklaoha baeng yaek prathet" [Candid interview with Sankamphaeng AFDD (Assembly for the Defense of Democracy) on secessionist accusation]. 4 March 2014 <http://prachatai.com/journal/2014/03/52127> (accessed 10 February 2017).

————. "Chat kitchakam 'lueaktang thi lak' na ho sin nakkitchakam don ruap lai rai" ['Stolen election' activity in front of art museum, several activists nabbed]. 14 February 2015 <http://www.prachatai.com/journal/2015/02/57936> (accessed 10 February 2017).

————. "To ro sop pakkham o mahasarakham songsai mue khwaen pai tan phadetkan nai mo" [Police storm in to question Mahasarakham University lecturer suspected of hanging anti-dictatorship banner on campus]. 5 March 2015 <http://prachatai.org/journal/2015/03/58226> (accessed 10 February 2017).

————. "Raingan ruchak san thahan rapru saphapkan phutongha phonlaruean" [Report: Getting to know the military court system and learning about the status of civilian suspects]. 19 March 2015 <http://prachatai.org/journal/2015/03/58472> (accessed 10 February 2017).

————. "Poet tua 'isan mai' isan thi cha mai sayopyom" ['New Isan' unveiled, vows never to surrender]. 20 March 2015 <http://www.prachatai.com/journal/2015/03/58493> (accessed 10 February 2017).

————. "Kep praden 'sue mai' tong kamkap? yangrai? doi khrai" [The issue of 'new media: Must it be controlled? How? By whom?]. 16 June 2015 <http://www.prachatai.com/journal/2015/06/59817> (accessed 22 March 2018).

————. "Po o tho triam sue rabop kwat khomun fetbuk – thawittoe – phanthip thiap rup profai kap maichap" [TCSD to buy big data software for Facebook-Twitter-Pantip to compare profile photo with arrest warrant]. 25 January 2016 <https://prachatai.com/journal/2016/01/63668> (accessed 24 April 2018).

————. "Kritpatchara Somanawat muea tulakan pen yai kanprakopsang attalak tulakan thai" [Kritpatchara Somanawat — when judges are powerful: The making of the identity of Thai judges]. 26 April 2016 <http://prachatai.com/journal/2016/04/65447> (accessed 16 February 2017).

Prachatai English. "3-Fingered Salute Khon Kaen Students: We're Not Red Shirts". 28 November 2014 <http://www.prachatai.com/english/node/4544> (accessed 10 February 2017).

————. "Anti-Junta Student Activists Detained in Khon Kaen". 22 May 2015 <http://www.prachatai.com/english/node/5085> (accessed 10 February 2017).

Prachatai Online. "Wa duai prawatsat 80 pi prachathippatai" [On the history of 80 years of democracy]. 21 June 2012 <http://www.prachatai.com/journal/2012/06/41173> (accessed 22 February 2018).

Prajak Kongkirati. "Counter-Movements in Democratic Transition: Thai Right-Wing Movements after the 1973 Popular Uprising". *Asian Review* 19 (2006): 1–33.

————. "Thailand: The Cultural Politics of Student Resistance". In *Student Activism in Asia: Between Protest and Powerlessness*, edited by Meredith L. Weiss and Edward Aspinall. Minneapolis: University of Minnesota Press, 2012.

————. "Bosses, Bullets, and Ballots: Electoral Violence and Democracy in Thailand

1975–2011". Doctoral dissertation, Department of Political and Social Change, Australian National University, 2013.

———. "The Rise and Fall of Electoral Violence in Thailand: Changing Rules, Structures and Power Landscapes, 1997–2011". *Contemporary Southeast Asia* 36, no. 3 (December 2014): 386–416.

———. "Thailand's Failed 2014 Election: The Anti-Election Movement, Violence and Democratic Breakdown". *Journal of Contemporary Asia* 46, no. 3 (2016): 467–85.

———. "Haunted Past, Uncertain Future: The Fragile Transition to Military-Guided Semi-Authoritarianism in Thailand". In *Southeast Asian Affairs 2018*, edited by Malcolm Cook and Daljit Singh, pp. 363–88. Singapore: ISEAS – Yusof Ishak Institute, 2018.

Prapas Pintoptaeng. "Kanlukkhuensu khong khon 'yotya' bot wikhro nai choengmitikanmueang" [The "grasstips" people's rise to struggle: A political analysis]. In *Daeng thamai?* [Why red?], edited by Pinyo Traisuriyadhamma, pp. 36–55. Bangkok: Open Books, 2010.

Prasong Lertrattanawisut. *Tulakanphiwat patiwat kanmueang thai* [Judicialization: Revolutionizing Thai politics]. Bangkok: Matichon Books, 2008.

Prayudh Payutto. *Good, Evil and Beyond: Kamma in the Buddha's Teaching*, translated by Bruce Evans. Bangkok: Buddha Dharma Education Association, 1993.

Preecha Piampongsan. "Thitsadi chonchan klang" [The theory of the middle class]. In *Chonchan klang bon krasae prachathippatai* [The middle class on the democratic wave], edited by Sungsidh Piriyarangsan and Pasuk Phongpaichit, pp. 80–87. Bangkok: Political Economy Centre, Chulalongkorn University, 1993.

Prime Minister's Office, Malaysia. "Perlantikan Fasilitator" [Appointment of facilitator]. Media statement, 13 March 2013 <http://www.pmo.gov.my/home.php?menu=news&news_id=11153&news_cat=4&page=1729&sort_year=2013&sort_month=03> (accessed 6 December 2017).

Prince, Martin, Anders Wimo, Maëlenn Guerchet, Gemma-Claire Ali, Yu-Tzu Wu, and Matthew Prina. *World Alzheimer Report 2015: The Global Impact of Dementia*. London: Alzheimer's Disease International, 2015.

Privy Council, Thailand. *Phrabatsomdetphrachaoyuhua kap khana ongkhamontri* [His Majesty the King and the Privy Council]. Bangkok: Amarin Printing, 2011.

Puangthong Pawakapan. "Protracted Period in Power Can Prove Perilous for Thailand's Military Government". *ISEAS Perspective* 2015, no. 65 (19 November 2015): 1–7.

Ramsey, Adam. "To Be or Not to Be: The Great Firewall of Thailand". *Al Jazeera America*, 7 October 2015 <http://america.aljazeera.com/articles/2015/10/7/great-firewall-thailand-internet.html> (accessed 22 March 2018).

"Ratchawong thi khachaichai phaeng thisut nai lok" [World's most expensive royal family]. *Fa diaokan* 6, no. 1 (2008): 21.

Reformthai. "Reform Thai Movement". Reform Thai Movement. n.d. <www.reformthai.com> (accessed 1 December 2015).

Reporters without Borders. "Internet Enemies Report 2012". 12 March 2012 <https://rsf.org/sites/default/files/rapport-internet2012_ang.pdf> (accessed 22 March 2018).

Research and Development Division, National Police Office, Thailand. *Panha lae itthiphon khong mue puen rap chang* [The problems and influence of hired gunmen]. Mimeographed. 2004.

———. *Panha nai kansuepsuan atchayakam mue puen rap chang* [Obstacles in the investigation of hired gunmen's crimes]. Mimeographed. 2005.

Restrepo, Helena E., and Manuel Rozental. "The Social Impact of Aging Populations: Some Major Issues". *Social Science & Medicine* 39, no. 9 (November 1994): 1323–38.

Reuters. "Indonesia Says Hosts Talks on Thai Muslim Insurgency". 21 September 2008.

———. "Thailand's King Given Full Control of Crown Property". 17 July 2017 <https://www.reuters.com/article/us-thailand-king-property/thailands-king-given-full-control-of-crown-property-idUSKBN1A20OX> (accessed 23 August 2018).

Rex, Brian. "Monarchy in Spotlight: Tensions that Threaten New Turmoil in Thailand". *The Independent*, 23 June 2011 <http://www.independent.co.uk/news/world/asia/monarchy-in-spotlight-tensions-that-threaten-new-turmoil-in-thailand-2301364.html> (accessed 27 February 2017).

———. "Thai Princess Uses Social Media to 'Declare War': Photos posted by Princess Chulabhorn Mahidol widely interpreted as a sign of her support for anti-government protesters". *The Independent*, 11 February 2014 <http://www.independent.co.uk/news/world/asia/thai-princess-uses-social-media-to-declare-war-photos-posted-by-princess-chulabhorn-mahidol-widely-9122267.html> (accessed 27 February 2017).

Rigg, Jonathan. "Grass-Roots Development in Rural Thailand: A Lost Cause?" *World Development* 19, nos. 2–3 (February–March 1991): 199–211.

Rigg, Jonathan, and Sakunee Nattapoolwat. "Embracing the Global in Thailand: Activism and Pragmatism in an Era of Deagrarianization". *World Development* 29, no. 6 (June 2001): 945–60.

Riggs, Fred W. *Thailand: The Modernization of a Bureaucratic Polity*. Honolulu: East-West Center Press, 1966.

Rodil, B.R. Rudy. *Kalinaw Mindanaw: The Story of the GRP-MNLF Peace Process 1975–1996*. Davao City: Alternative Forum for Research in Mindanao, 2000.

Romadon Panjor. "Kanmueang khong thoikham nai chaidaen tai/Patani kanprakopsang santiphap nai khwamkhatyaeng chattiphan kanmueang"

[Politics of Words in Pa(t)tani: Constructing "Peace" in Ethno-political Conflict]. Master's thesis, Faculty of Political Science, Thammasat University, 2015.

Royal Thai Government. *Thai nai samai sang chat* [Thailand in the age of nation-building] Bangkok: Royal Thai Government, 1941.

Rueschemeyer, Dietrich, Evelyne Huber Stephens, and John D. Stephens. *Capitalist Development and Democracy.* Chicago: University of Chicago Press, 1992.

Rungmani Meksophon. *Prachathippatai puean lueat muean ma klai tae mai pai thueng nai* [Blood-stained democracy seems far but not beyond]. Bangkok: Ban Phra Athit Press, 2010.

Rungrawee Chalermsripinyorat. "Thai Blasts a Wake up Call for Peace?" *New Mandala*, 14 August 2016 <http://www.newmandala.org/thai-blasts-wake-call-peace/> (accessed 6 December 2017).

Saichon Sattayanurak. "Kansang 'khwampenthai' krasae lak lae 'kwamching' thi 'khwampenthai' sang" [The construction of mainstream thought on "Thainess" and the "truth" constructed by "Thainess"]. *Fringer*, 2005 <http://www.fringer.org/wp-content/writings/thainess.pdf> (accessed 10 February 2017).

Saiyai Sakawee. "Facebook users in Thailand grew by 33% in 3 months to 24 million users (INFOGRAPHIC)". *Tech in Asia*, 6 September 2013 <http://www.techinasia.com/facebook-thailand-grows-to-24-million-users-infographic/> (accessed 22 March 2018).

Saksith Saiyasombat. "The Thai Junta's 2015 Draft Budget, Explained in 4 Graphs". *Asian Correspondent*, 19 August 2014 <http://asiancorrespondent.com/2014/08/thai-juntas-2015-draft-budget-infographics/> (accessed 16 February 2017).

Samret Srirai. *Fai tai mai lap luang phrang* [Southern fire no secret, illusion, concealment]. Privately published, n.d.

Sandhu, Kernial Singh. "Preface". *SOJOURN: Social Issues in Southeast Asia* 1, no. 1 (February 1986): iii–v.

Sangop Songmueang. "Wiwatthanakan kankhian prawatsat phak tai" [The evolution of the historiography of the southern region]. Unpublished research report, 1989.

Santisuk Sophonsiri. *Sathaban phramahakasat kap prachathippatai nai thatsana khong phrabatsomdetphrachaoyuhua ratchakan thi 7 ratthaburut awuso Pridi Phanomyong lae mo ro wo Seni Pramot* [The monarchy and democracy in the views of King Rama VII, Pridi Phanomyong and Seni Pramoj]. Bangkok: The Children's Foundation Press, 2012.

Saowanee T. Alexander. "Thai Citizens Do Live beyond the Boundary of the City of Angels: Some Commentaries of the Complete TRCT Report". *Prachatai English*, 16 October 2012 <http://www.prachatai.com/english/node/3405> (accessed 10 February 2017).

Saowanee T. Alexander and Duncan McCargo. "Diglossia and Identity in Northeast Thailand: Linguistic, Social, and Political Hierarchy". *Journal of Sociolinguistics* 18, no. 1 (February 2014): 60–86.

Saowapa Pornsiripongse, Thiraphong Bunraksa, and Suphaphon Ruedichamroen. "Phu sungayu thai sun wai yangmikhunkha lae saksi" [Thai elderly: Aging older with pride and dignity]. *Warasan phasa lae watthanatham* [Journal of language and culture] 26, no. 1–2 (2007): 132–43.

Sarinee Achavanuntakul. "Rakha khong kanpitkan intoenet thai praphet tonthun lae pramoen tonthun thang trong (bueangton)" [The price of Thai Internet obstruction: Types of capital and the direct evaluation of capital (an introduction)]. Thai Netizen Network, July 2012 <https://thainetizen.org/wp-content/uploads/2012/07/cost-censorship-prelim-201207.pdf> (accessed 22 March 2018).

Sasiwan Mokkhasen. "Junta Approves 20 Billion Baht for Internet Broadband, Gateway". *Khaosod English*, 20 January 2016 <http://www.khaosodenglish.com/detail.php?newsid=1453264665> (accessed 22 March 2018).

Sawatree Suksri, Siriphon Kusonsinwut, and Orapin Yingyongpathana. "Ngan wichai phonkrathop chak pho ro bo khomphiutoe 2550" [Research report on the impact of the Computer Crime Act of 2007]. *iLaw*, 7 January 2013 <https://ilaw.or.th/sites/default/files/ComputerCrimeResearch.pdf (accessed 21 March 2018).

———. "Khrongkanwichai phonkratop chak pho ro bo wa duai kankrathamphit kiaokap khomphiutoe 2550 lae nayobai khong rat kap sit lae seriphap nai kansadaeng khwamkhithen" [Research project on the impact of the Computer Crime Act of 2007 and on state policy and the right to freedom of expression]. *iLaw*, 2014 <http://ilaw.or.th/sites/default/files/CCA7Nov_0.pdf> (accessed 21 March 2018).

Saxer, Marc. *Building the Good Society in Thailand: Resolving Transformation Conflict through Inclusive Compromise*. Bangkok: Friedrich Ebert Stifung, 2014a.

———. *In the Vertigo of Change: How to Resolve Thailand's Transformation Crisis*. Bangkok: Friedrich Ebert Stiftung Thailand, 2014b.

———. "Middle Class Rage Threatens Democracy". *New Mandala*, 21 January 2014c <http://asiapacific.anu.edu.au/newmandala/2014/01/21/middle-class-rage-threatens-democracy/> (accessed 21 April 2017).

Sayam rat. "Natthawut to 'Aphisit' rueang 'khon lok phi' korani nirathotsakam kap 91 sop phan fetbuk" [Natthawut fires back at Abhisit for "lying to ghosts" in the case of amnesty for the 91 corpses via Facebook]. *Bangkok Voice*, 24 June 2011 <http://www.bangkokvoice.com/2011/06/24/ณัฐวุฒิโต้อภิสิทธิ์เ ร/> (accessed 22 March 2018).

———. "Ko po po so lae daeng patakan" [PDRC and Reds clash]. 11 January 2014.

Senft, Adam, Jakub Dalek, Irene Poetranto, Masashi Crete-Nishihata, and Aim Sinpeng. "Information Controls during Thailand's 2014 Coup". Citizen Lab, 9 July 2014 <https://citizenlab.ca/2014/07/information-controls-thailand-2014-coup/> (accessed 17 April 2018).

Serafin, Tatiana. "The World's Richest Royals". *Forbes*, 17 June 2007 <http://www.forbes.com/2009/06/17/monarchs-wealth-scandal-business-billionaires-richest-royals.html> (accessed 16 February 2017).

Seri Thai Forum. "Khabuankan serithai wep bot" [Seri Thai Movement web board]. n.d. <http://forum.serithai.net/viewforum.php?f=22&sid=88cb58c7c7eca57e 728d5b9453a7f44e> (accessed 22 March 2018).

Seri Thai Movement. "Khabuankan seri thai" [Seri Thai movement]. Facebook, n.d. <https://www.facebook.com/serithai.net/> (accessed 22 March 2018).

Sharp, Lauriston, and Lucien M. Hanks. *Bang Chan: Social History of a Rural Community in Thailand*. Ithaca: Cornell University Press, 1978.

Sharpe, Lawrence J. "Theories and Values of Local Government". *Political Studies* 18, no. 2 (June 1970): 153–74.

Shigetomi Shinichi. "Four Decades of Development in Thailand's Rural Sector and the Role of Government". In *Rural Development and Agricultural Growth in Indonesia, the Philippines and Thailand*, edited by Takamasa Akiyama and Donald F. Larson, pp. 294–379. Canberra: Asia Pacific Press and the World Bank, 2004.

Shirky, Clay. *Here Comes Everybody: The Power of Organizing without Organizations*. New York: Penguin Books, 2008.

Sidel, John T. "Siam and its Twin? Democratization and Bossism in Contemporary Thailand and the Philippines". *IDS Bulletin* 27, no. 2 (April 1996): 56–63.

Sila Vilavong. *Prawattisat lao* [History of Laos], 2nd ed., translated by Sommai Premchit. Bangkok: Matichon, 1992.

Siregar, Liston P. "Eksklusif: Pemberontak Muslim utama Thailand Selatan siap berunding" [Exclusive: Main Muslim rebel group in Southern Thailand ready to negotiate]. BBC Indonesia, 11 April 2017 <http://www.bbc.com/indonesia/dunia-39552781> (accessed 6 December 2017).

Sirilaksana Khoman. "Education Policy". In *The Thai Economy in Transition*, edited by Peter G. Warr, pp. 325–54. Cambridge: Cambridge University Press, 1993.

Sirirat Burinkun. "Botbat thahan mafia nai sangkhom thai" [The roles of mafia soldiers in Thailand]. Master's thesis, Faculty of Political Science, Thammasat University, 2005.

Siriwut Raweechaiwat. "'La maemot' bon lok onlai ... khrai khue yuea sangkhom?" ["Witch hunting" in the online world ... who are the social victims?]. *MGR Online*, 16 November 2012 <http://www.manager.co.th/QOL/ViewNews.aspx?NewsID=9550000139846> (accessed 22 March 2018).

Skidmore, Thomas. "Politics and Economic Policy-making in Authoritarian Brazil, 1937–1971". In *Authoritarian Brazil: Origins, Policies, and Future*, edited by Alfred Stepan, pp. 3–46. New Haven: Yale University Press, 1976.

Sluka, Jeffrey A. *Death Squad: The Anthropology of State Terror*. Philadelphia: University of Pennsylvania, 2000.

Smalley, William. *Linguistic Diversity and National Unity: Language Ecology in Thailand*. Chicago: University of Chicago Press, 1994.

Smith, Joy. *Chronic Diseases Related to Aging and Health Promotion and Disease Prevention*. Ottawa: House of Commons, 2012.

Somboon Siriprachai. *Industrialization with a Weak State: Thailand's Development in Historical Perspective*. Singapore: NUS Press, 2012.

Somchai Jitsuchon. "A Framework for Revised Official Poverty Lines for Thailand". Paper presented to the United Nations Development Programme and National Economic and Social Development Board for the Review of Thailand's Official Poverty Line Project, 2004.

———. "Thailand in a Middle-Income Trap". *TDRI Quarterly Review* 27, no. 2 (June 2012): 13–20.

———. "Income Inequality, Poverty and Labor Migration in Thailand". *Singapore Economic Review* 59, no. 1 (March 2014): 1–16.

Somchai Preechasilpakul. "Chak ongkhamontri su sapha thiprueksa nai phra-ong chamlaeng" [From Privy Council to the king's disguised personal advisors]. *Fa diaokan* 13, no. 2 (2015): 10–48.

Somkhit Lertphaitoon. "Kanpatirup kanpokkhrong suan thongthin tam ratthathammanun chabap patchuban" [The reform of local government according to the present constitution]. In *Ruam sara ratthathammanun chabap prachachon doi khana so so ro* [Collected notes on the people's constitution by the constitution drafting assembly], edited by Boonlert Kachayudhadej, pp. 361–402. Bangkok: Matichon, 1998.

Somkiat Onwimon. "Phrachaoyuhua pongkan nam thuam 2538" [The king prevents flooding, 1995]. YouTube, 28 October 2011 <https://www.youtube.com/watch?v=Uv5HO7nA5EQ> (accessed 16 February 2017).

Somkiat Tangkijwanich and Issakul Unnaket. "Kanprabbotbat phak rat nai kanhaiborikan satharana kankrachai amnat hai thongthin tatsinchai" [The adjustment of state roles in public service provision: Decentralization to local decision-making]. *Raingan thi di a ai* [TRDI report], no. 118 (August 2016). Thailand Development Research Institute, August 2016 <https://tdri.or.th/wp-content/uploads/2016/09/wb118.pdf> (accessed 22 February 2018).

Somkiat Tangkitvanich and Nonnarit Bisonyabut. "Toward High-quality Growth: Thailand's Challenges and Opportunities in the Next Three Decades". *TDRI Quarterly Review* 30, no. 1 (March 2015): 3–17.

Somkiat Tangkitvanich, Saowaruj Rattanakhamfu, Sunthorn Tunmuntong, and Ploy

Thammapiranon. "Thailand in the AEC: Myths, Realities, Opportunities, and Challenges". *TDRI Quarterly Review* 28, no. 3 (September 2013): 3–18.

Somkiat Wattana. *Botkhwam prakob kansammana kuengsattawat thammasat 2477–2527 prawattisatniphon thai samai mai* [Articles prepared for a seminar on a half-century of Thammasat University, 1934–84: Modern Thai histororiography]. Bangkok: Thammasat University, 1984.

Sompis Khiawkaew. "Luang Pu Phuttha-itsara bon wethi muan mahaprachachon ratchadamnoen wan thi 20 pho yo 2556" [Luang Pu Buddha Issara on the Ratchadamoen stage of the great mass of the people, 20 November 2013]. YouTube, 20 November 2013 <https://www.youtube.com/watch?v=RqYMghtoDYs> (accessed 1 December 2016).

Somporn Isvilaanonda and Mahabub Hossain. "Dynamics of Rice Farming in the Chao Phraya Delta: A Case Study of Three Villages in Suphan Buri Province". In *Thailand's Rice Bowl: Perspectives on Agricultural and Social Change in the Chao Phraya Delta*, edited by François Molle and Thippawal Srijantr, pp. 109–24. Bangkok: White Lotus, 2003.

Somsak Jeamteerasakul. "Phrabarami pokklao phrasurasiang rachini bon wethi phanthamit" [Her Royal Benevolence: The queen's voice on PAD's stage]. *Prachatai*, 12 August 2008 <http://prachatai.com/journal/2008/08/17688> (accessed 27 February 2017).

———. "Samnakngan sapsin suan phramahakasat khue arai?" [What is the Crown Property Bureau?]. *Phraphrom chuai amnuai hai chuencham setthakit kanmueang wa duai sapsin suan phramahakasat lang 2475* [The god Brahma helps make things juicy: The politics and economics of crown property since 1932], edited by Chaithawat Tulathon, pp. 205–43. Nonthaburi: Fa diaokan, 2014.

Songkhramchai Lithongdi. *Kanpramoen khwamkaona lae wikhro phonkrathop nai kandamnoenngan tam phaen krachai amnat dan sukkhaphap* [Implementation of health decentralization: Progress evaluation and impact analysis]. Nonthaburi: Health System Research Institute, 2012.

Sondhi Limthongkul and Sarocha Pornudomsak. *Mueang thai raisapda 1–3* [Thailand weekly, 1–3]. Bangkok: Ban Phra Athit Press, 2005a.

———. *Mueang thai raisapda sanchon* [Thailand weekly mobile]. Bangkok: Ban Phra Athit Press, 2005b.

———. *Mueang thai raisapda sanchon song* [Thailand weekly mobile two]. Bangkok: Ban Phra Athit Press, 2006.

Special Criminal News Unit. *Poet faem banchi dam! Mue puen ying thing* [Revealing the blacklist of ruthless gunmen]. Bangkok: Khletthai, 1993.

The Spectator. "The Thai King's Wish is His People's Command". 23 September 2006. In *The King of Thailand in World Focus*, edited by Denis D. Gray and Dominic Faulder, pp. 116–17. Singapore: Editions Didier Millet, 2008.

Srawooth Paitoonpong and Yongyuth Chalamwong. *Managing International Labour*

Migration in ASEAN: A Case of Thailand. Bangkok: Thailand Development Research Institute, 2012.

Stanton, Mark W., and Margaret Rutherford. "The High Concentration of U.S. Health Care Expenditures". *Research in Action*, no. 19 (June 2006).

Stengs, Irene. *Worshipping the Great Moderniser: King Chulalongkorn, Patron Saint of the Thai Middle Class*. Seattle: University of Washington Press, 2009.

Stepan, Alfred C. "The New Professionalism of Internal Warfare and Military Role Expansion". In *Authoritarian Brazil: Origins, Policies, and Future*, edited by Alfred Stepan, pp. 47–65. New Haven: Yale University Press, 1973.

―――. *Rethinking Military Politics Brazil and the Southern Cone*. Princeton, New Jersey: Princeton University Press, 1988.

―――. *Arguing Comparative Politics*. New York: Oxford University Press, 2001.

Streckfuss, David. *Truth on Trial in Thailand: Defamation, Treason and Lèse-majesté*. London: Routledge, 2011.

―――. "Freedom and Silencing under the Neo-absolutist Monarchy Regime in Thailand, 2006–2011". In *'Good Coup' Gone Bad: Thailand's Political Developments since Thaksin's Downfall*, edited by Pavin Chachavalpongpun, pp. 109–38. Singapore: Institute of Southeast Asian Studies, 2014.

Stuifbergen, Maria C., and Johannes J.M. Van Delden. "Filial Obligations to Elderly Parents: A Duty to Care?" *Medicine, Health Care, and Philosophy* 14, no. 1 (February 2011): 63–71.

Suchin Tantikul. *Ratthaprahan phutthasakkarat 2490* [The 1947 coup]. Bangkok: Matichon, 2014.

Suchit Bunbongkarn and Prudhisan Jumbala, eds. *Monarchy and Constitutional Rule in Democratizing Thailand*. Bangkok: Institute of Thai Studies, Chulalongkorn University, 2012.

Suchunya Aungkulanon, Margaret McCarron, Jongkol Lertiendumrong, Sonja J. Olsen, and Kanitta Bundhamcharoen. "Infectious Disease Mortality Rates, Thailand, 1958–2009". *Emerging Infectious Diseases* 18, no. 11 (November 2012): 1794–801.

Suehiro Akira. "Technocracy and Thaksinocracy in Thailand: Reform of the Public Sector and the Budget System under the Thaksin Government". *Southeast Asian Studies* 3, no. 2 (August 2014): 299–344.

Sujit Wongthet. *Boeng sangkhom lae watthanatham isan* [Observing Isan society and culture]. Bangkok: Matichon, 2000.

Sukritta Sanguanphan. "Ni khrua ruean" [Household debt]. *Bankers' Talk* 3, no. 1 (February 2015): 1–2. Bank of Thailand, 6 February 2015 <http://www. bot.or.th/Thai/FinancialInstitutions/Highlights/ASEANCommunity/ BankersTalk/Vol3Issue1.pdf> (accessed 16 October 2017).

The Sunday Nation. "Suthep Vows to End Regime". 30 March 2014 <http://www. nationmultimedia.com/politics/Suthep-vows-to-end-regime-30230445.html> (accessed 23 August 2018).

Supasawad Chardchawarn. "Local Governance in Thailand: The Politics of Decentralization and the Roles of Bureaucrats, Politicians, and the People". VRF Series, no. 459. Institute of Developing Economies, Japan External Trade Organization, March 2010 <http://www.ide.go.jp/library/English/Publish/Download/Vrf/pdf/459.pdf> (accessed 22 February 2018).

———. "Kanmueang nai krabuankan krachai amnat sueksa phan botbat khong nakwichakan kharatchakan nakkanmueang lae prachachon" [The politics of decentralization: Studying the roles of scholars, bureacrats, politicians and ordinary people]. *Warasan Thammasat* [Thammasat University journal] 32, no. 1 (2013): 57–90.

Supinya Klangnarong. "Lamdap hetkan khadi Supinya" [The chronology of Supinya's case]. 28 July 2005 <http://supinya.blogspot.com.au/2005/07/blog-post.html> (accessed 22 March 2018).

———. "An! raingan phiset chak wethi sewana toklom'chettanarom phruetsapha 35 kap naeothang kanpatirup sue nai yuk ko so tho cho'" [Read! Special report from a round-table seminar on "The intentions of May '92 and the process of media reform in the era of the National Broadcasting and Telecommunications Commission"]. 6 June 2013 <http://www.supinya.com/2013/06/อ่านรายงานพิเศษ-จากเวที/> (accessed 17 April 2018).

Supreme Court, Thailand. "Khamphiphaksa dika thi 6374–2556" [Appeals Court judgement no. 6374–2556]. 25 October 2015 <http://documents.tips/documents/-6374-2556.html> (accessed 16 February 2017).

Surachart Bamrungsuk. *United States Foreign Policy and Thai Military Rule, 1947–1977*. Bangkok: Duang Kamol, 1988.

———. "Thai kap punha kamphucha phonkrathop to nayobai khwammankhong lae tangprathet khong thai" [Thailand and the Cambodian problem: Impacts on Thailand's security and foreign policy]. In *Ha thotsawat kantangprathet thai chak khwamkhatyaeng su khwamruammue* [Five decades of Thai foreign affairs: From conflict to cooperation], edited by Chaichoke Chulasiriwong, pp. 183–93. Bangkok: Office of the National Culture Commission, and Faculty of Political Science, Chulalongkorn University, 1993.

———. *Thahan kap prachathippatai thai chak 14 tula su patchuban lae anakhot* [The military and Thai democracy: From 14 October to the present and the future]. Bangkok: Research and Publications Center, Krirk University, and American and Canadian Studies Program, Chulalongkorn University, 1998.

———. "From Dominance to Power Sharing: The Military and Politics in Thailand, 1973–1992". Doctoral dissertation, Columbia University, 1999.

———. *Thahan kap kanmueang thai nai satawat na phatthanakan lae khwamplianplaeng* [The military and Thai politics in the next century: Development and change]. Bangkok: Institute of Security and International Studies, Faculty of Political Science, Chulalongkorn University, 2000.

———. "Khwamsamphan phonlaruean-thahan khong thai" [Thailand's civil-military relations]. *Chulasan khwammankhongsueksa* [Security studies monographs], no. 9 (August 2006). Bangkok: Thailand Research Fund, 2006.

———. "Panha khetdaen thai chak 2484-patchuban" [Thai boundary problems: From 1941 to the present]. *Chulasan khwammankhongsueksa* [Security studies monographs], no. 65 (October 2009). Bangkok: Thailand Research Fund, 2009.

———. "*Tulakanthippatai nai kanmueang thai*" [Juristocracy in Thai politics]. *Matichon Weekly* 34, no. 1755 (4–10 April 2014): 36–37.

———. *Senathippatai ratthaprahan kap kanmueang thai* [Militocracy: Military coups and Thai politics]. Bangkok: Matichon, 2015.

Surin Maisrikrod. "Learning from the 19 September Coup: Advancing Thai-style Democracy?" In *Southeast Asian Affairs 2007*, edited by Daljit Singh and Lorraine C. Salazar, pp. 340–59. Singapore: Institute of Southeast Asian Studies, 2007.

Surin Pitsuwan. *Islam and Malay Nationalism: A Case Study of the Malay-Muslims of Southern Thailand*. Bangkok: Thai Khadi Research Institute, Thammasat University, 1985.

———. "Lessons in Democracy from the Streets of Bangkok". *The Nation*, 9 December 2013 <http://www.nationmultimedia.com/opinion/Lessons-in-Democracy-from-the-streets-of-Bangkok-30221613.html> (accessed 21 April 2017).

Suriyan Sakthaisong. *Senthang mafia* [Mafia paths]. Bangkok: Matichon, 1989.

Sutayut Osornprasop and Lars M. Sondergaard. *Closing the Health Gaps for the Elderly: Promoting Health Equity and Social Inclusion in Thailand: Promoting Health Equity and Social Inclusion in Thailand*. Washington, DC: The World Bank, 2016.

Suthachai Yimprasert, ed. *60 pi prachathippatai thai* [60 Years of Thai democracy]. Bangkok: The Committee on Sixty Years of the Fight for Thai Democracy, 1993.

———. *Saithan prawattisat prachathippatai thai* [Currents in the history of Thai democracy]. Bangkok: P. Press, 2008.

———. *Phaen chingchat thai wa duai rat lae kantotan rat samai chomphon Po Phibunsongkhram khrang thi song* [Political movements against Field Marshal Plaek Phibunsongkhram's second regime]. Bangkok: P. Press, 2010.

Suthichai Yoon. "Thai Journalists Fight an Unexpected Revival of Press Restrictions". *Nieman Reports*, 15 June 2012 <http://niemanreports.org/articles/thai-journalists-fight-an-unexpected-revival-of-press-restrictions> (accessed 22 March 2018).

Sutthichai Jitapunkul, Srichitra Bunnag, and Shan Ebrahim. "Health Care for Elderly People in Developing Countries: A Case Study of Thailand". *Age and Ageing* 22, no. 5 (September 1993): 377–81.

Suttinee Yuvejwattana. "Thailand's GDP Growth Slowed Last Quarter on Exports Decline". Bloomberg News, 18 May 2015 <http://www.bloomberg.com/news/articles/2015-05-18/thailand-s-economic-growth-slowed-last-quarter-on-export-decline> (accessed 9 November 2016).

Suwatsadi Photphan, ed. "Kabot baengyaek dindaen isan" [Isan separatists]. King Prajadhipok's Institute, n.d. <http://wiki.kpi.ac.th/index.php?title=กบฏแบ่ง แยกดินแดนอีสาน> (accessed 10 February 2017).

Suwit Thirasatsawat. *Prawattisat isan 2322–2488* [Isan history 1779–1945], vol. 2. Khon Kaen: Khlang nana, 2014.

Suwit Wibulpolprasert, ed. *Thailand Health Profile, 1999–2000*. Bangkok: Bureau of Policy and Strategy, Ministry of Public Health, 2002.

———, ed. *Thailand Health Profile, 2008–2010*. Bangkok: Bureau of Policy and Strategy, Ministry of Public Health, 2011.

The Sydney Morning Herald. "Thailand Elections: Opposition are Democrats in Name Only". 4 February 2004.

Tamada Yoshifumi. "Itthiphon and Amnat: An Informal Aspect of Thai Politics". *Southeast Asian Studies* 28, no. 4 (March 1991): 455–66.

Tambiah, Stanley J. "The Galactic Polity: The Structure of Traditional Kingdoms in Southeast Asia". *Annals of the New York Academy of Sciences* 293, no. 1 (July 1977): 69–97.

Tanet Charoenmuang. "Kankrachai amnat su thongthin" [The devolution of authority to localities]. In *Kankrachai amnat yangrai sang prachathippatai* [How to devolve power to build democracy], edited by Pasuk Phongpaichit and Sungsidh Piriyarangsan, pp. 59–76. Bangkok: Political Economy Center, Chulalongkorn University, 1994.

———. *Thailand: A Late Decentralizing Country*. Chiang Mai: Urban Development Institute Foundation, 2006.

———. *Prachathippatai nai sangkhom thai 19 kanyayon 2549–kumphaphan 2553* [Democracy in Thai society, 19 September 2006 – February 2010]. Chiang Mai: Faculty of Political Science and Public Administration, Chiang Mai University, 2011.

Tassana Choowattanapakorn. "The Social Situation in Thailand: The Impact on Elderly People". *International Journal of Nursing Practice* 5, no. 2 (June 1999): 95–99.

Tay, Simon. "Why ASEAN Hasn't Condemned Thailand". *The Nation*, 7 August 2014 <http://www.nationmultimedia.com/news/opinion/aec/30240378> (accessed 27 February 2017).

Taylor, Jim. "Larger than Life: 'Central World' and its Demise and Rebirth – Red Shirts and the Creation of an *Urban Cultural Myth* in Thailand". ARI Working Paper Series, no. 150 (March 2011) <http://www.ari.nus.edu.sg/wps/wps11_150.pdf> (accessed 22 March 2018).

Tej Bunnag. *The Provincial Administration of Siam, 1892–1915: The Ministry of the Interior under Prince Damrong Rajanubhab*. Kuala Lumpur: Oxford University Press, 1977.

Terwiel, B.J. *Thailand's Political History: From the 13th Century to Recent Times*, rev. ed. Bangkok: River Books, 2011.

Thai Civil Rights and Investigative Journalism. "On ro so to po hai thongthin mai khuep dai khae 51 chak 9,787 haeng" [Transferring sub-district health-promoting hospitals to local governments does not progress; only 51 out of 9,787 were transferred]. 10 Septermber 2017 <http://www.tcijthai.com/news/2017/9/scoop/7326> (accessed 22 February 2018).

Thai Free News. "Poet chomna chomfong mo 112 khondiao fong 16 rai phainai 1 pi" [Revealing the faces of those accused by single defamation plaintiff, 16 complaints in one year]. *Thai Free News*, 24 May 2012.

Thai Lawyers for Human Rights. "Chatakam phonlaruean nai san thahan tang changwat" [Fate of civilians in provincial military courts]. 21 June 2015 <https://tlhr2014.wordpress.com/2015/06/21/militarycourt_province/> (accessed 10 February 2017).

———. "Kandamnoen khadi 112 and phu puai chitphet lang ratthaprahan" [112 prosecutions and schizophrenics after the coup]. 28 June 2016 <http://www.tlhr2014.com/th/?p=712> (accessed 28 October 2016).

Thai Netizen Network, ed. "Raingan phonlamueang net: seriphap lae watthanatham intoenet thai pho so 2554" [Thai Netizen Report 2011: The Freedom and Culture of the Thai Internet in 2011]. 6 April 2012 <https://thainetizen.org/docs/netizen-report-2011/> (accessed 17 April 2018).

———. "Raingan phonlamueang net 2555: pi haeng kanphiphaksa" [Thai Netizen Report 2012: The Year of Judgement]. 31 October 2013 <https://thainetizen.org/docs/netizen-report-2012/> (accessed 17 April 2018).

———. "Raingan phonlamueang net 2556" [Thai Netizen Report 2013]. 16 June 2014 <https://thainetizen.org/docs/netizen-report-2013/> (accessed 17 April 2018).

———. "Raingan phonlamueang net 2557: pi haeng kansotnaem" [Thai netizen report 2014: The year of surveillance]". 1 June 2015*a* <https://thainetizen.org/docs/netizen-report-2014/> (accessed 17 April 2018).

———. "Wan pang pho ro bo khom chabap mai poet chong hai liang mattra 20 sang pit wep sai" [The new draft Computer Crime Act may open ways to avoid article 20 to shut down websites]. 19 October 2015*b* <https://thainetizen.org/2015/10/digital-economy-laws-update-sawatree/> (accessed 22 March 2018).

Thai PBS. "Thai PBS Issue Withdrawn from NBTC's Meeting Agenda". 6 July 2015 <http://englishnews.thaipbs.or.th/thai-pbs-issue-withdrawn-from-nbtcs-meeting-agenda> (accessed 22 March 2018).

———. "Somlak lae Wichan nom samnuk nai phramahakarunathikun" [Somlak and Wichan expressed gratitude for His Majesty's kindness]. YouTube, 18 October 2016 <https://www.youtube.com/watch?v=9MdaXGyvP-c> (accessed 16 February 2017).

Thai Post. "Aksara to kaennam BRN tok khabuan! din ruam cheracha" [Aksara says to BRN leadership that missed train, now wants to take part in dialogue]. 12 April 2017 <http://thaipost.net/?q='อักษรา'โต้แกนนำbrn-ตกขบวนดิ้นร่วมเจรจา> (accessed 6 December 2017).

Thai rat. "Samakhom nakkhao naknangsuephim haeng prathet thai chuea rat khukkham sue" [Journalists association believes government threatens media]. News Center Database, 3 January 2003 <http://www.infoquest.co.th/th/news-services/newscenter/> (accessed 2 June 2012).

———. "TOT chaeng sun ISOC chai ngop 43 lan yamriak kep ICT chon khrop" [TOT says ISOC spent 43 million and insists on collecting all ICT money]. News Center Database, 20 February 2009 <http://www.infoquest.co.th/th/news-services/newscenter/> (accessed 9 June 2015).

———. "Hai yu topai chon ayu 60 pi" [Staying alive until 60 years old]. 13 October 2012 <http://www.thairath.co.th/content/297989> (accessed 22 February 2018).

———. "Kho po tho buk di es ai thip phap Tharit" [STR force their way into DSI; kick 'Tarit's' portrait"]. 24 December 2013.

———. "Phon lueaktang 2 ko pho bok arai nai kanmueang thai" [What do the results of the 2 February 2014 election tell us about Thai politics?]. 6 February 2014 <http://www.thairath.co.th/content/401626> (accessed 24 April 2017).

———. "Ko o po tho rong thahan damnoen khadi no po cho ubon baengyaek dindaen" [Ubon people for the protection of the nation urges soldiers to prosecute Ubon UDD for separatism]. 14 March 2014 <http://www.thairath.co.th/content/409930> (accessed 10 February 2017).

———. "Kongthap daeng 'o pho po cho' suan sanam cho thi khorat" ["O Pho Po Cho" red army stages parade at Khorat]. 21 April 2014 <http://www.thairath.co.th/content/417865> (accessed 9 October 2017).

———. "Luea 55 khon yang khat khamsang mai ma raingan tua kho so cho" [55 still defy orders, do not report to NCPO]. 25 July 2014 <http://www.thairath.co.th/content/438944> (accessed 10 February 2017).

———. "San phiphaksa chamkhuk 2 pi 6 duean 'cha Prasit' than min bueang sung" [Court sentences 'Pol. Sgt. Maj. Prasit' to 2 years 6 months for insulting high institution]. 3 December 2014 <http://www.thairath.co.th/content/466995> (accessed 10 February 2017).

———. "Ko no o dan khet setthakit phiset phak tawan ok" [Estate Authority pushes Eastern Region special economic zone hard]. 31 May 2016 <http://www.thairath.co.th/content/628810> (accessed 9 November 2016).

Thailand. "Phraratchabanyat laksana pokkhrong thongthi pho so 2457" [Local Government Act 1914]. *Royal Gazette* 31 (17 July 1914): 229–74.

———. "Phraratchabanyat rabiap kharatchakan tulakan phutthasakkarat 2477" [The law on the judiciary commission and personnel 1934/5]. *Royal Gazette* 52 (30 April 1935): 251–80.

———. "Phraratchabanyat sapha tambon lae ongkan borihan suan tambon pho so 2537" [Sub-district Council and Sub-district Administrative Organization Act 1994]. *Royal Gazette* 111, no. 53 (2 December 1994): 1–35.

———. "Phraratchabanyat ongkan borihan suan changwat (o bo cho) pho so 2540" [Provincial Administrative Organization Act 1997]. *Royal Gazette* 114, no. 62 (31 October 1997): 1–23.

———. "Phraratchabanyat sapha tambon lae ongkan borihan suan tambon pho so 2542" [Sub-District Council and Sub-District Administrative Organization Act 1999]. *Royal Gazette* 116, no. 40 (20 May 1999a): 1–10.

———. "Phraratchabanyat kamnot phaen lae khanton kankrachai amnat hai kae ongkan pokkhrong suan thongthin pho so 2542" [Decentralization and Procedure Act 1999]. *Royal Gazette* 116, no. 114 (17 November 1999b): 48–66.

———. "Phraratchabanyat sapha tambon lae ongkan borihan suan tambon pho so 2546" [Sub-District Council and Sub-District Administrative Organization Act 2003]. *Royal Gazette* 120, no. 124 (22 December 2003): 16–37.

———. "Phraratchbanyat kamnot phaen lae khanton kankrachai amnat hai kae ongkan pokkhrong suan thongthin chabap thi song pho so 2549" [Decentralization Plan and Procedure Act No. 2 2006]. *Royal Gazette* 124, no. 2 (8 January 2006): 1–3.

———. "Ratthathammanun haeng ratcha-anachak thai pho so 2550" [Constitution of the Kingdom of Thailand 2007]. *Royal Gazette* 124, no. 47 (25 August 2007): 1–127.

———. "Phraratchabanyat laksana pokkhrong thongthi pho so 2457 kaekhai phoemtoem (chabap thi 11) pho so 2551" [Local Government Act of 1914, as amended in 2008]. *Royal Gazette* 125, no. 27 (5 February 2008a): 96–105.

———. "Kot krasuang baeng suan ratchakan krom songsoem kanpokkhrong thongthin pho so 2551" [Ministerial Regulation on Decentralization and Extension of Local Administration by the Ministry of Interior 2008]. *Royal Gazette* 125, no. 125 (26 November 2008b): 2–8.

———. "Prakat khana raksa khwamsangop haeng chat thi 85/2557 rueang kandaima sueng samachik sapha thongthin rue phu borihan thongthin pen kanchuakhrao" [Order of the National Council for Peace and Order 85/2014]. *Royal Gazette* 131, no. 134 (10 July 2014a): 12–14.

———. "Ratthathammanun haeng ratcha-anachak thai (chabap chuakhrao) phutthasakkarat pho so 2557" [Constitution of the Kingdom of Thailand (Interim) 2014]. *Royal Gazette* 131, no. 55 (22 July 2014b): 1–17.

———. "Khamsang khana raksa khwamsangop haeng chat thi 96/2557 rueang kantaengtang khanakammakan khapkhluean kankaekhaipanha changwat chai daen phak tai" [The 96/2557 order of the National Council for Peace and Order on the establishment of a steering committee to resolve problems in the southern border provinces]. *Royal Gazette* 131, special section 144N (30 July 2014c) <http://www.ratchakitcha.soc.go.th/DATA/PDF/2557/E/144/1.PDF> (accessed 6 December 2017).

———. "Prakat huana khana raksa khwamsangop haeng chat thi 16/2558 rueang mattrakan kae panha chaonathi khong rat thi yu rawang kanthuktruatsop lae kankamnot rop attra kamlang chuakhrao" [Order of the Head of the National Council for Peace and Order 16/2015 on officials under investigation and temporary staffing]. *Royal Gazette* 132, no. 112 (15 May 2015a): 1–2.

———. "Khamsang huana khana raksa khwamsangop haeng chat thi 19/2558 rueang taengtang hai chaonathi khong rat damrong damnaeng lae patibat nathi uen" [Order of the Head of the National Council for Peace and Order 19/2015 on the appointment of state officials to other posts and to perform other duties]. *Royal Gazette* 132, no. 145 (25 June 2015b): 8–9.

———. "Ratthathammanun haeng ratcha-anachak thai (chabap chuakhrao pho so 2557 kaekhai phoemtoem khrang thi 1" [Constitution of the Kingdom of Thailand (Interim) 2014, Amendment 1]. *Royal Gazette* 132, no. 64 (15 July 2015c): 5.

———. "Khamsang huana khana raksa khwamsangop haeng chat thi 1/2559 rueang prakat raichue chaonathi rat thi yu rawang kantruatsop phoem khrang thi 3" [Order of the Head of the National Council for Peace and Order 1/2016 announcing the list of names of state officials under investigation, third supplementary instalment]. *Royal Gazette* 133, no. 2 (5 January 2016a): 4–5.

———. "Khamsang huana khana raksa khwamsangop haeng chat thi 43/2559 rueang prakat raichue chaonathi khong rat thi yu rawang kantruatsop phoem khrang thi 4" [Order of the Head of the National Council for Peace and Order 43/2016 announcing the list of names of state officials under investigation, fourth supplementary instalment]. *Royal Gazette* 133, no. 161 (21 July 2016b): 11–12.

———. "Khamsang huana khana raksa khwamsangop haeng chat thi 44/2559 rueang prakat raichue chaonathi khong rat thi yu rawang kantruatsop phoem khrang thi 5" [Order of the Head of the National Council for Peace and Order 44/2016 announcing the list of names of state officials under investigation, fifth supplementary instalment]. *Royal Gazette* 133, no. 164 (26 July 2016c): 10.

———. "Khamsang huana khana raksa khwamsangop haeng chat thi 50/2559 rueang prakat raichue chaonathi khong rat thi yu rawang kantruatsop phoem khrang thi 6" [Order of the Head of the National Council for Peace and Order 50/2016 announcing the list of names of state officials under investigation, sixth supplementary instalment]. *Royal Gazette* 133, no. 188 (25 August 2016*d*): 17.

———. "Khamsang huana khana raksa khwamsangop haeng chat thi 52/2559 rueang prakat raichue chaonathi khong rat thi yu rawang kantruatsop phoem khrang thi 7" [Order of the Head of the National Council for Peace and Order 52/2016 announcing the list of names of state officials under investigation, seventh supplementary instalment]. *Royal Gazette* 133, no. 197 (2 September 2016*e*): 12–14.

———. "Khamsang huana khana raksa khwamsangop haeng chat thi 59/2559 rueang prakat raichue chaonathi khong rat thi yu rawang kantruatsop phoem khrang thi 8 lae kanprapprung kanborihan ngan bukkhon nai bang nuaingan khong rat" [Order of the Head of the National Council for Peace and Order 59/2016 announcing the list of names of state officials under investigation, eighth supplementary instalment, and adjusting personnel management in some state agencies]. *Royal Gazette* 133, no. 216 (27 September 2016*f*): 20–23.

———. "Ratthathammanun haeng ratcha-anachak thai" [Constitution of the Kingdom of Thailand]. *Royal Gazette* 134, section 40K (6 April 2017*a*) <http://www.ratchakitcha.soc.go.th/DATA/PDF/2560/A/040/1.PDF> (accessed 6 December 2017).

———. "Khamsang huana khana raksa khwamsangop haeng chat thi 35/2560 rueang prakat raichue chaonathi khong rat thi yu rawang kantruatsop phoem khrang thi 9" [Order of the Head of the National Council for Peace and Order 35/2017 announcing the list of names of state officials under investigation, ninth supplementary instalment]. *Royal Gazette* 133, no. 190 (25 July 2017*b*): 144–46.

———. "Khamsang huana khana raksa khwamsangop haeng chat thi 39/2560 rueang prakat raichue chaonathi khong rat thi yu rawang kantruatsop phoem khrang thi 10" [Order of the Head of the National Council for Peace and Order 39/2017 announcing the list of names of state officials under investigation, tenth supplementary instalment]. *Royal Gazette* 133, no. 221 (8 September 2017*c*): 62–63.

———. "Ratthathammanun haeng ratcha-anachak thai pho so 2560" [Constitution of the Kingdom of Thailand 2017]. *Royal Gazette* 134, no. 40 (6 April 2017*a*): 1–90.

Thailand Development Research Institute and Ministry for Social Development and Human Security. "Kanpraman kanngoppraman samrap phu sungayu lae laengthima khong ngoen" [An estimation of the budget for the elderly and source of the budget]. March 2012 <http://tdri.or.th/wp-content/uploads/2013/03/elder_a4_new.pdf> (accessed 16 October 2017).

Thailand Political Database. "Korani kabot aithiwi" [The case of the iTV rebellion].

Siam Intelligence Unit, 2008 <http://www.politicalbase.in.th/index.php?title
=%E0%B8%81%E0%B8%A3%E0%B8%93%E0%B8%B5%E0%B8%81%E0%B8%
9A%E0%B8%8E%E0%B9%84%E0%B8%AD%E0%B8%97%E0%B8%B5%E0%B
8%A7%E0%B8%B5> (accessed 24 March 2018).

Thak Chaloemtiarana. *Thailand: The Politics of Despotic Paternalism*. Bangkok: Social
Science Association of Thailand, 1979.

———. *Thailand: The Politics of Despotic Paternalism*, 2nd ed. Ithaca: Southeast Asia
Program Publications, Southeast Asia Program, Cornell University, 2007.

Thamrongsak Petchlert-anan. *2475 lae nueng pi lang kanpatiwat* [The 1932 revolution
and its aftermath]. Bangkok: Institute of Asian Studies, Chulalongkorn
University, 2000.

———. *"Kho ang" kanpatiwat-ratthaprahan kabot nai kanmueang thai patchuban botwikhro
lae ekkasan* ["Reasons" for coups in modern Thailand politics: Analysis and
documents]. Bangkok: The Foundation for the Promotion of Social Sciences
and Humanities Textbooks Project, 2007.

Thanapol Eawsakul. "Phumlang ongkhamontri tai phraboromaphothisomphan"
[Backgrounds of the Privy Councillors under royal hegemony]. *Fa diaokan* 13,
no. 2 (2015): 70–79.

Thanapol Eawsakul and Chaithawat Tulathon. "Khrai pen khrai nai ongkhamontri
haeng rabop prachathippatai an mi phramahakasat pen pramuk" [Who is
who among the privy councillors in the era of democracy with the king as
the head of the state]. *Fa diaokan* 13, no. 2 (2015): 50–69.

Thanathon Chuengrungrueangkit. "Yang mi honthang santiwithi yu ik rue?"
[Is there still a peaceful path?]. *MGR Online*, 6 July 2015 <http://www.
manager.co.th/Sport/ViewNews.aspx?NewsID=9580000076085> (accessed
23 October 2017).

Thawin Phaison. "Hetphon thi tong lueaktang phuwaratchakan changwat"
[Why we need elections for governors]. *Thai Post*, 16 July 2014.

Thippawal Srijantr. "Agrarian Transformations in the Chao Phraya Delta: A Case
Study in Tambon Thung Luk Nok". In *Thailand's Rice Bowl: Perspectives on
Agricultural and Social Change in the Chao Phraya Delta*, edited by François Molle
and Thippawal Srijantr, pp. 125–56. Bangkok: White Lotus, 2003.

Thirayuth Boonmee. "Kankrachai amnat khue thangok diao" [Decentralization is
the only solution]. *Sayam rat weekly* 40, no. 22 (1993): 13.

Thoettham Songthai. *Kha khue nakrop prachachon ku chat* [I am a people's national
warrior]. Bangkok: GPP Publication, 2008.

Thongchai Winichakul. "The Others Within: Travel and Ethno-Spatial Differentiation
of Siamese Subjects 1885–1910". In *Civility and Savagery: Social Identity in Tai
States*, edited by Andrew Turton, pp. 38–62. Richmond: Curzon Press, 2000.

———. "Prawattisat thai baep rachachatniyom chak yuk ananikom amphrang su
rachachatniyom mai rue latthi sadetpho khong kradumphi thai nai patchuban"

[Thai royal-nationalist Thai history, from the era of crypto-colonialism to the new royal-nationalism of the royal father cult of the contemporary Thai bourgeoisie]. *Sinlapa watthanatham* [Art and culture] 23, no. 1 (November 2001): 56–65.

———. "Toppling Democracy". *Journal of Contemporary Asia* 38, no. 1 (February 2008): 11–37.

———. "Siam's Colonial Conditions and the Birth of Thai History". In *Unraveling Myths in Southeast Asian Historiography*, edited by Volker Grabowsky. Bangkok: Rivers Books, 2011.

———. "The Monarchy and Anti-Monarchy: Two Elephants in the Room of Thai Politics and the State of Denial". In *'Good Coup' Gone Bad: Thailand's Political Developments since Thaksin's Downfall*, edited by Pavin Chachavalpongpun, pp. 79–108. Singapore: Institute of Southeast Asian Studies, 2014.

———. *Thailand's Hyper-Royalism: Its Past Success and Present Predicament*. Trends in Southeast Asia, no. 7/2016. Singapore: ISEAS – Yusof Ishak Insitute, 2016.

Tilly, Charles. *The Politics of Collective Violence*. New York: Cambridge University Press, 2003.

Time. "A Monarchy Fights for Freedom". 27 May 1966. In *The King of Thailand in World Focus*, edited by Denis D. Gray and Dominic Faulder, pp. 53–56. Singapore: Editions Didier Millet, 2008.

———. "Democracy Rising". 1 June 1992. In *The King of Thailand in World Focus*, edited by Denis D. Gray and Dominic Faulder, pp. 100–103. Singapore: Editions Didier Millet, 2008.

Todaro, Michael. P. "A Model for Labour Migration and Urban Unemployment in Less Developed Countries". *American Economic Review* 59, no. 1 (1969): 138–48.

Tourism Authority of Thailand. *Thailand Tourism Statistics*. Bangkok: Ministry of Tourism and Sport, n.d. (various years).

Tsuneishi Takao. "Thailand's Economic Cooperation with Neighboring Countries and Its Effects on Economic Development within Thailand". IDE Discussion Papers, no. 115 (August 2007).

———. "Development of Border Economic Zones in Thailand: Expansion of Border Trade and Formation of Border Economic Zones". IDE Discussion Papers, no. 153 (May 2008).

Ubonrat Siriyuvasak. "Limited Competition without Re-Regulating the Media: The Case of the Broadcasting Industry in Thailand". *Asian Journal of Communication* 7, no. 2 (1997): 57–74.

———. "Yuk pit hu pit ta pit pak sitthiseriphap nai mue thurakit kanmueang sue" [The era of closed eyes and closed ears and closed mouths: Media rights and the political economy of media]. Midnight University, June 2002 <http://v1.midnightuniv.org/midnight2545/document9640.html> (accessed 15 December 2015).

Ünaldi, Serhat. "Thailand, A Coup, the Crown and the Two Middle Classes". *The Diplomat*, 23 May 2014*a*.

————. "The Tyranny of SE Asia's Establishment". *The Diplomat*, 8 November 2014*b* <http://thediplomat.com/2014/11/the-tyranny-of-se-asias-establishment/> (accessed 21 April 2017).

————. "Working towards the Monarchy and its Discontents: Anti-royal Graffiti in Downtown Bangkok". *Journal of Contemporary Asia* 44, no. 3 (2014*c*): 377–403.

————. "Thailand in 2015: The Waiting Game". In *Southeast Asian Affairs 2016*, edited by Malcolm Cook and Daljit Singh, pp. 317–30. Singapore: ISEAS – Yusof Ishak Institute, 2016*a*.

————. *Working towards the Monarchy: The Politics of Space in Downtown Bangkok*. Honolulu: University of Hawai'i Press, 2016*b*.

UNICEF. "Thailand: Statistics". 31 December 2013 <http://www.unicef.org/infobycountry/Thailand_statistics.html> (accessed 9 November 2016).

United Nations. *World Population Aging: 1950–2050*. New York: Population Division, United Nations Department of Economic and Social Affairs, 2002.

————. *World Population Prospects: The 2006 Revision*. New York: Population Division, United Nations Department of Economic and Social Affairs, 2007.

————. *World Population Aging 2013*. New York: Population Division, United Nations Department of Economic and Social Affairs, 2013*a*.

————. *World Population Prospects: The 2012 Revision*. New York: Population Division, United Nations Department of Economic and Social Affairs, 2013*b*.

————. "World Population Ageing Highlights". New York: Department of Economic and Social Affairs, United Nations, 2015.

United Nations Population Fund. *Population Ageing in Thailand: Prognosis and Policy Response*. New York: United Nations Population Fund, 2006.

————. *Ageing in the Twenty-First Century: A Celebration and a Challenge*. New York: United Nations Population Fund and HelpAge International, 2012.

————. *World Population Prospects: The 2015 Revision, Key Findings and Advance Tables*. New York: Population Division United Nations Department of Economic and Social Affairs, 2015.

Vatikiotis, Michael. "Malaysia Can help to Secure Peace". *Bangkok Post*, 2 March 2013.

Viengrat Nethipo. "Chao pho uppatham rue rat uppatham" [Godfather patronage or state patronage]. *Warasan sangkomsat* [Social science journal] 33, no. 1 (2003): 444–56.

————. "Kankrachai amnat kap baepphaen mai khong khrueakhai itthiphon" [Decentralization and the new pattern of networks of influence]. In *Kao (mai) phon prachaniyom krachai amnat su thongthin* [(Not) beyond populism: Decentralization], edited by Narong Phetprasert, pp. 59–106. Bangkok: Political Economy Center, Chulalongkorn University, 2008.

————. "The Political Process of Public Health Decentralization in Thailand: Studying the Case of Primary Care Units". Health Systems Research Institute, 2011 <http://kb.hsri.or.th/dspace/handle/11228/3099> (accessed 22 February 2018).

————. *Hipbat kap bunkhun kanmueang kanlueaktang lae kanplianplaeng khrueakhai uppatham* [Ballots and gratitude: Electoral politics and the dynamics of clentelistic networks]. Chiang Mai: Centre for ASEAN Studies, Chiang Mai University, 2015a.

————. "Thailand's Divided Civil Society at a Time of Crisis". In *Civil Society and Democracy in Southeast Asia and Turkey*, edited by N. Ganesan and Colin Dürkop, pp. 160–97. Ankara: Konrad-Adenauer-Stiftung, 2015b.

Volkov, Vadim. *Violent Entrepreneurs: The Use of Force in the Making of Russian Capitalism*. Ithaca: Cornell University Press, 2002.

Voravidh Charoenlert. "Chonchan klang kap hetkan pruetsaphakhom" [The middle class and the May events]. In *Chonchan klang bon krasae prachathippatai* [The middle class on the democratic wave], edited by Sungsidh Piriyarangsan and Pasuk Phongpaichit, pp. 117–54. Bangkok: Political Economy Centre, Chulalongkorn University, 1993.

Wada Taizo, Wada Chizu, Ishine Masayuki, Okumiya Kiyohito, Kawakita Toshiko, Fushida Mutsuko, Kita Toru, Mizuno Kosuke, and Matsubayashi Kozo. "Comprehensive Geriatric Assessment for Community-Dwelling Elderly in Asia Compared with Those in Japan: V. West Java in Indonesia". *Geriatrics and Gerontology International* 5, no. 3 (September 2005): 168–75.

Wahari, Hata. "Southern Thailand: Rebels Commit to Peace Talks Despite BRN Rift". *BenarNews*, 14 October 2015 <http://www.benarnews.org/english/news/thai/thai-peace-talks-10142015181608.html> (accessed 6 December 2017).

Walker, Andrew. *Thailand's Political Peasants: Power in the Modern Rural Economy*. Madison: University of Wisconsin Press, 2012.

The Wall Street Journal. "Thailand's Disloyal Opposition". 23 December 2013 <www.wsj.com/articles/SB10001424052702304020704579275631180950354> (accessed 27 February 2017).

————. "Thailand Votes for Democracy". 3 February 2014 <www.wsj.com/articles/SB10001424052702303442704579360272255058790> (accessed 27 February 2017).

————. "Thailand's Aristocratic Dead-Enders". 7 May 2014 <www.wsj.com/articles/SB10001424052702304431104579547340574302518> (accessed 27 February 2017).

Warr, Peter. "Boom, Bust and Beyond". In *Thailand beyond the Crisis*, edited by Peter Warr, pp. 3–65. Abingdon: RoutledgeCurzon, 2005.

Warr, Peter G., and Bhanupong Nidhiprabha. *Thailand's Macroeconomic Miracle: Stable Adjustment and Sustained Growth*. Washington, DC: World Bank, 1996.

The Washington Post. "As Ever, the Last Word in Thailand: Resolution of Election Crisis Affirms Enduring Influence of Long-serving King". 28 May 2006. In *The King of Thailand in World Focus,* edited by Denis D. Gray and Dominic Faulder, pp. 112–13. Singapore: Editions Didier Millet, 2008.

Wassana Nanuam. *Lap luang phrang phak 2: son rup patiwat hak liam hot* [Secrets, deceit, and camouflage, part 2: The concealed coup and ruthless double-cross]. Bangkok: Matichon, 2009.

———. *Lap luang phrang phak 3: The Last War kongthap tang si suek sai lueat cho po ro* [Secrets, deceit, and camouflage, part 3: The last war, armies of different colours and conflict among *cho pho ro* lineages]. Bangkok: Matichon, 2010.

———. *Lap luang phrang awasan Yinglak* [Secrets, deceit and camouflage: The end of Yingluck], 3rd ed. Bangkok: Matichon, 2014.

Weaver, Matthew, and Adam Gabatt. "Thailand Protests: Crackdown against Redshirts — As it Happened". *The Guardian,* 19 May 2010 <http://www.theguardian.com/news/blog/2010/may/19/thailand-crackdown-redshirts> (accessed 22 March 2018).

Webster, Douglas. "Urbanization: New Driver, New Outcomes". In *Thailand beyond the Crisis,* edited by Peter Warr, pp. 285–314. Abingdon: RoutledgeCurzon, 2005.

Weerasak Krueathep. "Local Government Initiatives in Thailand: Cases and Lessons Learned". *Asia Pacific Journal of Public Administration* 26, no. 2 (2004): 217–39.

Weist, Dana. "Thailand's decentralization: Progress and prospects". Paper presented at KPI Annual Congress III on Decentralization and Local Government, 10–11 November 2001, Bangkok <https://pdfs.semanticscholar.org/b636/be18984797d169b9a65e9f37ddb2912f3dc2.pdf> (accessed 22 February 2018).

Weng Tojirakarn. Facebook, 7 July 2015 <https://www.facebook.com/wengtojirakarn/posts/774127082686108> (accessed 23 October 2017).

Wichit Chantanusornsiri. "Benefit Hike for Retirees Considered Monthly Allowance Increase of 100 Baht". *Bangkok Post,* 26 January 2017 <http://www.bangkokpost.com/print/1187021/> (accessed 17 October 2017).

Wiener, Joshua M., and Jane Tilly. "Population Ageing in the United States of America: Implications for Public Programmes". *International Journal of Epidemiology* 31, no. 4 (August 2002): 776–81.

Wigell, Mikael. "Mapping 'Hybrid Regimes': Regime Types and Concepts in Comparative Politics". *Democratization* 15, no. 2 (April 2008): 230–50.

Wilkinson, Steven I. *Votes and Violence: Electoral Competition and Ethnic Riots in India.* New York: Cambridge University Press, 2004.

Wilson, David A. *Politics in Thailand.* Ithaca: Cornell University Press, 1962.

Wimo, Anders, and Martin Prince. *World Alzheimer Report 2010: The Global Economic*

Impact of Dementia. Alzheimer's Disease International, 21 September 2010 <http://www.alz.org/documents/national/world_alzheimer_report_2010.pdf> (accessed 17 October 2017).

Wimonphan Pitathawatchai. *Sanya Thammasak khon khong phaendin* [Sanya Thammasak: A man of the country]. Bangkok: Sanya Thammasak Foundation, 2003.

Worawat Worawatthana. "Krabuankan klaipen mue puen rap chang atchayakon mue achip" [The process of becoming a hired gunman: Professional criminals]. Doctoral dissertation, Krirk University, 2010.

World Bank. *East Asia and Pacific Economic Update (April 2015): Adjusting to a Changing World*. Washington, DC: World Bank, 2015*a*.

———. "International Tourism, Number of Arrivals". 2015*b* <http://data.worldbank.org/indicator/ST.INT.ARVL> (accessed 9 November 2016).

World Health Organization. *World Health Report 2003 — Shaping the Future*. Geneva: World Health Organization, 2003.

———. *Preventing Chronic Disease: A Vital Investment*. Geneva: World Health Organization, 2005.

———. "Dementia". September 2017 <http://www.who.int/mediacentre/factsheets/fs362/en/> (accessed 24 October 2017).

World Travel and Tourism Council. "Benchmarking Travel & Tourism in Thailand: How does Travel & Tourism Compare to Other Sectors? Summary of Findings, November 2013". November 2013 <http://www.wttc.org/-/media/files/reports/benchmark%20reports/country%20results/thailand%20benchmarking%202013.pdf> (accessed 9 November 2016).

Wright, Tom. "Thai Monarchy Is a Factor in Dispute". *The Wall Street Journal*, 23 May 2014 <https://www.wsj.com/articles/SB10001424052702303980004579580240531749422> (accessed 27 February 2017).

Yongyut Chuwaen. "Botnam" [Introduction]. In *Khapsamut thai nai ratcha-anachak sayam* [The Thai Peninsula in the Siamese Kingdom], edited by Yongyut Chuwaen, pp. 19–16. Bangkok: Nakhon Press, 2007.

Zarembka, Paul. *Toward a Theory of Economic Development*. San Francisco: Holden-Day, 1972.

Zarrow, Peter. *China in War and Revolution, 1895–1949*. New York: Routledge, 2005.

Index

CPSIA information can be obtained
at www.ICGtesting.com
Printed in the USA
LVHW081055110920
665691LV00016B/1094